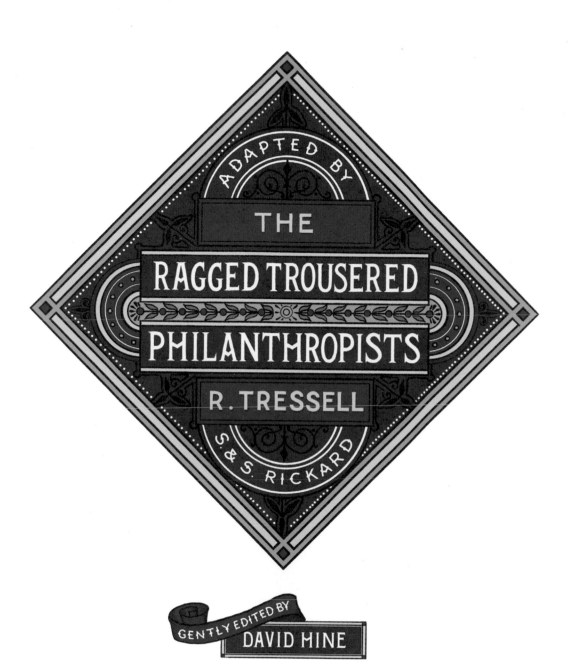

ADAPTED BY

THE

RAGGED TROUSERED

PHILANTHROPISTS

R. TRESSELL

S & S. RICKARD

GENTLY EDITED BY DAVID HINE

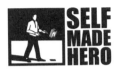

First published in English in 2020
by SelfMadeHero
139–141 Pancras Road
London NW1 1UN
www.selfmadehero.com

Original Author Robert Tressell
Text adapted by Sophie Rickard
Drawn by Scarlett Rickard
Edited by David Hine
Textual Consultant Nick de Somogyi

Publishing Director Emma Hayley
Editorial & Production Director Guillaume Rater
Publishing Assistant Stefano Mancin
UK Publicist Paul Smith

A CIP record for this book is available from the British Library

ISBN: 978-1-910593-92-9

10 9 8 7 6 5 4 3 2

Printed and bound in China

MIX
Paper from responsible sources
FSC® C008047

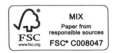

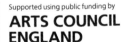

Supported using public funding by ARTS COUNCIL ENGLAND

For Tim and Dan,
whose patience and support
made this possible.

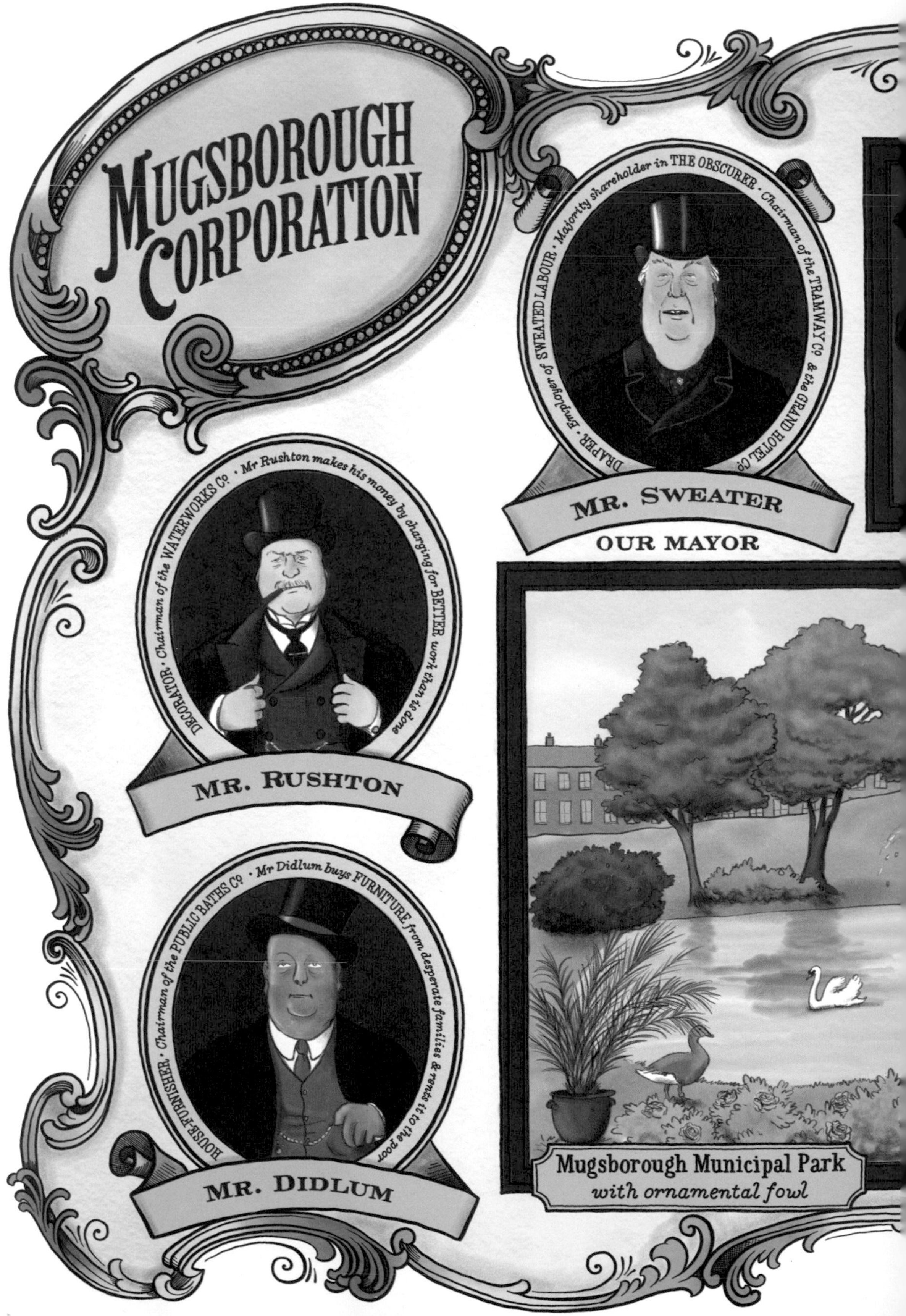
MUGSBOROUGH CORPORATION
DRAPER · Employer of SWEATED LABOUR · Majority shareholder in THE OBSCURER · Chairman of the TRAMWAY Co. & the GRAND HOTEL Co.
MR. SWEATER
OUR MAYOR
DECORATOR · Chairman of the WATERWORKS Co. · Mr Rushton makes his money by charging for BETTER work than is done
MR. RUSHTON
HOUSE-FURNISHER · Chairman of the PUBLIC BATHS Co. · Mr Didlum buys FURNITURE from desperate families & rents it to the poor
MR. DIDLUM
Mugsborough Municipal Park
with ornamental fowl

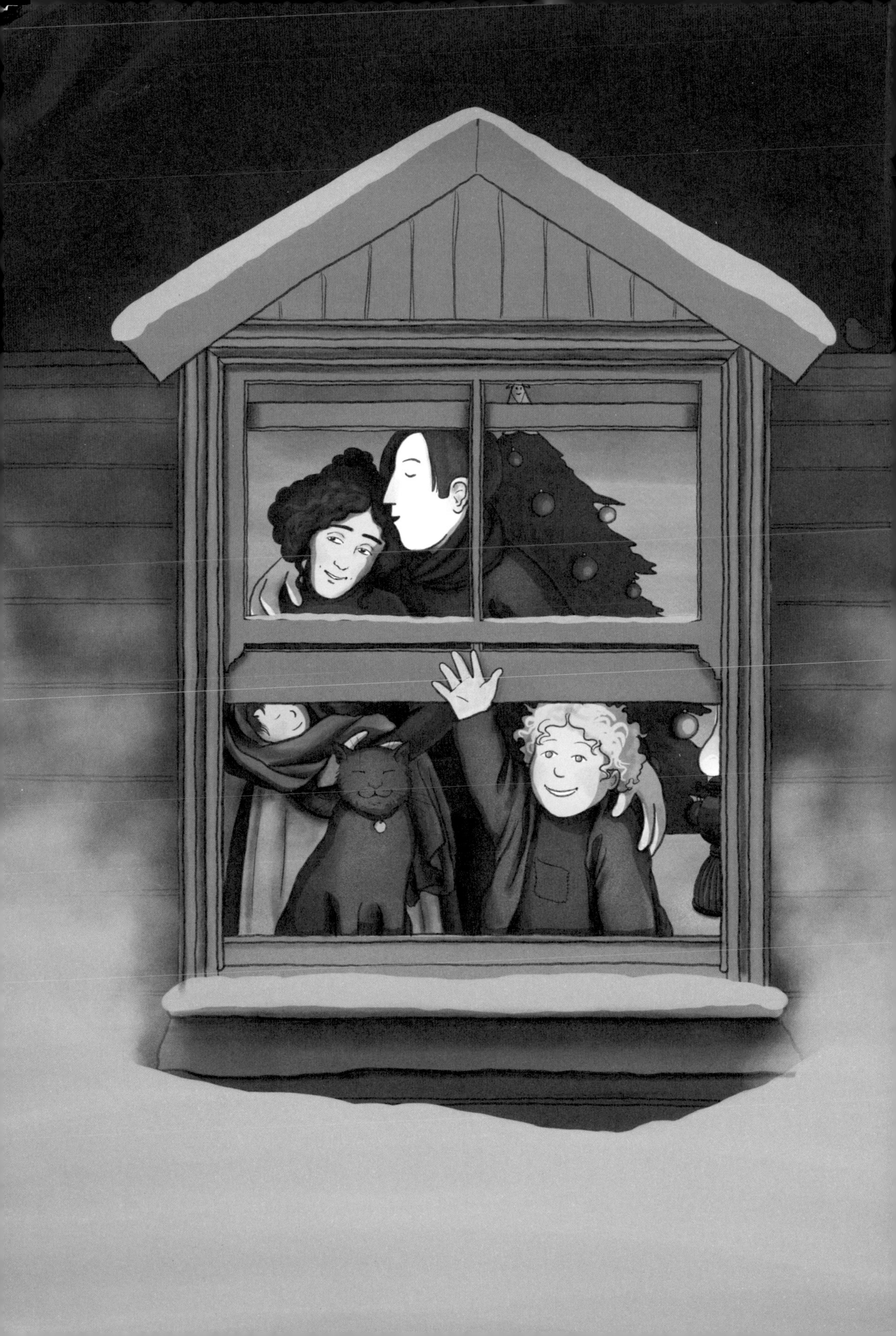

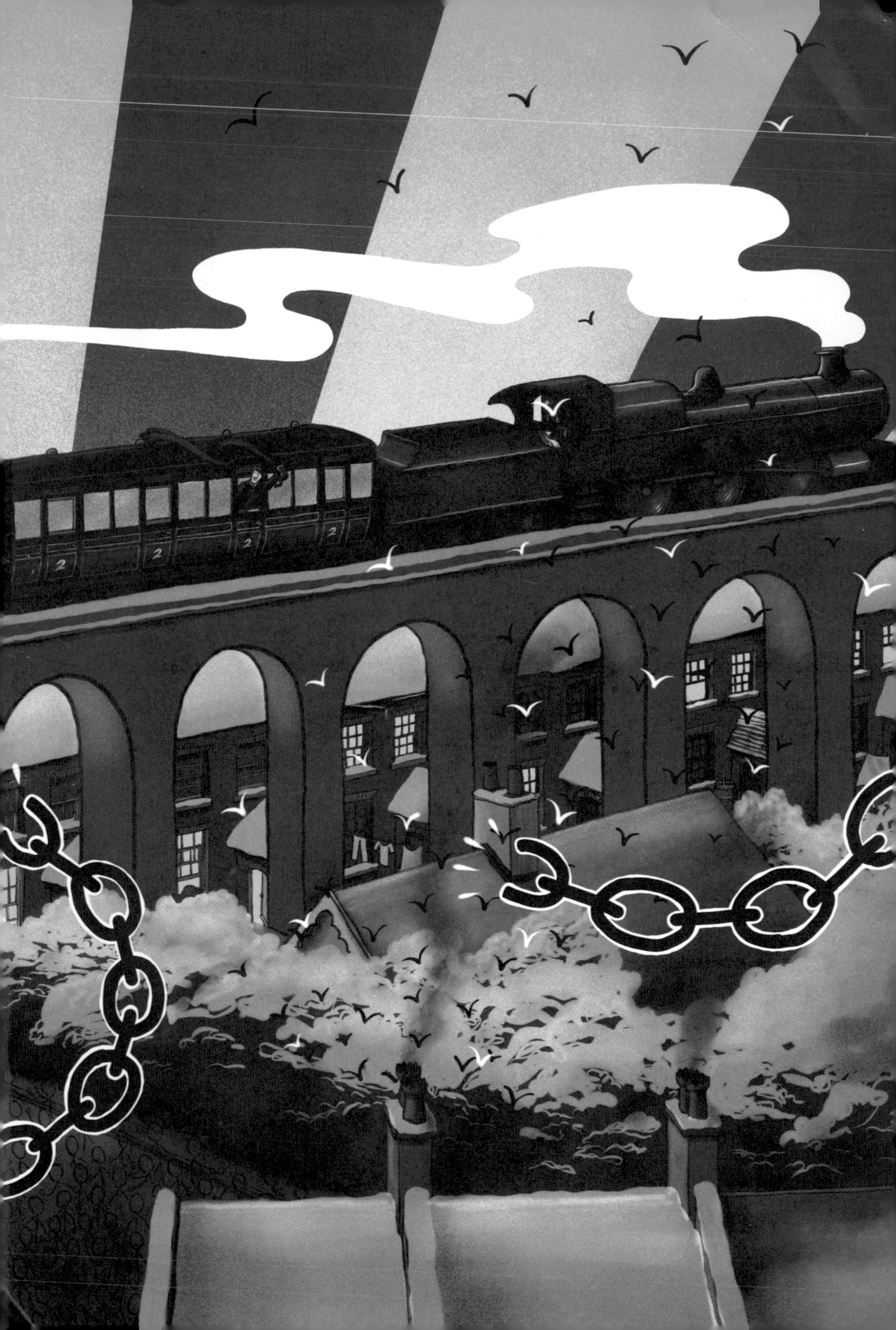

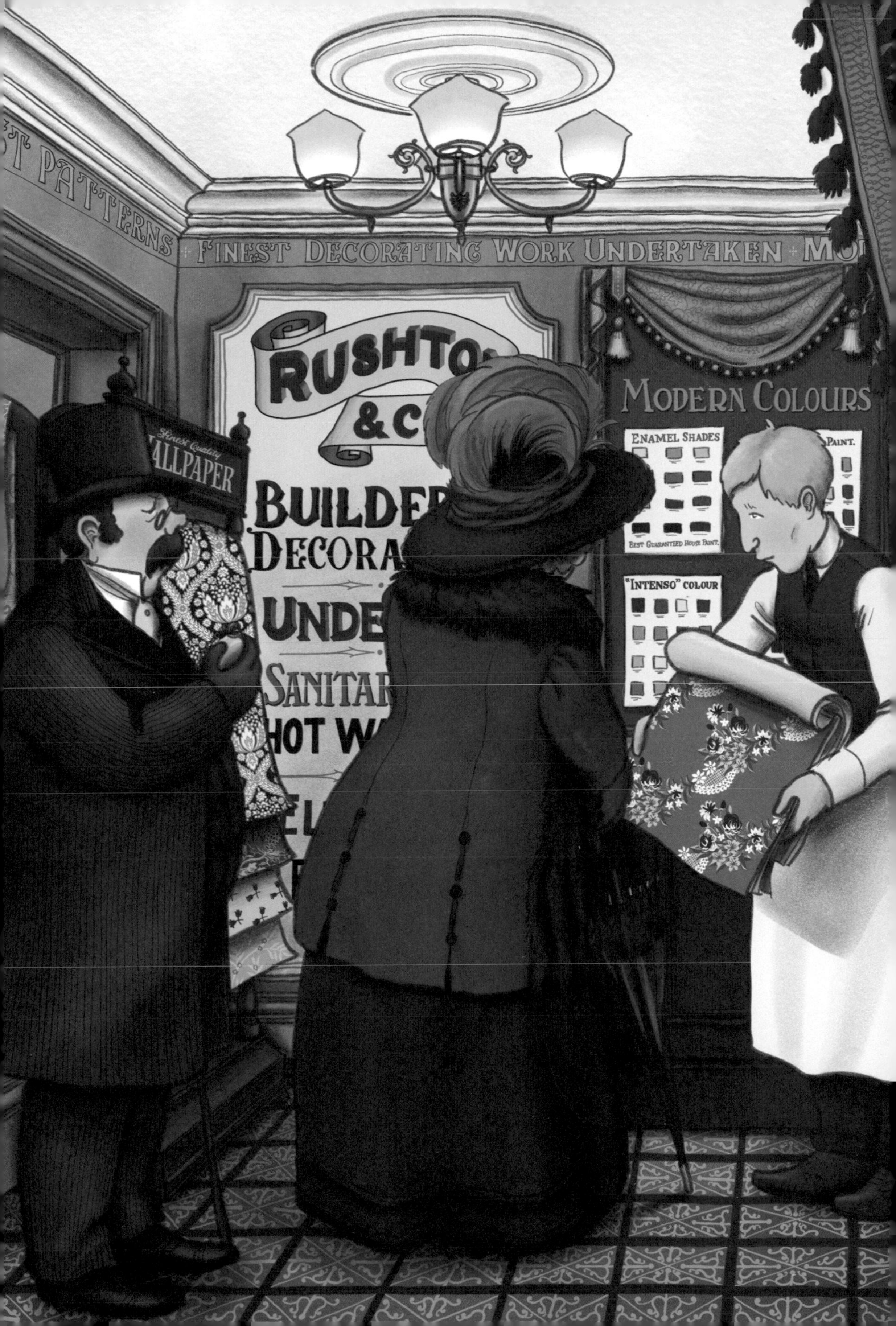

T PATTERNS
FINEST DECORATING WORK UNDERTAKEN
RUSHTO
&C
BUILDE
DECORA
UNDE
SANITAR
HOT W
Finest Quality
ALLPAPER
MODERN COLOURS
ENAMEL SHADES
PAINT.
BEST GUARANTEED HOUSE PAINT.
"INTENSO" COLOUR

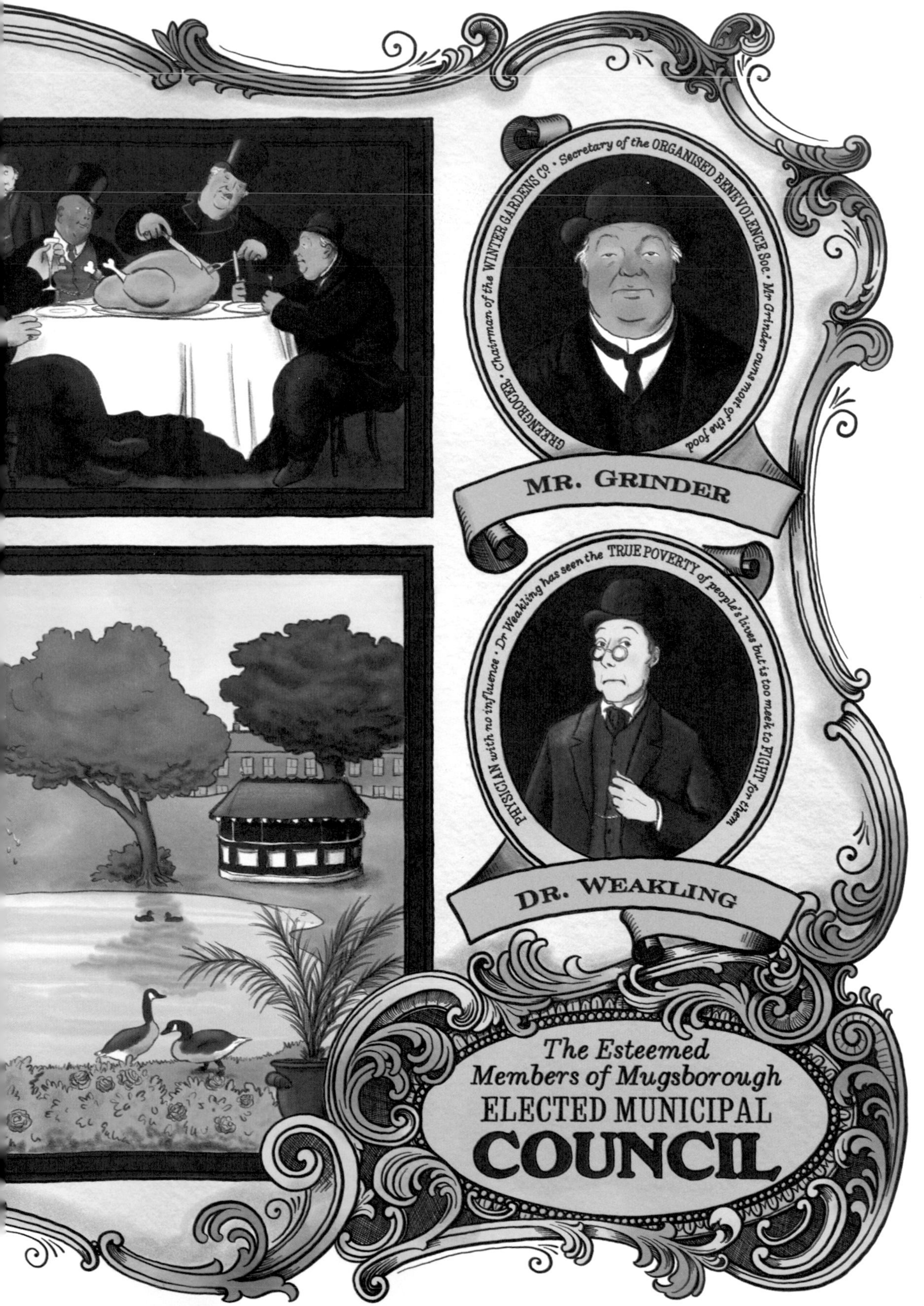
GREENGROCER • Chairman of the WINTER GARDENS Co. • Secretary of the ORGANISED BENEVOLENCE Soc. • Mr Grinder owns most of the food
MR. GRINDER
PHYSICIAN with no influence • Dr Weakling has seen the TRUE POVERTY of people's lives but is too meek to FIGHT for them
DR. WEAKLING
The Esteemed
Members of Mugsborough
ELECTED MUNICIPAL
COUNCIL

AFTERWORD

By the time *The Ragged Trousered Philanthropists* was posthumously published in 1914, under the pen-name Robert Tressell, it had been rejected by several publishers and (allegedly) thrown in the fire by its exasperated creator. It is the kind of book people feel they ought to have read, but have never quite got round to. Of those who have tried, many (like the PM's girlfriend in Chris Mullin's play *A Very British Coup*) "struggled through the first fifty pages, and then gave up".

Tressell's chosen name comes from the folding wooden stands associated with the decorator's trade. He was Irish, born in Dublin in 1870 as Robert Croker. His father, Samuel Croker, was an elderly retired police officer and magistrate with an adult family of his own, who never married Robert's mother, Mary Noonan. They had two more children together, and Croker left his mistress and her children the wealth of significant property when he died. Robert must have grown up conscious of the social status afforded to his father's "real" family, and of the contrasting position of his own mother and sisters.

It seems that Tressell may have refused an opportunity to attend Trinity College in Dublin on principle. Robert later told his daughter that he began a painting apprenticeship at sixteen, but there's no record of it. At some point he emigrated to London, then Liverpool (via a six-month prison sentence for selling stolen goods, though it's unclear who was really responsible), and then to South Africa, where he made a good living as a talented sign writer and decorator.

At the age of twenty-one, Robert (now using his mother's name, Noonan) married eighteen-year-old Elizabeth Hartell, and they had a baby daughter. By 1896 Robert and the child were living alone in Johannesburg, and little Kathleen had been told that her mother was dead. Robert's circumstances were later explored in *The Ragged Trousered Philanthropists*: Noonan seems to have neglected Elizabeth's emotional needs and taken her for granted, thereby allowing a maleficent lodger to take advantage of her, impregnating her before moving on. This is the story arc given to Ruth and Easton in the novel, where Tressell holds Easton to account for Ruth's suffering.

By 1902 Noonan and his daughter were living in the English seaside town of Hastings, where he struggled to earn a living as a decorator during a deep and painful building slump. He was well-travelled, politically aware, talented, versatile and experienced. Yet he was often unemployed, and it was during this period that he worked on *The Ragged Trousered Philanthropists*. The manuscript was unlike anything that had been seen before,

and it was rejected by several publishers. This devastated Robert, by now ill with bronchial pneumonia, also known as tuberculosis — the death sentence that his protagonist, Owen, lives with throughout the novel.

In 1910, he was living in Liverpool, trying to earn and save enough to emigrate to Canada. He died the following year, aged just forty. Kathleen, now nineteen, was working as a governess in the house of Jessie Pope, the pro-war columnist and opinion writer to whom Wilfred Owen would dedicate "Dulce et Decorum Est" seven years later. Kathleen, having rescued her father's manuscript from the fire and hidden it under her bed, showed it to Pope, who recommended *The Ragged Trousered Philanthropists* to her publisher, Grant Richards. He commissioned Pope to "edit" the text into a much safer working-class tragedy of about one-third the length of the original. Tressell's political ideology was the first victim of the mutilation. Kathleen sold it for £25 (about three months' pay), and began a new life in Canada. The book has never been out of print since.

It wasn't until after the Second World War that Kathleen returned to Britain and discovered the success of her father's work. The full 250,000-word edition was published in 1955, and the original manuscript donated to the TUC library, where it can still be seen, including Tressell's lettering on the front cover: "the story of twelve months in Hell, told by one of the damned."

This book is known as *the* socialist novel, regarded for its intimate and realist depictions of working-class people, and the relentless exploitation they endured. But Tressell points the finger, not at the government or the aristocracy, but at the working classes themselves. If it hadn't been for his commitment to record what he saw around him, and Kathleen's preservation of his life's work, we would never have heard of him. He would have been just another nameless, itinerant working man who died prematurely, of a disease directly related to his working conditions and "the present system".

The Ragged Trousered Philanthropists has been cited as an inspiration to many an active socialist over the last century, and yet it has never been so current. Perhaps this continued relevance, more than any literary criticism, provides the most persuasive evidence that the book's exasperating message — that the working class continues to elect capitalists — might be a valid point.

SCARLETT & SOPHIE RICKARD

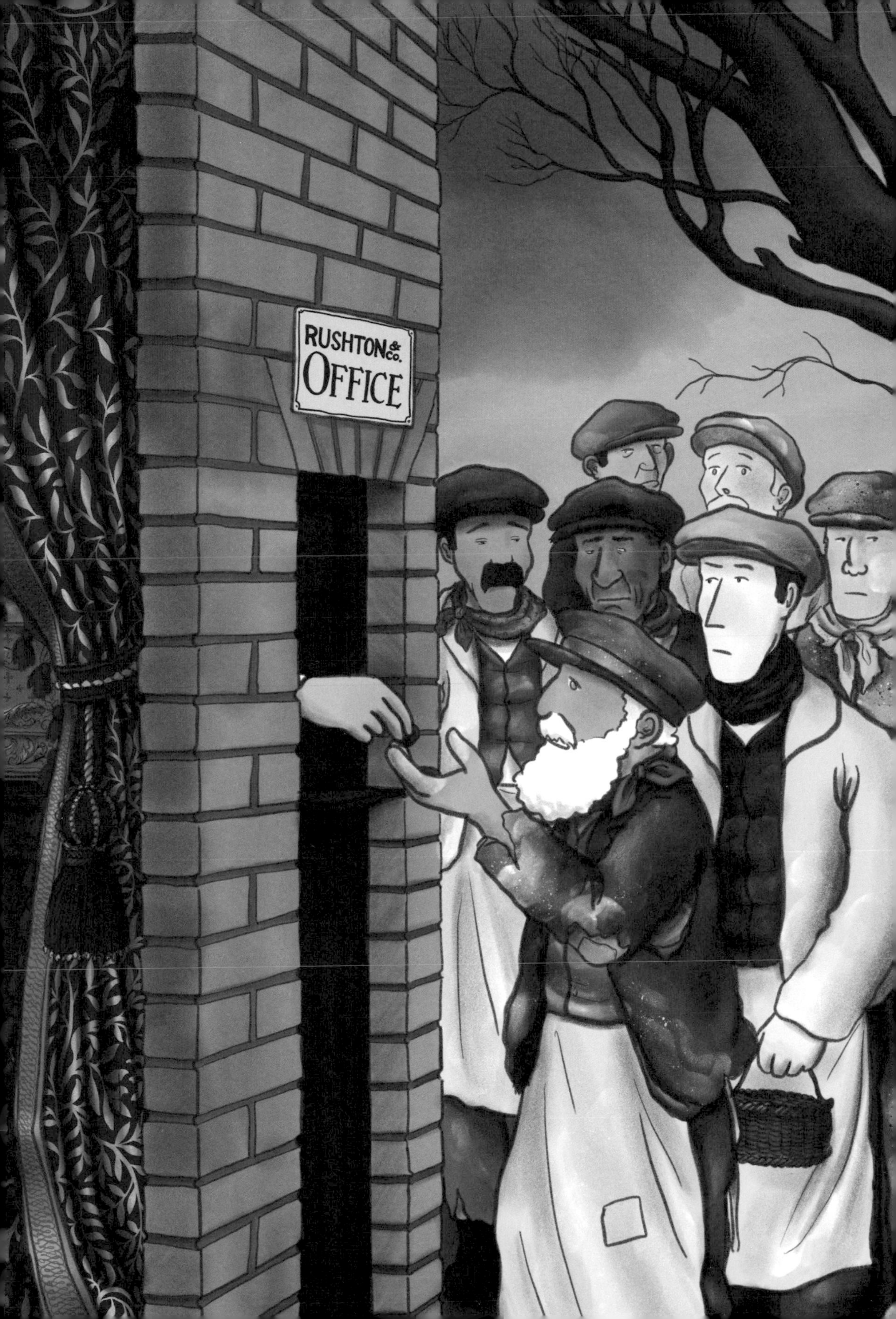
RUSHTON & Co.
OFFICE

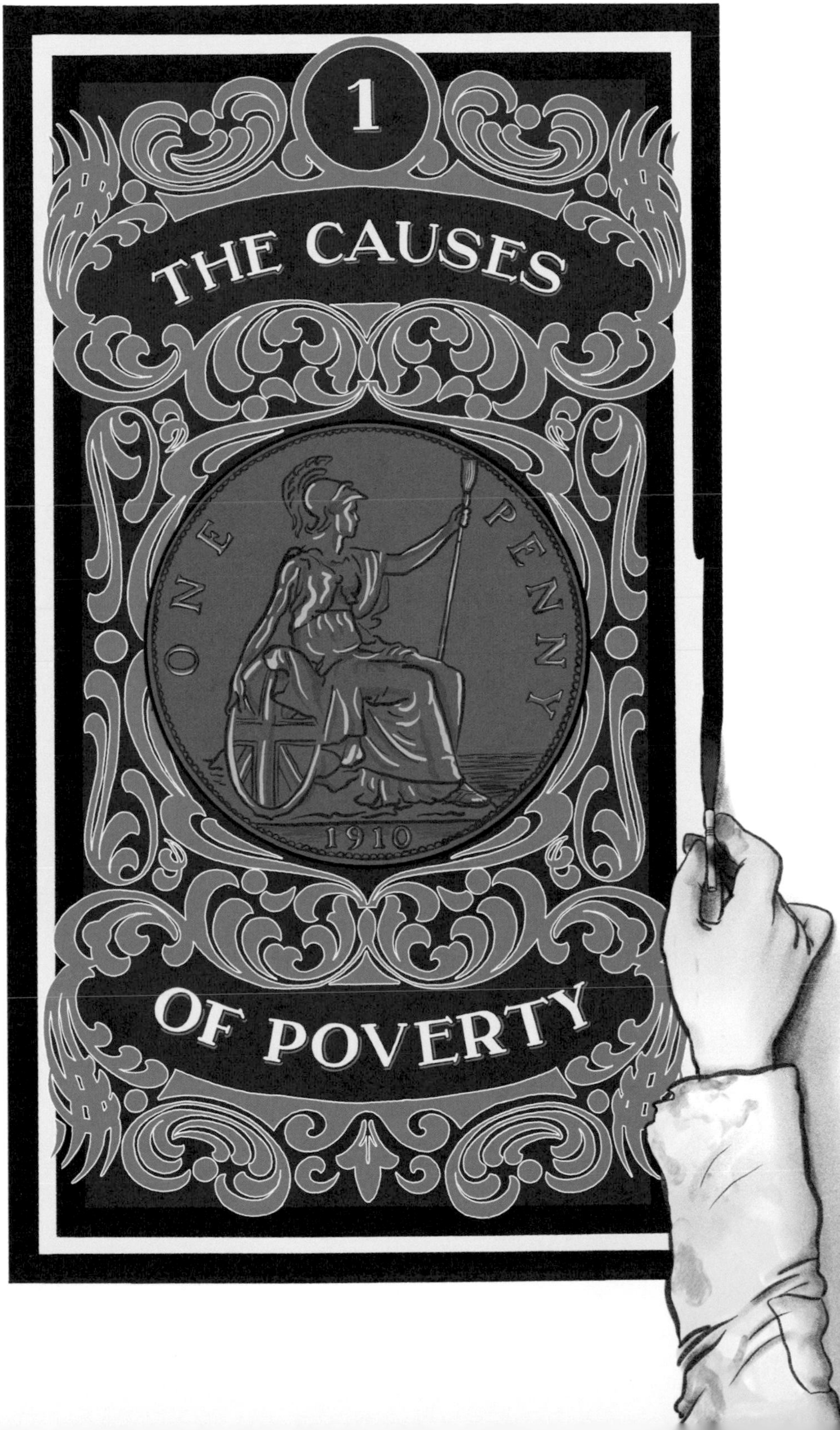
1
THE CAUSES
ONE PENNY
1910
OF POVERTY

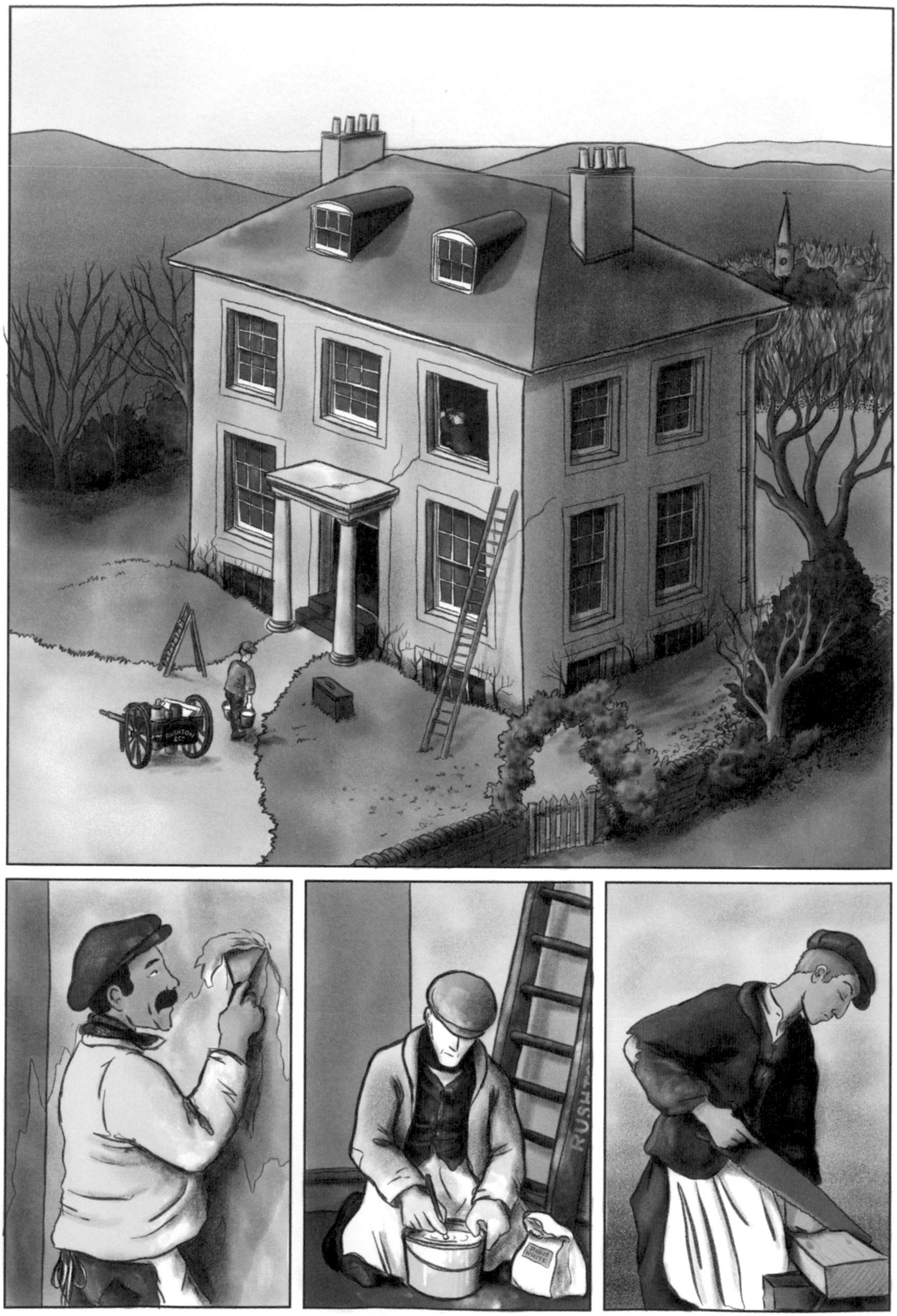
RUSHTON
&Co
PARIS
WHITE

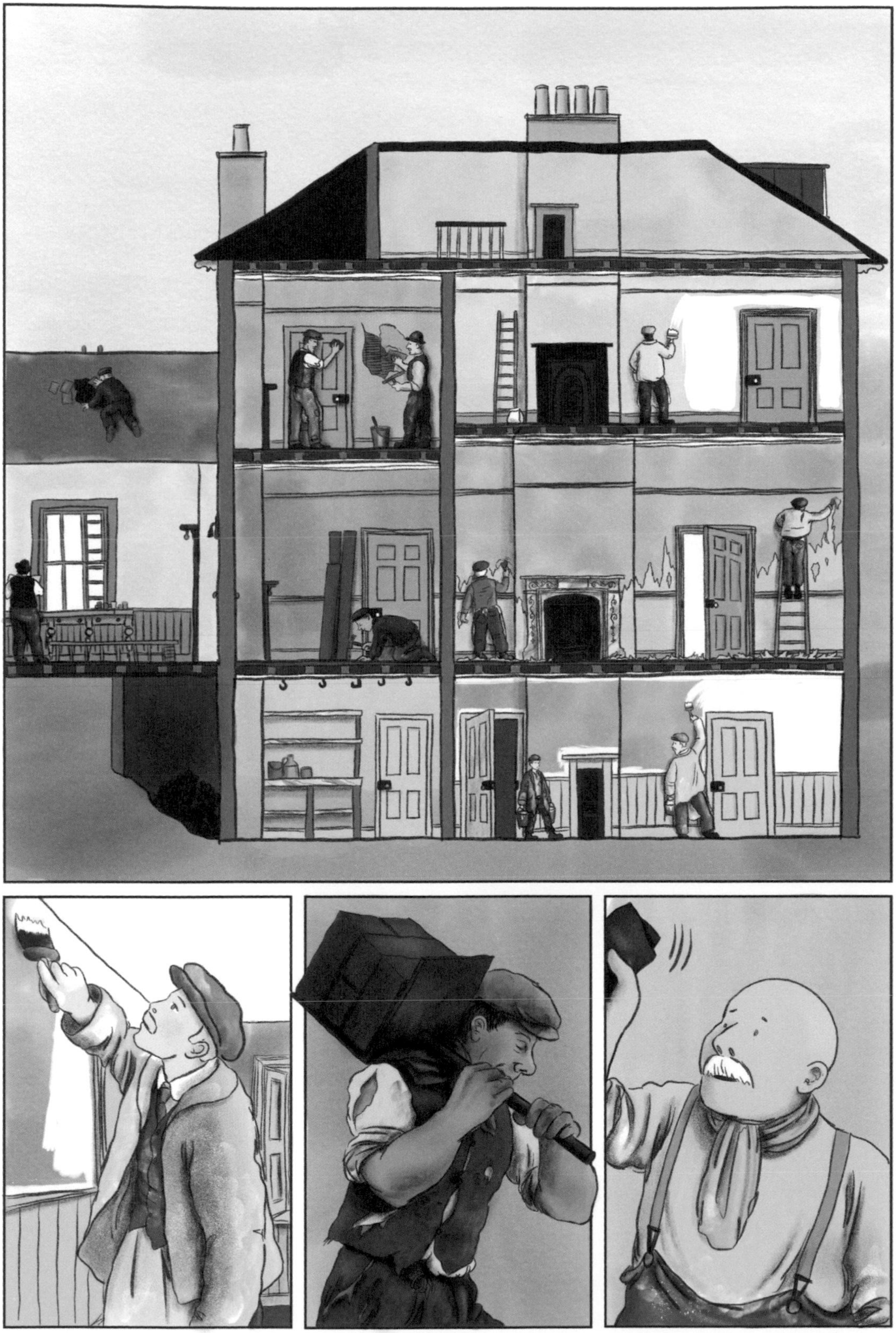

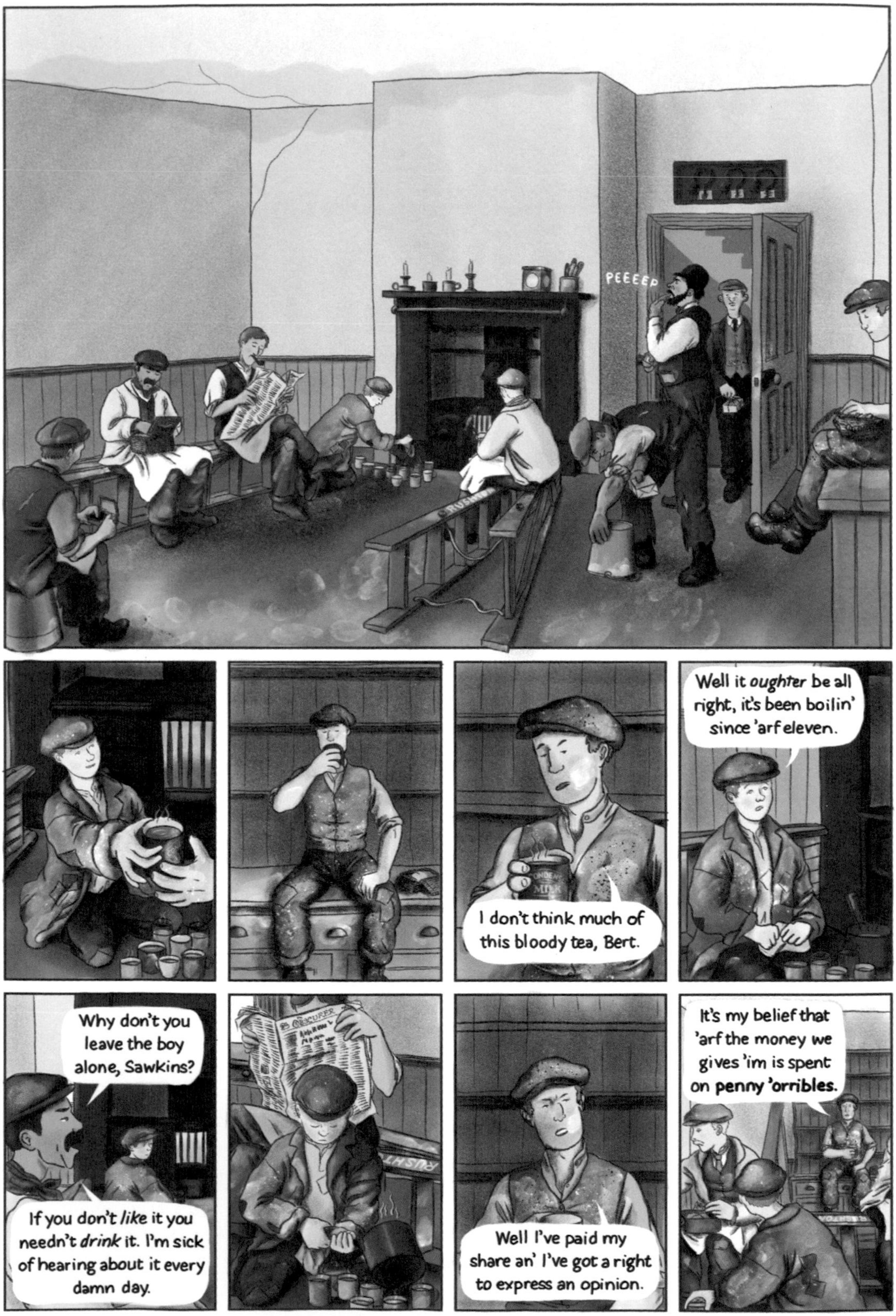
PEEEEP
I don't think much of this bloody tea, Bert.
Well it *oughter* be all right, it's been boilin' since 'arf eleven.
Why don't you leave the boy alone, Sawkins?
If you don't *like* it you needn't *drink* it. I'm sick of hearing about it every damn day.
Well I've paid my share an' I've got a right to express an opinion.
It's my belief that 'arf the money we gives 'im is spent on **penny 'orribles.**

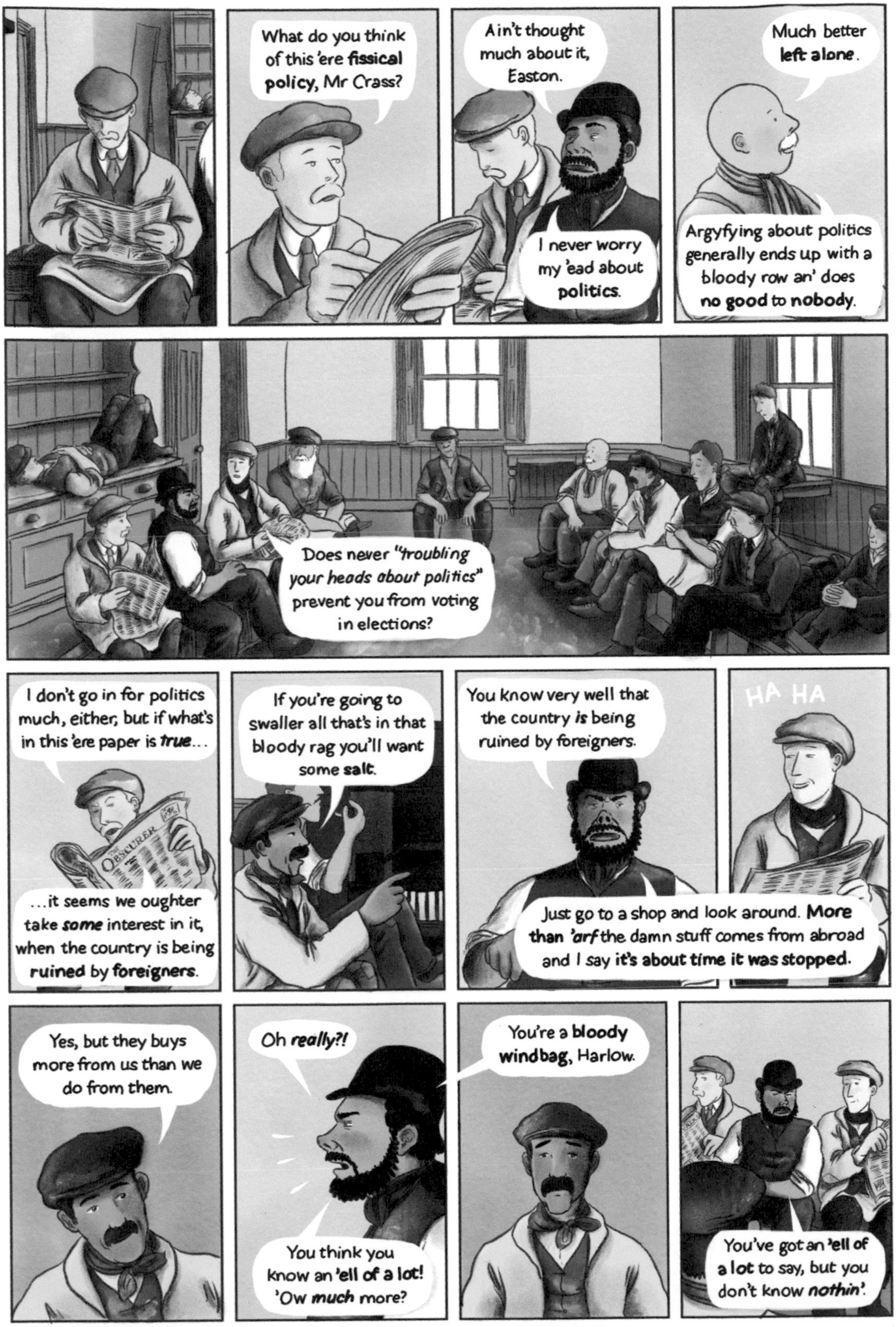
What do you think of this 'ere fissical policy, Mr Crass?
Ain't thought much about it, Easton.
I never worry my 'ead about politics.
Much better left alone.
Argyfying about politics generally ends up with a bloody row an' does no good to nobody.
Does never "troubling your heads about politics" prevent you from voting in elections?
I don't go in for politics much, either, but if what's in this 'ere paper is true...
...it seems we oughter take some interest in it, when the country is being ruined by foreigners.
If you're going to swaller all that's in that bloody rag you'll want some salt.
You know very well that the country is being ruined by foreigners.
Just go to a shop and look around. More than 'arf the damn stuff comes from abroad and I say it's about time it was stopped.
HA HA
Yes, but they buys more from us than we do from them.
Oh really?!
You think you know an 'ell of a lot! 'Ow much more?
You're a bloody windbag, Harlow.
You've got an 'ell of a lot to say, but you don't know nothin'.

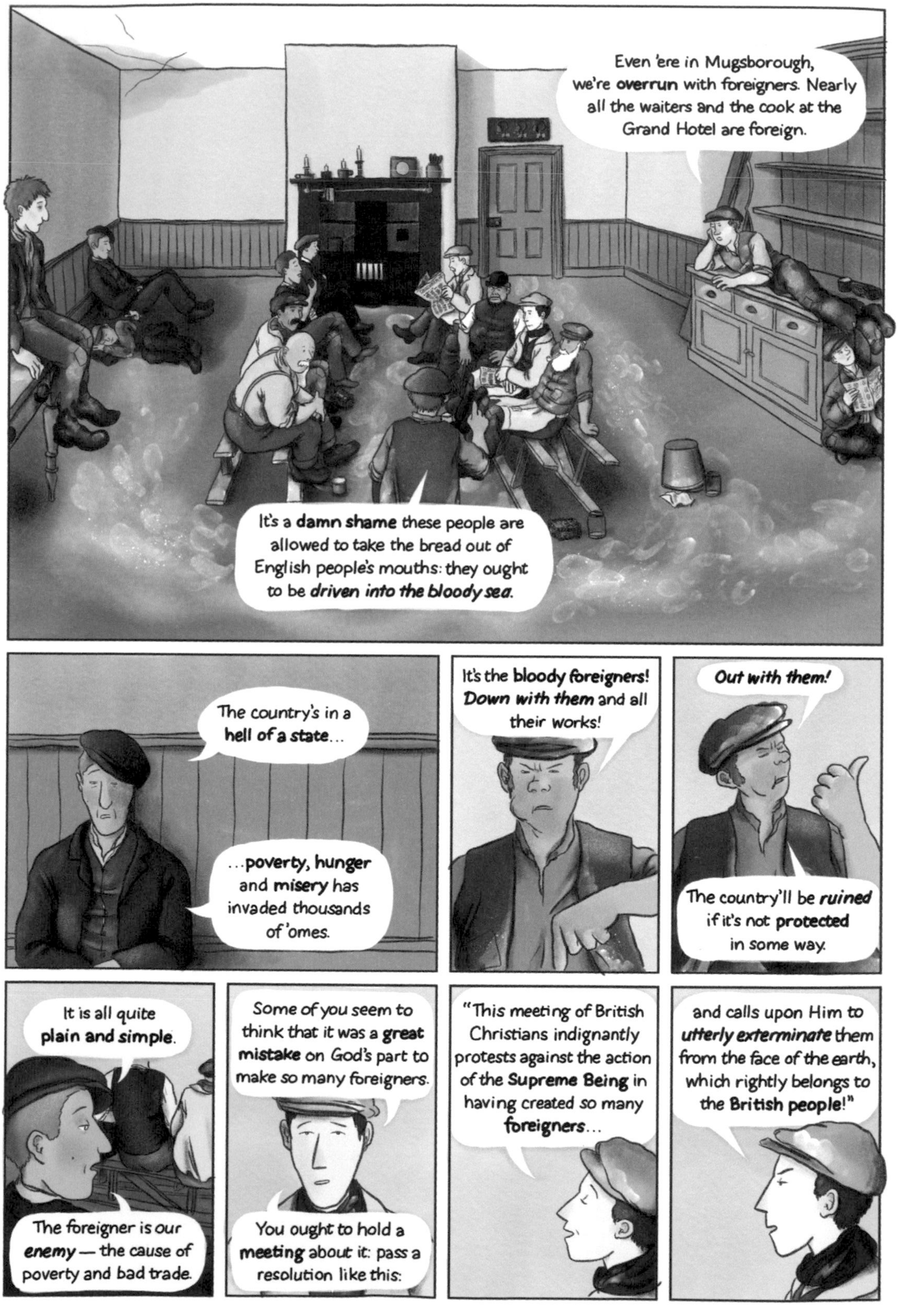
Even 'ere in Mugsborough, we're overrun with foreigners. Nearly all the waiters and the cook at the Grand Hotel are foreign.
It's a damn shame these people are allowed to take the bread out of English people's mouths: they ought to be driven into the bloody sea.
The country's in a hell of a state...
...poverty, hunger and misery has invaded thousands of 'omes.
It's the bloody foreigners! Down with them and all their works!
Out with them!
The country'll be ruined if it's not protected in some way.
It is all quite plain and simple.
The foreigner is our enemy — the cause of poverty and bad trade.
Some of you seem to think that it was a great mistake on God's part to make so many foreigners.
You ought to hold a meeting about it: pass a resolution like this:
"This meeting of British Christians indignantly protests against the action of the Supreme Being in having created so many foreigners...
and calls upon Him to utterly exterminate them from the face of the earth, which rightly belongs to the British people!"

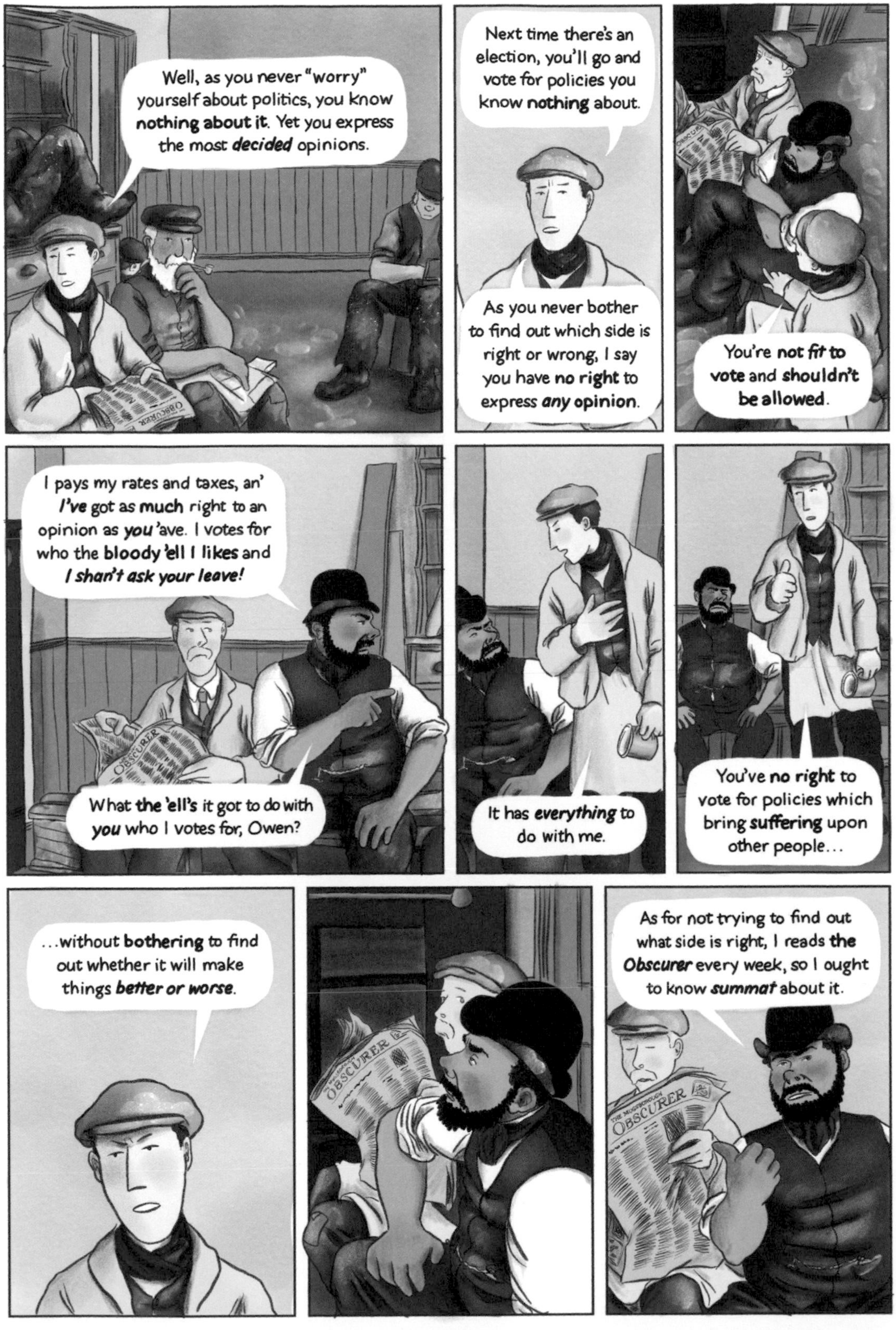
Well, as you never "worry" yourself about politics, you know **nothing about it**. Yet you express the most ***decided*** opinions.
Next time there's an election, you'll go and vote for policies you know **nothing** about.
As you never bother to find out which side is right or wrong, I say you have **no right** to express ***any* opinion**.
You're **not *fit* to vote** and **shouldn't be allowed**.
I pays my rates and taxes, an' ***I've*** got as **much** right to an opinion as ***you*** 'ave. I votes for who the **bloody 'ell I likes** and ***I shan't ask your leave!***
What **the 'ell's** it got to do with ***you*** who I votes for, Owen?
It has ***everything*** to do with me.
You've **no right** to vote for policies which bring **suffering** upon other people...
...without **bothering** to find out whether it will make things ***better or worse***.
As for not trying to find out what side is right, I reads **the *Obscurer*** every week, so I ought to know ***summat*** about it.

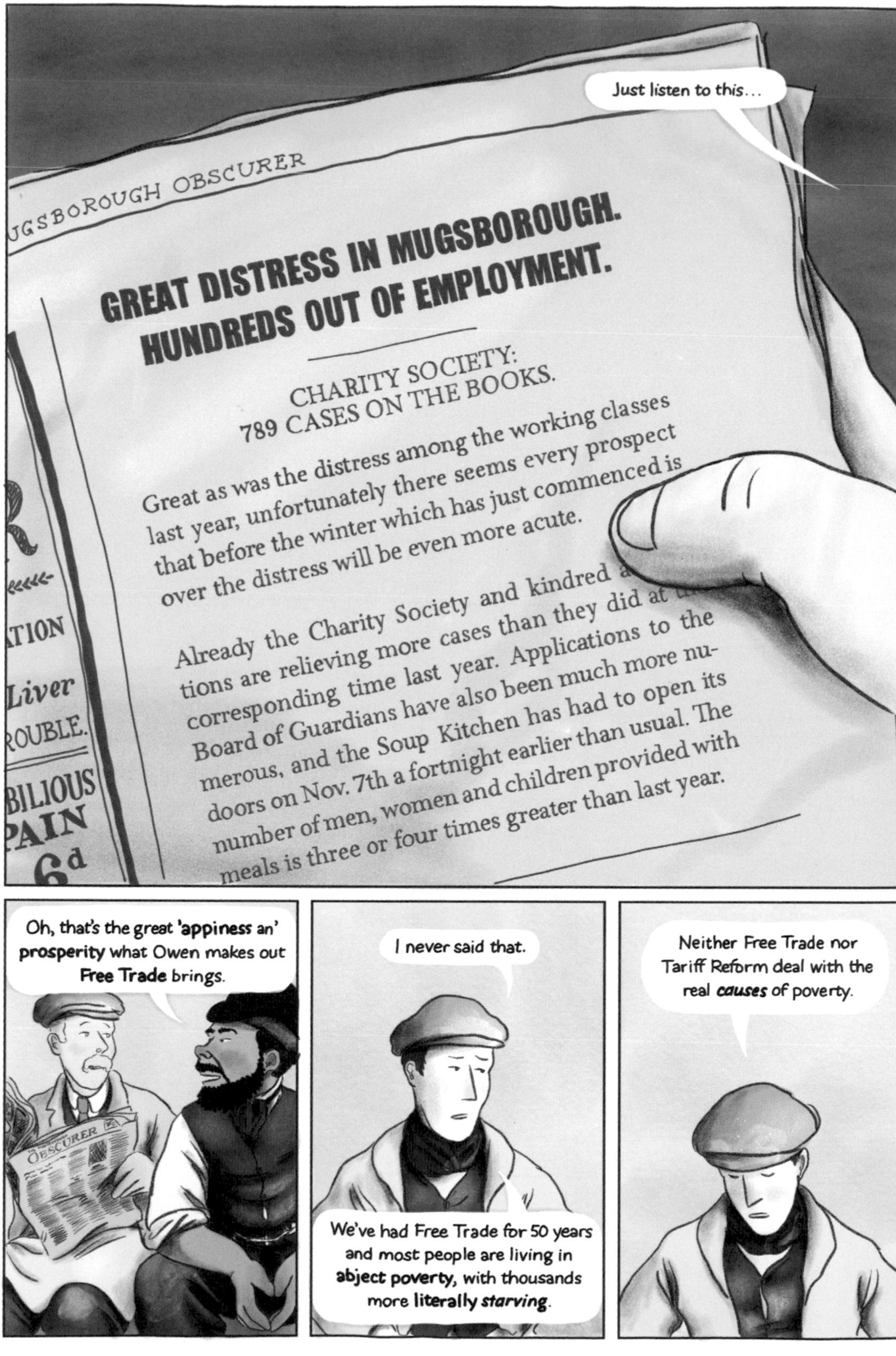
Just listen to this...
UGSBOROUGH OBSCURER
GREAT DISTRESS IN MUGSBOROUGH.
HUNDREDS OUT OF EMPLOYMENT.
CHARITY SOCIETY:
789 CASES ON THE BOOKS.
Great as was the distress among the working classes last year, unfortunately there seems every prospect that before the winter which has just commenced is over the distress will be even more acute.
Already the Charity Society and kindred
tions are relieving more cases than they did at
corresponding time last year. Applications to the Board of Guardians have also been much more numerous, and the Soup Kitchen has had to open its doors on Nov. 7th a fortnight earlier than usual. The number of men, women and children provided with meals is three or four times greater than last year.
TION
Liver
ROUBLE.
BILIOUS
PAIN
6d
Oh, that's the great 'appiness an' prosperity what Owen makes out Free Trade brings.
OBSCURER
I never said that.
We've had Free Trade for 50 years and most people are living in abject poverty, with thousands more literally starving.
Neither Free Trade nor Tariff Reform deal with the real causes of poverty.

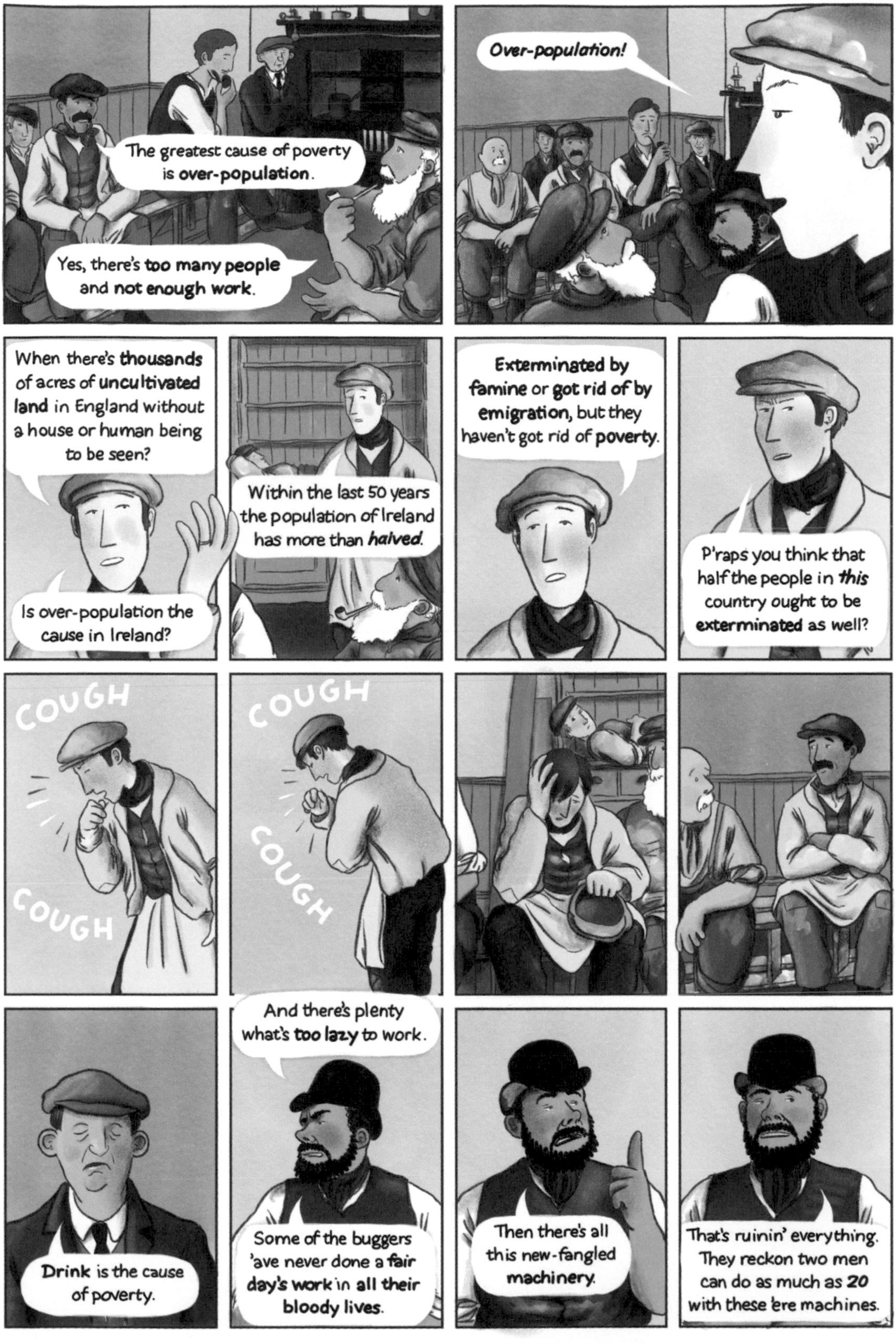
The greatest cause of poverty is over-population.
Yes, there's too many people and not enough work.
Over-population!
When there's thousands of acres of uncultivated land in England without a house or human being to be seen?
Is over-population the cause in Ireland?
Within the last 50 years the population of Ireland has more than halved.
Exterminated by famine or got rid of by emigration, but they haven't got rid of poverty.
P'raps you think that half the people in this country ought to be exterminated as well?
COUGH
COUGH
COUGH
COUGH
Drink is the cause of poverty.
And there's plenty what's too lazy to work.
Some of the buggers 'ave never done a fair day's work in all their bloody lives.
Then there's all this new-fangled machinery.
That's ruinin' everything. They reckon two men can do as much as 20 with these 'ere machines.

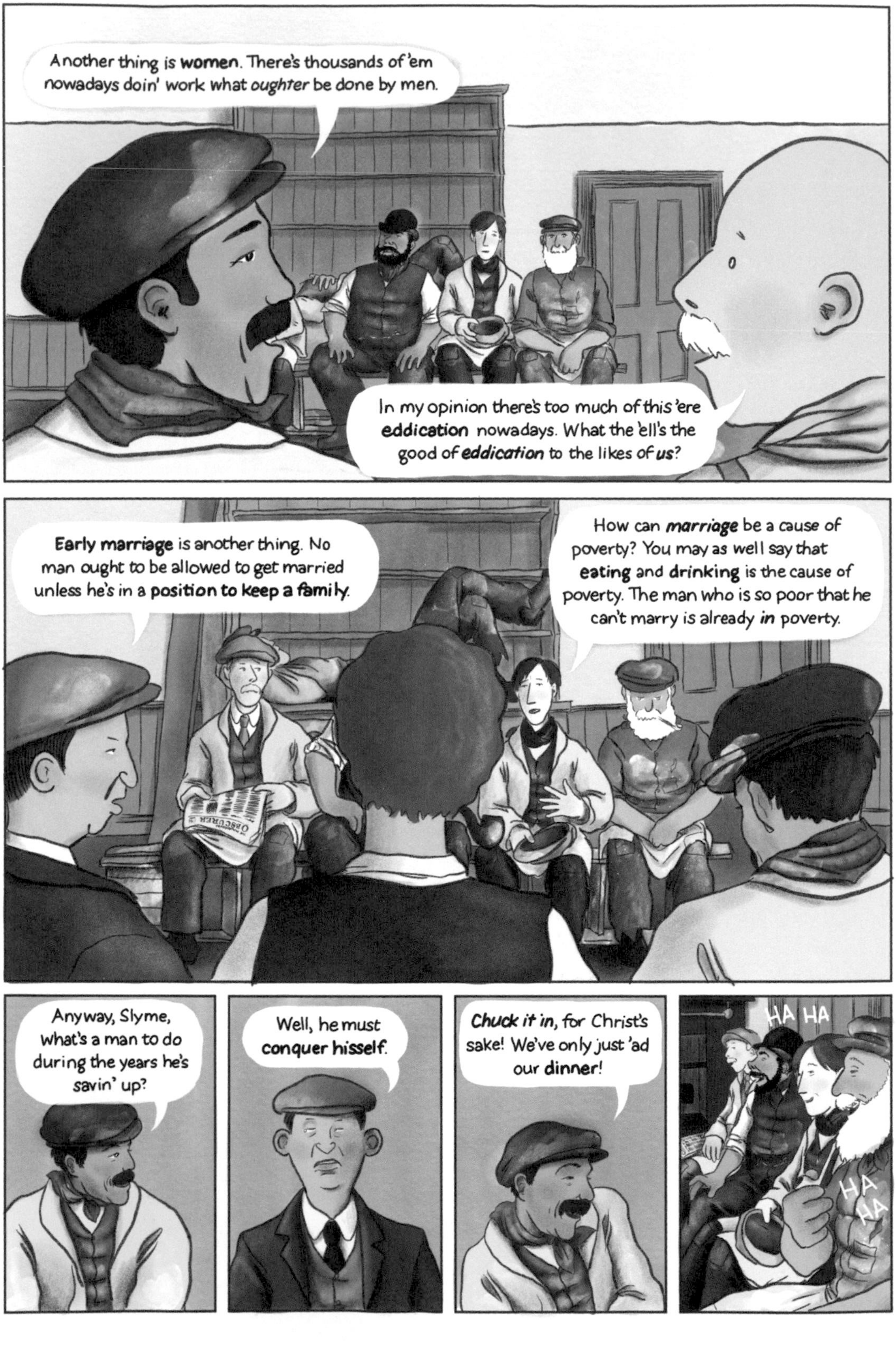
Another thing is **women**. There's thousands of 'em nowadays doin' work what *oughter* be done by men.
In my opinion there's too much of this 'ere **eddication** nowadays. What the 'ell's the good of ***eddication*** to the likes of ***us***?
Early marriage is another thing. No man ought to be allowed to get married unless he's in a **position to keep a family**.
How can ***marriage*** be a cause of poverty? You may as well say that **eating** and **drinking** is the cause of poverty. The man who is so poor that he can't marry is already ***in*** poverty.
Anyway, Slyme, what's a man to do during the years he's savin' up?
Well, he must **conquer hisself**.
Chuck it in, for Christ's sake! We've only just 'ad our **dinner**!
HA HA
HA HA

And what about **drink**?

'Ear, 'ear, **that's** the bleedin' talk.

I wouldn't mind 'arf a pint **now**, if someone'll pay for it!

Don't blame **drink** or **laziness**, because they've **nothing** to do with it.

If all the drunks and skives were transformed into sober, industrious and skilled workers tomorrow, it would be **even worse** for us, because there isn't enough work **now**.

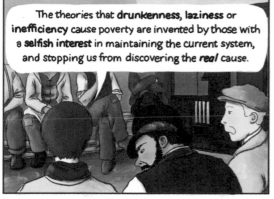

The theories that **drunkenness**, **laziness** or **inefficiency** cause poverty are invented by those with a **selfish interest** in maintaining the current system, and stopping us from discovering the **real** cause.

Well, since **we're all wrong**, p'raps **you** can tell us what the **real** cause is?

And how it's to be **altered**?

Yes, I think I can tell you...

It can't **never** be altered.

There's **always** been **rich and poor** in the world, and there **always** will be.

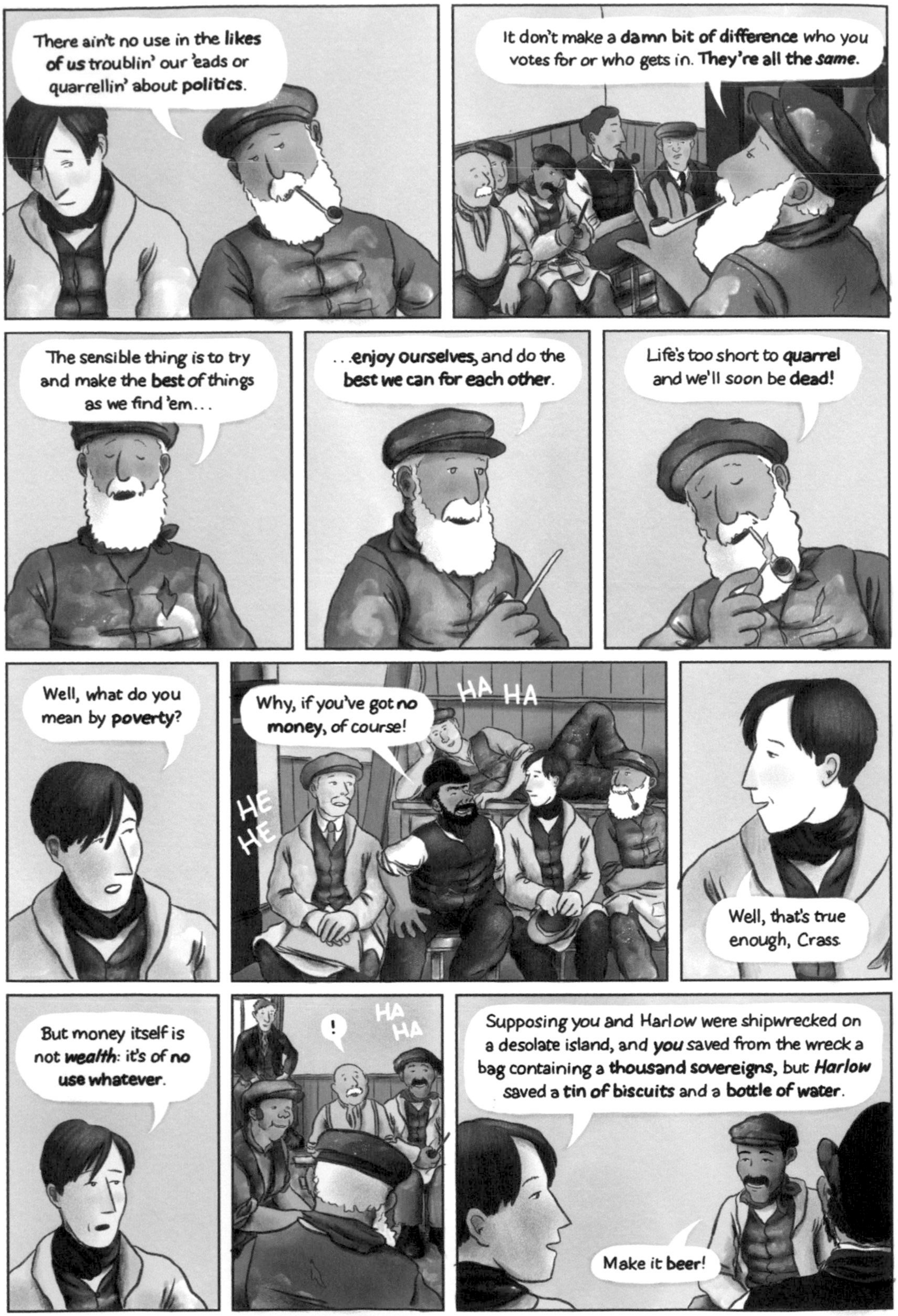
There ain't no use in the likes of us troublin' our 'eads or quarrellin' about politics.
It don't make a damn bit of difference who you votes for or who gets in. They're all the same.
The sensible thing is to try and make the best of things as we find 'em...
...enjoy ourselves, and do the best we can for each other.
Life's too short to quarrel and we'll soon be dead!
Well, what do you mean by poverty?
Why, if you've got no money, of course!
HA HA
HE HE
Well, that's true enough, Crass.
But money itself is not wealth: it's of no use whatever.
!
HA HA
Supposing you and Harlow were shipwrecked on a desolate island, and you saved from the wreck a bag containing a thousand sovereigns, but Harlow saved a tin of biscuits and a bottle of water.
Make it beer!

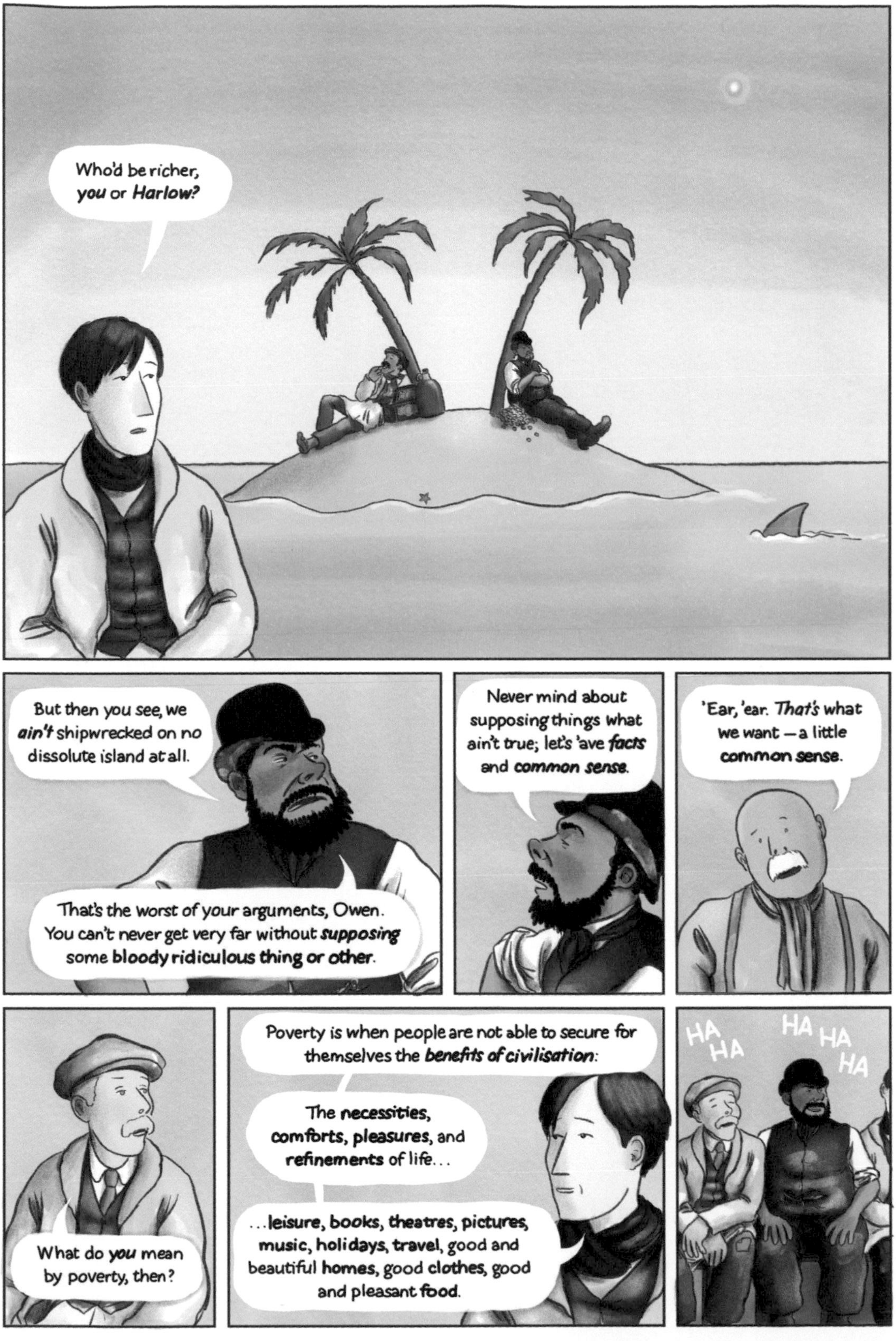
Who'd be richer, you or Harlow?
But then you see, we ain't shipwrecked on no dissolute island at all.
That's the worst of your arguments, Owen. You can't never get very far without supposing some bloody ridiculous thing or other.
Never mind about supposing things what ain't true; let's 'ave facts and common sense.
'Ear, 'ear. That's what we want — a little common sense.
What do you mean by poverty, then?
Poverty is when people are not able to secure for themselves the benefits of civilisation:
The necessities, comforts, pleasures, and refinements of life...
...leisure, books, theatres, pictures, music, holidays, travel, good and beautiful homes, good clothes, good and pleasant food.
HA HA
HA HA HA

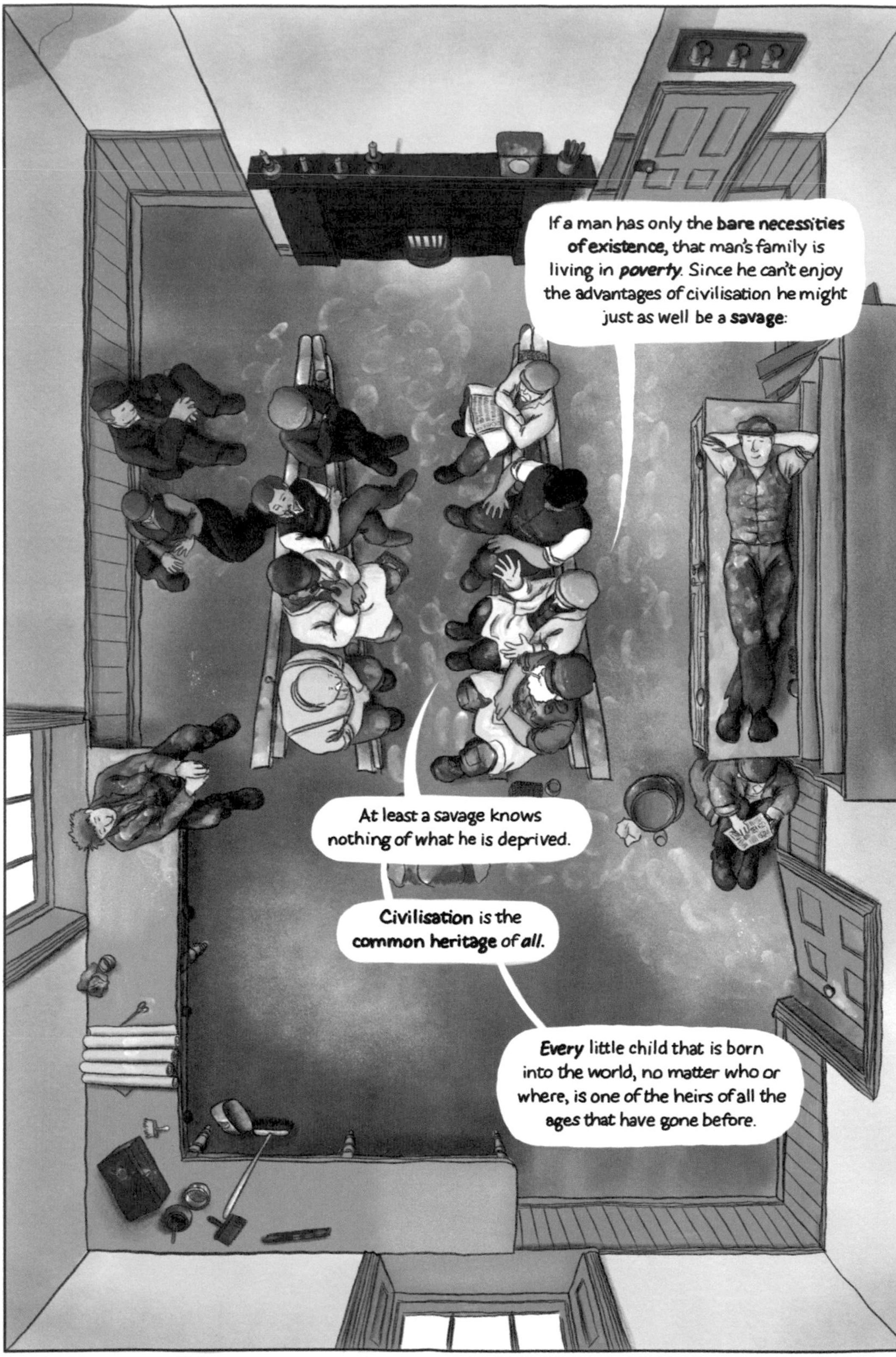
If a man has only the bare necessities of existence, that man's family is living in poverty. Since he can't enjoy the advantages of civilisation he might just as well be a savage.
At least a savage knows nothing of what he is deprived.
Civilisation is the common heritage of all.
Every little child that is born into the world, no matter who or where, is one of the heirs of all the ages that have gone before.

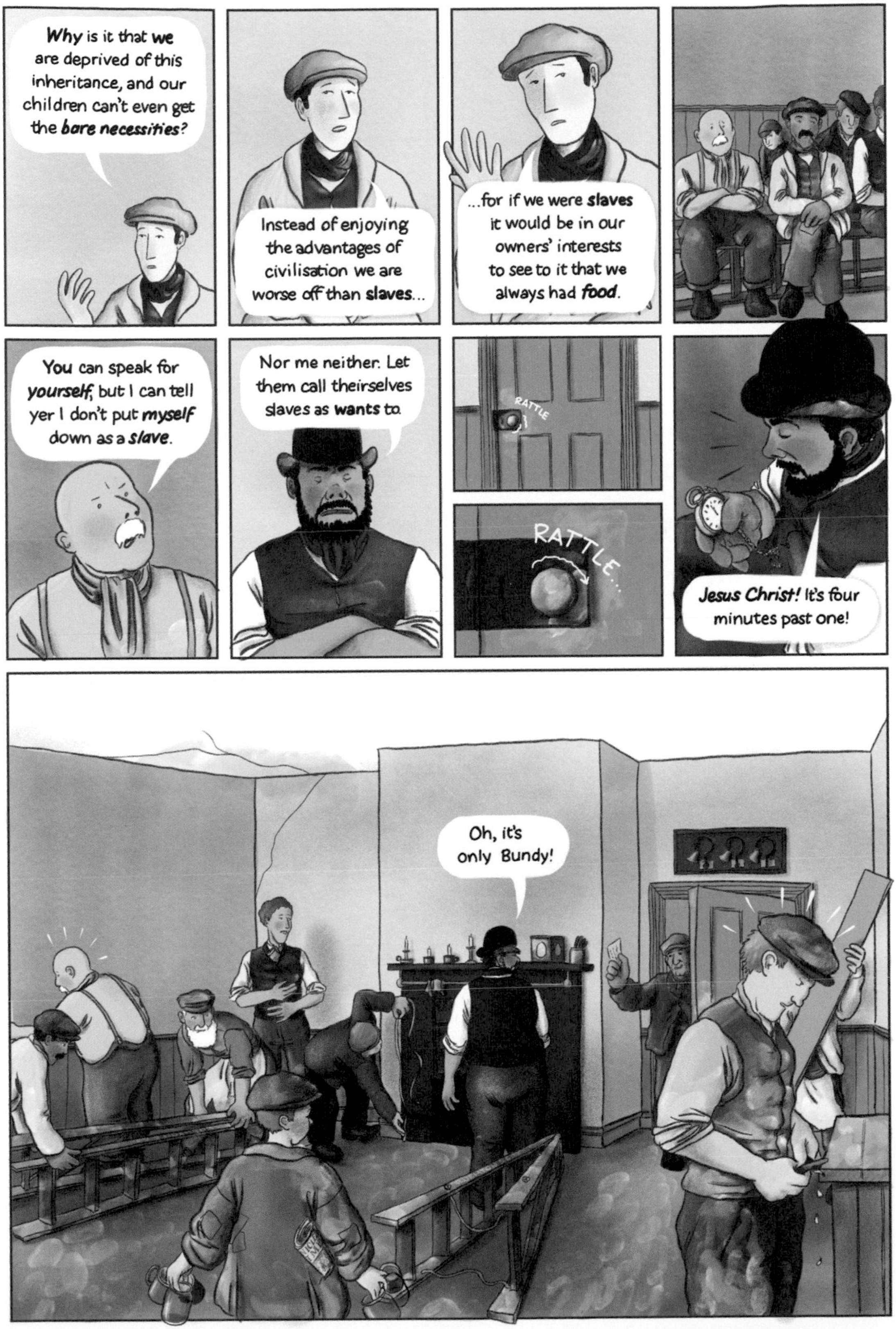
Why is it that we are deprived of this inheritance, and our children can't even get the bare necessities?
Instead of enjoying the advantages of civilisation we are worse off than slaves...
...for if we were slaves it would be in our owners' interests to see to it that we always had food.
You can speak for yourself, but I can tell yer I don't put myself down as a slave.
Nor me neither. Let them call theirselves slaves as wants to.
RATTLE
RATTLE...
Jesus Christ! It's four minutes past one!
Oh, it's only Bundy!

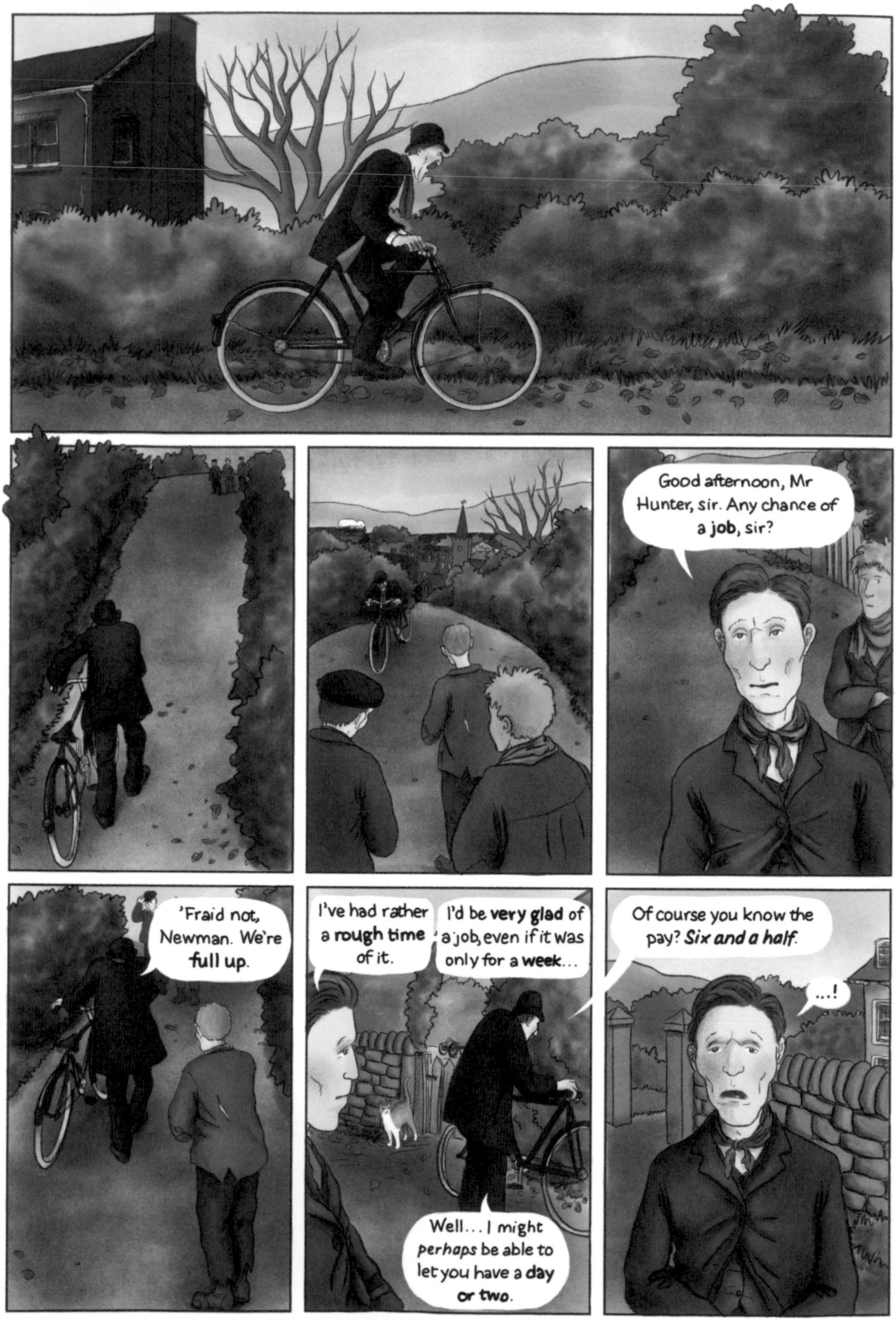
Good afternoon, Mr Hunter, sir. Any chance of a **job**, sir?
'Fraid not, Newman. We're **full up**.
I've had rather a **rough time** of it.
I'd be **very glad** of a job, even if it was only for a **week**...
Well... I might *perhaps* be able to let you have a **day or two**.
Of course you know the pay? ***Six and a half***.
...!

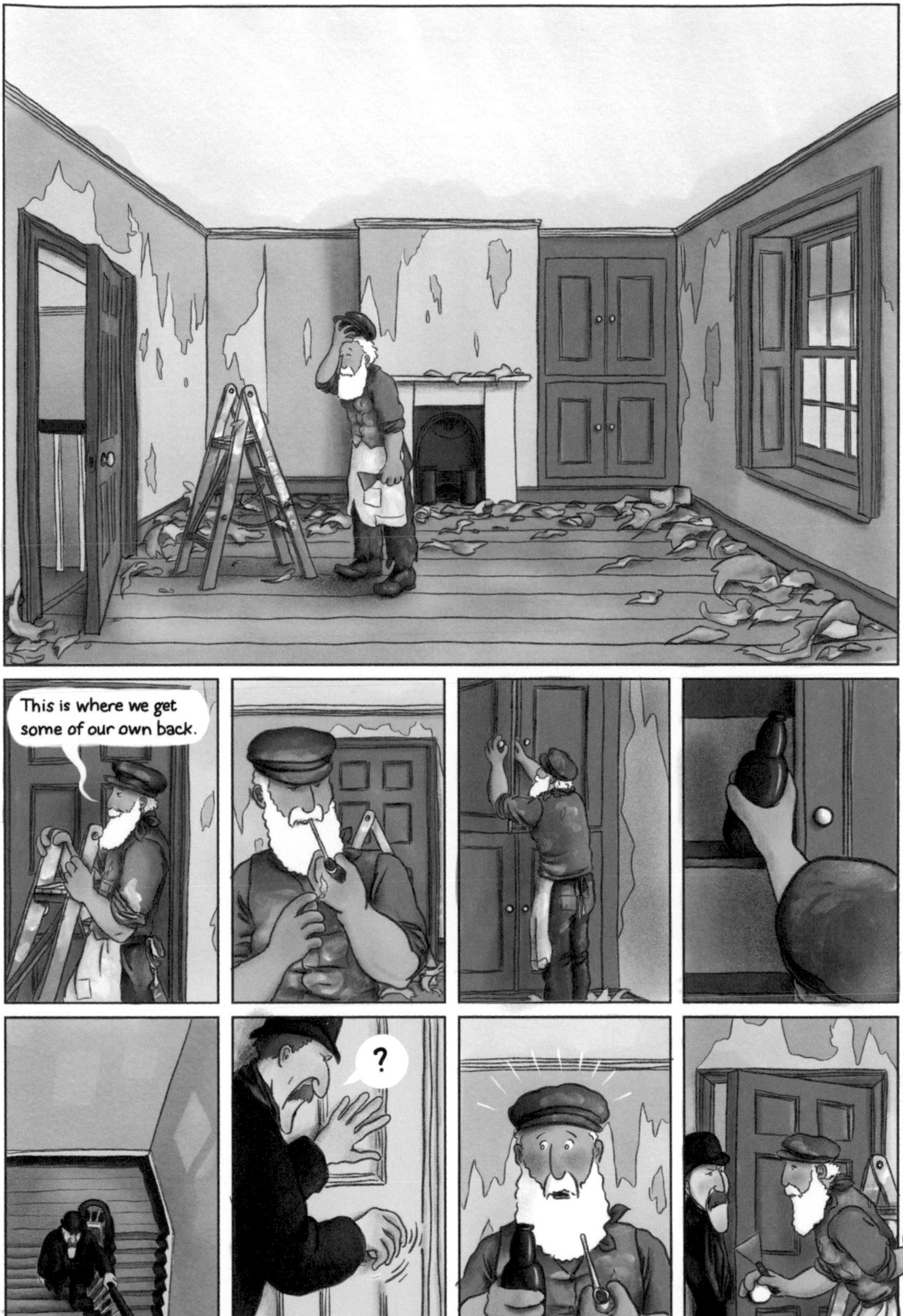
This is where we get some of our own back.
?

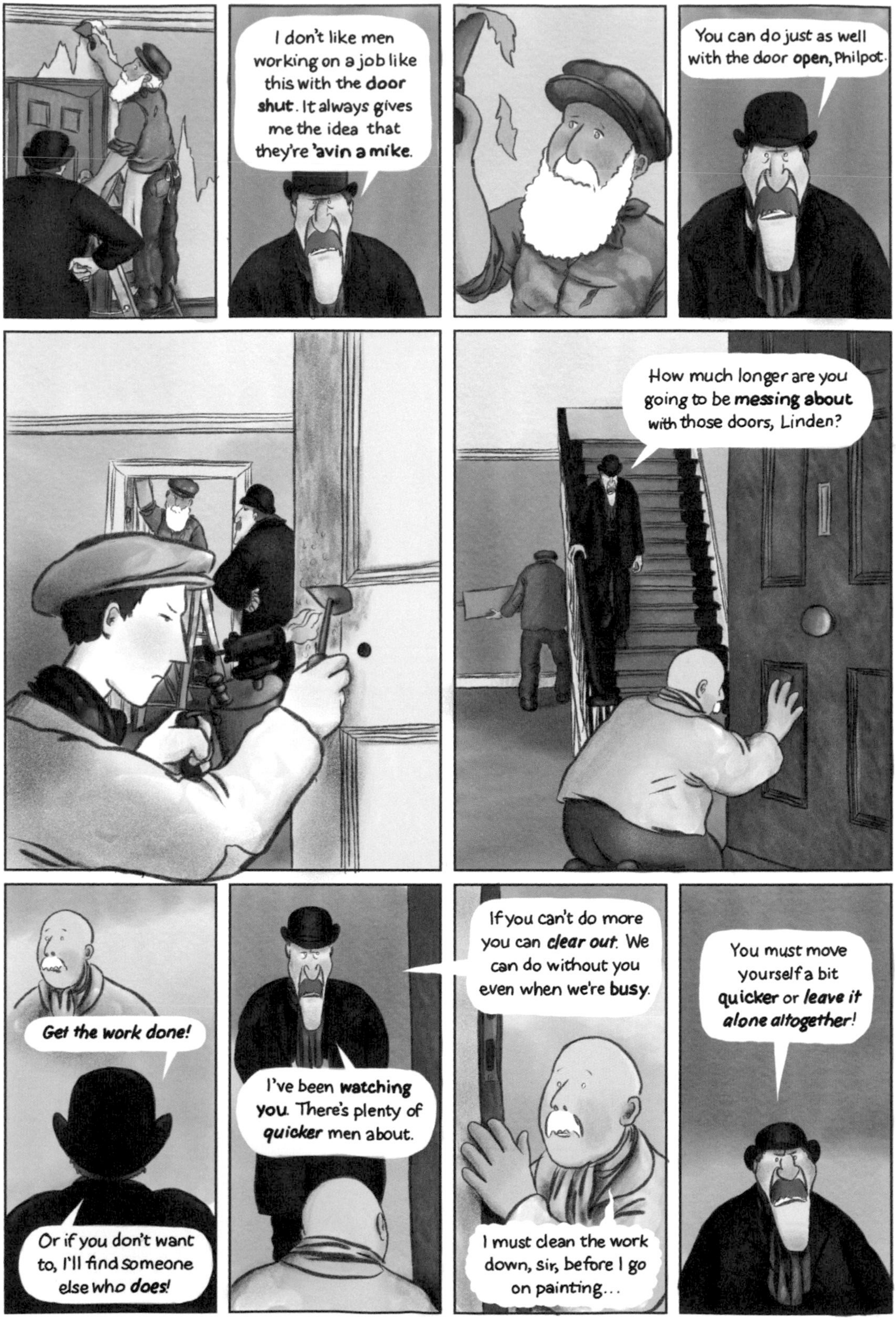
I don't like men working on a job like this with the door shut. It always gives me the idea that they're 'avin a mike.
You can do just as well with the door open, Philpot.
How much longer are you going to be messing about with those doors, Linden?
Get the work done!
Or if you don't want to, I'll find someone else who does!
I've been watching you. There's plenty of quicker men about.
If you can't do more you can clear out. We can do without you even when we're busy.
I must clean the work down, sir, before I go on painting...
You must move yourself a bit quicker or leave it alone altogether!

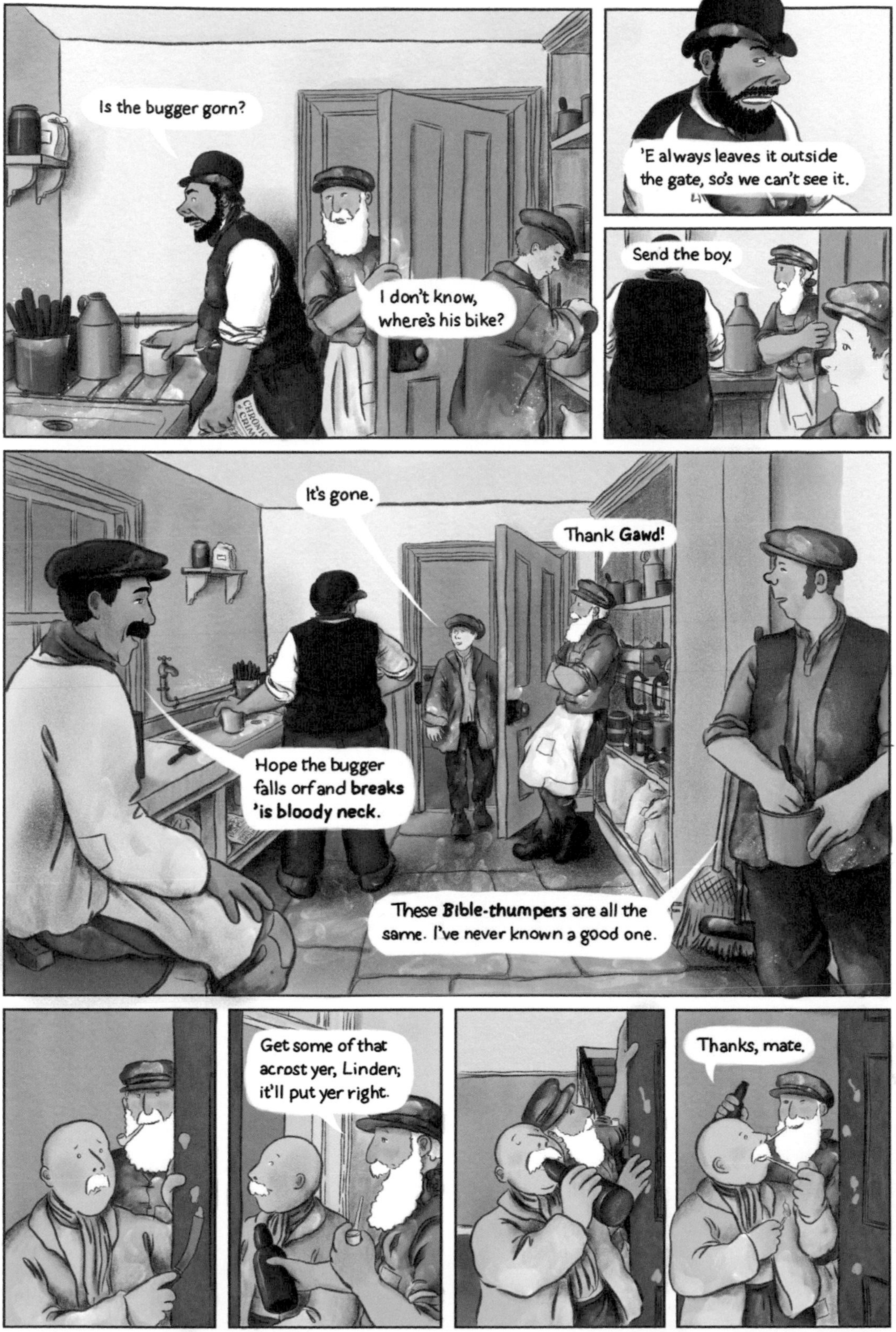
Is the bugger gorn?
I don't know, where's his bike?
'E always leaves it outside the gate, so's we can't see it.
Send the boy.
It's gone.
Thank **Gawd!**
Hope the bugger falls orf and **breaks 'is bloody neck.**
These **Bible-thumpers** are all the same. I've never known a good one.
Get some of that acrost yer, Linden; it'll put yer right.
Thanks, mate.

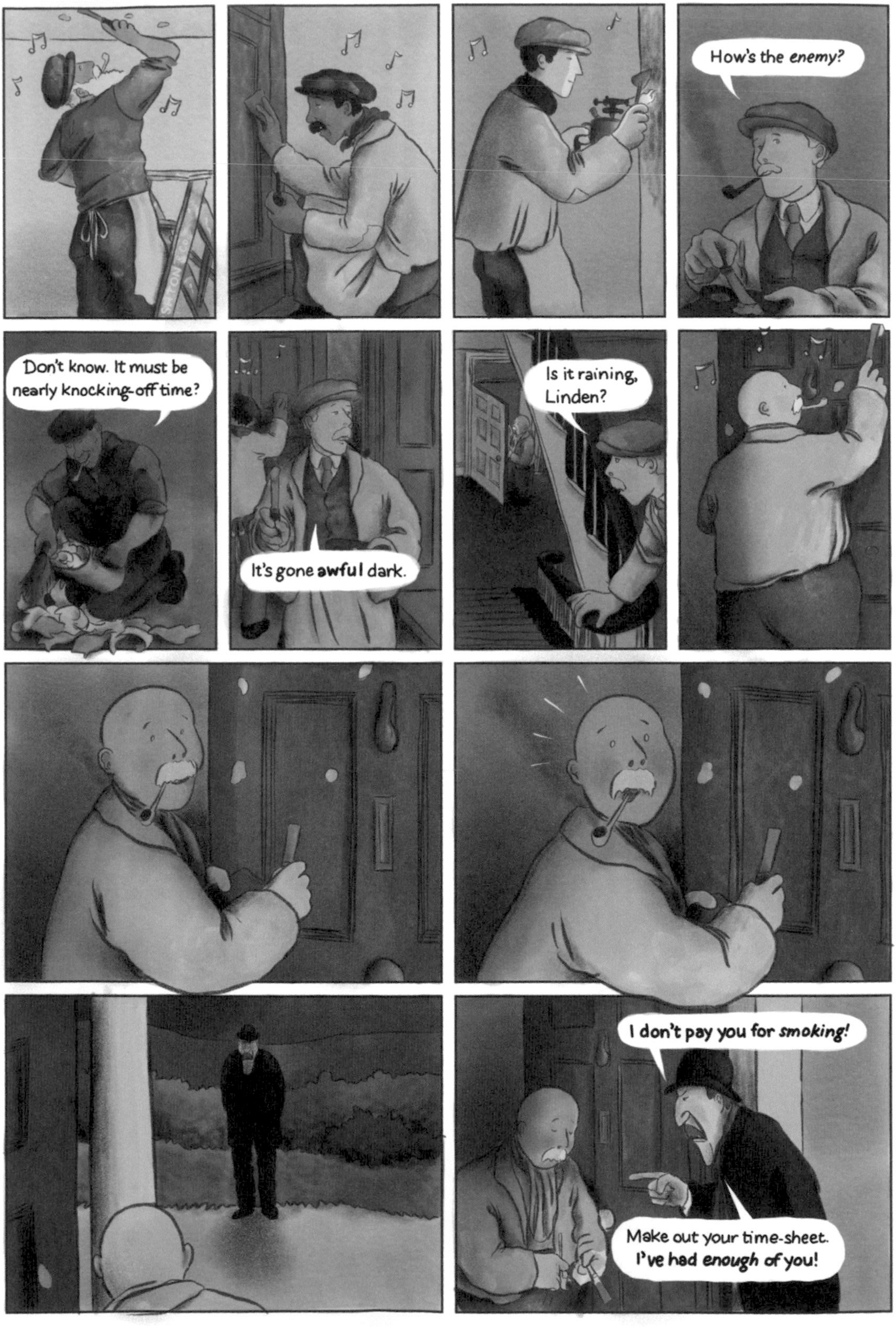
How's the *enemy?*
Don't know. It must be nearly knocking-off time?
It's gone **awful** dark.
Is it raining, Linden?
I don't pay you for *smoking!*
Make out your time-sheet.
I've had *enough* of you!

2

The LORD our

Shapherd

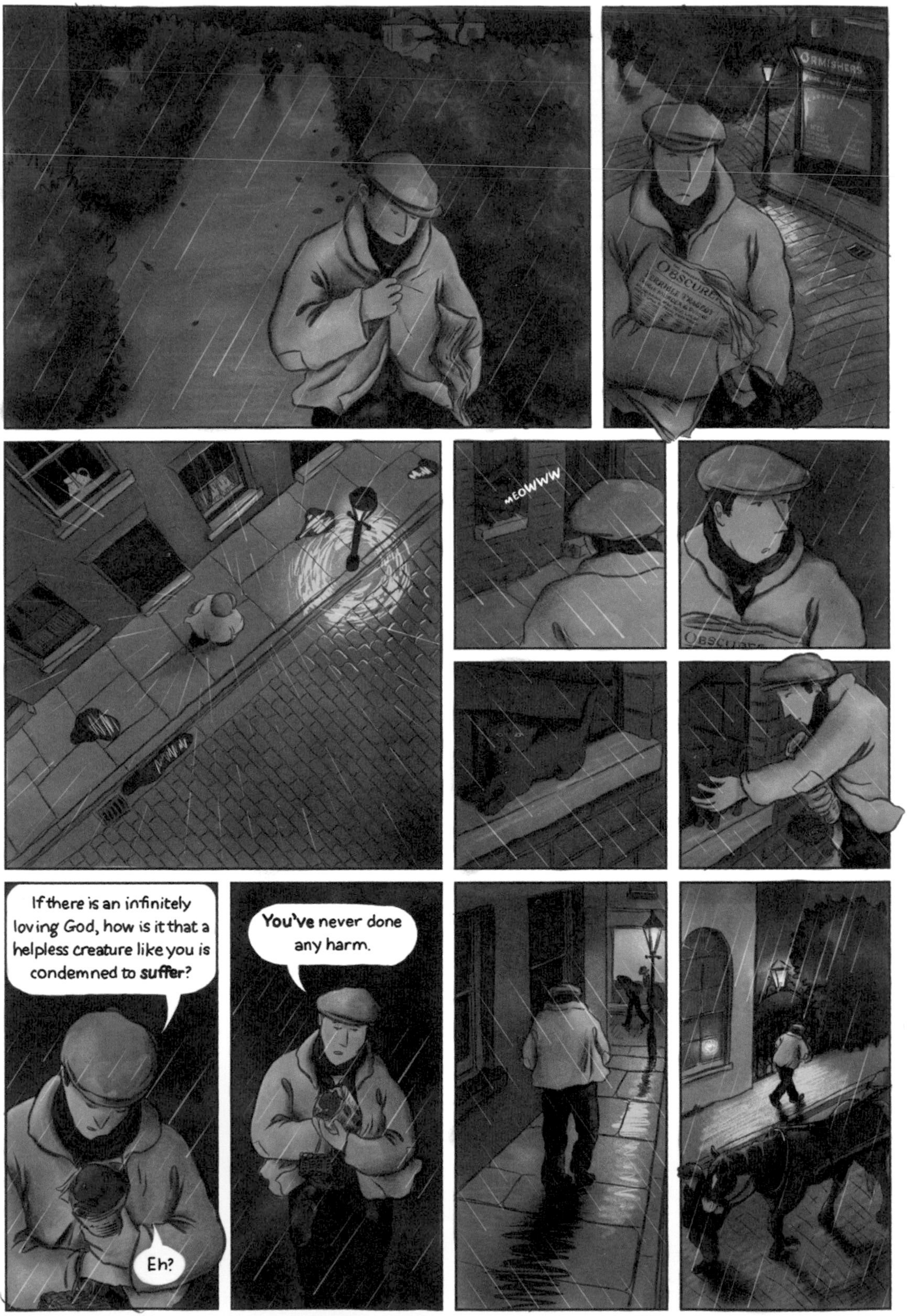
ORMISHERS
OBSCURER
TERRIBLE TRAGEDY
MEOWWW
If there is an infinitely loving God, how is it that a helpless creature like you is condemned to suffer?
Eh?
You've never done any harm.

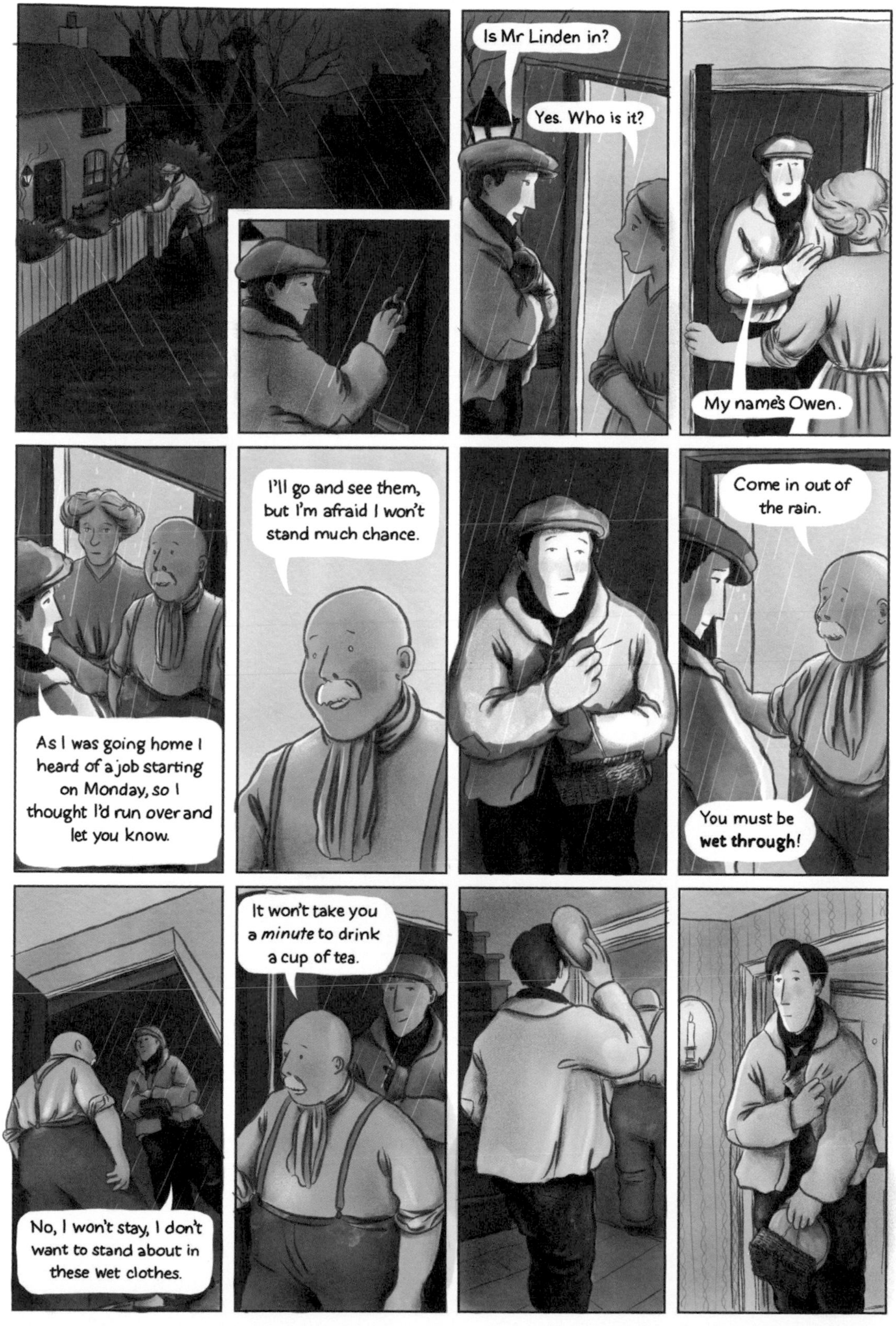
Is Mr Linden in?
Yes. Who is it?
My name's Owen.
As I was going home I heard of a job starting on Monday, so I thought I'd run over and let you know.
I'll go and see them, but I'm afraid I won't stand much chance.
Come in out of the rain.
You must be **wet through**!
No, I won't stay, I don't want to stand about in these wet clothes.
It won't take you a *minute* to drink a cup of tea.

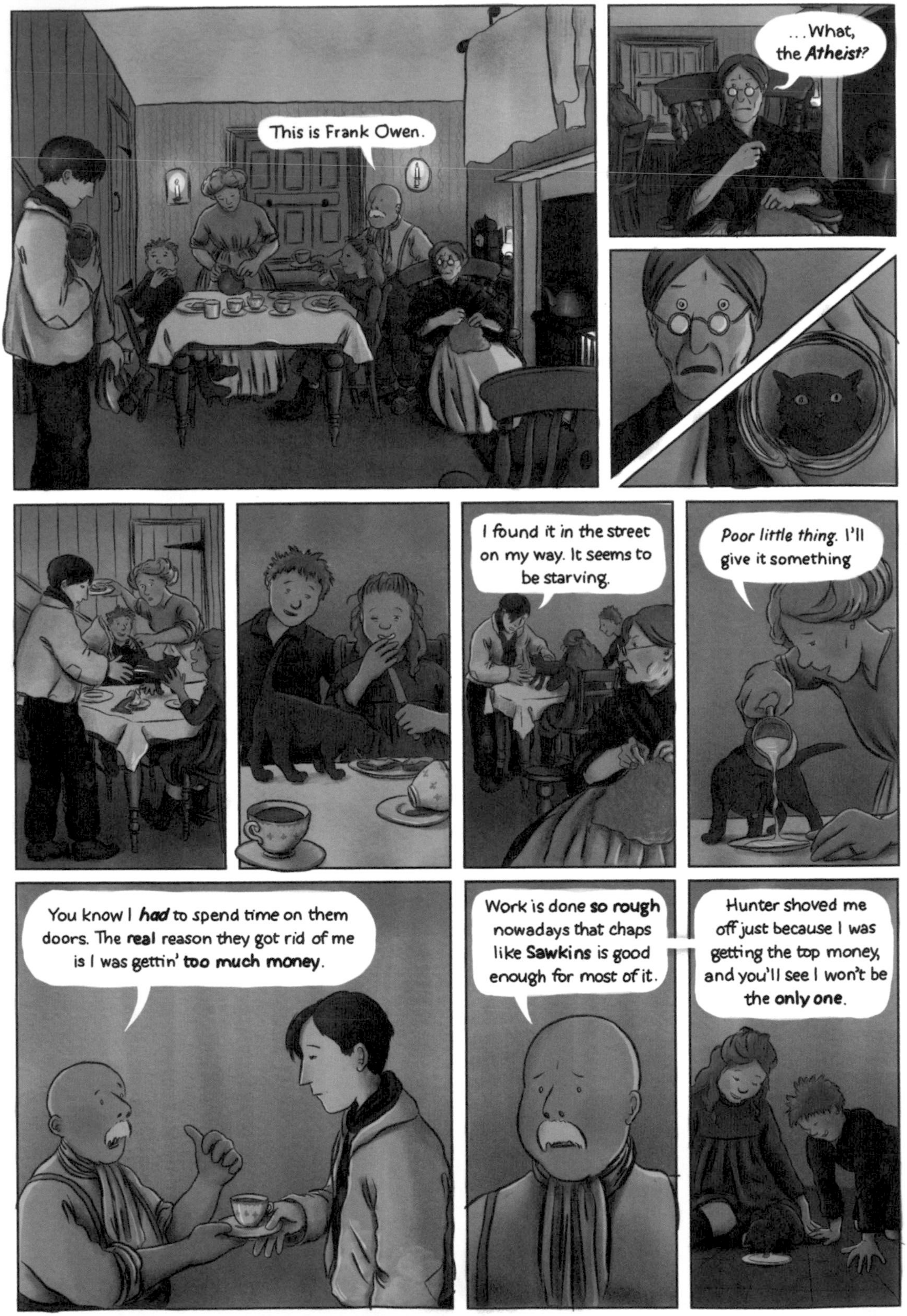
This is Frank Owen.
...What, the *Atheist?*
I found it in the street on my way. It seems to be starving.
Poor little thing. I'll give it something
You know I ***had*** to spend time on them doors. The **real** reason they got rid of me is I was gettin' **too much money**.
Work is done **so rough** nowadays that chaps like **Sawkins** is good enough for most of it.
Hunter shoved me off just because I was getting the top money, and you'll see I won't be the **only one**.

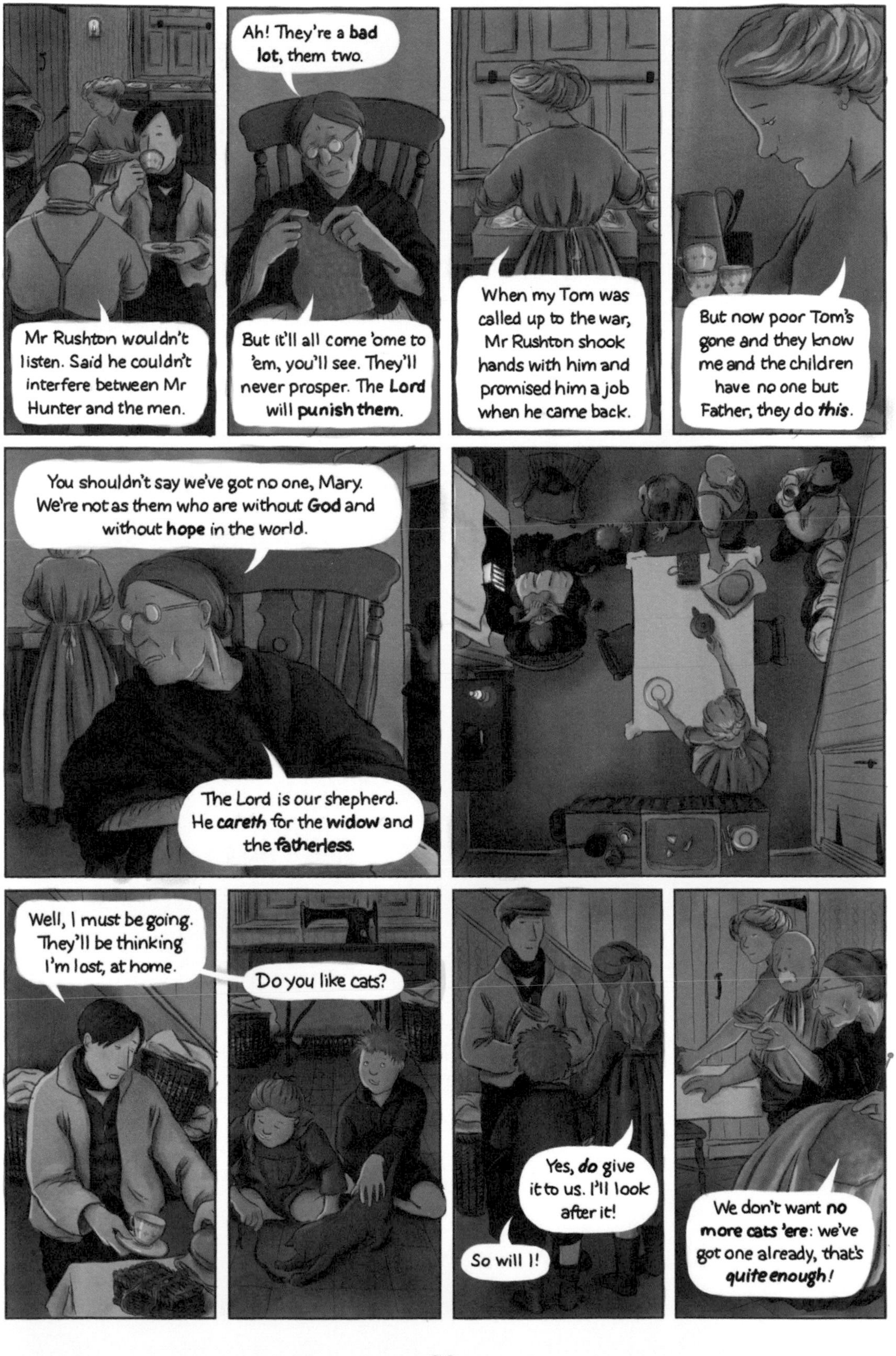
Mr Rushton wouldn't listen. Said he couldn't interfere between Mr Hunter and the men.
Ah! They're a **bad lot**, them two.
But it'll all come 'ome to 'em, you'll see. They'll never prosper. The **Lord** will **punish them**.
When my Tom was called up to the war, Mr Rushton shook hands with him and promised him a job when he came back.
But now poor Tom's gone and they know me and the children have no one but Father, they do ***this***.
You shouldn't say we've got no one, Mary. We're not as them who are without **God** and without **hope** in the world.
The Lord is our shepherd. He ***careth*** for the **widow** and the ***fatherless***.
Well, I must be going. They'll be thinking I'm lost, at home.
Do you like cats?
Yes, ***do*** give it to us. I'll look after it!
So will I!
We don't want **no more cats 'ere**: we've got one already, that's ***quite enough!***

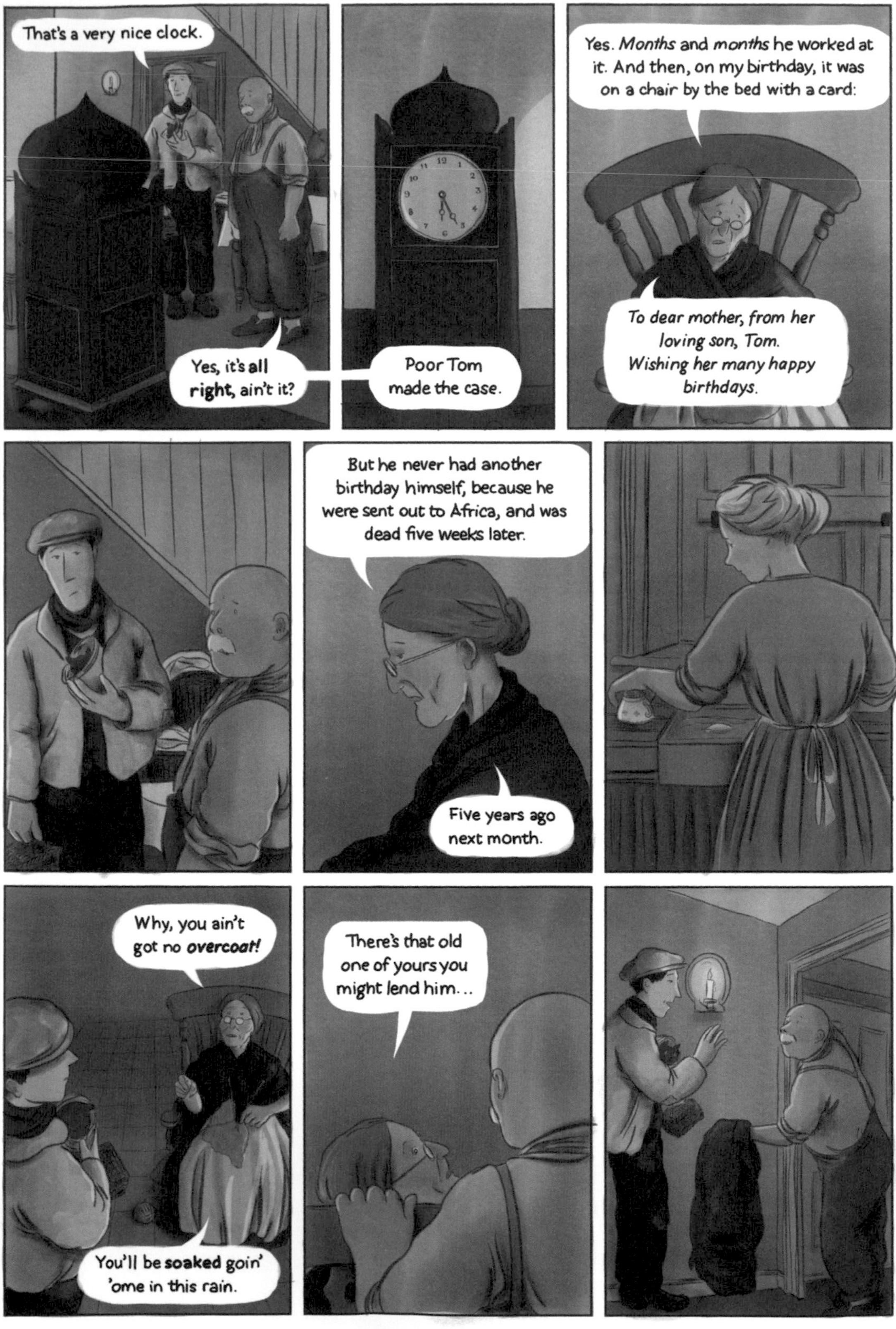
That's a very nice clock.
Yes, it's **all right**, ain't it?
Poor Tom made the case.
Yes. *Months* and *months* he worked at it. And then, on my birthday, it was on a chair by the bed with a card:
To dear mother, from her loving son, Tom. Wishing her many happy birthdays.
But he never had another birthday himself, because he were sent out to Africa, and was dead five weeks later.
Five years ago next month.
Why, you ain't got no ***overcoat!***
You'll be **soaked** goin' 'ome in this rain.
There's that old one of yours you might lend him...

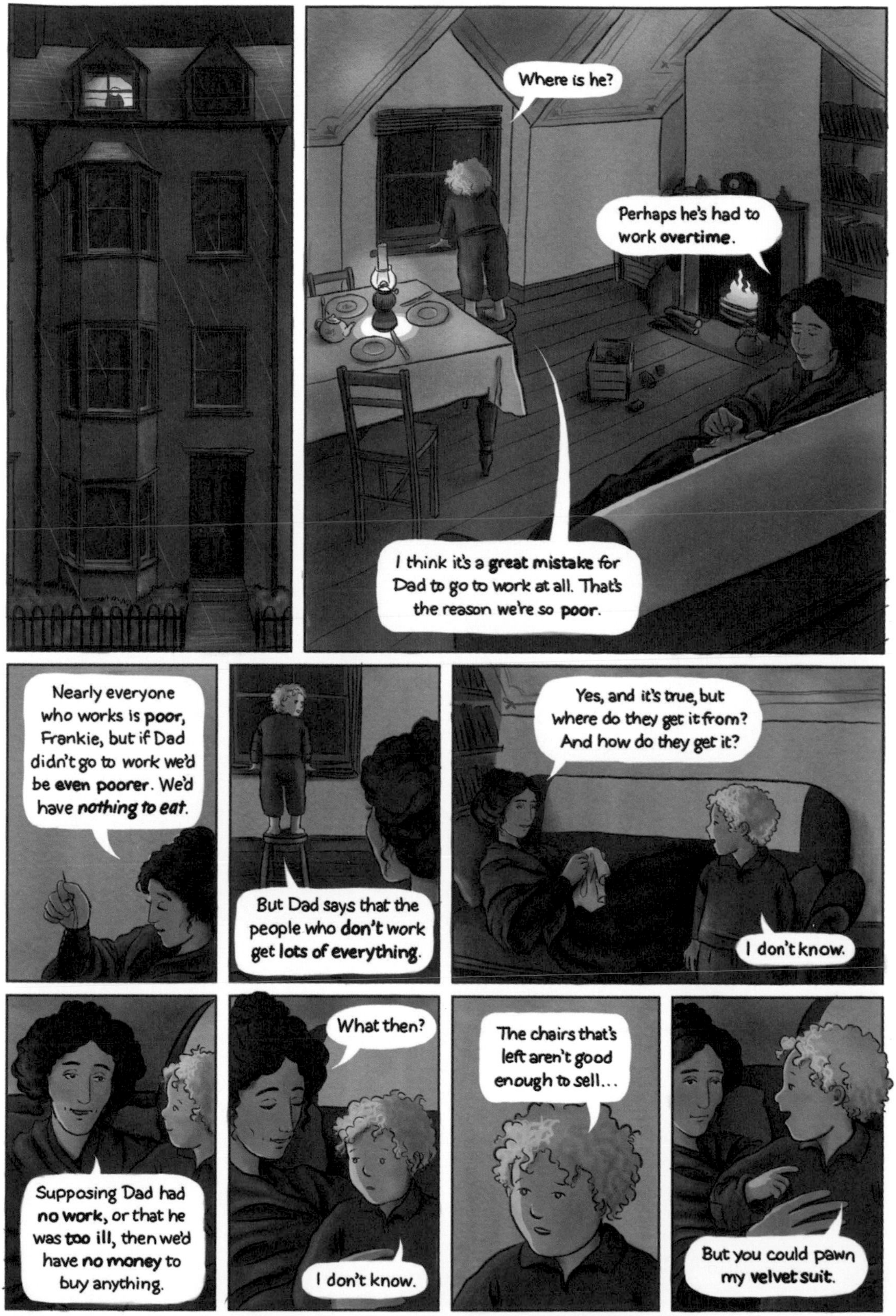
Where is he?
Perhaps he's had to work overtime.
I think it's a great mistake for Dad to go to work at all. That's the reason we're so poor.
Nearly everyone who works is poor, Frankie, but if Dad didn't go to work we'd be even poorer. We'd have nothing to eat.
But Dad says that the people who don't work get lots of everything.
Yes, and it's true, but where do they get it from? And how do they get it?
I don't know.
Supposing Dad had no work, or that he was too ill, then we'd have no money to buy anything.
What then?
I don't know.
The chairs that's left aren't good enough to sell...
But you could pawn my velvet suit.

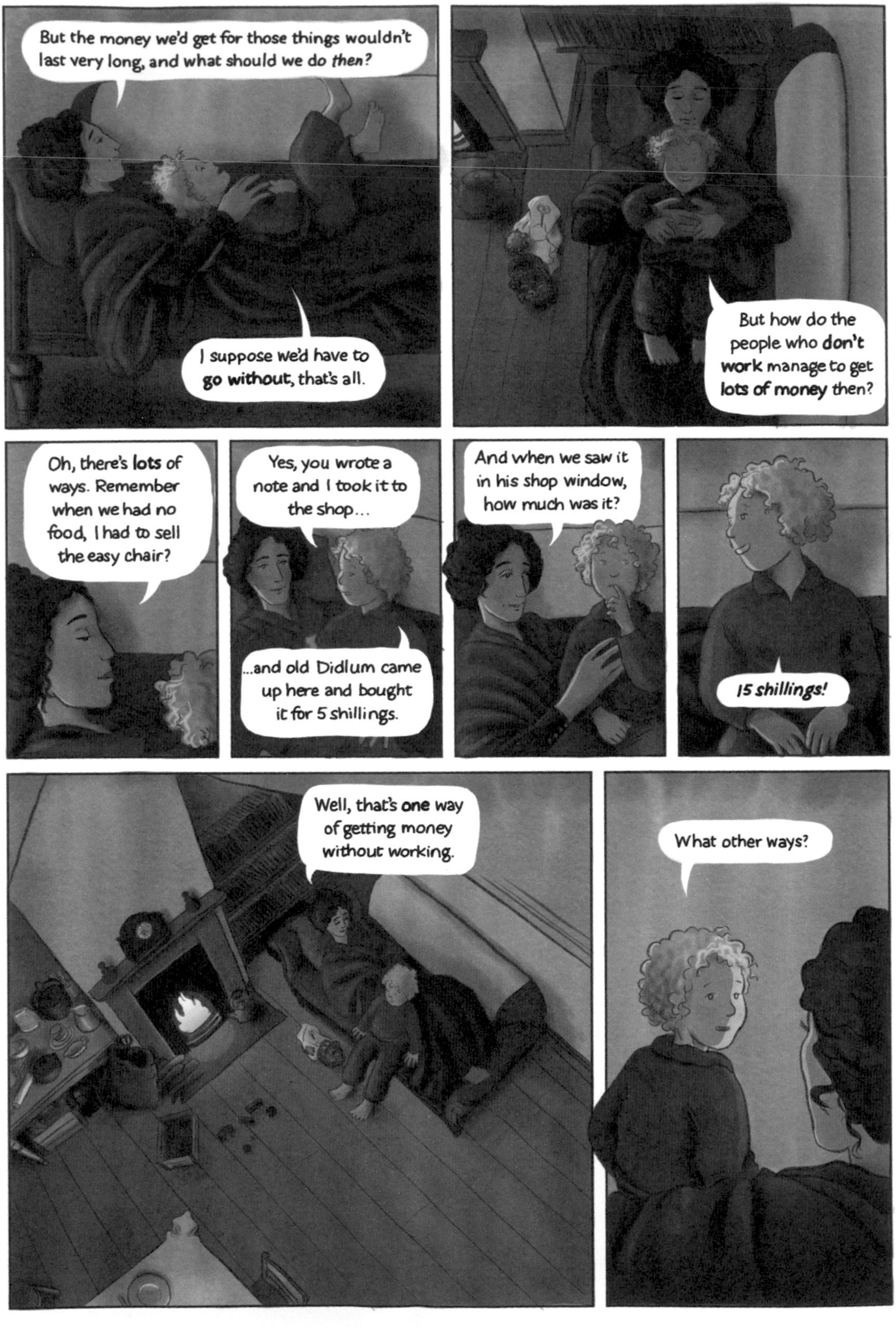
But the money we'd get for those things wouldn't last very long, and what should we do *then?*
I suppose we'd have to **go without**, that's all.
But how do the people who **don't work** manage to get **lots of money** then?
Oh, there's **lots** of ways. Remember when we had no food, I had to sell the easy chair?
Yes, you wrote a note and I took it to the shop...
...and old Didlum came up here and bought it for 5 shillings.
And when we saw it in his shop window, how much was it?
15 shillings!
Well, that's **one** way of getting money without working.
What other ways?

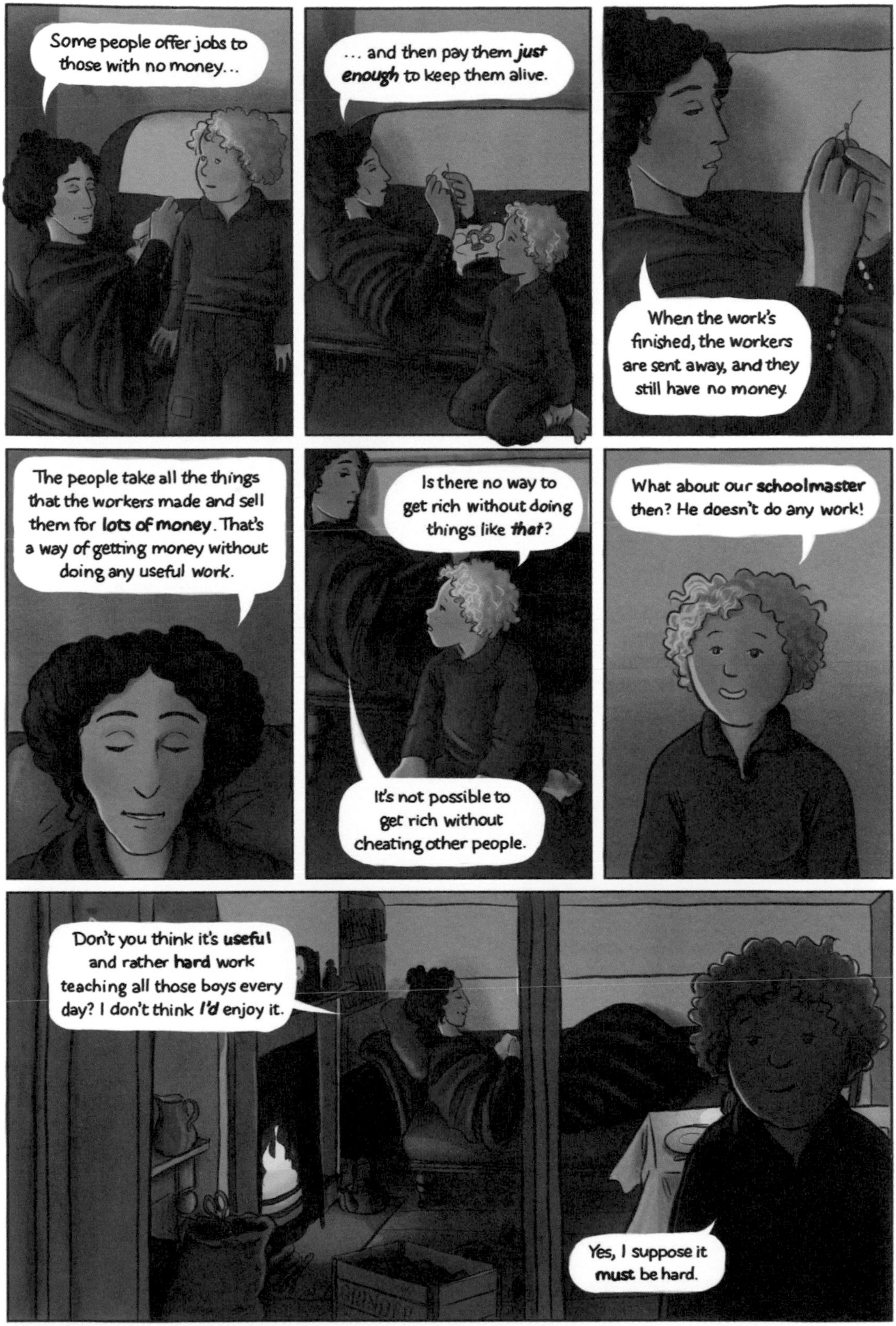
Some people offer jobs to those with no money...
... and then pay them just enough to keep them alive.
When the work's finished, the workers are sent away, and they still have no money.
The people take all the things that the workers made and sell them for lots of money. That's a way of getting money without doing any useful work.
Is there no way to get rich without doing things like that?
It's not possible to get rich without cheating other people.
What about our schoolmaster then? He doesn't do any work!
Don't you think it's useful and rather hard work teaching all those boys every day? I don't think I'd enjoy it.
Yes, I suppose it must be hard.

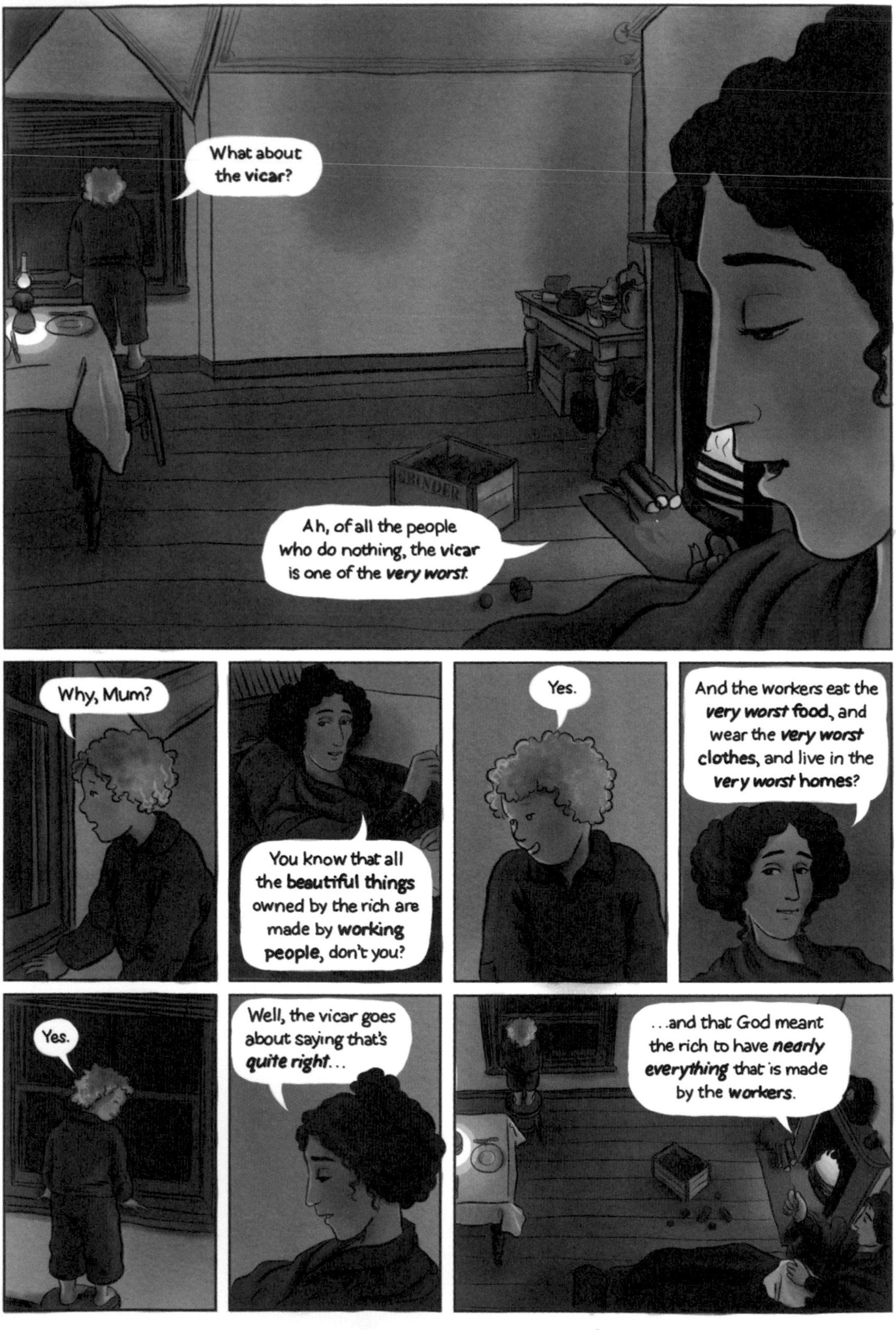
What about the vicar?
Ah, of all the people who do nothing, the vicar is one of the very worst.
GRINDER
Why, Mum?
You know that all the beautiful things owned by the rich are made by working people, don't you?
Yes.
And the workers eat the very worst food, and wear the very worst clothes, and live in the very worst homes?
Yes.
Well, the vicar goes about saying that's quite right...
...and that God meant the rich to have nearly everything that is made by the workers.

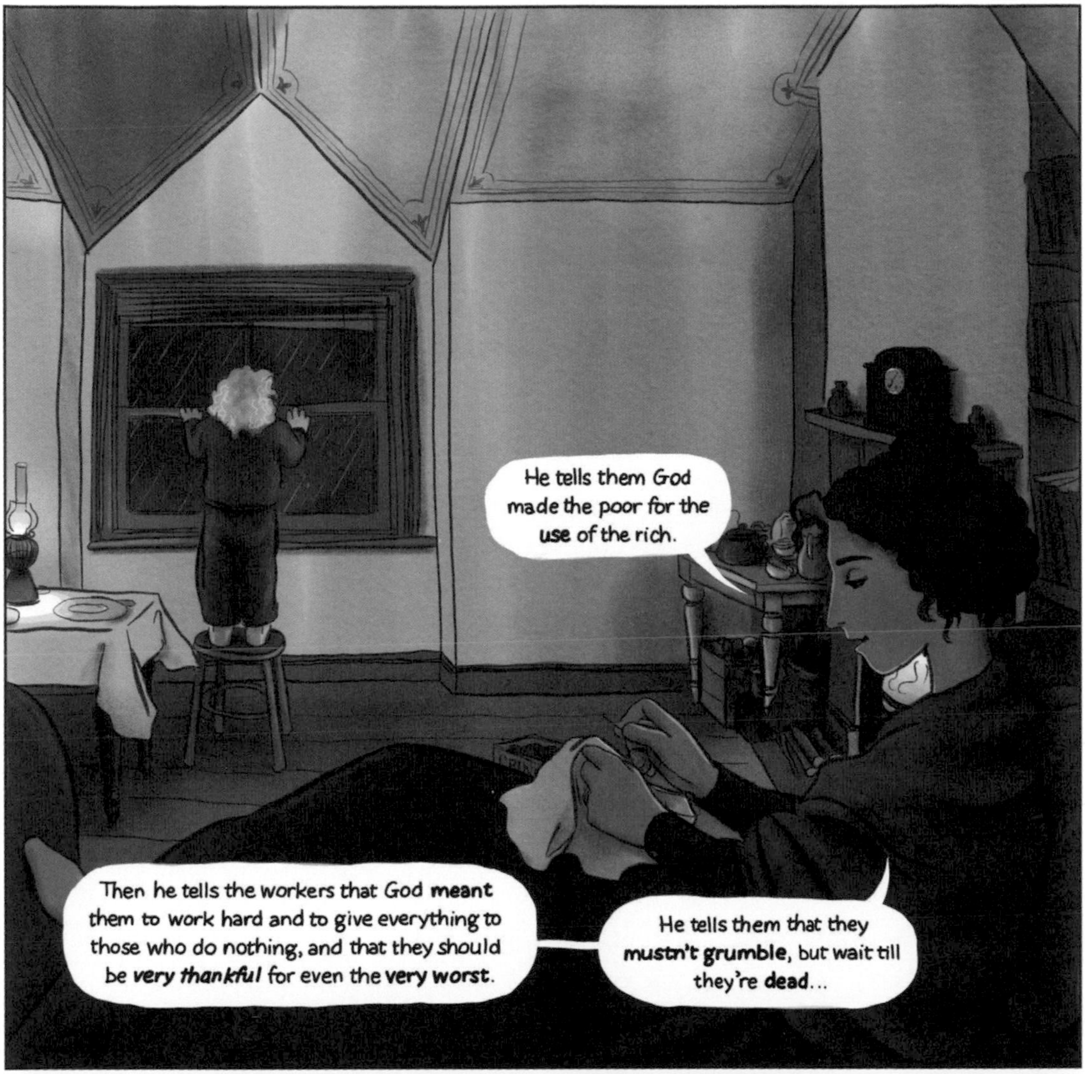
He tells them God made the poor for the **use** of the rich.
Then he tells the workers that God **meant** them to work hard and to give everything to those who do nothing, and that they should be ***very thankful*** for even the **very worst**.
He tells them that they **mustn't grumble**, but wait till they're **dead**...

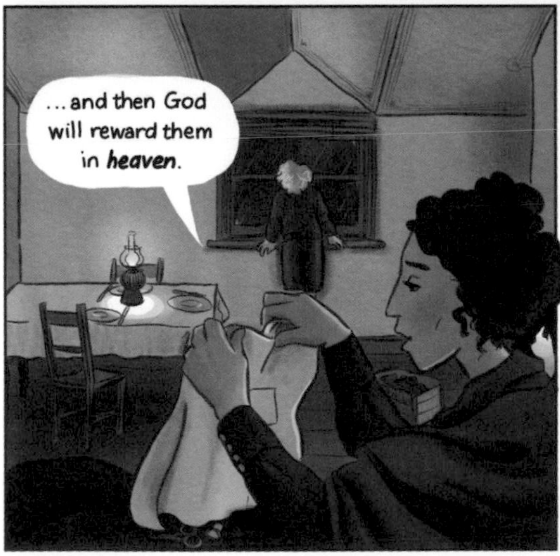
...and then God will reward them in ***heaven***.

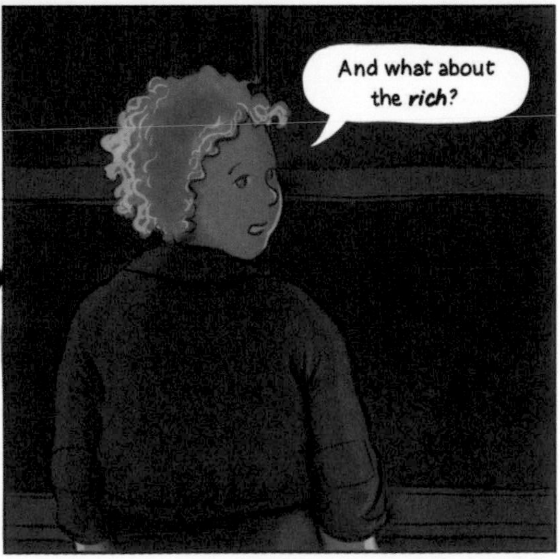
And what about the ***rich***?

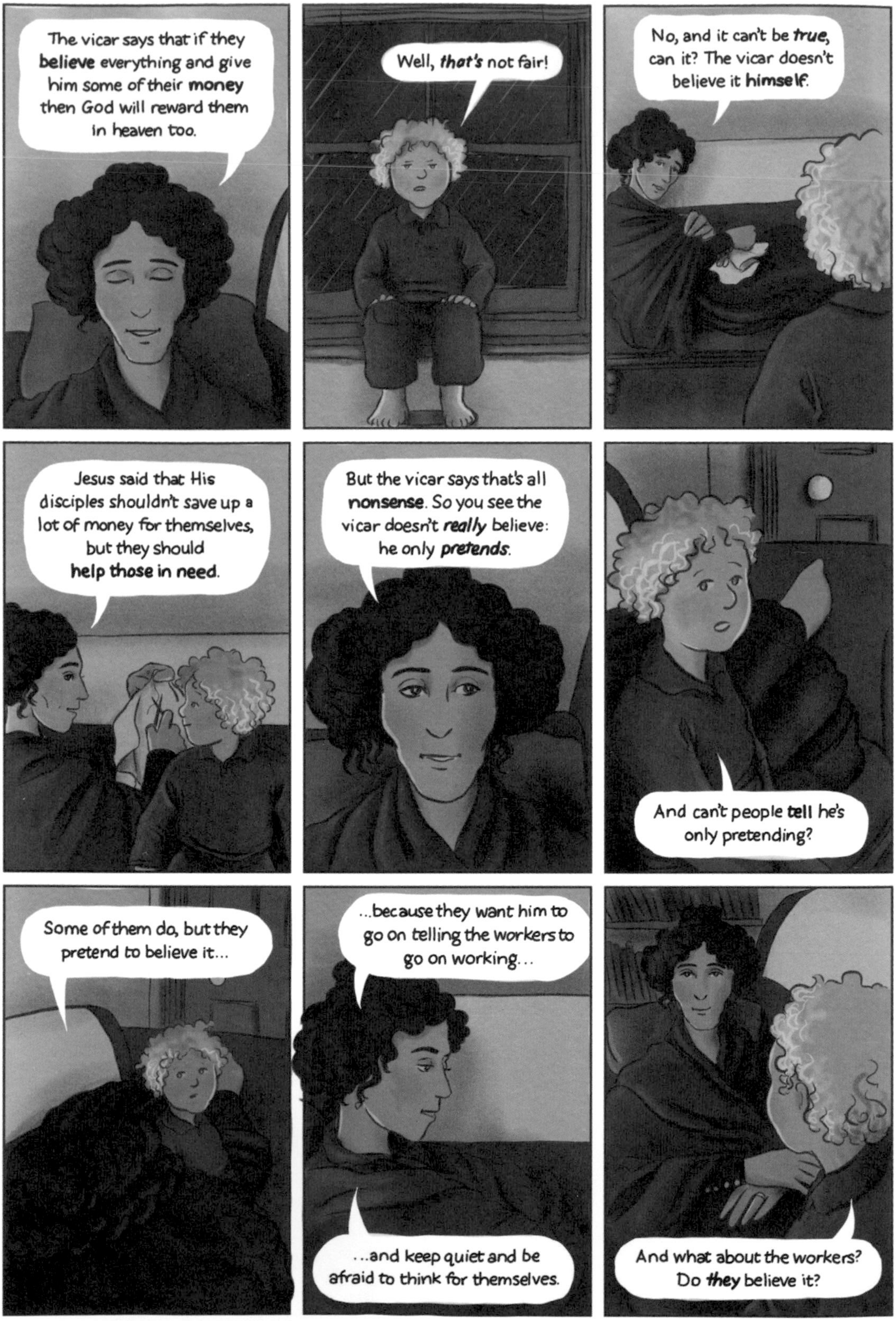
The vicar says that if they believe everything and give him some of their money then God will reward them in heaven too.
Well, that's not fair!
No, and it can't be true, can it? The vicar doesn't believe it himself.
Jesus said that His disciples shouldn't save up a lot of money for themselves, but they should help those in need.
But the vicar says that's all nonsense. So you see the vicar doesn't really believe: he only pretends.
And can't people tell he's only pretending?
Some of them do, but they pretend to believe it...
...because they want him to go on telling the workers to go on working...
...and keep quiet and be afraid to think for themselves.
And what about the workers? Do they believe it?

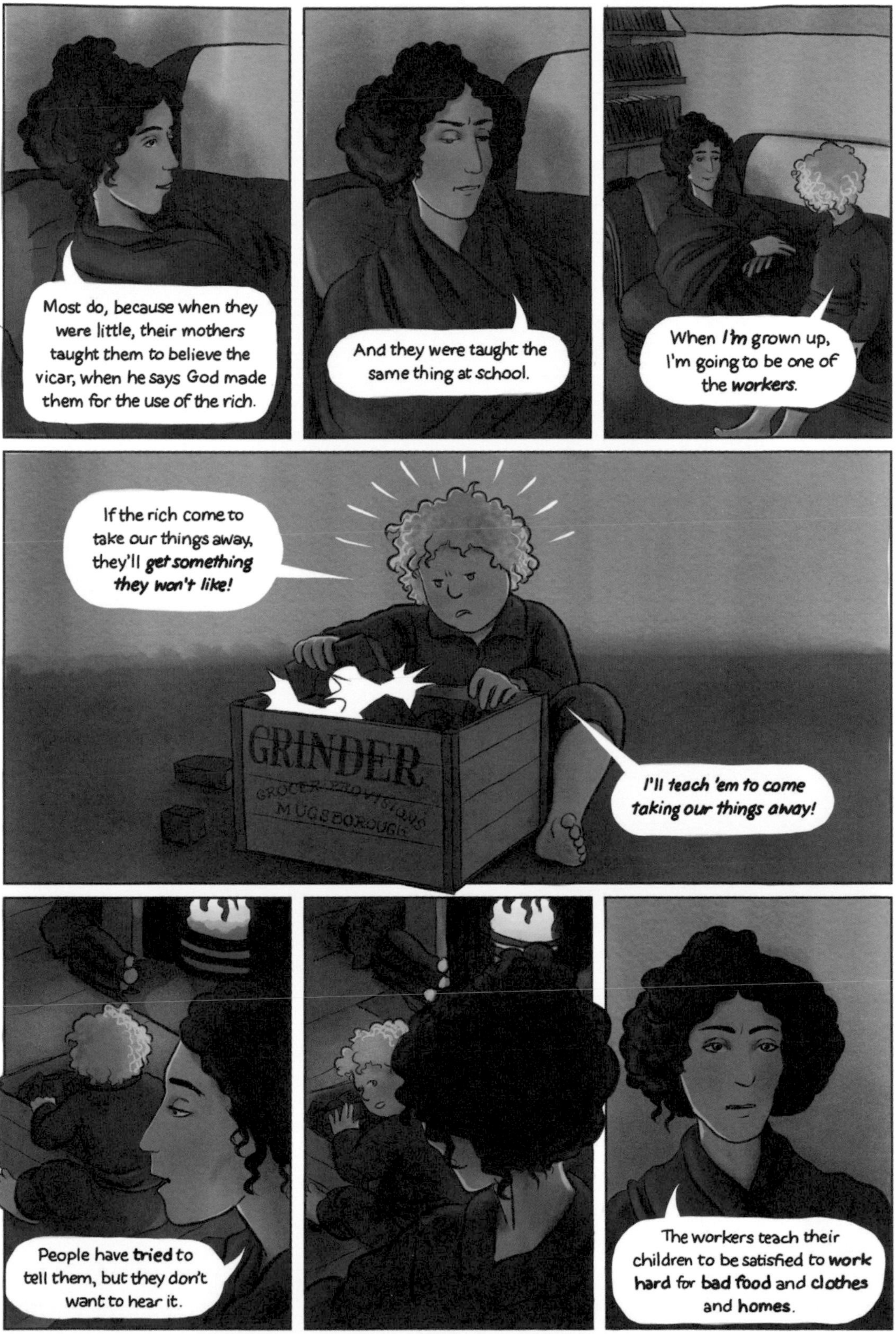
Most do, because when they were little, their mothers taught them to believe the vicar, when he says God made them for the use of the rich.
And they were taught the same thing at school.
When *I'm* grown up, I'm going to be one of the **workers**.
If the rich come to take our things away, they'll ***get something they won't like!***
GRINDER
GROCER PROVISIONS
MUGSBOROUGH
I'll teach 'em to come taking our things away!
People have **tried** to tell them, but they don't want to hear it.
The workers teach their children to be satisfied to **work hard** for **bad food** and **clothes** and **homes**.

Then the workers should be *jolly ashamed of themselves!*

But that's what they've always been **taught**, Frankie.

First, their mothers and fathers told them so, then their schoolteachers, and then the vicar and the Sunday school teacher.

So you can't be surprised that they now **really believe** that God made them and their children to make things for the rich.

But you'd think their *own sense* would tell them!

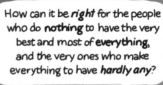

How can it be *right* for the people who do **nothing** to have the very best and most of **everything**, and the very ones who make everything to have **hardly any**?

Even *I* know better than that, and I'm only six **and a half**.

Listen!

Dad!

Hullo!

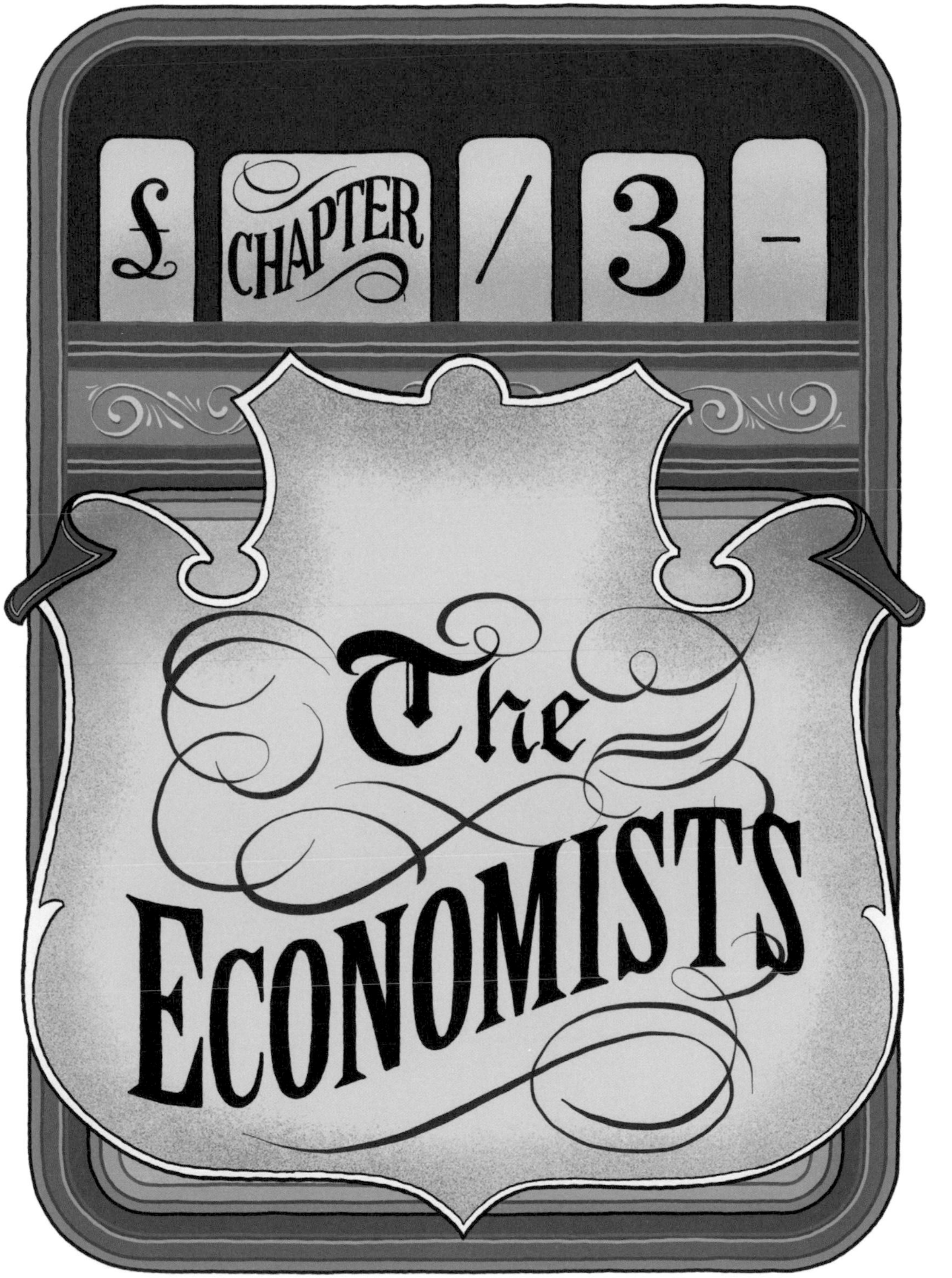
£
CHAPTER
/
3
-
The
ECONOMISTS

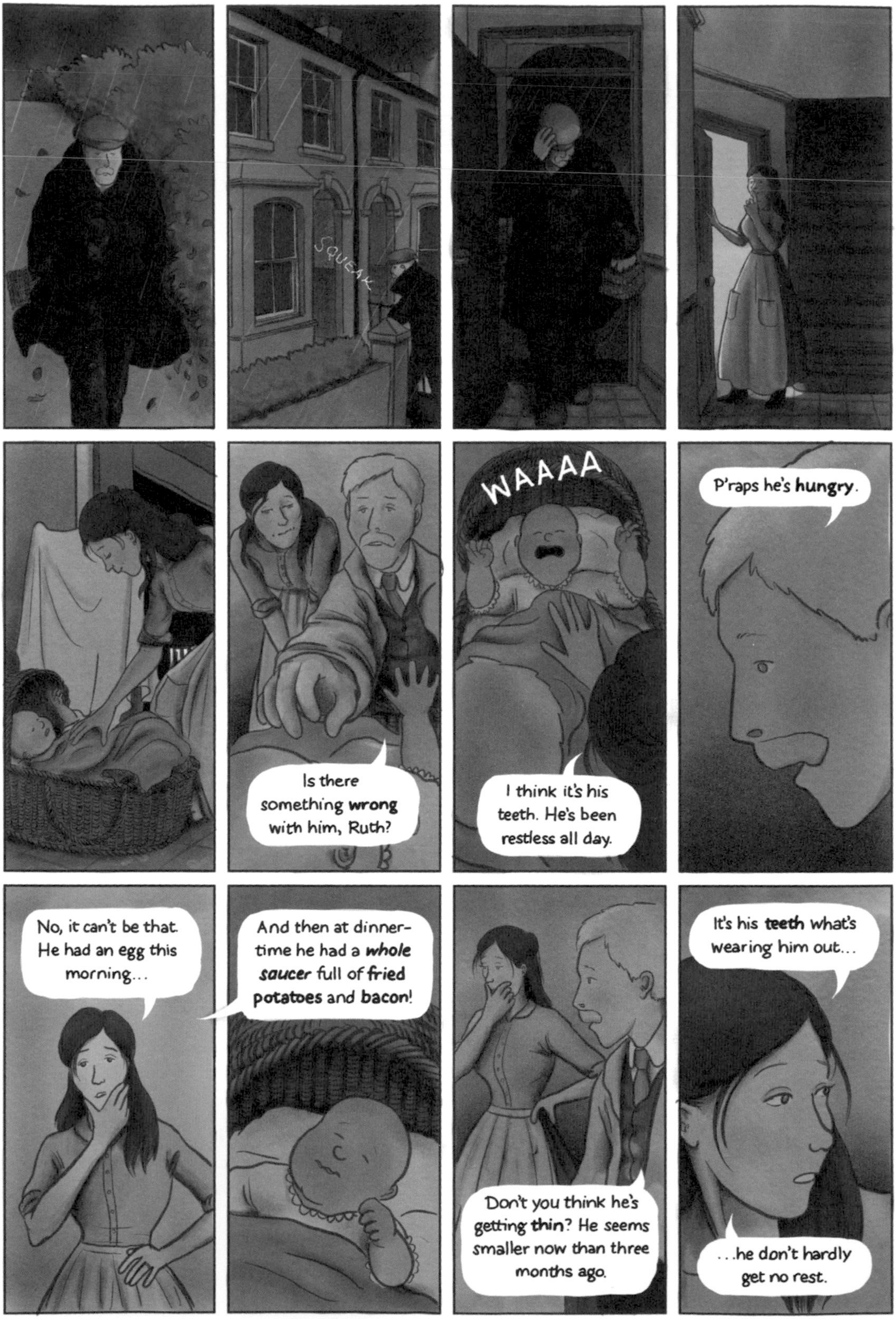
SQUEAK
WAAAA
Is there something wrong with him, Ruth?
I think it's his teeth. He's been restless all day.
P'raps he's hungry.
No, it can't be that. He had an egg this morning...
And then at dinner-time he had a whole saucer full of fried potatoes and bacon!
Don't you think he's getting thin? He seems smaller now than three months ago.
It's his teeth what's wearing him out...
...he don't hardly get no rest.

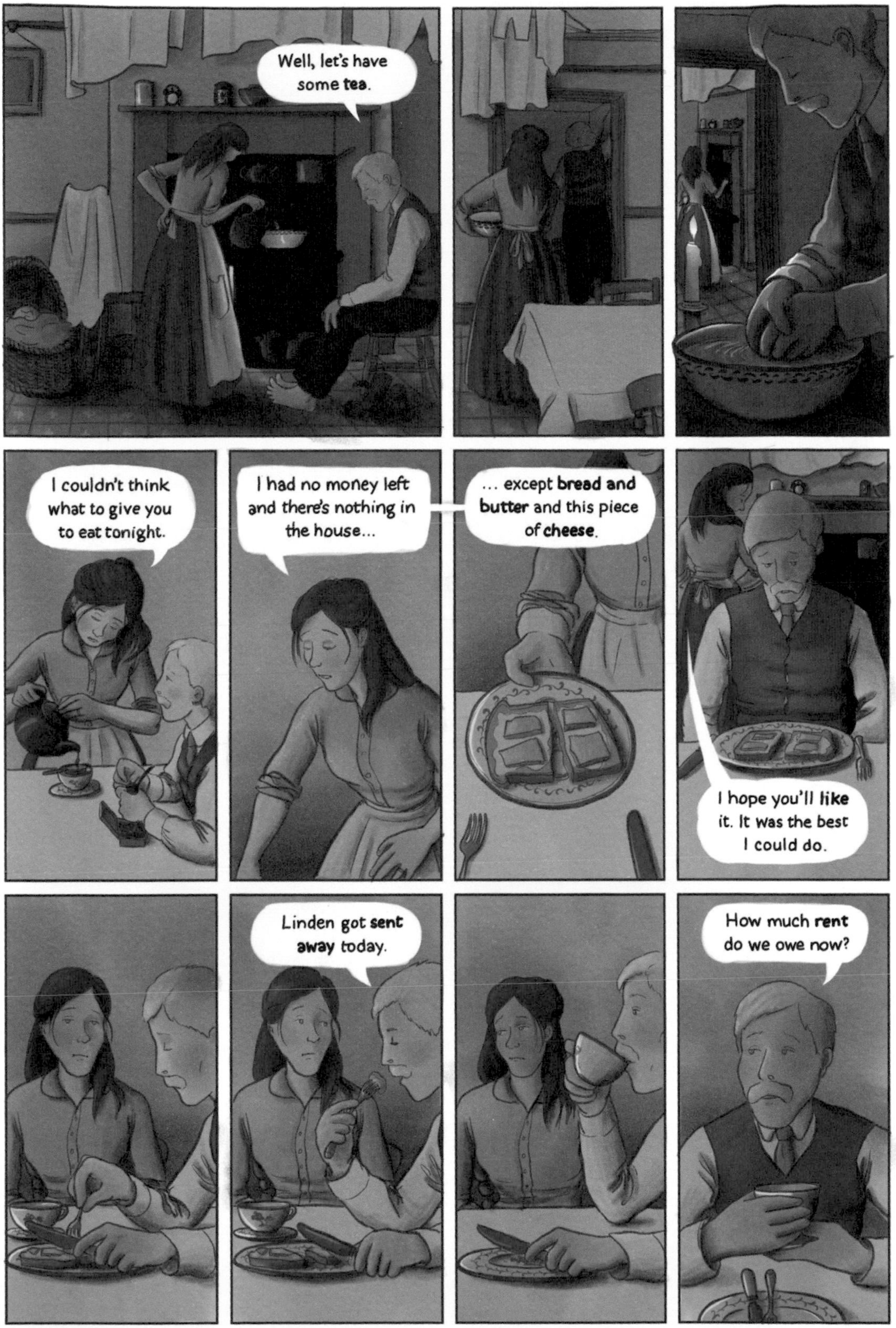
Well, let's have some tea.
I couldn't think what to give you to eat tonight.
I had no money left and there's nothing in the house...
... except bread and butter and this piece of cheese.
I hope you'll like it. It was the best I could do.
Linden got sent away today.
How much rent do we owe now?

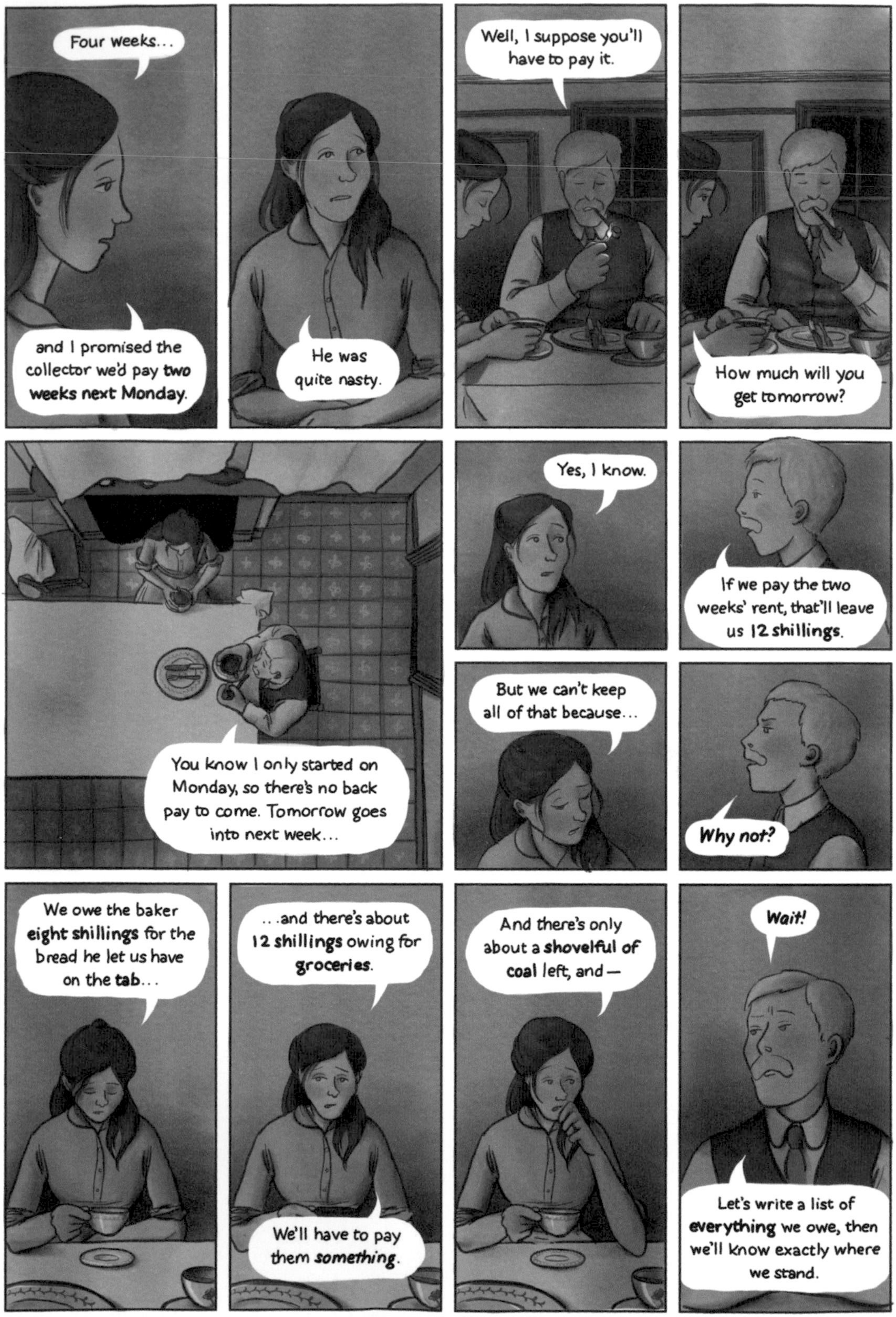
Four weeks...
and I promised the collector we'd pay two weeks next Monday.
He was quite nasty.
Well, I suppose you'll have to pay it.
How much will you get tomorrow?
You know I only started on Monday, so there's no back pay to come. Tomorrow goes into next week...
Yes, I know.
If we pay the two weeks' rent, that'll leave us 12 shillings.
But we can't keep all of that because...
Why not?
We owe the baker eight shillings for the bread he let us have on the tab...
...and there's about 12 shillings owing for groceries.
We'll have to pay them something.
And there's only about a shovelful of coal left, and—
Wait!
Let's write a list of everything we owe, then we'll know exactly where we stand.

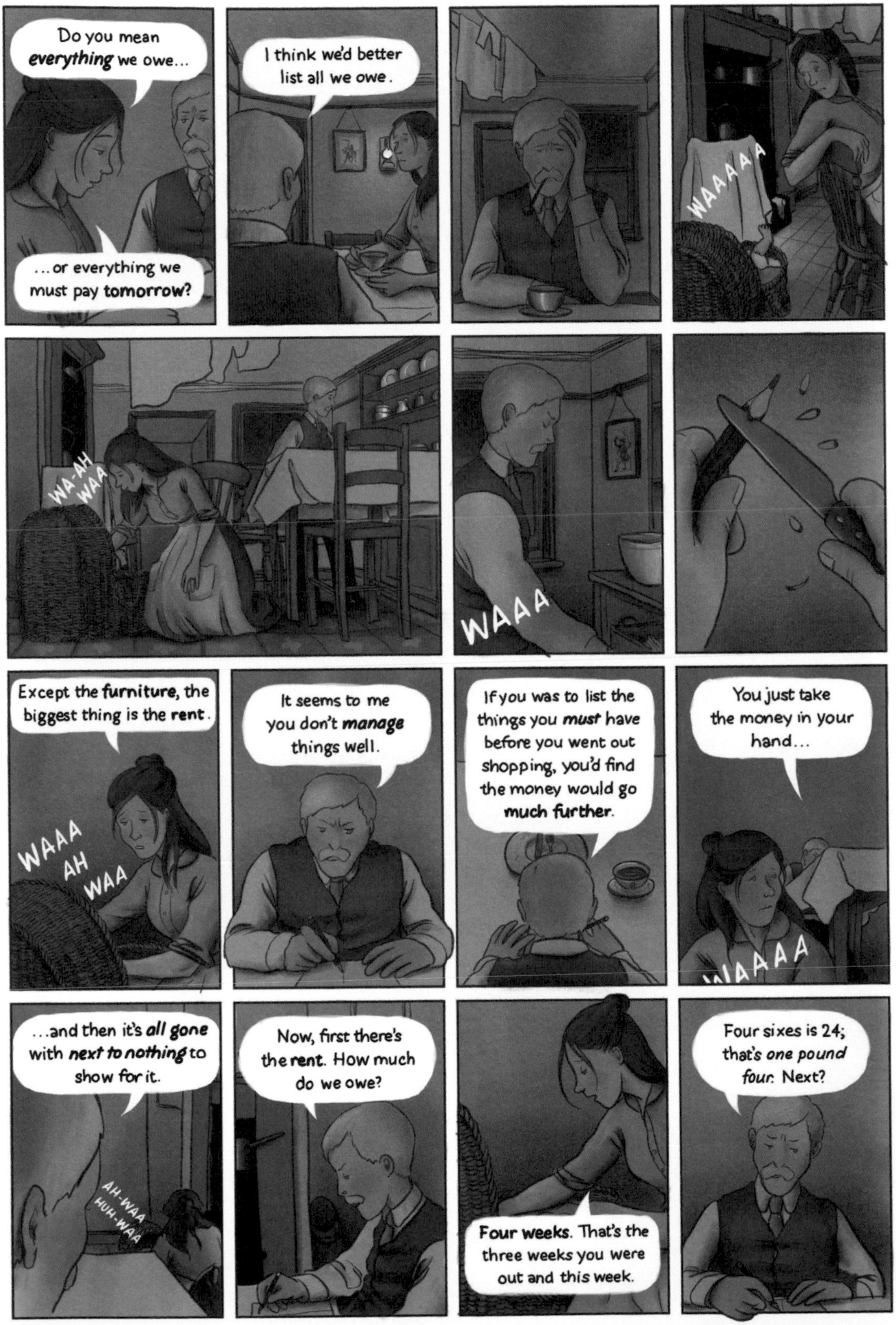
Do you mean everything we owe...
...or everything we must pay tomorrow?
I think we'd better list all we owe.
WAAAAAA
WA-AH WAA
WAAA
Except the furniture, the biggest thing is the rent.
WAAA AH WAA
It seems to me you don't manage things well.
If you was to list the things you must have before you went out shopping, you'd find the money would go much further.
You just take the money in your hand...
WAAAA
...and then it's all gone with next to nothing to show for it.
AH-WAA HUH-WAA
Now, first there's the rent. How much do we owe?
Four weeks. That's the three weeks you were out and this week.
Four sixes is 24; that's one pound four. Next?

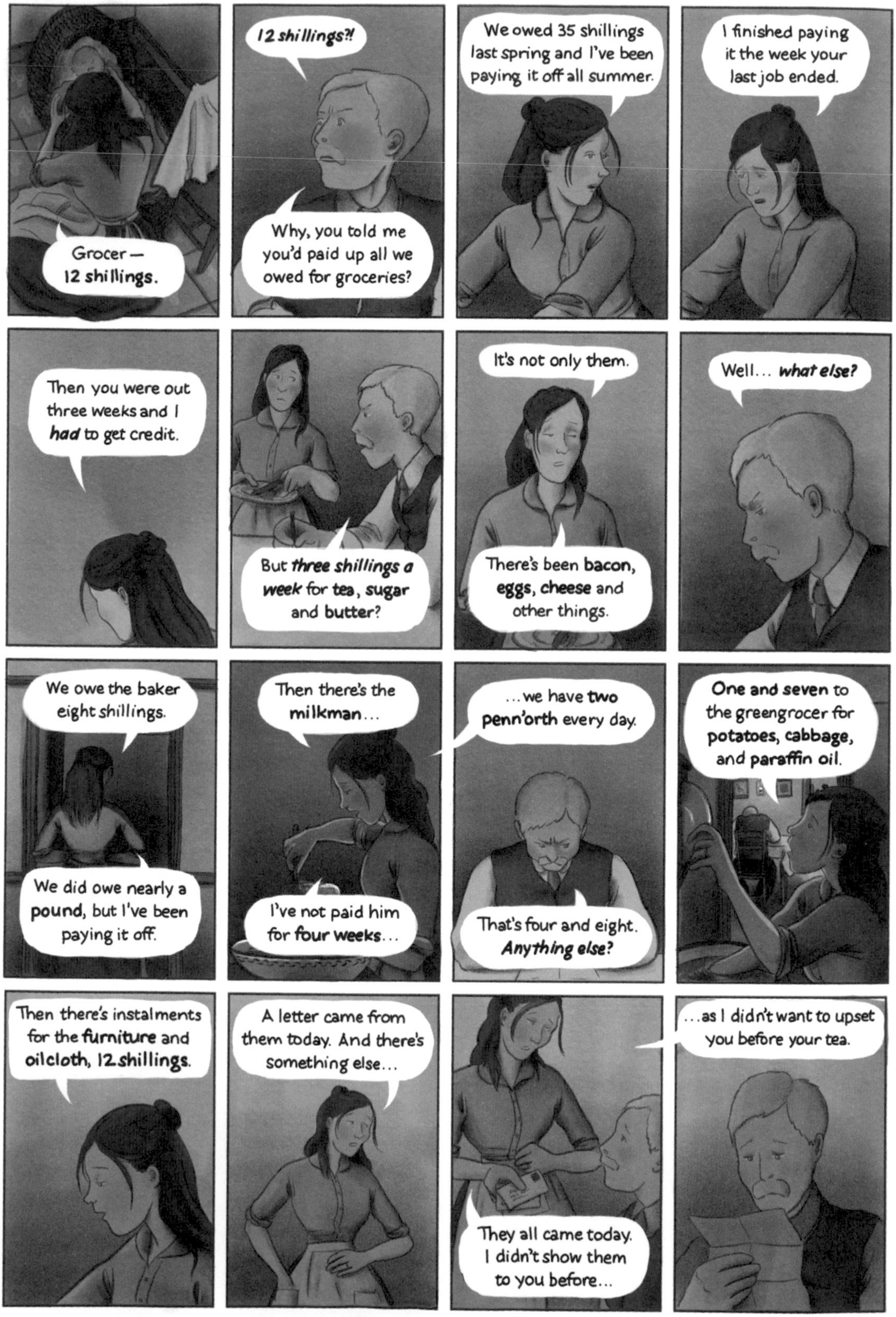
Grocer — 12 shillings.
12 shillings?!
Why, you told me you'd paid up all we owed for groceries?
We owed 35 shillings last spring and I've been paying it off all summer.
I finished paying it the week your last job ended.
Then you were out three weeks and I had to get credit.
But three shillings a week for tea, sugar and butter?
It's not only them.
There's been bacon, eggs, cheese and other things.
Well... what else?
We owe the baker eight shillings.
We did owe nearly a pound, but I've been paying it off.
Then there's the milkman...
I've not paid him for four weeks...
...we have two penn'orth every day.
That's four and eight. Anything else?
One and seven to the greengrocer for potatoes, cabbage, and paraffin oil.
Then there's instalments for the furniture and oilcloth, 12 shillings.
A letter came from them today. And there's something else...
They all came today. I didn't show them to you before...
...as I didn't want to upset you before your tea.

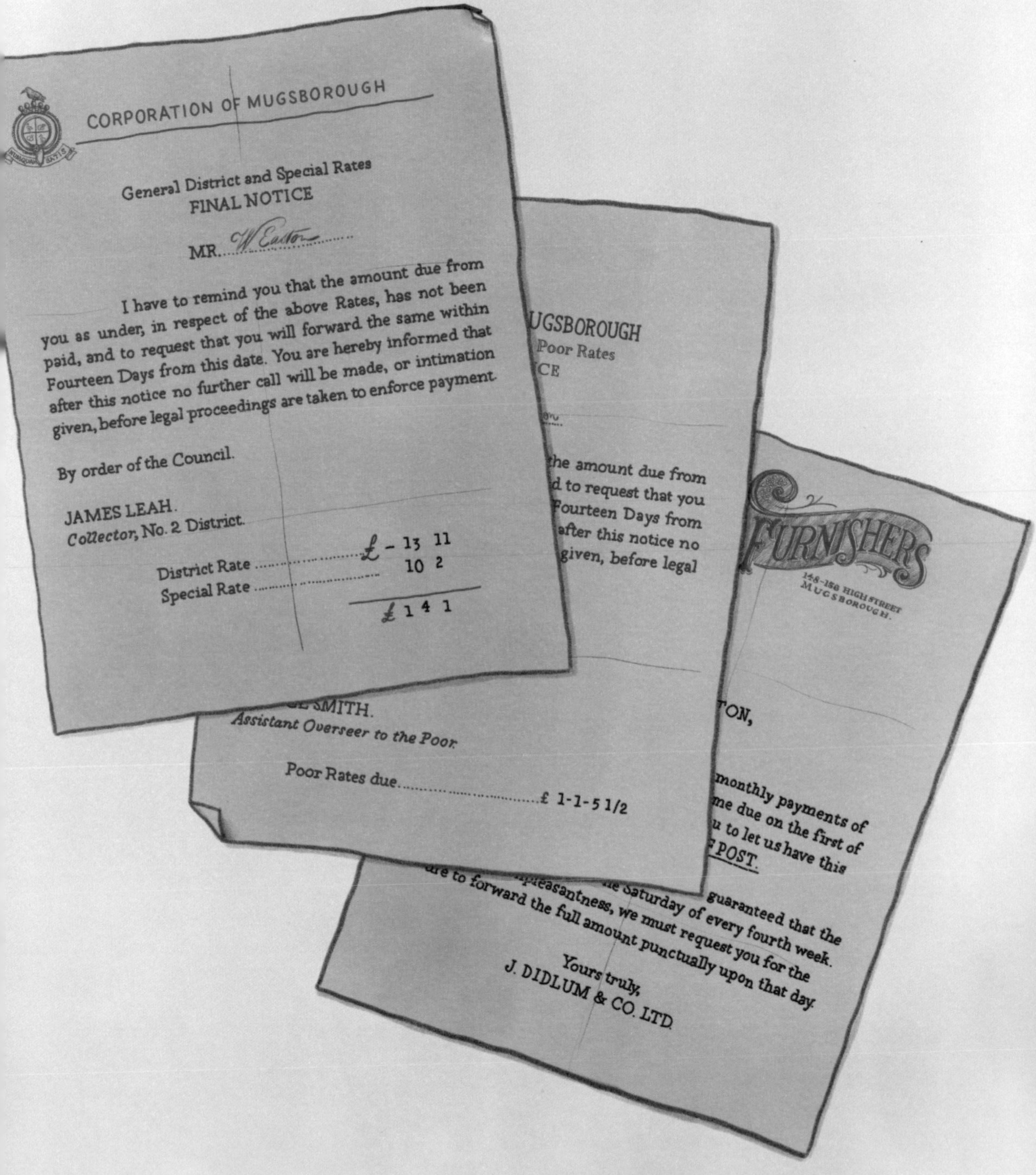
CORPORATION OF MUGSBOROUGH
General District and Special Rates
FINAL NOTICE
MR. W Easton
I have to remind you that the amount due from you as under, in respect of the above Rates, has not been paid, and to request that you will forward the same within Fourteen Days from this date. You are hereby informed that after this notice no further call will be made, or intimation given, before legal proceedings are taken to enforce payment.
By order of the Council.
JAMES LEAH.
Collector, No. 2 District.
District Rate £ - 13 11
Special Rate 10 2
£ 1 4 1
UGSBOROUGH
Poor Rates
CE
the amount due from
d to request that you
Fourteen Days from
after this notice no
given, before legal
SMITH.
Assistant Overseer to the Poor.
Poor Rates due £ 1-1-5 1/2
FURNISHERS
146-150 HIGH STREET
MUGSBOROUGH.
TON,
monthly payments of
me due on the first of
u to let us have this
POST.
guaranteed that the
Saturday of every fourth week.
unpleasantness, we must request you for the
ure to forward the full amount punctually upon that day.
Yours truly,
J. DIDLUM & CO. LTD.

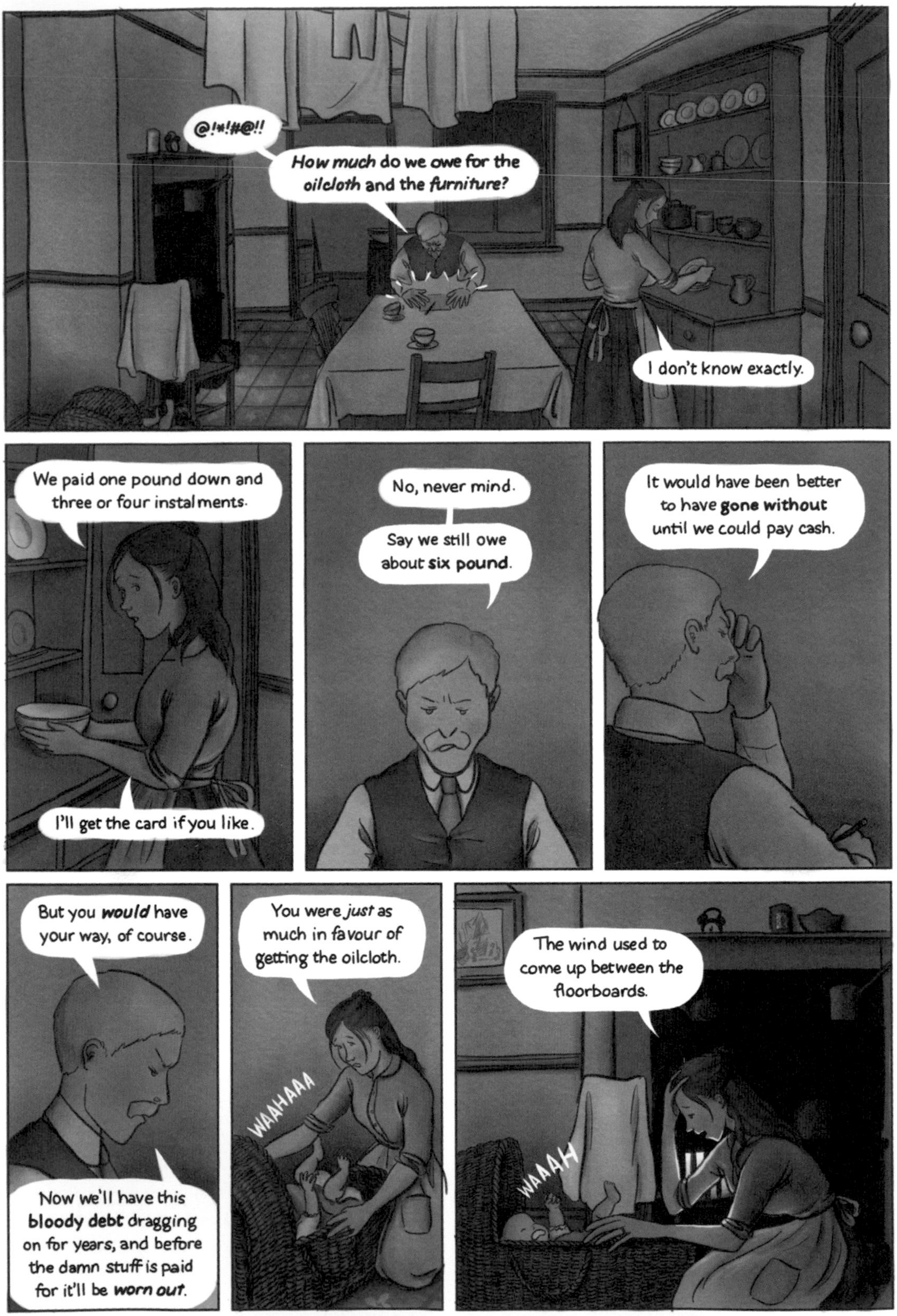
@!*!#@!!
How much do we owe for the oilcloth and the furniture?
I don't know exactly.
We paid one pound down and three or four instalments.
I'll get the card if you like.
No, never mind.
Say we still owe about six pound.
It would have been better to have gone without until we could pay cash.
But you would have your way, of course.
Now we'll have this bloody debt dragging on for years, and before the damn stuff is paid for it'll be worn out.
You were just as much in favour of getting the oilcloth.
WAAHAAA
The wind used to come up between the floorboards.
WAAAH

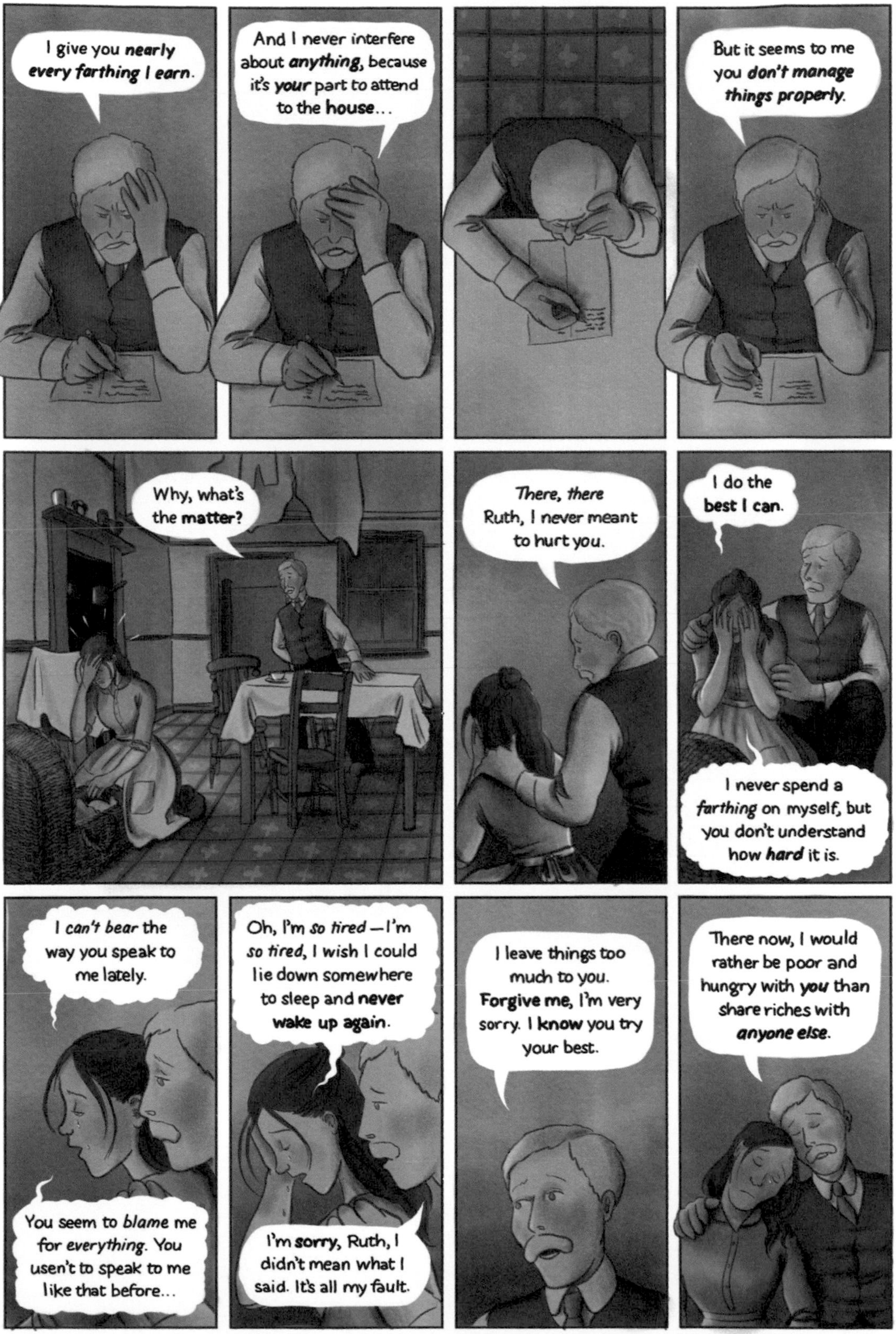
I give you nearly every farthing I earn.
And I never interfere about anything, because it's your part to attend to the house...
But it seems to me you don't manage things properly.
Why, what's the matter?
There, there Ruth, I never meant to hurt you.
I do the best I can.
I never spend a farthing on myself, but you don't understand how hard it is.
I can't bear the way you speak to me lately.
You seem to blame me for everything. You usen't to speak to me like that before...
Oh, I'm so tired—I'm so tired, I wish I could lie down somewhere to sleep and never wake up again.
I'm sorry, Ruth, I didn't mean what I said. It's all my fault.
I leave things too much to you. Forgive me, I'm very sorry. I know you try your best.
There now, I would rather be poor and hungry with you than share riches with anyone else.

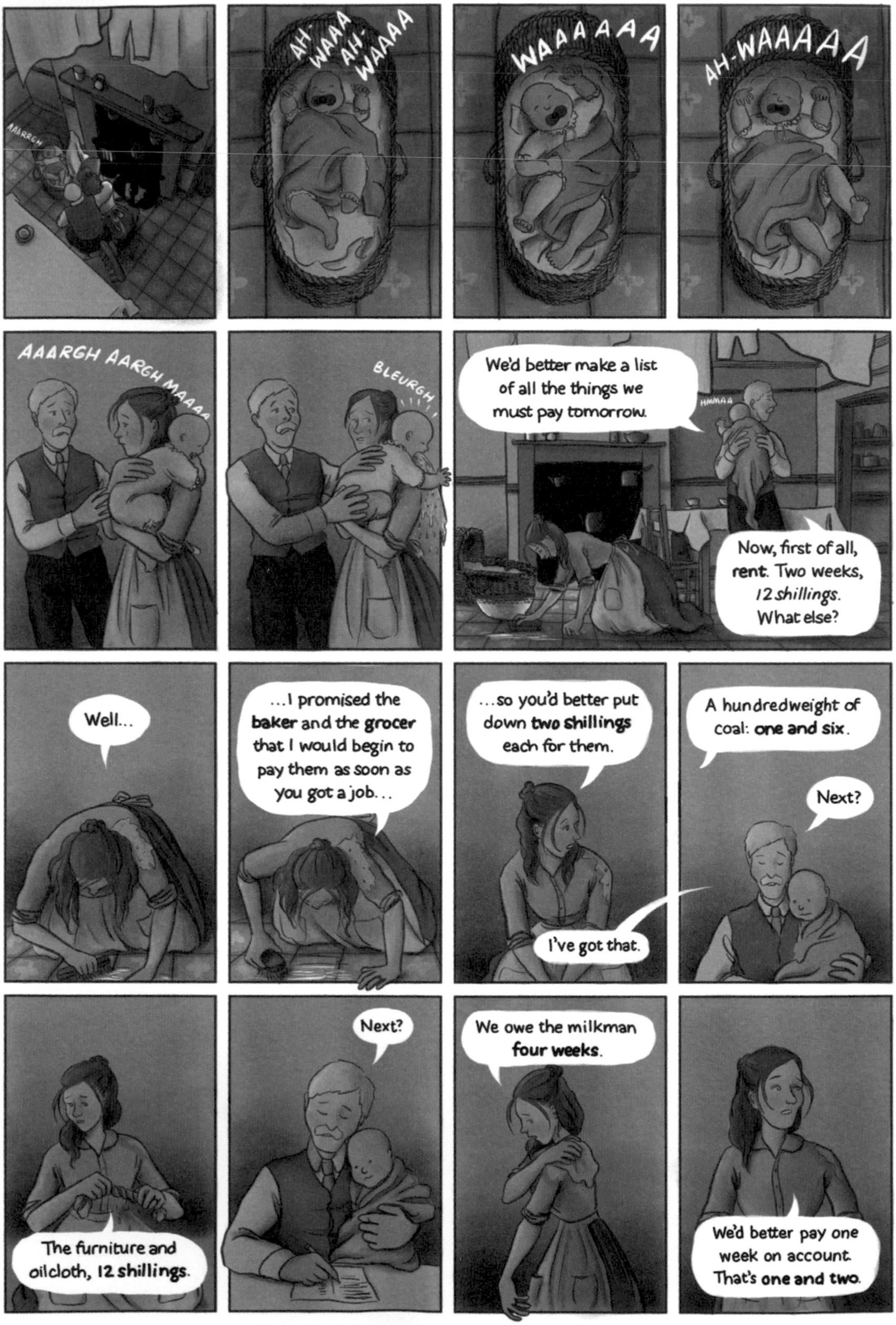
AAARRGH
AH-WAAA AH-WAAAA
WAAAAAA
AH-WAAAAA
AAARGH AARGH MAAAA
BLEURGH
We'd better make a list of all the things we must pay tomorrow.
HMMAA
Now, first of all, rent. Two weeks, 12 shillings. What else?
Well...
...I promised the baker and the grocer that I would begin to pay them as soon as you got a job...
...so you'd better put down two shillings each for them.
I've got that.
A hundredweight of coal: one and six.
Next?
The furniture and oilcloth, 12 shillings.
Next?
We owe the milkman four weeks.
We'd better pay one week on account. That's one and two.

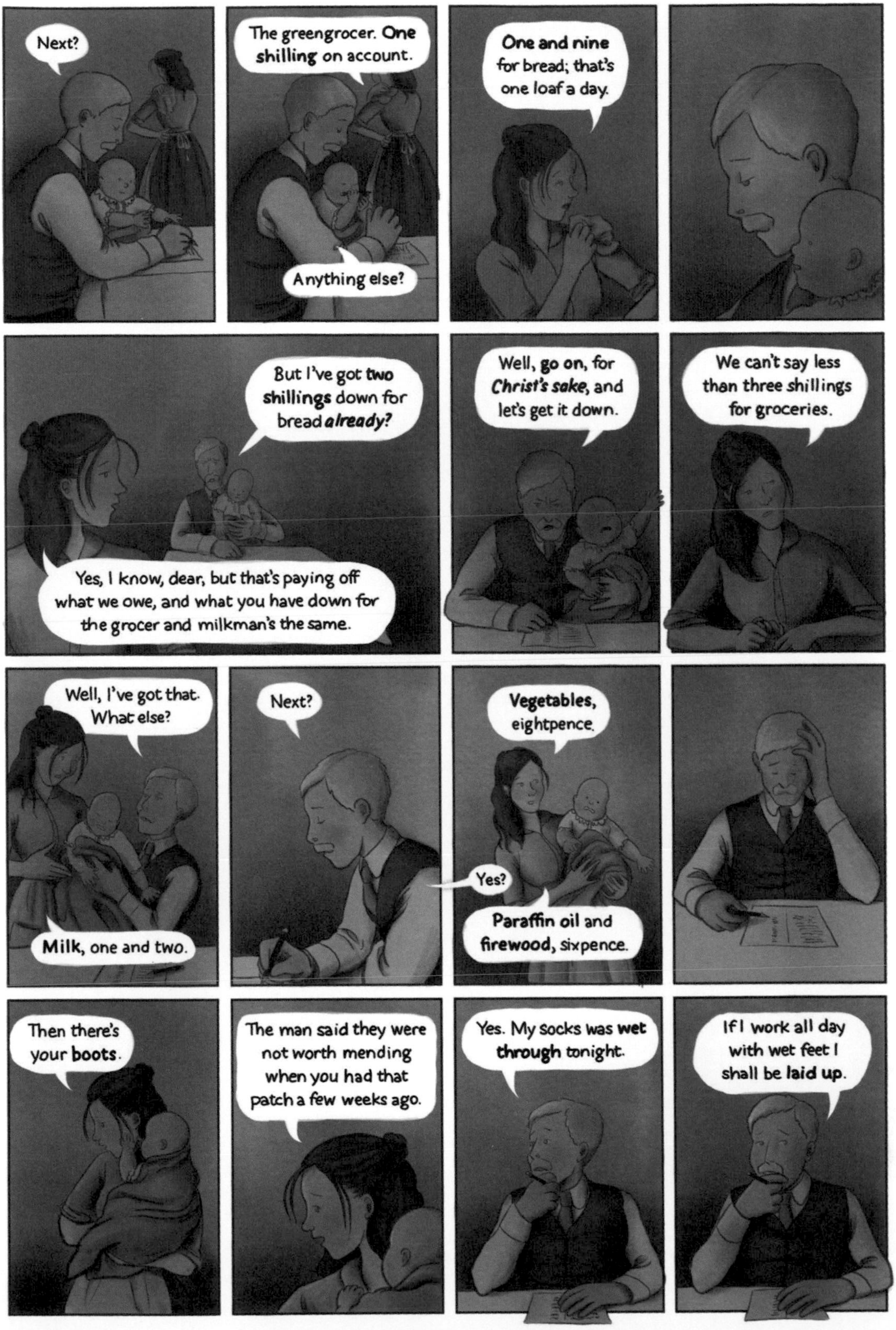
Next?
The greengrocer. One shilling on account.
Anything else?
One and nine for bread; that's one loaf a day.
But I've got two shillings down for bread already?
Yes, I know, dear, but that's paying off what we owe, and what you have down for the grocer and milkman's the same.
Well, go on, for Christ's sake, and let's get it down.
We can't say less than three shillings for groceries.
Well, I've got that. What else?
Milk, one and two.
Next?
Vegetables, eightpence.
Yes?
Paraffin oil and firewood, sixpence.
Then there's your boots.
The man said they were not worth mending when you had that patch a few weeks ago.
Yes. My socks was wet through tonight.
If I work all day with wet feet I shall be laid up.

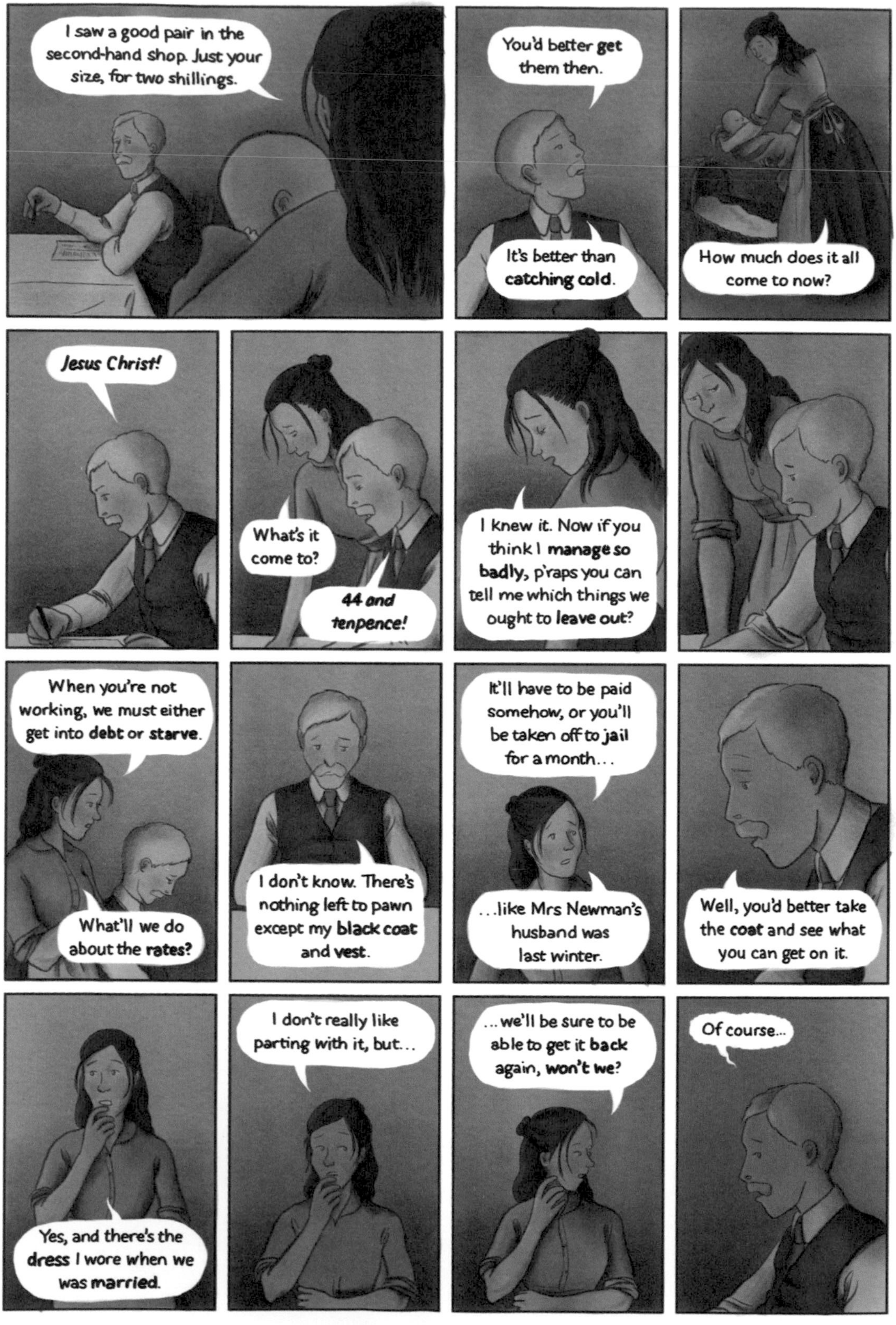
I saw a good pair in the second-hand shop. Just your size, for two shillings.
You'd better get them then.
It's better than catching cold.
How much does it all come to now?
Jesus Christ!
What's it come to?
44 and tenpence!
I knew it. Now if you think I manage so badly, p'raps you can tell me which things we ought to leave out?
When you're not working, we must either get into debt or starve.
What'll we do about the rates?
I don't know. There's nothing left to pawn except my black coat and vest.
It'll have to be paid somehow, or you'll be taken off to jail for a month...
...like Mrs Newman's husband was last winter.
Well, you'd better take the coat and see what you can get on it.
Yes, and there's the dress I wore when we was married.
I don't really like parting with it, but...
...we'll be sure to be able to get it back again, won't we?
Of course...

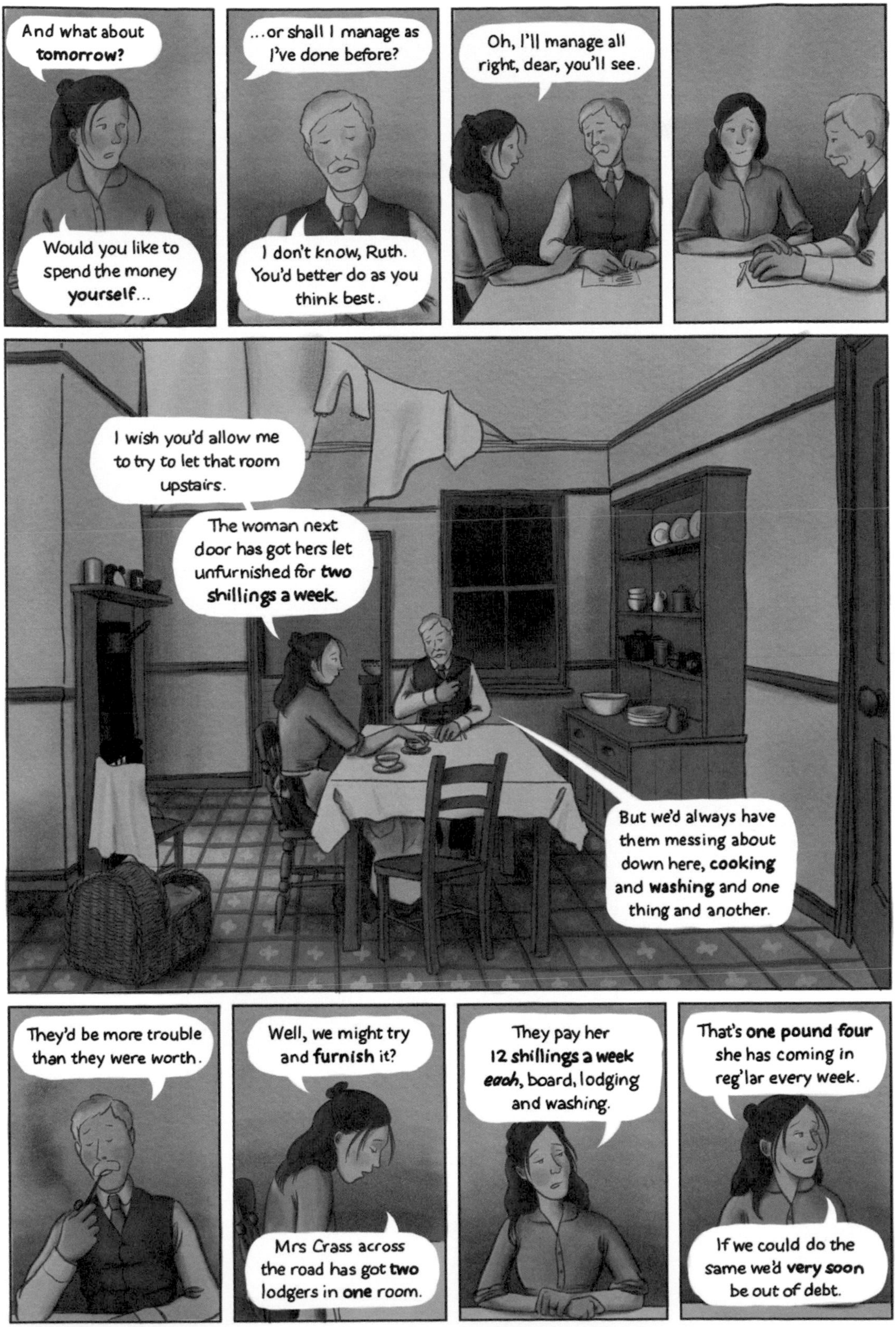
And what about tomorrow?
Would you like to spend the money yourself...
...or shall I manage as I've done before?
I don't know, Ruth. You'd better do as you think best.
Oh, I'll manage all right, dear, you'll see.
I wish you'd allow me to try to let that room upstairs.
The woman next door has got hers let unfurnished for two shillings a week.
But we'd always have them messing about down here, cooking and washing and one thing and another.
They'd be more trouble than they were worth.
Well, we might try and furnish it?
Mrs Crass across the road has got two lodgers in one room.
They pay her 12 shillings a week each, board, lodging and washing.
That's one pound four she has coming in reg'lar every week.
If we could do the same we'd very soon be out of debt.

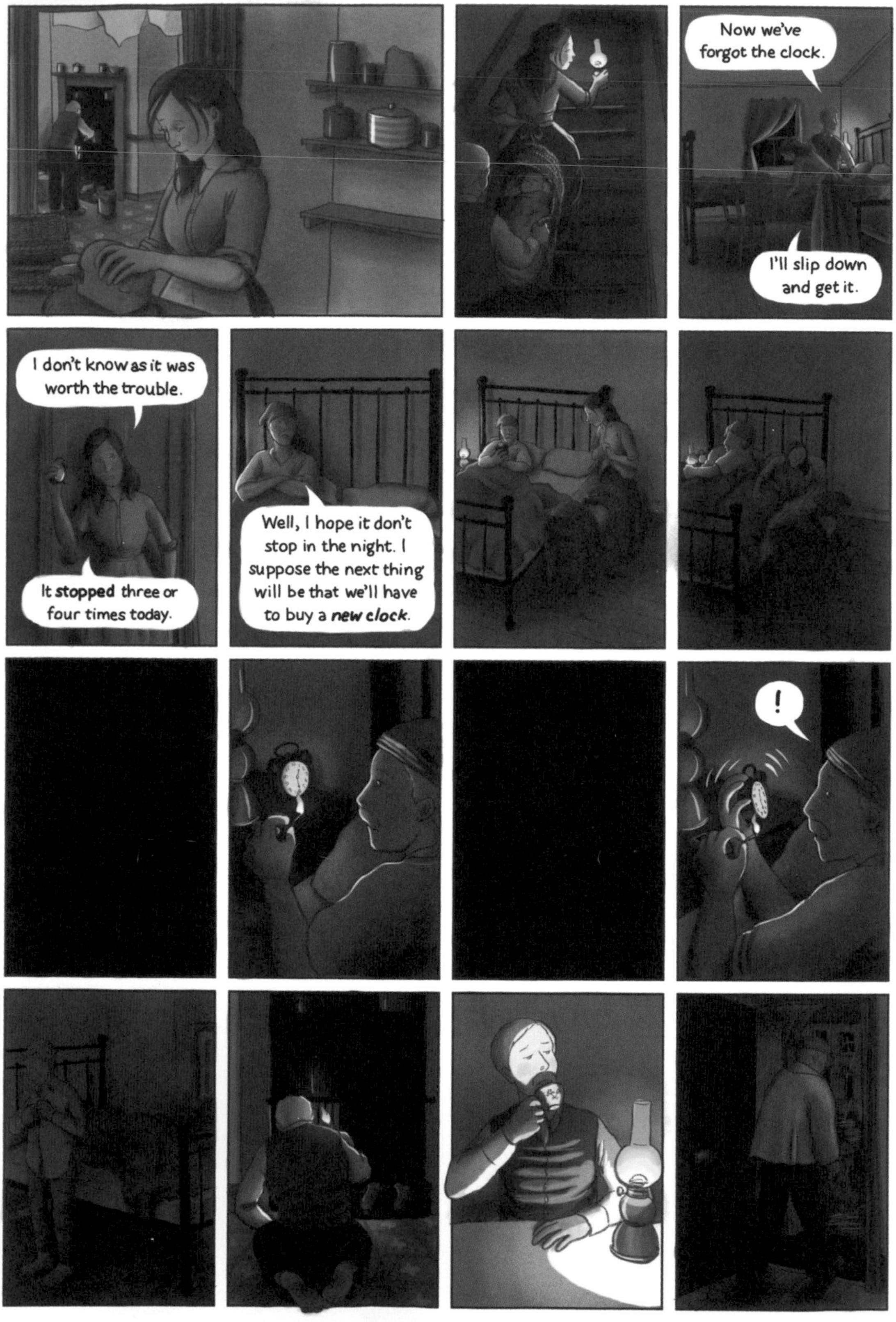
Now we've forgot the clock.
I'll slip down and get it.
I don't know as it was worth the trouble.
It stopped three or four times today.
Well, I hope it don't stop in the night. I suppose the next thing will be that we'll have to buy a new clock.
!

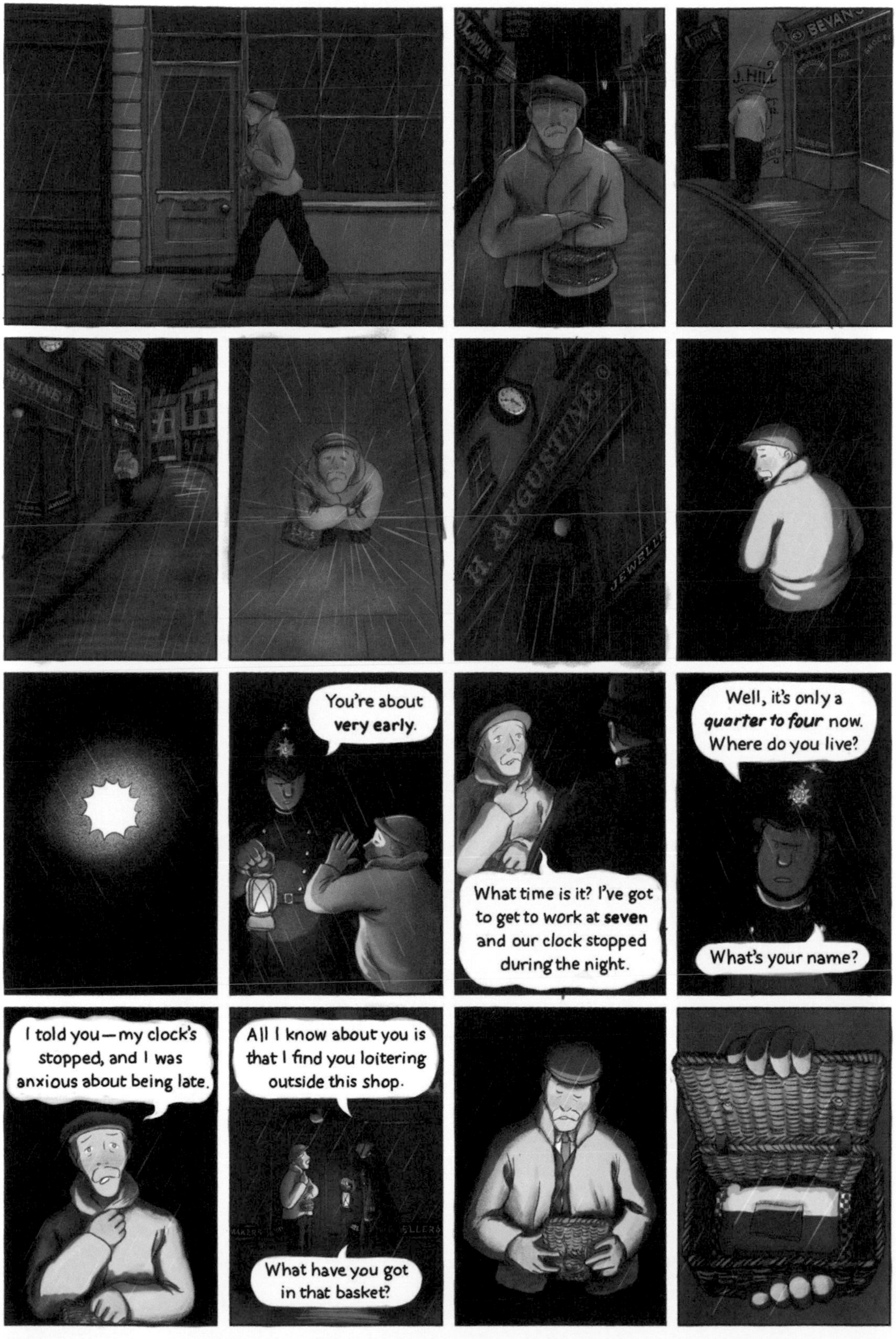

D. LAVIN
BEVAN
J. HILL
H. AUGUSTINE
JEWELLE
You're about **very early**.
What time is it? I've got to get to work at **seven** and our clock stopped during the night.
Well, it's only a ***quarter to four*** now. Where do you live?
What's your name?
I told you—my clock's stopped, and I was anxious about being late.
All I know about you is that I find you loitering outside this shop.
What have you got in that basket?

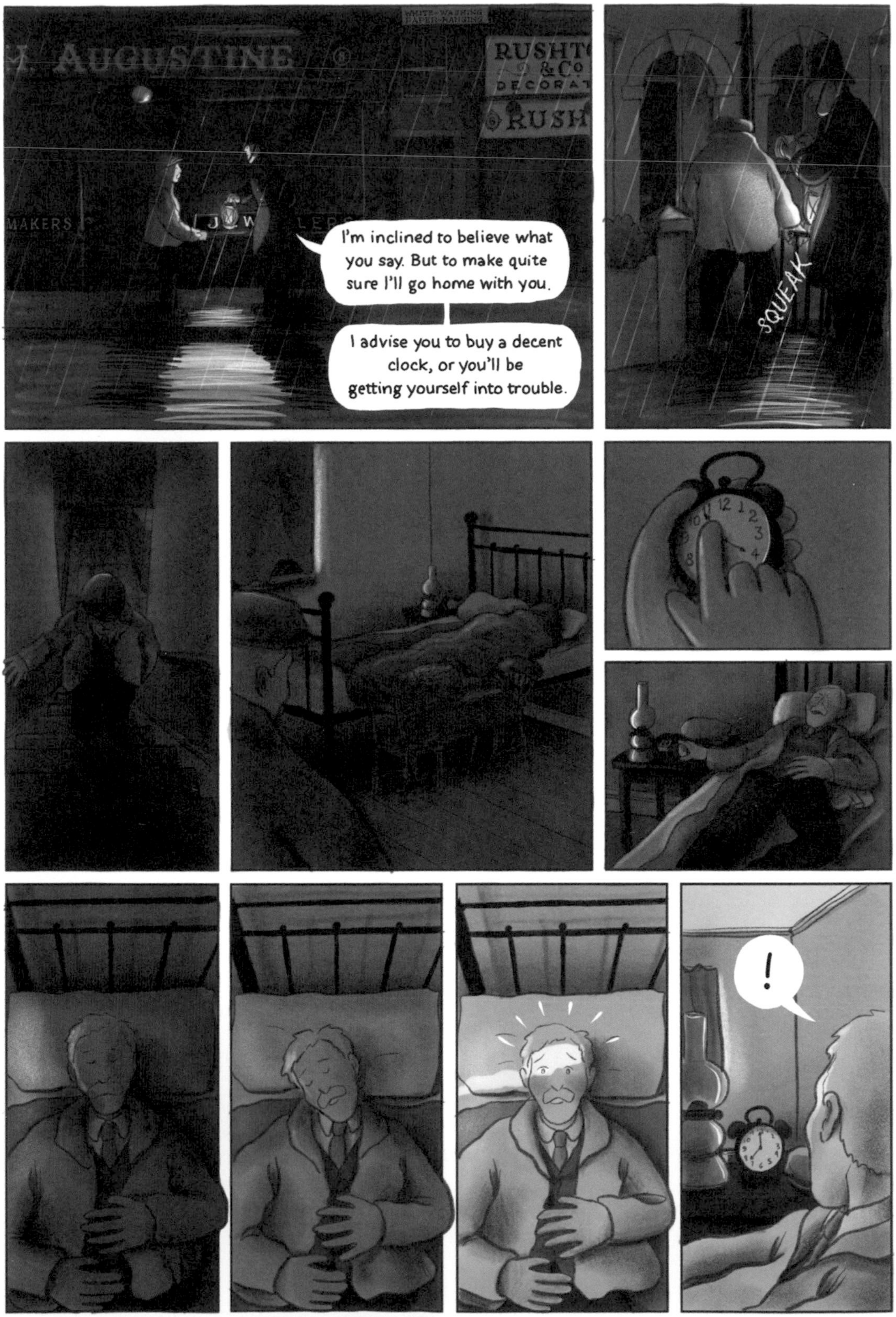
I'm inclined to believe what you say. But to make quite sure I'll go home with you.
I advise you to buy a decent clock, or you'll be getting yourself into trouble.
SQUEAK
!

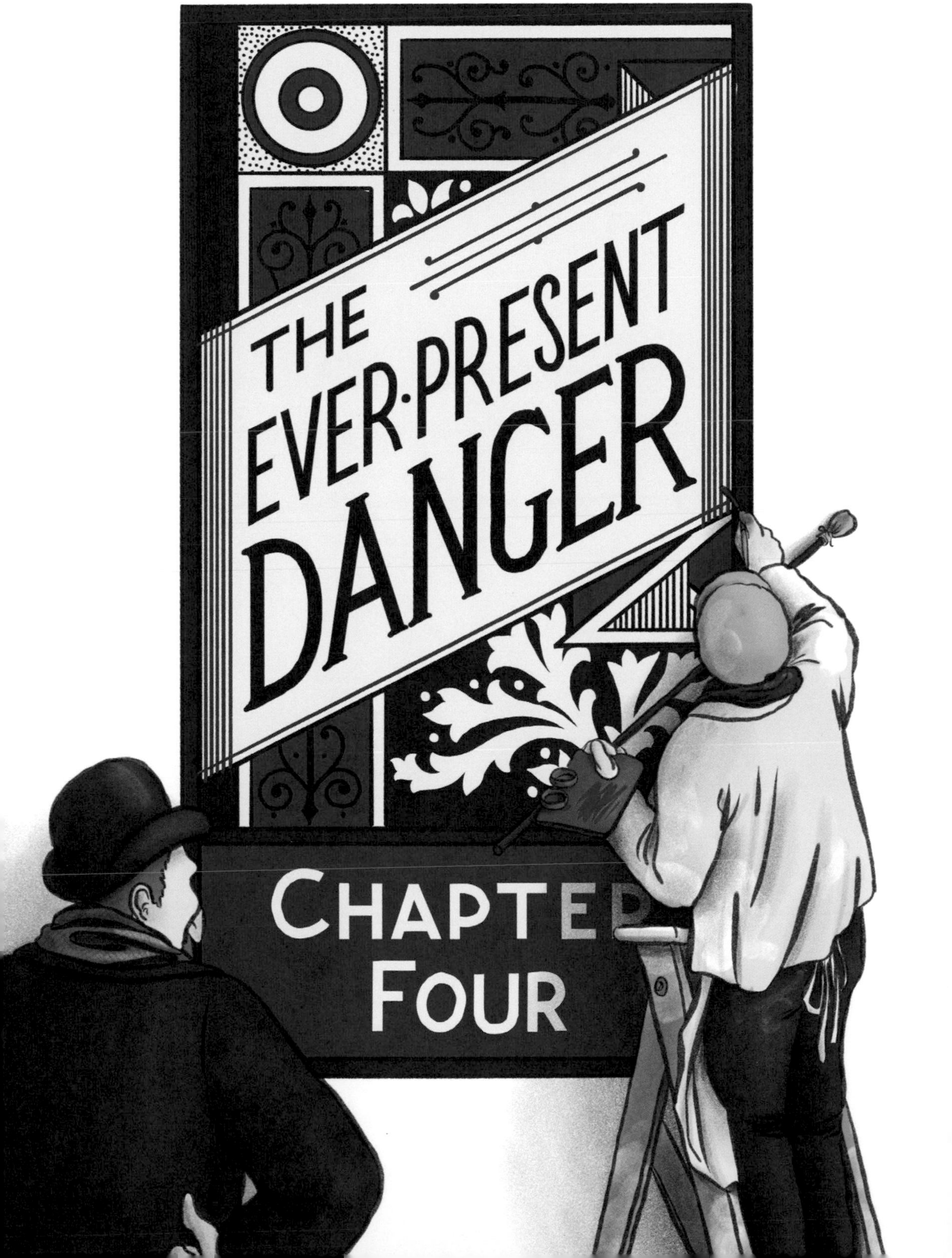
THE EVER-PRESENT DANGER
CHAPTE
FOUR

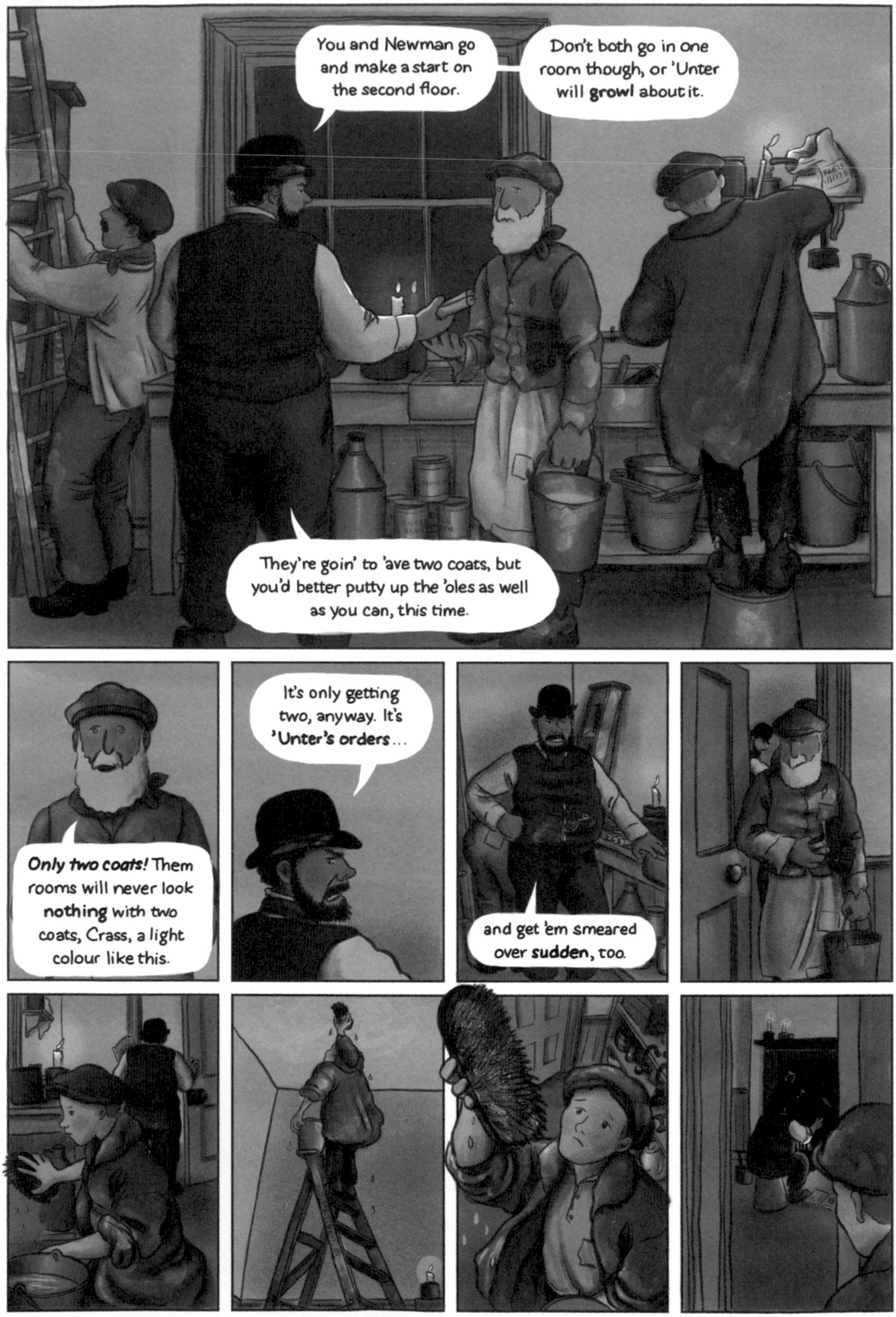
You and Newman go and make a start on the second floor.
Don't both go in one room though, or 'Unter will **growl** about it.
They're goin' to 'ave two coats, but you'd better putty up the 'oles as well as you can, this time.
Only two coats! Them rooms will never look **nothing** with two coats, Crass, a light colour like this.
It's only getting two, anyway. It's **'Unter's orders**...
and get 'em smeared over **sudden**, too.

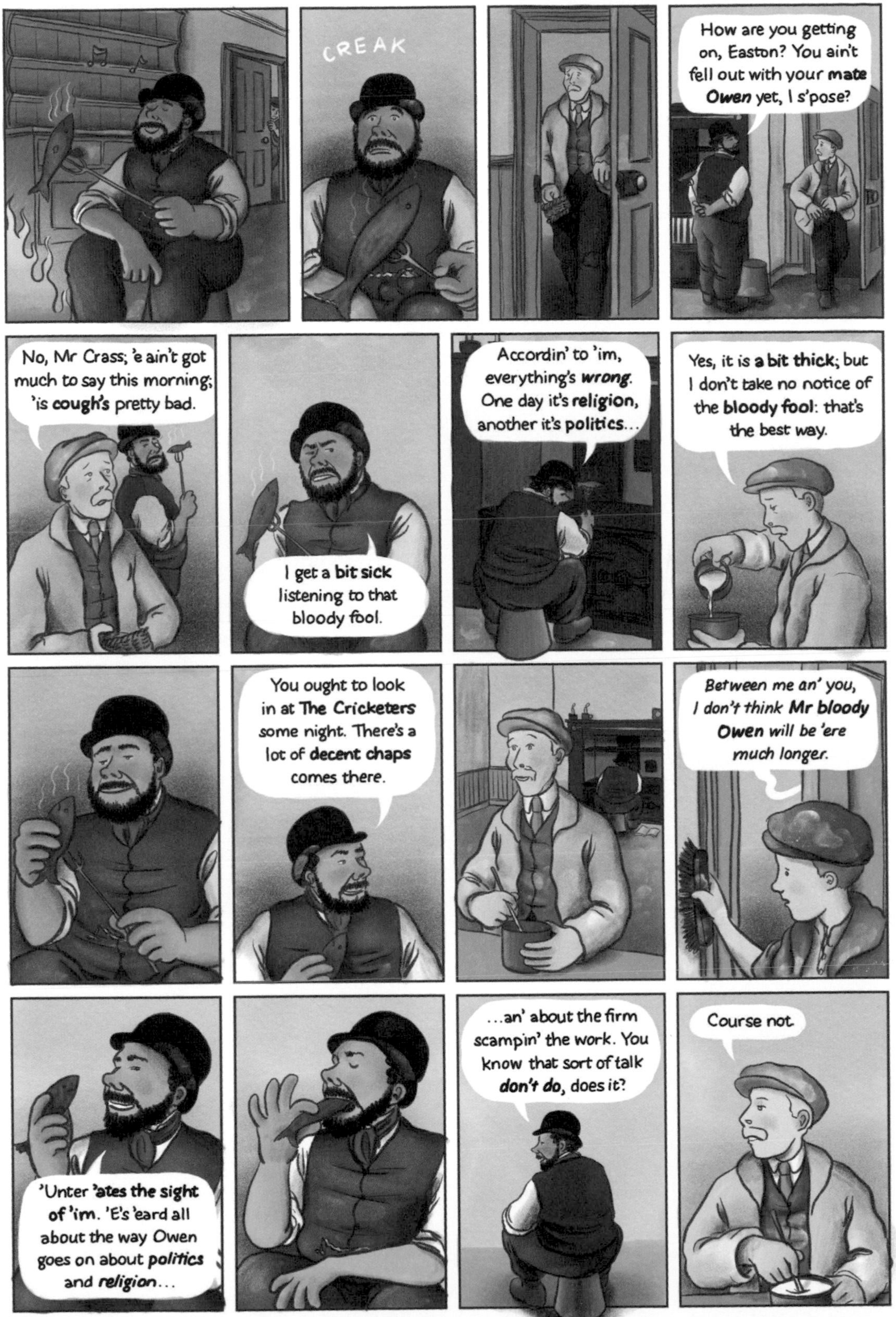
CREAK
How are you getting on, Easton? You ain't fell out with your mate Owen yet, I s'pose?
No, Mr Crass; 'e ain't got much to say this morning; 'is cough's pretty bad.
I get a bit sick listening to that bloody fool.
Accordin' to 'im, everything's wrong. One day it's religion, another it's politics...
Yes, it is a bit thick; but I don't take no notice of the bloody fool: that's the best way.
You ought to look in at The Cricketers some night. There's a lot of decent chaps comes there.
Between me an' you, I don't think Mr bloody Owen will be 'ere much longer.
'Unter 'ates the sight of 'im. 'E's 'eard all about the way Owen goes on about politics and religion...
...an' about the firm scampin' the work. You know that sort of talk don't do, does it?
Course not.

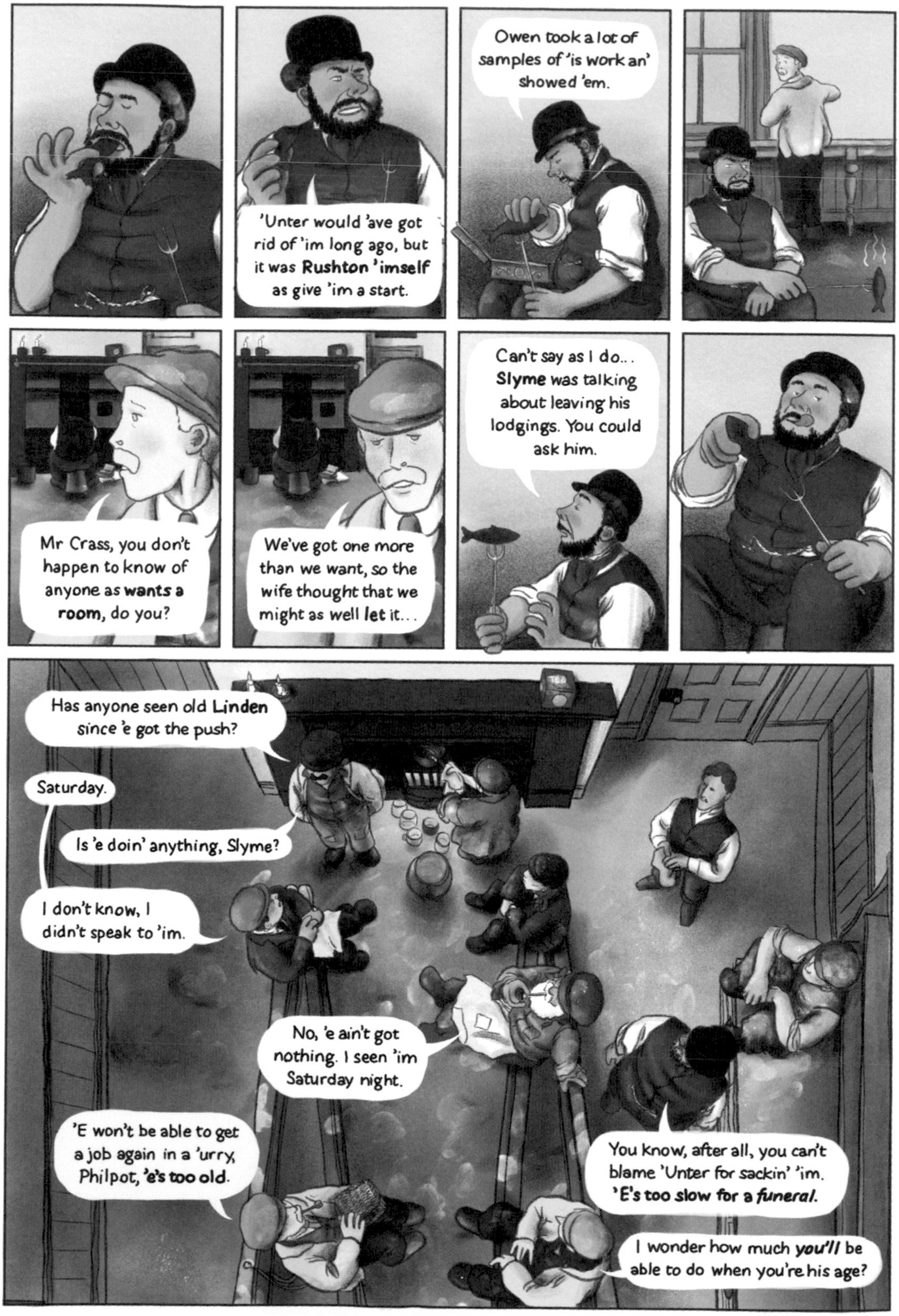
'Unter would 'ave got rid of 'im long ago, but it was **Rushton 'imself** as give 'im a start.
Owen took a lot of samples of 'is work an' showed 'em.
Mr Crass, you don't happen to know of anyone as **wants a room**, do you?
We've got one more than we want, so the wife thought that we might as well **let** it...
Can't say as I do... **Slyme** was talking about leaving his lodgings. You could ask him.
Has anyone seen old **Linden** since 'e got the push?
Saturday.
Is 'e doin' anything, Slyme?
I don't know, I didn't speak to 'im.
No, 'e ain't got nothing. I seen 'im Saturday night.
'E won't be able to get a job again in a 'urry, Philpot, **'e's too old**.
You know, after all, you can't blame 'Unter for sackin' 'im. **'E's too slow for a *funeral*.**
I wonder how much ***you'll*** be able to do when you're his age?

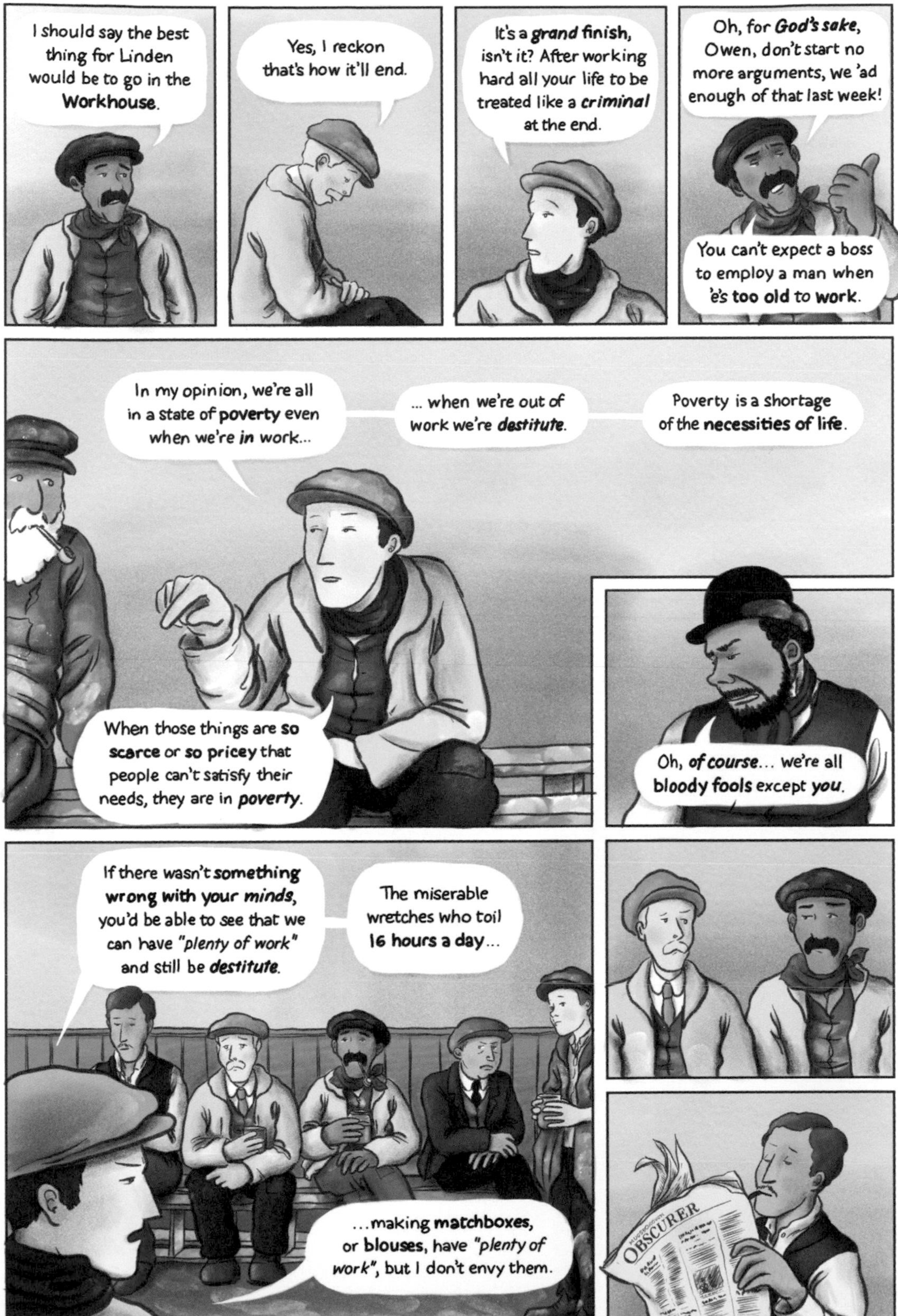
I should say the best thing for Linden would be to go in the **Workhouse**.
Yes, I reckon that's how it'll end.
It's a ***grand* finish**, isn't it? After working hard all your life to be treated like a ***criminal*** at the end.
Oh, for ***God's sake***, Owen, don't start no more arguments, we 'ad enough of that last week!
You can't expect a boss to employ a man when 'e's **too old** to **work**.
In my opinion, we're all in a state of **poverty** even when we're ***in*** work...
... when we're out of work we're ***destitute***.
Poverty is a shortage of the **necessities of life**.
When those things are **so scarce** or **so pricey** that people can't satisfy their needs, they are in ***poverty***.
Oh, ***of course***... we're all **bloody fools** except ***you***.
If there wasn't **something wrong with your *minds***, you'd be able to see that we can have *"plenty of work"* and still be ***destitute***.
The miserable wretches who toil **16 hours a day**...
...making **matchboxes**, or **blouses**, have *"plenty of work"*, but I don't envy them.
OBSCURER

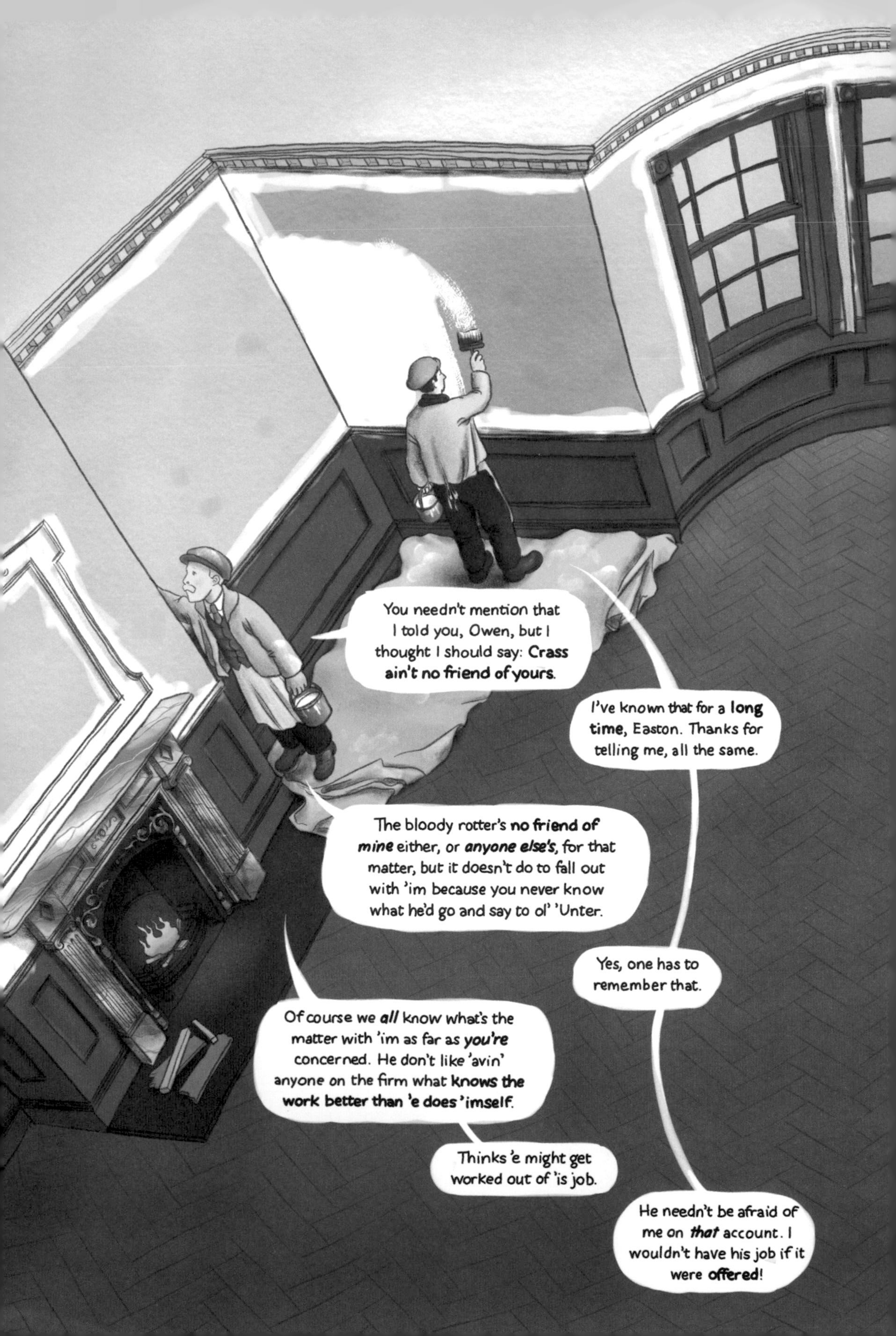
You needn't mention that I told you, Owen, but I thought I should say: **Crass ain't no friend of yours**.
I've known that for a **long time**, Easton. Thanks for telling me, all the same.
The bloody rotter's **no friend of *mine*** either, or ***anyone else's***, for that matter, but it doesn't do to fall out with 'im because you never know what he'd go and say to ol' 'Unter.
Yes, one has to remember that.
Of course we ***all*** know what's the matter with 'im as far as ***you're*** concerned. He don't like 'avin' anyone on the firm what **knows the work better than 'e does 'imself**.
Thinks 'e might get worked out of 'is job.
He needn't be afraid of me on ***that*** account. I wouldn't have his job if it were **offered**!

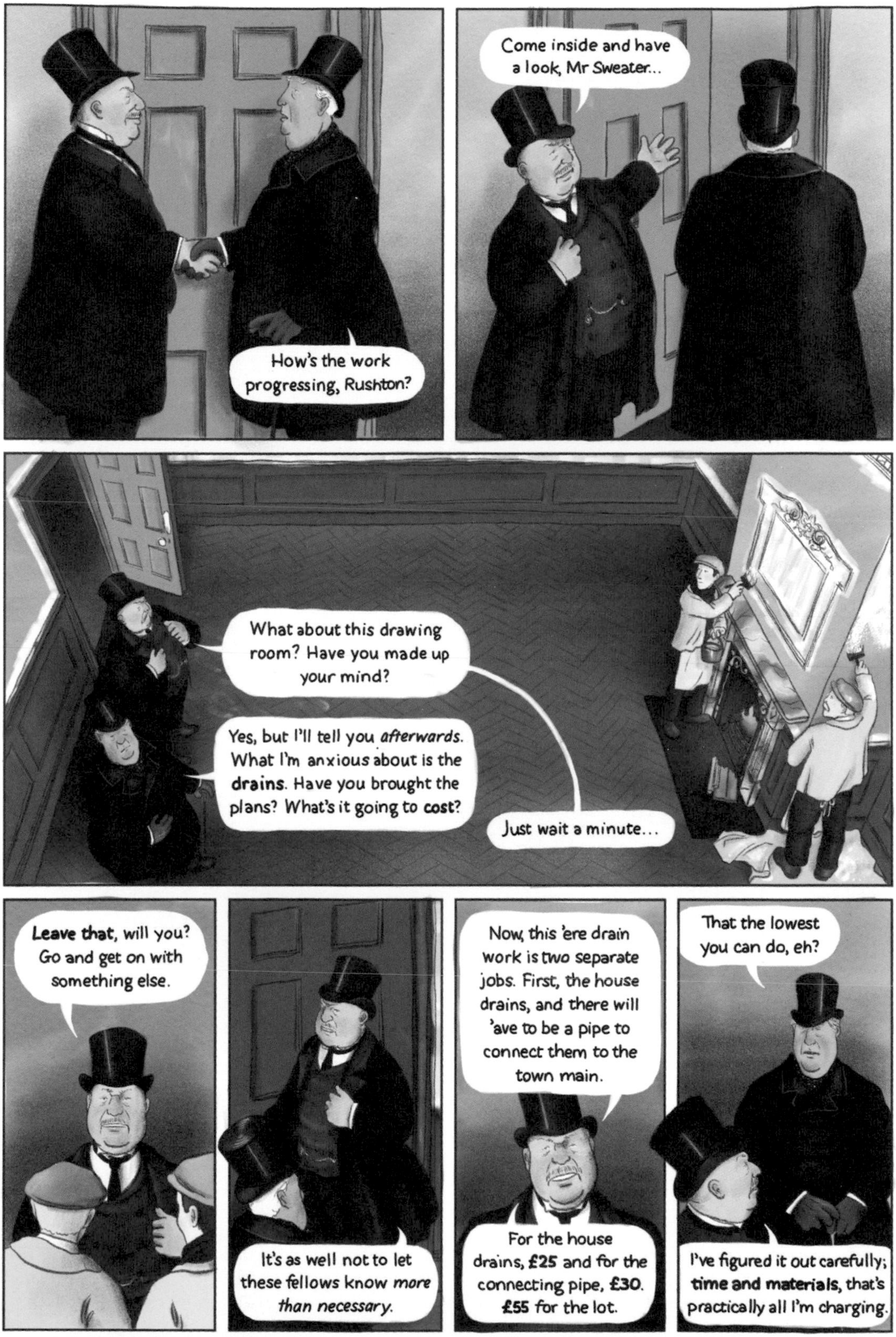
How's the work progressing, Rushton?
Come inside and have a look, Mr Sweater...
What about this drawing room? Have you made up your mind?
Yes, but I'll tell you *afterwards*. What I'm anxious about is the **drains**. Have you brought the plans? What's it going to **cost**?
Just wait a minute...
Leave that, will you? Go and get on with something else.
It's as well not to let these fellows know *more than necessary*.
Now, this 'ere drain work is two separate jobs. First, the house drains, and there will 'ave to be a pipe to connect them to the town main.
For the house drains, **£25** and for the connecting pipe, **£30**. **£55** for the lot.
That the lowest you can do, eh?
I've figured it out carefully; **time and materials**, that's practically all I'm charging.

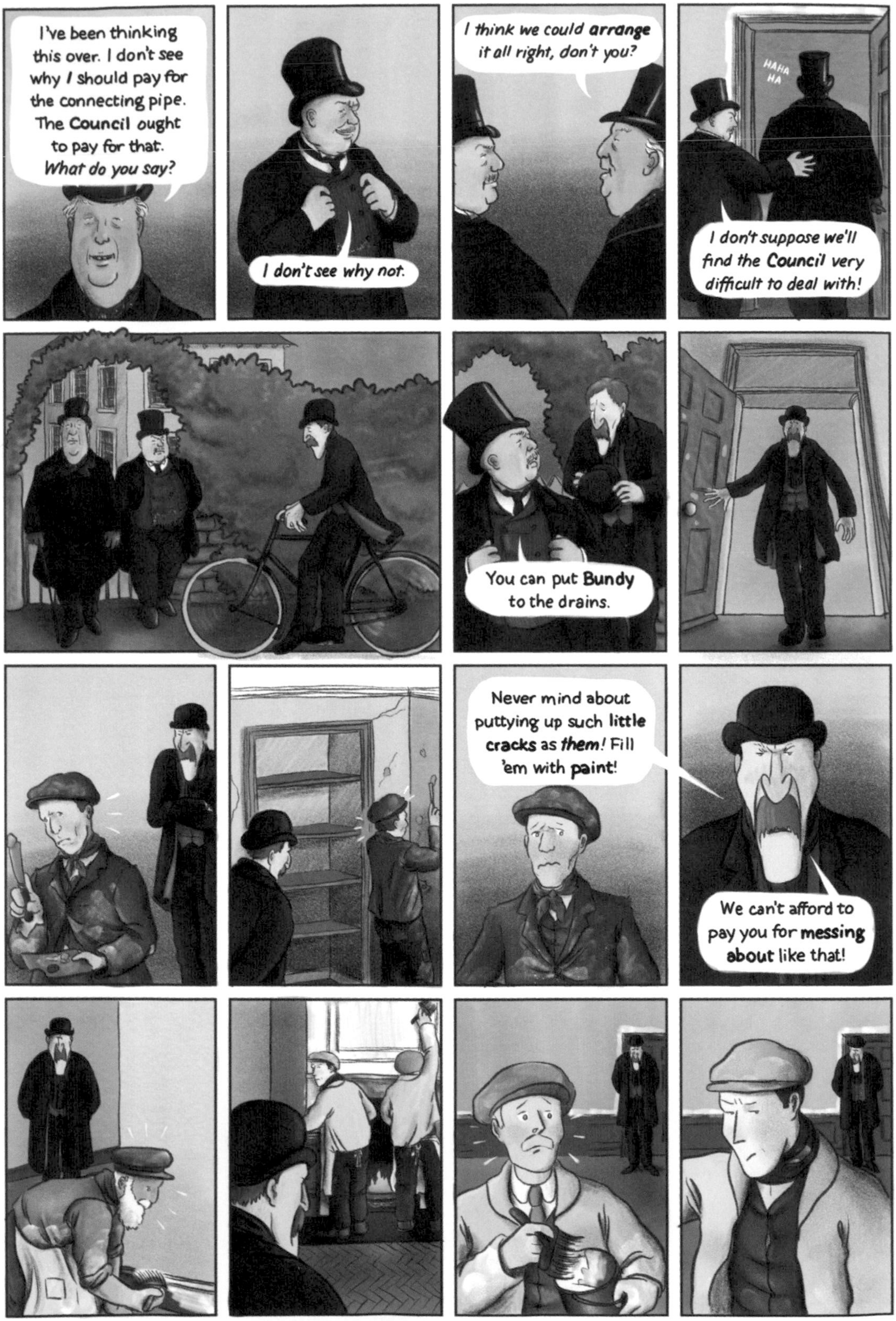
I've been thinking this over. I don't see why *I* should pay for the connecting pipe. The **Council** ought to pay for that. *What do you say?*
I don't see why not.
*I think we could **arrange** it all right, don't you?*
HAHA HA
*I don't suppose we'll find the **Council** very difficult to deal with!*
You can put **Bundy** to the drains.
Never mind about puttying up such **little cracks** as ***them***! Fill 'em with **paint**!
We can't afford to pay you for **messing about** like that!

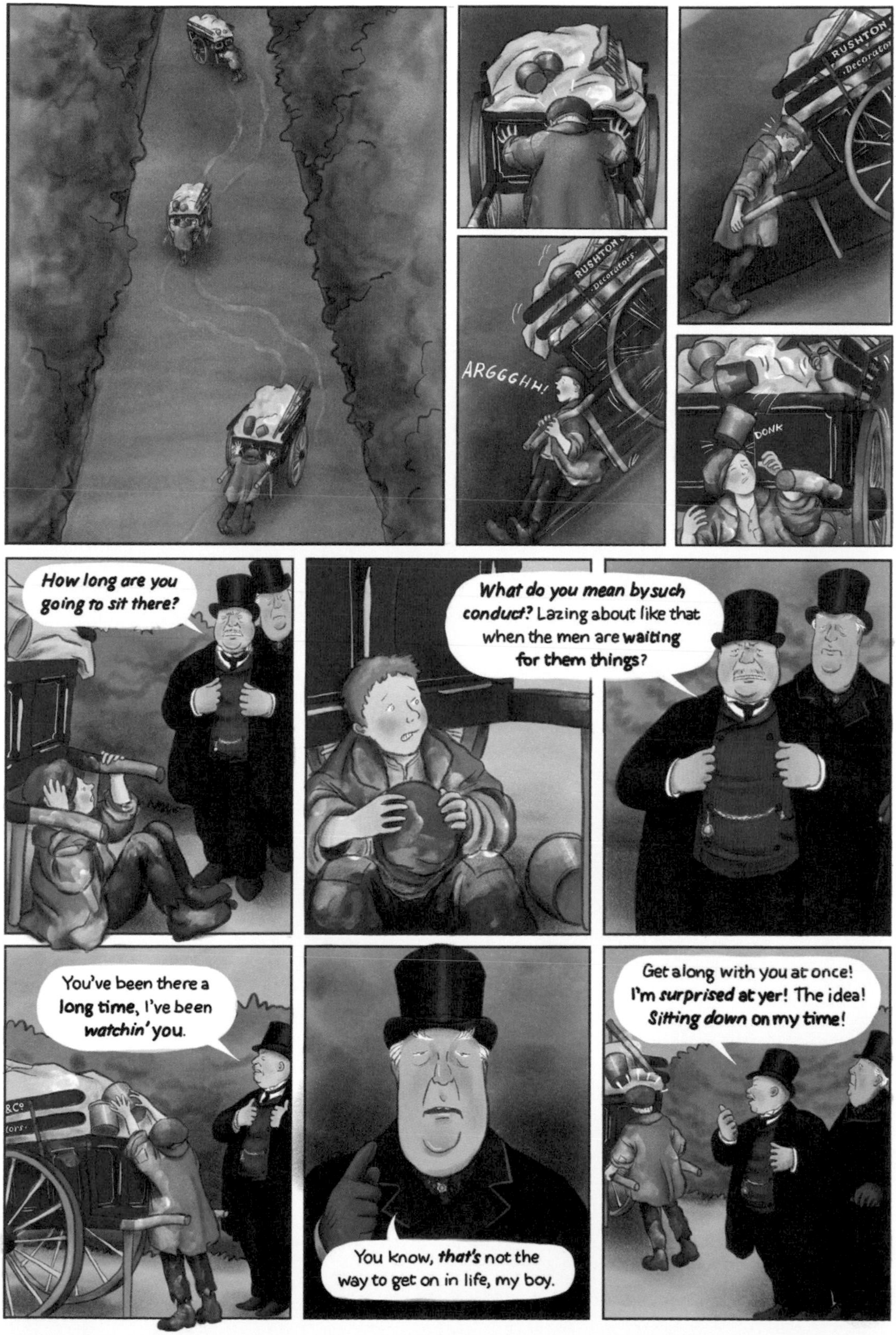
RUSHTON
Decorators
RUSHTON
Decorators
ARGGGHH!
DONK
How long are you going to sit there?
What do you mean by such conduct? Lazing about like that when the men are waiting for them things?
You've been there a long time, I've been watchin' you.
You know, that's not the way to get on in life, my boy.
Get along with you at once! I'm surprised at yer! The idea! Sitting down on my time!

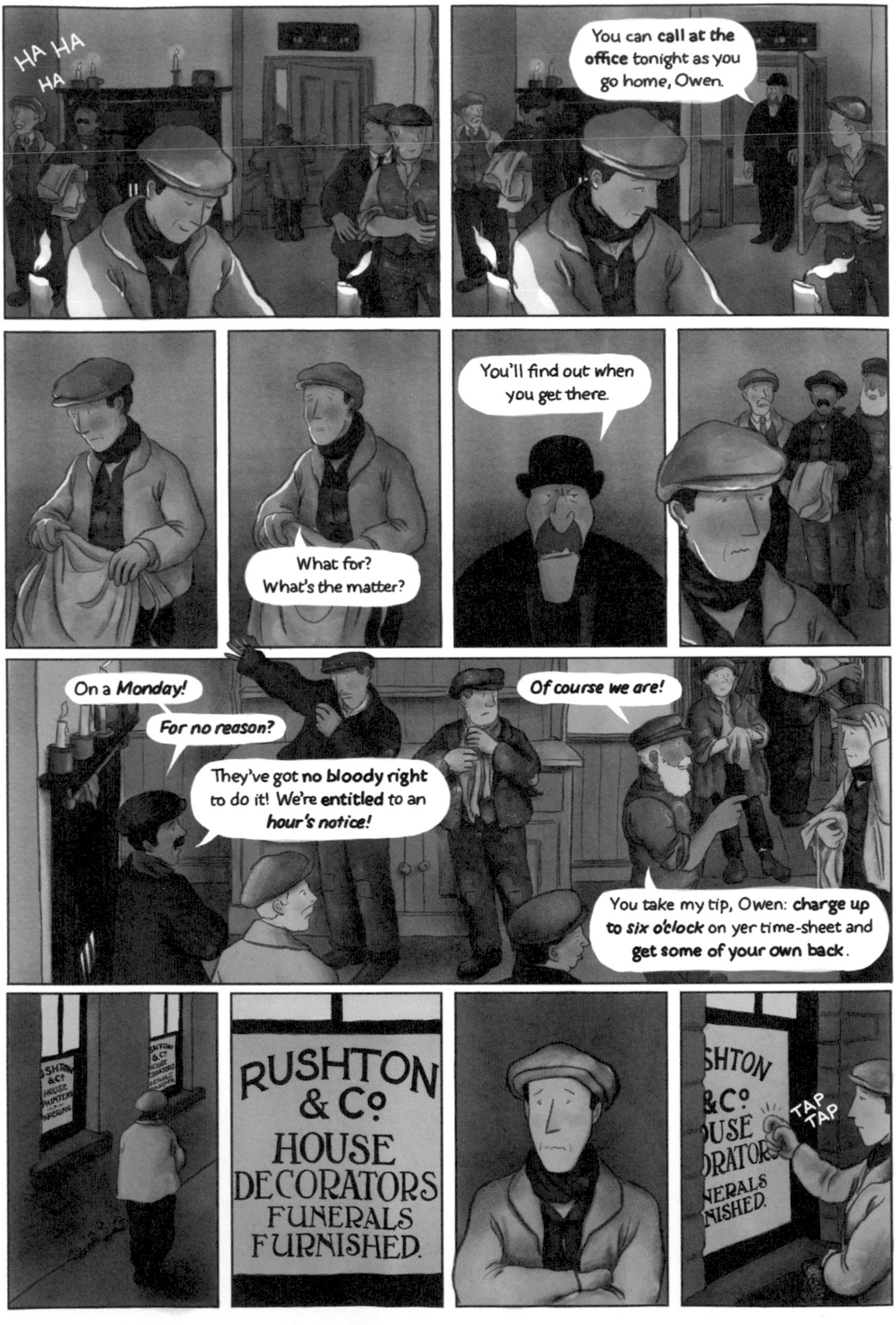
HA HA HA
You can call at the office tonight as you go home, Owen.
What for? What's the matter?
You'll find out when you get there.
On a Monday!
For no reason?
They've got no bloody right to do it! We're entitled to an hour's notice!
Of course we are!
You take my tip, Owen: charge up to six o'clock on yer time-sheet and get some of your own back.
RUSHTON & Co HOUSE DECORATORS FUNERALS FURNISHED.
TAP TAP

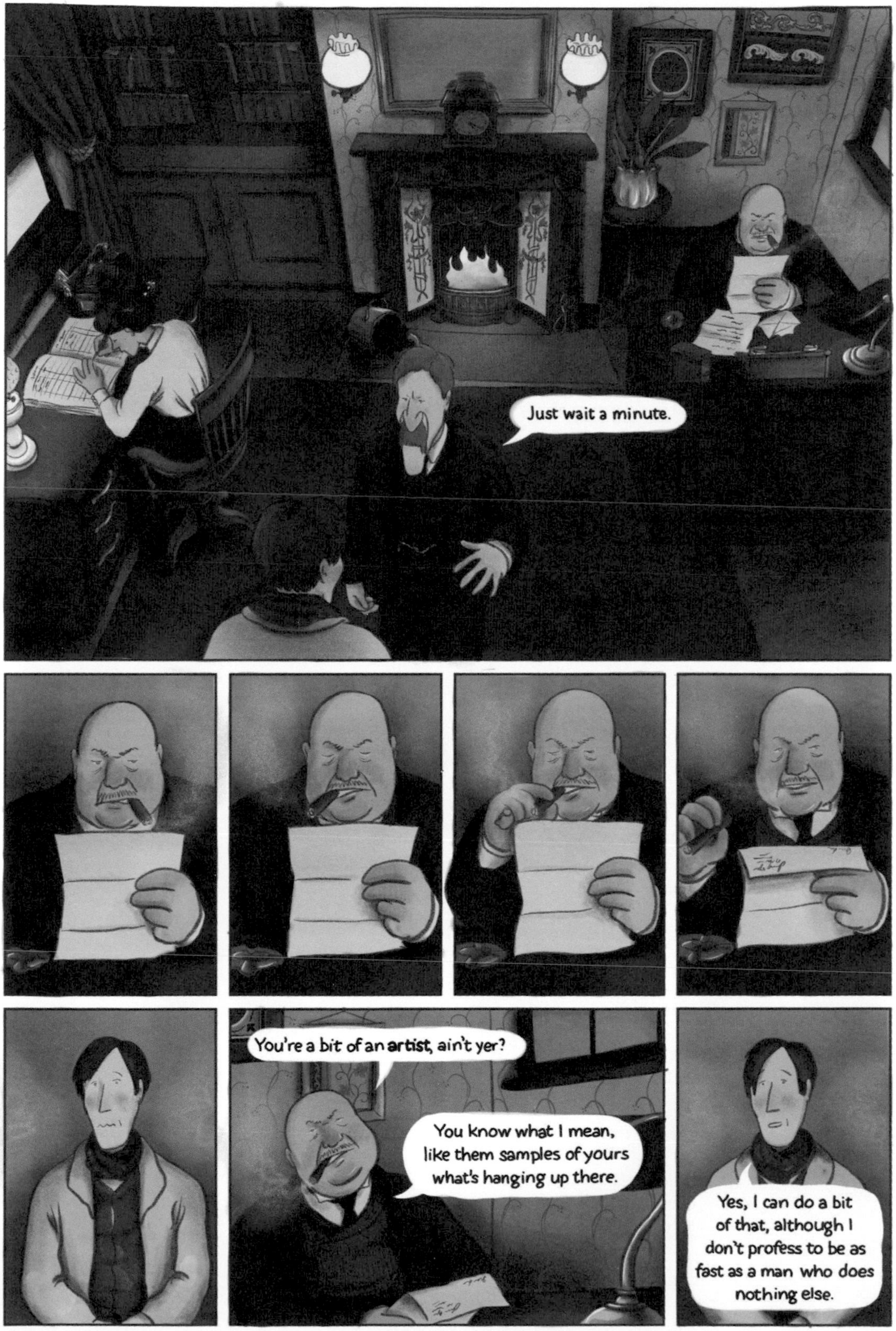
Just wait a minute.
You're a bit of an **artist**, ain't yer?
You know what I mean, like them samples of yours what's hanging up there.
Yes, I can do a bit of that, although I don't profess to be as fast as a man who does nothing else.

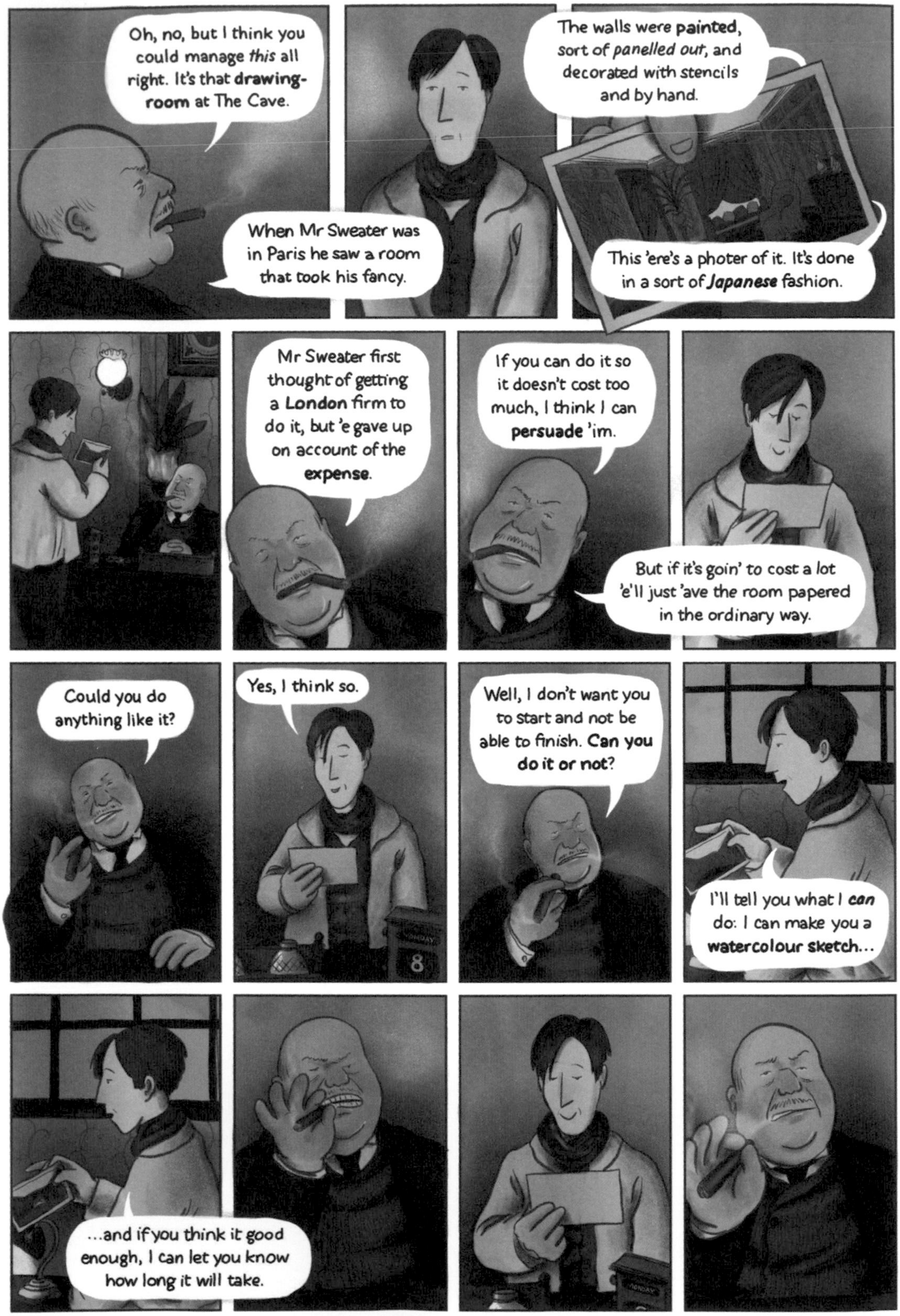
Oh, no, but I think you could manage *this* all right. It's that **drawing-room** at The Cave.
When Mr Sweater was in Paris he saw a room that took his fancy.
The walls were **painted**, *sort of panelled out*, and decorated with stencils and by hand.
This 'ere's a photer of it. It's done in a sort of ***Japanese*** fashion.
Mr Sweater first thought of getting a **London** firm to do it, but 'e gave up on account of the **expense**.
If you can do it so it doesn't cost too much, I think I can **persuade** 'im.
But if it's goin' to cost a lot 'e'll just 'ave the room papered in the ordinary way.
Could you do anything like it?
Yes, I think so.
Well, I don't want you to start and not be able to finish. **Can you do it or not**?
I'll tell you what I ***can*** do: I can make you a **watercolour sketch**...
...and if you think it good enough, I can let you know how long it will take.

What if I let you spend a lot of time on it and then Mr Sweater doesn't approve your design?

How about if I draw the design at home in my **own time**?

If it's accepted, I'll charge you for the time I've spent.

If it's not suitable, I won't charge at all.

All right, but don't pile it on **too** thick.

If it's going to cost a great deal 'e won't 'ave it done at all.

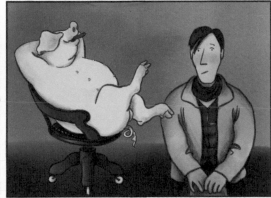

Can you get the drawings done **tonight**?

I'm afraid not. It will need a little **thinking about**

When **can** you do 'em then?

Well, say Friday morning?

I'm afraid that if we keeps 'im waiting all that time we may lose the job altogether.

I can't get them done any quicker in my spare time.

If you let me stay home tomorrow and charge the same as if I had gone to work...

...I could go to my ordinary work on Wednesday and let you have the drawings on Thursday morning.

Oh, all right.

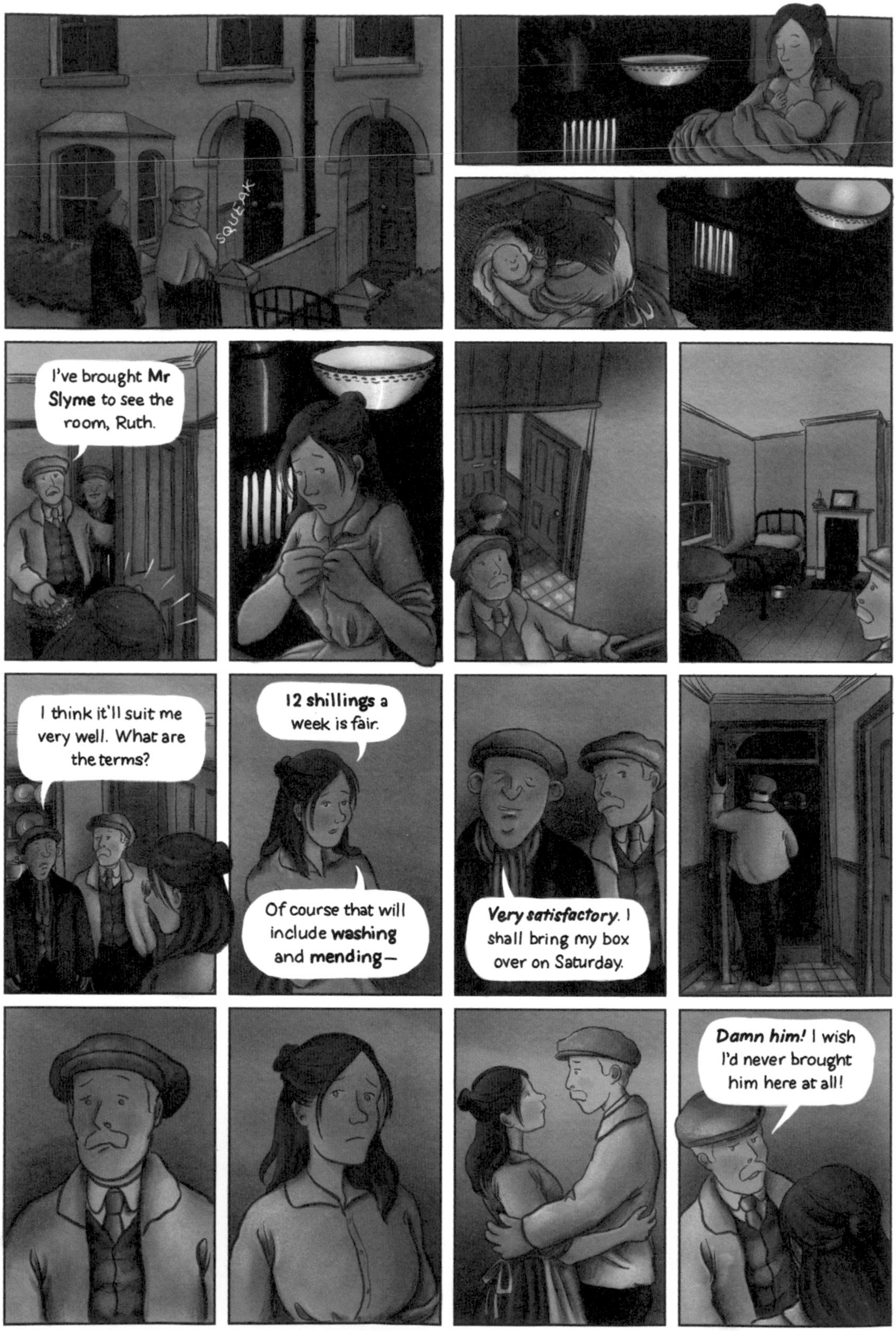
SQUEAK
I've brought Mr Slyme to see the room, Ruth.
I think it'll suit me very well. What are the terms?
12 shillings a week is fair.
Of course that will include washing and mending—
Very satisfactory. I shall bring my box over on Saturday.
Damn him! I wish I'd never brought him here at all!

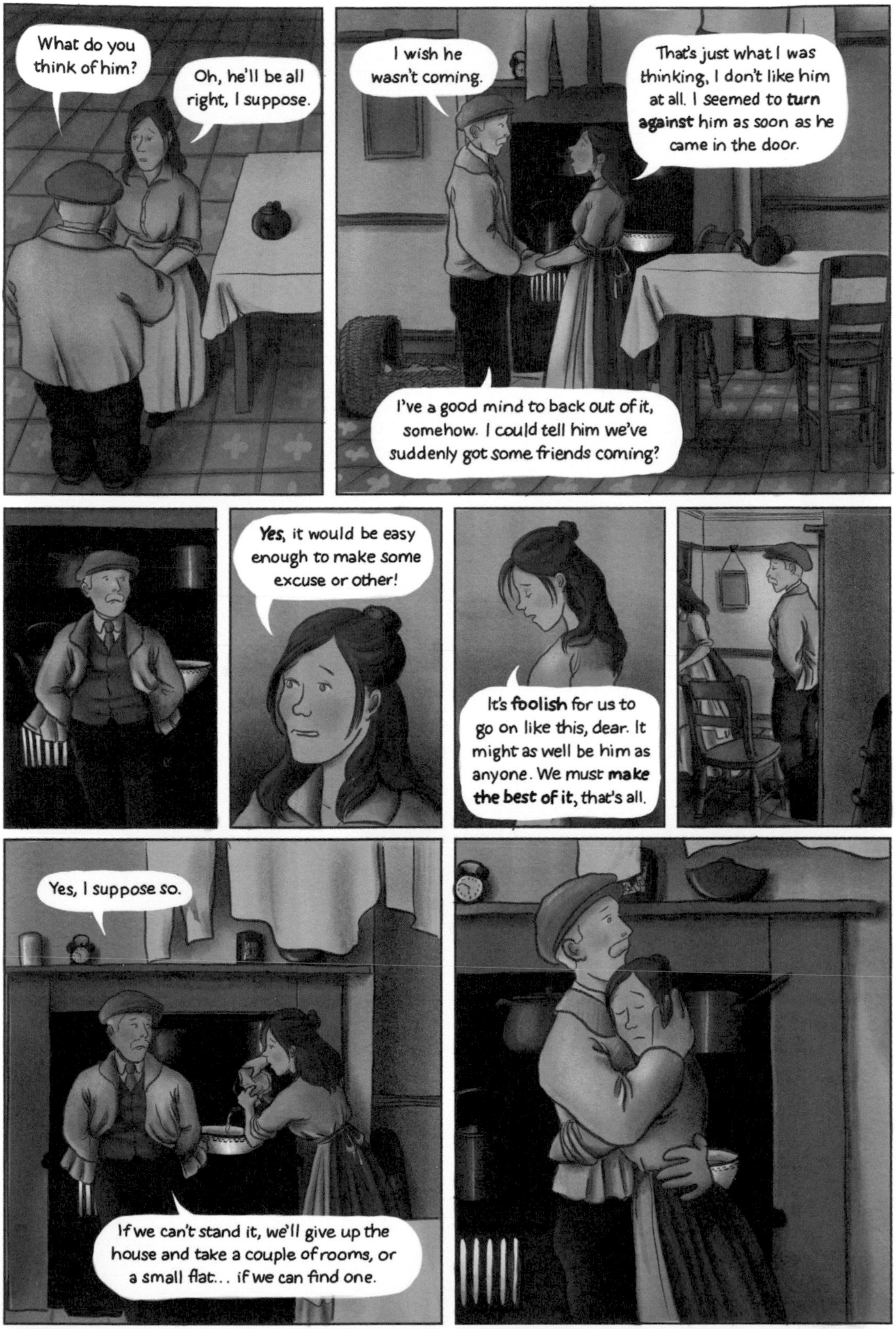
What do you think of him?
Oh, he'll be all right, I suppose.
I wish he wasn't coming.
That's just what I was thinking, I don't like him at all. I seemed to **turn against** him as soon as he came in the door.
I've a good mind to back out of it, somehow. I could tell him we've suddenly got some friends coming?
Yes, it would be easy enough to make some excuse or other!
It's **foolish** for us to go on like this, dear. It might as well be him as anyone. We must **make the best of it**, that's all.
Yes, I suppose so.
If we can't stand it, we'll give up the house and take a couple of rooms, or a small flat... if we can find one.

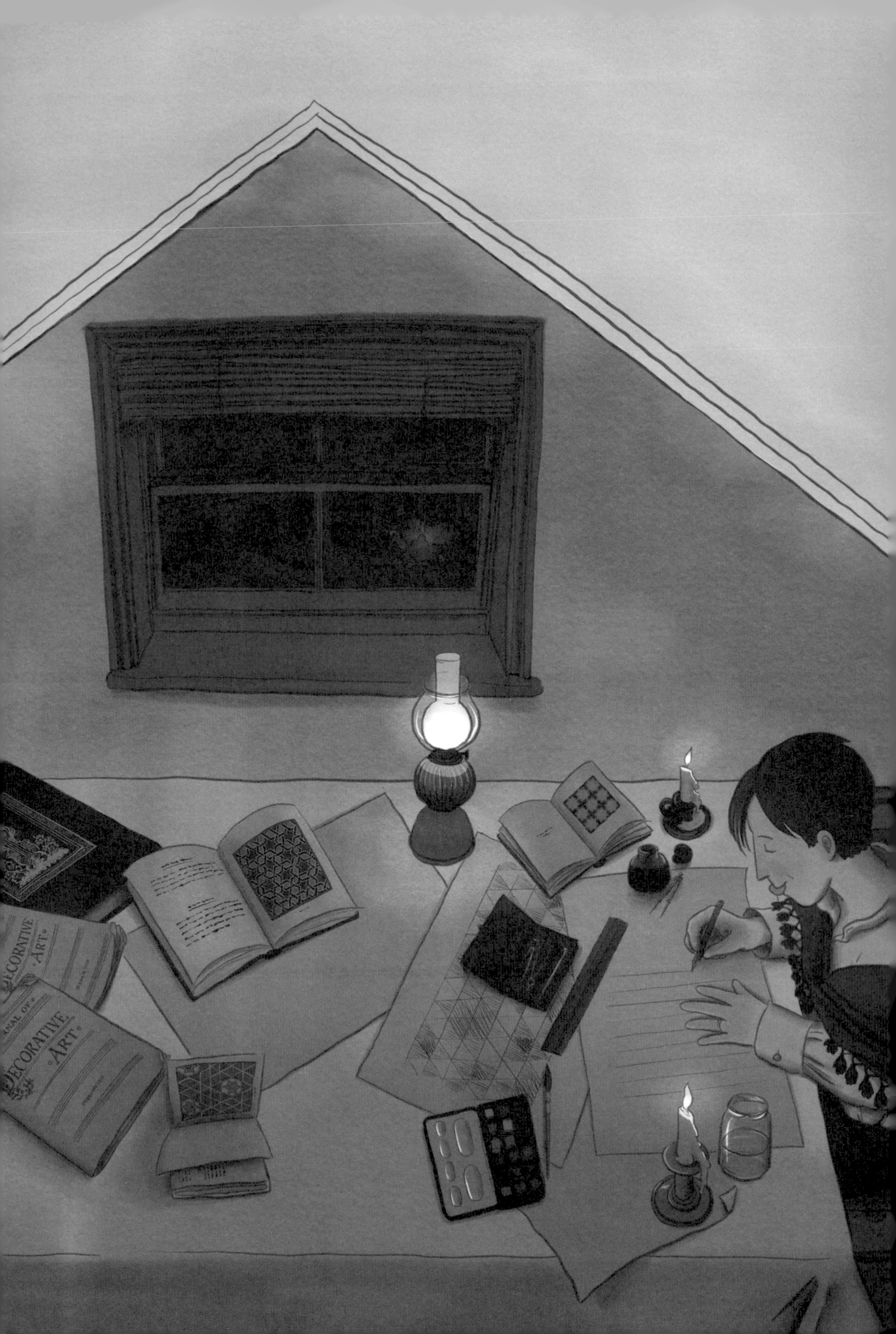
DECORATIVE
ART
DECORATIVE
ART

CHAPTER

5

THE ROOM

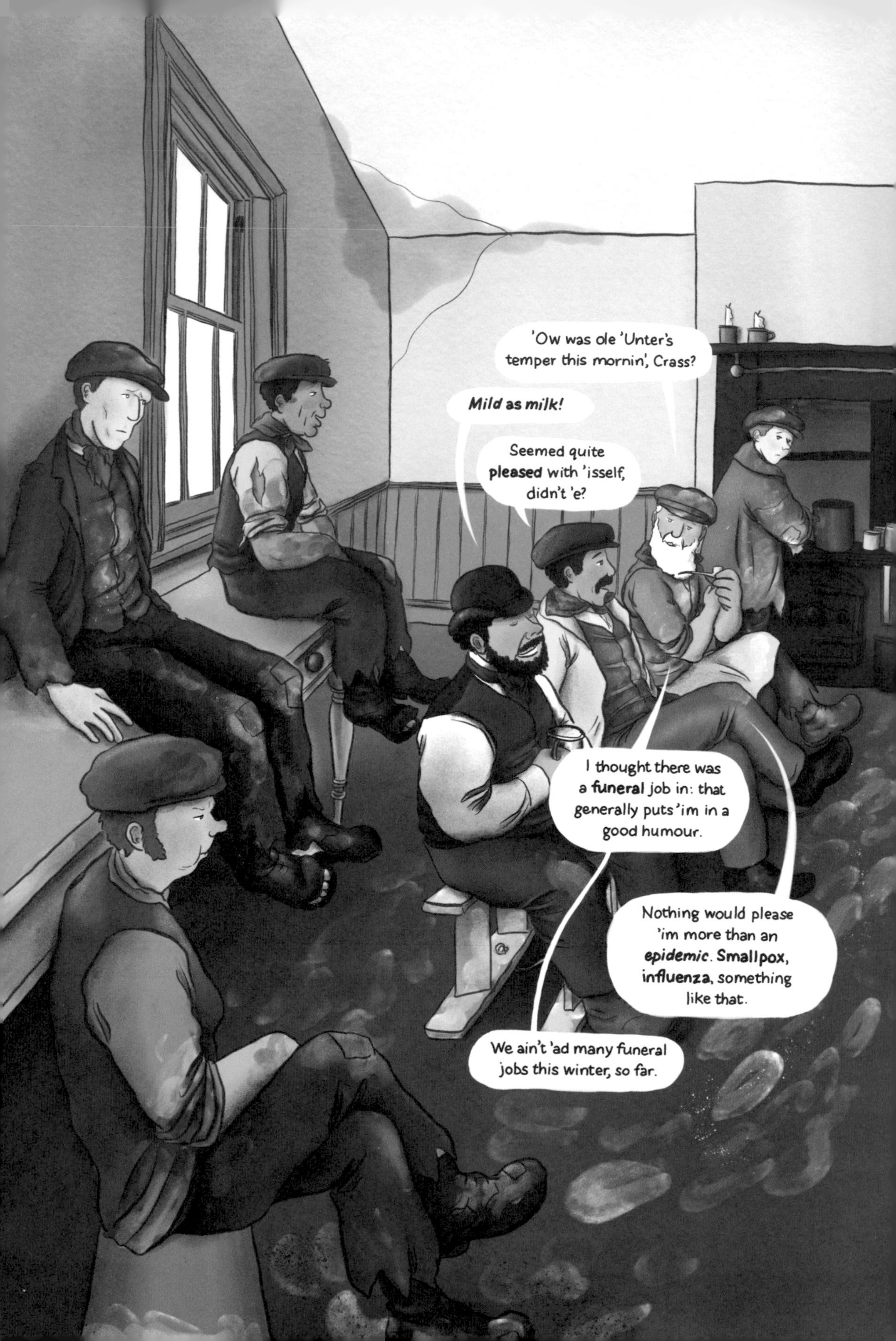
'Ow was ole 'Unter's temper this mornin', Crass?
Mild as milk!
Seemed quite pleased with 'isself, didn't 'e?
I thought there was a funeral job in: that generally puts 'im in a good humour.
Nothing would please 'im more than an epidemic. Smallpox, influenza, something like that.
We ain't 'ad many funeral jobs this winter, so far.

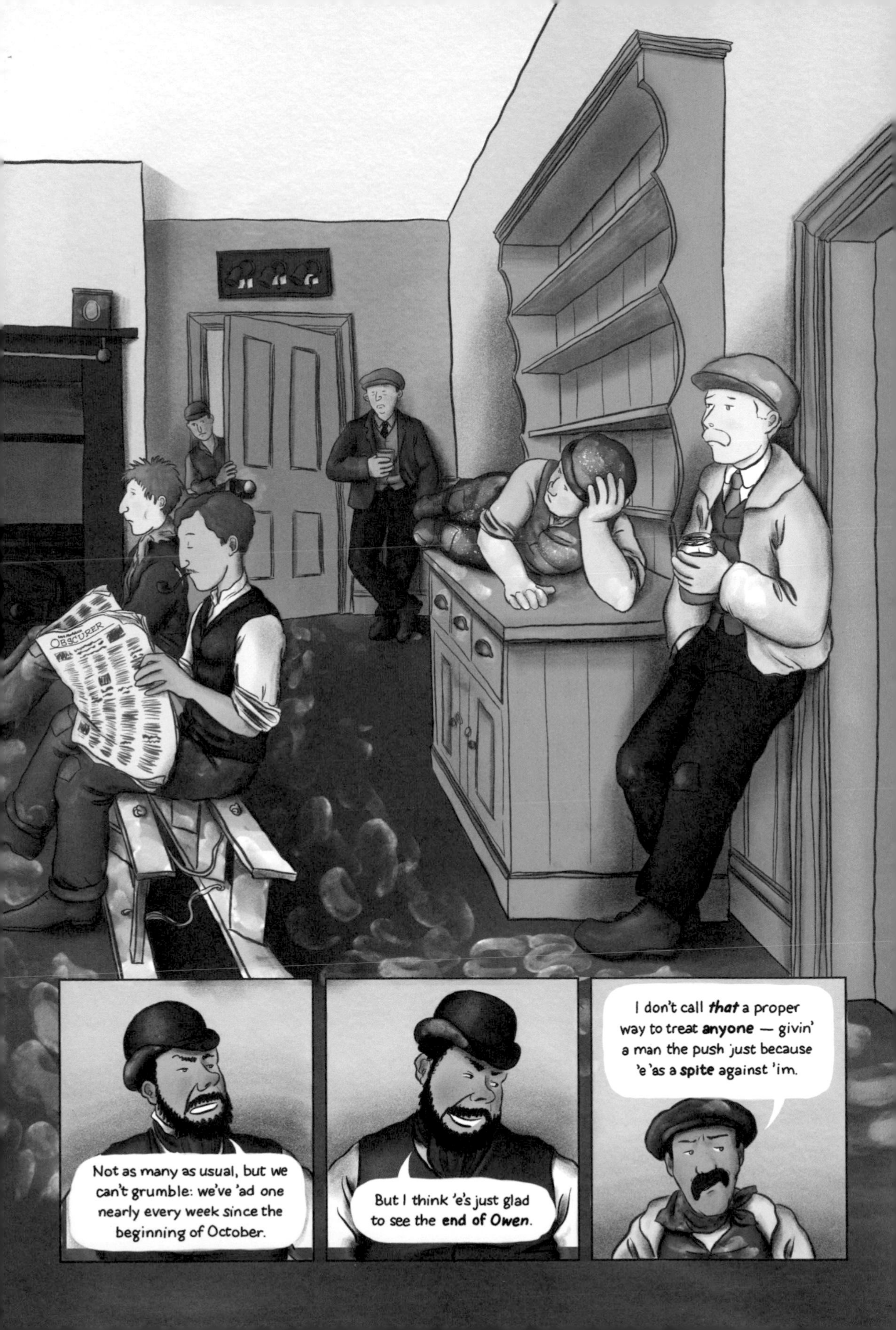
OBSCURER
Not as many as usual, but we can't grumble: we've 'ad one nearly every week since the beginning of October.
But I think 'e's just glad to see the end of Owen.
I don't call *that* a proper way to treat **anyone** — givin' a man the push just because 'e 'as a **spite** against 'im.

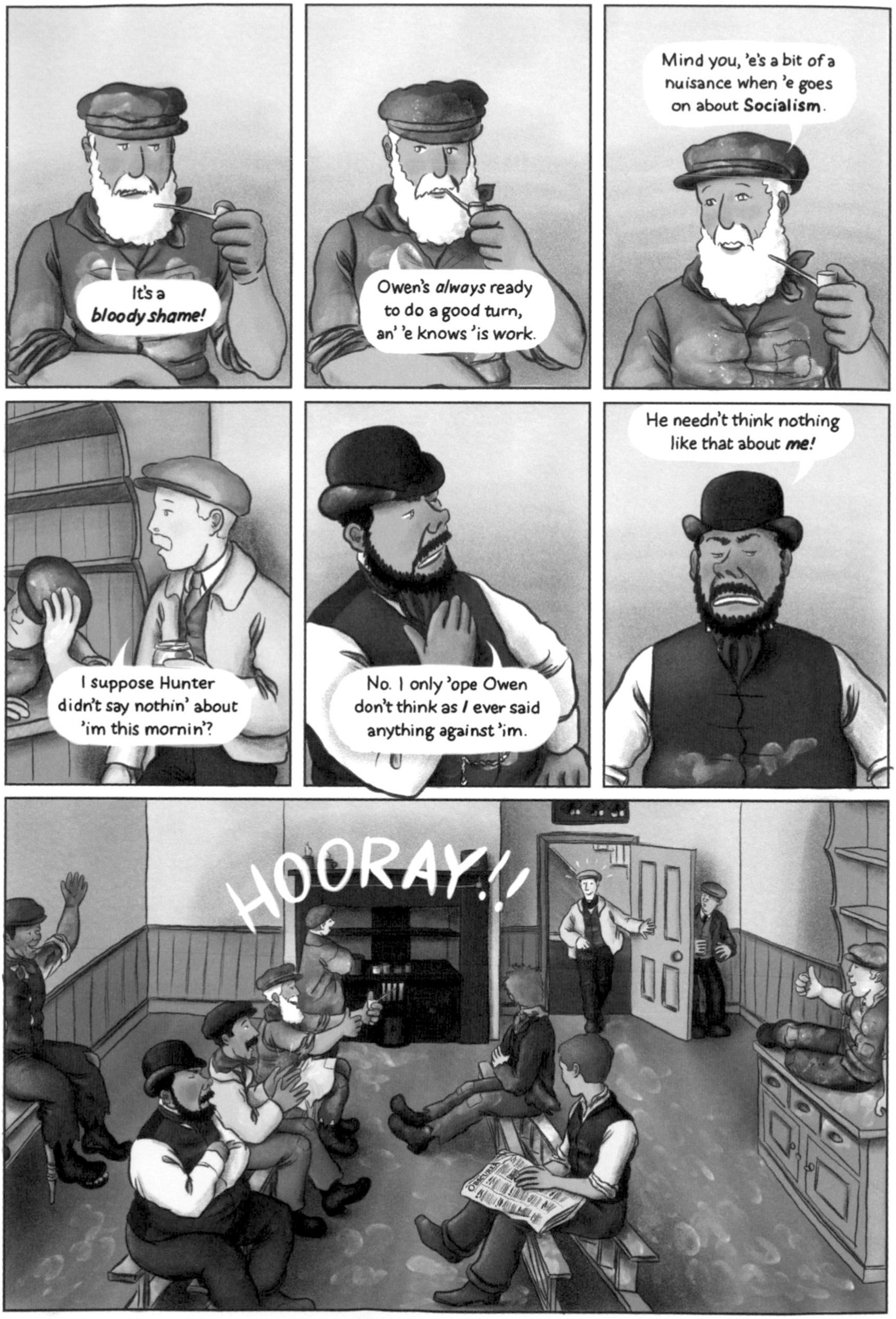
It's a
bloody shame!
Owen's *always* ready to do a good turn, an' 'e knows 'is work.
Mind you, 'e's a bit of a nuisance when 'e goes on about **Socialism**.
I suppose Hunter didn't say nothin' about 'im this mornin'?
No. I only 'ope Owen don't think as *I* ever said anything against 'im.
He needn't think nothing like that about *me!*
HOORAY!!

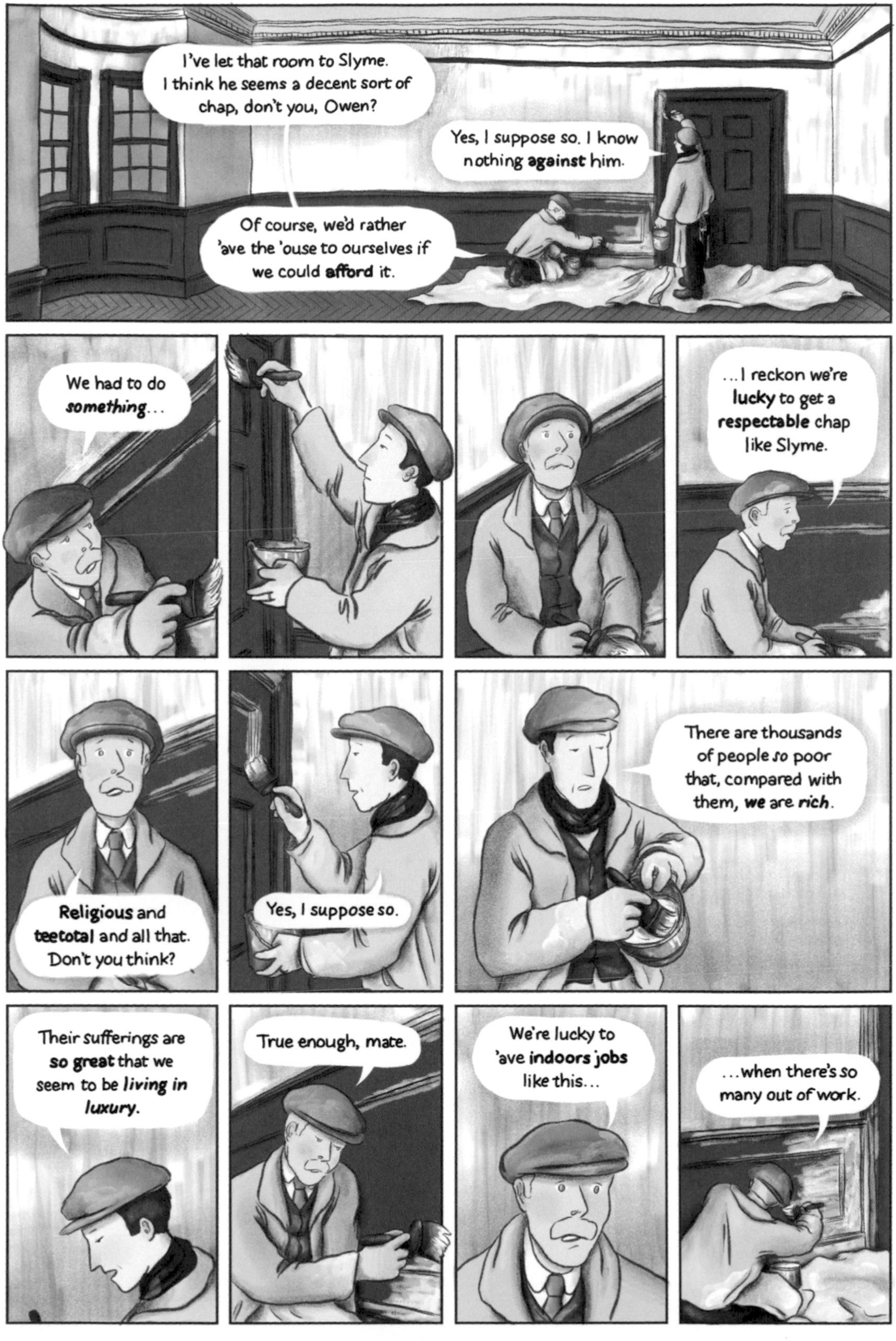
I've let that room to Slyme. I think he seems a decent sort of chap, don't you, Owen?
Yes, I suppose so. I know nothing **against** him.
Of course, we'd rather 'ave the 'ouse to ourselves if we could **afford** it.
We had to do ***something***...
...I reckon we're **lucky** to get a **respectable** chap like Slyme.
Religious and **teetotal** and all that. Don't you think?
Yes, I suppose so.
There are thousands of people *so* poor that, compared with them, ***we*** are ***rich***.
Their sufferings are **so great** that we seem to be ***living in luxury***.
True enough, mate.
We're lucky to 'ave **indoors jobs** like this...
...when there's so many out of work.

Yes, we're *lucky!*

Although we're in **abject, miserable poverty,** we feel *lucky* that we're not actually *starving.*

D'you think it's **right** for us to tamely make up our minds to live like this?

No. But things'll get **better.**

A few years ago there was so much work that we was putting in **16 hours a day.**

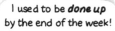

I used to be **done up** by the end of the week!

Don't you think it's worth trying to find out how we could live like **civilised human beings** without being alternately **worked or starved to *death*?**

I don't see how we're goin' to alter things. Work is scarce everywhere. We can't **make** work, can we?

Do you think the affairs of the world are like the **weather...**

...altogether beyond our control?

And we can do **nothing** but just **sit and wait** for it to improve?

Well, if the people with money won't spend it, the likes of **me** and **you** can't make 'em, can we?

I suppose you're about 26? So you've another **30 years** to live.

Of course, if you had **proper food** and **clothes** and **working hours,** you could live for another **50 years.**

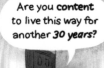

Are you **content** to live this way for another **30 years?**

If you committed a crime, and were sentenced to 10 years' hard labour, you'd probably think your fate very pitiable...

...yet you submit **quite cheerfully** to this other sentence, to die a **premature death** after another 30 years of this.

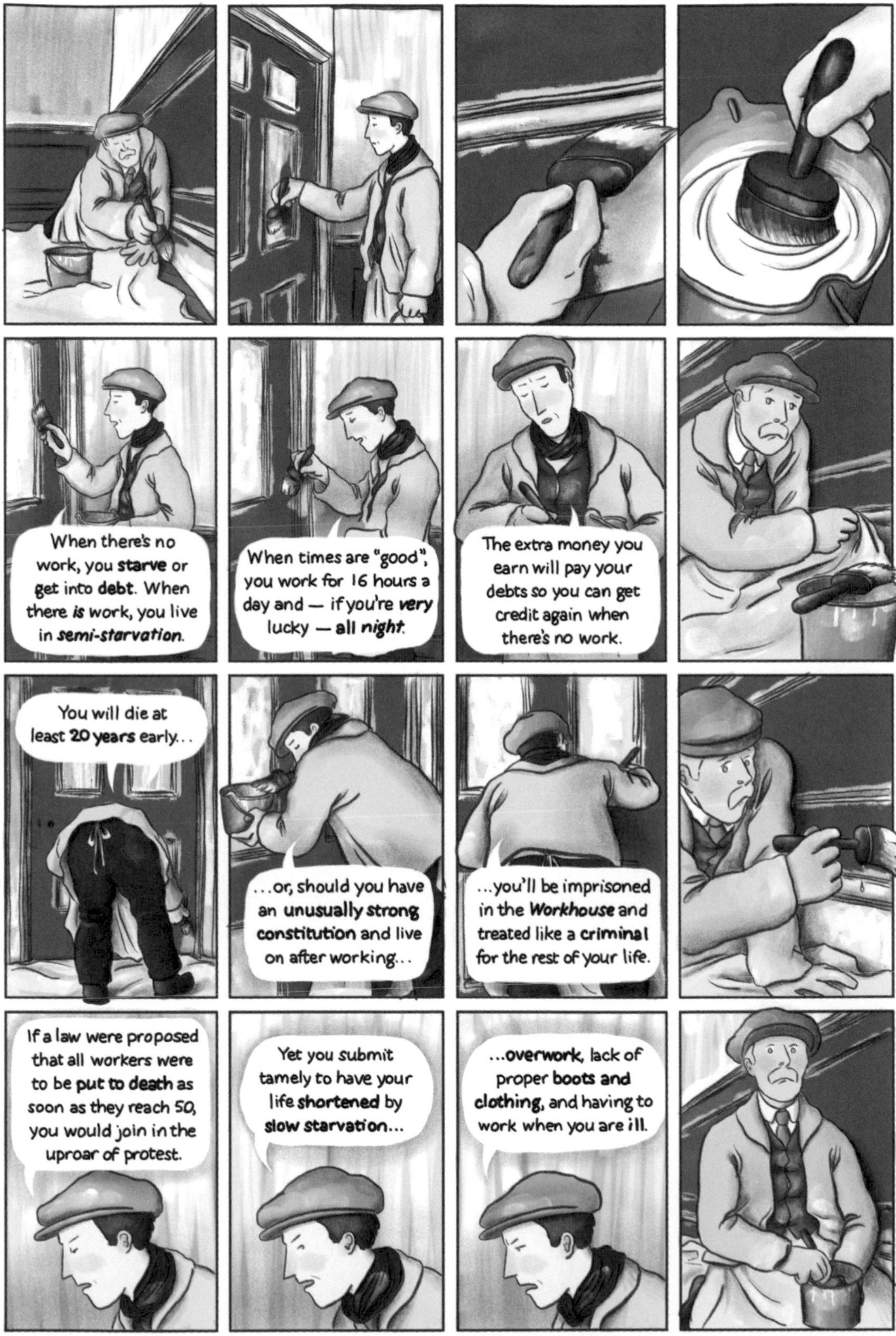
When there's no work, you starve or get into debt. When there is work, you live in semi-starvation.
When times are "good", you work for 16 hours a day and — if you're very lucky — all night.
The extra money you earn will pay your debts so you can get credit again when there's no work.
You will die at least 20 years early...
...or, should you have an unusually strong constitution and live on after working...
...you'll be imprisoned in the Workhouse and treated like a criminal for the rest of your life.
If a law were proposed that all workers were to be put to death as soon as they reach 50, you would join in the uproar of protest.
Yet you submit tamely to have your life shortened by slow starvation...
...overwork, lack of proper boots and clothing, and having to work when you are ill.

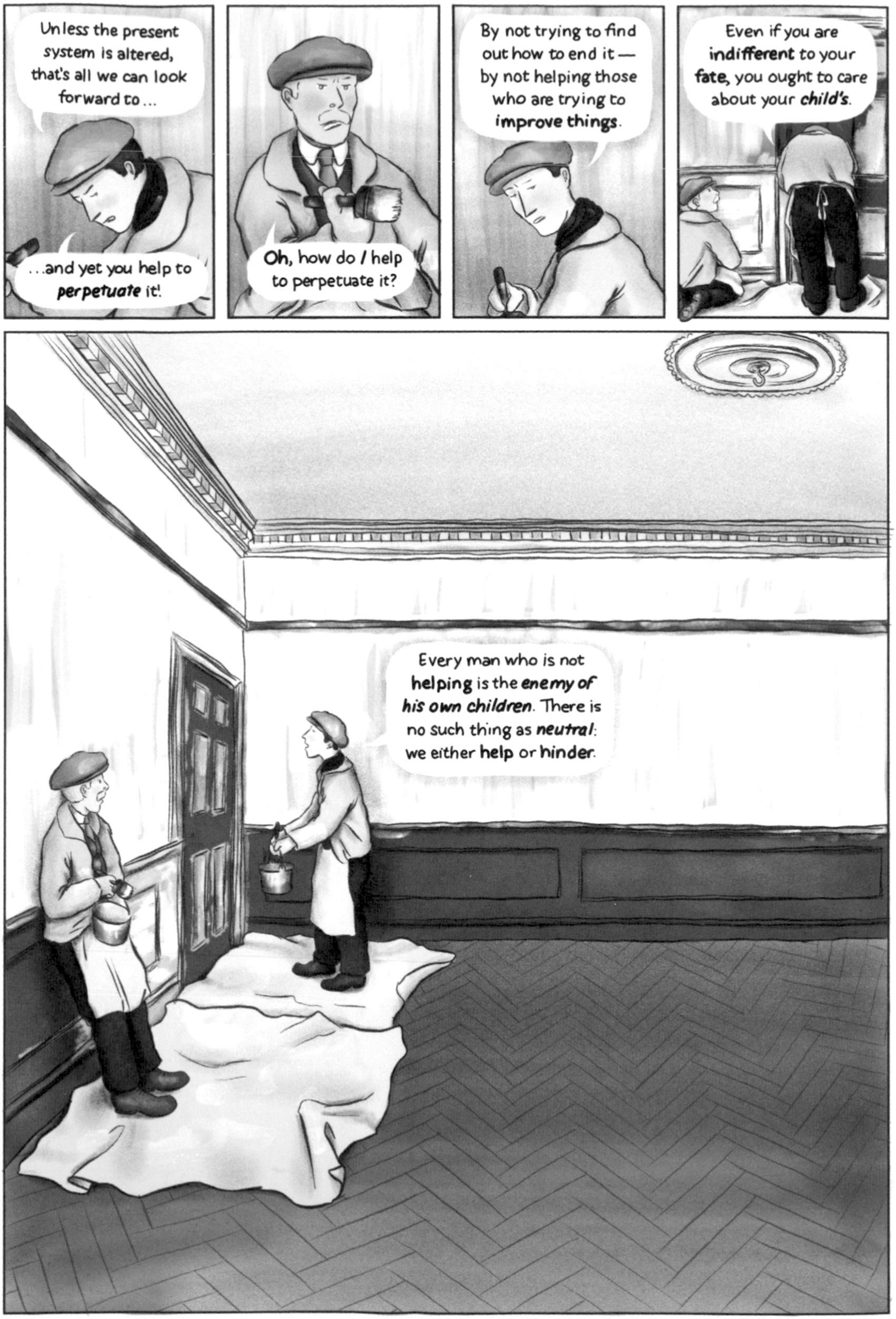
Unless the present system is altered, that's all we can look forward to...
...and yet you help to **perpetuate** it!
Oh, how do **I** help to perpetuate it?
By not trying to find out how to end it — by not helping those who are trying to **improve things**.
Even if you are **indifferent** to your **fate**, you ought to care about your ***child's***.
Every man who is not **helping** is the ***enemy of his own children***. There is no such thing as ***neutral***: we either **help** or **hinder**.

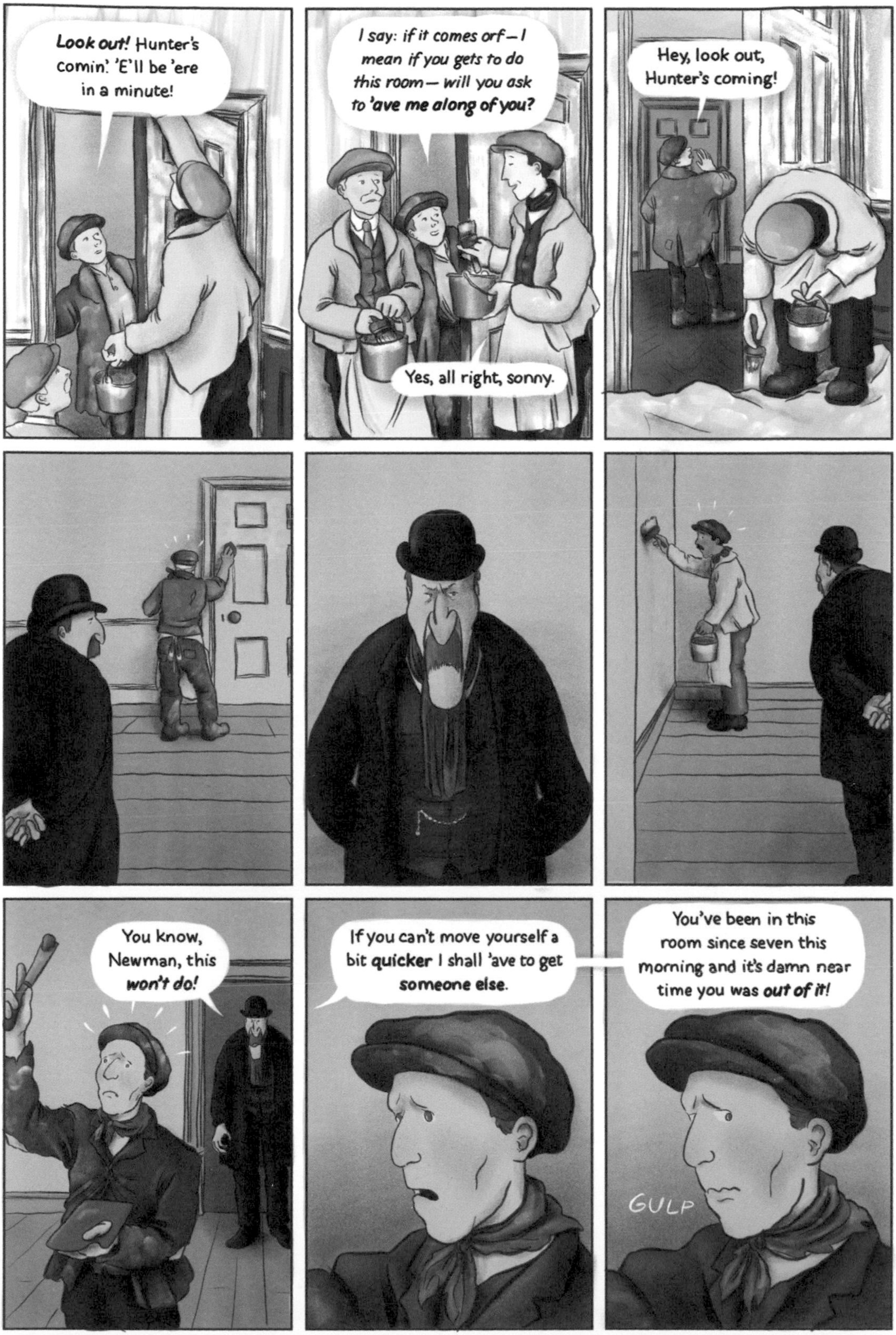
Look out! Hunter's comin'. 'E'll be 'ere in a minute!
I say: if it comes orf — I mean if you gets to do this room — will you ask to 'ave me along of you?
Yes, all right, sonny.
Hey, look out, Hunter's coming!
You know, Newman, this won't do!
If you can't move yourself a bit quicker I shall 'ave to get someone else.
You've been in this room since seven this morning and it's damn near time you was out of it!
GULP

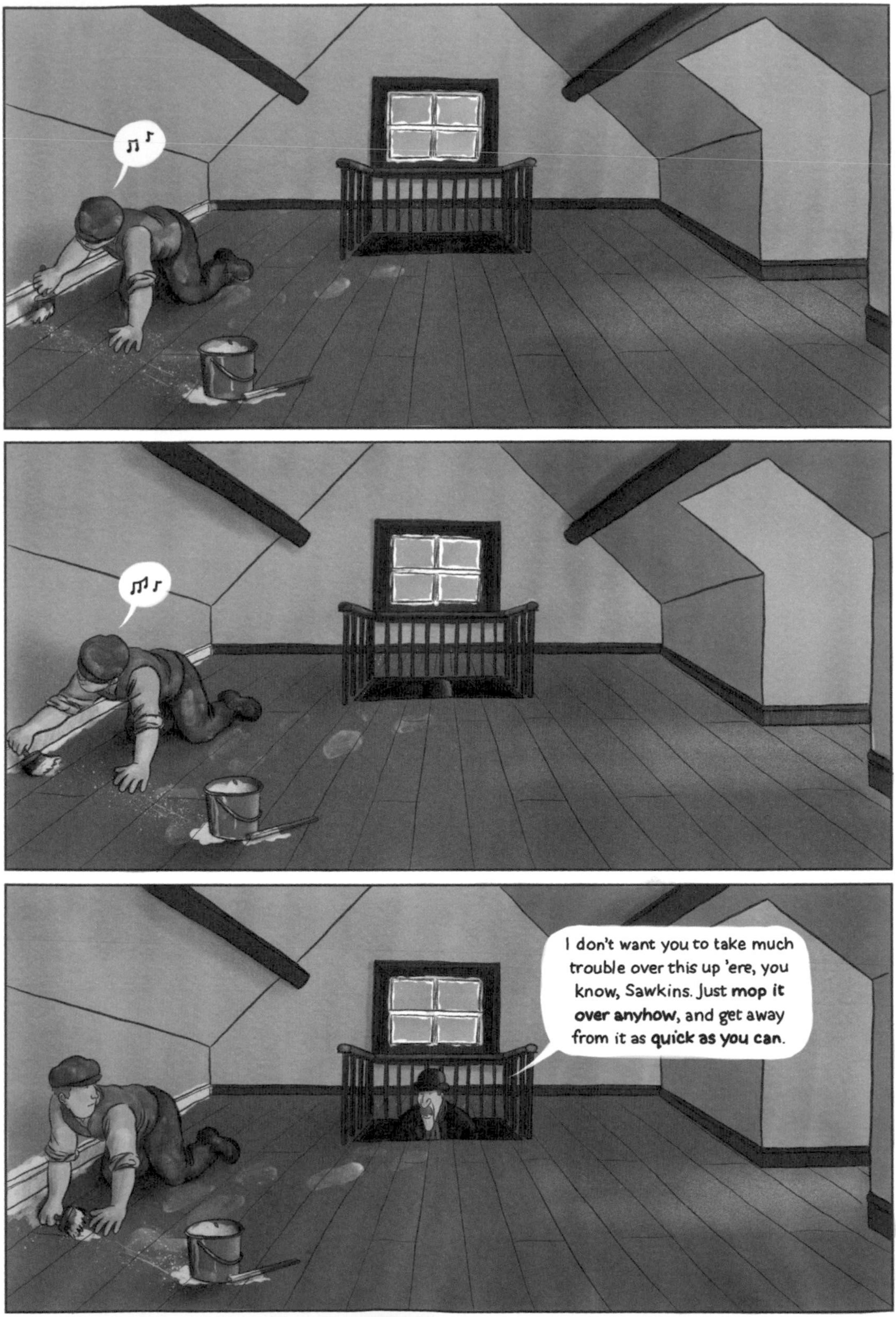
I don't want you to take much trouble over this up 'ere, you know, Sawkins. Just **mop it over anyhow**, and get away from it as **quick as you can**.

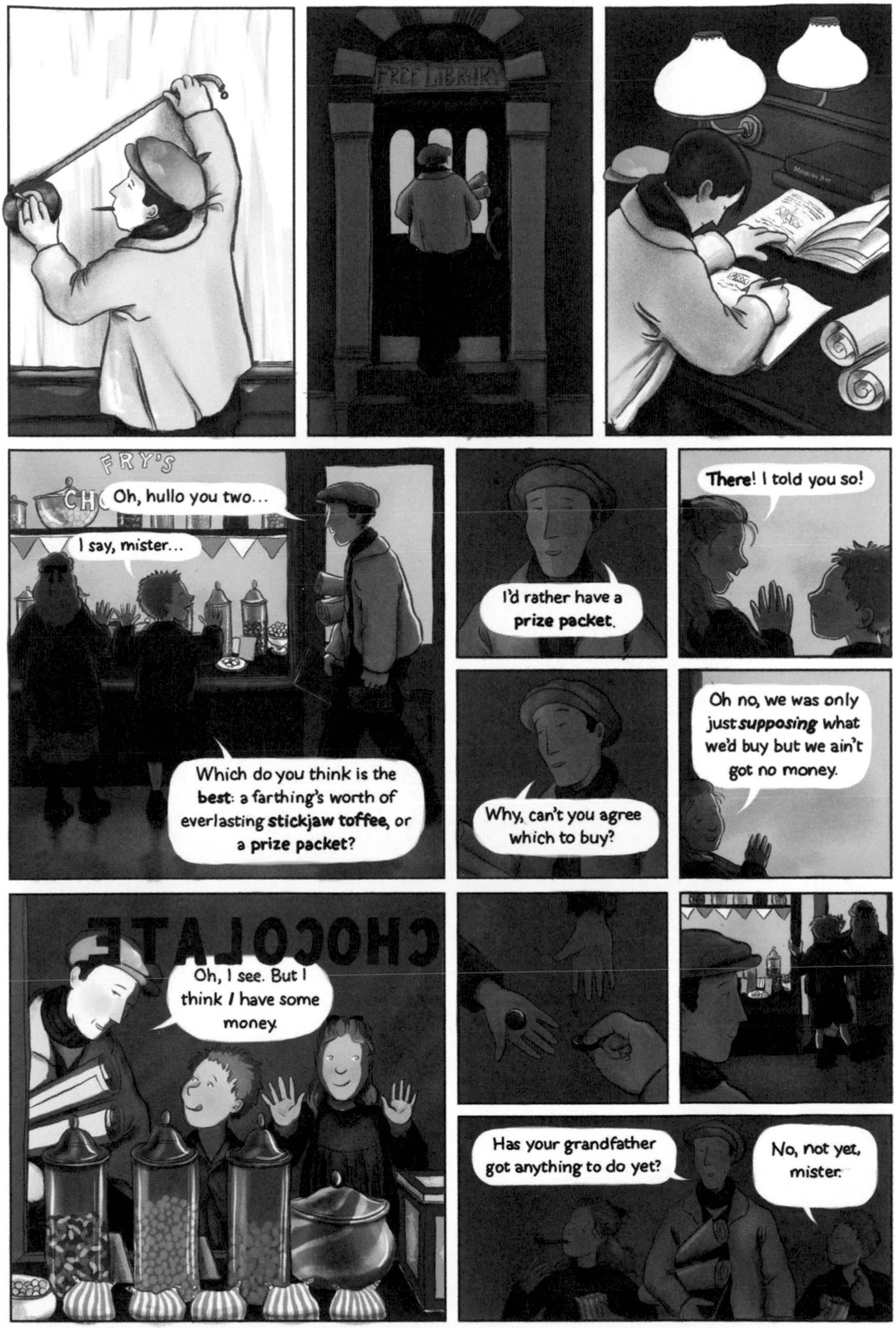
FREE LIBRARY
FRY'S
Oh, hullo you two...
I say, mister...
Which do you think is the **best**: a farthing's worth of everlasting **stickjaw toffee**, or a **prize packet**?
I'd rather have a **prize packet**.
There! I told you so!
Why, can't you agree which to buy?
Oh no, we was only just ***supposing*** what we'd buy but we ain't got no money.
CHOCOLATE
Oh, I see. But I think *I* have some money.
Has your grandfather got anything to do yet?
No, not yet, mister.

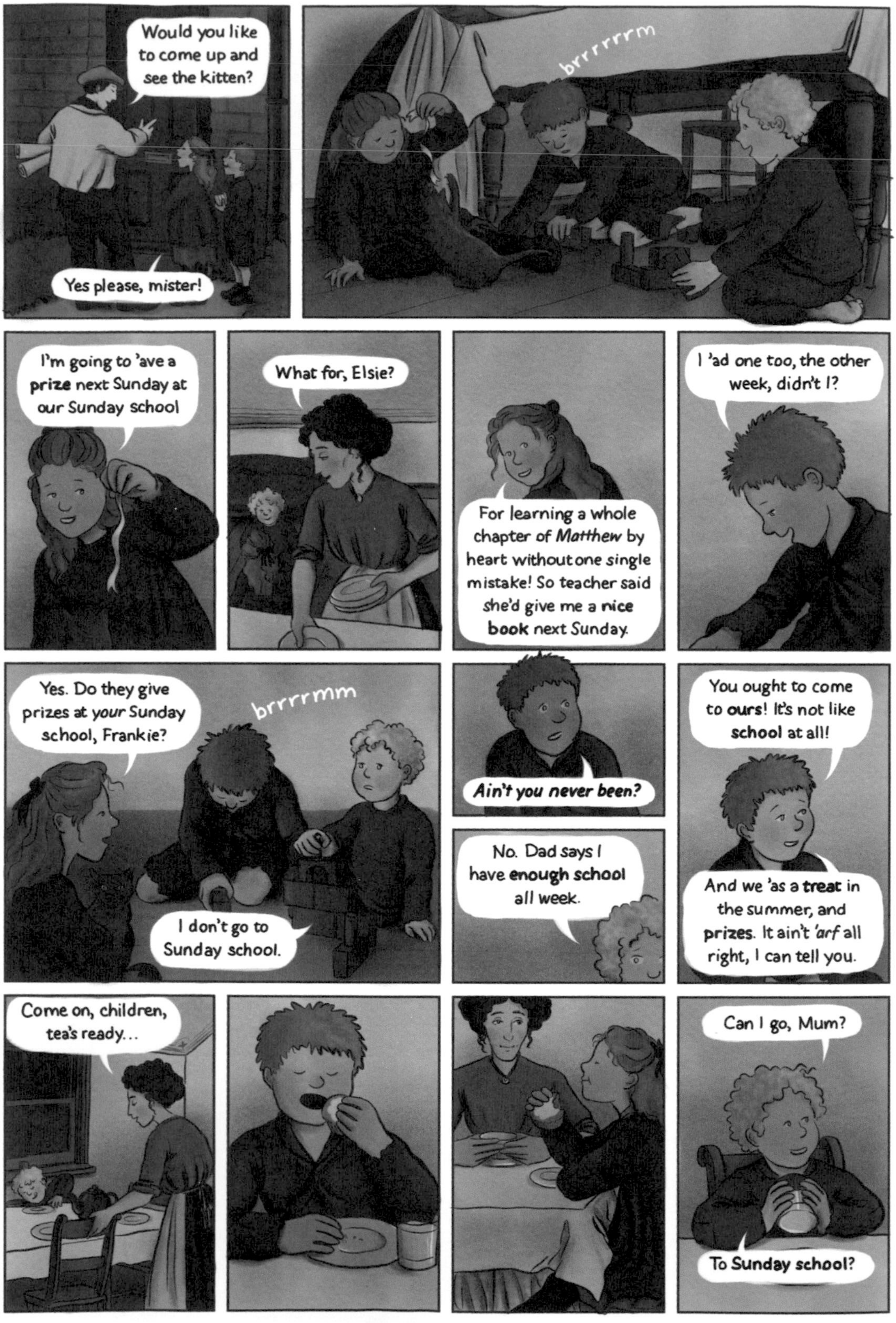
Would you like to come up and see the kitten?
Yes please, mister!
brrrrrrm
I'm going to 'ave a **prize** next Sunday at our Sunday school
What for, Elsie?
For learning a whole chapter of *Matthew* by heart without one *single* mistake! So teacher said *she'd* give me a **nice book** next Sunday.
I 'ad one too, the other week, didn't I?
Yes. Do they give prizes at *your* Sunday school, Frankie?
brrrrmm
I don't go to Sunday school.
Ain't you never been?
No. Dad says I have **enough school** all week.
You ought to come to **ours**! It's not like **school** at all!
And we 'as a **treat** in the summer, and **prizes**. It ain't *'arf* all right, I can tell you.
Come on, children, tea's ready...
Can I go, Mum?
To Sunday school?

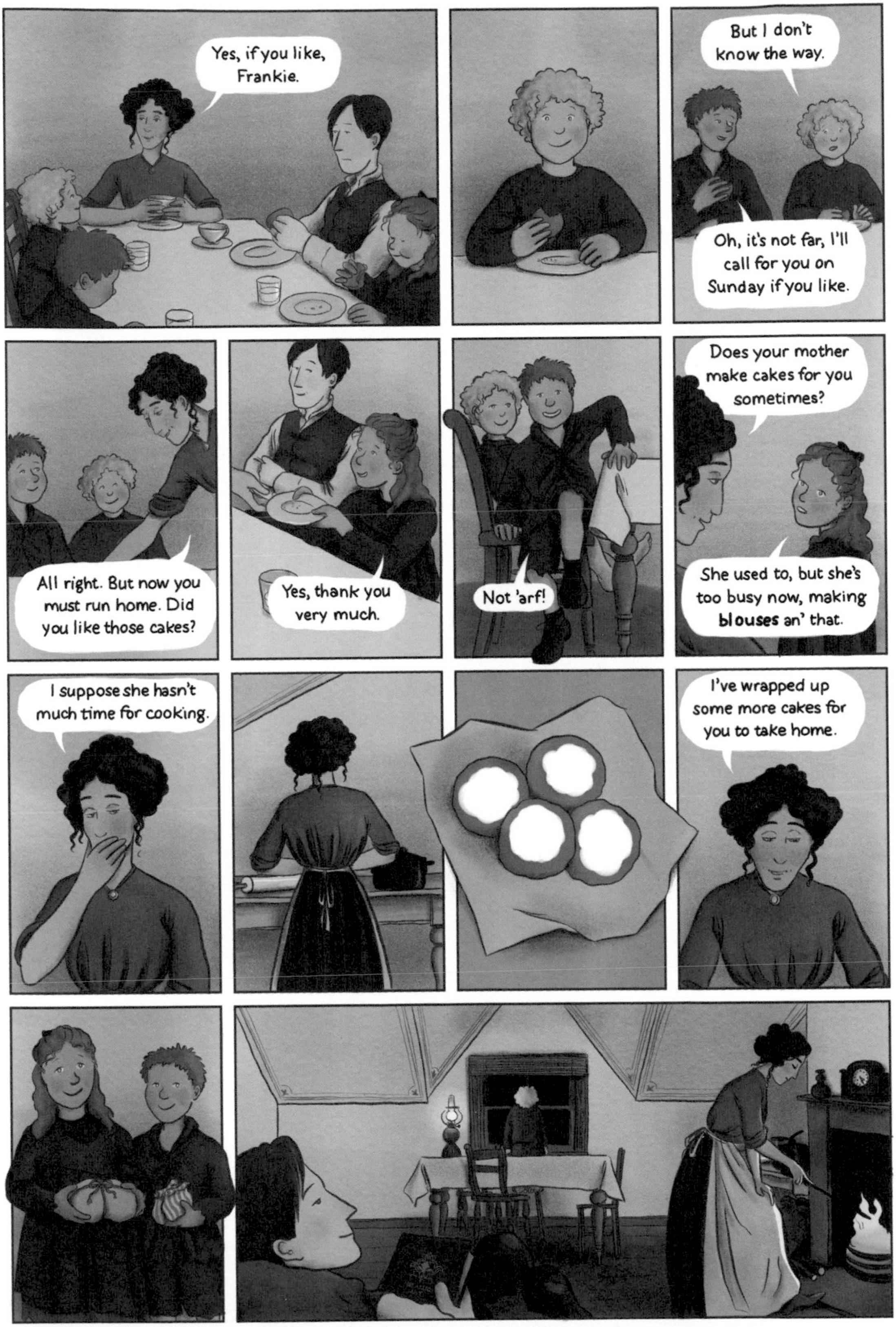
Yes, if you like, Frankie.
But I don't know the way.
Oh, it's not far, I'll call for you on Sunday if you like.
All right. But now you must run home. Did you like those cakes?
Yes, thank you very much.
Not 'arf!
Does your mother make cakes for you sometimes?
She used to, but she's too busy now, making **blouses** an' that.
I suppose she hasn't much time for cooking.
I've wrapped up some more cakes for you to take home.

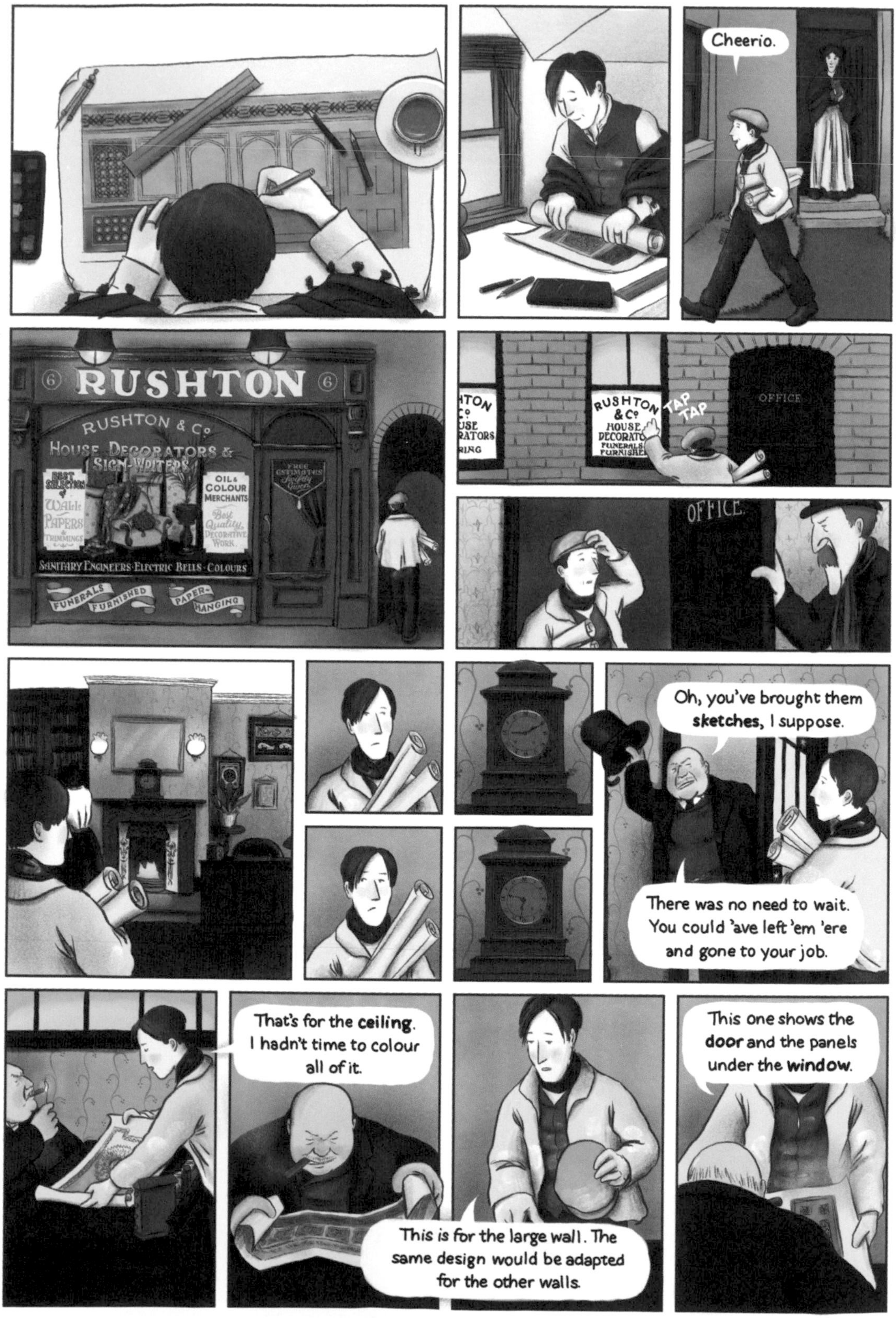
Cheerio.
RUSHTON
RUSHTON & Co
HOUSE DECORATORS & SIGN-WRITERS
OIL & COLOUR MERCHANTS
SANITARY ENGINEERS · ELECTRIC BELLS · COLOURS
FUNERALS FURNISHED
PAPER-HANGING
RUSHTON & Co HOUSE DECORATORS FUNERALS FURNISHED
TAP TAP
OFFICE
OFFICE
Oh, you've brought them sketches, I suppose.
There was no need to wait. You could 'ave left 'em 'ere and gone to your job.
That's for the ceiling. I hadn't time to colour all of it.
This is for the large wall. The same design would be adapted for the other walls.
This one shows the door and the panels under the window.

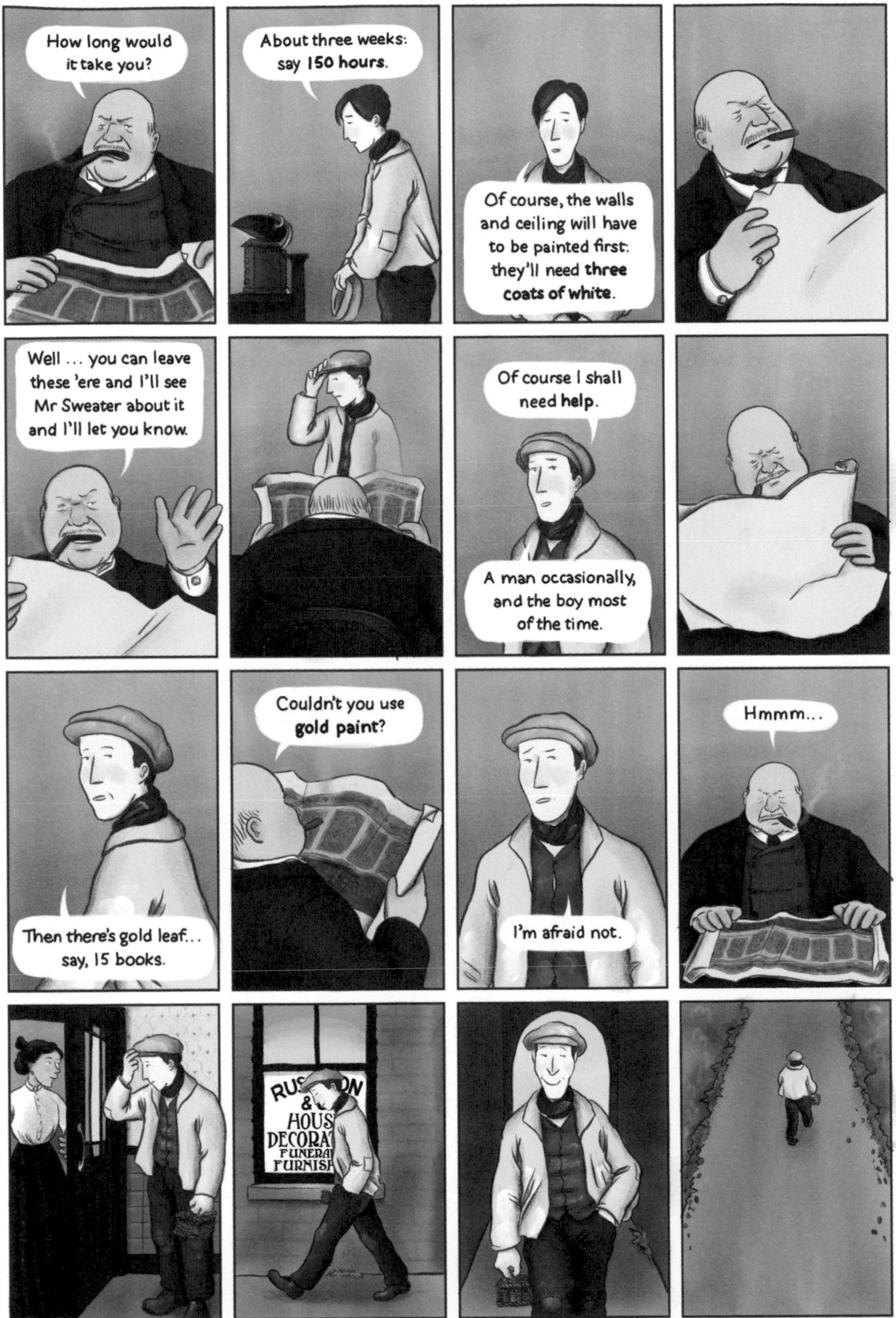
How long would it take you?
About three weeks: say **150 hours**.
Of course, the walls and ceiling will have to be painted first: they'll need **three coats of white**.
Well ... you can leave these 'ere and I'll see Mr Sweater about it and I'll let you know.
Of course I shall need **help**.
A man occasionally, and the boy most of the time.
Then there's gold leaf... say, 15 books.
Couldn't you use **gold paint**?
I'm afraid not.
Hmmm...
RUS
ON
&
HOUS
DECORA
FUNERA
FURNISH

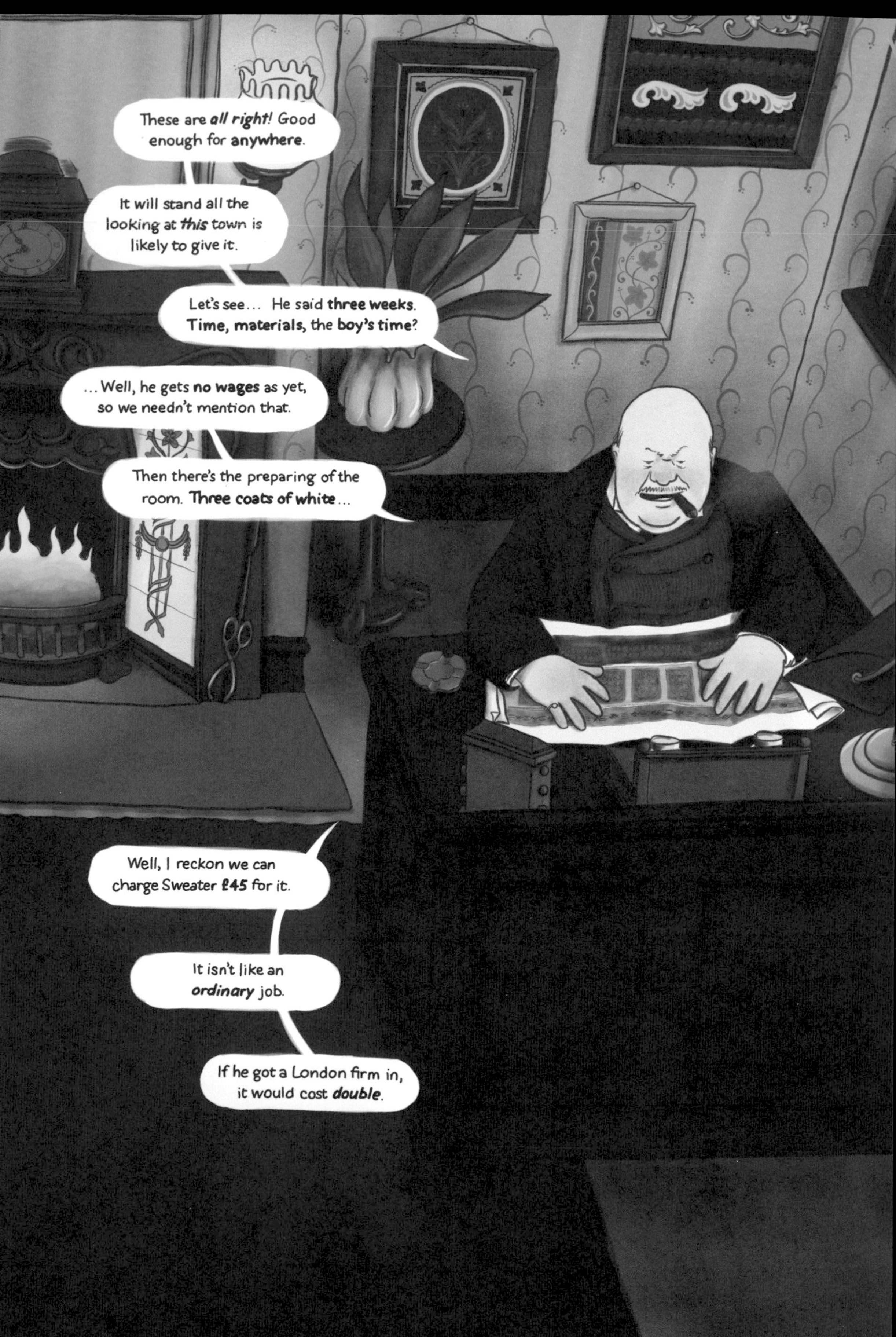
These are *all right!* Good enough for **anywhere**.
It will stand all the looking at ***this*** town is likely to give it.
Let's see... He said **three weeks**. **Time, materials,** the **boy's time**?
...Well, he gets **no wages** as yet, so we needn't mention that.
Then there's the preparing of the room. **Three coats of white**...
Well, I reckon we can charge Sweater **£45** for it.
It isn't like an ***ordinary*** job.
If he got a London firm in, it would cost ***double***.

CHAPTER
6
THE
TRUTH

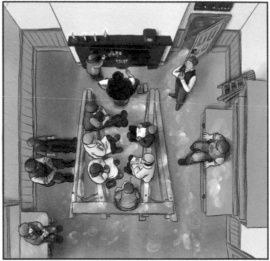

If God made everything for some useful purpose, what the hell's the use of **bugs** and **fleas** and the like?

To teach people to keep theirselves **clean**, of course.

That's *funny*, ain't it, Slyme?

They say diseases is caused by **little insects**.

If God 'adn't made no **cancer germs** there wouldn't be no *cancer*.

That's one of the proofs that there *isn't a God*.

If we believe that the universe was created by God, then we must also believe that He made disease for the purpose of **torturing** His creatures.

You can't tell me a bloody yarn like that, Owen. There's a **Ruler** over us, mate, and so you're likely to **find out**.

If God didn't create the world, 'ow did it **come 'ere**?

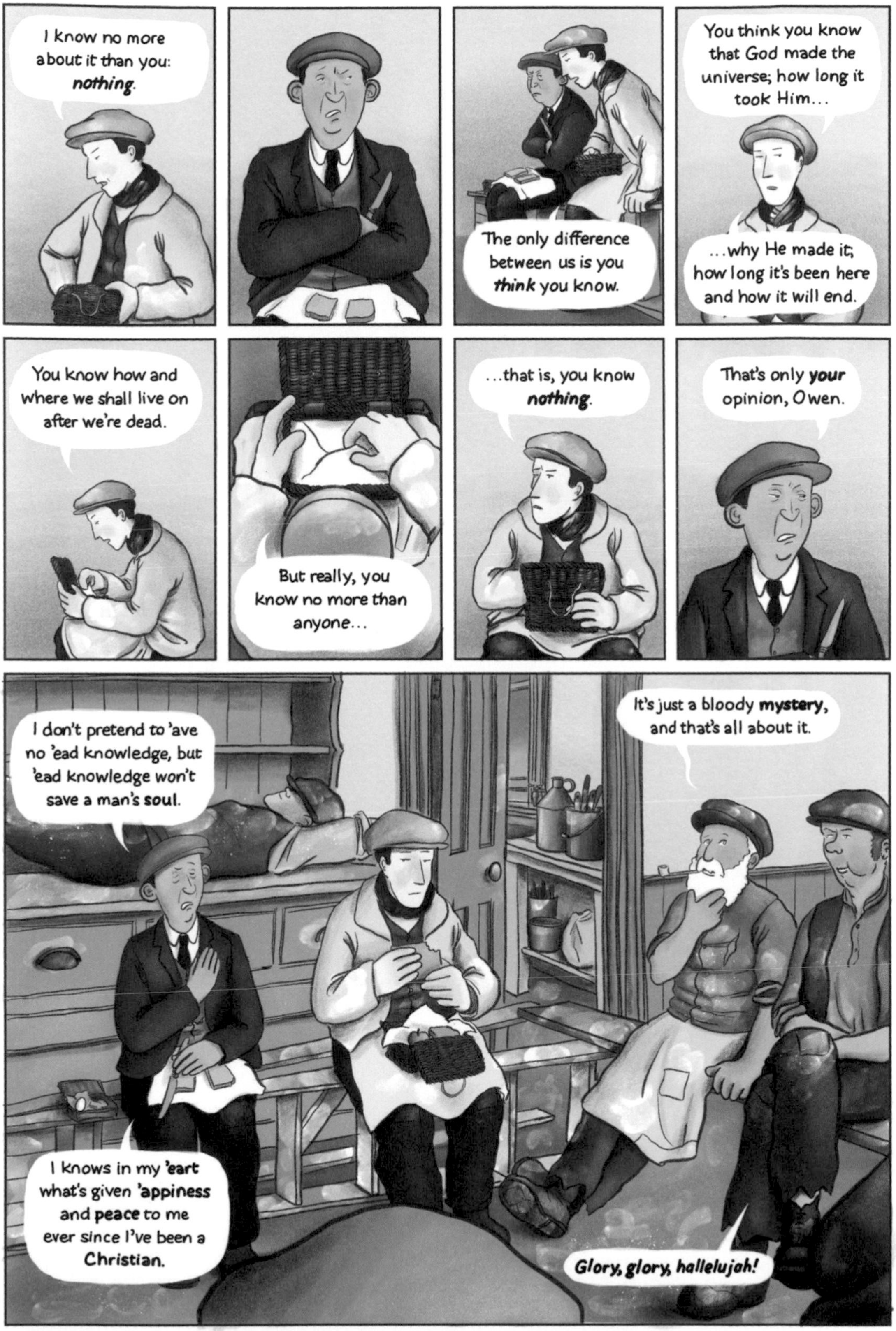
I know no more about it than you: ***nothing***.
The only difference between us is you ***think*** you know.
You think you know that God made the universe; how long it took Him...
...why He made it; how long it's been here and how it will end.
You know how and where we shall live on after we're dead.
But really, you know no more than anyone...
...that is, you know ***nothing***.
That's only ***your*** opinion, Owen.
I don't pretend to 'ave no 'ead knowledge, but 'ead knowledge won't save a man's **soul**.
I knows in my **'eart** what's given **'appiness** and **peace** to me ever since I've been a **Christian**.
It's just a bloody **mystery**, and that's all about it.
Glory, glory, hallelujah!

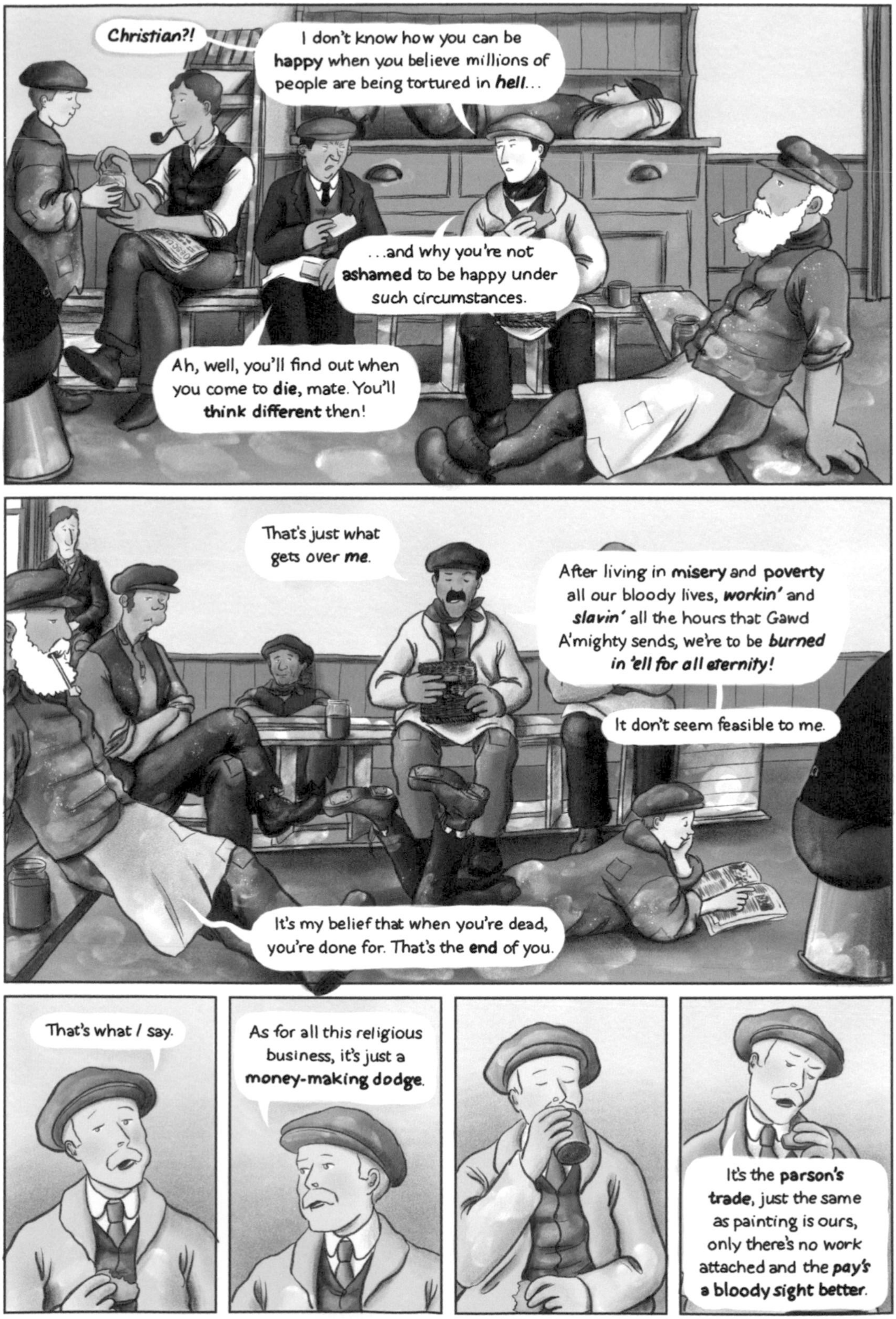
Christian?!
I don't know how you can be happy when you believe millions of people are being tortured in hell...
...and why you're not ashamed to be happy under such circumstances.
Ah, well, you'll find out when you come to die, mate. You'll think different then!
That's just what gets over me.
After living in misery and poverty all our bloody lives, workin' and slavin' all the hours that Gawd A'mighty sends, we're to be burned in 'ell for all eternity!
It don't seem feasible to me.
It's my belief that when you're dead, you're done for. That's the end of you.
That's what I say.
As for all this religious business, it's just a money-making dodge.
It's the parson's trade, just the same as painting is ours, only there's no work attached and the pay's a bloody sight better.

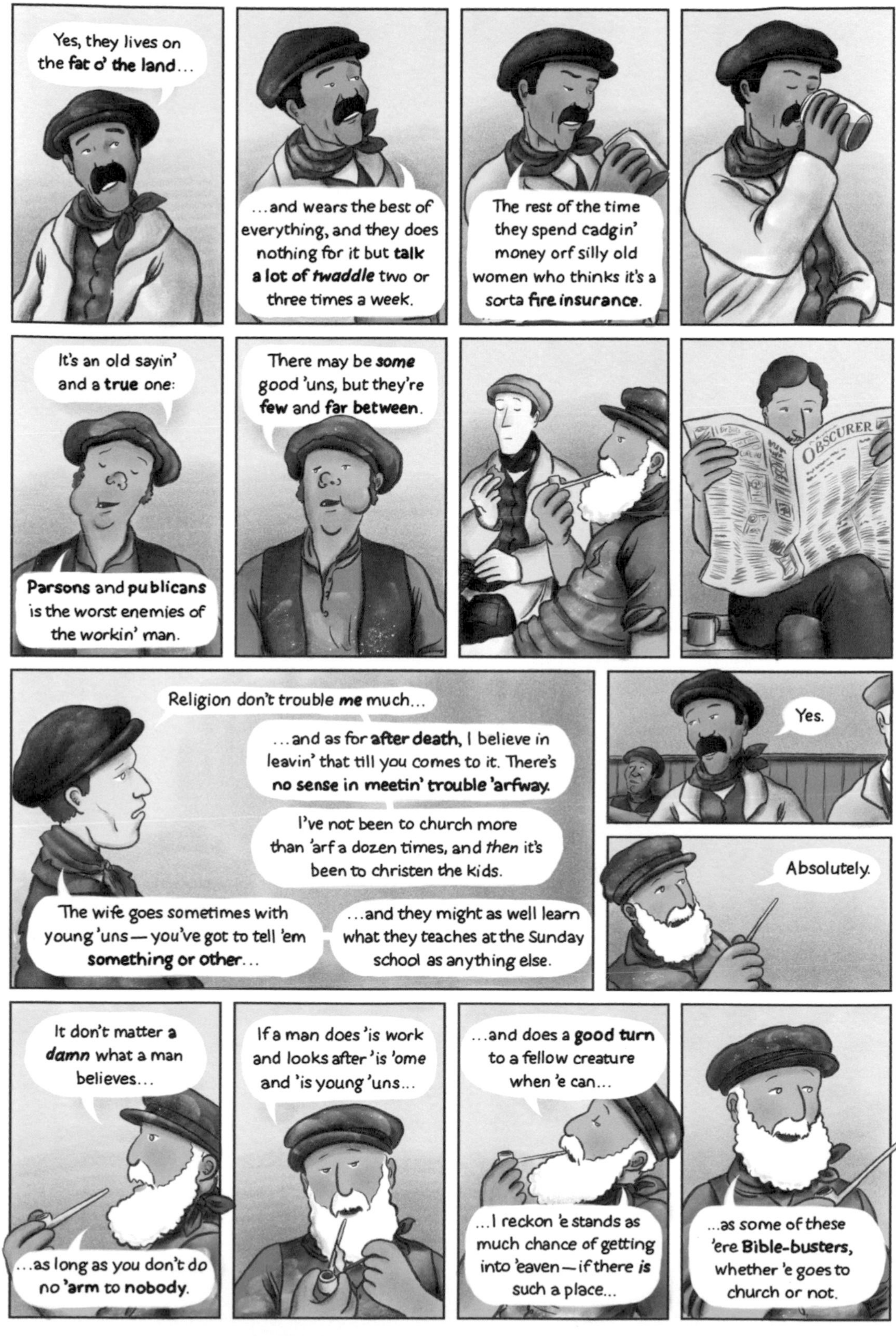
Yes, they lives on the **fat o' the land**...
...and wears the best of everything, and they does nothing for it but **talk a lot of *twaddle*** two or three times a week.
The rest of the time they spend cadgin' money orf silly old women who thinks it's a sorta **fire insurance**.
It's an old sayin' and a **true** one:
Parsons and **publicans** is the worst enemies of the workin' man.
There may be ***some*** good 'uns, but they're **few** and **far between**.
OBSCURER
Religion don't trouble ***me*** much...
...and as for **after death**, I believe in leavin' that till you comes to it. There's **no sense in meetin' trouble 'arfway**.
I've not been to church more than 'arf a dozen times, and *then* it's been to christen the kids.
The wife goes sometimes with young 'uns — you've got to tell 'em **something or other**...
...and they might as well learn what they teaches at the Sunday school as anything else.
Yes.
Absolutely.
It don't matter **a *damn*** what a man believes...
...as long as you don't do no **'arm** to **nobody**.
If a man does 'is work and looks after 'is 'ome and 'is young 'uns...
...and does a **good turn** to a fellow creature when 'e can...
...I reckon 'e stands as much chance of getting into 'eaven — if there ***is*** such a place...
...as some of these 'ere **Bible-busters**, whether 'e goes to church or not.

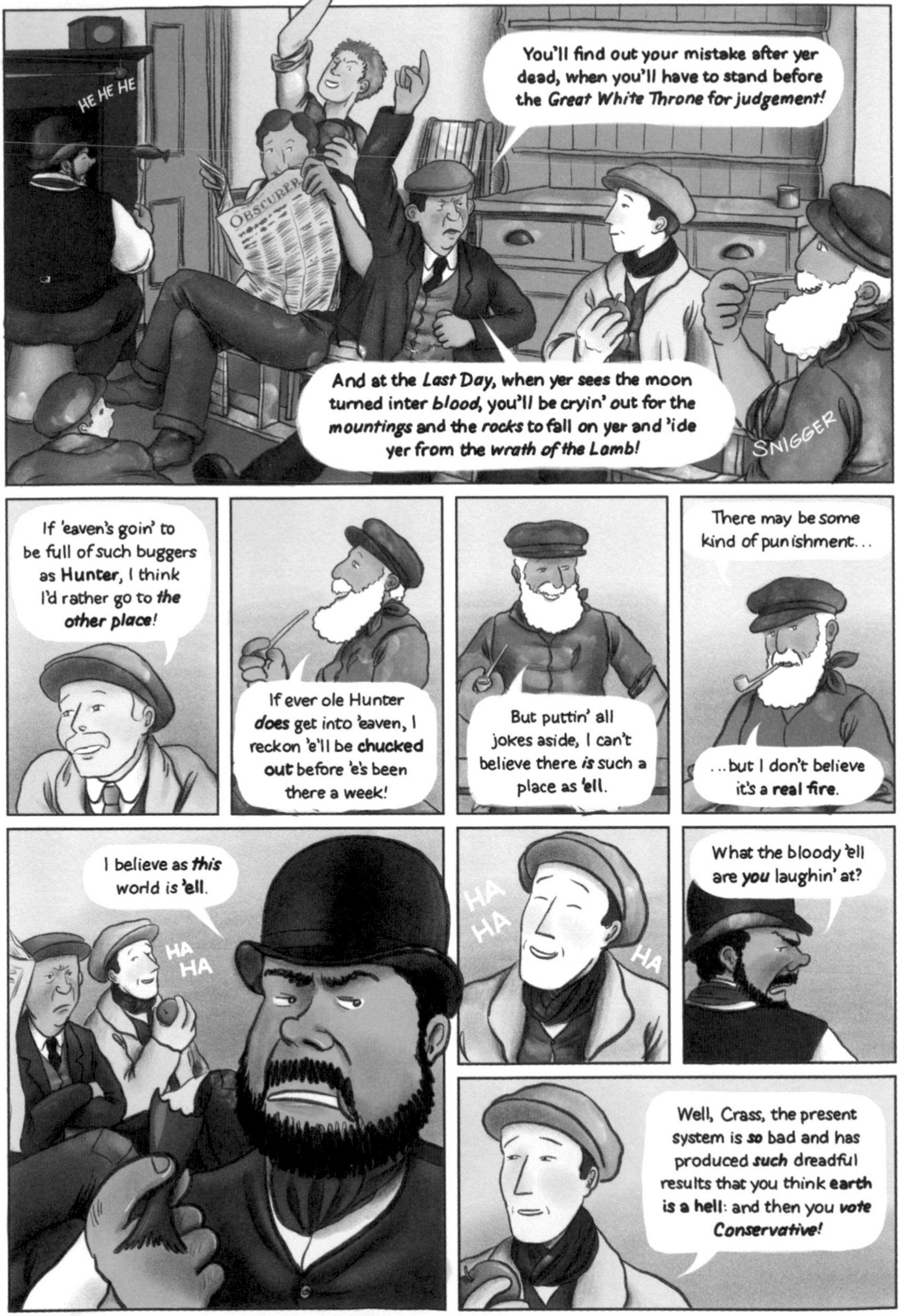
HE HE HE
You'll find out your mistake after yer dead, when you'll have to stand before the *Great White Throne* for judgement!
OBSCURER
And at the *Last Day*, when yer sees the moon turned inter *blood*, you'll be cryin' out for the *mountings* and the *rocks* to fall on yer and 'ide yer from the *wrath of the Lamb!*
SNIGGER
If 'eaven's goin' to be full of such buggers as **Hunter**, I think I'd rather go to ***the other place***!
If ever ole Hunter ***does*** get into 'eaven, I reckon 'e'll be **chucked out** before 'e's been there a week!
But puttin' all jokes aside, I can't believe there *is* such a place as **'ell**.
There may be some kind of punishment...
...but I don't believe it's a **real fire**.
I believe as ***this*** world is **'ell**.
HA HA
HA HA
HA
What the bloody 'ell are *you* laughin' at?
Well, Crass, the present system is ***so*** bad and has produced ***such*** dreadful results that you think **earth is a hell**: and then you ***vote Conservative!***

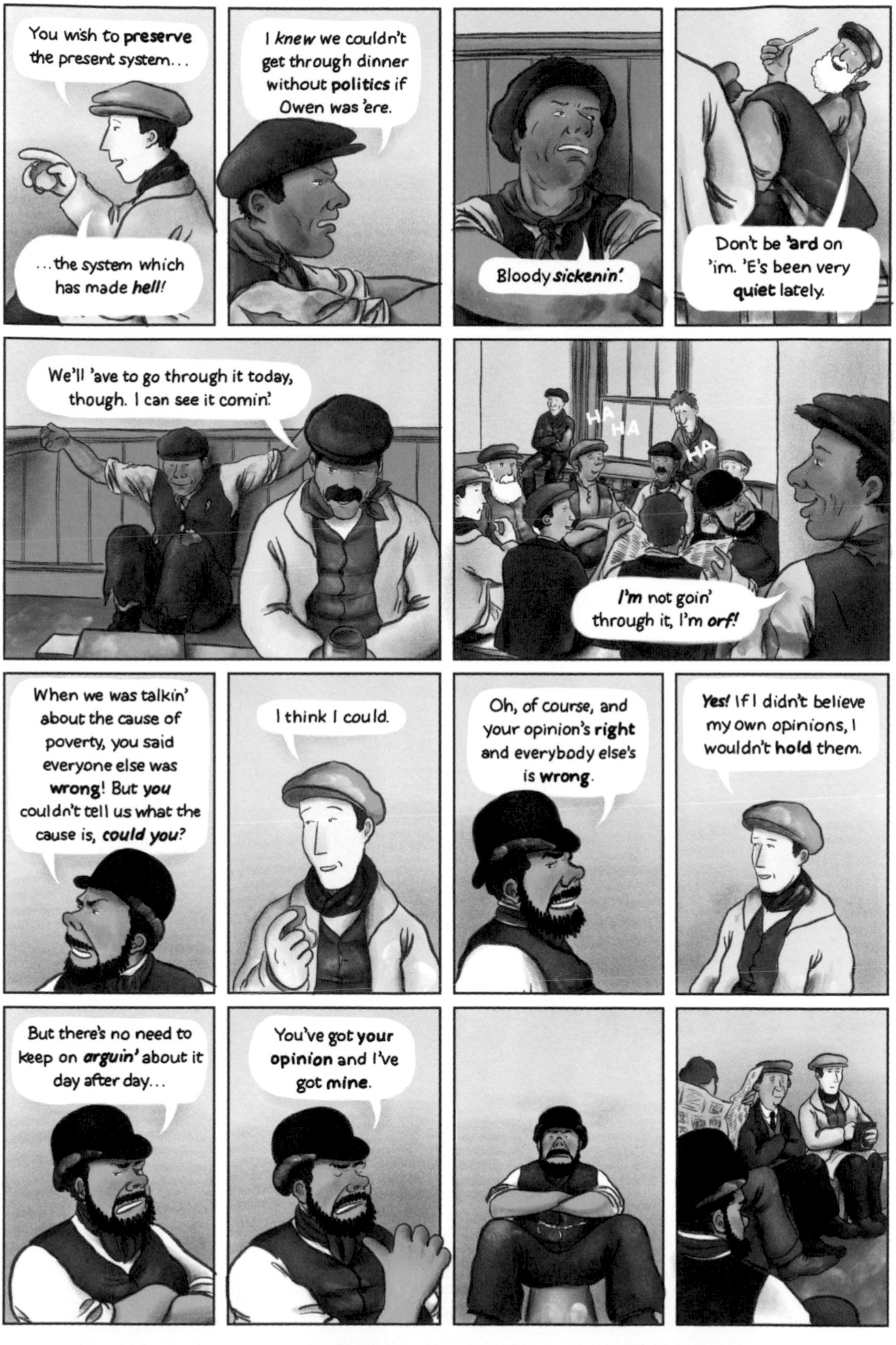
You wish to **preserve** the present system...
...the system which has made ***hell!***
I *knew* we couldn't get through dinner without **politics** if Owen was 'ere.
Bloody ***sickenin'***.
Don't be **'ard** on 'im. 'E's been very **quiet** lately.
We'll 'ave to go through it today, though. I can see it comin'.
HA
HA
HA
I'm not goin' through it, I'm ***orf!***
When we was talkin' about the cause of poverty, you said everyone else was **wrong**! But ***you*** couldn't tell us what the cause is, ***could you?***
I think I could.
Oh, of course, and your opinion's **right** and everybody else's is **wrong**.
Yes! If I didn't believe my own opinions, I wouldn't **hold** them.
But there's no need to keep on ***arguin'*** about it day after day...
You've got **your opinion** and I've got **mine**.

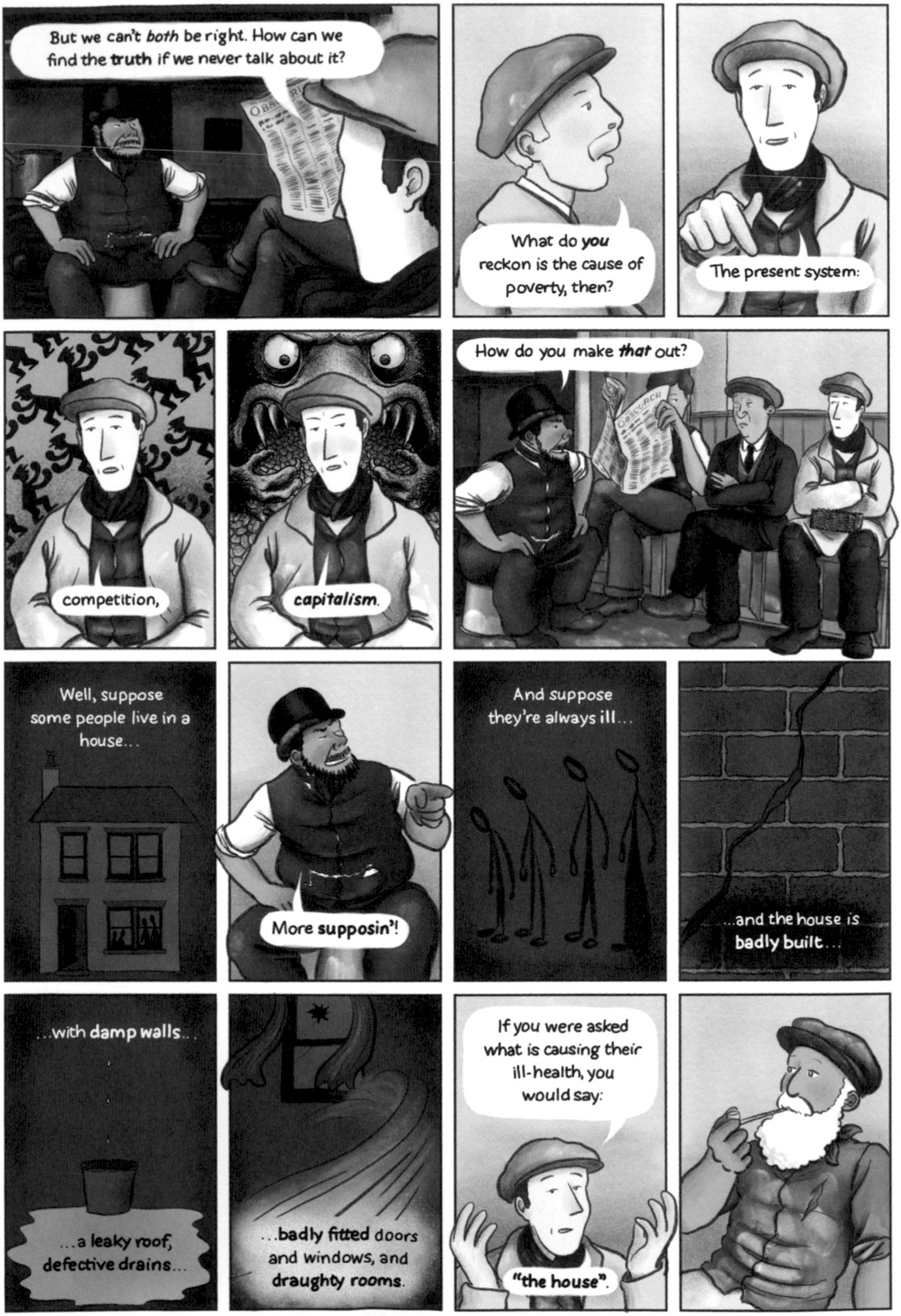
But we can't *both* be right. How can we find the **truth** if we never talk about it?
What do *you* reckon is the cause of poverty, then?
The present system:
competition,
capitalism.
How do you make *that* out?
Well, suppose some people live in a house...
More **supposin'**!
And suppose they're always ill...
...and the house is **badly built**...
...with **damp walls**...
...a **leaky roof**, **defective drains**...
...**badly fitted** doors and windows, and **draughty rooms**.
If you were asked what is causing their ill-health, you would say:
"the house".

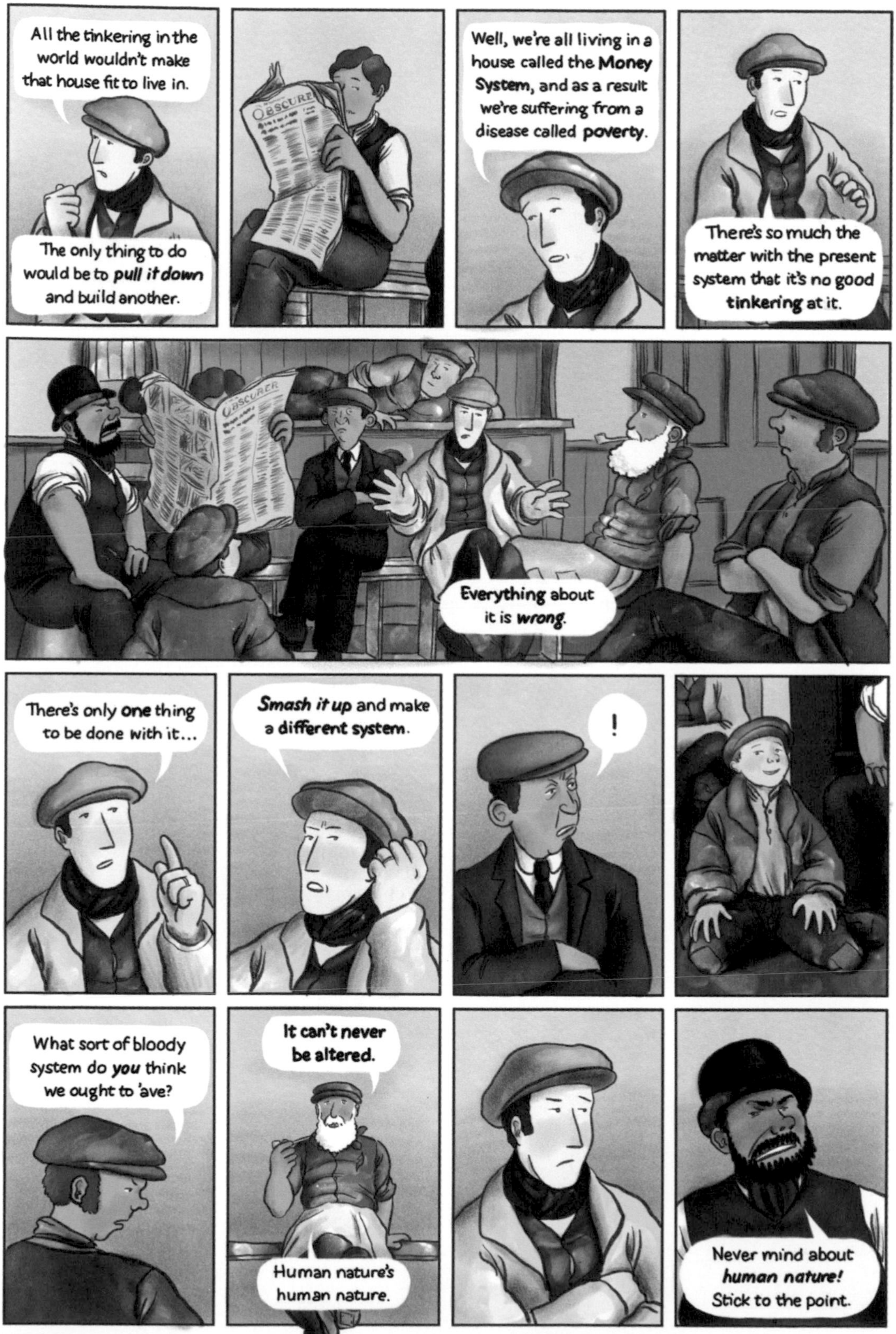
All the tinkering in the world wouldn't make that house fit to live in.
The only thing to do would be to *pull it down* and build another.
Well, we're all living in a house called the **Money System**, and as a result we're suffering from a disease called **poverty**.
There's so much the matter with the present system that it's no good **tinkering** at it.
Everything about it is *wrong*.
There's only **one** thing to be done with it...
Smash it up and make a **different system**.
!
What sort of bloody system do *you* think we ought to 'ave?
It can't never be altered.
Human nature's human nature.
Never mind about *human nature!* Stick to the point.

What's the **cause** of poverty?

Oh, **bugger** the **cause of poverty**! I've 'ad **enough** of this bloody row.

There are **many** causes, but they are all part of the system.

To do away with poverty we must **destroy the causes**...

...to do away with the causes we must **destroy the system.**

But one of the causes is **money**.

HA HA

I always thought it was the **lack** of it!

Well, I'll try to show you.

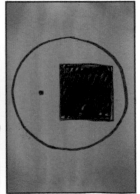

This circle represents **England**.

Oh, **I see**. I thought there'd be **supposin'**.

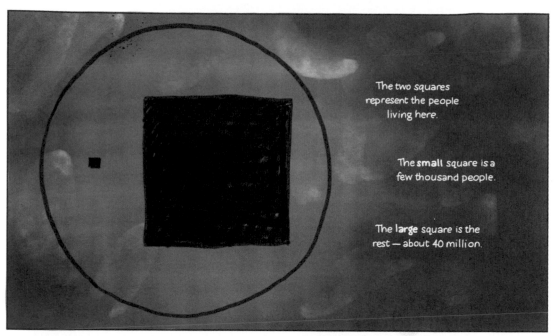

The two squares represent the people living here.

The **small** square is a few thousand people.

The **large** square is the rest — about 40 million.

The majority in the large square **work** for their living...

...and in return they get **money**: some more, some less than others.

I suppose you think they should all get the **same**!

Do you think it's right that a **sweeper** should get as much as a **painter**?

I'm not talking about that now, I'm trying to show you the **causes of poverty**.

Shut up, can't you, Harlow? We can't all talk at once.

I know, but 'e takes such a 'ell of a time to say what 'e's got to say.

First people need a **place to live**...

Well! I should never o' **thought** it!

HA HA HA

HE HE

Bloody rot!

Who the bloody 'ell does 'e think 'e is? A **schoolmaster?**

They must live on the land and that's the trouble, because the land belongs to a *few*...

...those in the **small square**.

If it would pay them, and they felt like it...

...these few people have a perfect right...

...to order everyone else to **clear out!**

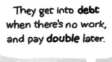

But they let them stay on condition they pay **rent** for the privilege of living in the *land of their birth*.

The rent is so high...

...that most have to do without the **comforts** and **necessities** of life.

For the working classes the rent takes **one-third** of their earnings...

...and rent **must be** paid, whether they are employed or not.

They get into **debt** when there's no work, and pay **double** later.

The majority work hard and live in **poverty**...

...so that the few can live in **luxury** without working at all.

The fools agree to live with incessant slavery and want, simply to pay rent, and are grateful to the few for letting them *exist at all*.

Hogswallop!

Stuff and nonsense!

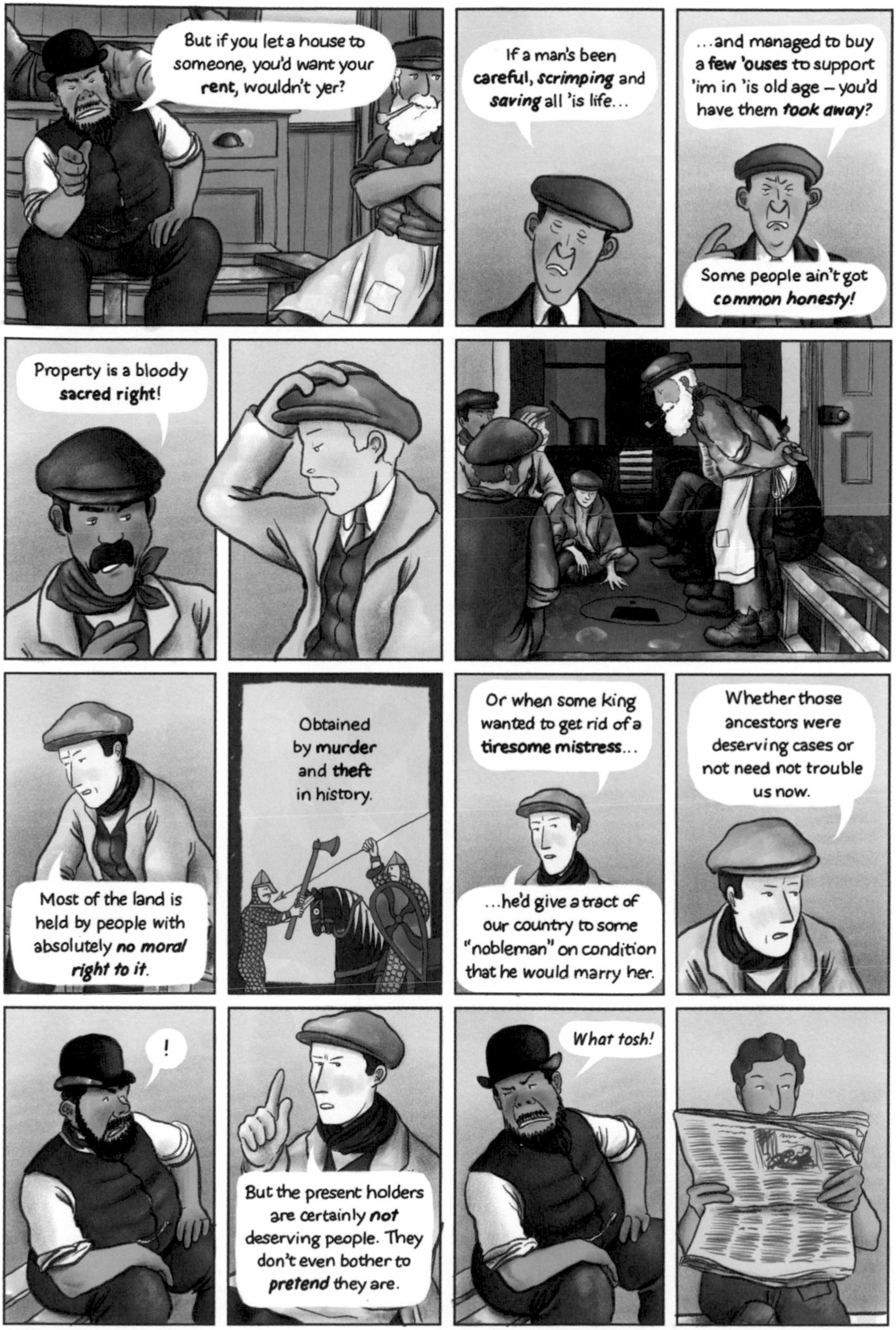
But if you let a house to someone, you'd want your rent, wouldn't yer?
If a man's been careful, scrimping and saving all 'is life...
...and managed to buy a few 'ouses to support 'im in 'is old age – you'd have them took away?
Some people ain't got common honesty!
Property is a bloody sacred right!
Most of the land is held by people with absolutely no moral right to it.
Obtained by murder and theft in history.
Or when some king wanted to get rid of a tiresome mistress...
...he'd give a tract of our country to some "nobleman" on condition that he would marry her.
Whether those ancestors were deserving cases or not need not trouble us now.
!
But the present holders are certainly not deserving people. They don't even bother to pretend they are.
What tosh!

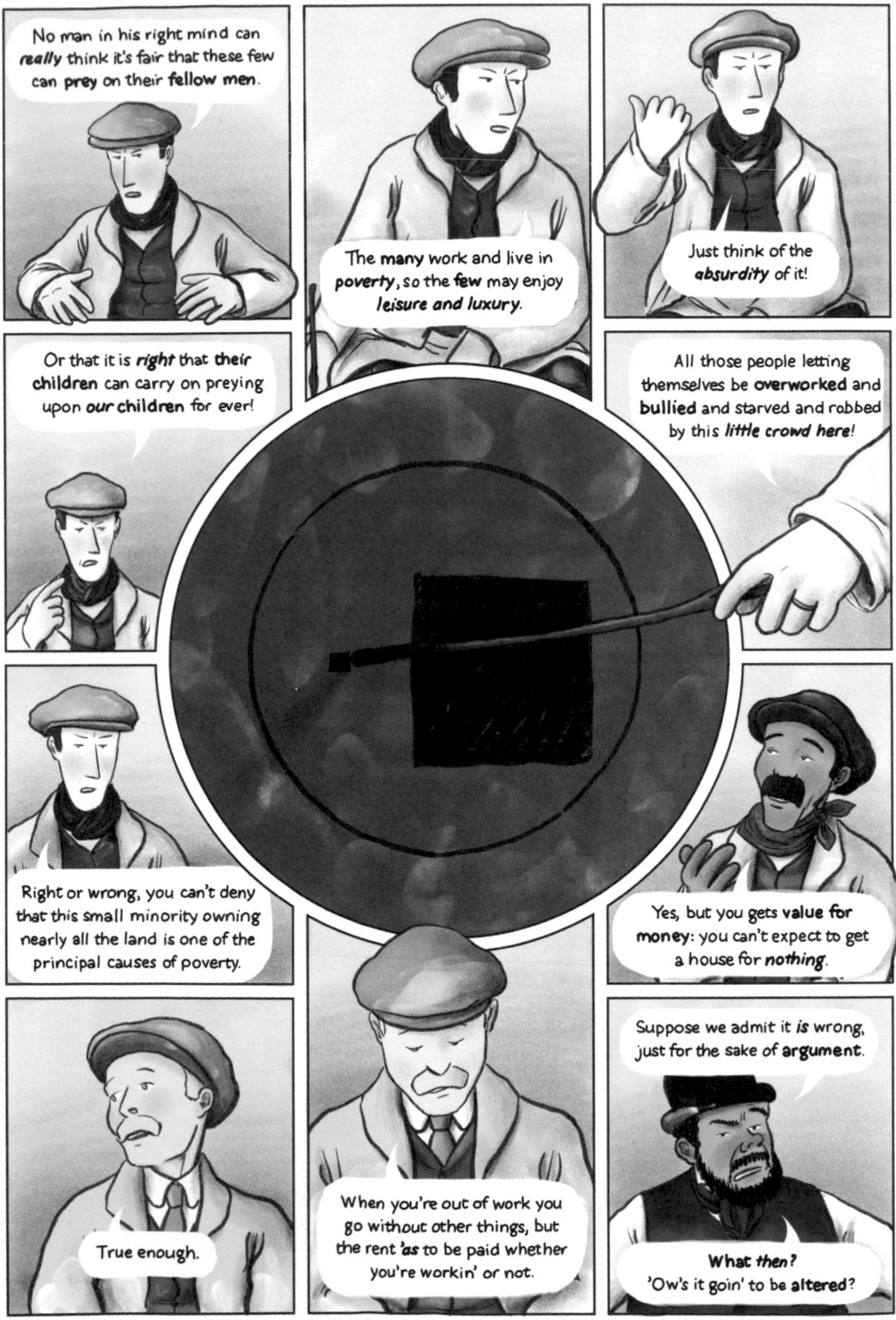
No man in his right mind can really think it's fair that these few can prey on their fellow men.
The many work and live in poverty, so the few may enjoy leisure and luxury.
Just think of the absurdity of it!
Or that it is right that their children can carry on preying upon our children for ever!
All those people letting themselves be overworked and bullied and starved and robbed by this little crowd here!
Right or wrong, you can't deny that this small minority owning nearly all the land is one of the principal causes of poverty.
Yes, but you gets value for money: you can't expect to get a house for nothing.
True enough.
When you're out of work you go without other things, but the rent 'as to be paid whether you're workin' or not.
Suppose we admit it is wrong, just for the sake of argument.
What then?
'Ow's it goin' to be altered?

Yes! **That's** the bloody question!

It can't be done!

Whether it can be altered or not, whether it's right or wrong...

...**landlordism** is one of the causes of poverty.

Poverty is not caused by marriage

or machinery

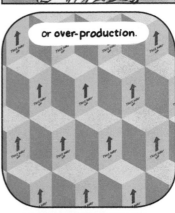

or over-production.

It's not caused by **drink**

or **laziness**

or **over-population.**

It's caused by **private monopoly**, the present system.

They have **monopolised** everything possible: they've got the **whole earth**, the **minerals** in it and the **streams** that water it.

The only reason they've not monopolised the **daylight** and air is that it isn't yet possible.

And if it **was** possible, you'd see people dying for want of air, as thousands now are dying for want of the other necessities of life.

You would see people going about **gasping for breath**...

...and telling each other that the **likes of them** could not expect to have **air** to breathe unless they had **money to pay for it.**

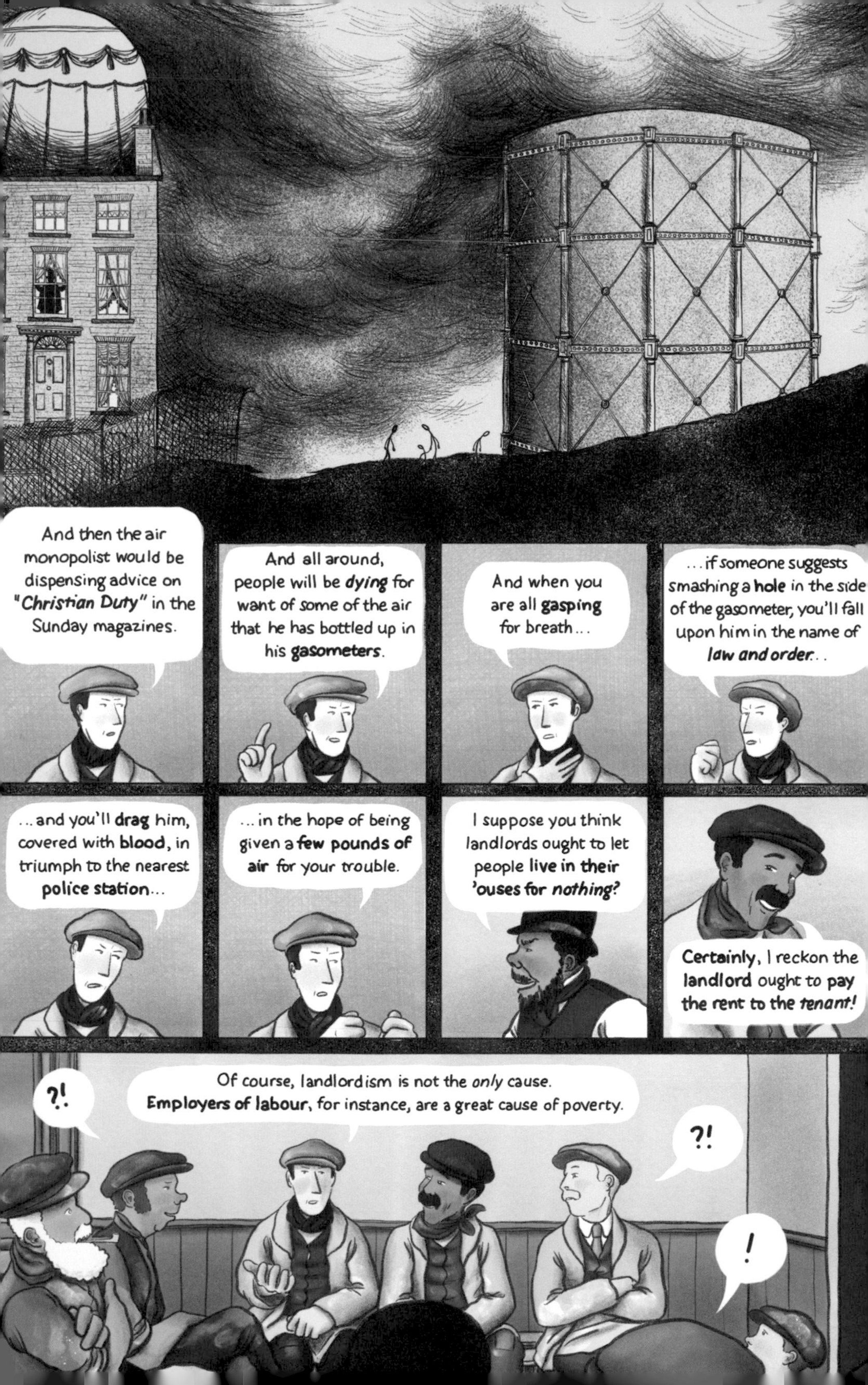
And then the air monopolist would be dispensing advice on "Christian Duty" in the Sunday magazines.
And all around, people will be dying for want of some of the air that he has bottled up in his gasometers.
And when you are all gasping for breath...
...if someone suggests smashing a hole in the side of the gasometer, you'll fall upon him in the name of law and order...
...and you'll drag him, covered with blood, in triumph to the nearest police station...
...in the hope of being given a few pounds of air for your trouble.
I suppose you think landlords ought to let people live in their 'ouses for nothing?
Certainly, I reckon the landlord ought to pay the rent to the tenant!
?!
Of course, landlordism is not the only cause. Employers of labour, for instance, are a great cause of poverty.
?!
!

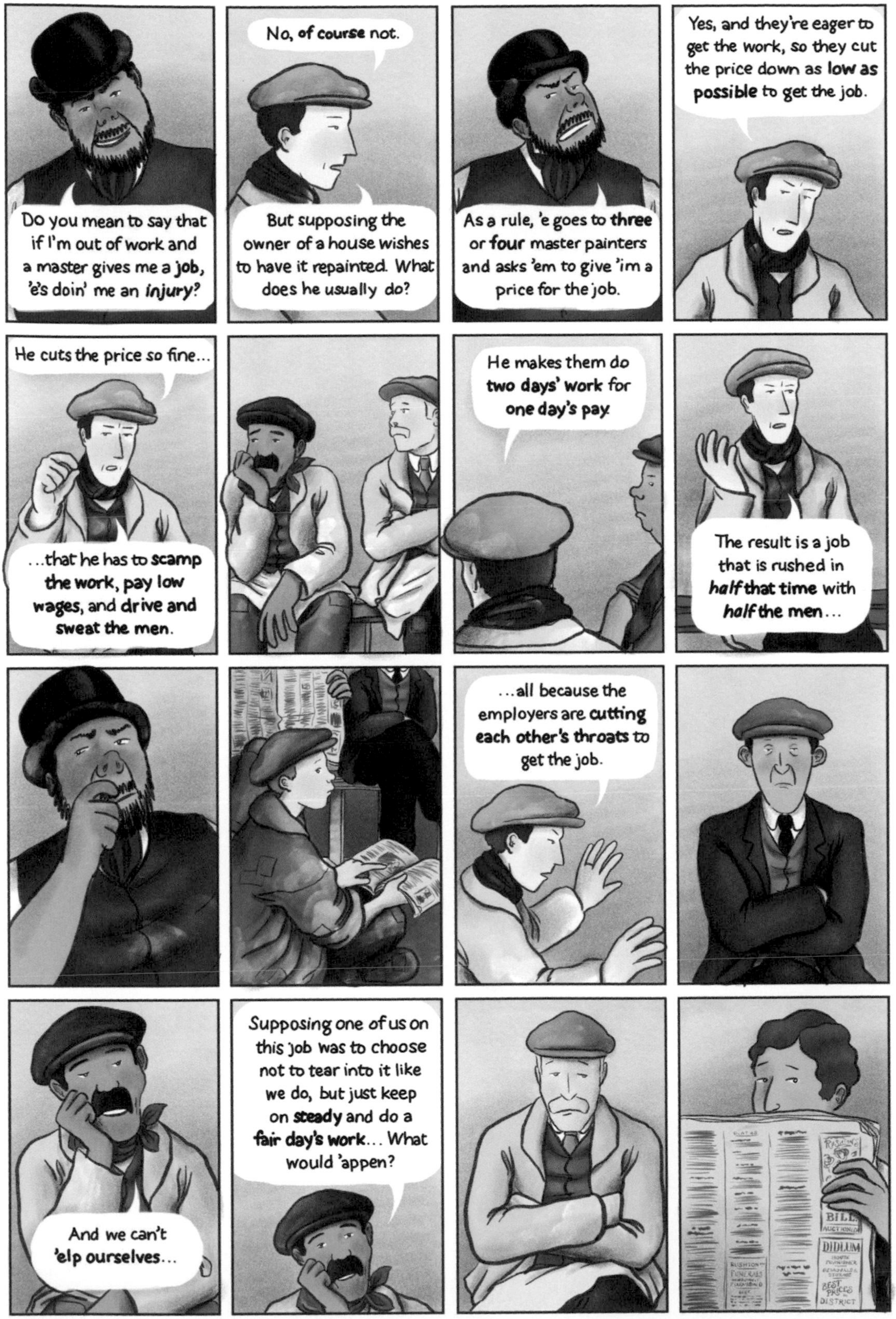
Do you mean to say that if I'm out of work and a master gives me a job, 'e's doin' me an injury?
No, of course not.
But supposing the owner of a house wishes to have it repainted. What does he usually do?
As a rule, 'e goes to three or four master painters and asks 'em to give 'im a price for the job.
Yes, and they're eager to get the work, so they cut the price down as low as possible to get the job.
He cuts the price so fine...
...that he has to scamp the work, pay low wages, and drive and sweat the men.
He makes them do two days' work for one day's pay.
The result is a job that is rushed in half that time with half the men...
...all because the employers are cutting each other's throats to get the job.
And we can't 'elp ourselves...
Supposing one of us on this job was to choose not to tear into it like we do, but just keep on steady and do a fair day's work... What would 'appen?

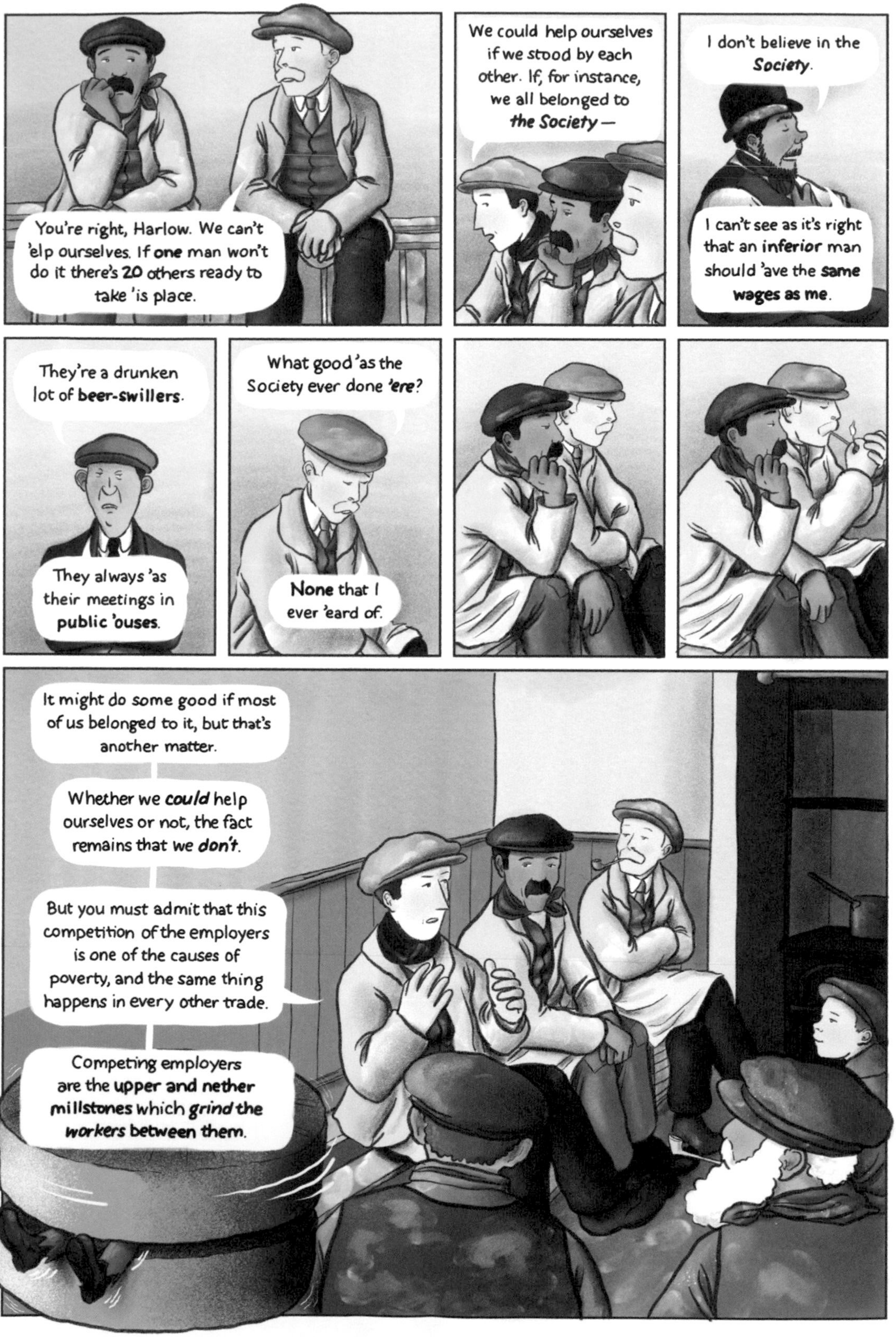
You're right, Harlow. We can't 'elp ourselves. If **one** man won't do it there's **20** others ready to take 'is place.
We could help ourselves if we stood by each other. If, for instance, we all belonged to ***the Society*** —
I don't believe in the ***Society***.
I can't see as it's right that an ***inferior*** man should 'ave the **same wages as me**.
They're a drunken lot of **beer-swillers**.
They always 'as their meetings in **public 'ouses**.
What good 'as the Society ever done ***'ere***?
None that I ever 'eard of.
It might do some good if most of us belonged to it, but that's another matter.
Whether we ***could*** help ourselves or not, the fact remains that we ***don't***.
But you must admit that this competition of the employers is one of the causes of poverty, and the same thing happens in every other trade.
Competing employers are the **upper and nether millstones** which ***grind*** the ***workers*** **between them**.

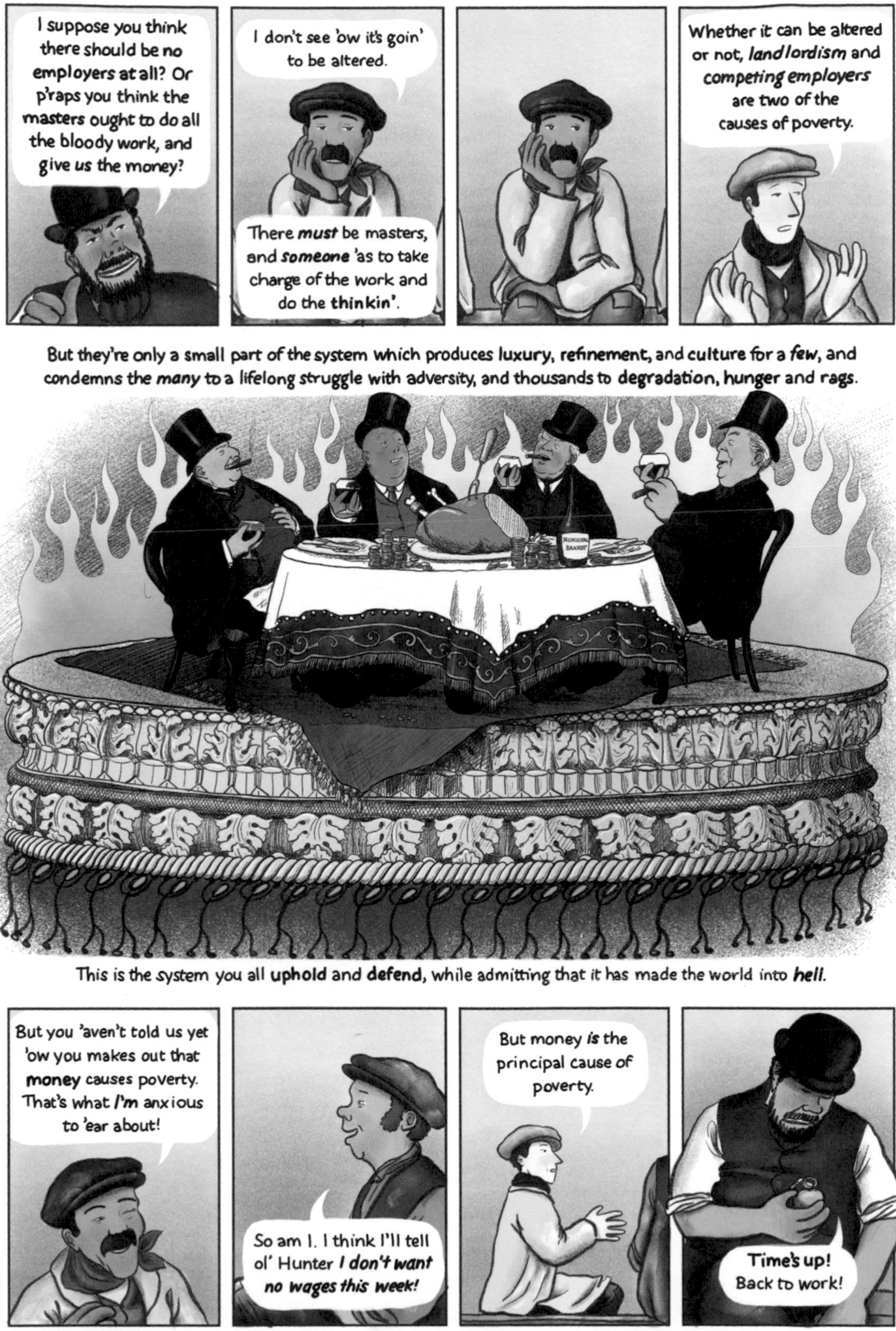
I suppose you think there should be no employers at all? Or p'raps you think the masters ought to do all the bloody work, and give us the money?
I don't see 'ow it's goin' to be altered.
There must be masters, and someone 'as to take charge of the work and do the thinkin'.
Whether it can be altered or not, landlordism and competing employers are two of the causes of poverty.
But they're only a small part of the system which produces luxury, refinement, and culture for a few, and condemns the many to a lifelong struggle with adversity, and thousands to degradation, hunger and rags.
This is the system you all uphold and defend, while admitting that it has made the world into hell.
But you 'aven't told us yet 'ow you makes out that money causes poverty. That's what I'm anxious to 'ear about!
So am I. I think I'll tell ol' Hunter I don't want no wages this week!
But money is the principal cause of poverty.
Time's up! Back to work!

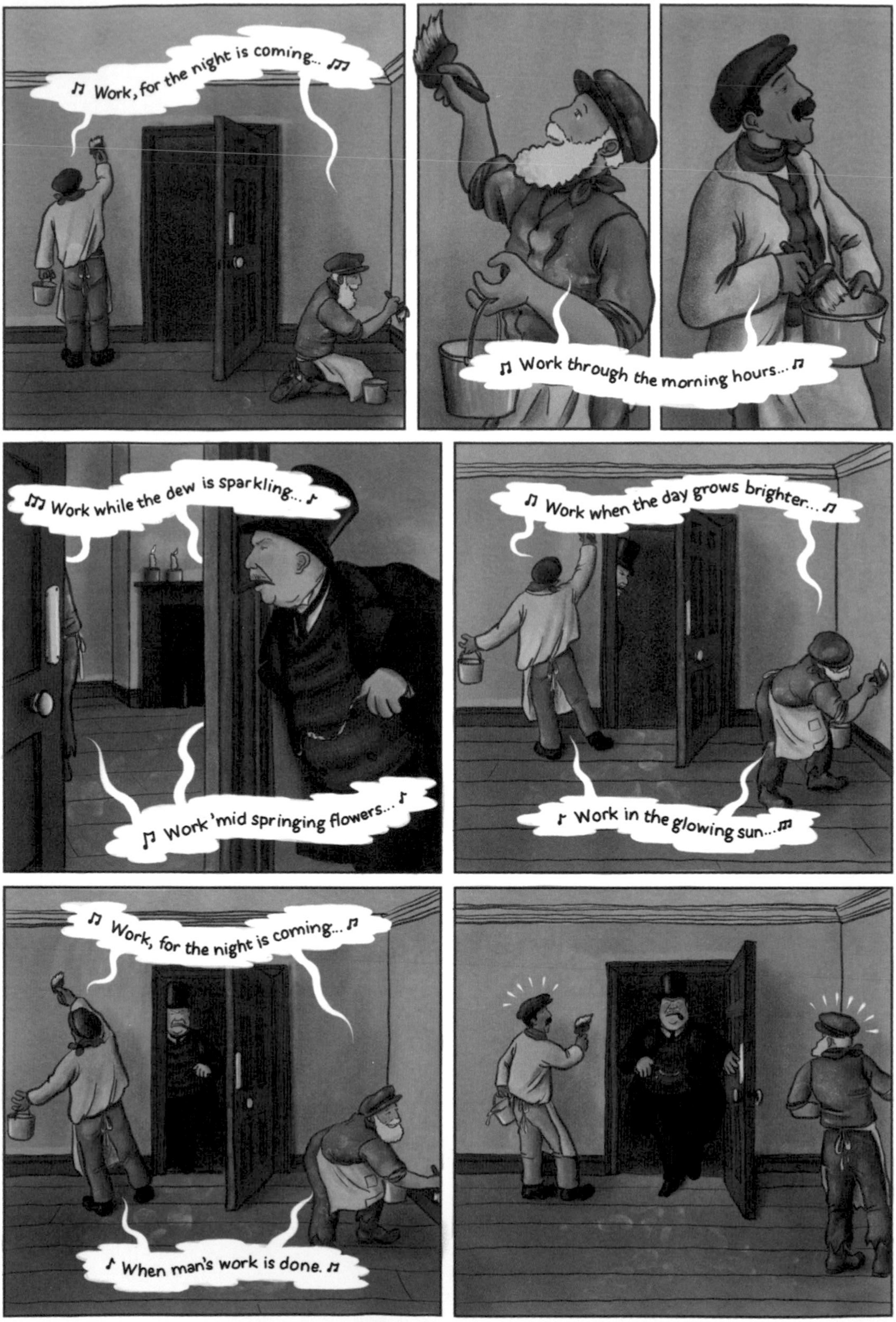
Work, for the night is coming...
Work through the morning hours...
Work while the dew is sparkling...
Work 'mid springing flowers...
Work when the day grows brighter...
Work in the glowing sun...
Work, for the night is coming...
When man's work is done.

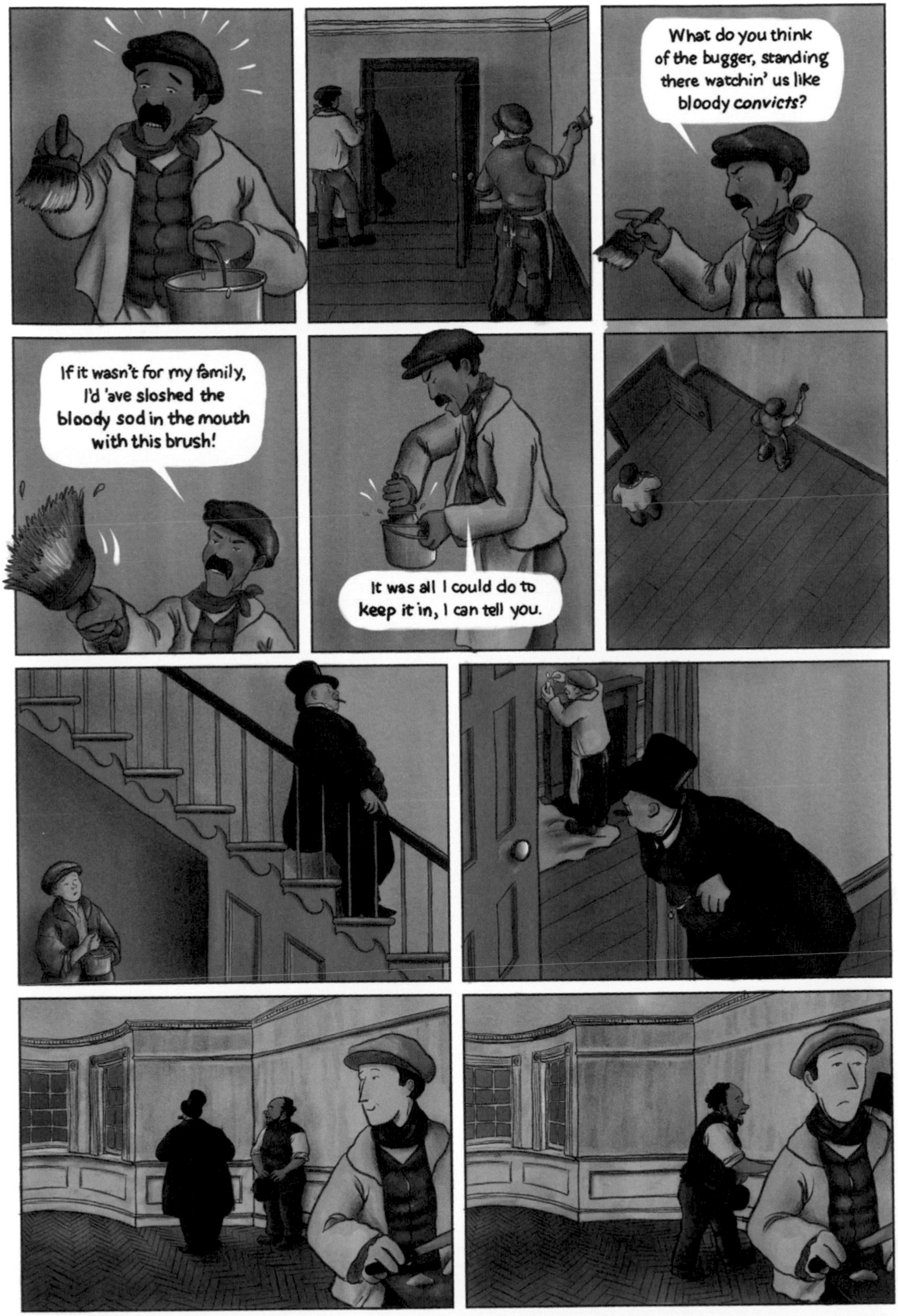
What do you think of the bugger, standing there watchin' us like bloody *convicts*?
If it wasn't for my family, I'd 'ave sloshed the bloody sod in the mouth with this brush!
It was all I could do to keep it in, I can tell you.

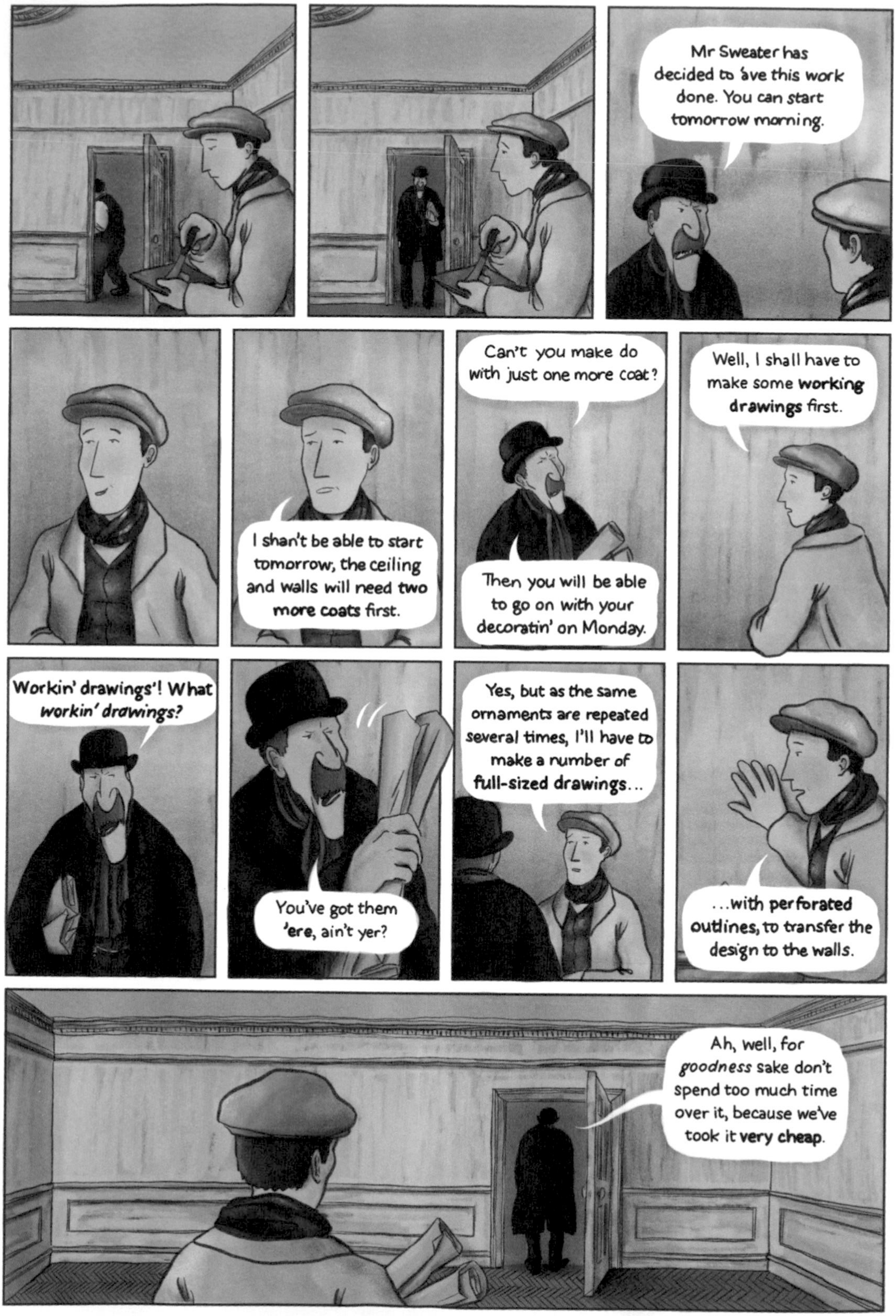
Mr Sweater has decided to 'ave this work done. You can start tomorrow morning.
I shan't be able to start tomorrow, the ceiling and walls will need two more coats first.
Can't you make do with just one more coat?
Then you will be able to go on with your decoratin' on Monday.
Well, I shall have to make some working drawings first.
Workin' drawings'! What workin' drawings?
You've got them 'ere, ain't yer?
Yes, but as the same ornaments are repeated several times, I'll have to make a number of full-sized drawings...
...with perforated outlines, to transfer the design to the walls.
Ah, well, for goodness sake don't spend too much time over it, because we've took it very cheap.

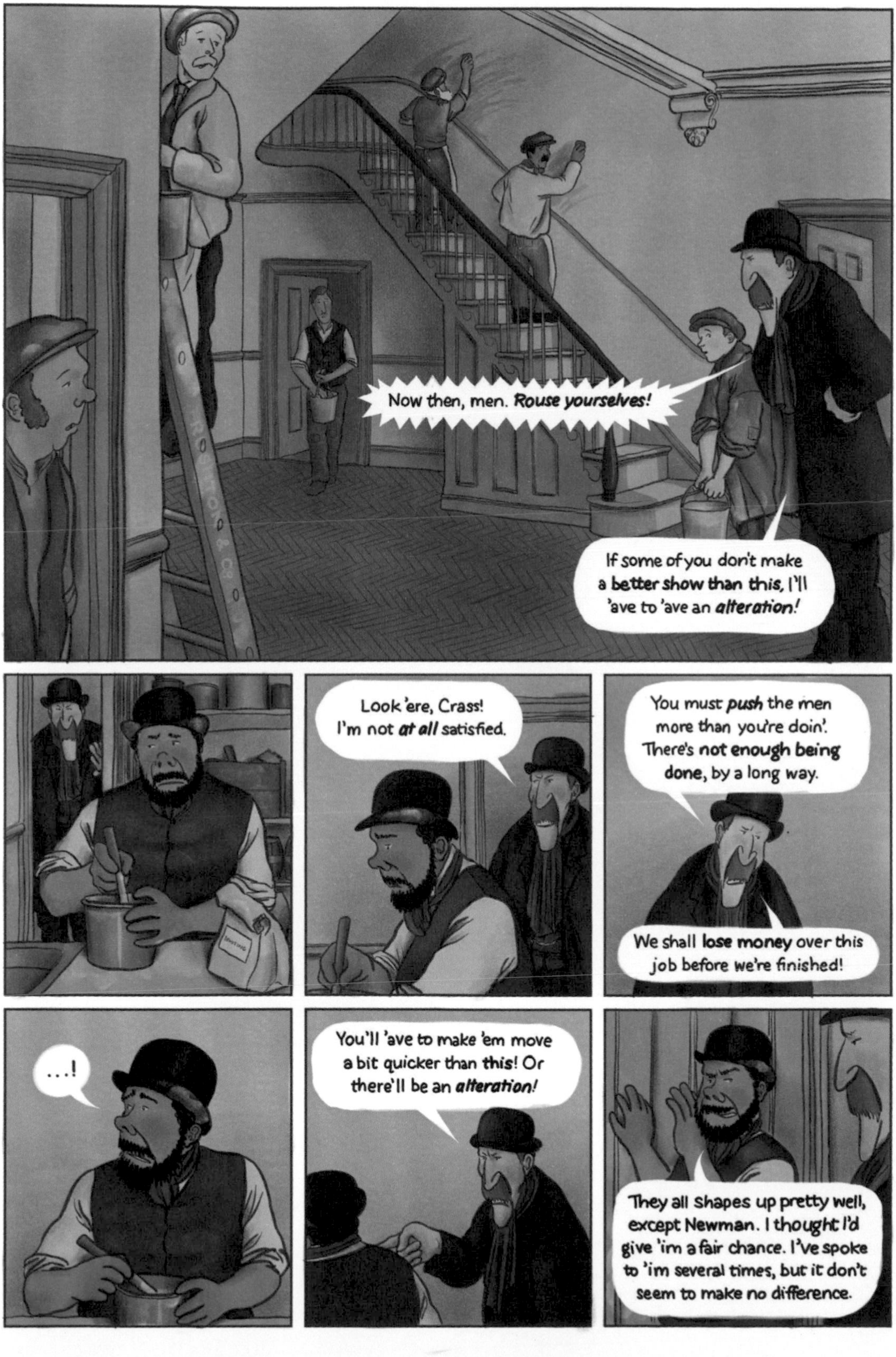
Now then, men. Rouse yourselves!
If some of you don't make a better show than this, I'll 'ave to 'ave an alteration!
Look 'ere, Crass! I'm not at all satisfied.
You must push the men more than you're doin'. There's not enough being done, by a long way.
We shall lose money over this job before we're finished!
...!
You'll 'ave to make 'em move a bit quicker than this! Or there'll be an alteration!
They all shapes up pretty well, except Newman. I thought I'd give 'im a fair chance. I've spoke to 'im several times, but it don't seem to make no difference.

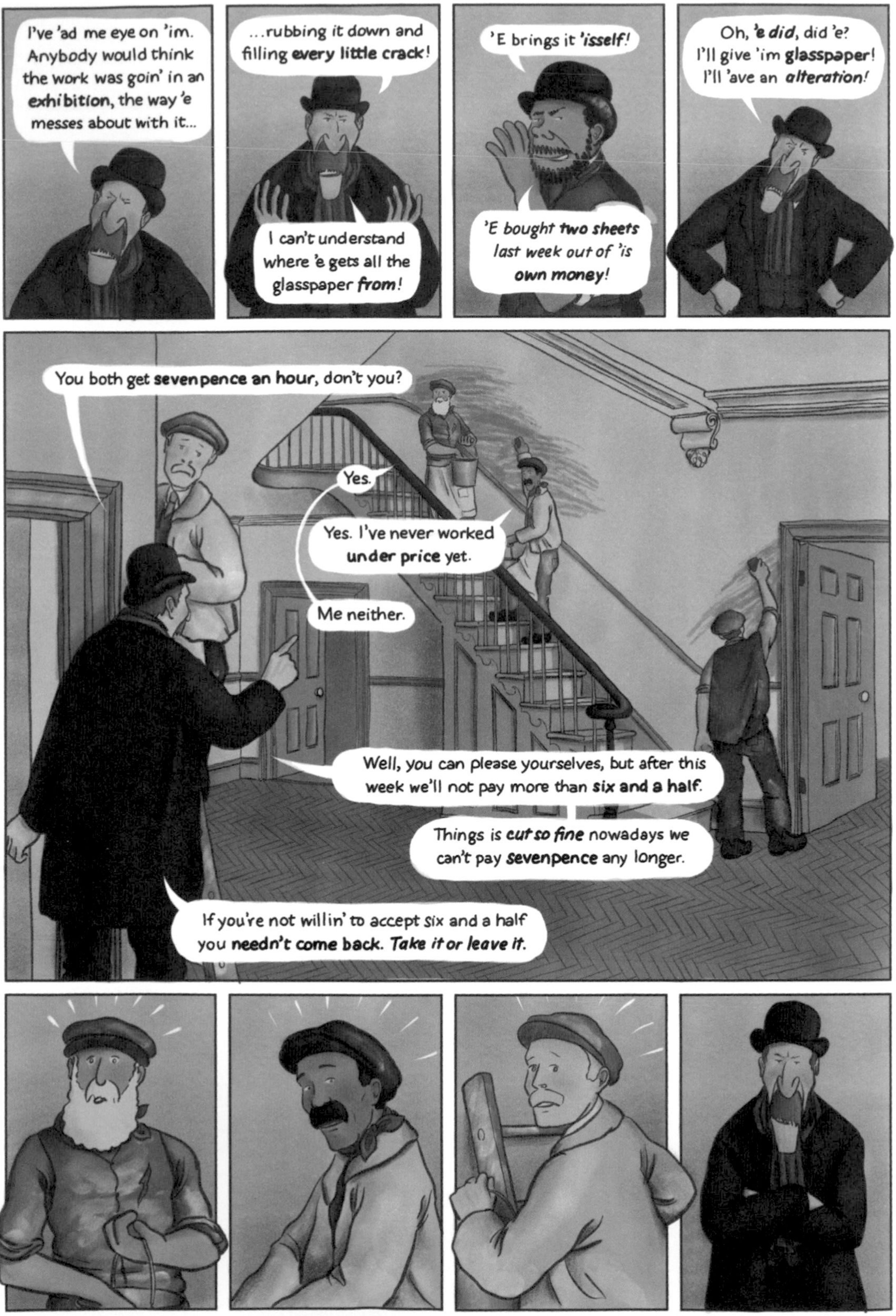
I've 'ad me eye on 'im. Anybody would think the work was goin' in an exhibition, the way 'e messes about with it...
...rubbing it down and filling every little crack!
I can't understand where 'e gets all the glasspaper from!
'E brings it 'isself!
'E bought two sheets last week out of 'is own money!
Oh, 'e did, did 'e? I'll give 'im glasspaper! I'll 'ave an alteration!
You both get sevenpence an hour, don't you?
Yes.
Yes. I've never worked under price yet.
Me neither.
Well, you can please yourselves, but after this week we'll not pay more than six and a half.
Things is cut so fine nowadays we can't pay sevenpence any longer.
If you're not willin' to accept six and a half you needn't come back. Take it or leave it.

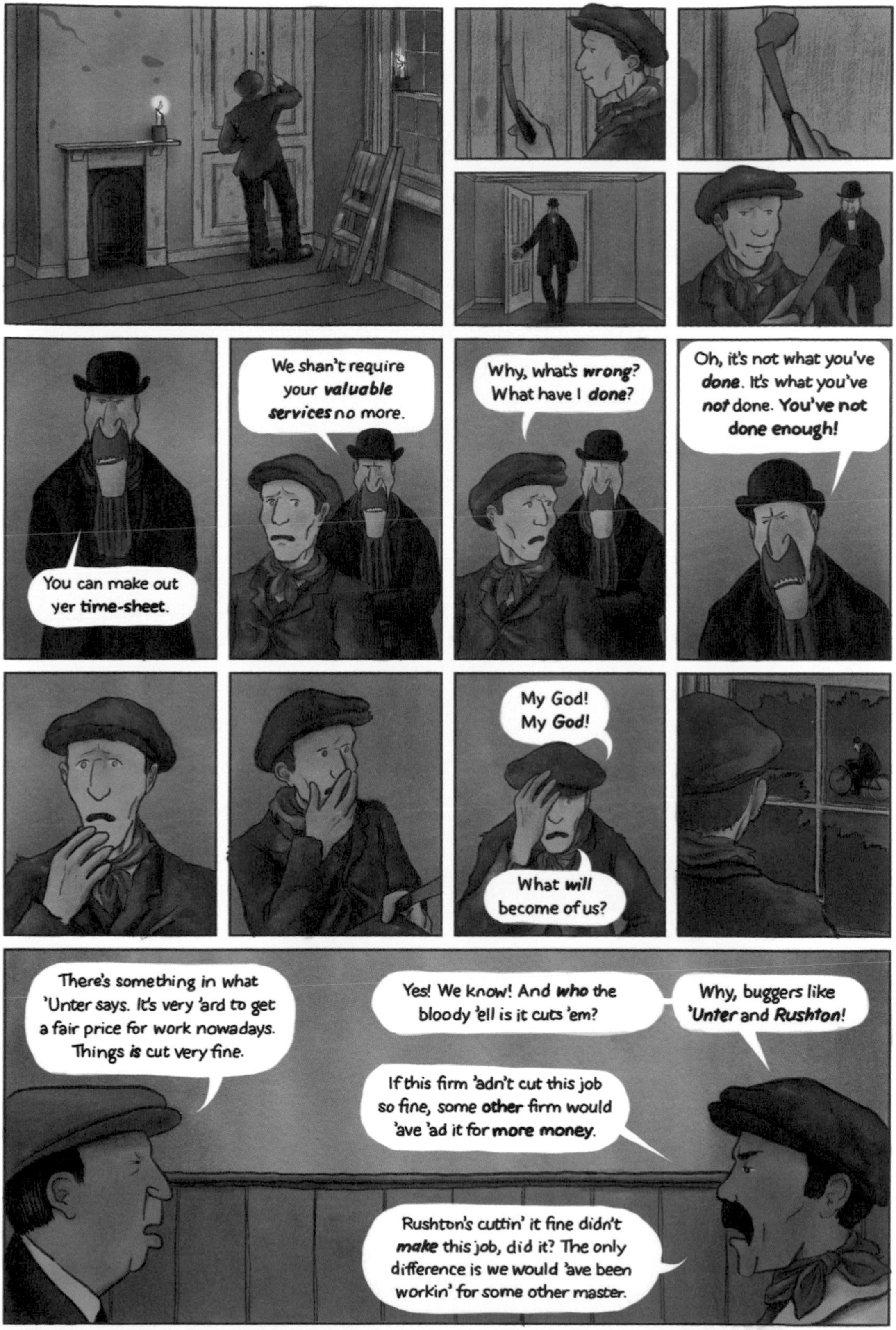
You can make out yer time-sheet.
We shan't require your valuable services no more.
Why, what's wrong? What have I done?
Oh, it's not what you've done. It's what you've not done. You've not done enough!
My God! My God!
What will become of us?
There's something in what 'Unter says. It's very 'ard to get a fair price for work nowadays. Things is cut very fine.
Yes! We know! And who the bloody 'ell is it cuts 'em?
Why, buggers like 'Unter and Rushton!
If this firm 'adn't cut this job so fine, some other firm would 'ave 'ad it for more money.
Rushton's cuttin' it fine didn't make this job, did it? The only difference is we would 'ave been workin' for some other master.

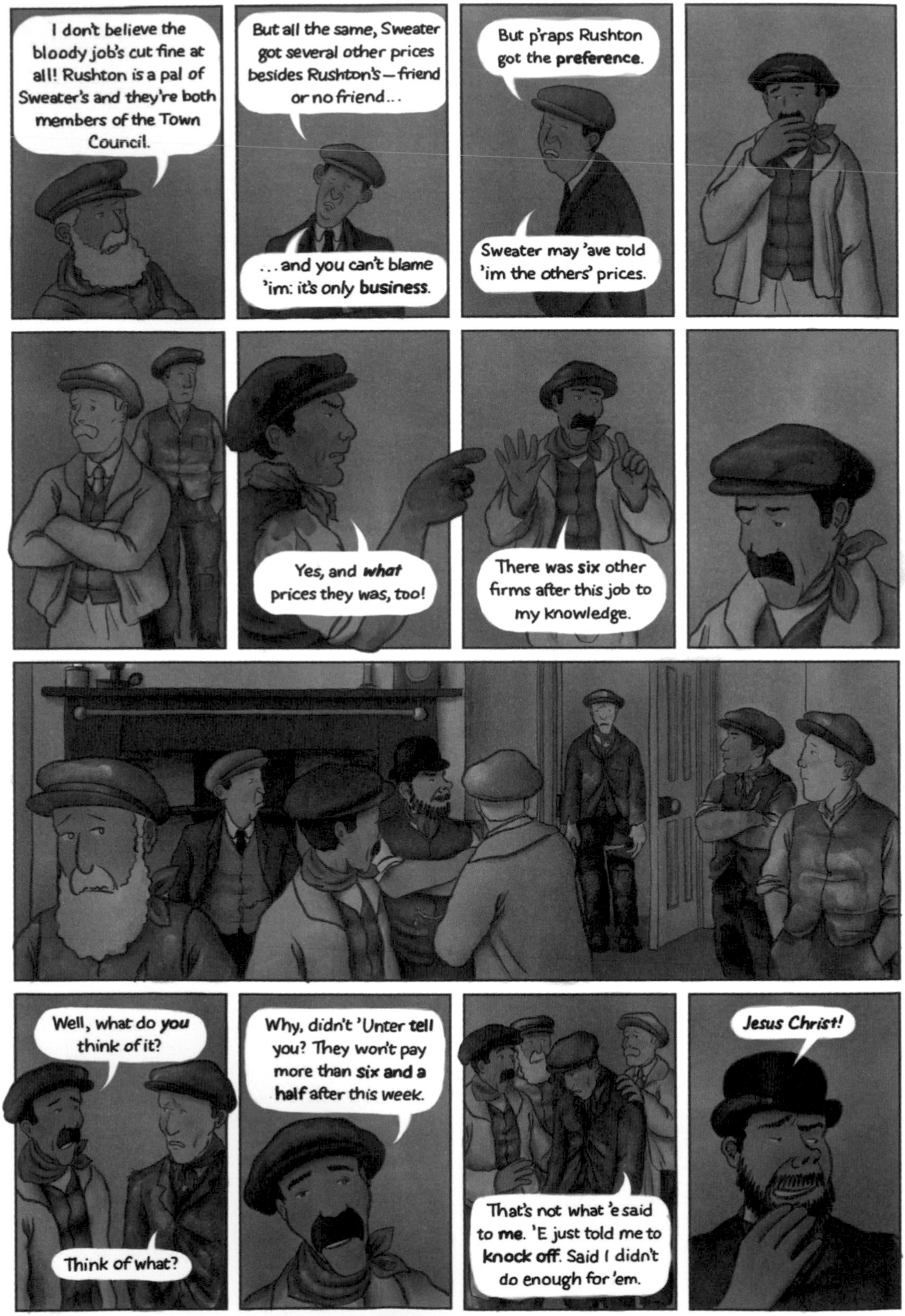
I don't believe the bloody job's cut fine at all! Rushton is a pal of Sweater's and they're both members of the Town Council.
But all the same, Sweater got several other prices besides Rushton's — friend or no friend...
...and you can't blame 'im: it's only **business**.
But p'raps Rushton got the **preference**.
Sweater may 'ave told 'im the others' prices.
Yes, and ***what*** prices they was, too!
There was **six** other firms after this job to my knowledge.
Well, what do ***you*** think of it?
Think of what?
Why, didn't 'Unter tell you? They won't pay more than **six and a half** after this week.
That's not what 'e said to **me**. 'E just told me to **knock off**. Said I didn't do enough for 'em.
Jesus Christ!

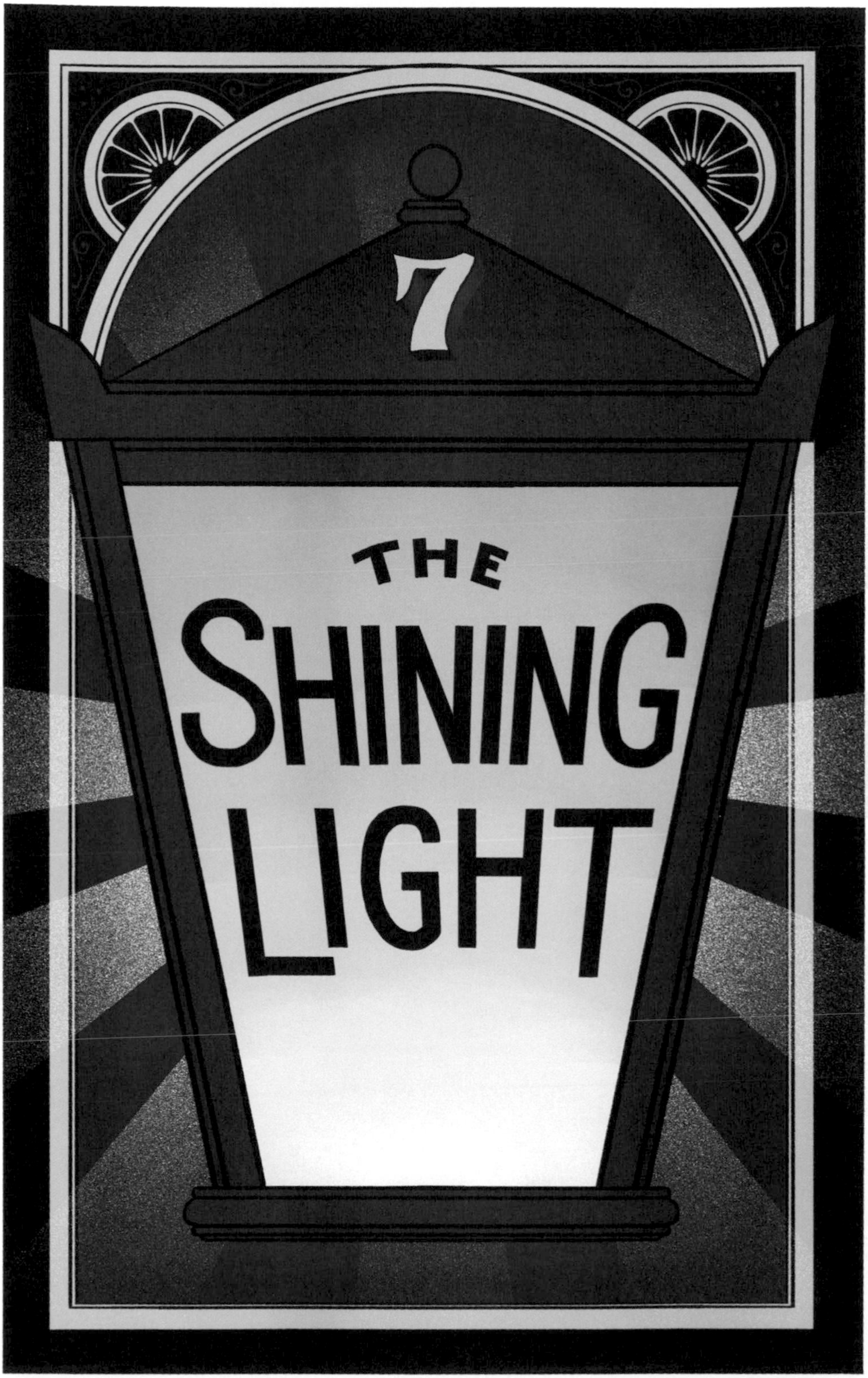
7
THE
SHINING
LIGHT

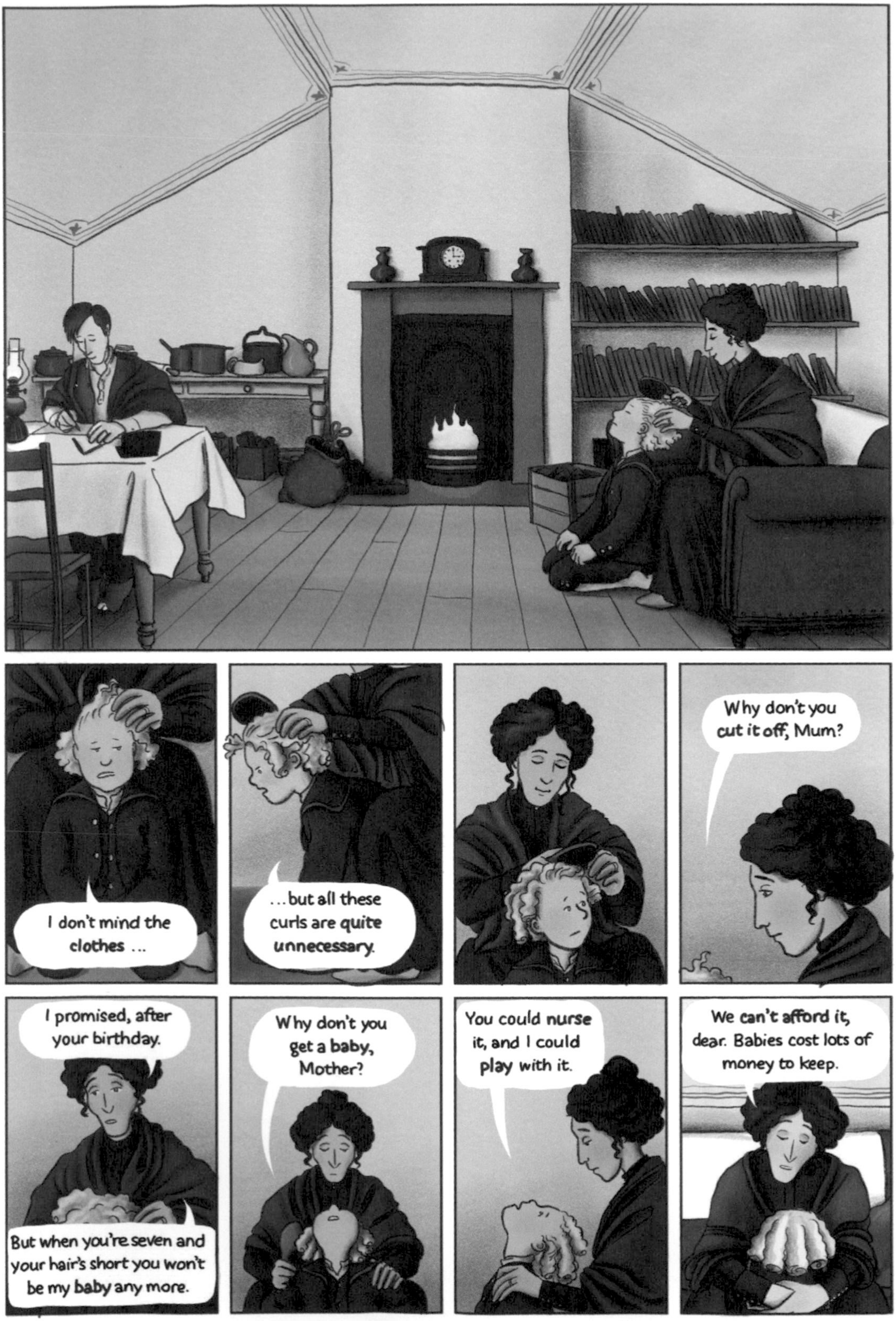
I don't mind the clothes ...
...but all these curls are quite unnecessary.
Why don't you cut it off, Mum?
I promised, after your birthday.
But when you're seven and your hair's short you won't be my baby any more.
Why don't you get a baby, Mother?
You could nurse it, and I could play with it.
We can't afford it, dear. Babies cost lots of money to keep.

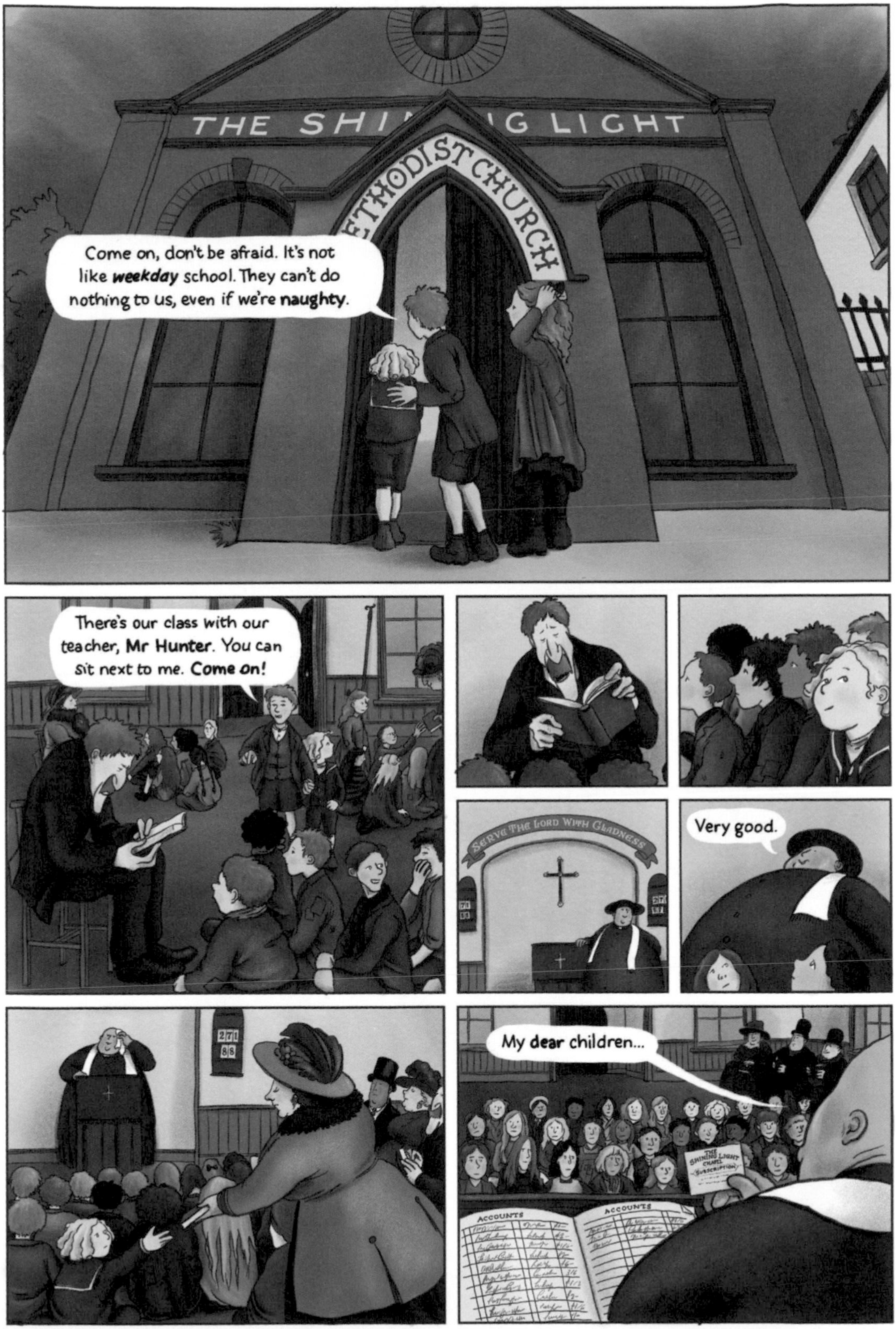
Come on, don't be afraid. It's not like **weekday** school. They can't do nothing to us, even if we're **naughty**.
There's our class with our teacher, **Mr Hunter**. You can sit next to me. **Come on**!
SERVE THE LORD WITH GLADNESS
Very good.
My dear children...
ACCOUNTS
ACCOUNTS

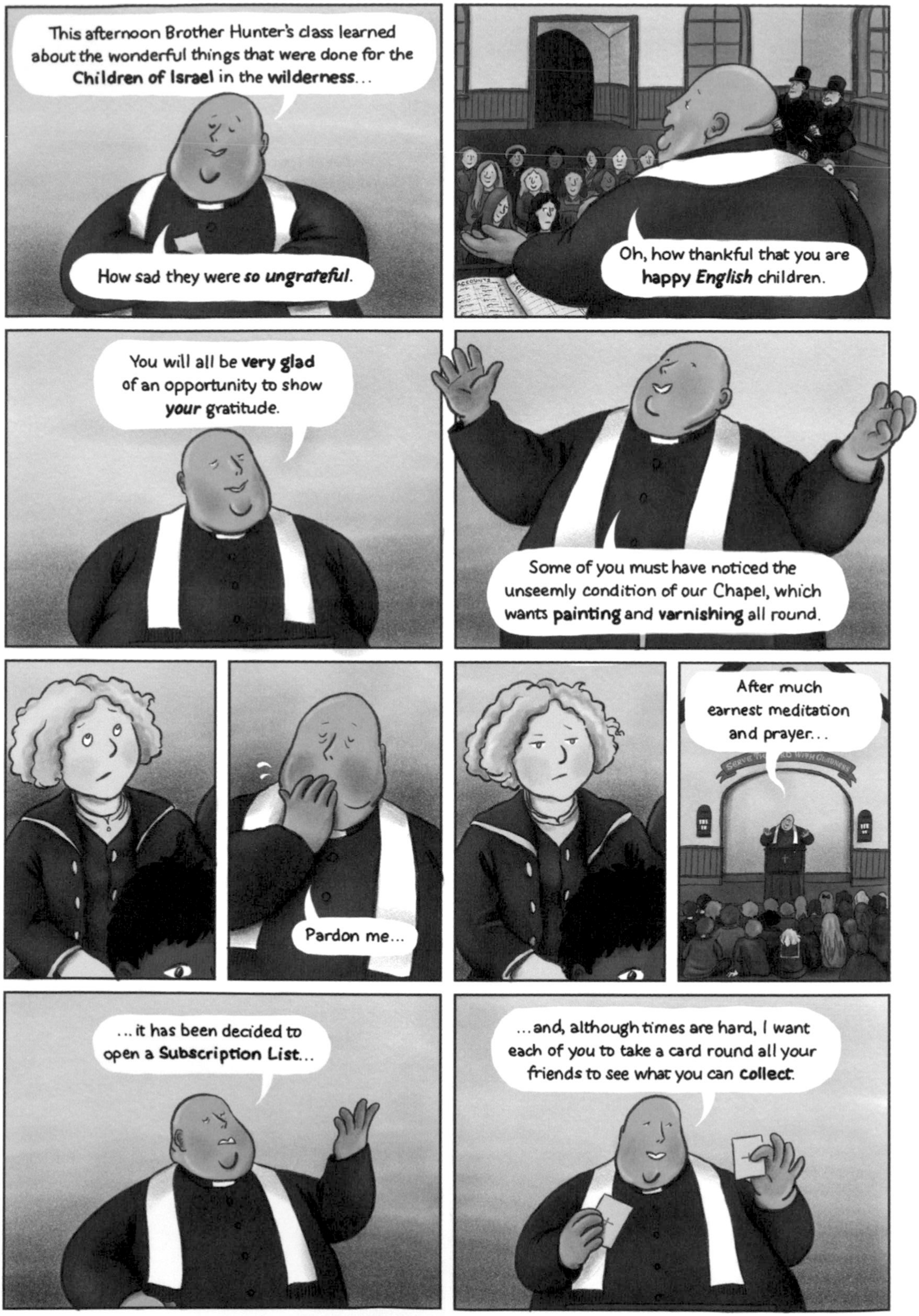
This afternoon Brother Hunter's class learned about the wonderful things that were done for the Children of Israel in the wilderness...
How sad they were so ungrateful.
Oh, how thankful that you are happy English children.
You will all be very glad of an opportunity to show your gratitude.
Some of you must have noticed the unseemly condition of our Chapel, which wants painting and varnishing all round.
Pardon me...
After much earnest meditation and prayer...
...it has been decided to open a Subscription List...
...and, although times are hard, I want each of you to take a card round all your friends to see what you can collect.

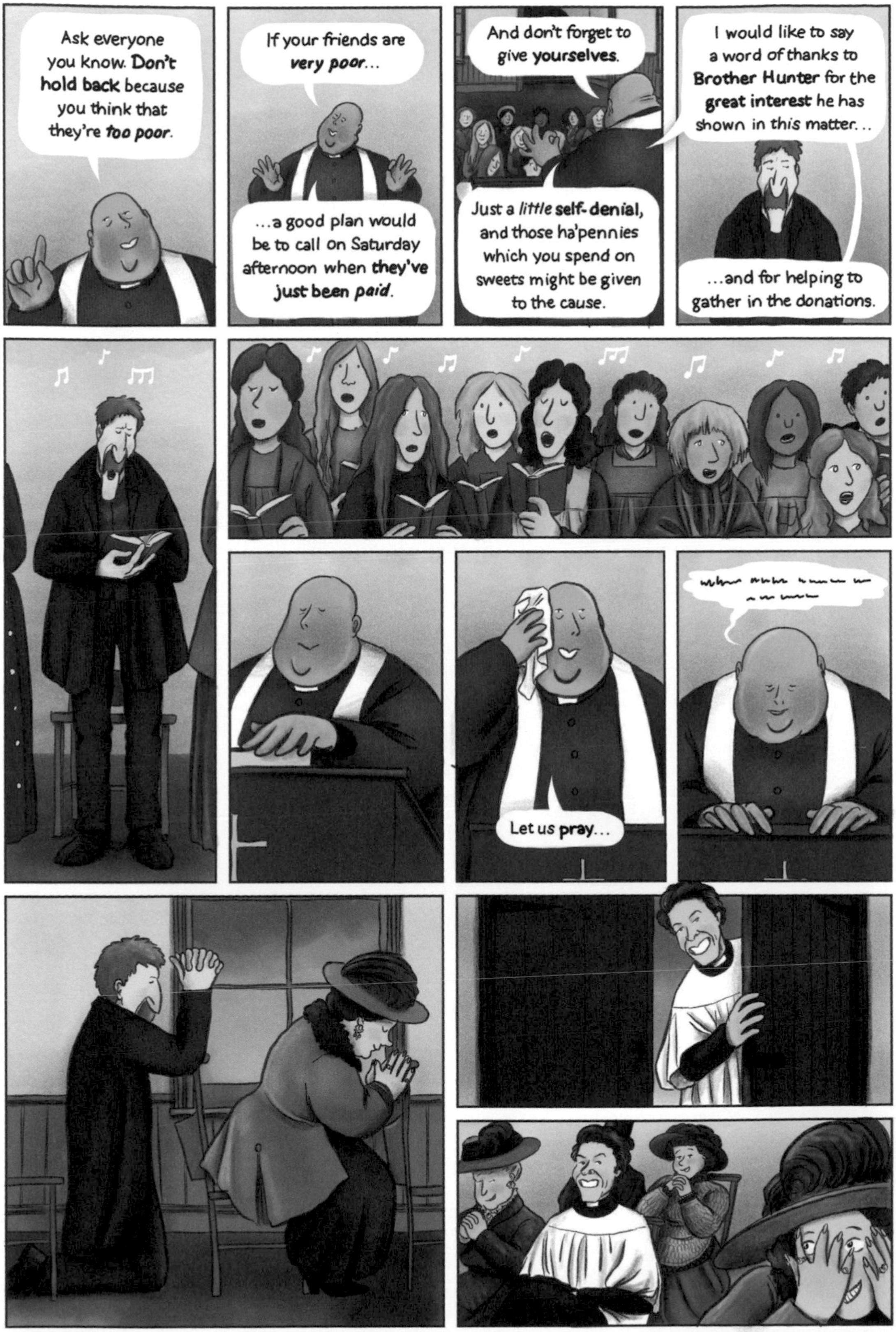
Ask everyone you know. **Don't hold back** because you think that they're ***too poor***.
If your friends are ***very poor***...
...a good plan would be to call on Saturday afternoon when **they've just been *paid***.
And don't forget to give **yourselves**.
Just a *little* **self-denial**, and those ha'pennies which you spend on sweets might be given to the cause.
I would like to say a word of thanks to **Brother Hunter** for the **great interest** he has shown in this matter...
...and for helping to gather in the donations.
Let us **pray**...

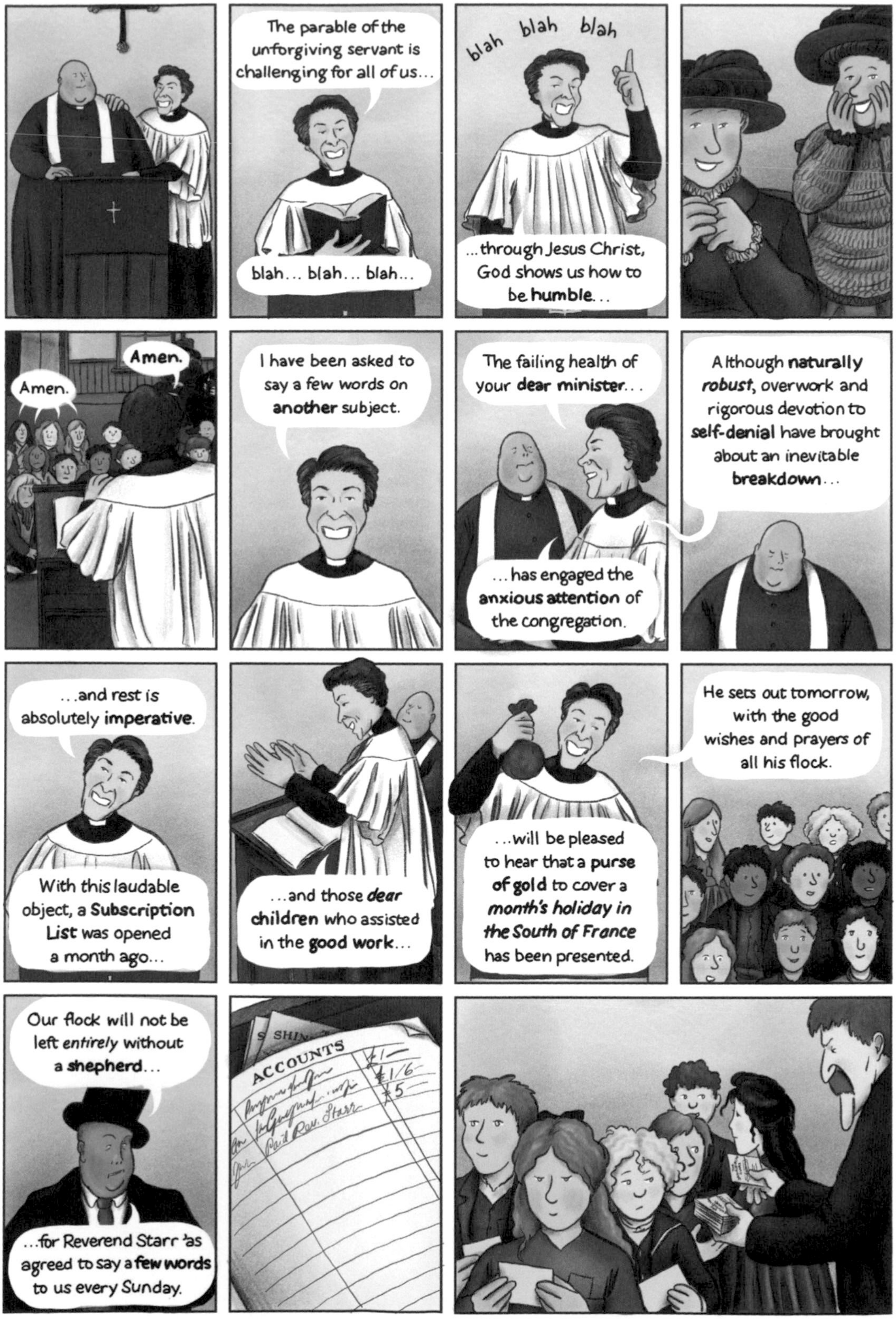
The parable of the unforgiving servant is challenging for all of us...
blah... blah... blah...
blah blah blah
...through Jesus Christ, God shows us how to be **humble**...
Amen.
Amen.
I have been asked to say a few words on **another** subject.
The failing health of your **dear minister**...
...has engaged the **anxious attention** of the congregation.
Although **naturally** ***robust***, overwork and rigorous devotion to **self-denial** have brought about an inevitable **breakdown**...
...and rest is absolutely **imperative**.
With this laudable object, a **Subscription List** was opened a month ago...
...and those ***dear*** **children** who assisted in the **good work**...
...will be pleased to hear that a **purse of gold** to cover a ***month's holiday in the South of France*** has been presented.
He sets out tomorrow, with the good wishes and prayers of all his flock.
Our flock will not be left *entirely* without a **shepherd**...
...for Reverend Starr 'as agreed to say a **few words** to us every Sunday.
ACCOUNTS
Paid Rev. Starr
£5

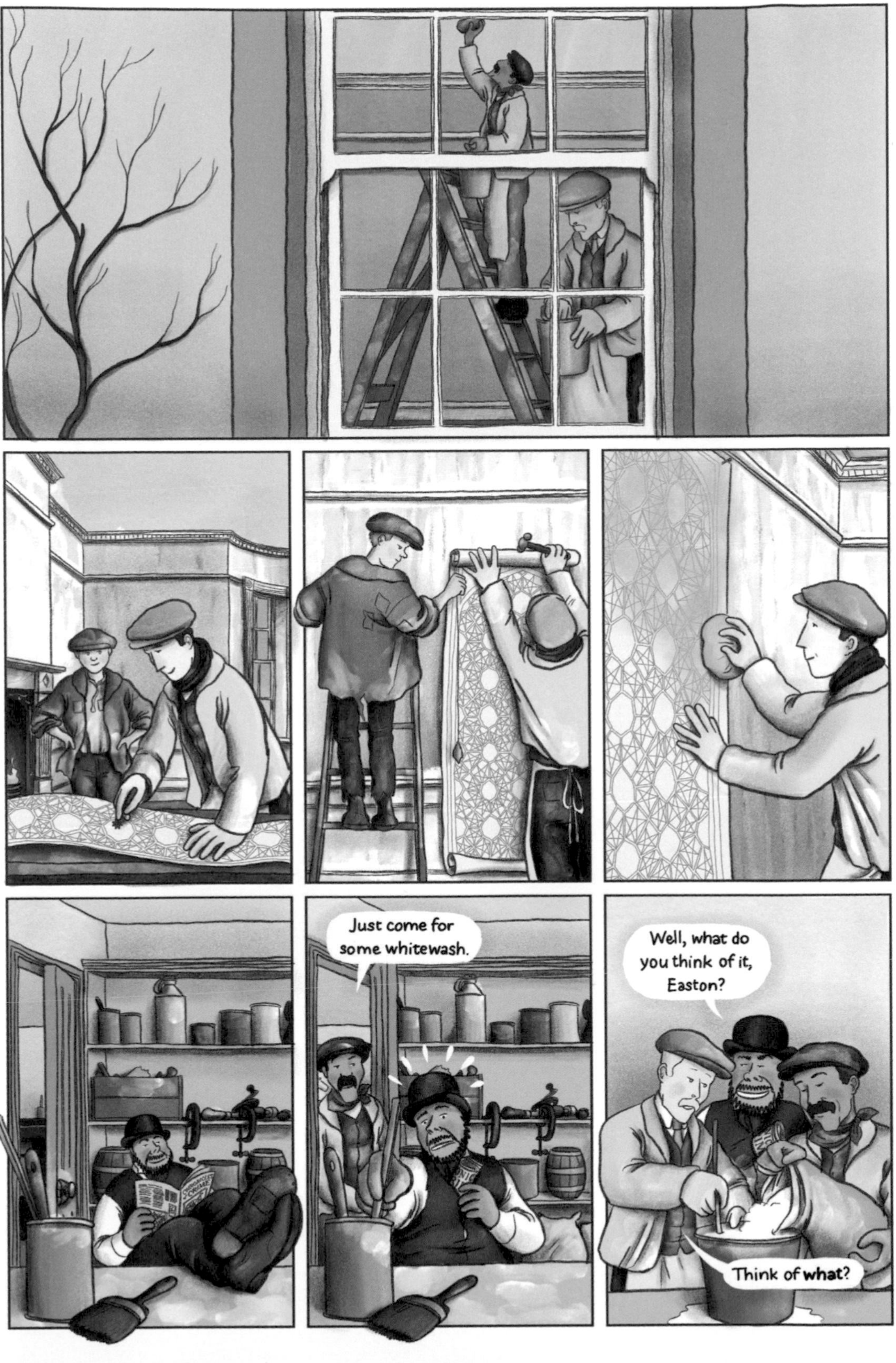
Just come for some whitewash.
Well, what do you think of it, Easton?
Think of what?

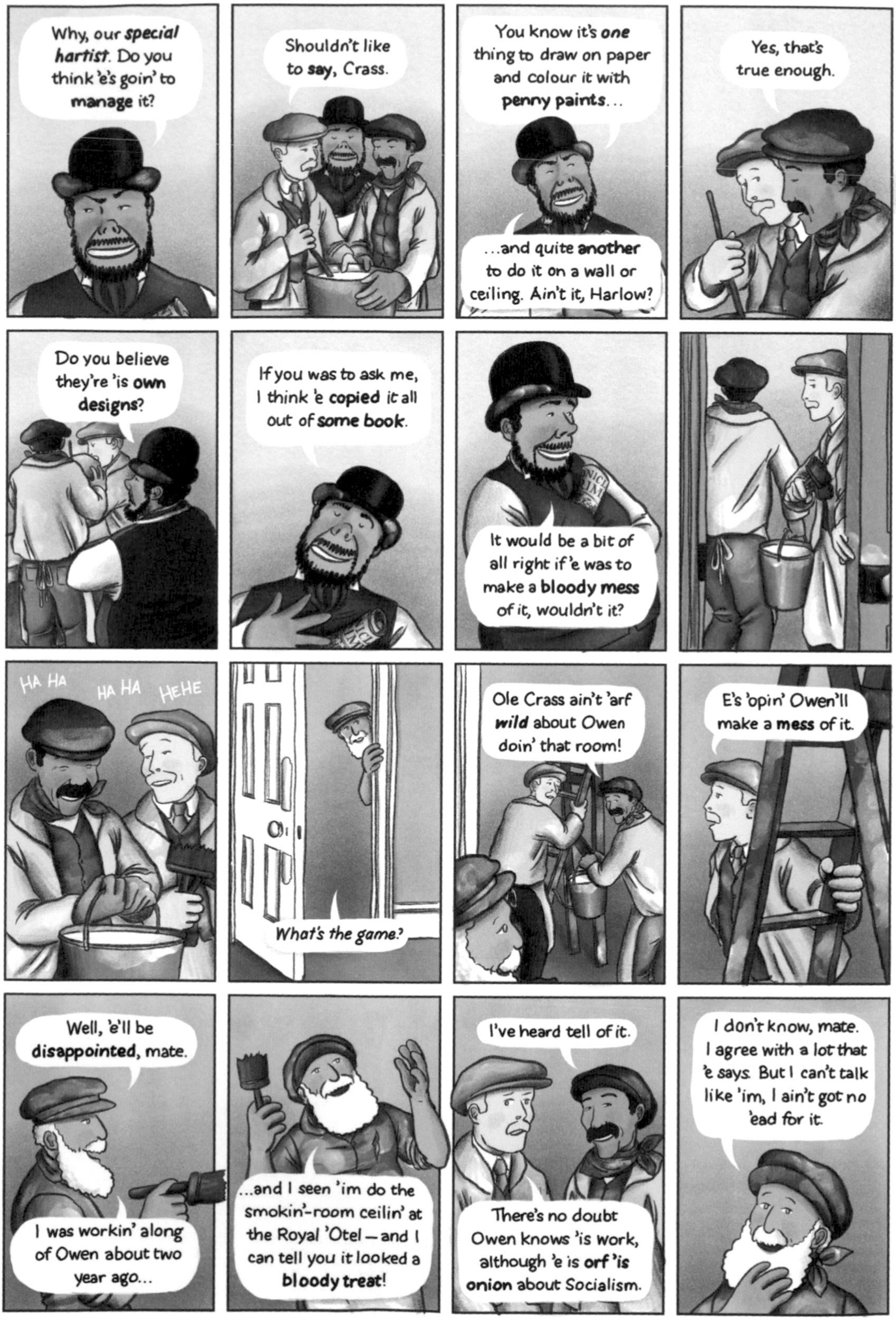
Why, our **special hartist**. Do you think 'e's goin' to **manage** it?
Shouldn't like to **say**, Crass.
You know it's ***one*** thing to draw on paper and colour it with **penny paints**...
...and quite **another** to do it on a wall or ceiling. Ain't it, Harlow?
Yes, that's true enough.
Do you believe they're 'is **own designs**?
If you was to ask me, I think 'e **copied** *it* all out of **some book**.
It would be a bit of all right if 'e was to make a **bloody mess** of it, wouldn't it?
HA HA
HA HA
HEHE
What's the game?
Ole Crass ain't 'arf ***wild*** about Owen doin' that room!
E's 'opin' Owen'll make a **mess** of it.
Well, 'e'll be **disappointed**, mate.
I was workin' along of Owen about two year ago...
...and I seen 'im do the smokin'-room ceilin' at the Royal 'Otel — and I can tell you it looked a **bloody treat**!
I've heard tell of it.
There's no doubt Owen knows 'is work, although 'e is **orf 'is onion** about Socialism.
I don't know, mate. I agree with a lot that 'e says. But I can't talk like 'im, I ain't got no 'ead for it.

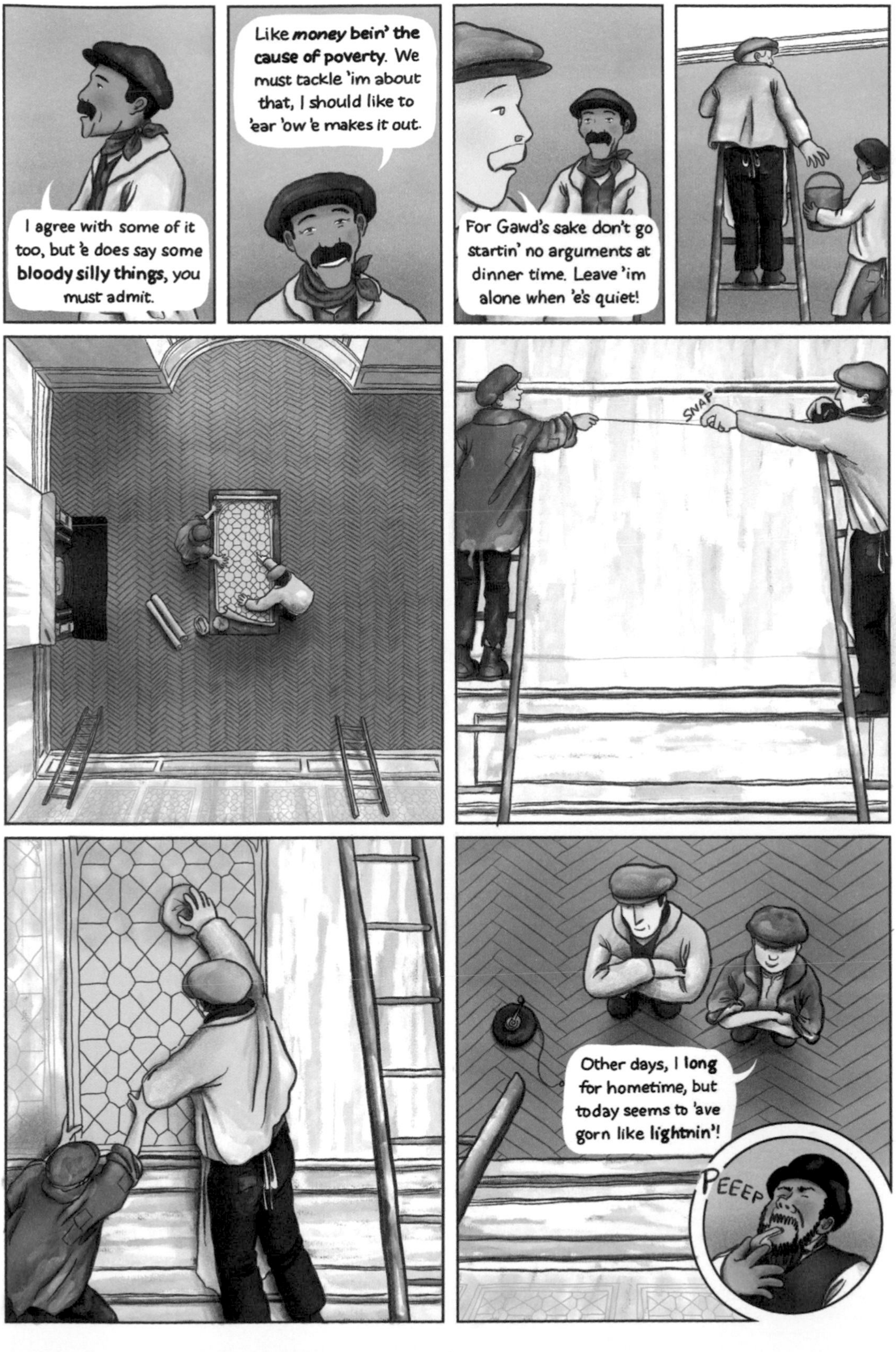
I agree with some of it too, but 'e does say some **bloody silly things**, you must admit.
Like ***money* bein' the cause of poverty**. We must tackle 'im about that, I should like to 'ear 'ow 'e makes it out.
For Gawd's sake don't go startin' no arguments at dinner time. Leave 'im alone when 'e's quiet!
SNAP
Other days, I **long** for hometime, but today seems to 'ave gorn like **lightnin'**!
PEEEP

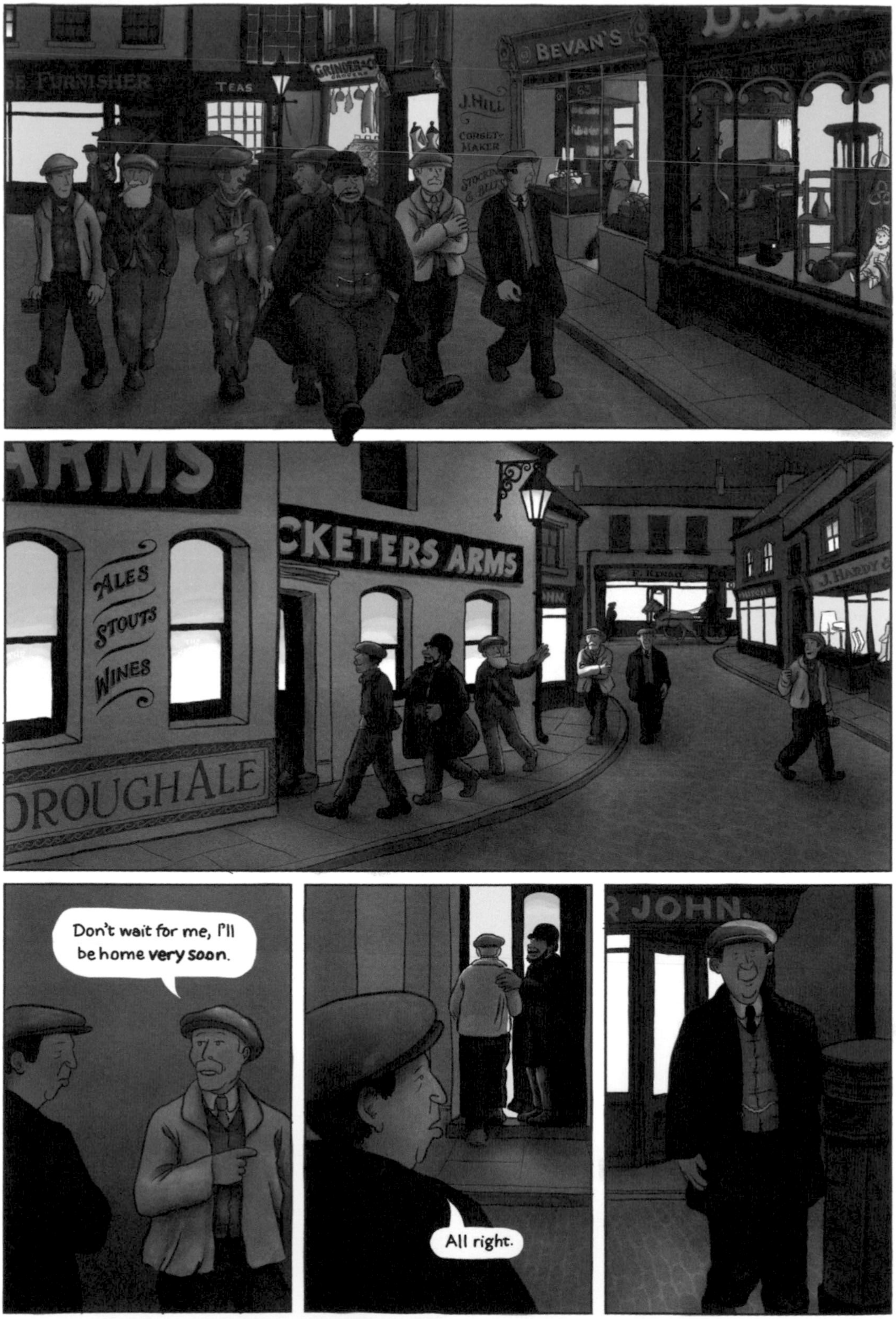
BEVAN'S
TEAS
J. HILL
CORSET-MAKER
ARMS
CKETERS ARMS
ALES
STOUTS
WINES
ROUGHALE
Don't wait for me, I'll be home very soon.
All right.
JOHN

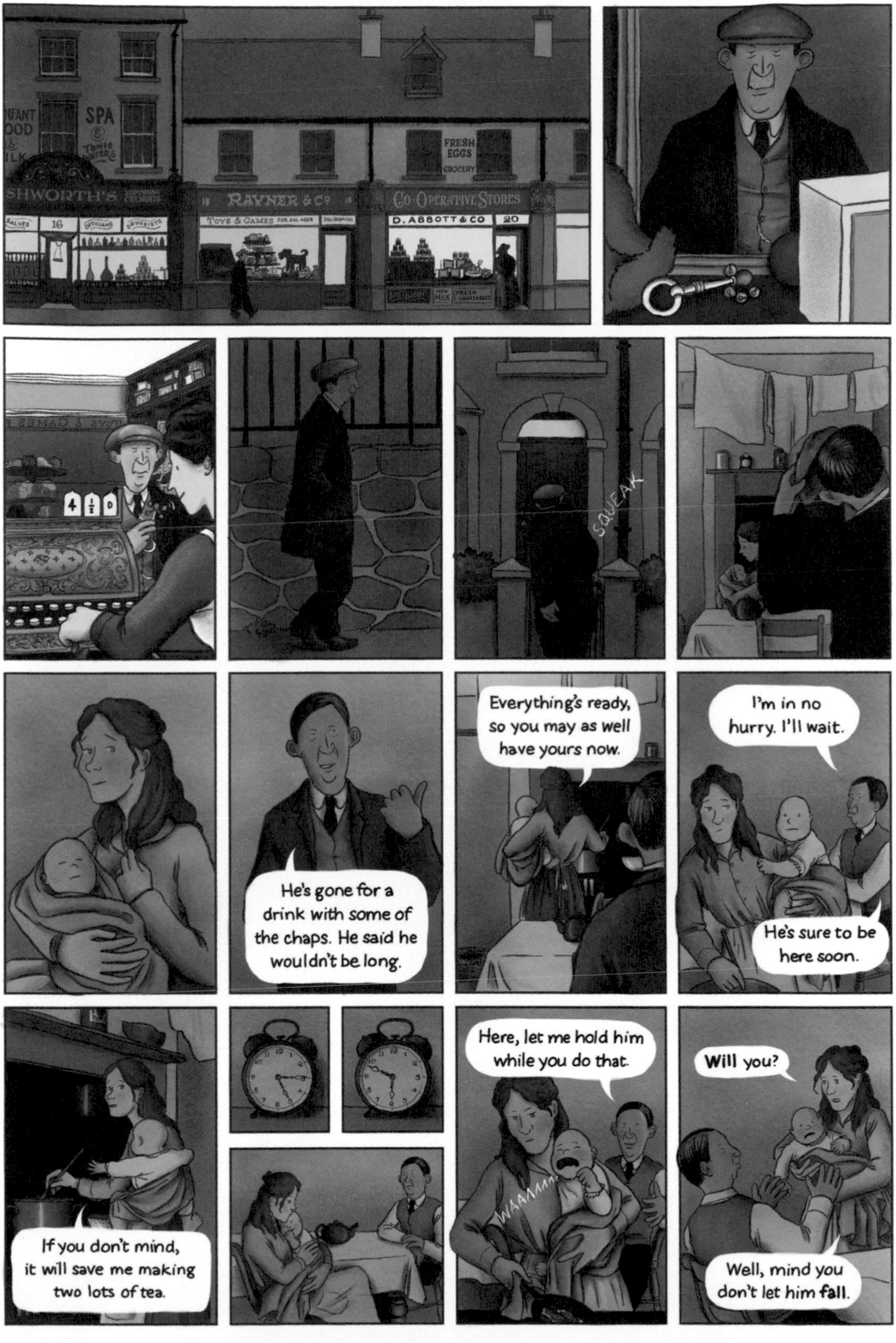
INFANT FOOD & MILK
SPA & Tonic Waters
SHWORTH'S
SALVES
16
OPTICIANS
DRUGGISTS
COLOGNES
RAYNER & Co
TOYS & GAMES FOR ALL AGES
DOLL HOSPITAL
FRESH EGGS
GROCERY
CO-OPERATIVE STORES
D. ABBOTT & CO
20
NEW MILK
FRESH VEGETABLES
4 1/2 D
SQUEAK
He's gone for a drink with some of the chaps. He said he wouldn't be long.
Everything's ready, so you may as well have yours now.
I'm in no hurry. I'll wait.
He's sure to be here soon.
If you don't mind, it will save me making two lots of tea.
Here, let me hold him while you do that.
WAAAAAA
Will you?
Well, mind you don't let him fall.

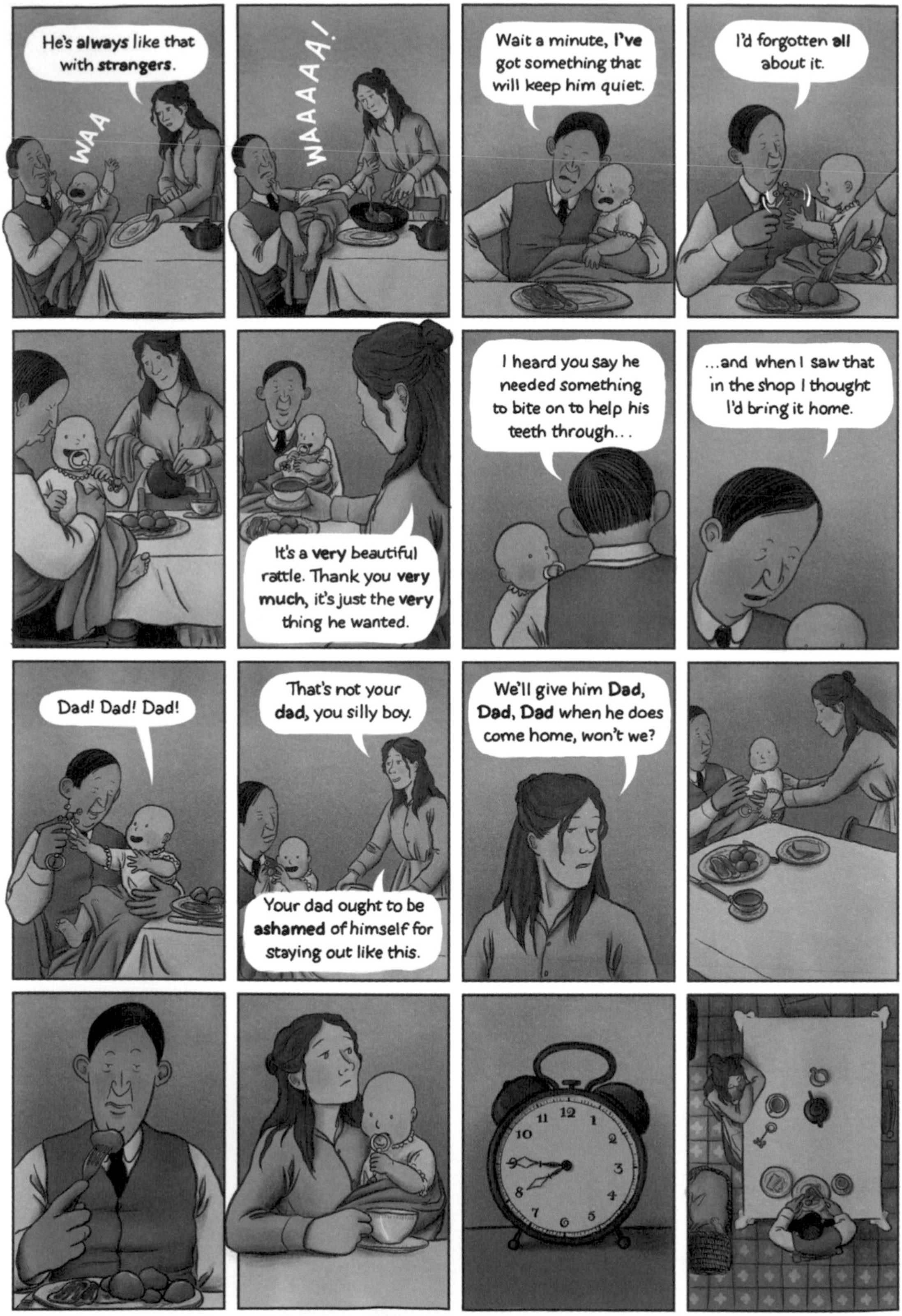
He's always like that with strangers.
WAA
WAAAAA!
Wait a minute, I've got something that will keep him quiet.
I'd forgotten all about it.
It's a very beautiful rattle. Thank you very much, it's just the very thing he wanted.
I heard you say he needed something to bite on to help his teeth through...
...and when I saw that in the shop I thought I'd bring it home.
Dad! Dad! Dad!
That's not your dad, you silly boy.
Your dad ought to be ashamed of himself for staying out like this.
We'll give him Dad, Dad, Dad when he does come home, won't we?

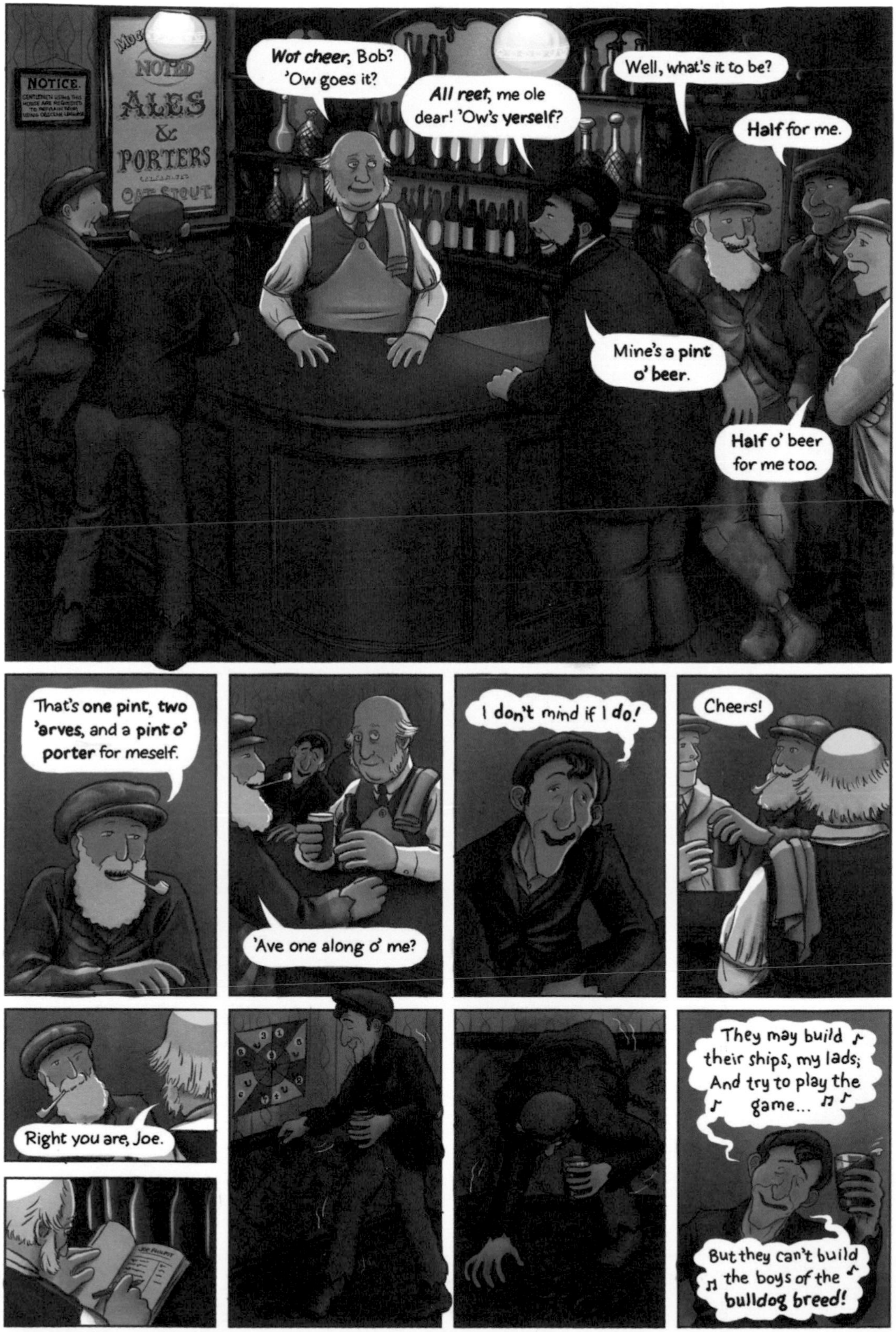
NOTICE
NOTED
ALES
&
PORTERS
Wot cheer, Bob? 'Ow goes it?
All reet, me ole dear! 'Ow's yerself?
Well, what's it to be?
Half for me.
Mine's a pint o' beer.
Half o' beer for me too.
That's one pint, two 'arves, and a pint o' porter for meself.
'Ave one along o' me?
I don't mind if I do!
Cheers!
Right you are, Joe.
They may build their ships, my lads; And try to play the game...
But they can't build the boys of the bulldog breed!

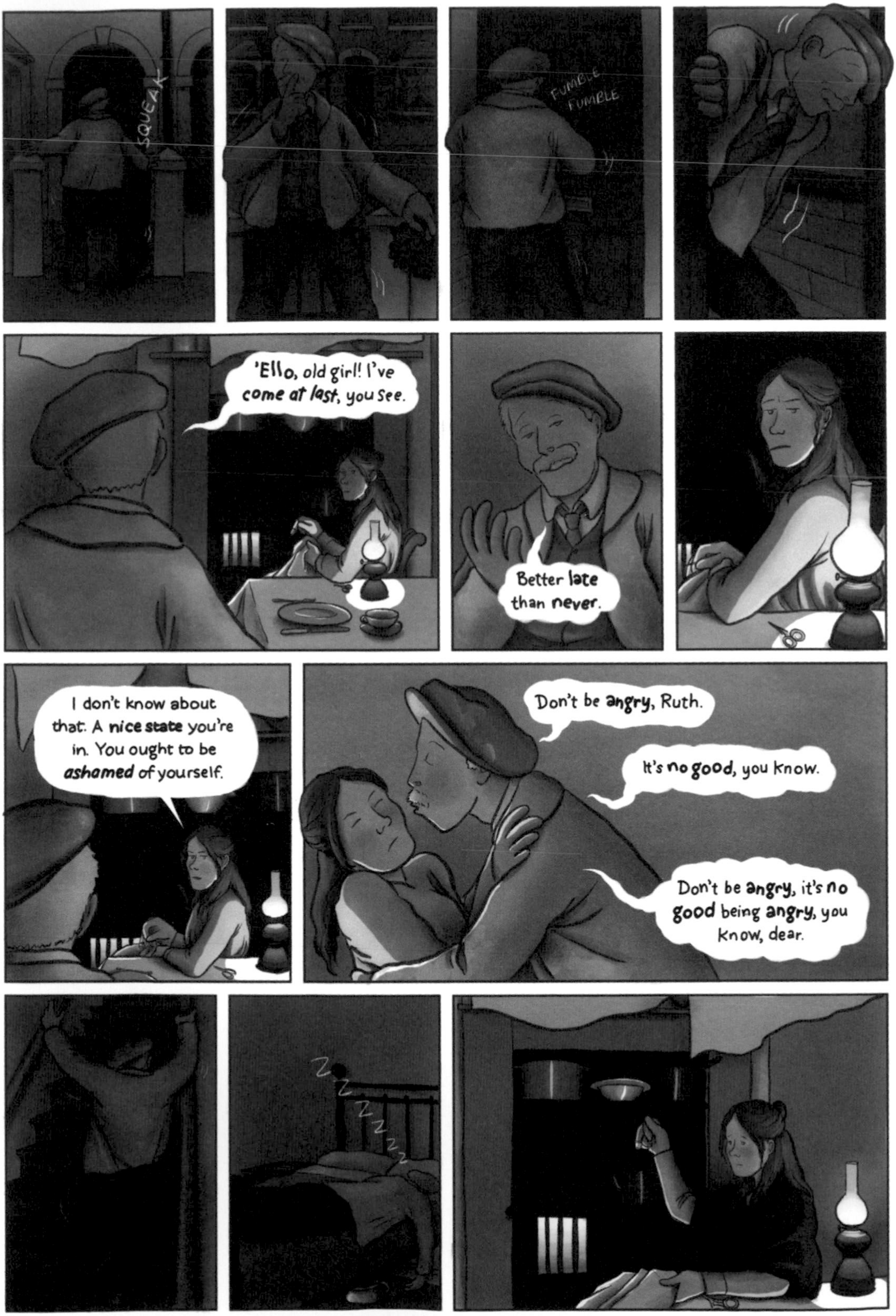
SQUEAK
FUMBLE FUMBLE
'Ello, old girl! I've come at last, you see.
Better late than never.
I don't know about that. A nice state you're in. You ought to be ashamed of yourself.
Don't be angry, Ruth.
It's no good, you know.
Don't be angry, it's no good being angry, you know, dear.

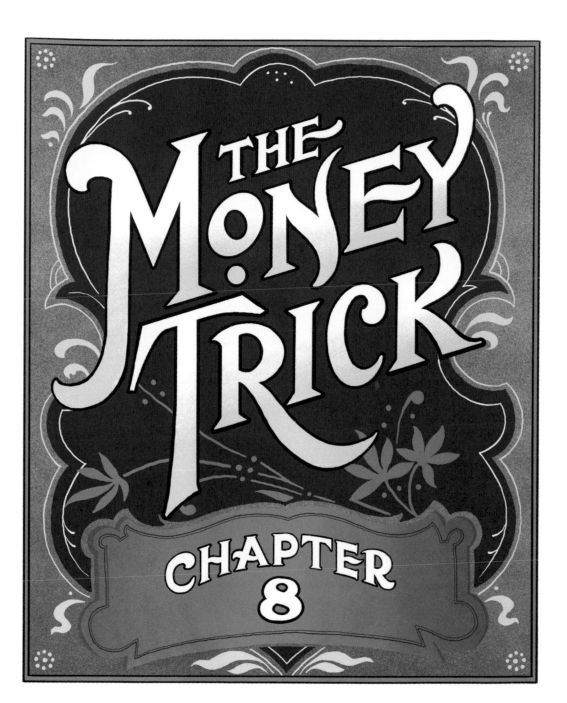

THE MONEY TRICK

CHAPTER 8

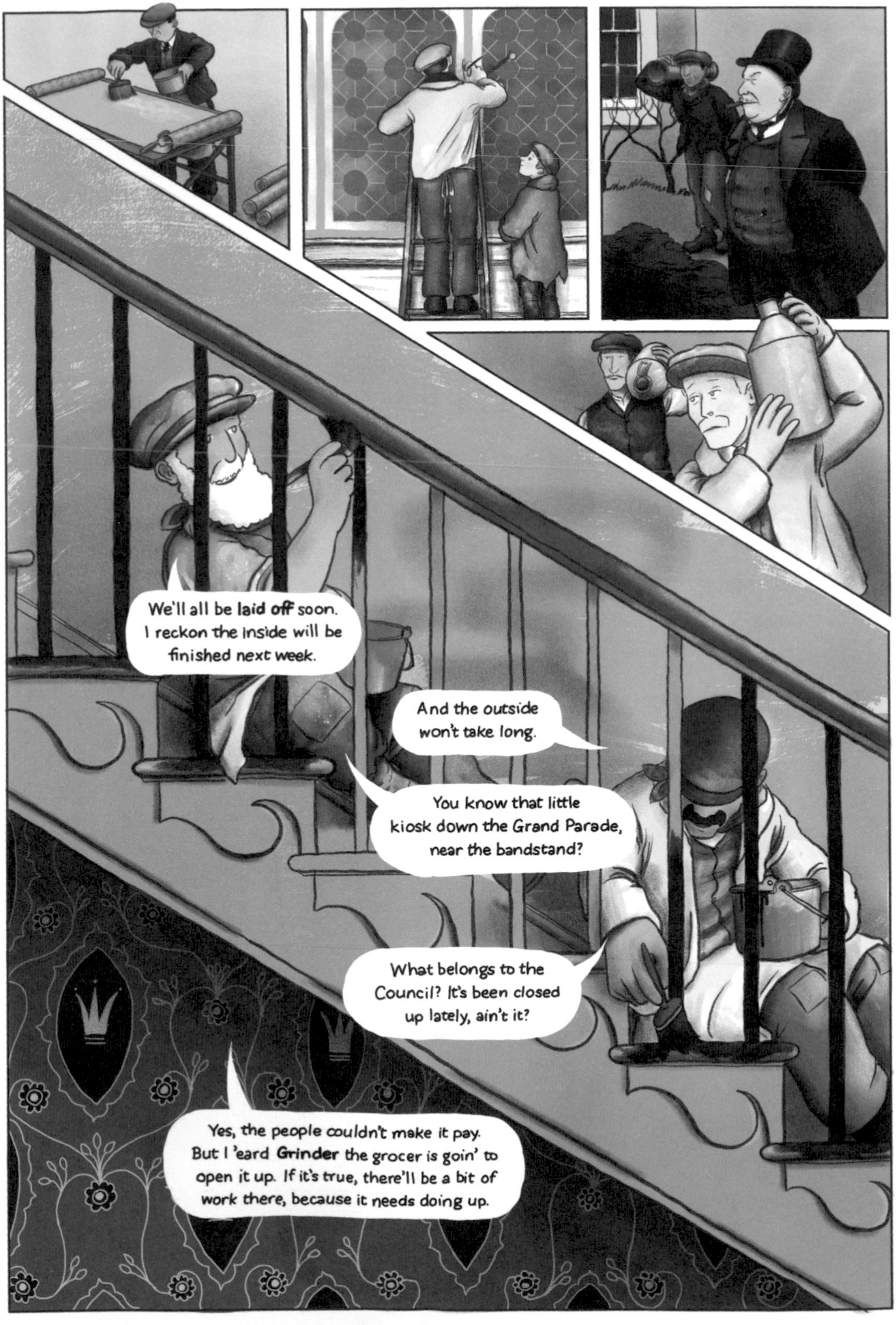

We'll all be **laid off** soon. I reckon the inside will be finished next week.
And the outside won't take long.
You know that little kiosk down the Grand Parade, near the bandstand?
What belongs to the Council? It's been closed up lately, ain't it?
Yes, the people couldn't make it pay. But I 'eard **Grinder** the grocer is goin' to open it up. If it's true, there'll be a bit of work there, because it needs doing up.

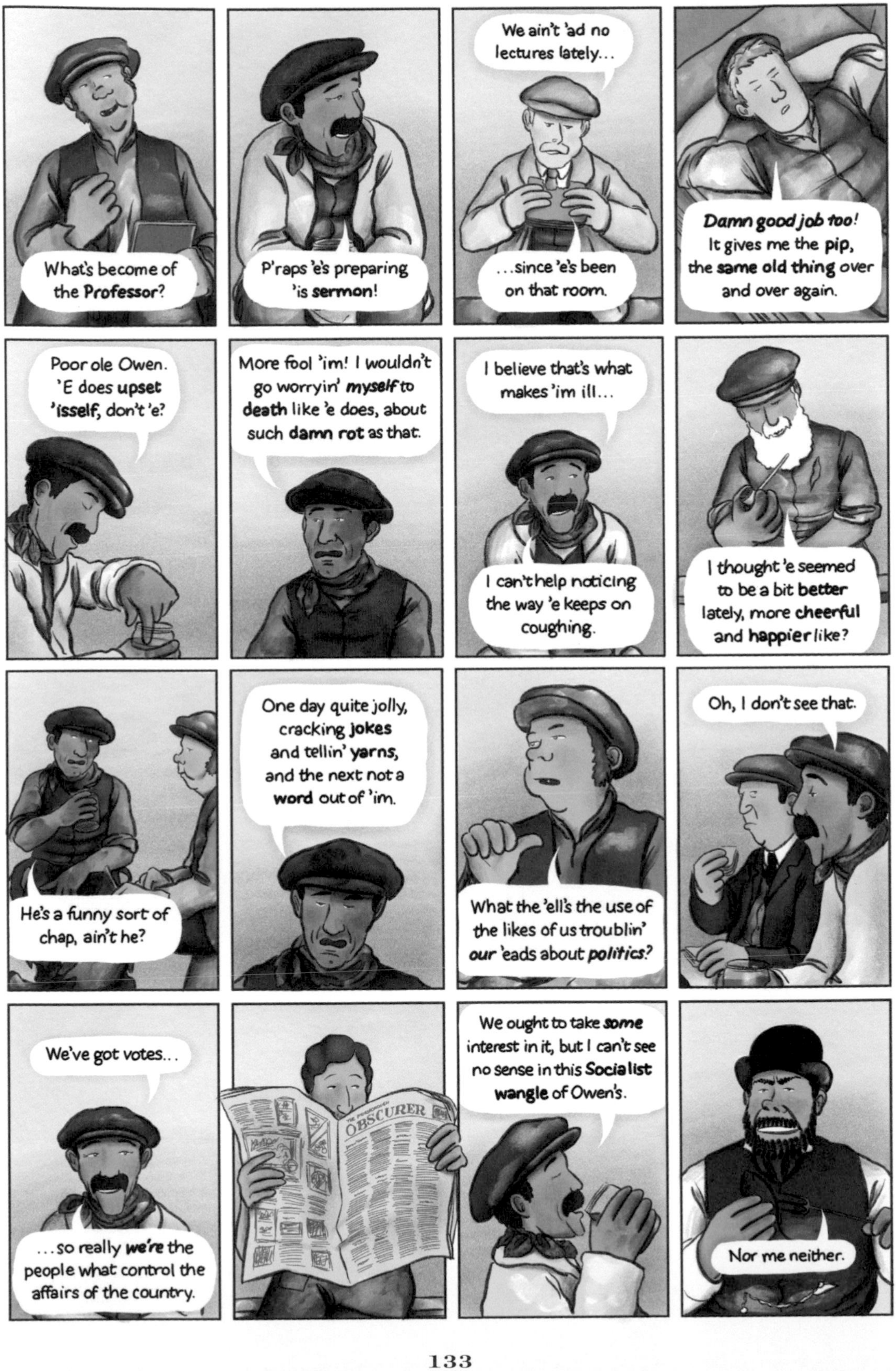
What's become of the Professor?
P'raps 'e's preparing 'is sermon!
We ain't 'ad no lectures lately...
...since 'e's been on that room.
Damn good job too! It gives me the pip, the same old thing over and over again.
Poor ole Owen. 'E does upset 'isself, don't 'e?
More fool 'im! I wouldn't go worryin' myself to death like 'e does, about such damn rot as that.
I believe that's what makes 'im ill...
I can't help noticing the way 'e keeps on coughing.
I thought 'e seemed to be a bit better lately, more cheerful and happier like?
He's a funny sort of chap, ain't he?
One day quite jolly, cracking jokes and tellin' yarns, and the next not a word out of 'im.
What the 'ell's the use of the likes of us troublin' our 'eads about politics?
Oh, I don't see that.
We've got votes...
...so really we're the people what control the affairs of the country.
OBSCURER
We ought to take some interest in it, but I can't see no sense in this Socialist wangle of Owen's.
Nor me neither.

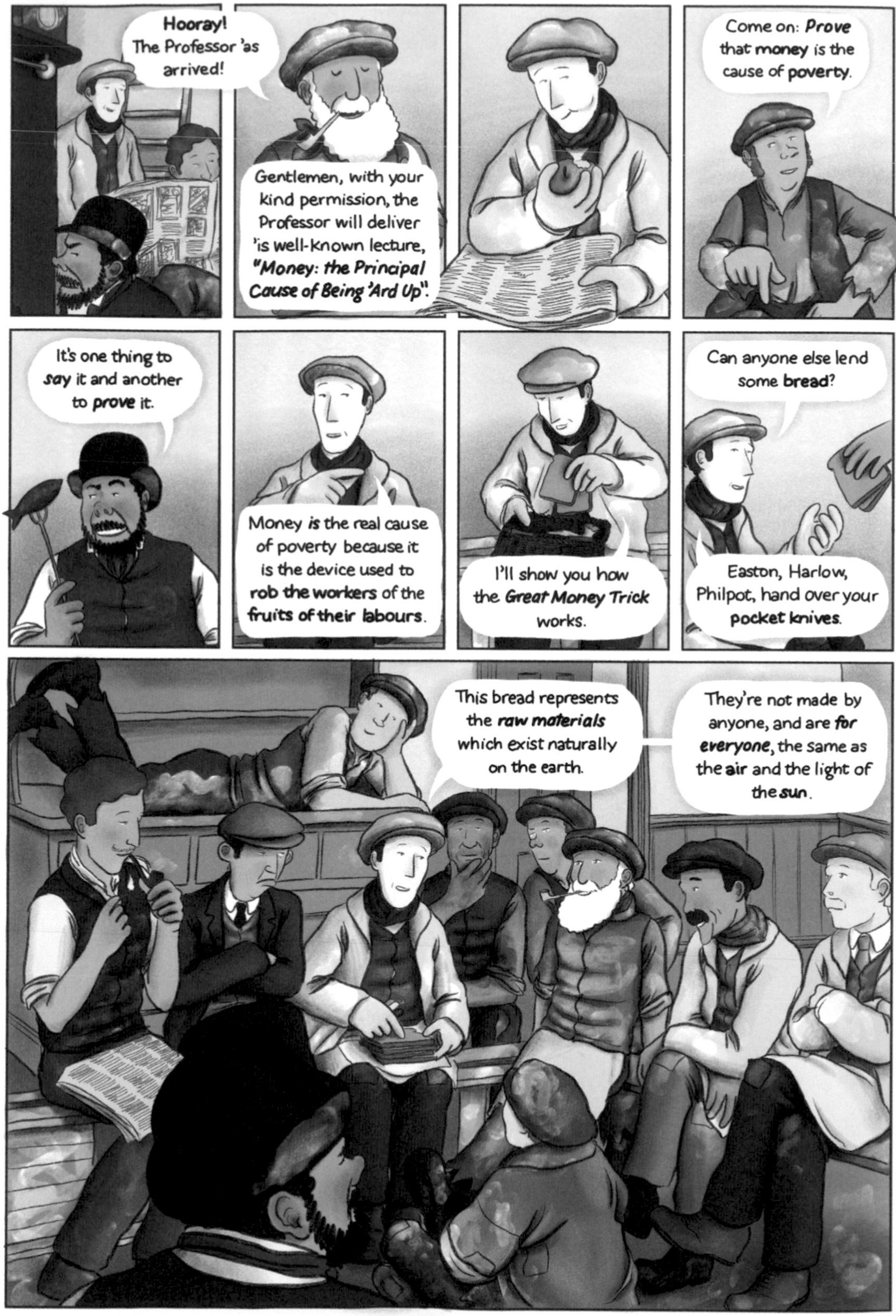
Hooray! The Professor 'as arrived!
Gentlemen, with your kind permission, the Professor will deliver 'is well-known lecture, "Money: the Principal Cause of Being 'Ard Up".
Come on: Prove that money is the cause of poverty.
It's one thing to say it and another to prove it.
Money is the real cause of poverty because it is the device used to rob the workers of the fruits of their labours.
I'll show you how the Great Money Trick works.
Can anyone else lend some bread?
Easton, Harlow, Philpot, hand over your pocket knives.
This bread represents the raw materials which exist naturally on the earth.
They're not made by anyone, and are for everyone, the same as the air and the light of the sun.

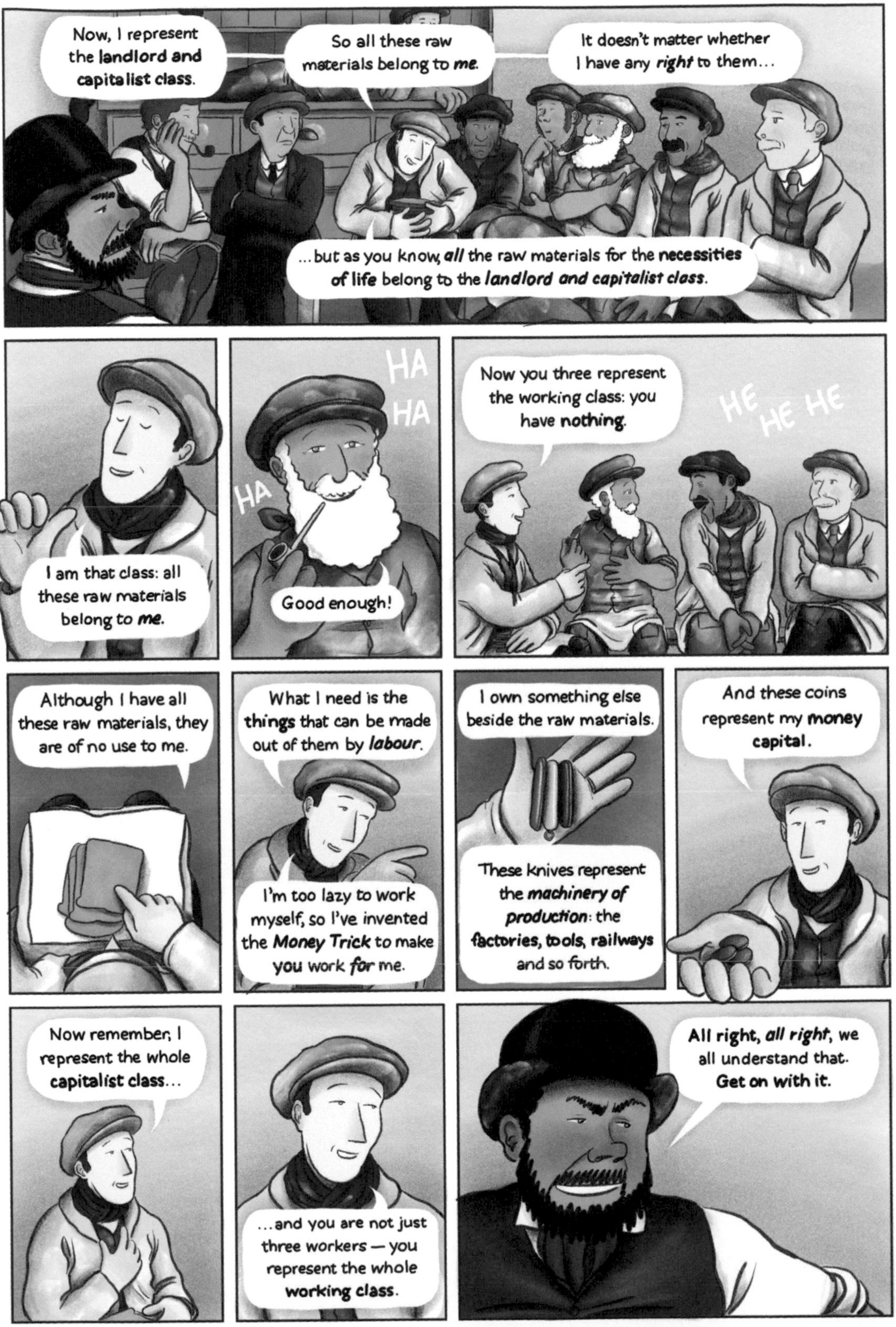
Now, I represent the **landlord and capitalist class**.
So all these raw materials belong to ***me***.
It doesn't matter whether I have any ***right*** to them...
...but as you know, ***all*** the raw materials for the **necessities of life** belong to the ***landlord and capitalist class***.
I am that class: all these raw materials belong to ***me***.
HA HA HA
Good enough!
Now you three represent the working class: you have **nothing**.
HE HE HE
Although I have all these raw materials, they are of no use to me.
What I need is the **things** that can be made out of them by ***labour***.
I'm too lazy to work myself, so I've invented the ***Money Trick*** to make **you** work ***for*** me.
I own something else beside the raw materials.
These knives represent the ***machinery of production***: the **factories, tools, railways** and so forth.
And these coins represent my **money capital**.
Now remember, I represent the whole **capitalist class**...
...and you are not just three workers — you represent the whole **working class**.
All right, *all right*, we all understand that. Get on with it.

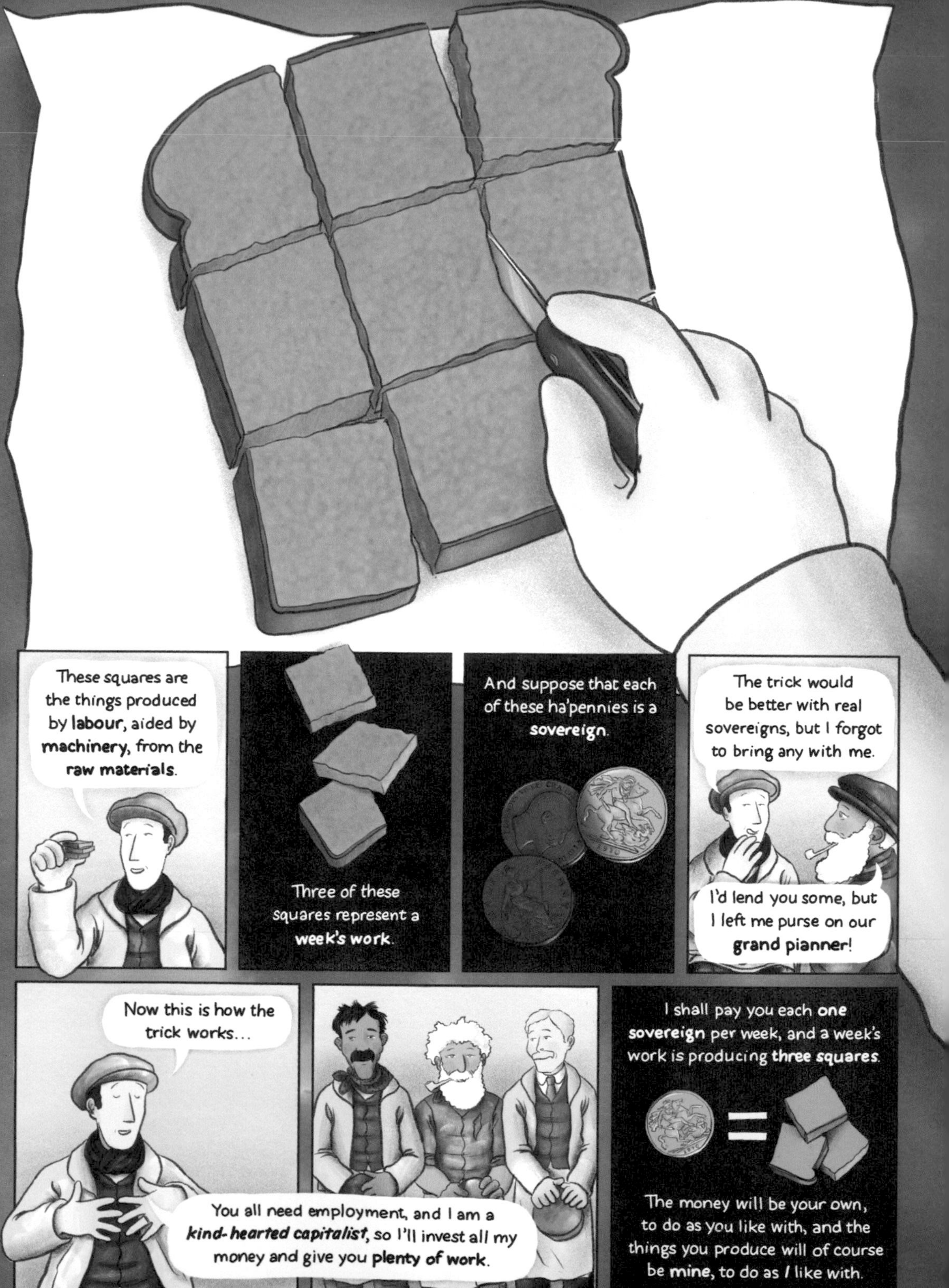
These squares are the things produced by **labour**, aided by **machinery**, from the **raw materials**.
Three of these squares represent a **week's work**.
And suppose that each of these ha'pennies is a **sovereign**.
The trick would be better with real sovereigns, but I forgot to bring any with me.
I'd lend you some, but I left me purse on our **grand pianner**!
Now this is how the trick works...
You all need employment, and I am a ***kind-hearted capitalist***, so I'll invest all my money and give you **plenty of work**.
I shall pay you each **one sovereign** per week, and a week's work is producing **three squares**.
The money will be your own, to do as you like with, and the things you produce will of course be **mine**, to do as ***I*** like with.

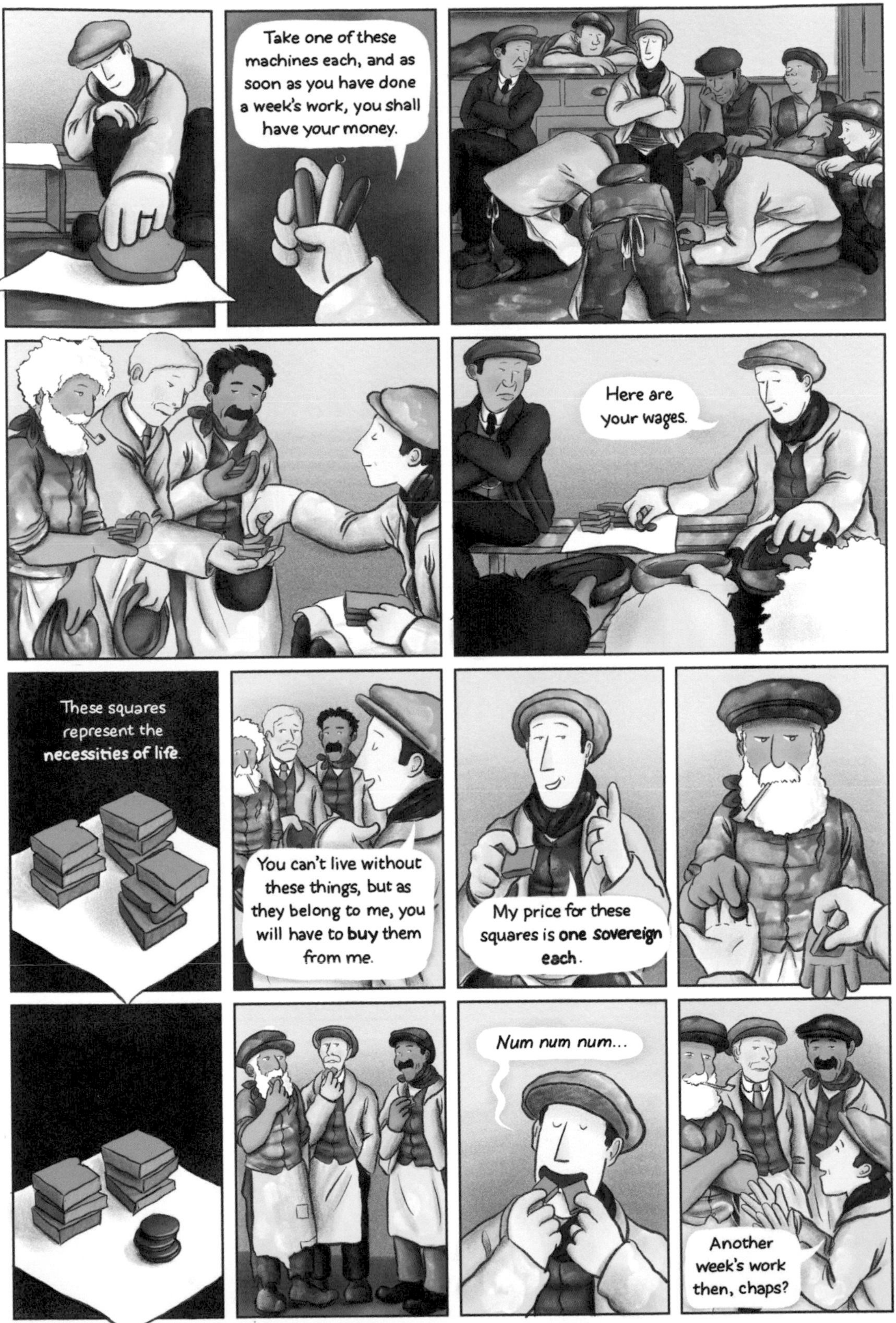
Take one of these machines each, and as soon as you have done a week's work, you shall have your money.
Here are your wages.
These squares represent the necessities of life.
You can't live without these things, but as they belong to me, you will have to buy them from me.
My price for these squares is one sovereign each.
Num num num...
Another week's work then, chaps?

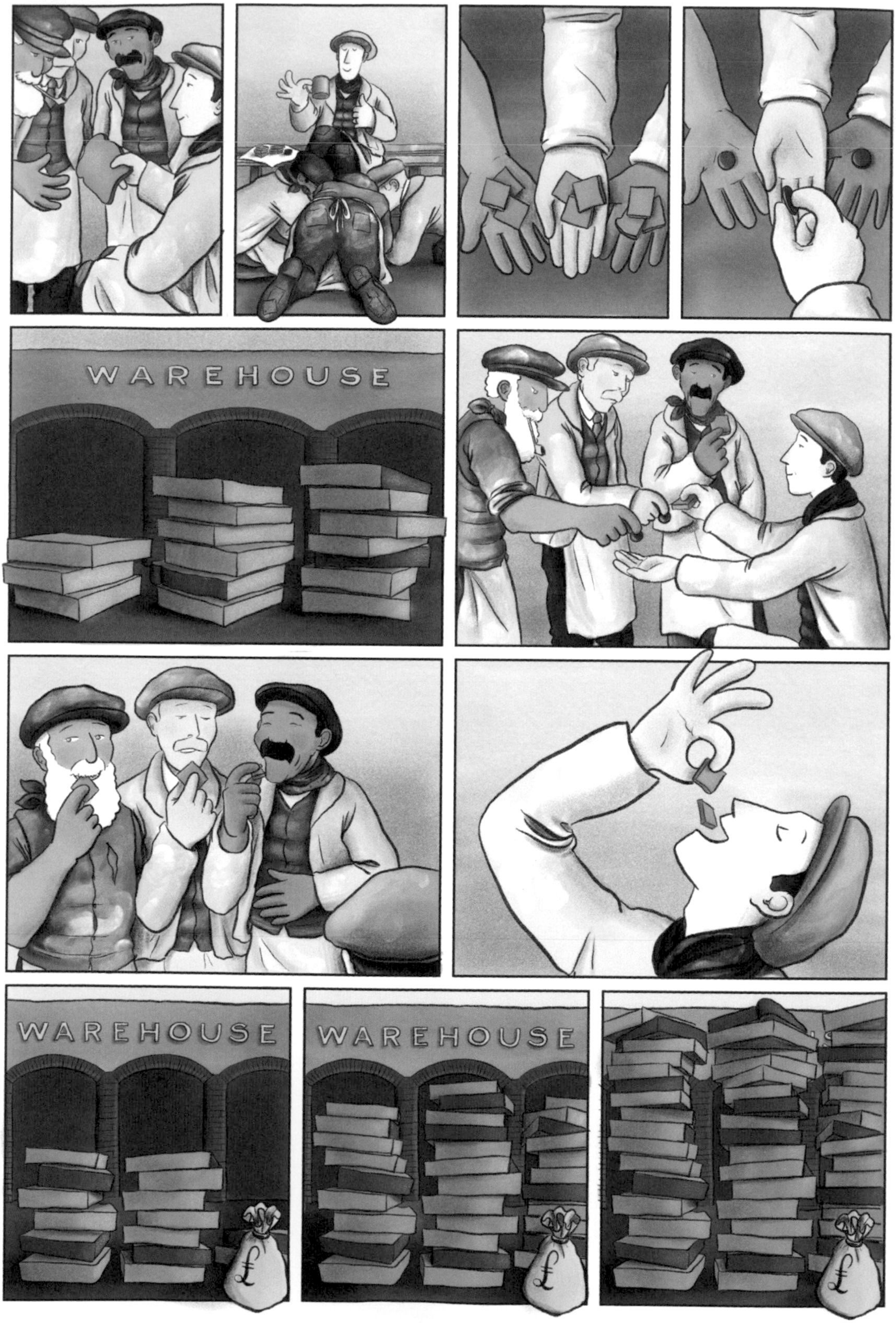
WAREHOUSE
WAREHOUSE
WAREHOUSE

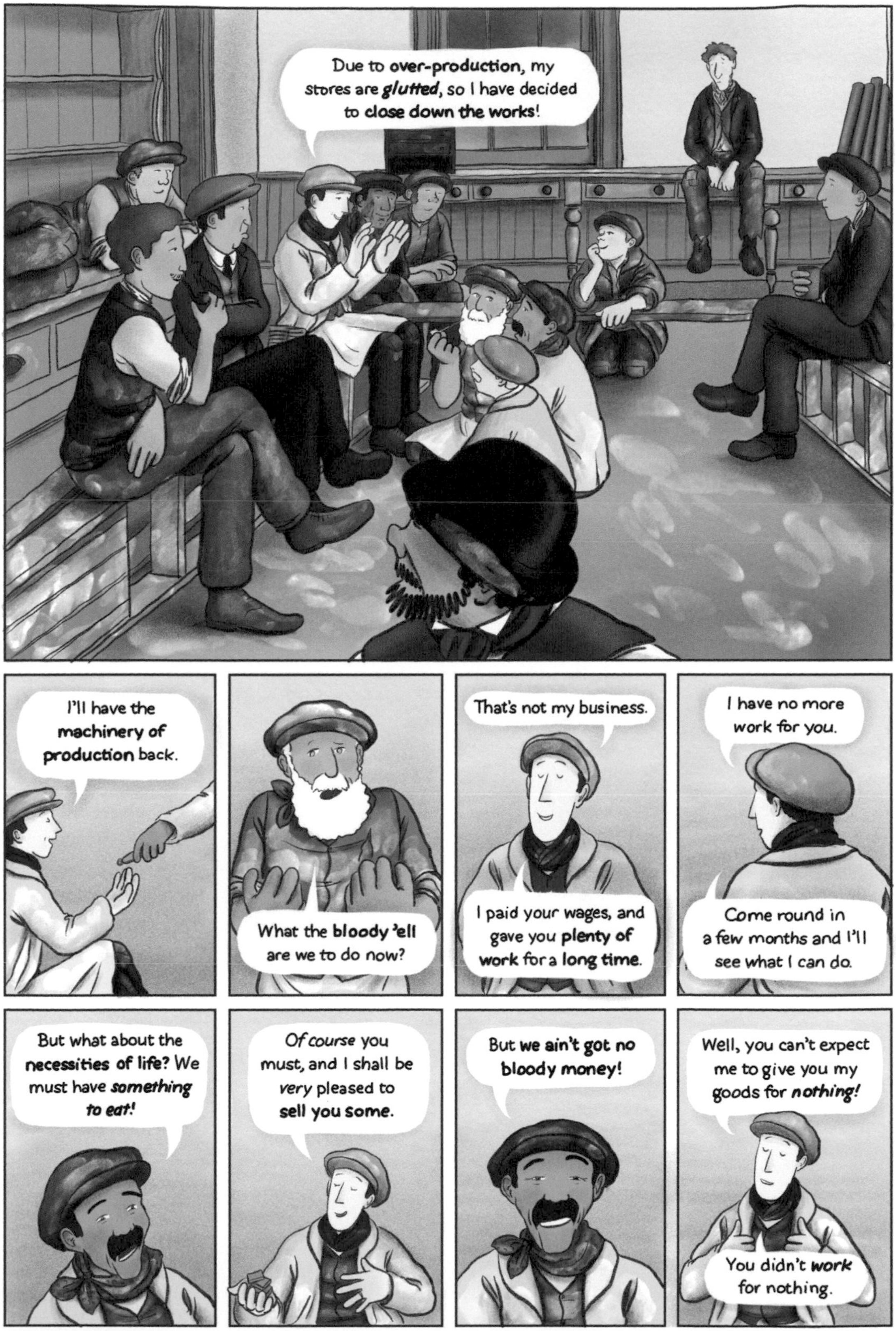
Due to over-production, my stores are glutted, so I have decided to close down the works!
I'll have the machinery of production back.
What the bloody 'ell are we to do now?
That's not my business.
I paid your wages, and gave you plenty of work for a long time.
I have no more work for you.
Come round in a few months and I'll see what I can do.
But what about the necessities of life? We must have something to eat!
Of course you must, and I shall be very pleased to sell you some.
But we ain't got no bloody money!
Well, you can't expect me to give you my goods for nothing!
You didn't work for nothing.

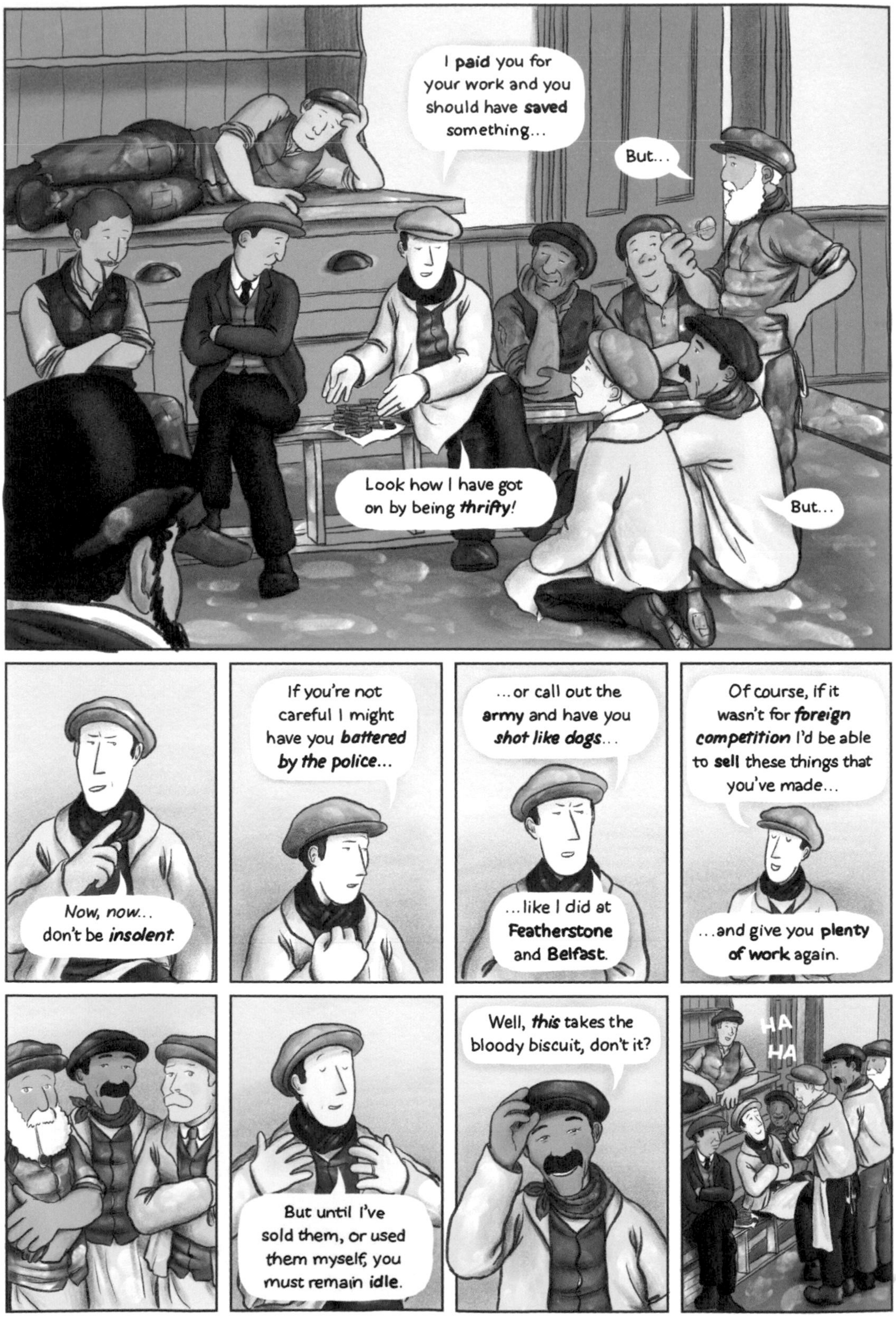
I paid you for your work and you should have saved something...
But...
Look how I have got on by being thrifty!
But...
Now, now... don't be insolent.
If you're not careful I might have you battered by the police...
...or call out the army and have you shot like dogs...
...like I did at Featherstone and Belfast.
Of course, if it wasn't for foreign competition I'd be able to sell these things that you've made...
...and give you plenty of work again.
But until I've sold them, or used them myself, you must remain idle.
Well, this takes the bloody biscuit, don't it?
HA
HA

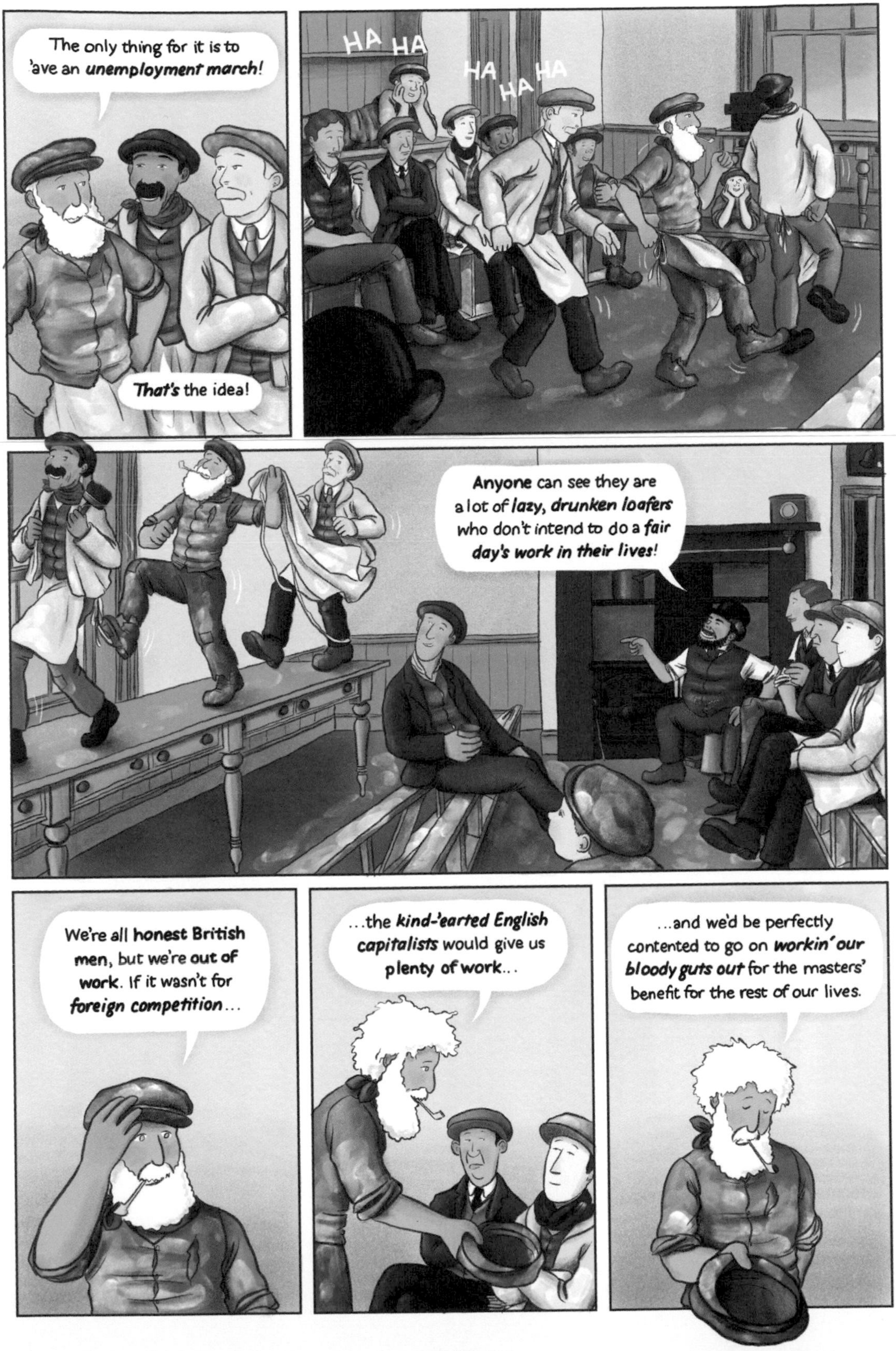
The only thing for it is to 'ave an *unemployment march!*
That's the idea!
HA HA HA HA HA
Anyone can see they are a lot of *lazy, drunken loafers* who don't intend to do a *fair day's work in their lives!*
We're all **honest British men**, but we're **out of work**. If it wasn't for *foreign competition*...
...the *kind-'earted English capitalists* would give us **plenty of work**...
...and we'd be perfectly contented to go on *workin' our bloody guts out* for the masters' benefit for the rest of our lives.

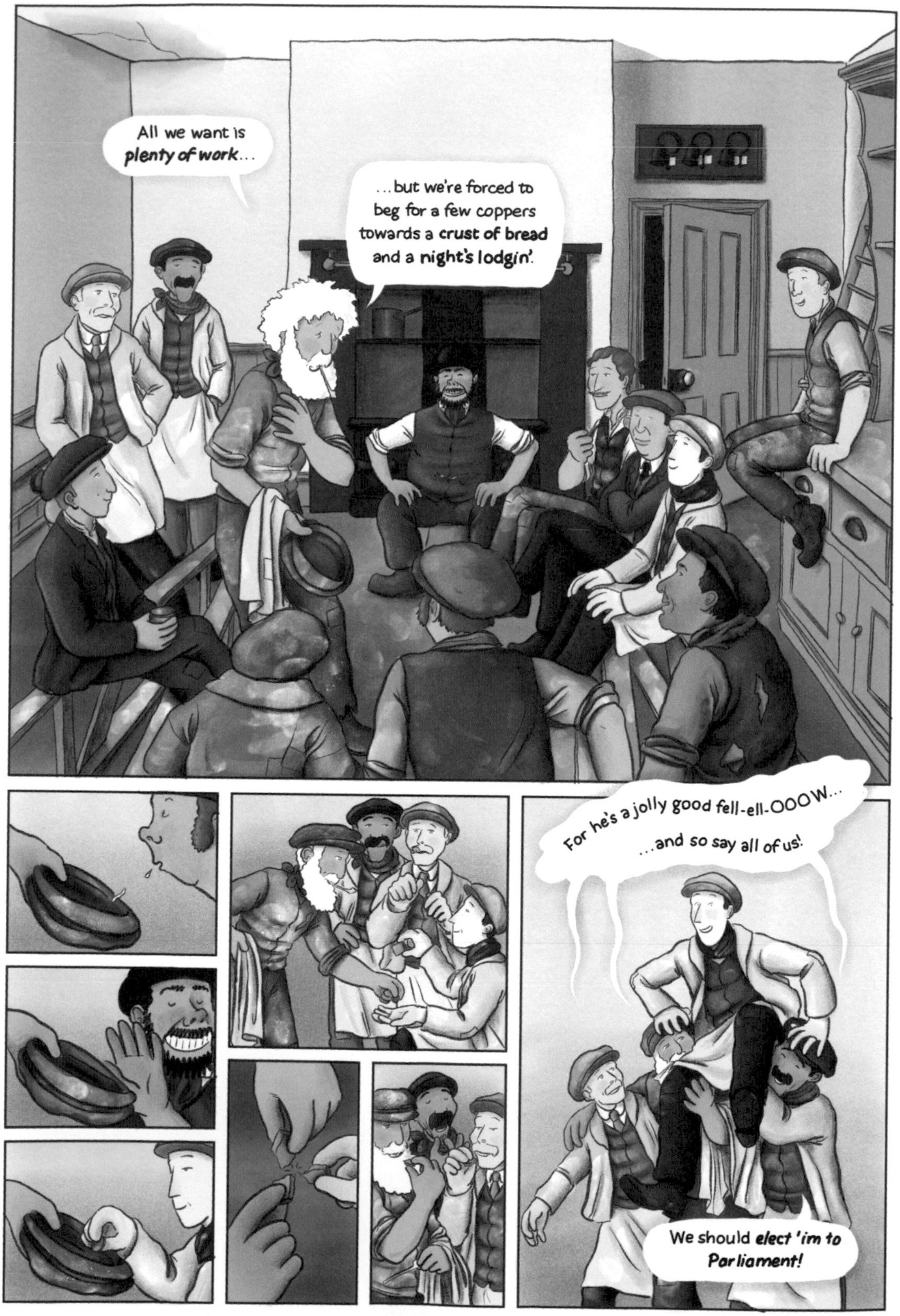
All we want is plenty of work...
...but we're forced to beg for a few coppers towards a crust of bread and a night's lodgin'.
For he's a jolly good fell-ell-OOOW...
...and so say all of us!
We should elect 'im to Parliament!

CHAPTER

THE

CRICKETERS

NINE

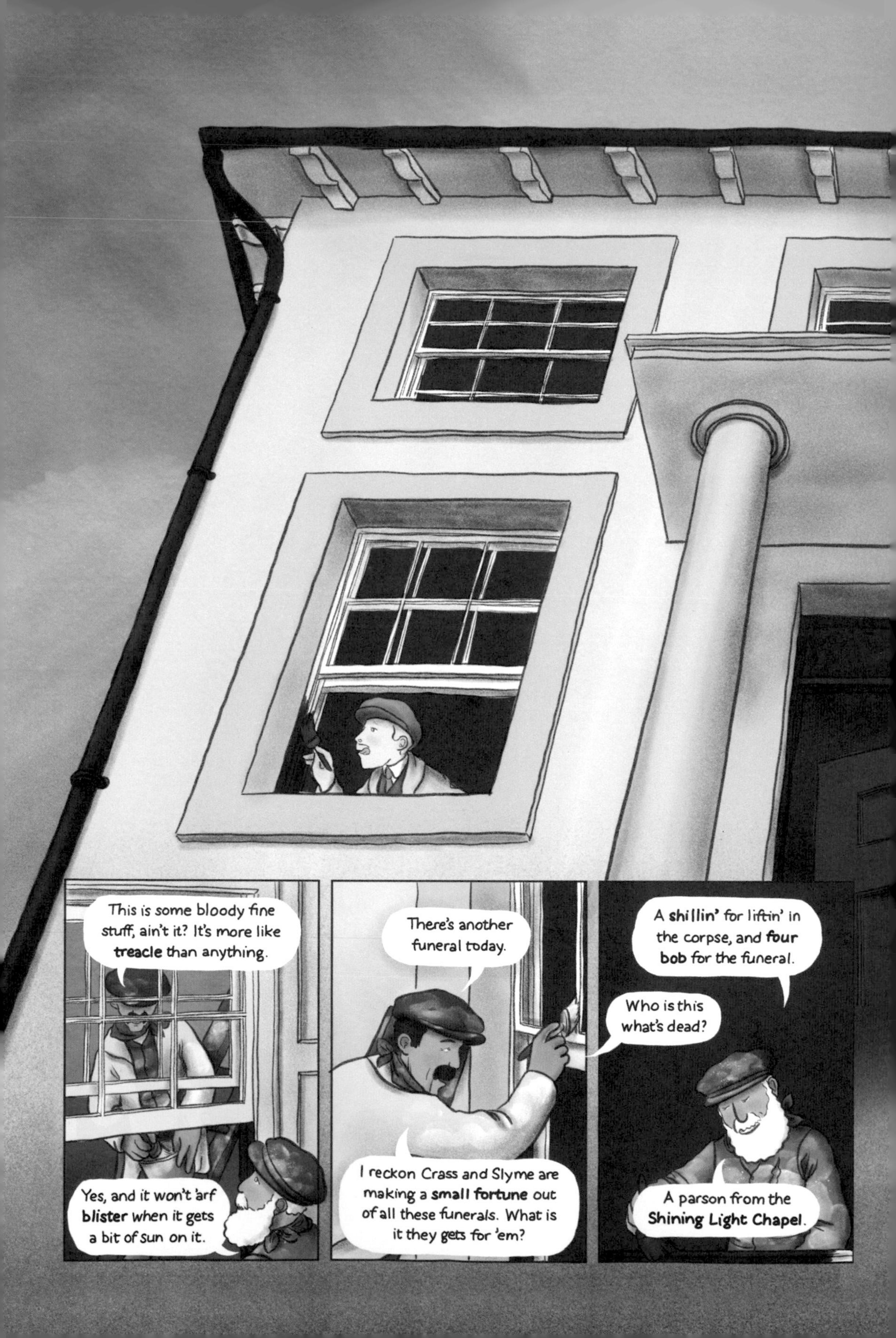
This is some bloody fine stuff, ain't it? It's more like **treacle** than anything.
Yes, and it won't 'arf **blister** when it gets a bit of sun on it.
There's another funeral today.
I reckon Crass and Slyme are making a **small fortune** out of all these funerals. What is it they gets for 'em?
A **shillin'** for liftin' in the corpse, and **four bob** for the funeral.
Who is this what's dead?
A parson from the **Shining Light Chapel**.

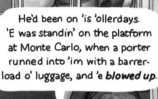

Blowed up?

Yes. *Blowed up! Exploded!* All into **pieces**. Reverend Belcher. A very **fat** chap.

Oh, *I* know the bloke!

He'd been on 'is 'ollerdays. 'E was standin' on the platform at Monte Carlo, when a porter runned into 'im with a barrer-load o' luggage, and 'e *blowed up.*

My youngsters brought 'ome a subscription to send 'im away because 'e was ill, and I gave 'em a penny each so they didn't feel **mean** in front of the others.

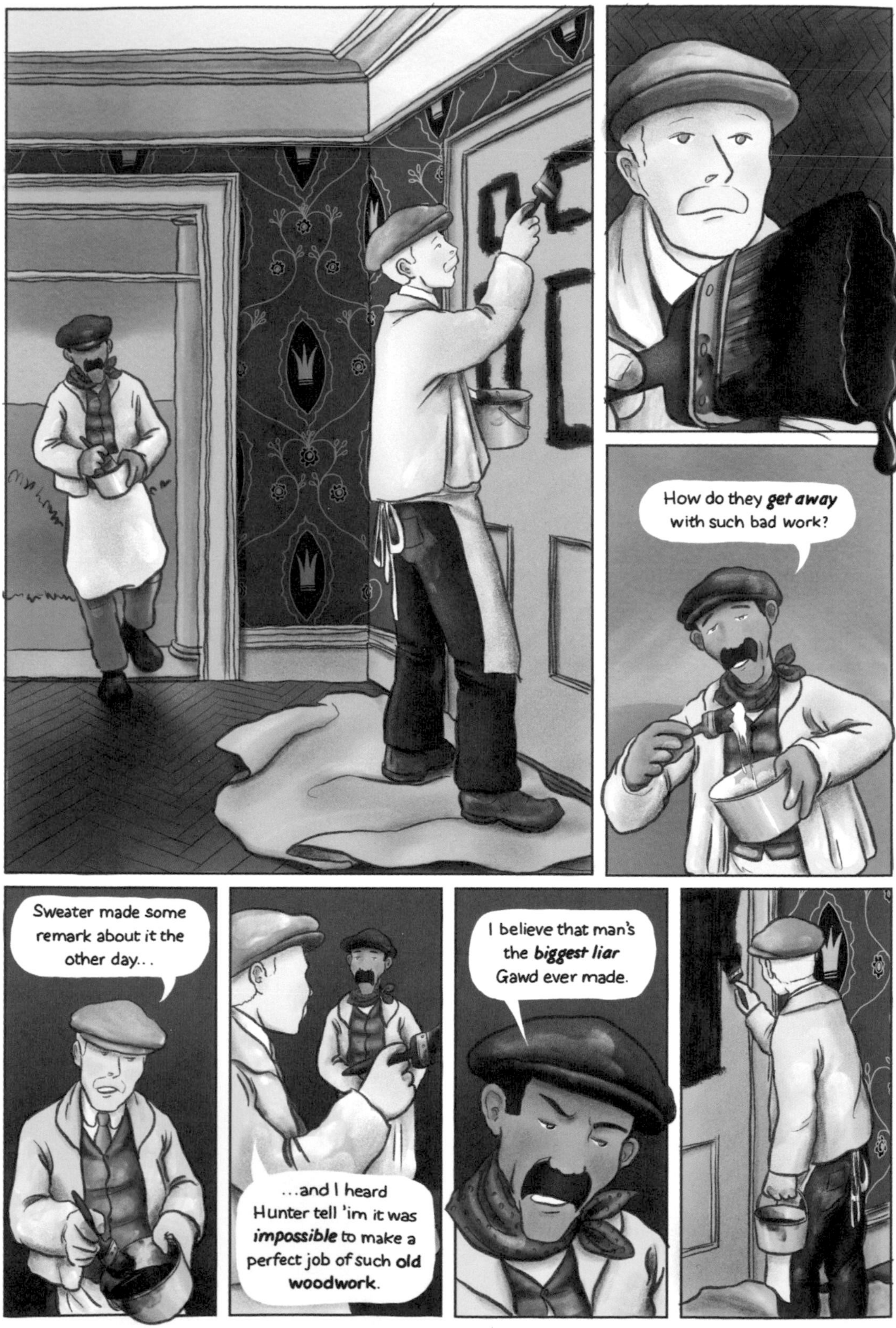
How do they **get away** with such bad work?
Sweater made some remark about it the other day...
...and I heard Hunter tell 'im it was **impossible** to make a perfect job of such **old woodwork**.
I believe that man's the **biggest liar** Gawd ever made.

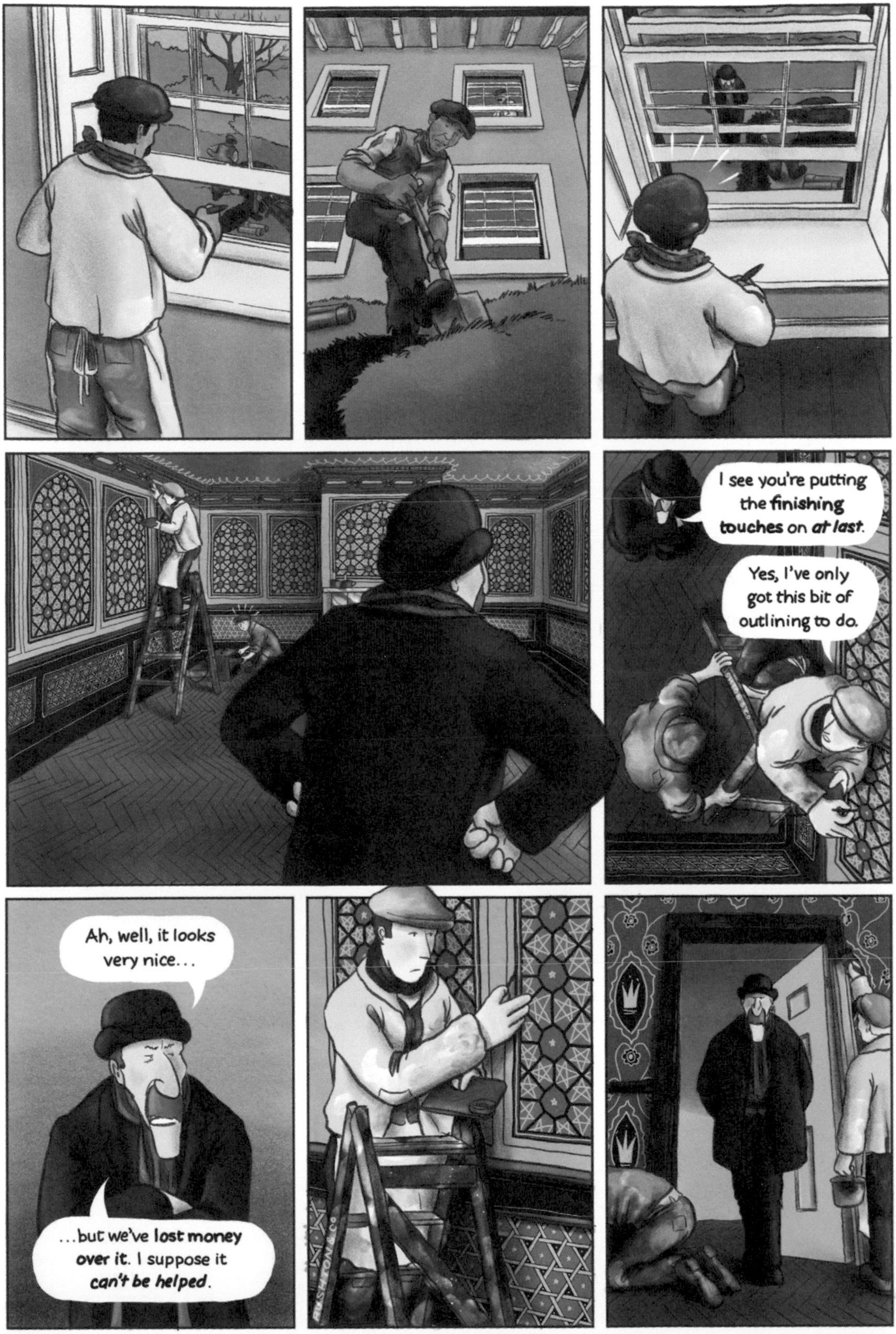
I see you're putting the finishing touches on at last.
Yes, I've only got this bit of outlining to do.
Ah, well, it looks very nice...
...but we've lost money over it. I suppose it can't be helped.

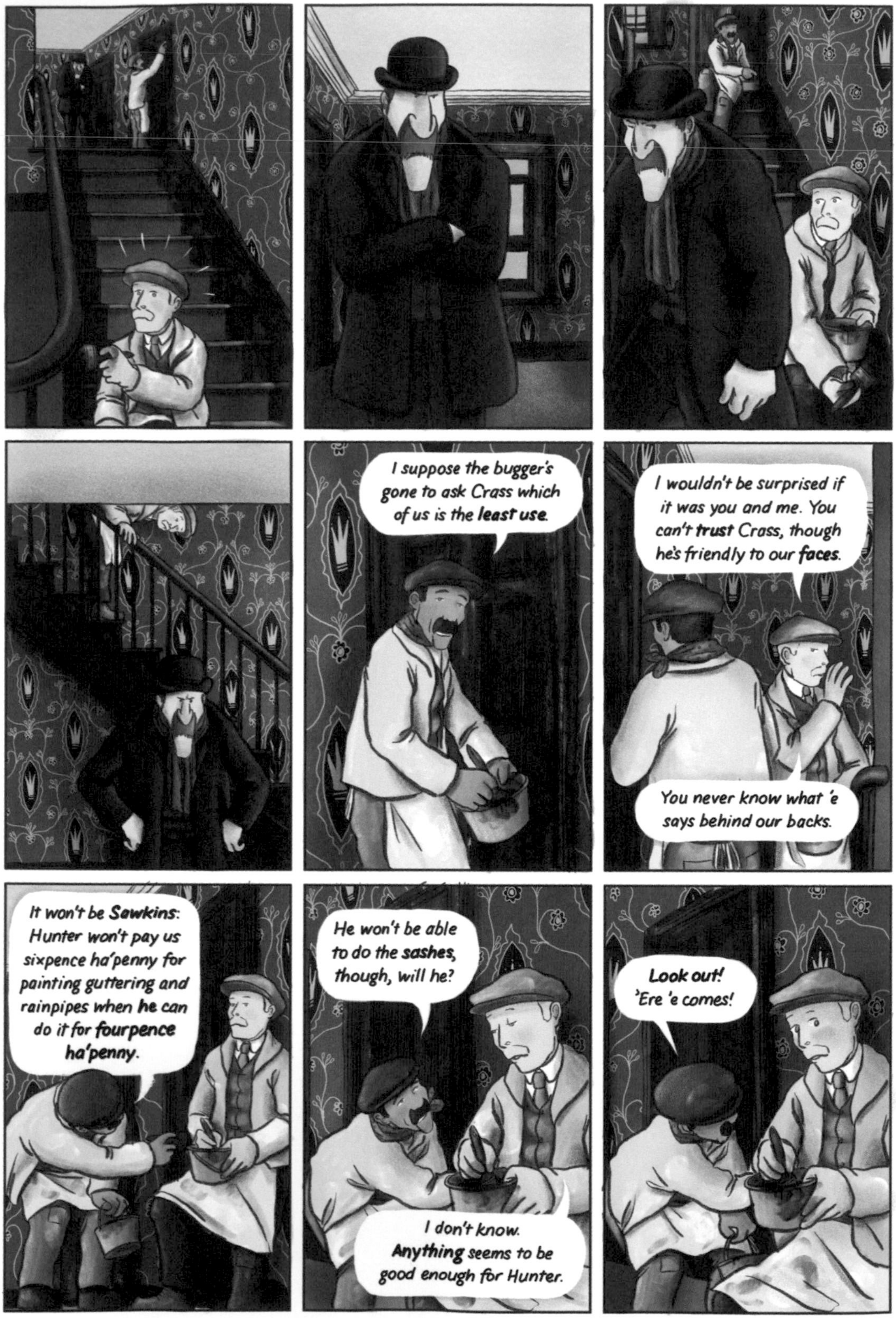
I suppose the bugger's gone to ask Crass which of us is the **least use**.
I wouldn't be surprised if it was you and me. You can't **trust** Crass, though he's friendly to our **faces**.
You never know what 'e says behind our backs.
It won't be **Sawkins**: Hunter won't pay us sixpence ha'penny for painting guttering and rainpipes when **he** can do it for **fourpence ha'penny**.
He won't be able to do the **sashes**, though, will he?
I don't know. **Anything** seems to be good enough for Hunter.
Look out! 'Ere 'e comes!

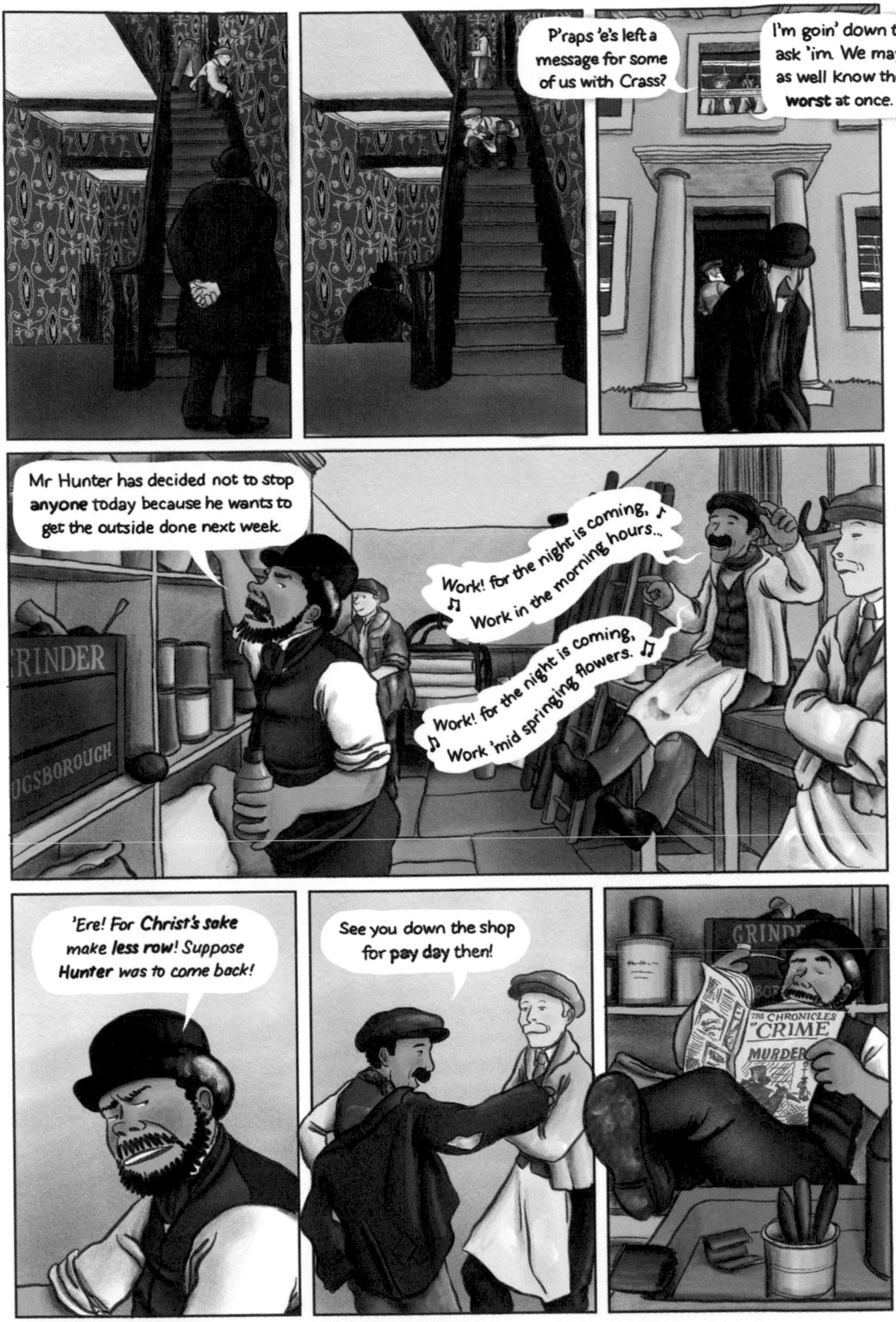
P'raps 'e's left a message for some of us with Crass?
I'm goin' down to ask 'im. We may as well know the **worst** at once.
Mr Hunter has decided not to stop **anyone** today because he wants to get the outside done next week.
Work! for the night is coming, ♪ Work in the morning hours...
Work! for the night is coming, ♫ Work 'mid springing flowers. ♫
GRINDER
UGSBOROUGH
'Ere! For **Christ's sake** make **less row**! Suppose **Hunter** was to come back!
See you down the shop for **pay day** then!
THE CHRONICLES OF CRIME
MURDER

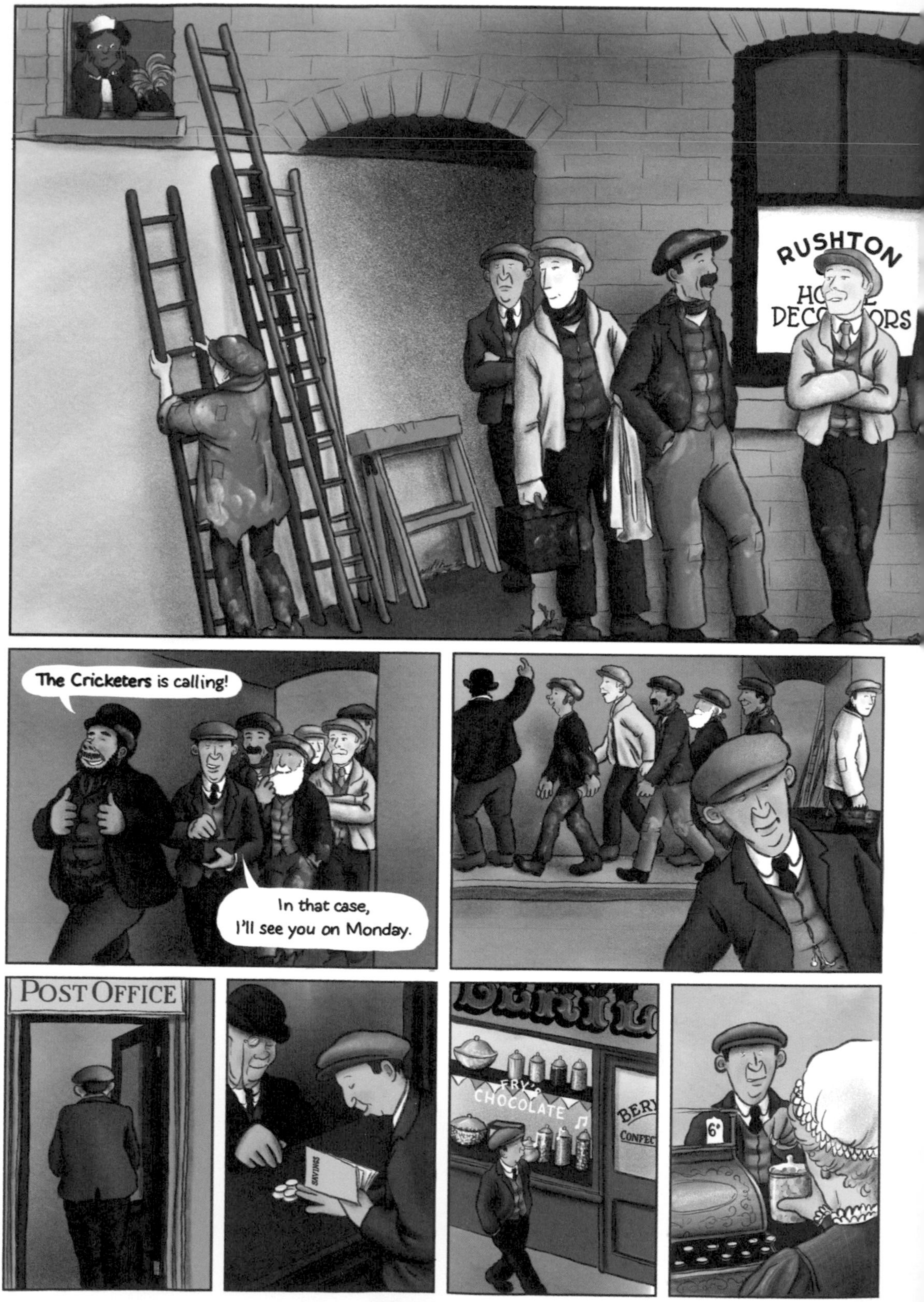
RUSHTON
The Cricketers is calling!
In that case,
I'll see you on Monday.
POST OFFICE
SAVINGS
FRY'S
CHOCOLATE
6d

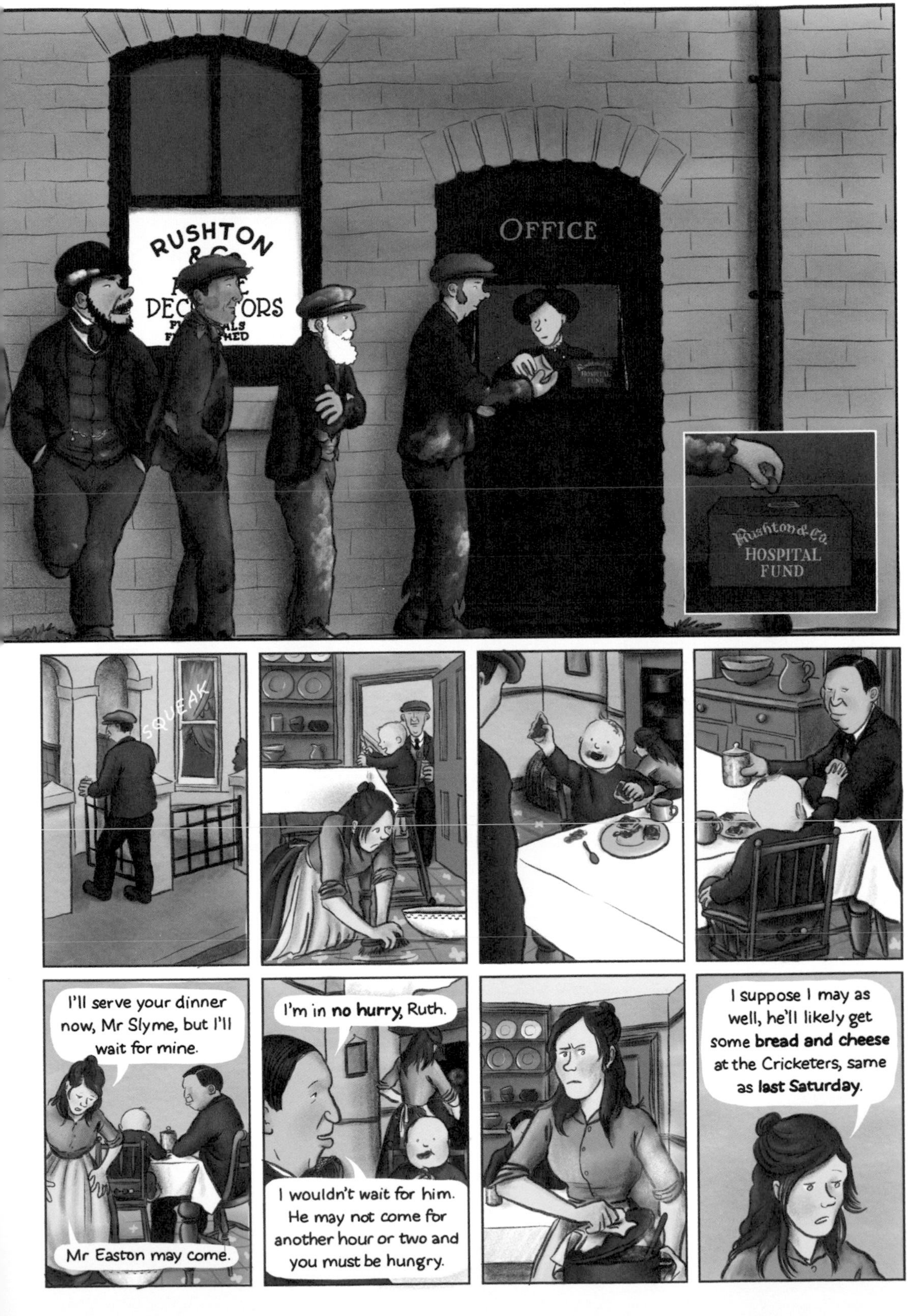
RUSHTON & Co.
DEC ORS
OFFICE
HOSPITAL FUND
Rushton & Co.
HOSPITAL
FUND
SQUEAK
I'll serve your dinner now, Mr Slyme, but I'll wait for mine.
Mr Easton may come.
I'm in no hurry, Ruth.
I wouldn't wait for him. He may not come for another hour or two and you must be hungry.
I suppose I may as well, he'll likely get some bread and cheese at the Cricketers, same as last Saturday.

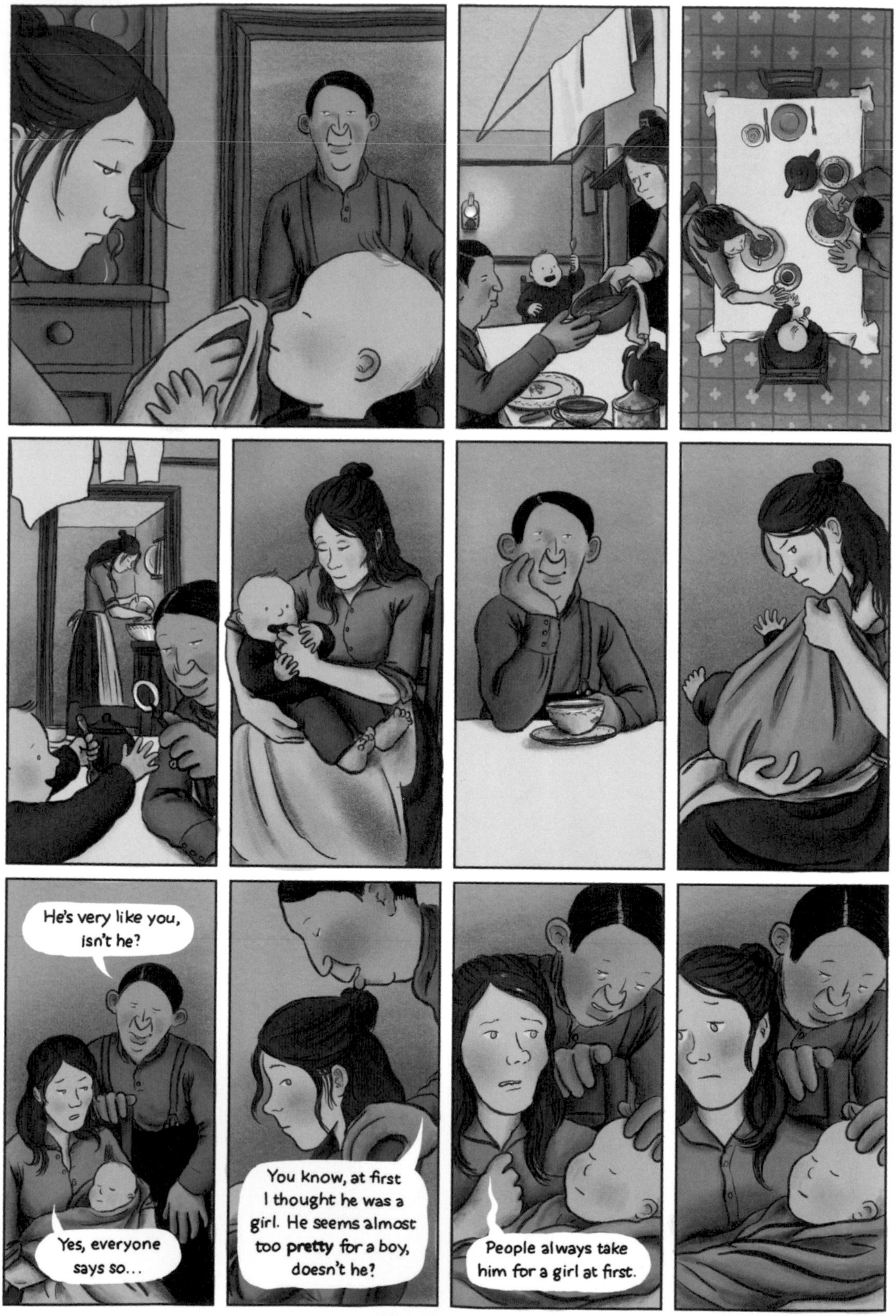
He's very like you, isn't he?
Yes, everyone says so...
You know, at first I thought he was a girl. He seems almost too pretty for a boy, doesn't he?
People always take him for a girl at first.

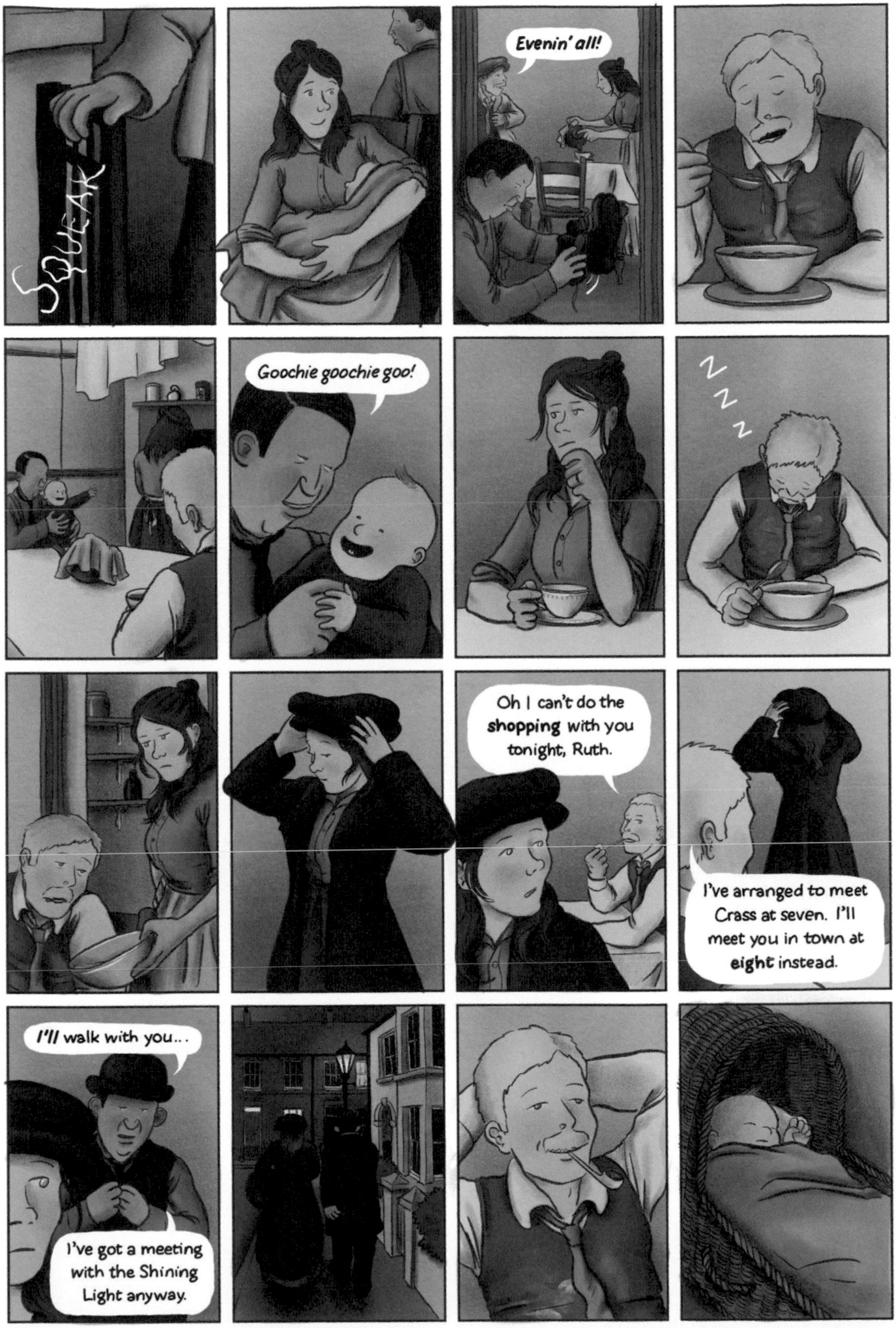
SQUEAK
Evenin' all!
Goochie goochie goo!
Z Z Z
Oh I can't do the shopping with you tonight, Ruth.
I've arranged to meet Crass at seven. I'll meet you in town at eight instead.
I'll walk with you...
I've got a meeting with the Shining Light anyway.

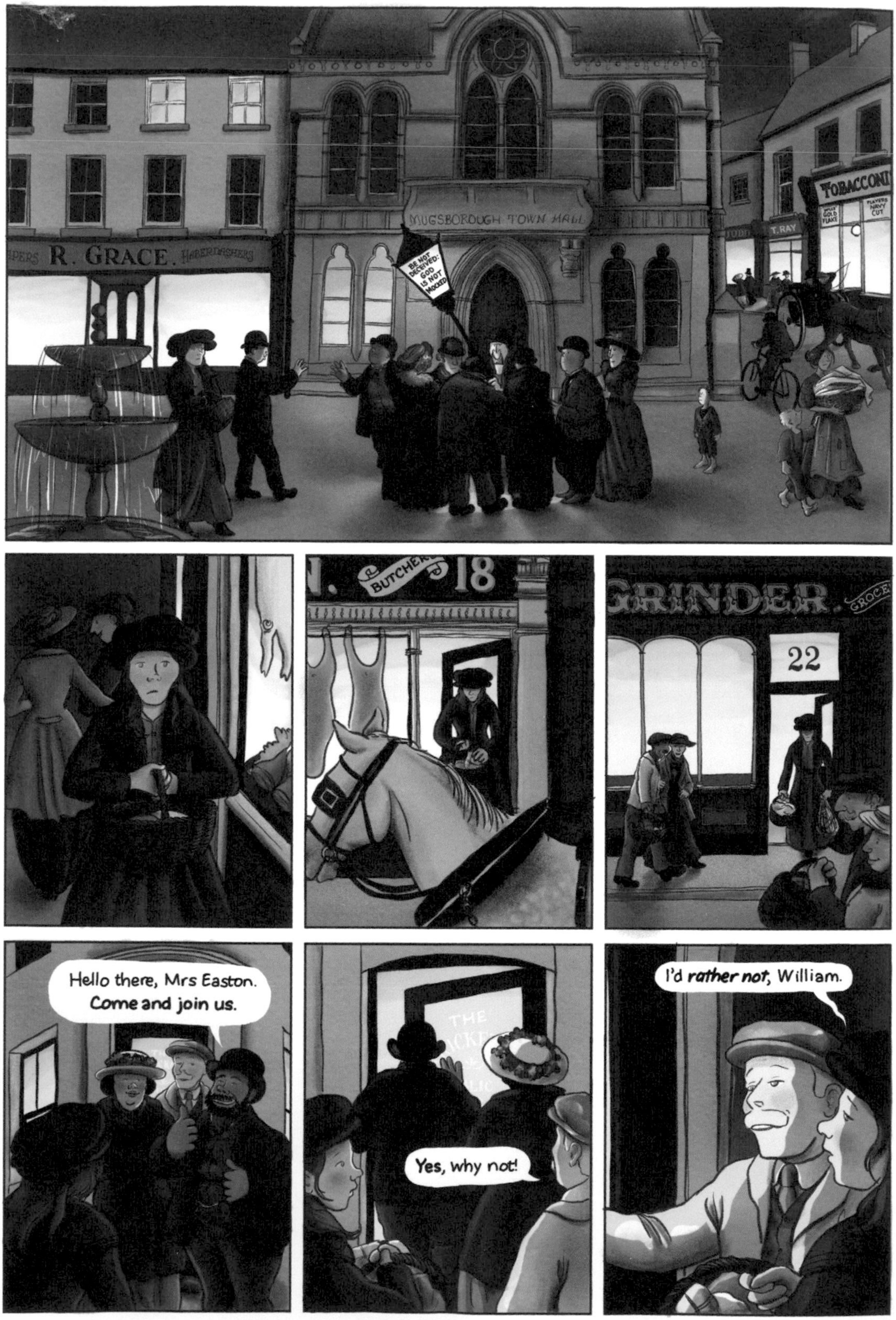
R. GRACE. HABERDASHERS
BE NOT DECEIVED: GOD IS NOT MOCKED
MUGSBOROUGH TOWN HALL
T. RAY
TOBACCONI
BUTCHERS
18
GRINDER.
22
Hello there, Mrs Easton. Come and join us.
Yes, why not!
I'd *rather not*, William.

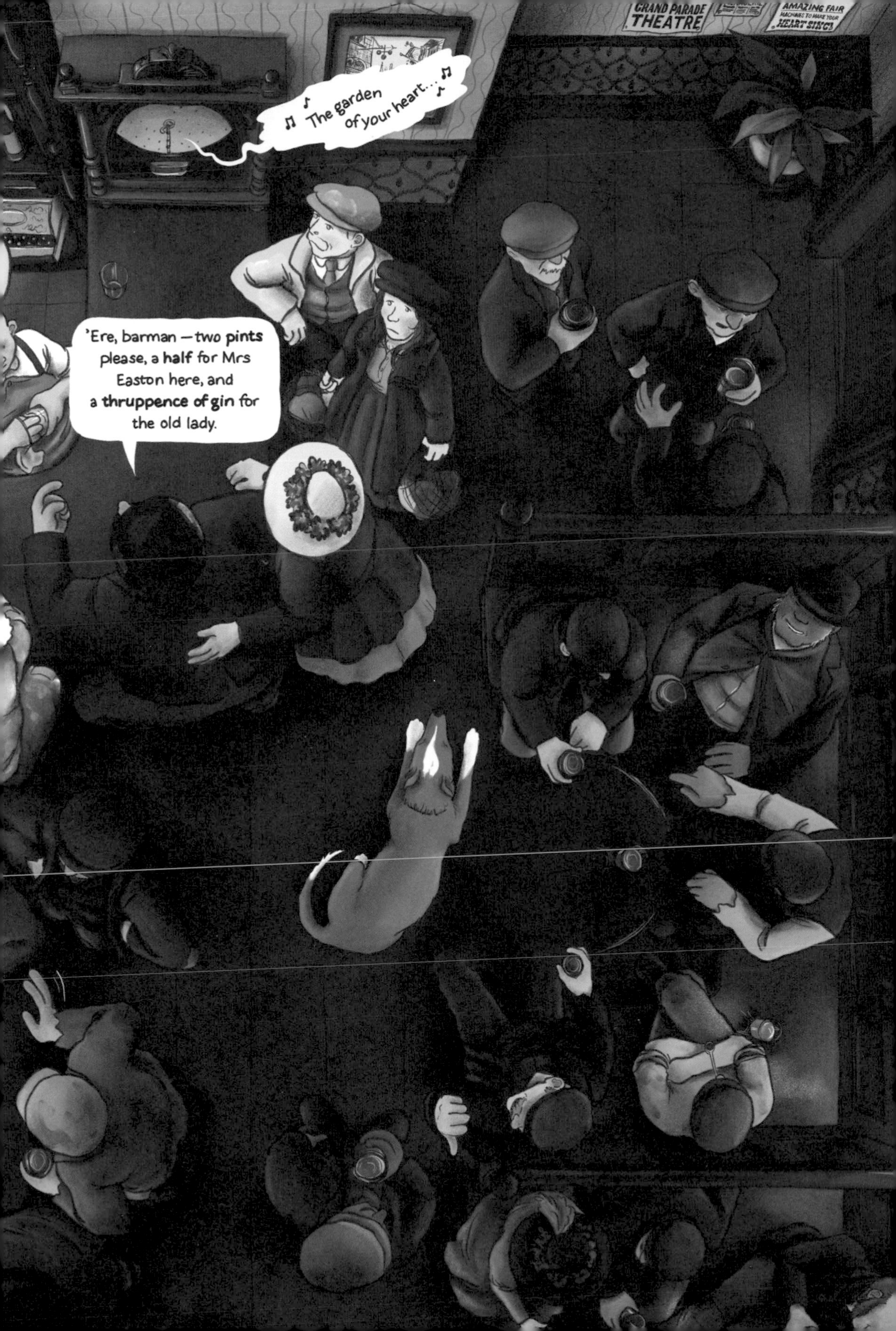
GRAND PARADE THEATRE
AMAZING FAIR MACHINES TO MAKE YOUR HEART SING!
♫ The garden of your heart... ♫
'Ere, barman — two **pints** please, a **half** for Mrs Easton here, and a **thruppence of gin** for the old lady.

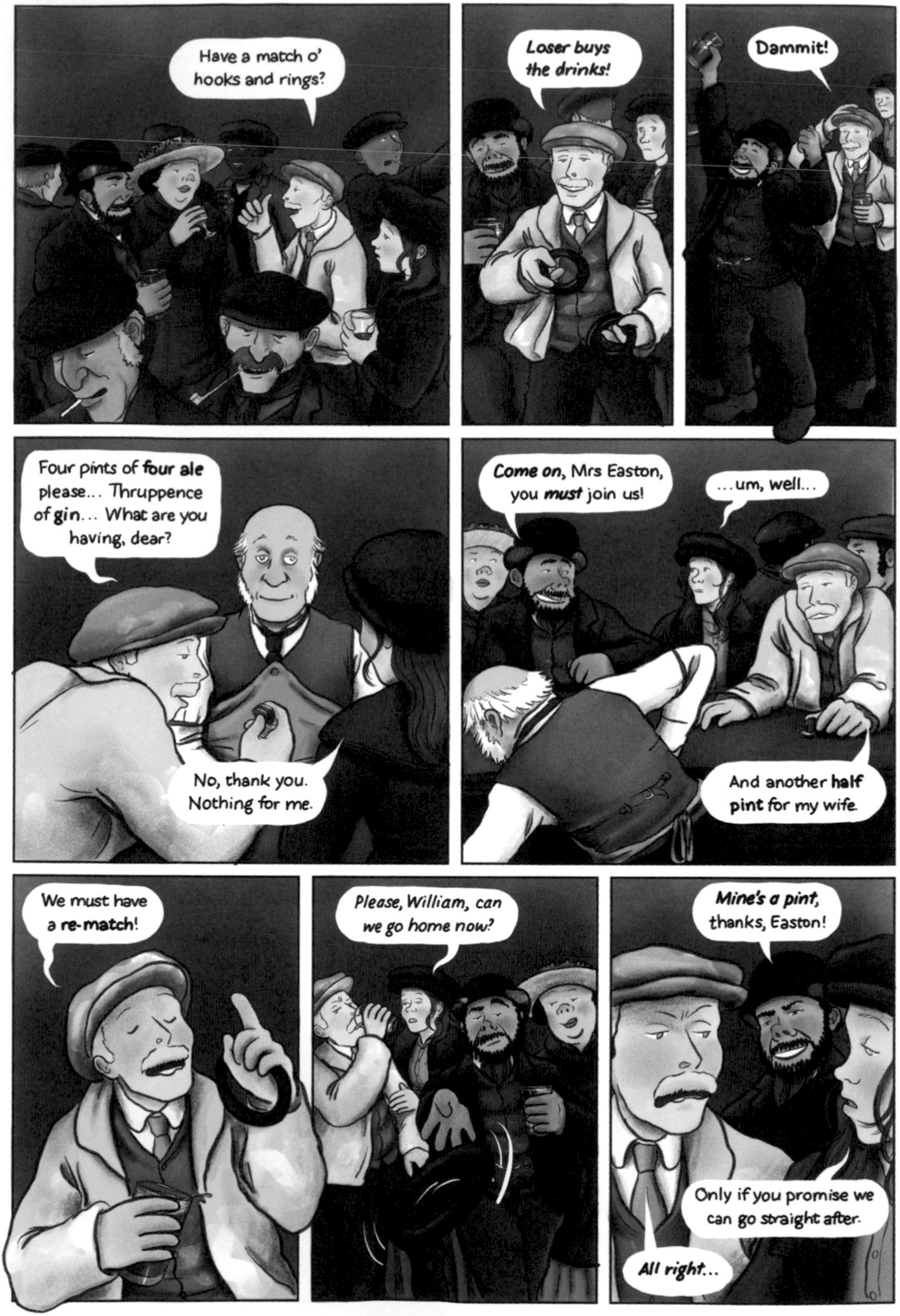
Have a match o' hooks and rings?
Loser buys the drinks!
Dammit!
Four pints of four ale please... Thruppence of gin... What are you having, dear?
No, thank you. Nothing for me.
Come on, Mrs Easton, you must join us!
...um, well...
And another half pint for my wife.
We must have a re-match!
Please, William, can we go home now?
Mine's a pint, thanks, Easton!
Only if you promise we can go straight after.
All right...

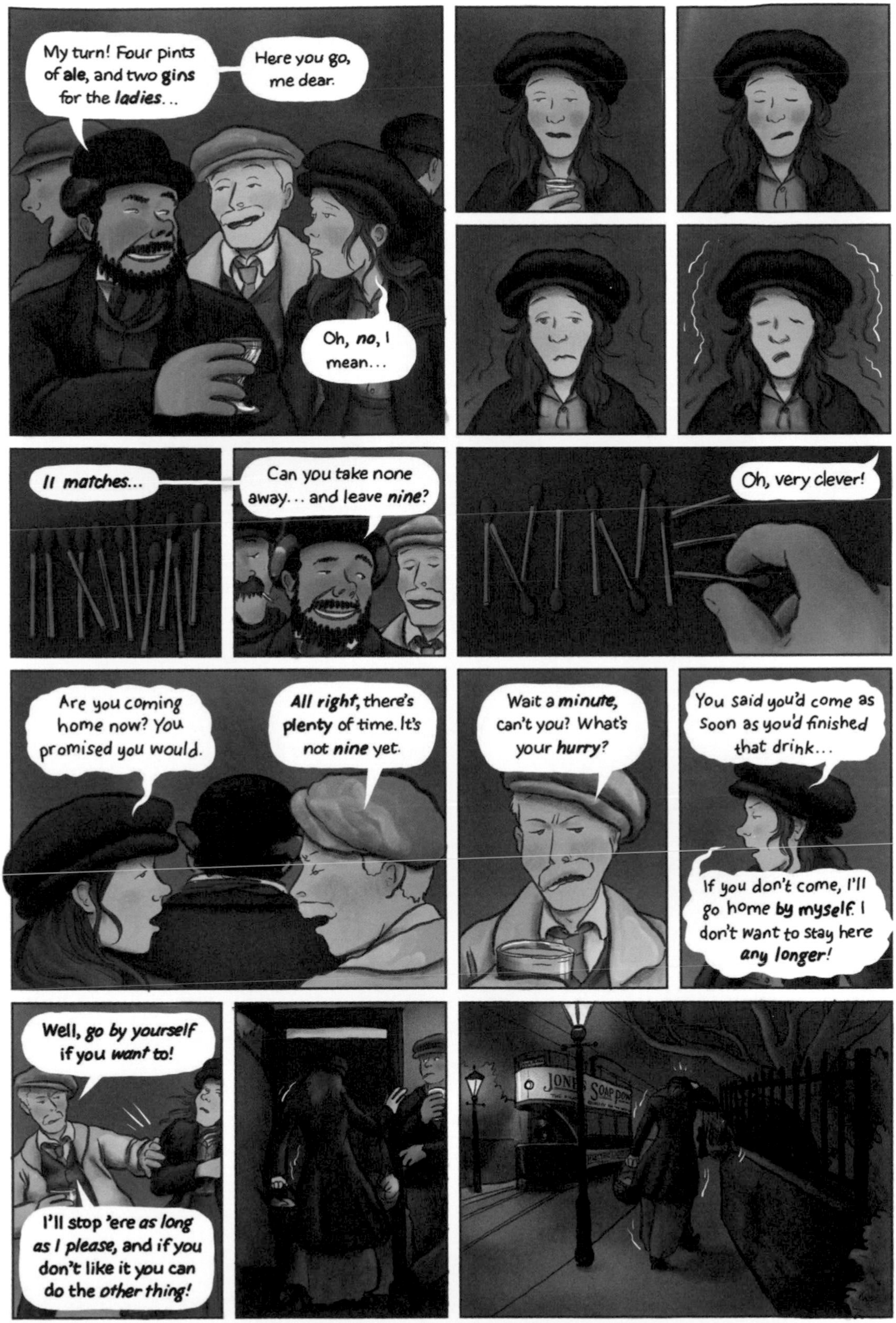
My turn! Four pints of ale, and two gins for the ladies...
Here you go, me dear.
Oh, no, I mean...
11 matches...
Can you take none away... and leave nine?
Oh, very clever!
Are you coming home now? You promised you would.
All right, there's plenty of time. It's not nine yet.
Wait a minute, can't you? What's your hurry?
You said you'd come as soon as you'd finished that drink...
If you don't come, I'll go home by myself. I don't want to stay here any longer!
Well, go by yourself if you want to!
I'll stop 'ere as long as I please, and if you don't like it you can do the other thing!
JONES SOAP

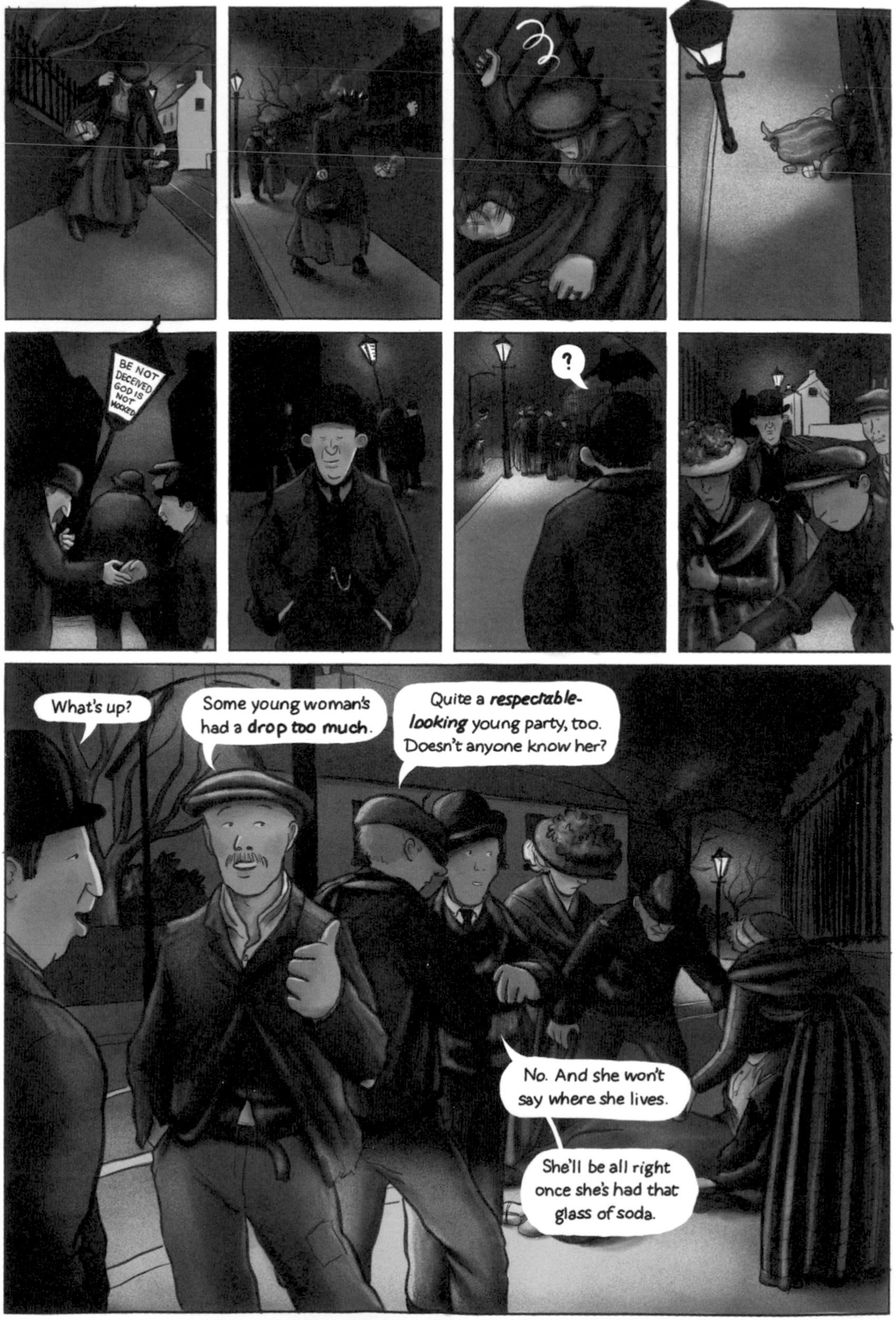
BE NOT DECEIVED GOD IS NOT MOCKED
?
What's up?
Some young woman's had a drop too much.
Quite a respectable-looking young party, too. Doesn't anyone know her?
No. And she won't say where she lives.
She'll be all right once she's had that glass of soda.

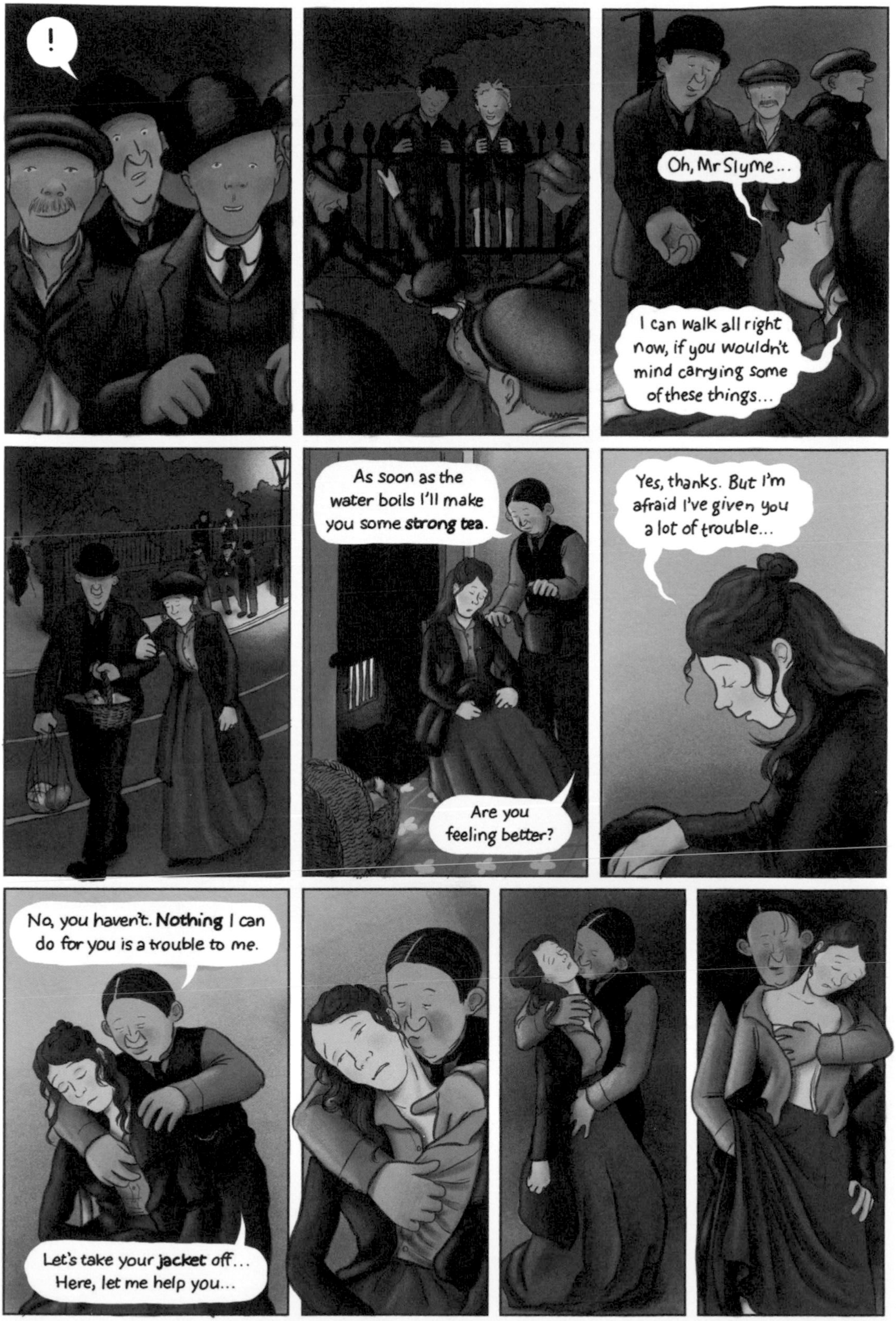
!
Oh, Mr Slyme...
I can walk all right now, if you wouldn't mind carrying some of these things...
As soon as the water boils I'll make you some strong tea.
Are you feeling better?
Yes, thanks. But I'm afraid I've given you a lot of trouble...
No, you haven't. Nothing I can do for you is a trouble to me.
Let's take your jacket off... Here, let me help you...

CHAPTER

The CHRISTMAS

PARTY

TEN

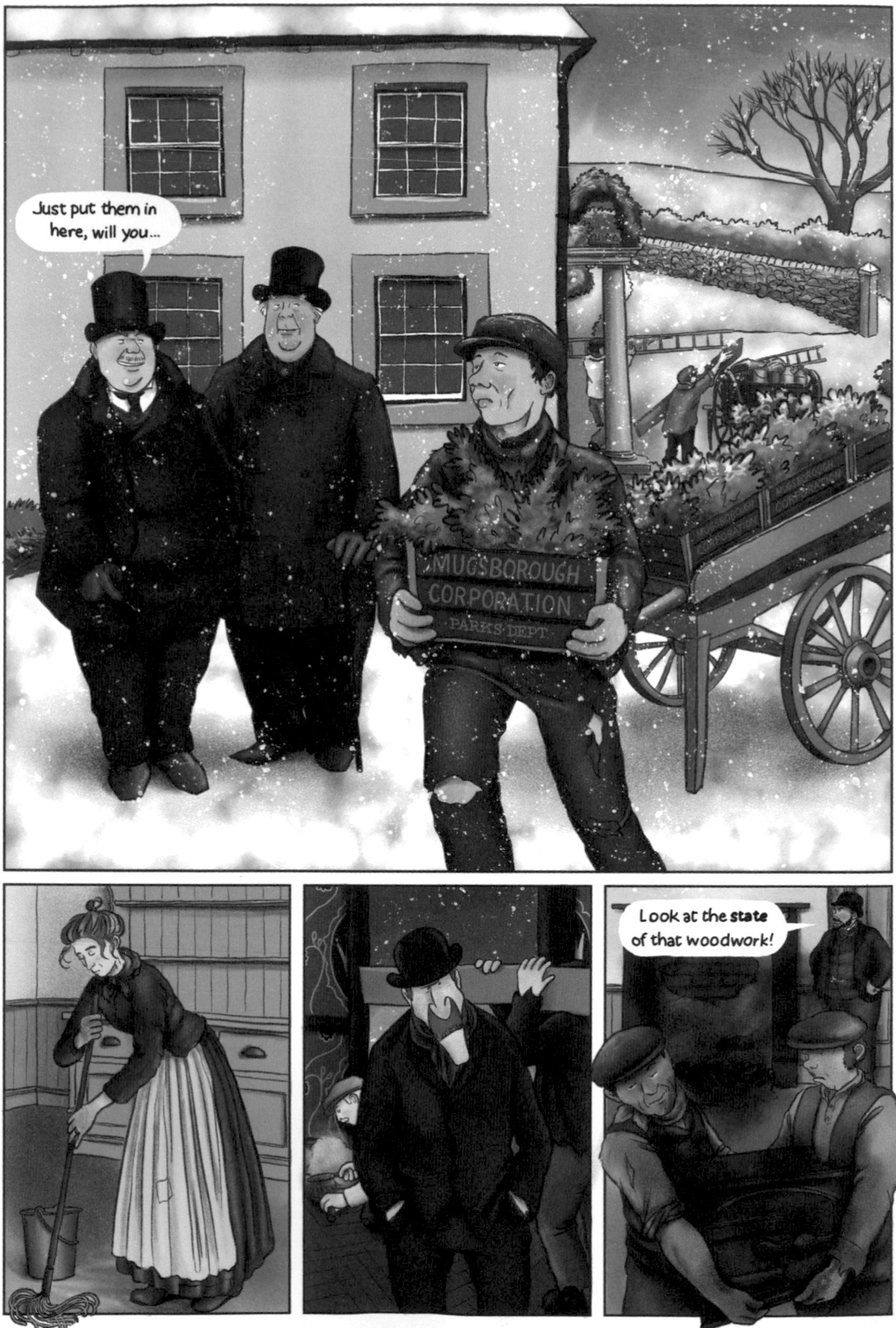
Just put them in here, will you...
MUGSBOROUGH
CORPORATION
PARKS DEPT
Look at the state of that woodwork!

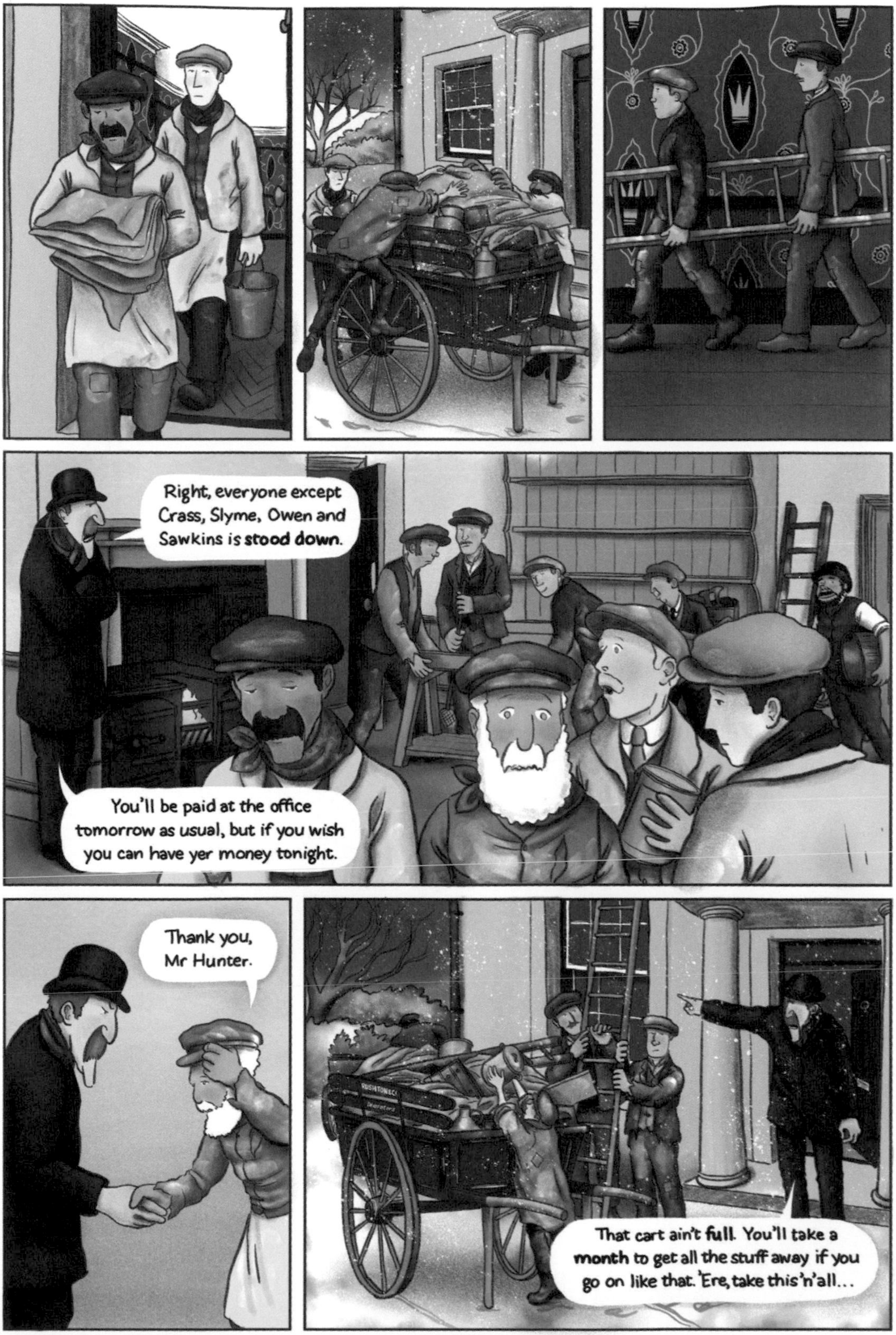
Right, everyone except Crass, Slyme, Owen and Sawkins is stood down.
You'll be paid at the office tomorrow as usual, but if you wish you can have yer money tonight.
Thank you, Mr Hunter.
That cart ain't full. You'll take a month to get all the stuff away if you go on like that. 'Ere, take this'n'all...

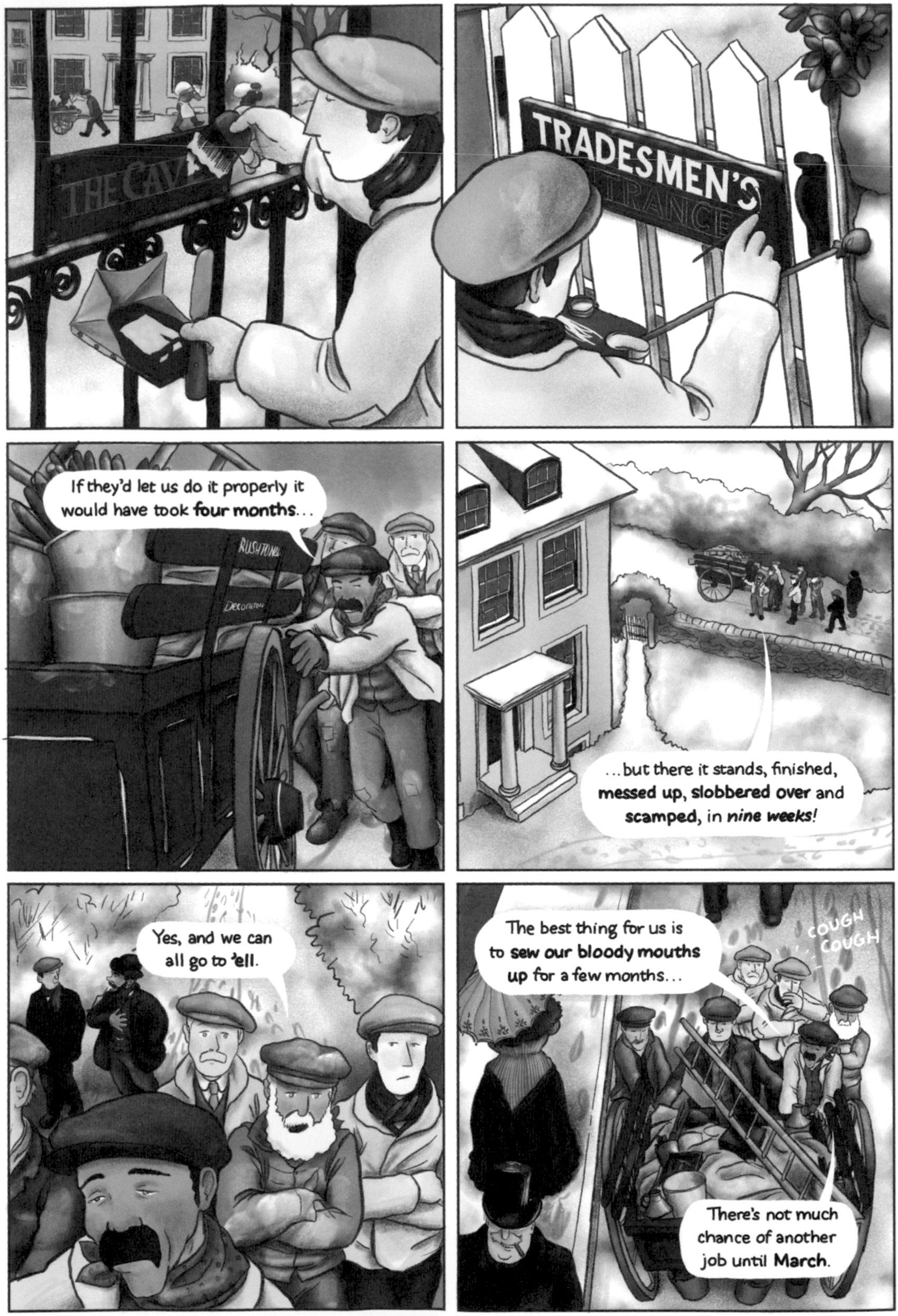
TRADESMEN'S
If they'd let us do it properly it would have took **four months**...
...but there it stands, finished, **messed up, slobbered over** and **scamped**, in ***nine weeks!***
Yes, and we can all go to **'ell**.
The best thing for us is to **sew our bloody mouths up** for a few months...
COUGH COUGH
There's not much chance of another job until **March**.

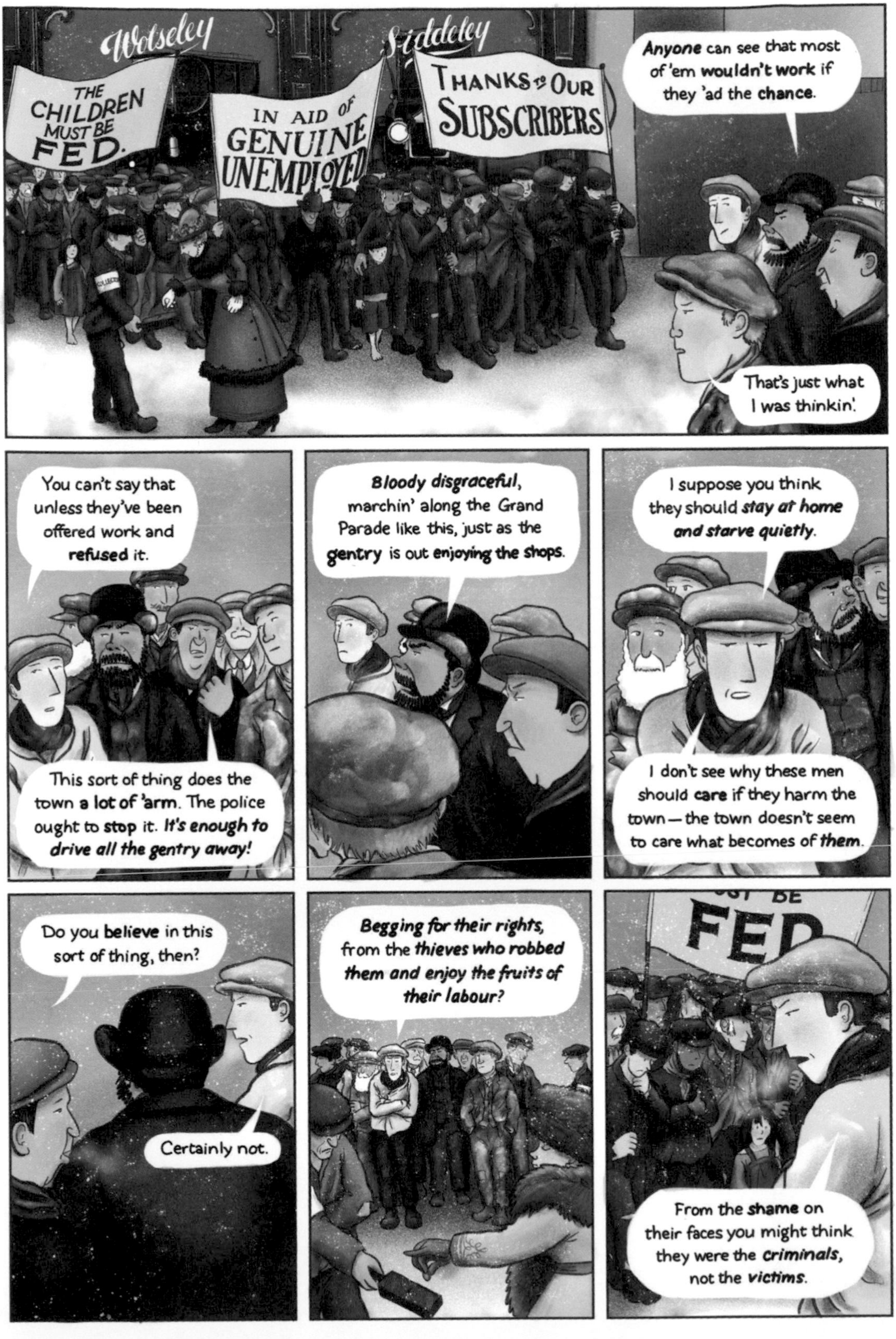
Wolseley
Siddeley
THE CHILDREN MUST BE FED.
IN AID OF GENUINE UNEMPLOYED
THANKS TO OUR SUBSCRIBERS
Anyone can see that most of 'em wouldn't work if they 'ad the chance.
That's just what I was thinkin'.
You can't say that unless they've been offered work and refused it.
This sort of thing does the town a lot of 'arm. The police ought to stop it. It's enough to drive all the gentry away!
Bloody disgraceful, marchin' along the Grand Parade like this, just as the gentry is out enjoying the shops.
I suppose you think they should stay at home and starve quietly.
I don't see why these men should care if they harm the town — the town doesn't seem to care what becomes of them.
Do you believe in this sort of thing, then?
Certainly not.
Begging for their rights, from the thieves who robbed them and enjoy the fruits of their labour?
FED
From the shame on their faces you might think they were the criminals, not the victims.

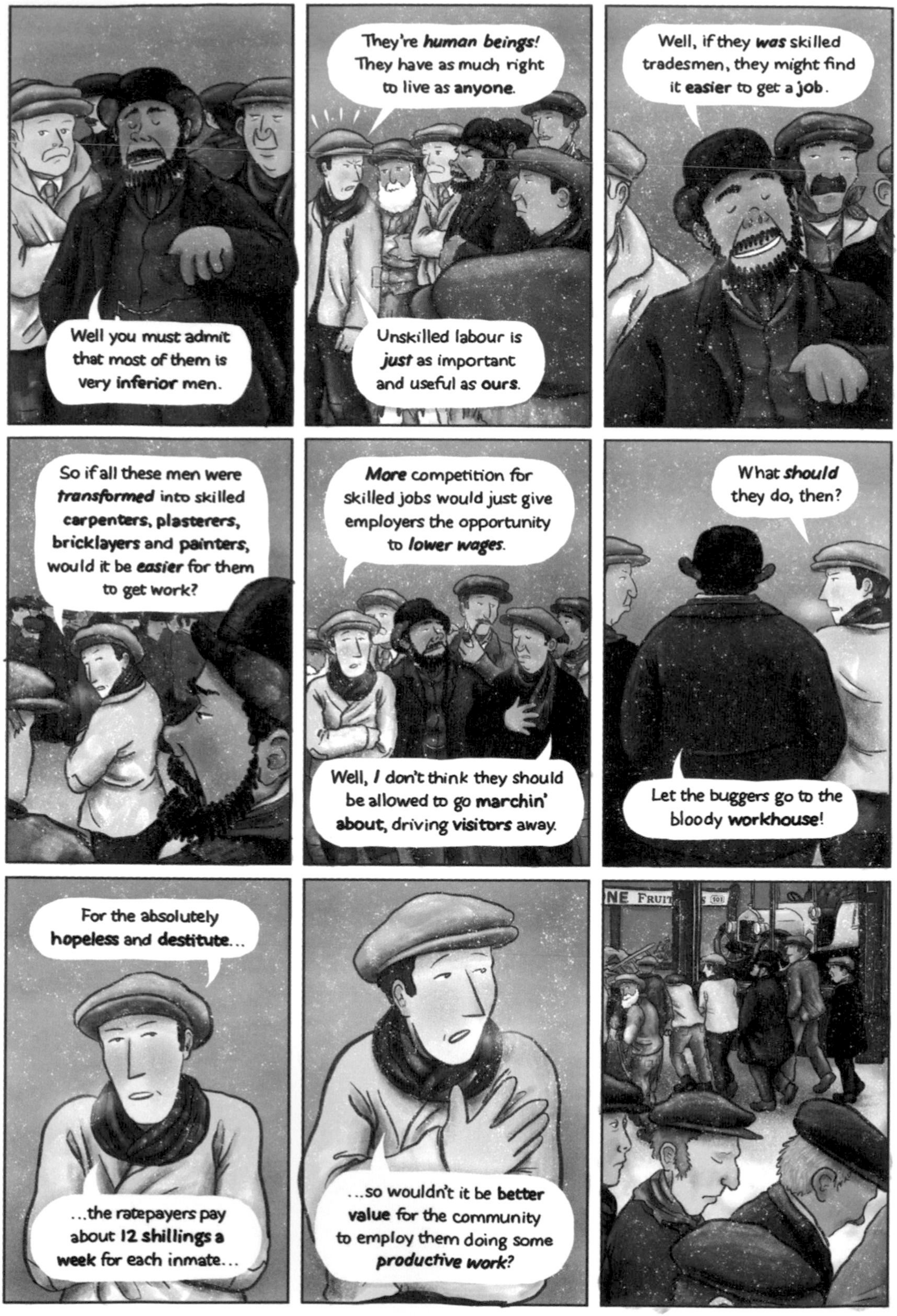
Well you must admit that most of them is very **inferior** men.
They're ***human beings!*** They have as much right to live as **anyone**.
Unskilled labour is ***just*** as important and useful as **ours**.
Well, if they ***was*** skilled tradesmen, they might find it **easier** to get a **job**.
So if all these men were ***transformed*** into skilled **carpenters, plasterers, bricklayers** and **painters**, would it be ***easier*** for them to get work?
More competition for skilled jobs would just give employers the opportunity to ***lower wages***.
Well, ***I*** don't think they should be allowed to go **marchin' about**, driving **visitors** away.
What ***should*** they do, then?
Let the buggers go to the bloody **workhouse**!
For the absolutely **hopeless** and **destitute**...
...the ratepayers pay about **12 shillings a week** for each inmate...
...so wouldn't it be **better value** for the community to employ them doing some ***productive work?***
NE FRUIT

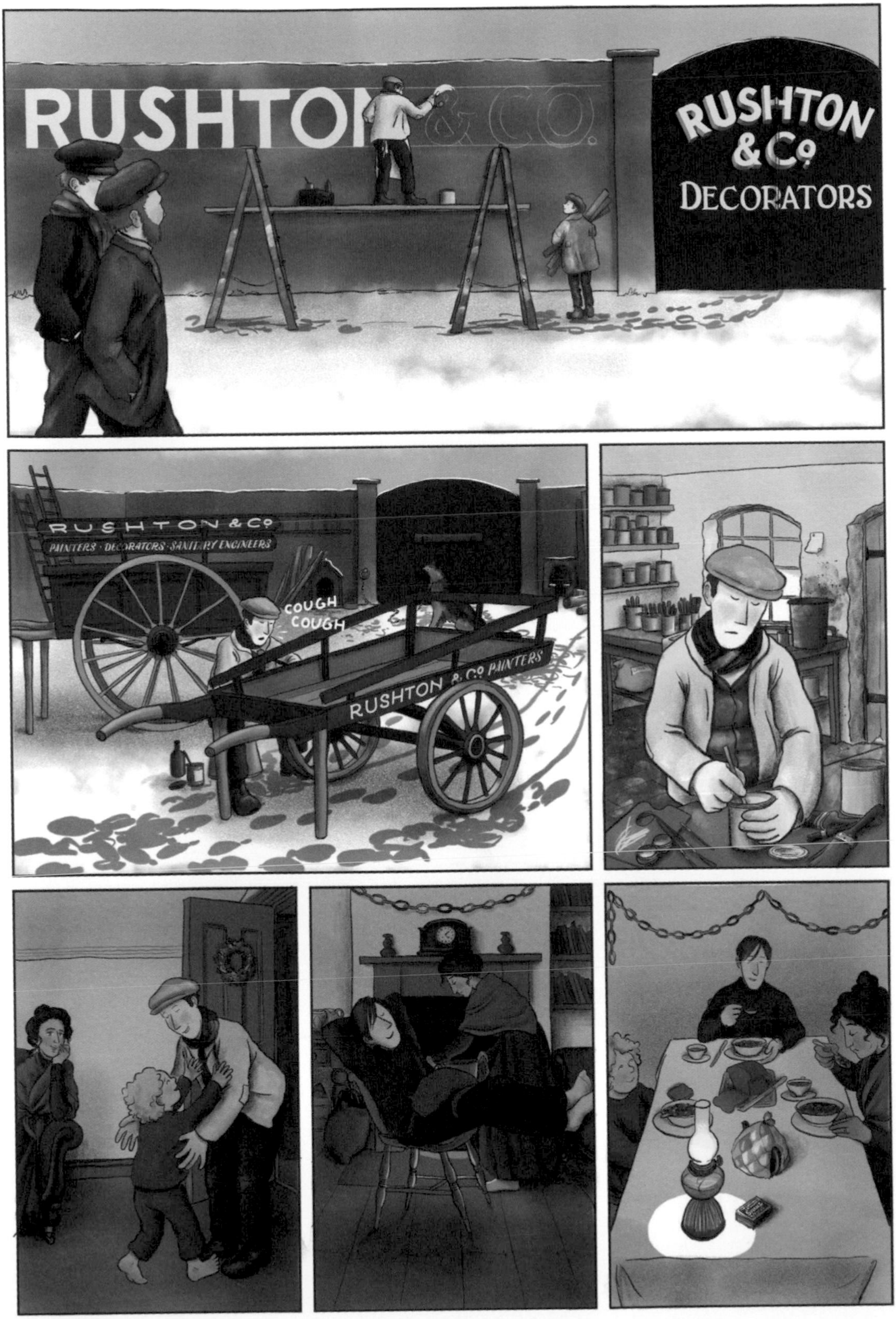
RUSHTON & CO.
RUSHTON & Co
DECORATORS
RUSHTON & Co
PAINTERS · DECORATORS · SANITARY ENGINEERS
COUGH
COUGH
RUSHTON & Co PAINTERS

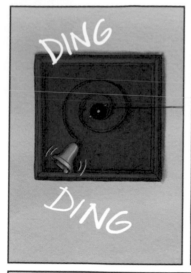

Coffin plate, Mr Owen...

...to be written at once, I've been told to wait for it.

Bert, I'm going to have a **Christmas party**. Mother said I could invite you.

All right, and I'll bring my **Pandorama**.

What's **that**? Is it **alive**?

No, **of course not**. It's a **show**, like at the **Hippodrome**. I made it myself from a sugar-box.

There's a **band** as well. I do that part with **this**.

Play something!

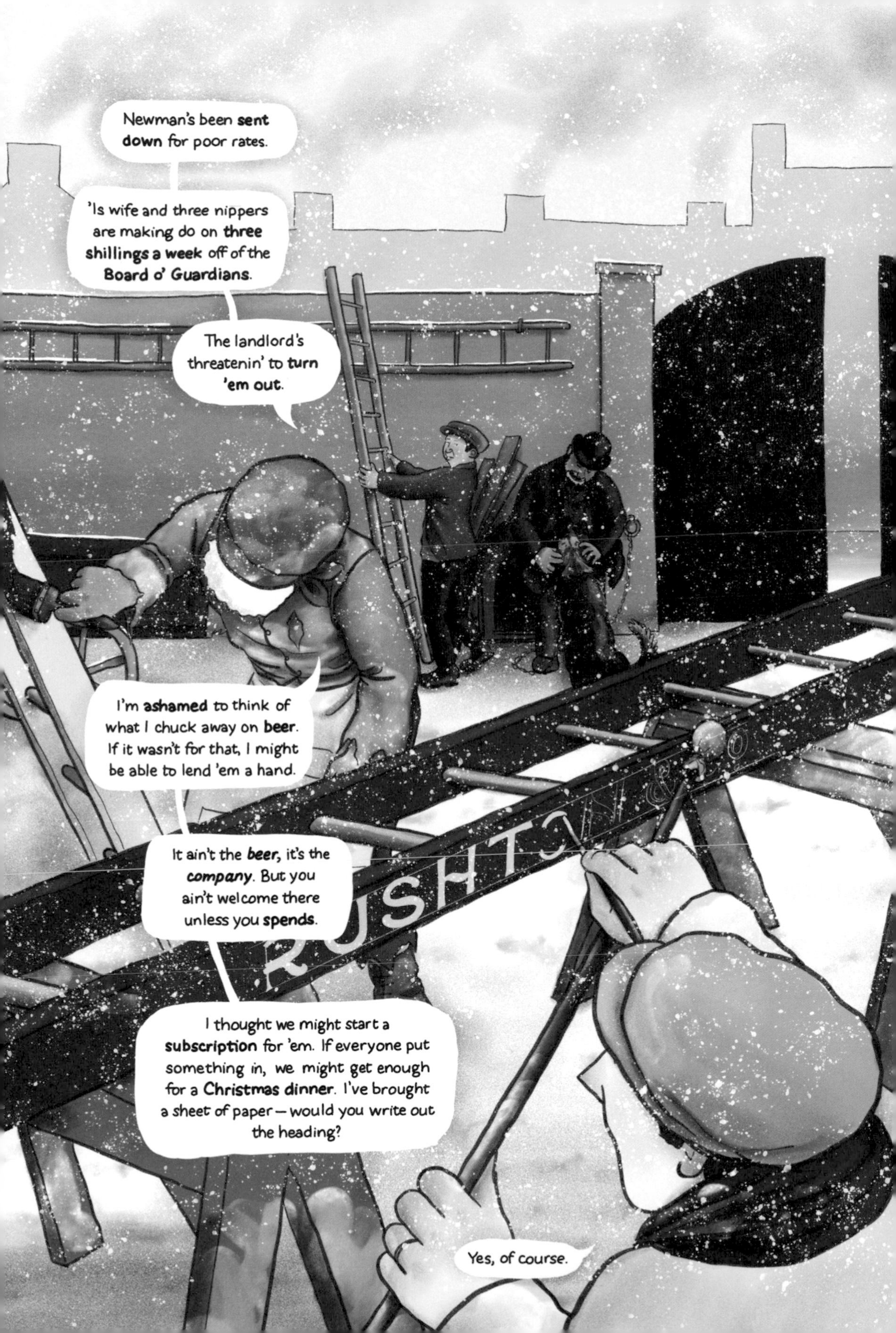
Newman's been **sent down** for poor rates.
'Is wife and three nippers are making do on **three shillings a week** off of the **Board o' Guardians**.
The landlord's threatenin' to **turn 'em out**.
I'm **ashamed** to think of what I chuck away on **beer**. If it wasn't for that, I might be able to lend 'em a hand.
It ain't the ***beer***, it's the ***company***. But you ain't welcome there unless you **spends**.
I thought we might start a **subscription** for 'em. If everyone put something in, we might get enough for a **Christmas dinner**. I've brought a sheet of paper – would you write out the heading?
Yes, of course.
RUSHTO

Mr Philpot's come for his tea.

Subscription
OF FRIENDS & WELLWISHERS
Frank Owen

Would you like to join us for **Christmas dinner** next week?

And come to my **party** too?

Please put your names down for Newman's family.

RUSHTON & C DECORATORS

FUNERALS FURNISHED

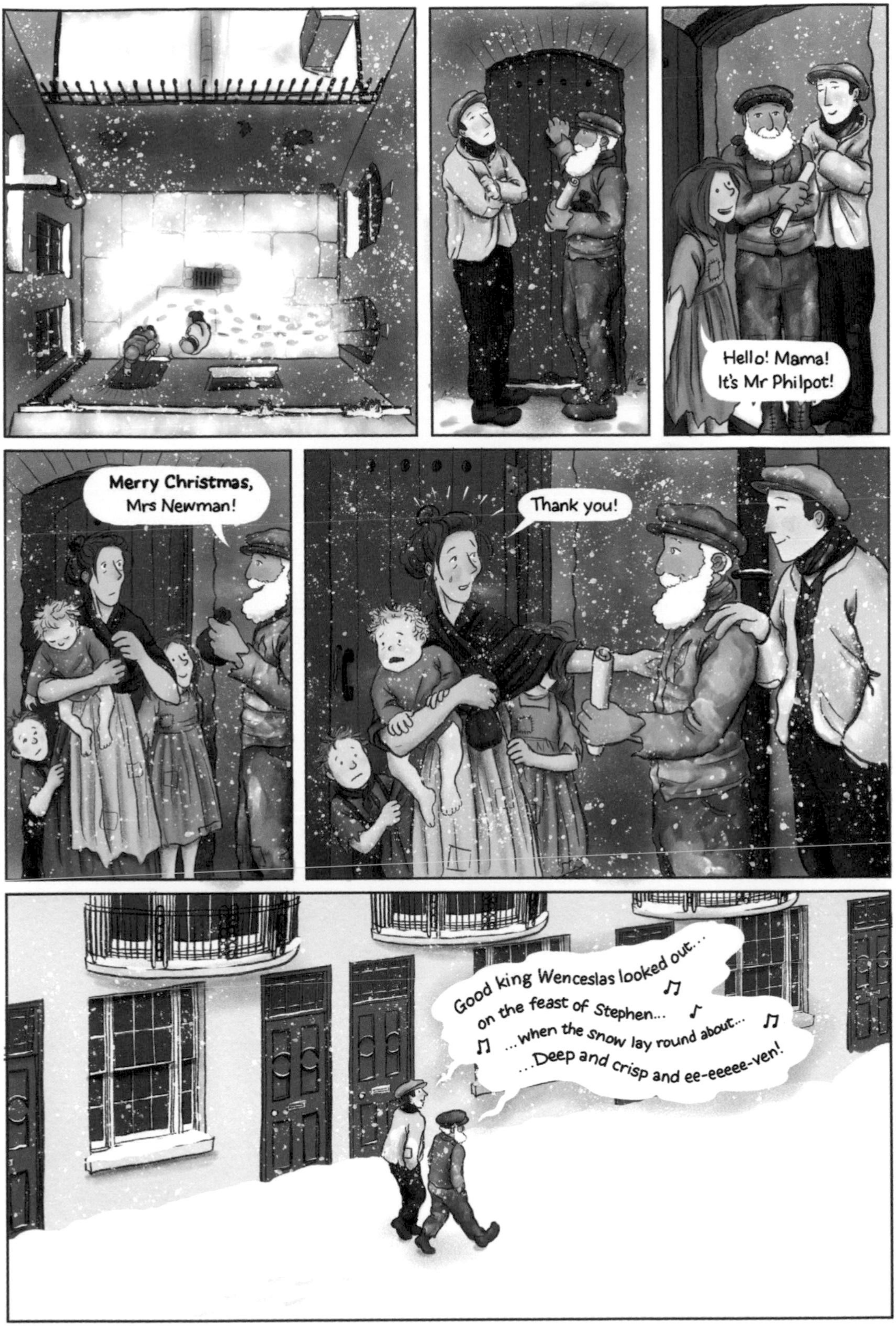
Hello! Mama!
It's Mr Philpot!
Merry Christmas,
Mrs Newman!
Thank you!
Good king Wenceslas looked out...
on the feast of Stephen...
...when the snow lay round about...
...Deep and crisp and ee-eeeee-ven!

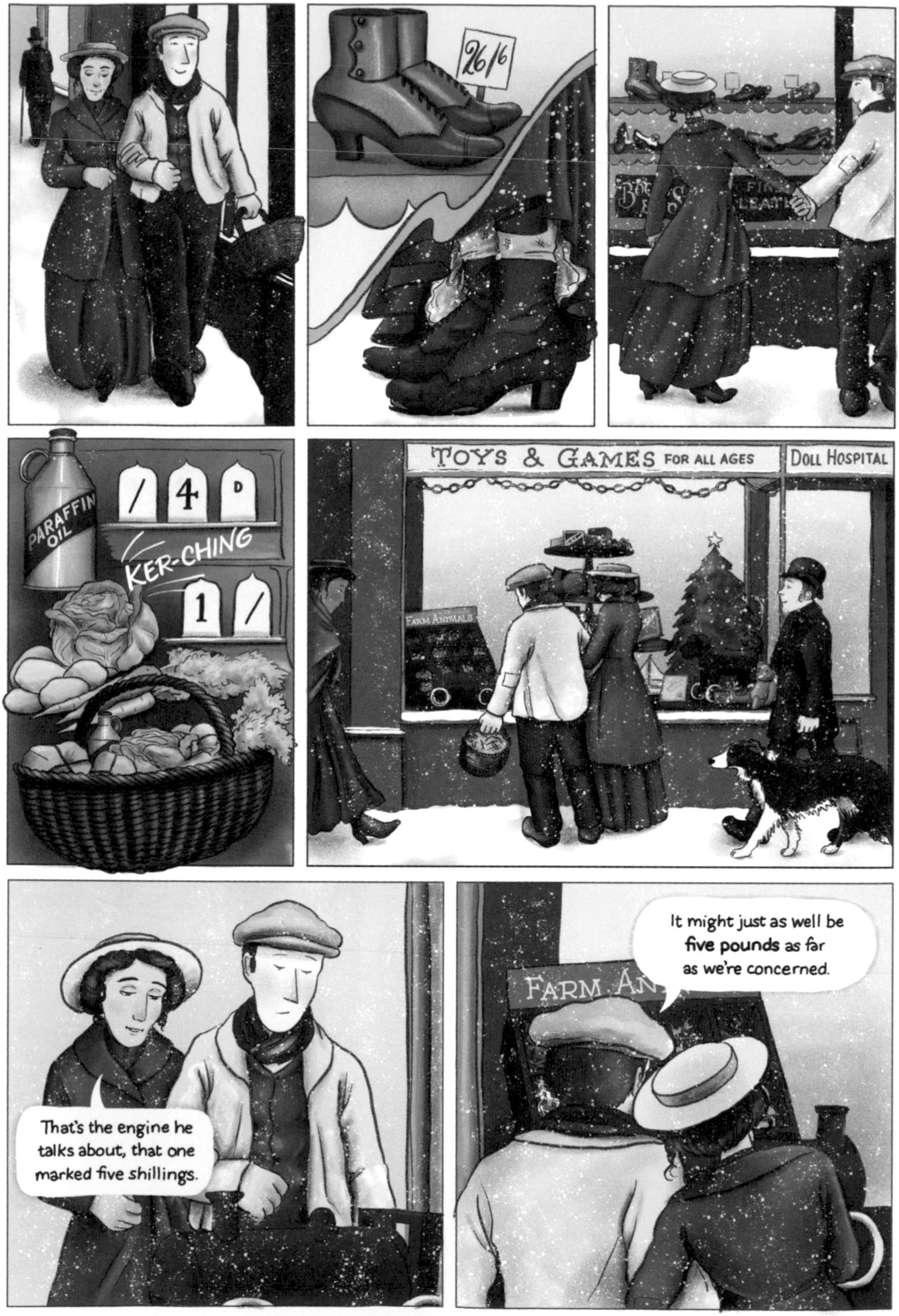
26/6
PARAFFIN OIL
/4 D
KER-CHING
1/
TOYS & GAMES FOR ALL AGES
DOLL HOSPITAL
FARM ANIMALS
That's the engine he talks about, that one marked five shillings.
It might just as well be five pounds as far as we're concerned.

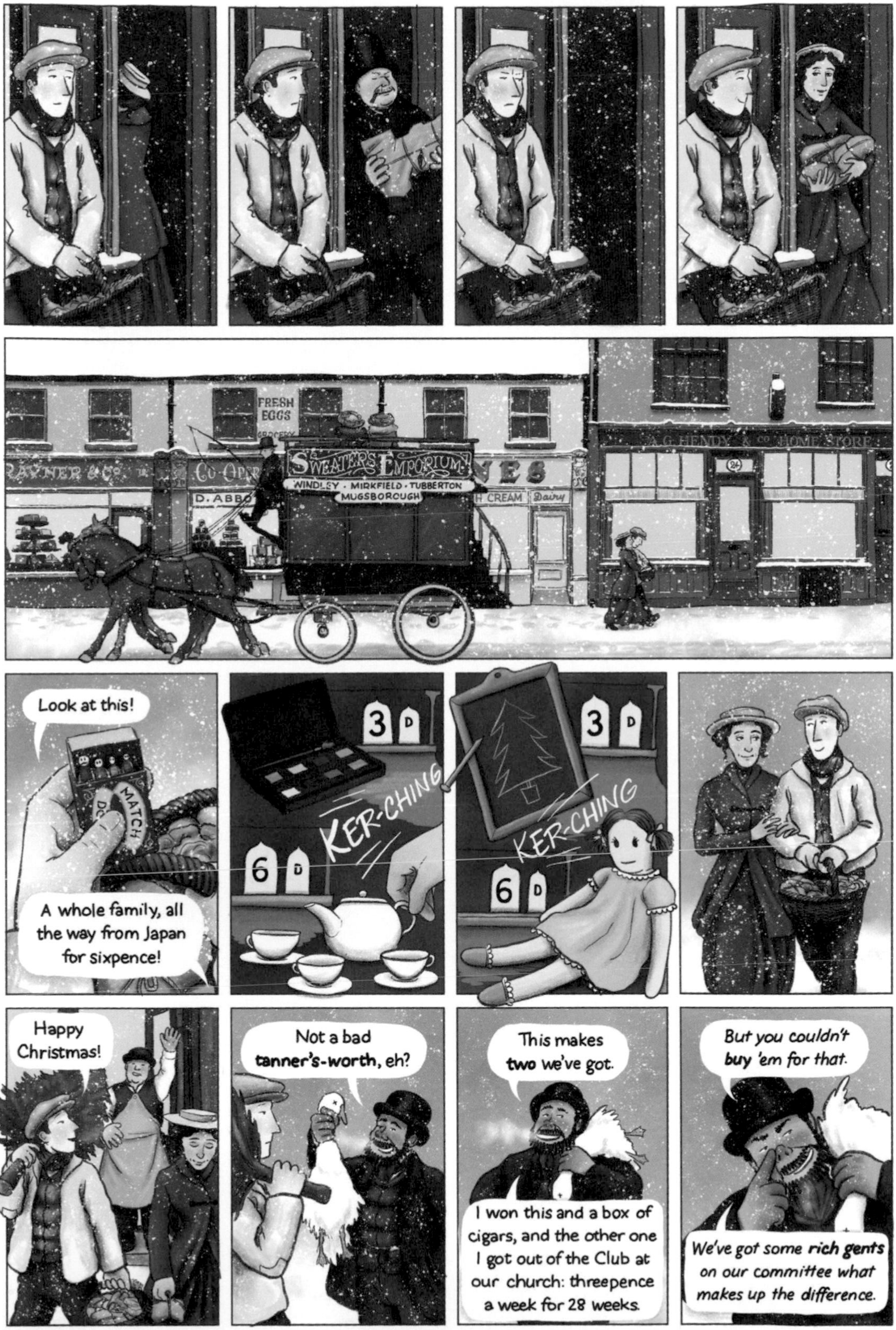
FRESH EGGS
SWEATERS EMPORIUM
WINDLEY · MIRKFIELD · TUBBERTON
MUGSBOROUGH
A.G. HENDY & Co HOME STORE
Look at this!
MATCH
A whole family, all the way from Japan for sixpence!
3 D
6 D
KER-CHING
KER-CHING
Happy Christmas!
Not a bad tanner's-worth, eh?
This makes two we've got.
I won this and a box of cigars, and the other one I got out of the Club at our church: threepence a week for 28 weeks.
But you couldn't buy 'em for that.
We've got some rich gents on our committee what makes up the difference.

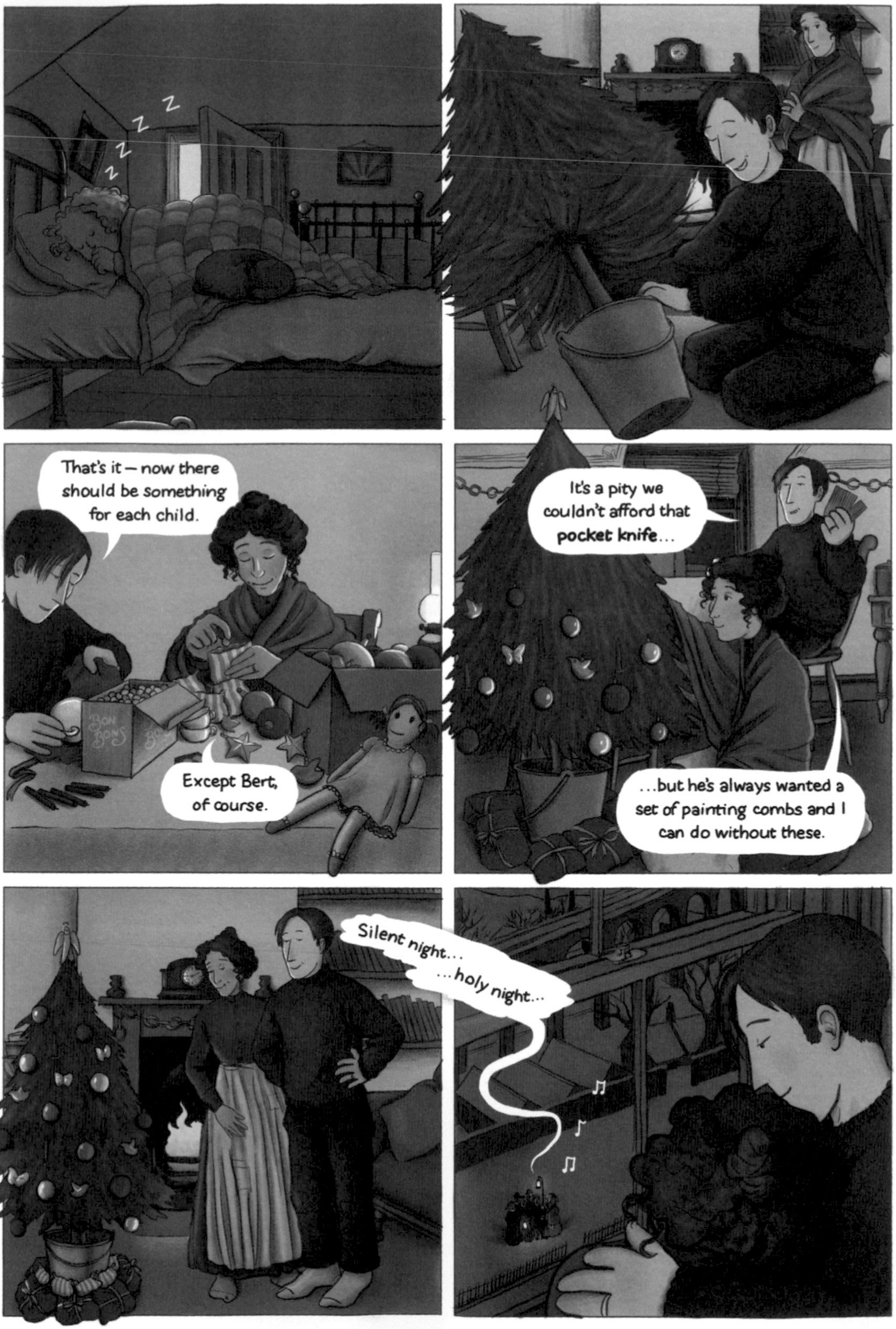

Z Z Z Z
That's it — now there should be something for each child.
BON BONS
Except Bert, of course.
It's a pity we couldn't afford that pocket knife…
…but he's always wanted a set of painting combs and I can do without these.
Silent night…
…holy night…

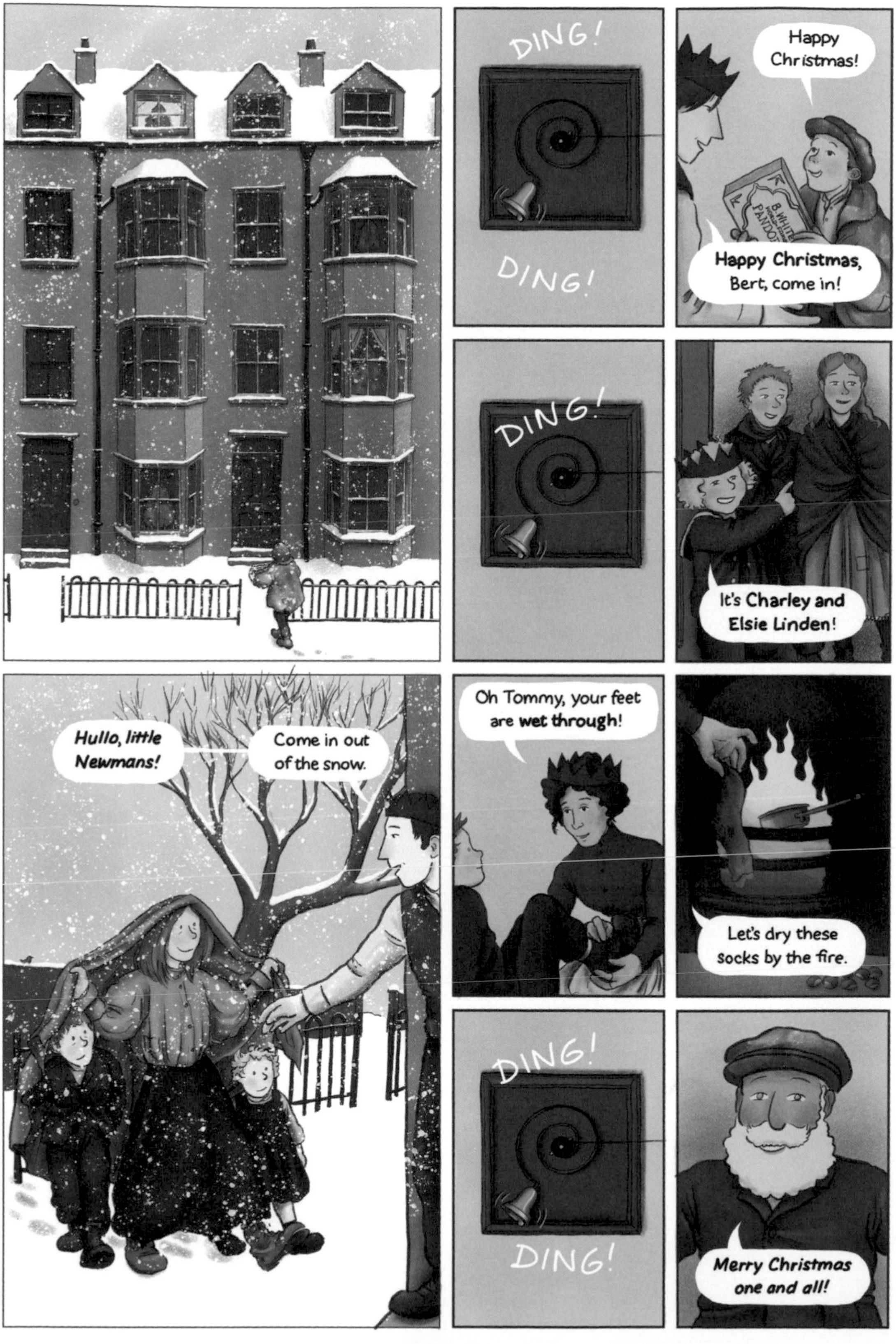
DING!
DING!
Happy Christmas!
Happy Christmas, Bert, come in!
DING!
It's Charley and Elsie Linden!
Hullo, little Newmans!
Come in out of the snow.
Oh Tommy, your feet are wet through!
Let's dry these socks by the fire.
DING!
DING!
Merry Christmas one and all!

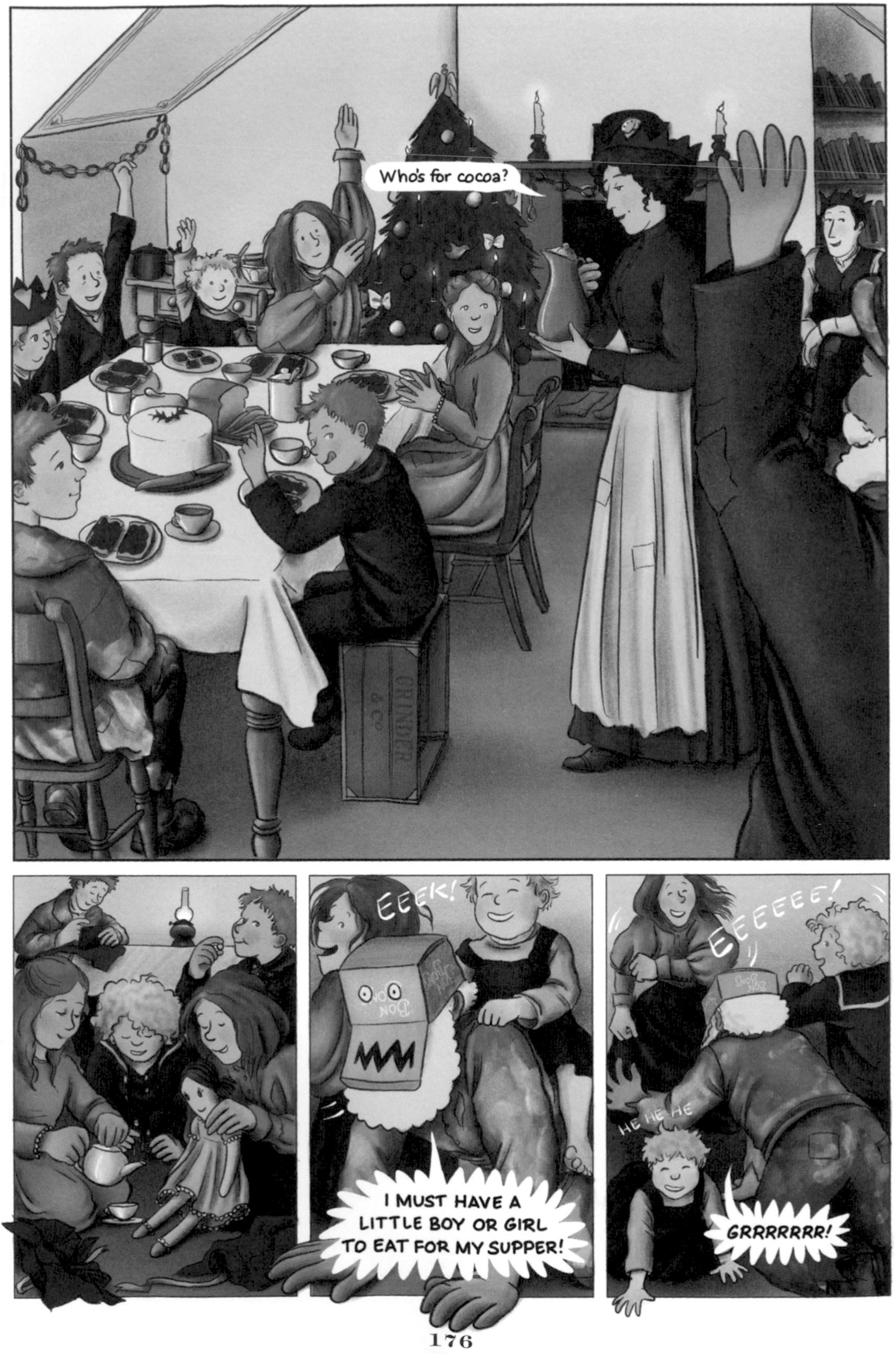
Who's for cocoa?
EEEK!
I MUST HAVE A LITTLE BOY OR GIRL TO EAT FOR MY SUPPER!
EEEEEE!
HE HE HE
GRRRRRRRR!

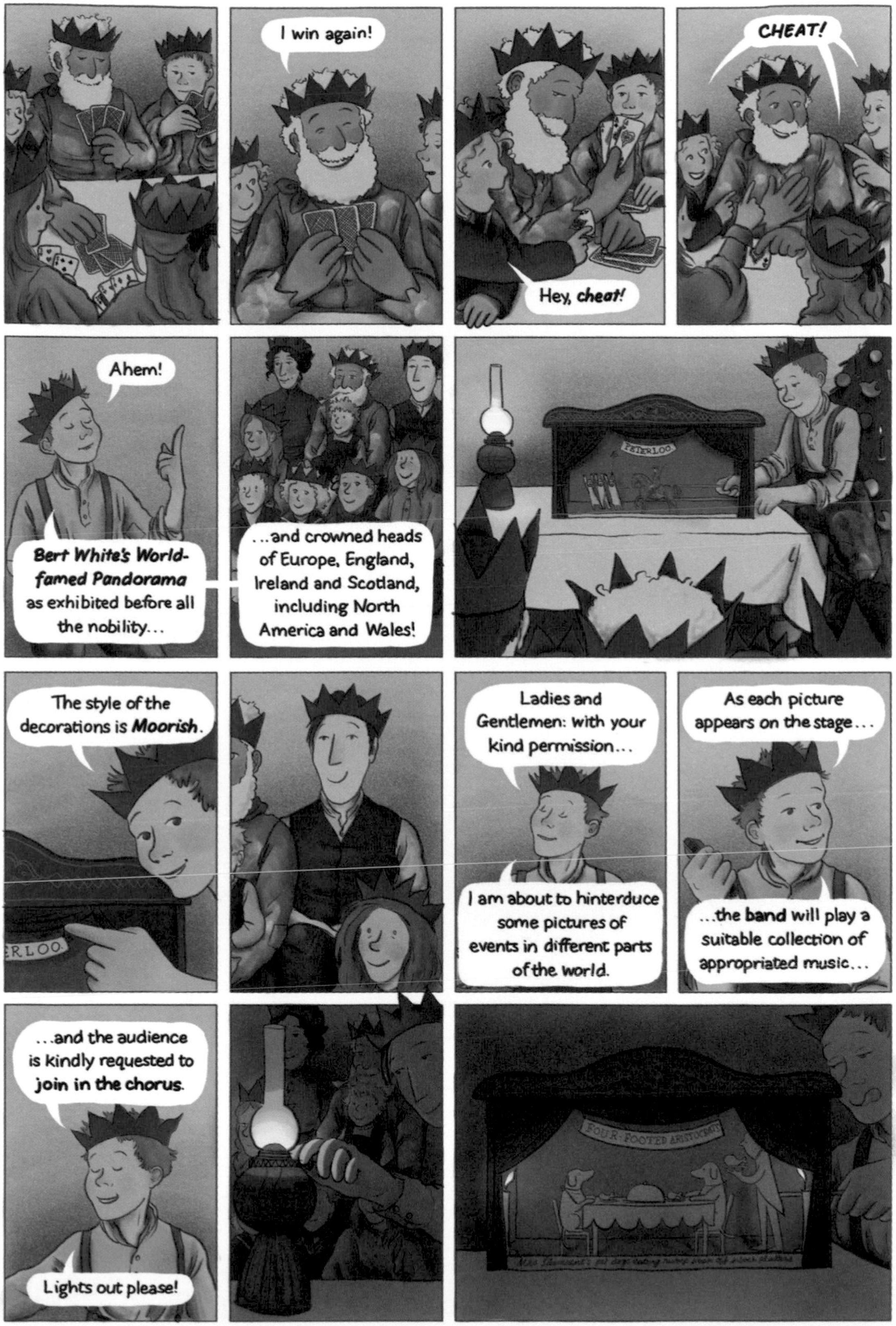
I win again!
Hey, *cheat!*
CHEAT!
Ahem!
Bert White's World-famed Pandorama as exhibited before all the nobility...
...and crowned heads of Europe, England, Ireland and Scotland, including North America and Wales!
PETERLOO
The style of the decorations is ***Moorish***.
Ladies and Gentlemen: with your kind permission...
I am about to hinterduce some pictures of events in different parts of the world.
As each picture appears on the stage...
...the **band** will play a suitable collection of appropriated music...
...and the audience is kindly requested to **join in the chorus**.
Lights out please!

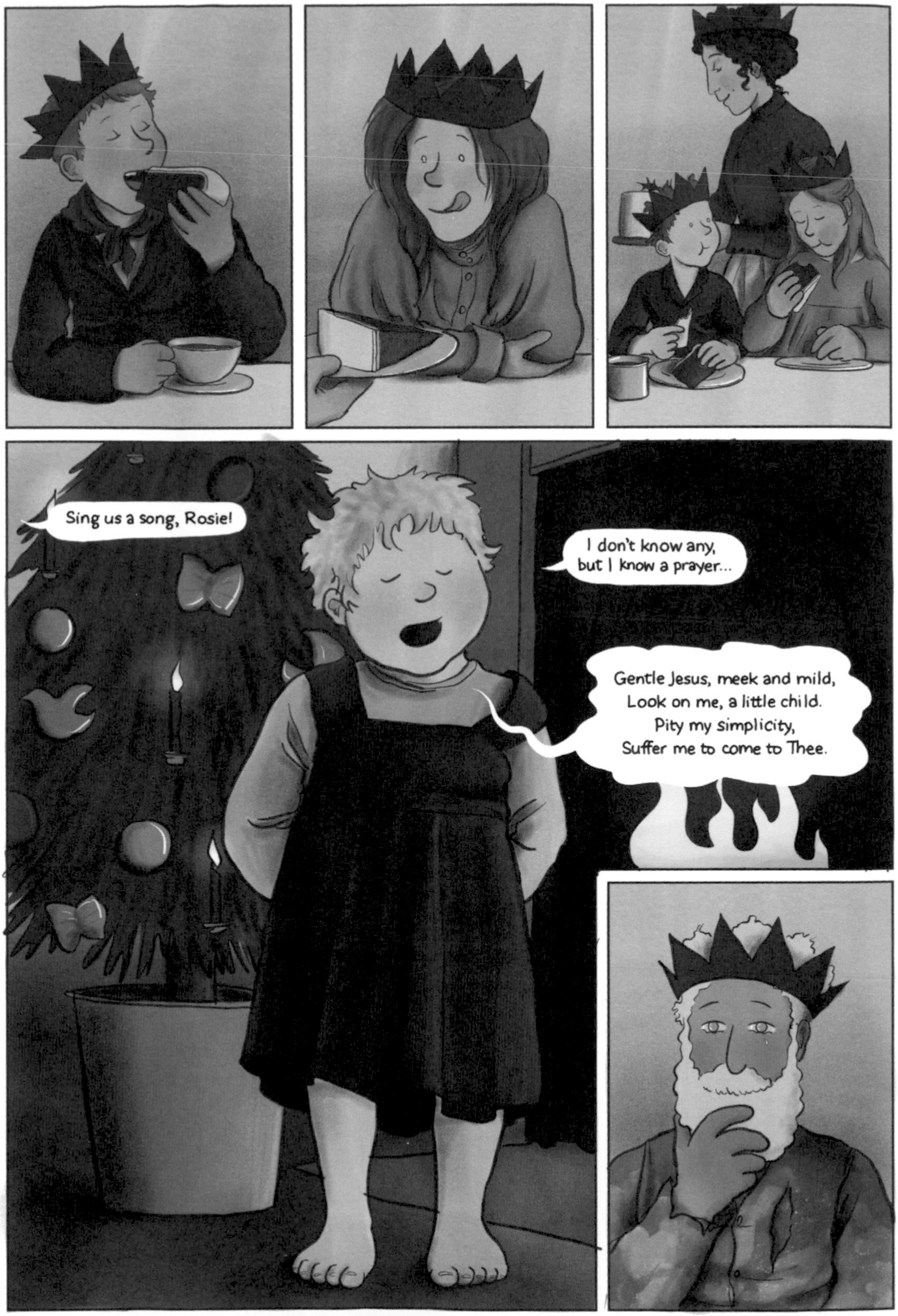
Sing us a song, Rosie!
I don't know any, but I know a prayer...
Gentle Jesus, meek and mild,
Look on me, a little child.
Pity my simplicity,
Suffer me to come to Thee.

CHAPTER

The COUNCIL

ELEVEN

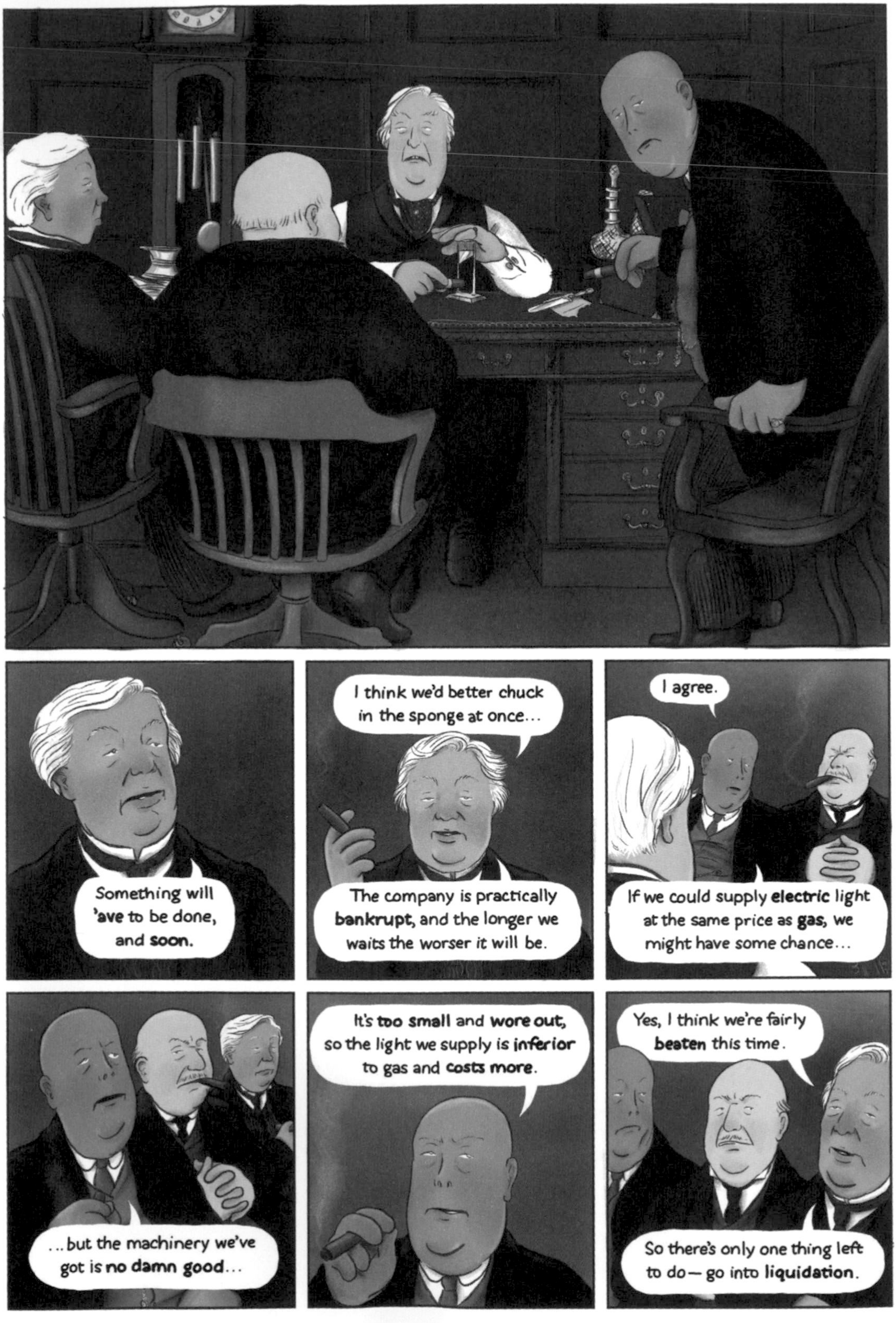
Something will 'ave to be done, and soon.
I think we'd better chuck in the sponge at once...
The company is practically bankrupt, and the longer we waits the worser it will be.
I agree.
If we could supply electric light at the same price as gas, we might have some chance...
...but the machinery we've got is no damn good...
It's too small and wore out, so the light we supply is inferior to gas and costs more.
Yes, I think we're fairly beaten this time.
So there's only one thing left to do — go into liquidation.

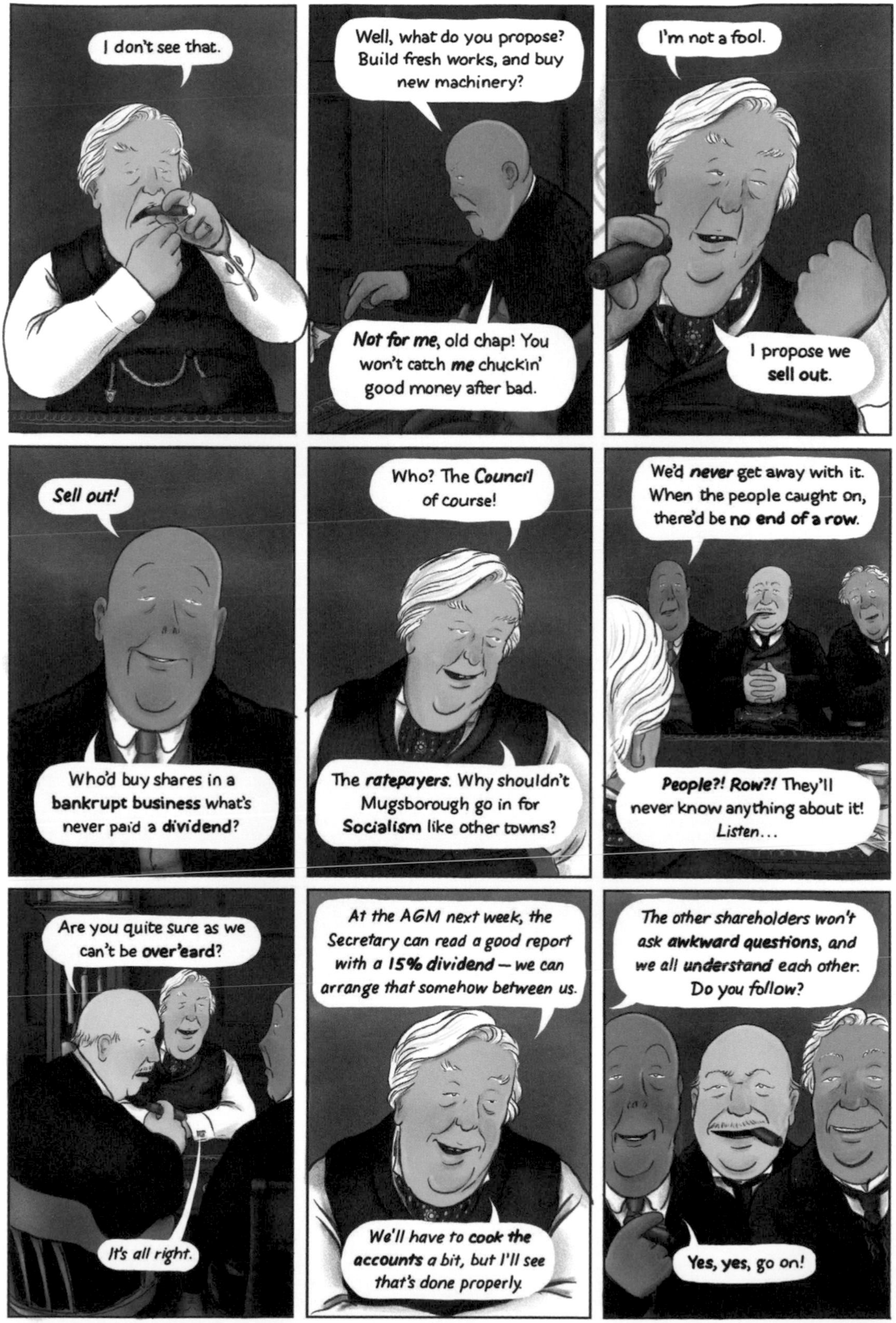
I don't see that.
Well, what do you propose? Build fresh works, and buy new machinery?
Not for me, old chap! You won't catch me chuckin' good money after bad.
I'm not a fool.
I propose we sell out.
Sell out!
Who'd buy shares in a bankrupt business what's never paid a dividend?
Who? The Council of course!
The ratepayers. Why shouldn't Mugsborough go in for Socialism like other towns?
We'd never get away with it. When the people caught on, there'd be no end of a row.
People?! Row?! They'll never know anything about it! Listen...
Are you quite sure as we can't be over'eard?
It's all right.
At the AGM next week, the Secretary can read a good report with a 15% dividend – we can arrange that somehow between us.
We'll have to cook the accounts a bit, but I'll see that's done properly.
The other shareholders won't ask awkward questions, and we all understand each other. Do you follow?
Yes, yes, go on!

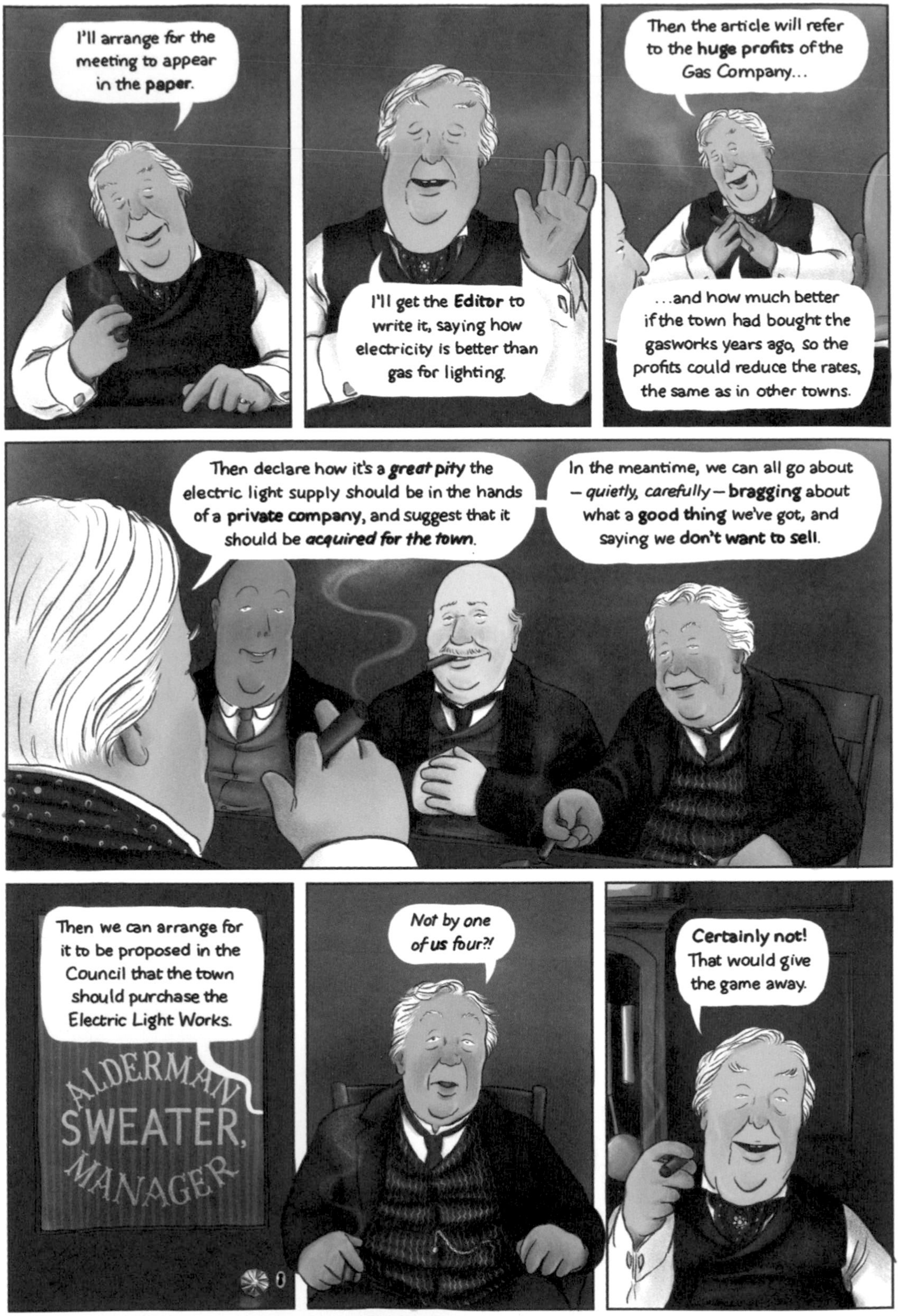
I'll arrange for the meeting to appear in the **paper**.
I'll get the **Editor** to write it, saying how electricity is better than gas for lighting.
Then the article will refer to the **huge profits** of the Gas Company...
...and how much better if the town had bought the gasworks years ago, so the profits could reduce the rates, the same as in other towns.
Then declare how it's a ***great pity*** the electric light supply should be in the hands of a **private company**, and suggest that it should be ***acquired for the town***.
In the meantime, we can all go about – *quietly, carefully* – **bragging** about what a **good thing** we've got, and saying we **don't want to sell**.
Then we can arrange for it to be proposed in the Council that the town should purchase the Electric Light Works.
ALDERMAN SWEATER, MANAGER
*Not by one of **us** four?!*
Certainly not! That would give the game away.

We'll pretend to be against selling, and **stick out** for our price...

...and when we **do** agree, we'll make out we are **sacrificing our interests** for the good of the town.

We'll rush the whole business through before the ratepayers have time to **realise**.

Not that we need worry much about **them**. Most take **no interest,** and it won't matter once we've got the **money**.

It'll be a **nine days' wonder** and we'll hear no more of it.

Well, what do you think?

Splendid! Couldn't be **better!**

If we can get away with it, it'll be one of the *smartest things we've ever done.*

Smart ain't the word for it!

And I've just thought of something else that might be done to **help it along**.

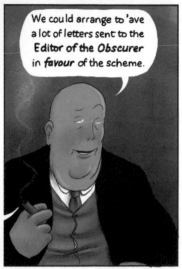

We could arrange to 'ave a lot of letters sent to the **Editor of the Obscurer** in **favour** of the scheme.

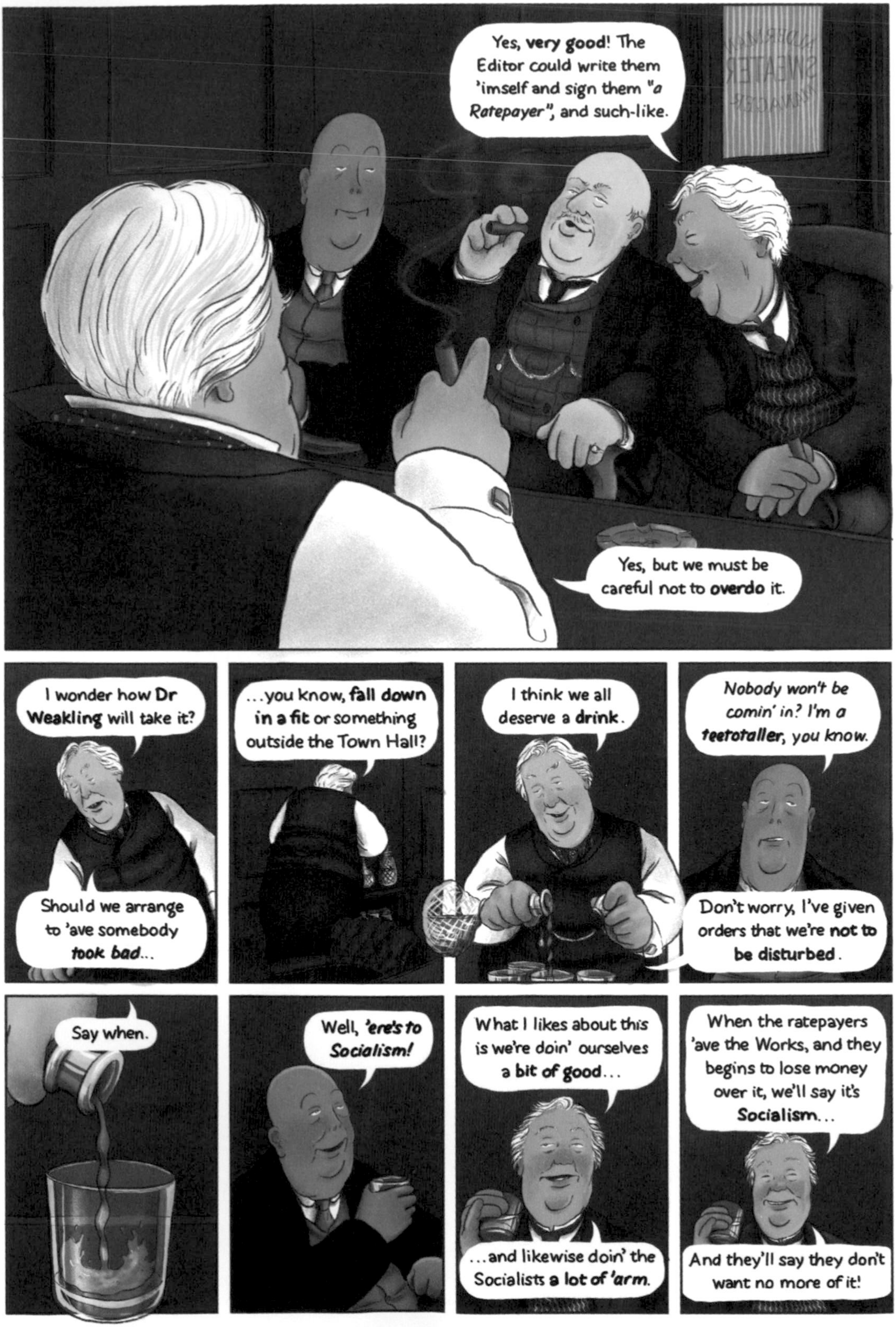
Yes, very good! The Editor could write them 'imself and sign them "a Ratepayer", and such-like.
Yes, but we must be careful not to overdo it.
I wonder how Dr Weakling will take it?
Should we arrange to 'ave somebody took bad...
...you know, fall down in a fit or something outside the Town Hall?
I think we all deserve a drink.
Nobody won't be comin' in? I'm a teetotaller, you know.
Don't worry, I've given orders that we're not to be disturbed.
Say when.
Well, 'ere's to Socialism!
What I likes about this is we're doin' ourselves a bit of good...
...and likewise doin' the Socialists a lot of 'arm.
When the ratepayers 'ave the Works, and they begins to lose money over it, we'll say it's Socialism...
And they'll say they don't want no more of it!

Chapter 12

THE BEGINNING OF THE END

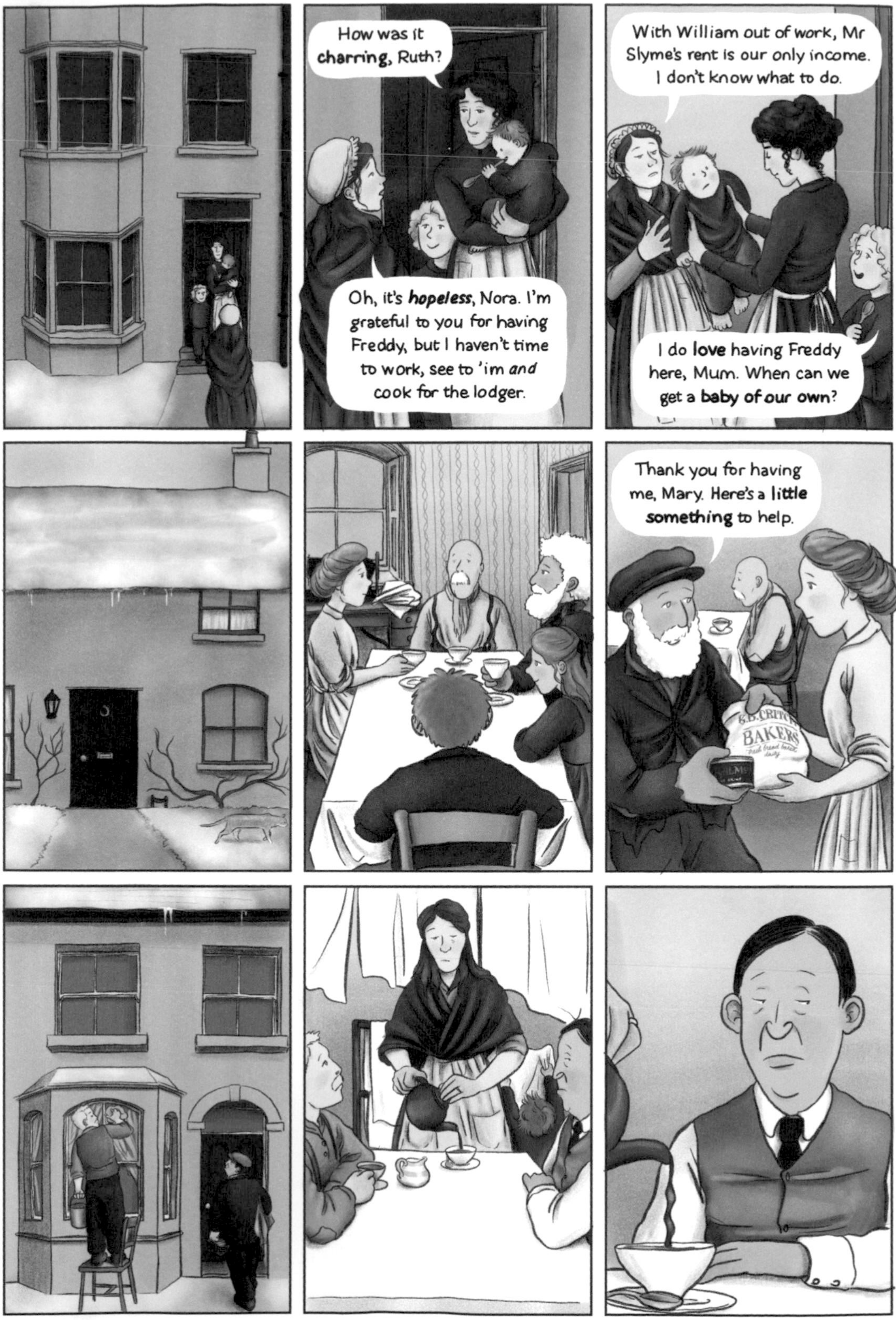
How was it charring, Ruth?
Oh, it's hopeless, Nora. I'm grateful to you for having Freddy, but I haven't time to work, see to 'im and cook for the lodger.
With William out of work, Mr Slyme's rent is our only income. I don't know what to do.
I do love having Freddy here, Mum. When can we get a baby of our own?
Thank you for having me, Mary. Here's a little something to help.
BAKERS

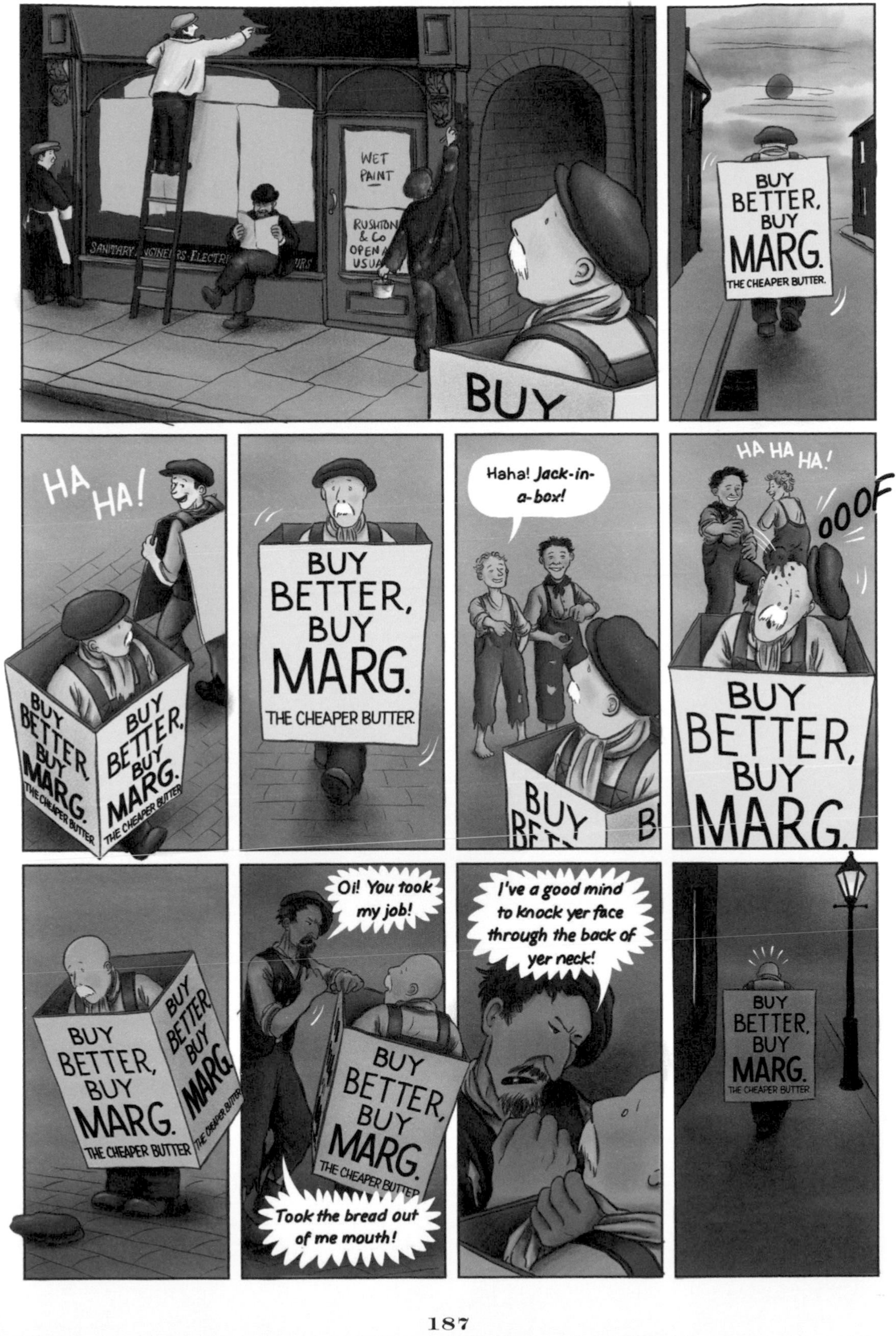
WET PAINT
RUSHTON & Co OPEN A USUA
SANITARY ENGINEERS ELECTRI URS
BUY
BUY BETTER, BUY MARG. THE CHEAPER BUTTER.
HA HA!
BUY BETTER, BUY MARG. THE CHEAPER BUTTER
BUY BETTER, BUY MARG. THE CHEAPER BUTTER
Haha! Jack-in-a-box!
HA HA HA!
OOOF
BUY BETTER, BUY MARG.
BUY BETTER, BUY MARG. THE CHEAPER BUTTER
Oi! You took my job!
Took the bread out of me mouth!
I've a good mind to knock yer face through the back of yer neck!
BUY BETTER, BUY MARG. THE CHEAPER BUTTER

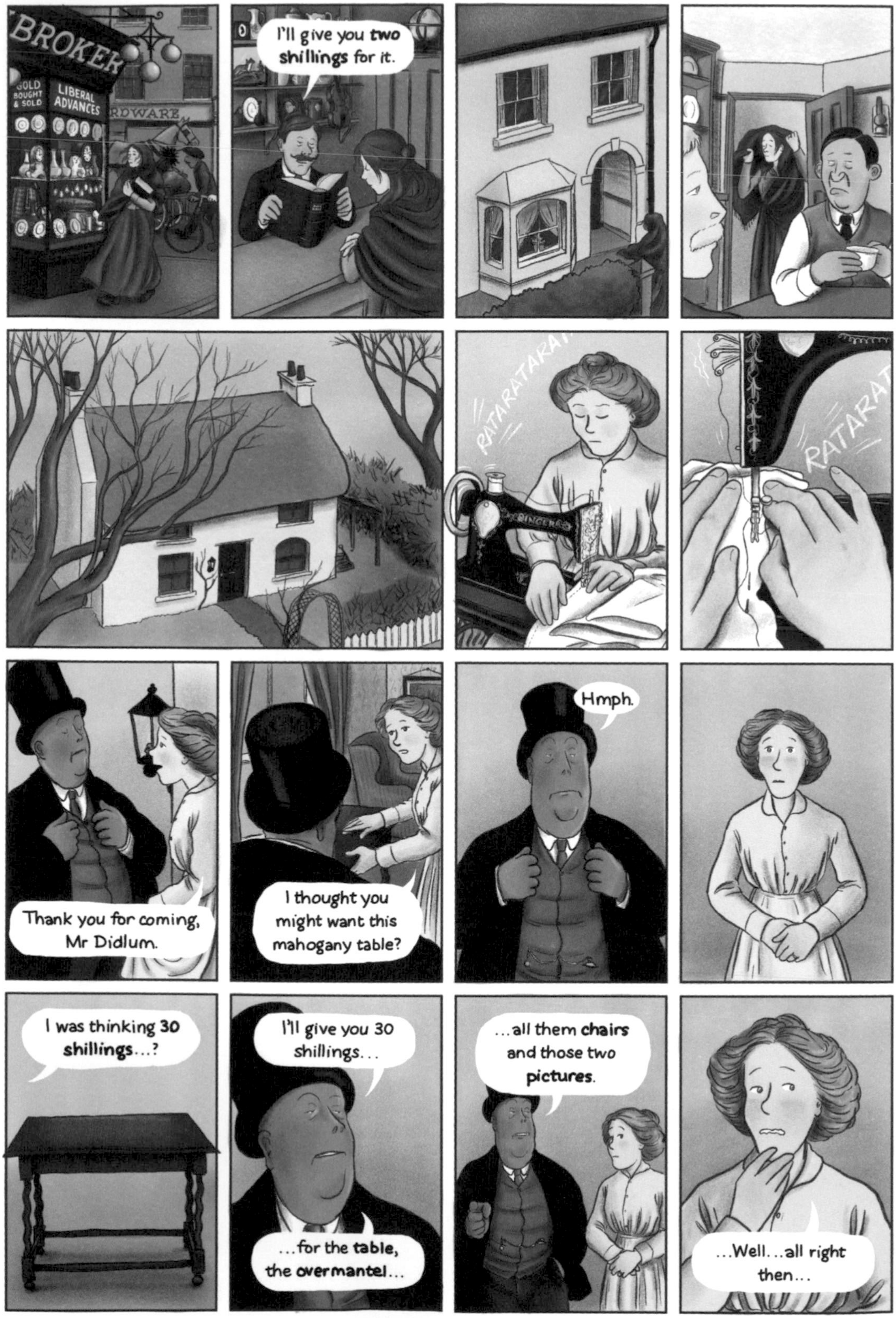
BROKER
GOLD BOUGHT & SOLD
LIBERAL ADVANCES
RDWARE
I'll give you two shillings for it.
RATARATARAT
RATARAT
Thank you for coming, Mr Didlum.
I thought you might want this mahogany table?
Hmph.
I was thinking 30 shillings...?
I'll give you 30 shillings...
...for the table, the overmantel...
...all them chairs and those two pictures.
...Well...all right then...

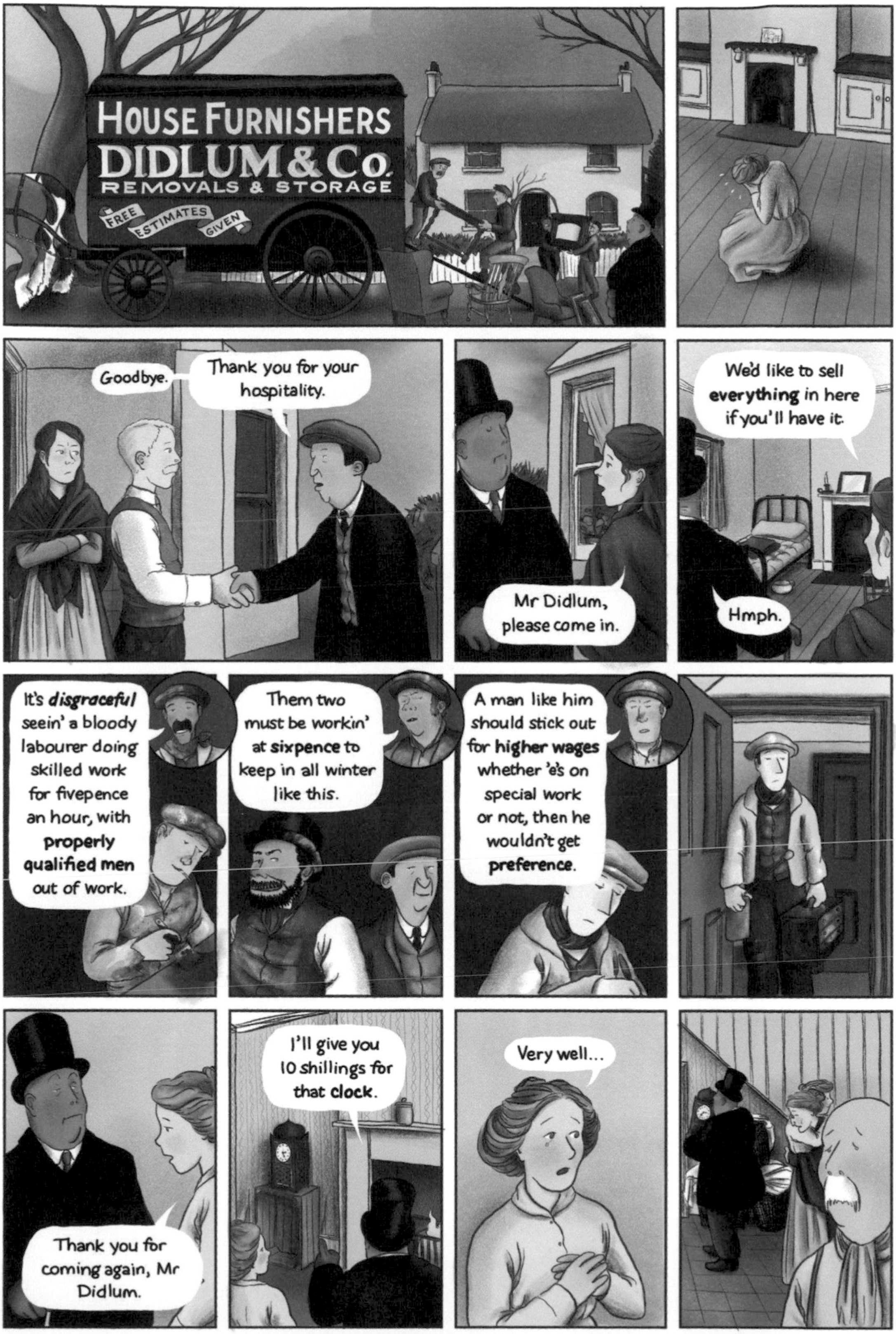
HOUSE FURNISHERS
DIDLUM & Co.
REMOVALS & STORAGE
FREE ESTIMATES GIVEN
Goodbye.
Thank you for your hospitality.
Mr Didlum, please come in.
We'd like to sell everything in here if you'll have it.
Hmph.
It's disgraceful seein' a bloody labourer doing skilled work for fivepence an hour, with properly qualified men out of work.
Them two must be workin' at sixpence to keep in all winter like this.
A man like him should stick out for higher wages whether 'e's on special work or not, then he wouldn't get preference.
Thank you for coming again, Mr Didlum.
I'll give you 10 shillings for that clock.
Very well...

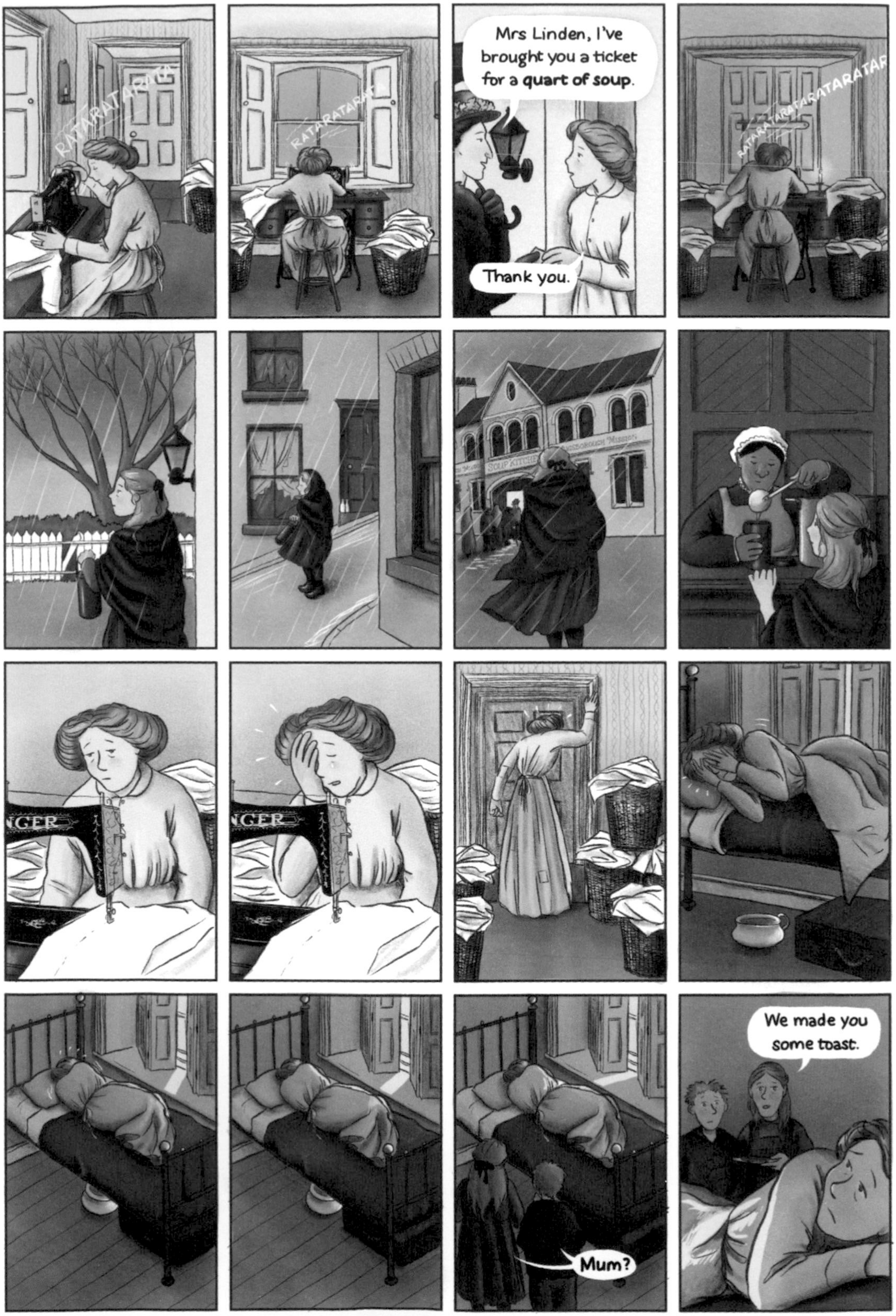
RATARATARATA
RATARATARATA
Mrs Linden, I've brought you a ticket for a quart of soup.
Thank you.
RATARATARATARATARATA
SOUP KITCHEN
NGER
NGER
Mum?
We made you some toast.

I shall be a **teacher** and bring money home to you.

I shall have a **grocer's shop.**

With a grocer's shop, there is always plenty to eat...

...even if you've no money, you can have **good stuff**...

...tins of **salmon, jam, sardines, eggs, cakes, biscuits** and all those sorts of things.

I shall deliver the groceries with a horse 'n' cart and give rides to all the boys I know...

...and after work when the shop's shut...

...you and Elsie and Granny can come for long rides into the **country**.

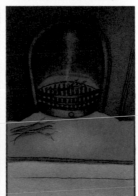

I'm going to try to sell some of these books.

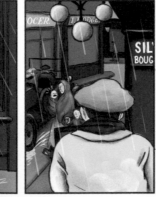

GOLD & SILVER
BOUGHT & APPRAISED

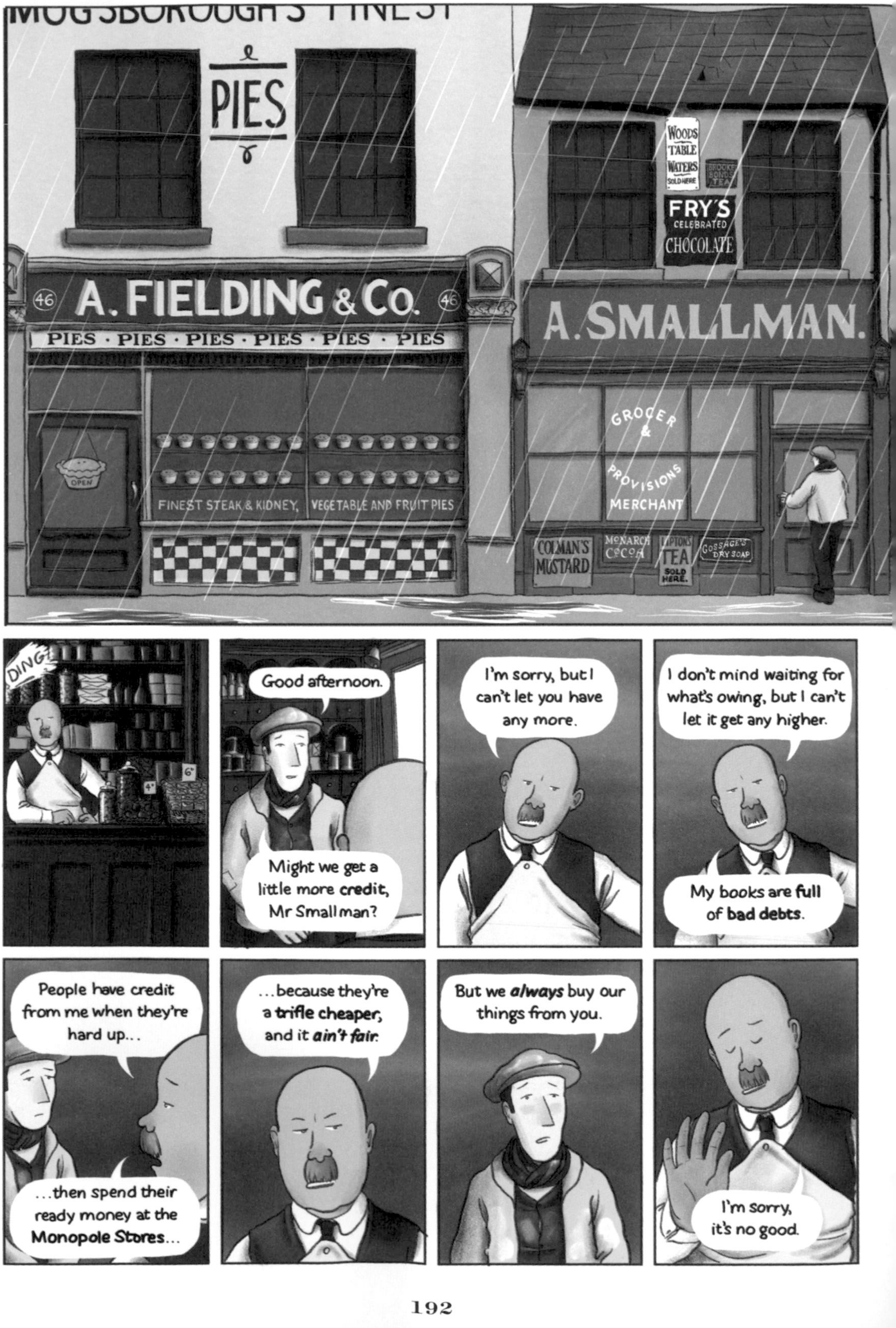
PIES
46 A. FIELDING & Co. 46
PIES · PIES · PIES · PIES · PIES · PIES
OPEN
FINEST STEAK & KIDNEY, VEGETABLE AND FRUIT PIES
WOODS TABLE WATERS SOLD HERE
FRY'S CELEBRATED CHOCOLATE
A. SMALLMAN.
GROCER & PROVISIONS MERCHANT
COLMAN'S MUSTARD
LIPTONS TEA SOLD HERE.
GOSSAGE'S DRY SOAP
DING
Good afternoon.
Might we get a little more **credit**, Mr Smallman?
I'm sorry, but I can't let you have any more.
I don't mind waiting for what's owing, but I can't let it get any higher.
My **books** are **full** of **bad debts**.
People have credit from me when they're hard up...
...then spend their ready money at the **Monopole Stores**...
...because they're a **trifle cheaper**, and it ***ain't fair***.
But we ***always*** buy our things from you.
I'm sorry, it's no good.

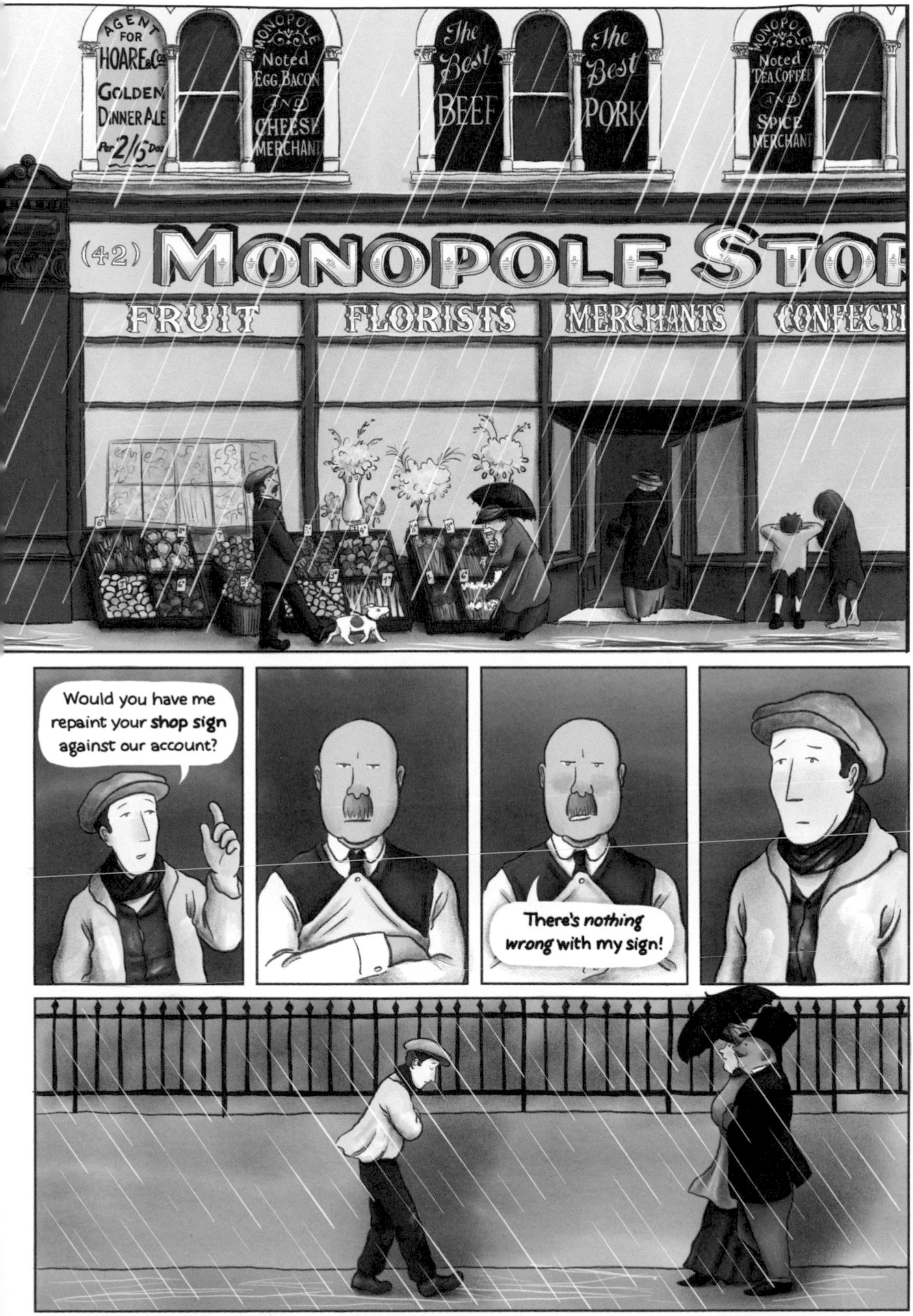
AGENT FOR HOARE & Co's GOLDEN DINNER ALE Per 2/6 Doz
MONOPOLE Noted EGG BACON AND CHEESE MERCHANTS
The Best BEEF
The Best PORK
MONOPOLE Noted TEA COFFEE AND SPICE MERCHANTS
(42) MONOPOLE STOR
FRUIT
FLORISTS
MERCHANTS
CONFECTI
Would you have me repaint your shop sign against our account?
There's nothing wrong with my sign!

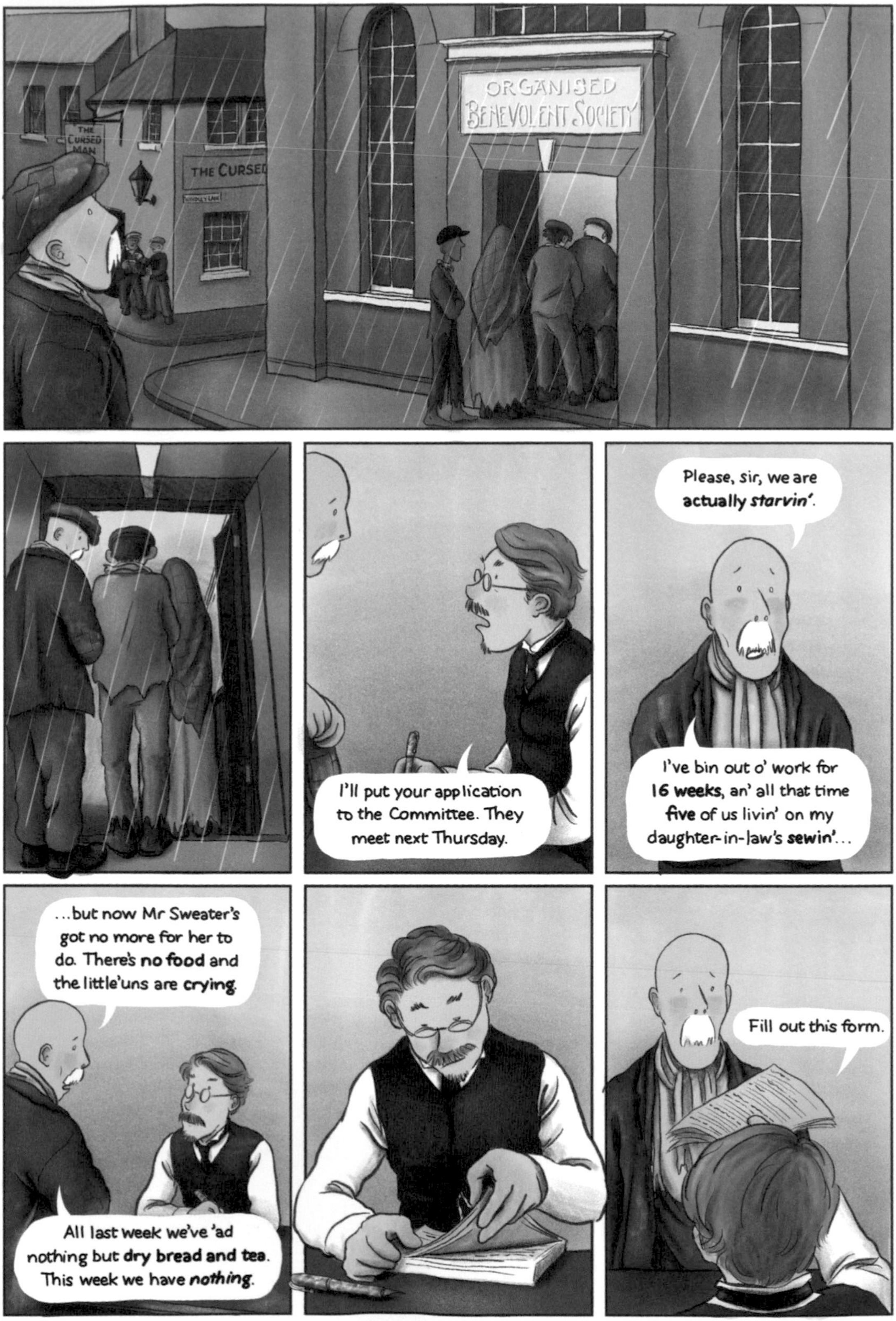
THE CURSED MAN
THE CURSED
ORGANISED BENEVOLENT SOCIETY
I'll put your application to the Committee. They meet next Thursday.
Please, sir, we are **actually *starvin'***.
I've bin out o' work for **16 weeks**, an' all that time **five** of us livin' on my daughter-in-law's **sewin'**...
...but now Mr Sweater's got no more for her to do. There's **no food** and the little'uns are **crying**.
All last week we've 'ad nothing but **dry bread and tea**. This week we have ***nothing***.
Fill out this form.

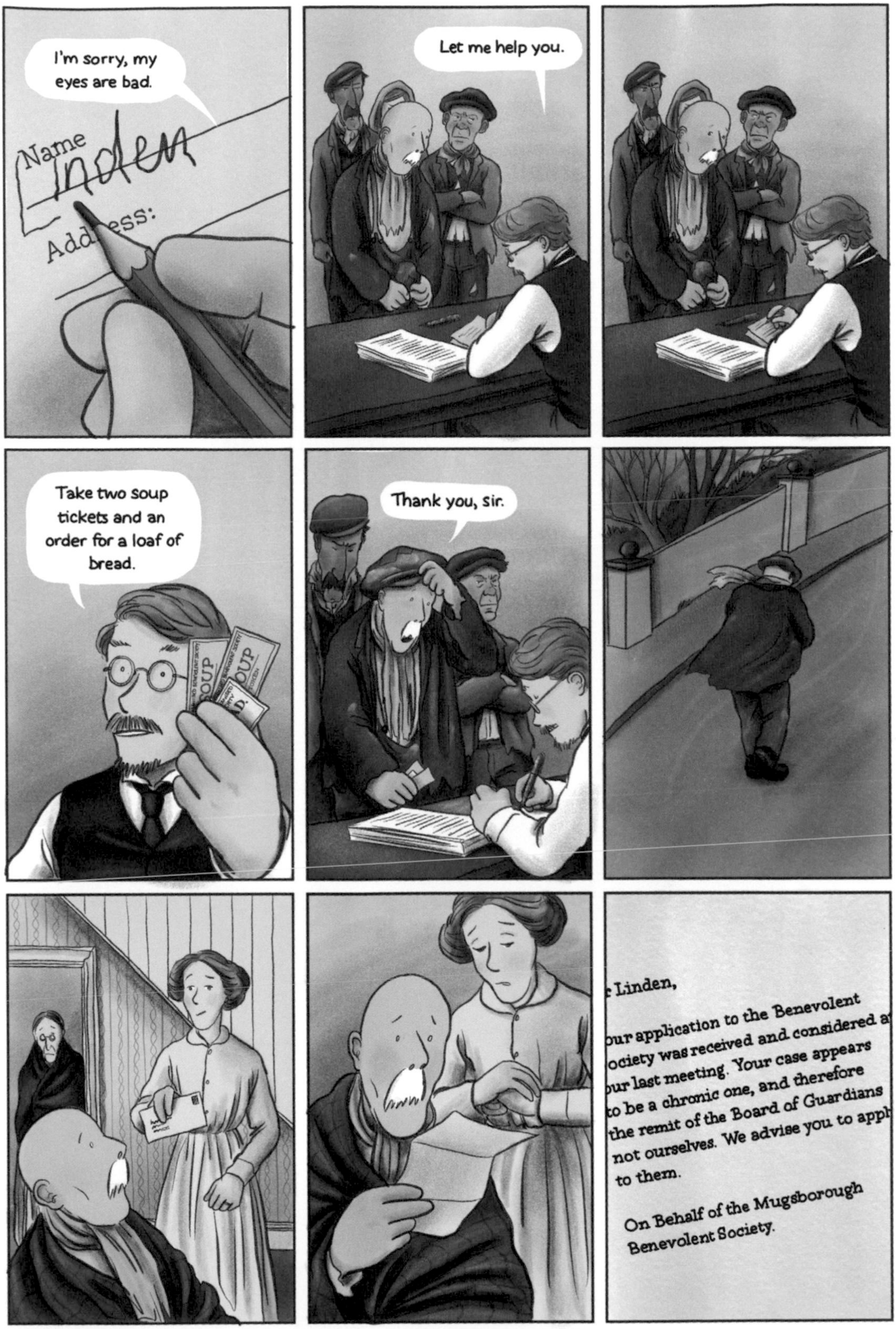
I'm sorry, my eyes are bad.
Name Linden
Address:
Let me help you.
Take two soup tickets and an order for a loaf of bread.
SOUP
SOUP
Thank you, sir.
Linden,
our application to the Benevolent
ociety was received and considered at
our last meeting. Your case appears
to be a chronic one, and therefore
the remit of the Board of Guardians
not ourselves. We advise you to appl
to them.
On Behalf of the Mugsborough
Benevolent Society.

MUGSBOROUGH DISTRICT

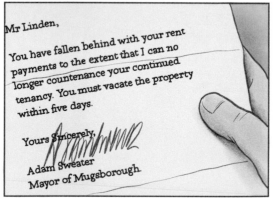

Mr Linden,

You have fallen behind with your rent payments to the extent that I can no longer countenance your continued tenancy. You must vacate the property within five days.

Yours Sincerely,

Adam Sweater
Mayor of Mugsborough.

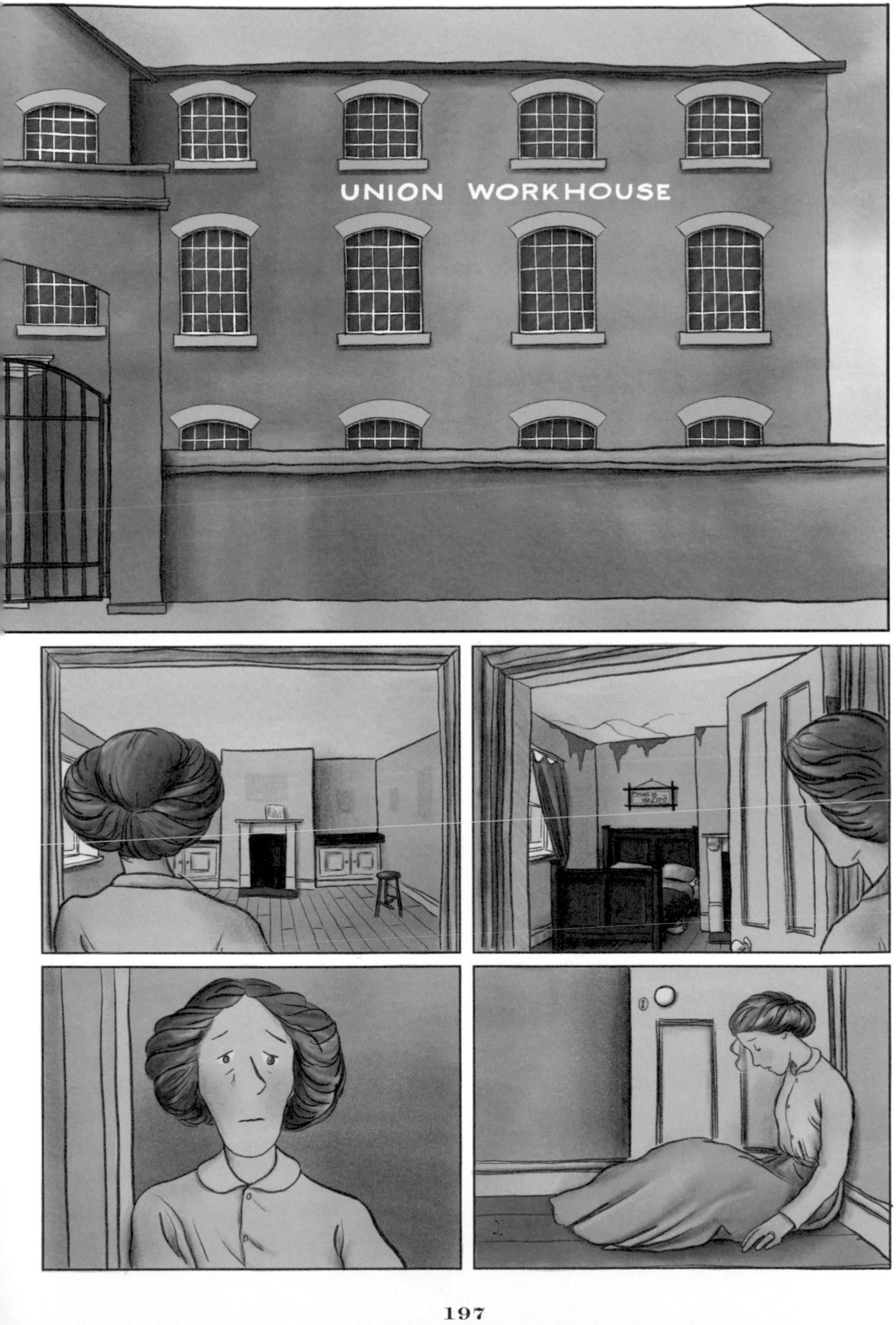
UNION WORKHOUSE
Trust in the Lord

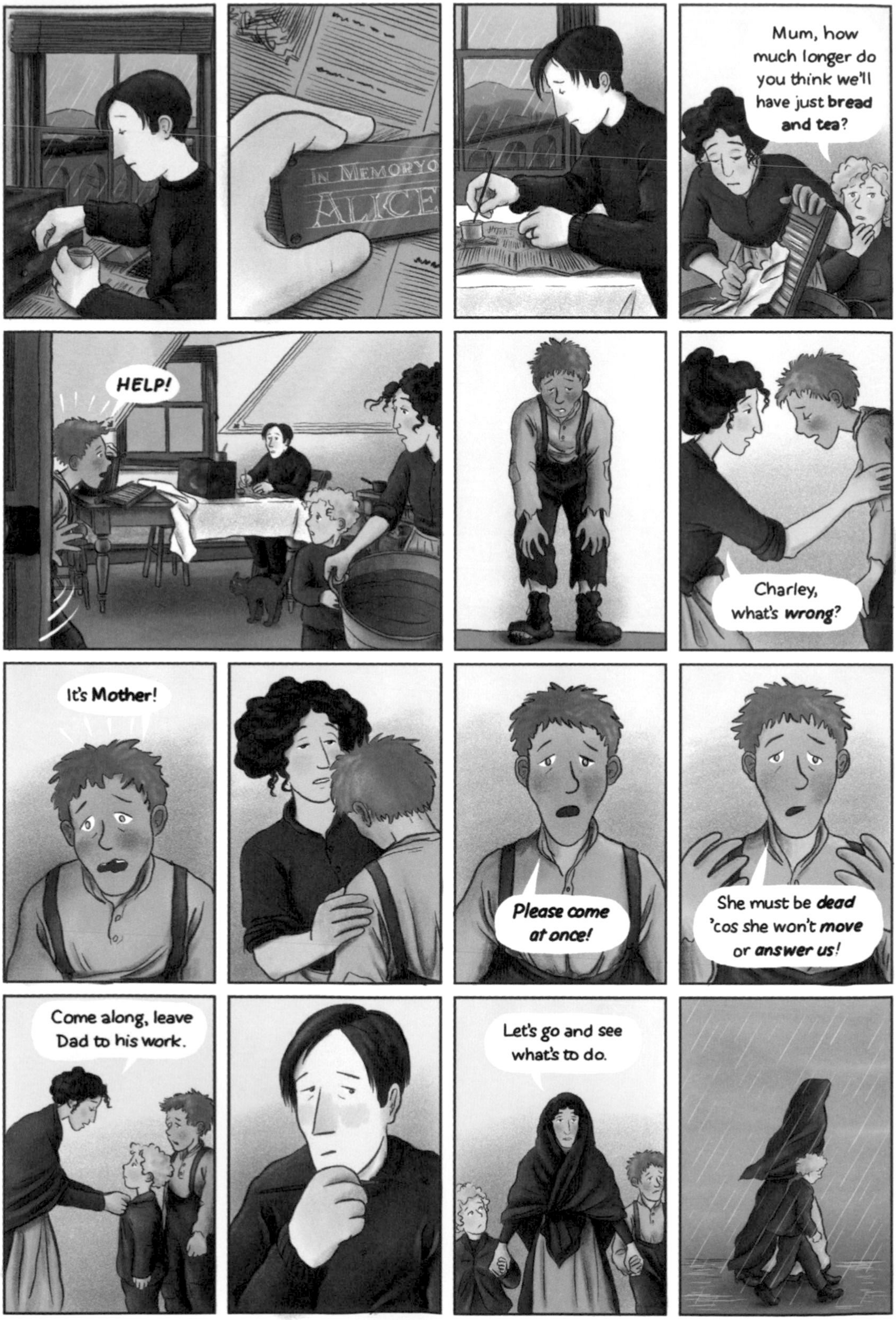
IN MEMORY O
ALICE
Mum, how much longer do you think we'll have just **bread and tea**?
HELP!
Charley, what's ***wrong***?
It's **Mother**!
Please come at once!
She must be ***dead*** 'cos she won't ***move*** or ***answer us***!
Come along, leave Dad to his work.
Let's go and see what's to do.

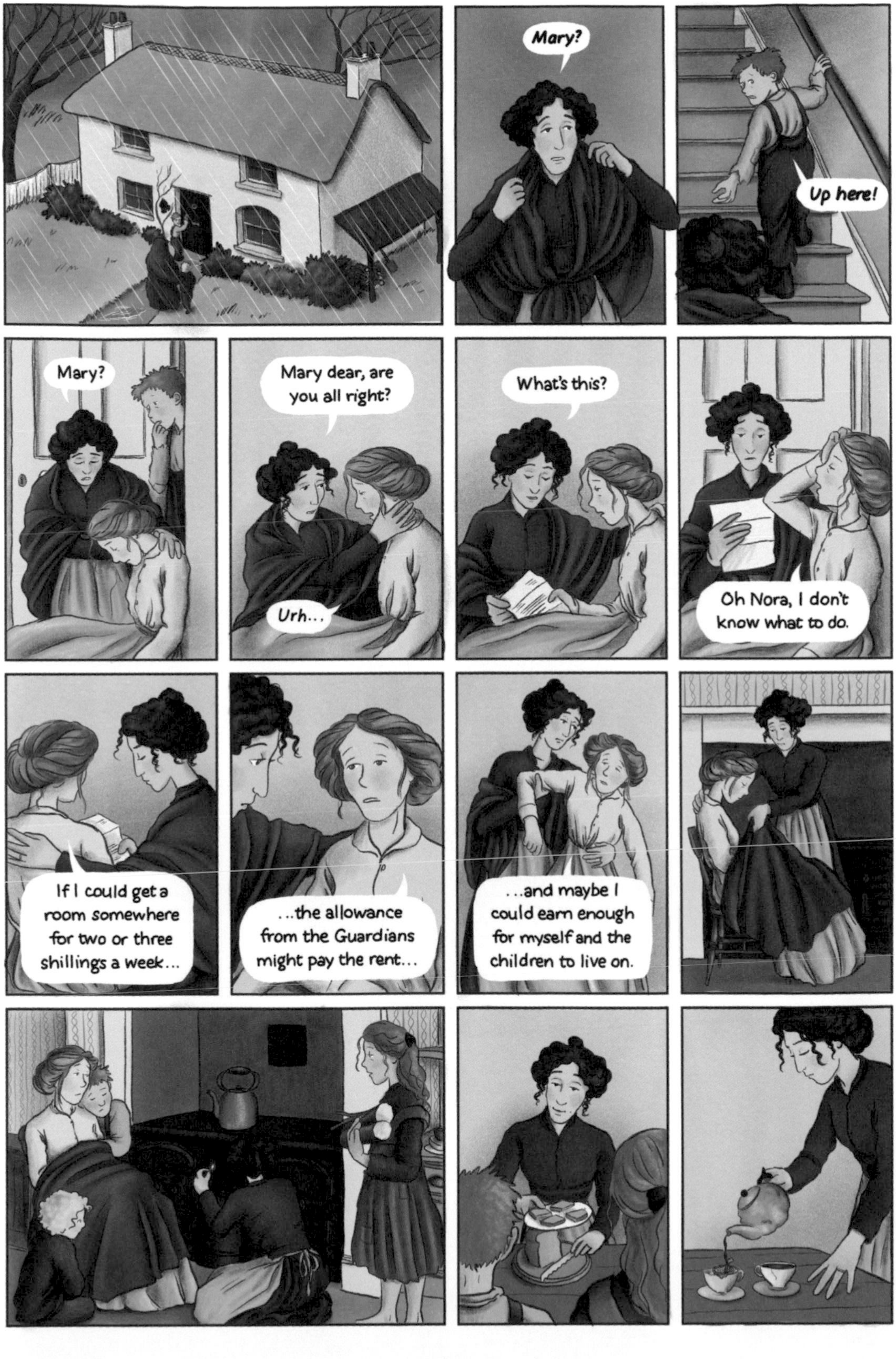
Mary?
Up here!
Mary?
Mary dear, are you all right?
Urh...
What's this?
Oh Nora, I don't know what to do.
If I could get a room somewhere for two or three shillings a week...
...the allowance from the Guardians might pay the rent...
...and maybe I could earn enough for myself and the children to live on.

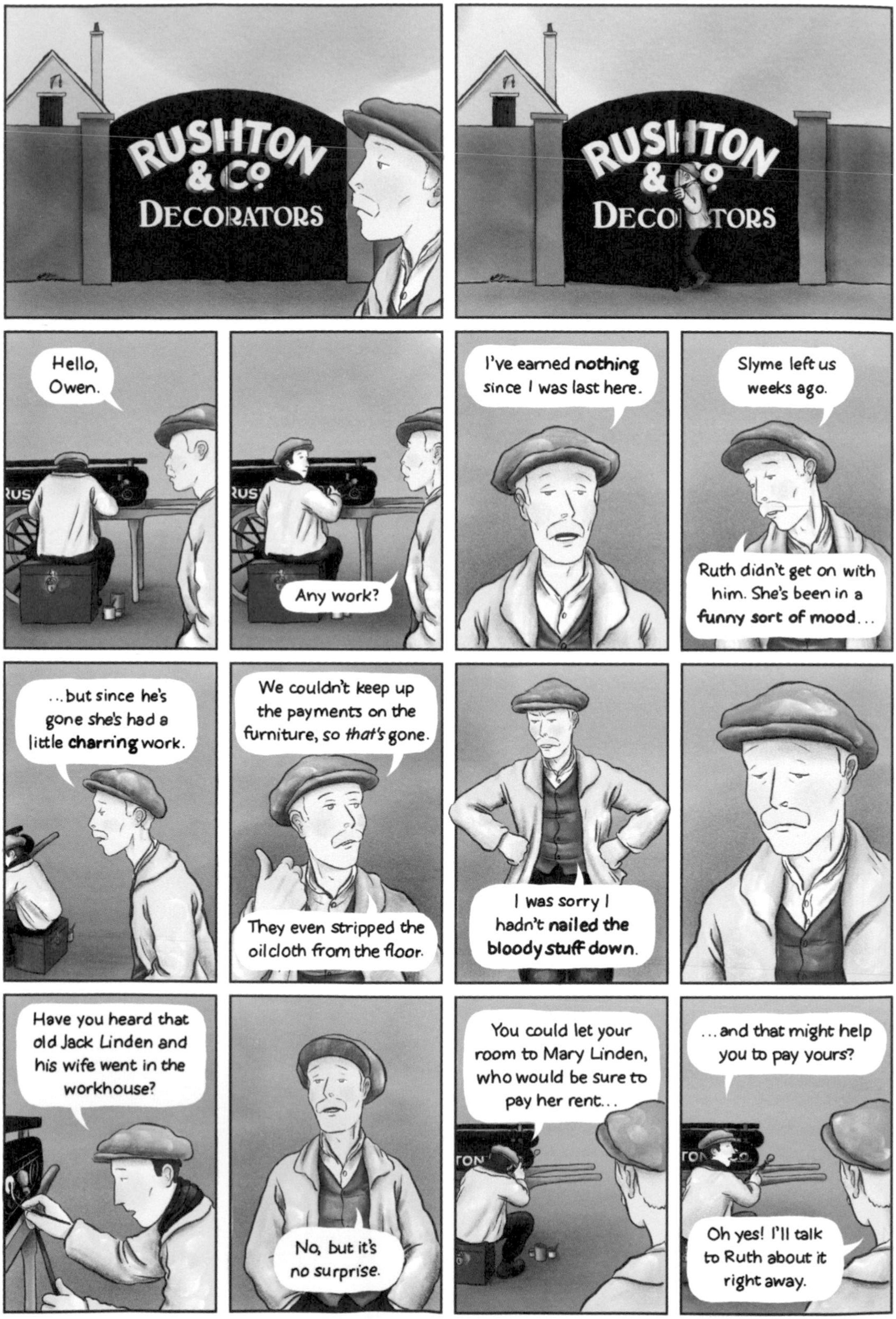
RUSHTON & Co DECORATORS
RUSHTON & Co DECORATORS
Hello, Owen.
Any work?
I've earned **nothing** since I was last here.
Slyme left us weeks ago.
Ruth didn't get on with him. She's been in a **funny sort of mood**...
...but since he's gone *she's* had a little **charring** work.
We couldn't keep up the payments on the furniture, so *that's* gone.
They even stripped the oilcloth from the floor.
I was sorry I hadn't **nailed the bloody stuff down**.
Have you heard that old Jack Linden and his wife went in the workhouse?
No, but it's no surprise.
You could let your room to Mary Linden, who would be sure to pay her rent...
...and that might help you to pay yours?
Oh yes! I'll talk to Ruth about it right away.

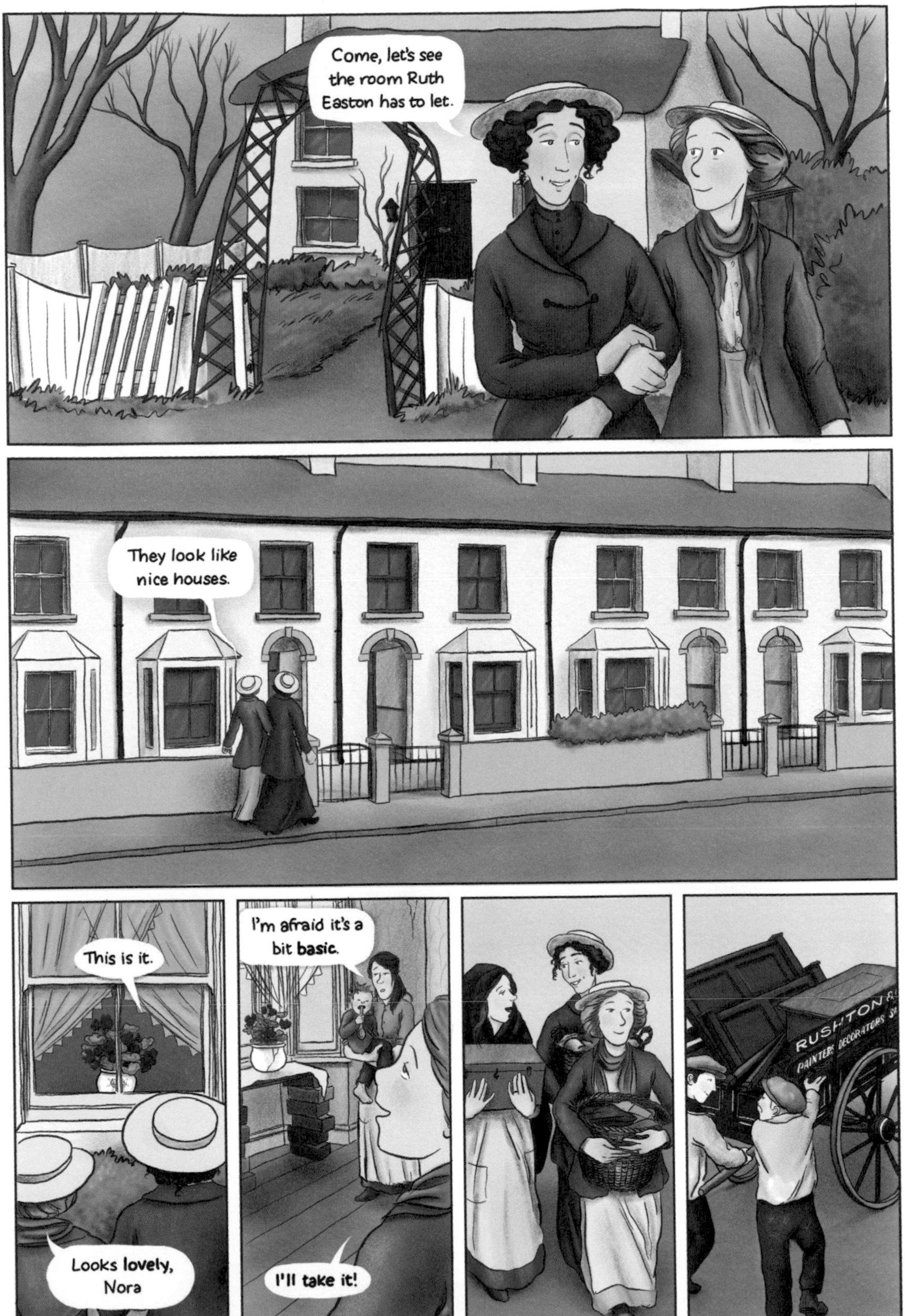
Come, let's see the room Ruth Easton has to let.
They look like nice houses.
This is it.
Looks lovely, Nora
I'm afraid it's a bit basic.
I'll take it!
RUSHTON
PAINTERS DECORATORS

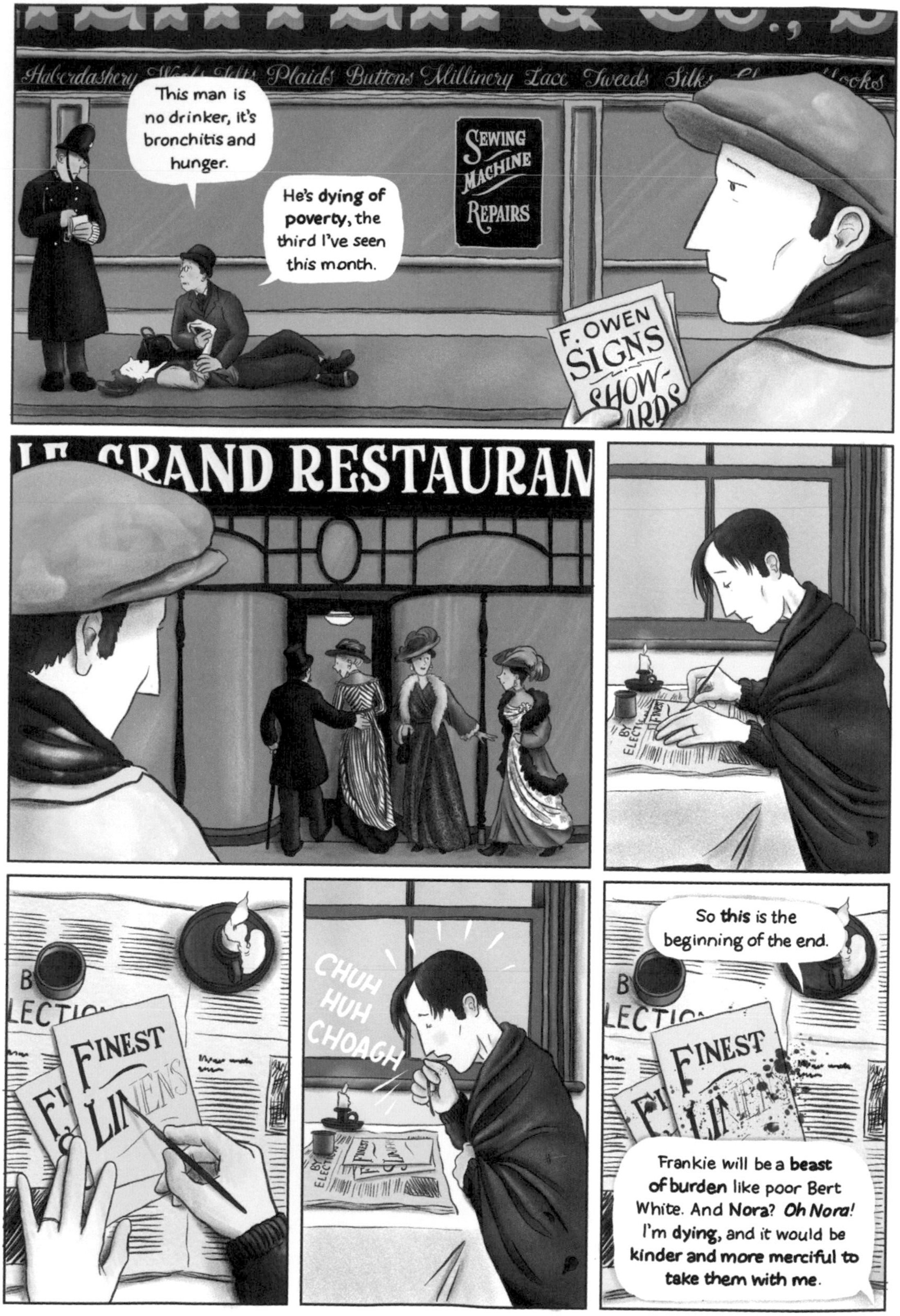
Haberdashery Plaids Buttons Millinery Lace Tweeds Silks
This man is no drinker, it's bronchitis and hunger.
He's dying of poverty, the third I've seen this month.
SEWING MACHINE REPAIRS
F. OWEN SIGNS
GRAND RESTAURAN
FINEST
CHUH HUH CHOAGH
So this is the beginning of the end.
Frankie will be a beast of burden like poor Bert White. And Nora? Oh Nora! I'm dying, and it would be kinder and more merciful to take them with me.

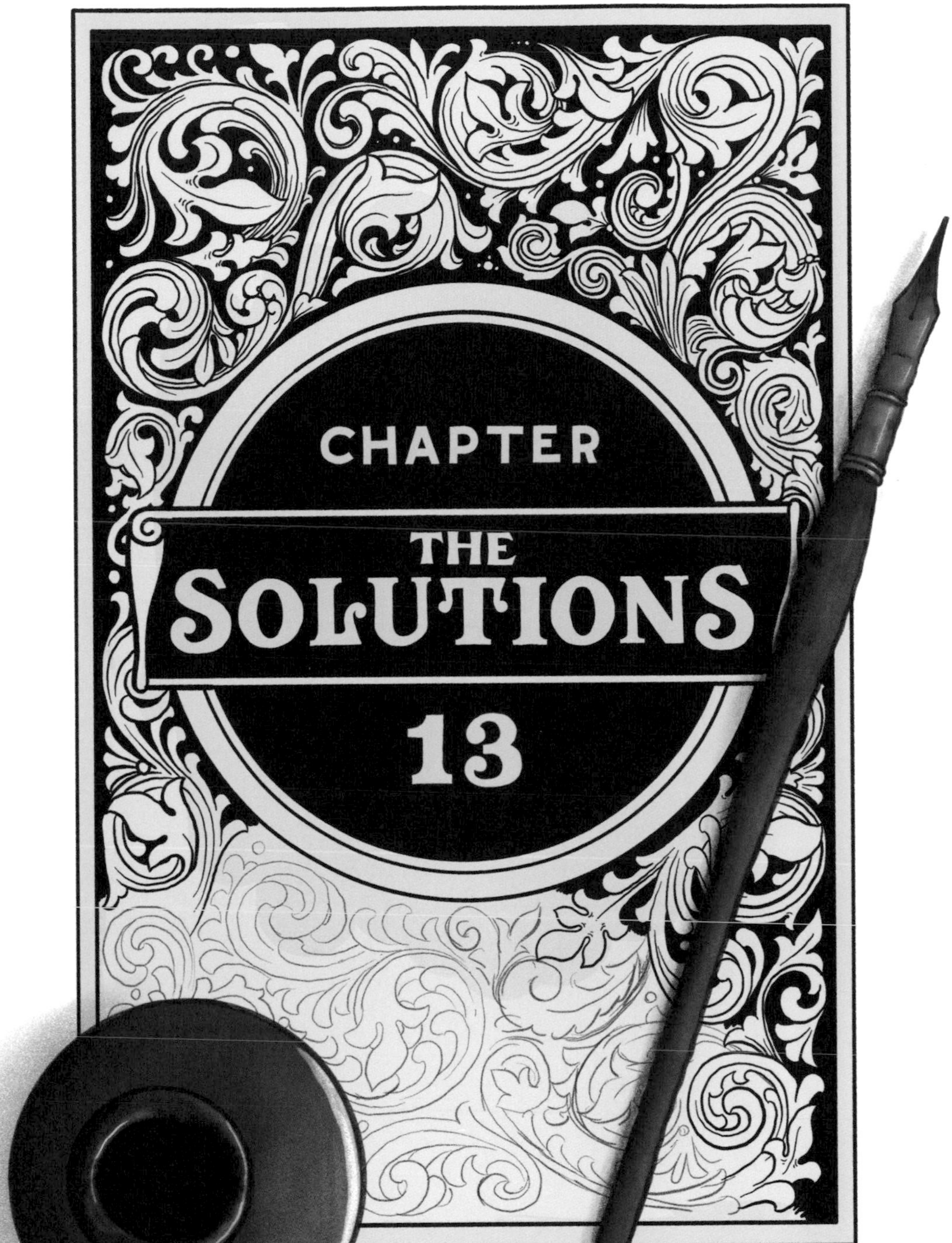
CHAPTER
THE
SOLUTIONS
13

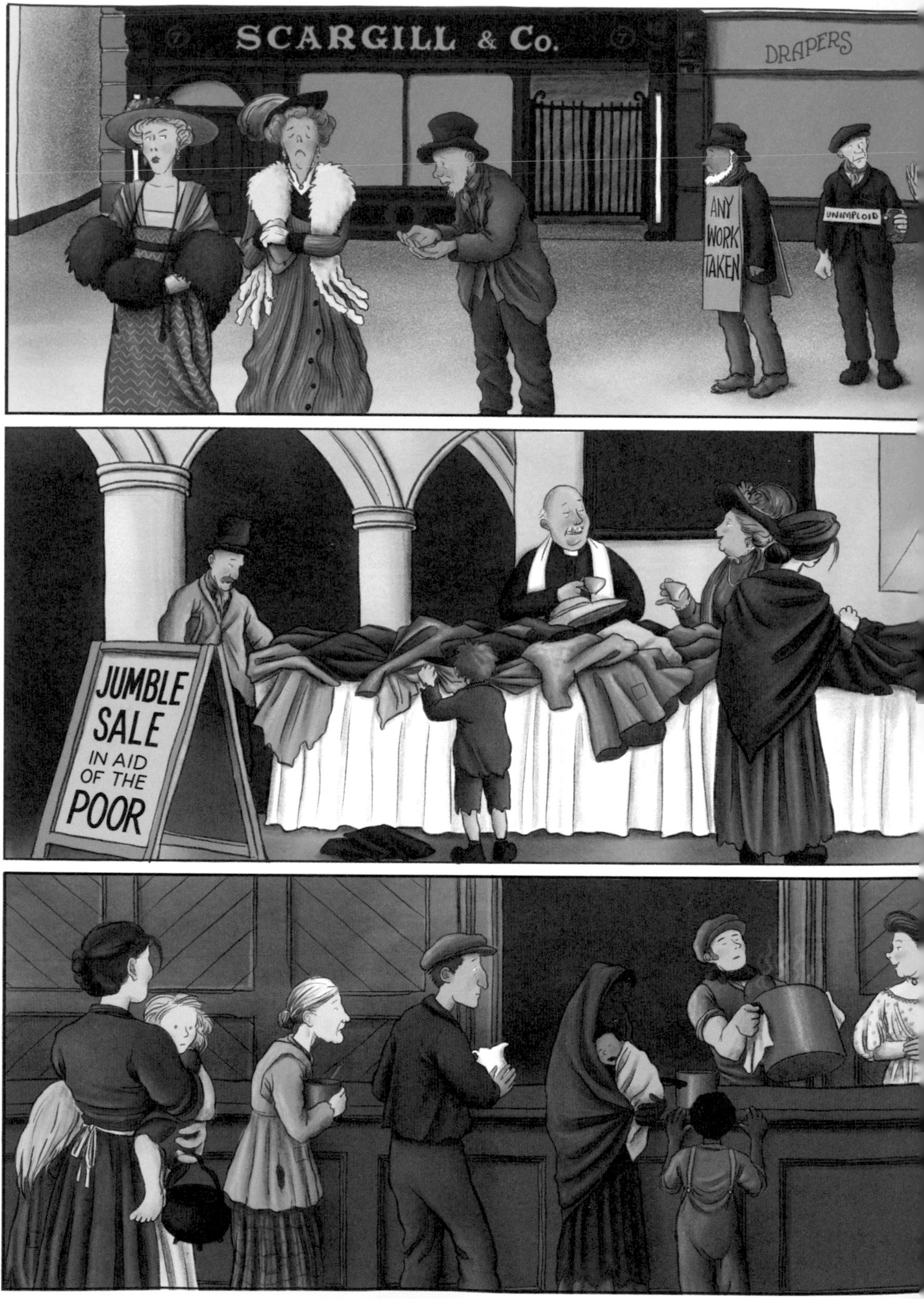
SCARGILL & Co.
DRAPERS
ANY WORK TAKEN
UNIMPLOID
JUMBLE SALE IN AID OF THE POOR

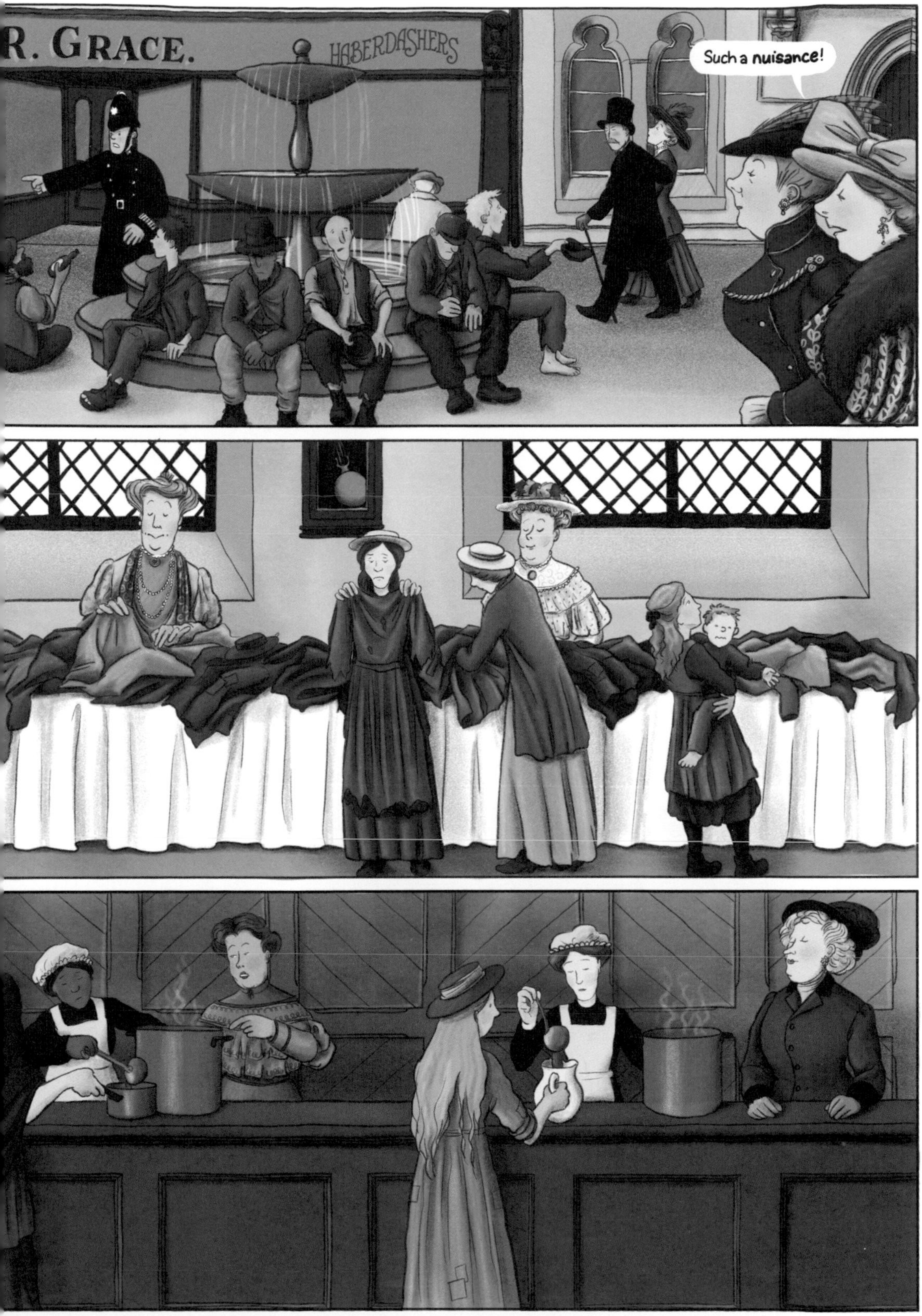
R. GRACE.
HABERDASHERS
Such a nuisance!

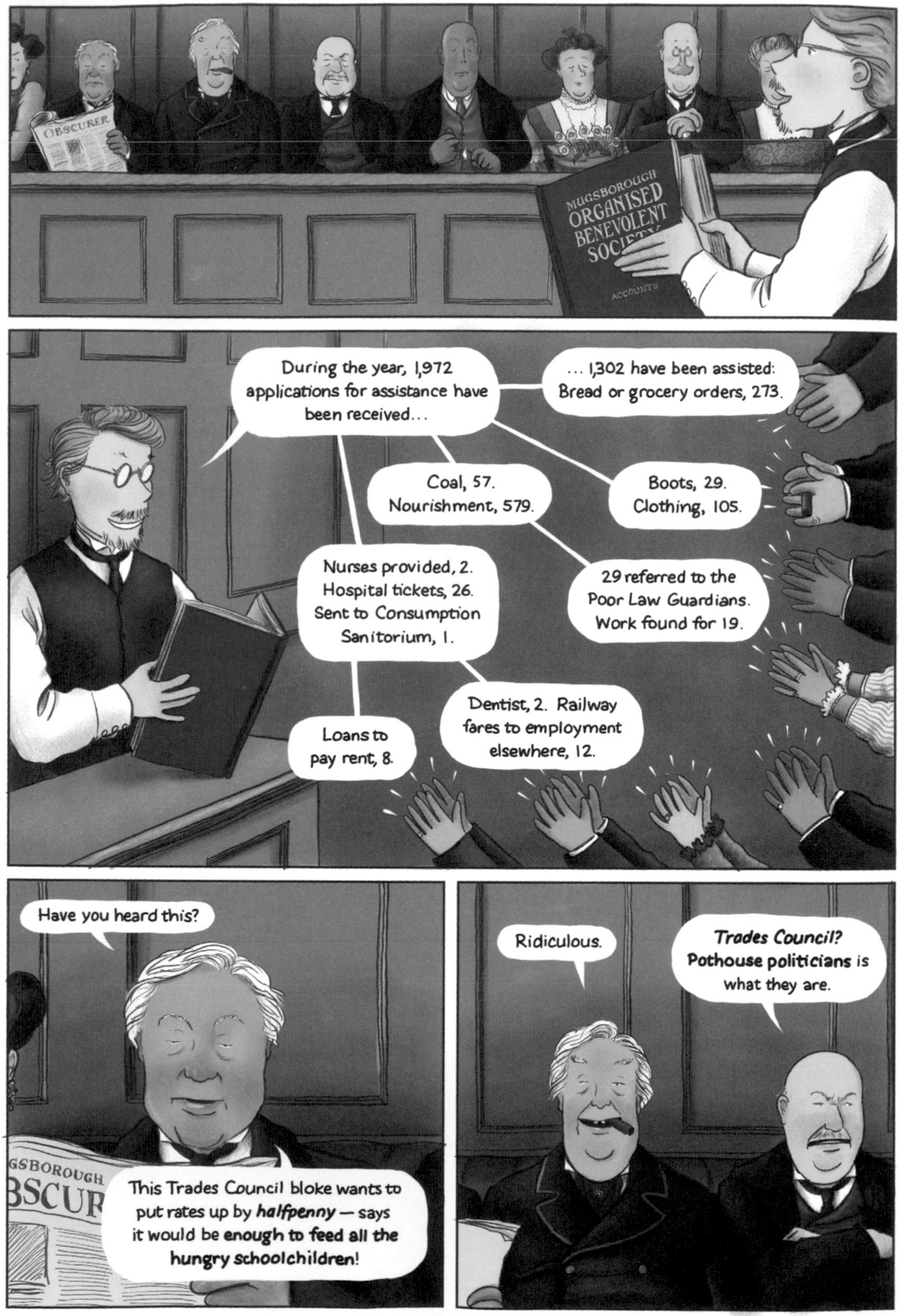
OBSCURER
MUGSBOROUGH ORGANISED BENEVOLENT SOCI
ACCOUNTS
During the year, 1,972 applications for assistance have been received...
... 1,302 have been assisted: Bread or grocery orders, 273.
Coal, 57. Nourishment, 579.
Boots, 29. Clothing, 105.
Nurses provided, 2. Hospital tickets, 26. Sent to Consumption Sanitorium, 1.
29 referred to the Poor Law Guardians. Work found for 19.
Loans to pay rent, 8.
Dentist, 2. Railway fares to employment elsewhere, 12.
Have you heard this?
GSBOROUGH BSCUR
This Trades Council bloke wants to put rates up by *halfpenny* — says it would be **enough to feed all the hungry schoolchildren**!
Ridiculous.
Trades Council? **Pothouse politicians** is what they are.

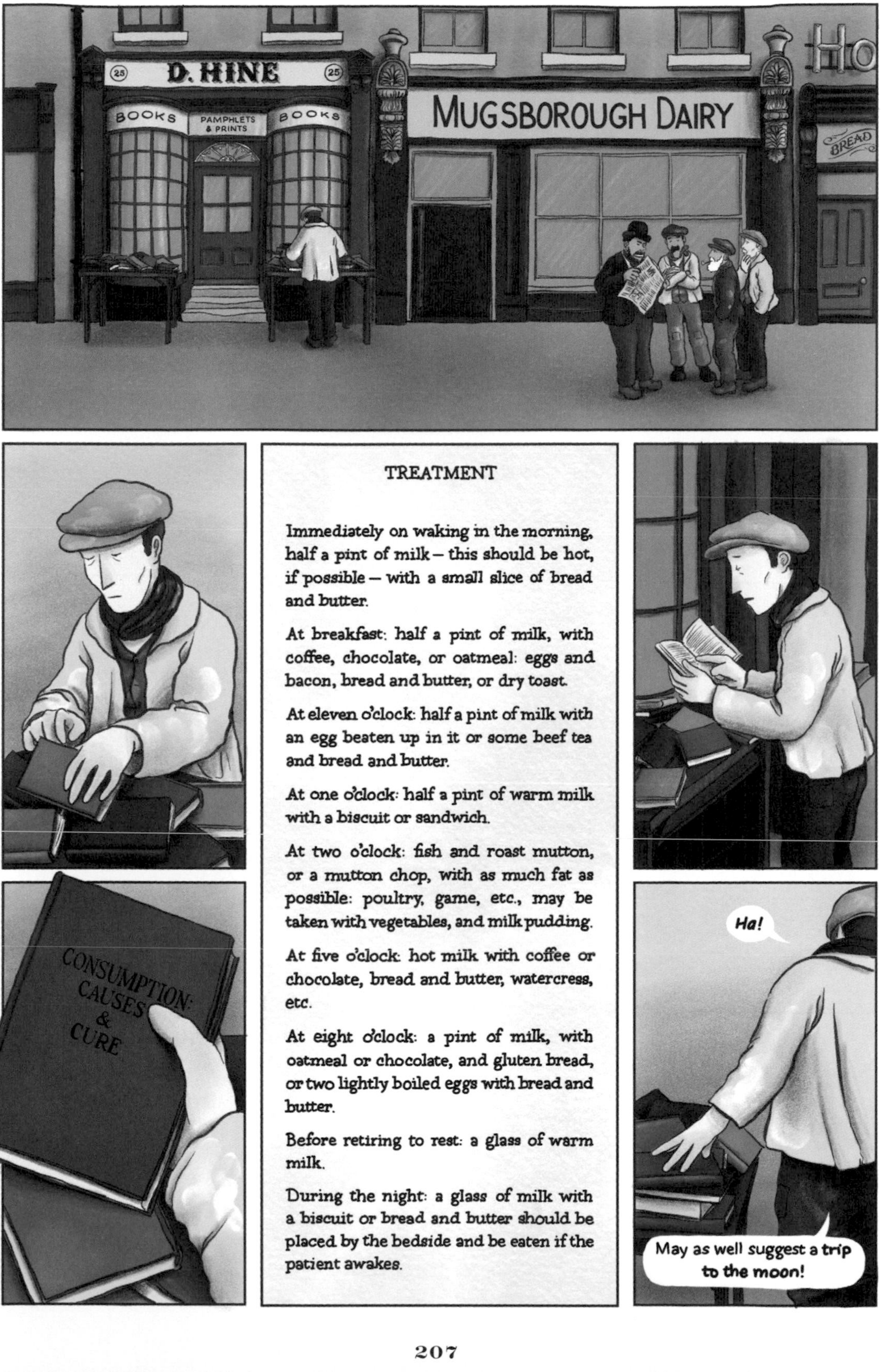
D. HINE
25
BOOKS
PAMPHLETS & PRINTS
BOOKS
MUGSBOROUGH DAIRY
BREAD
TREATMENT
Immediately on waking in the morning, half a pint of milk – this should be hot, if possible – with a small slice of bread and butter.
At breakfast: half a pint of milk, with coffee, chocolate, or oatmeal: eggs and bacon, bread and butter, or dry toast.
At eleven o'clock: half a pint of milk with an egg beaten up in it or some beef tea and bread and butter.
At one o'clock: half a pint of warm milk with a biscuit or sandwich.
At two o'clock: fish and roast mutton, or a mutton chop, with as much fat as possible: poultry, game, etc., may be taken with vegetables, and milk pudding.
At five o'clock: hot milk with coffee or chocolate, bread and butter, watercress, etc.
At eight o'clock: a pint of milk, with oatmeal or chocolate, and gluten bread, or two lightly boiled eggs with bread and butter.
Before retiring to rest: a glass of warm milk.
During the night: a glass of milk with a biscuit or bread and butter should be placed by the bedside and be eaten if the patient awakes.
CONSUMPTION: CAUSES & CURE
Ha!
May as well suggest a trip to the moon!

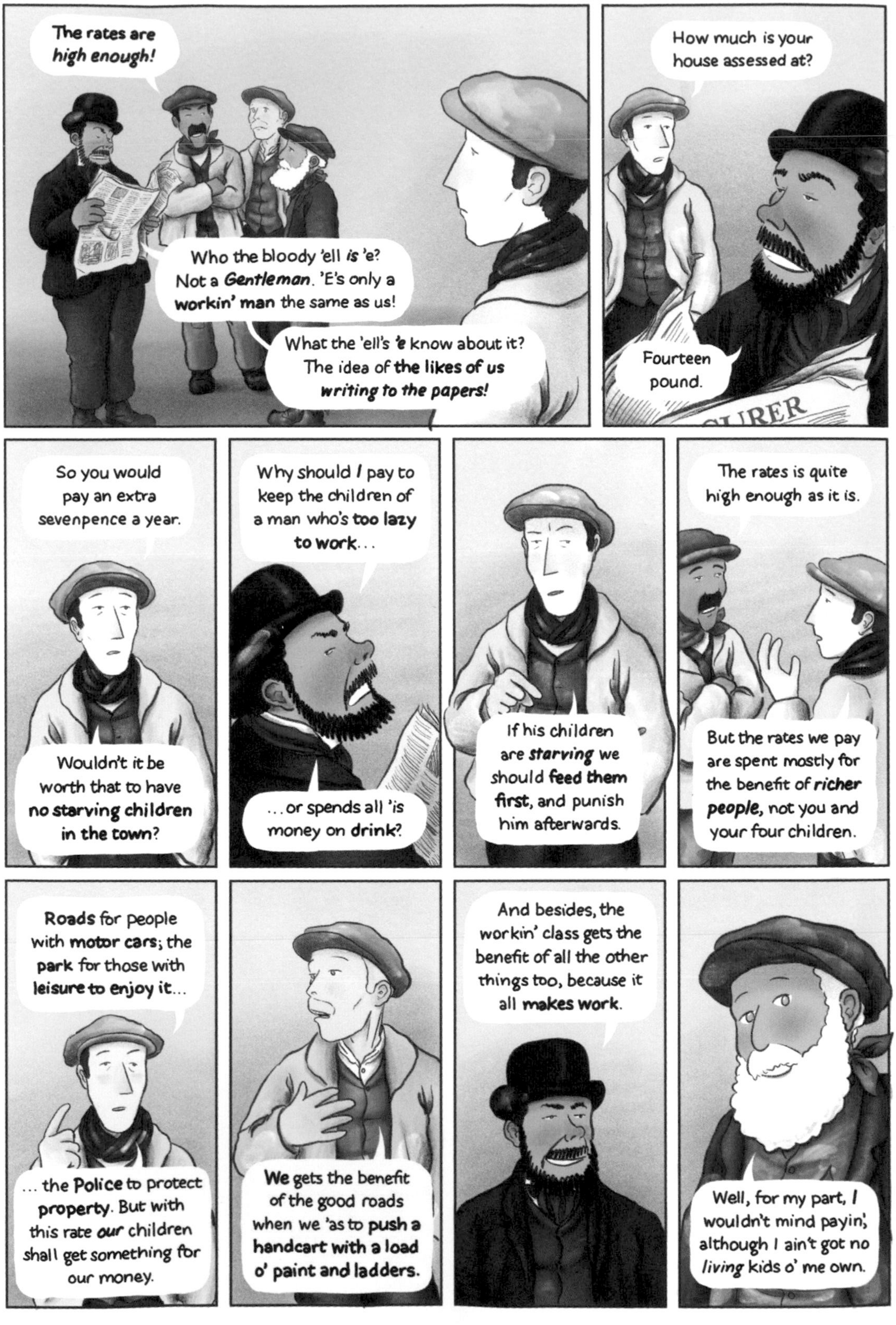
The rates are high enough!
Who the bloody 'ell is 'e? Not a Gentleman. 'E's only a workin' man the same as us!
What the 'ell's 'e know about it? The idea of the likes of us writing to the papers!
How much is your house assessed at?
Fourteen pound.
RER
So you would pay an extra sevenpence a year.
Wouldn't it be worth that to have no starving children in the town?
Why should I pay to keep the children of a man who's too lazy to work...
...or spends all 'is money on drink?
If his children are starving we should feed them first, and punish him afterwards.
The rates is quite high enough as it is.
But the rates we pay are spent mostly for the benefit of richer people, not you and your four children.
Roads for people with motor cars; the park for those with leisure to enjoy it...
...the Police to protect property. But with this rate our children shall get something for our money.
We gets the benefit of the good roads when we 'as to push a handcart with a load o' paint and ladders.
And besides, the workin' class gets the benefit of all the other things too, because it all makes work.
Well, for my part, I wouldn't mind payin', although I ain't got no living kids o' me own.

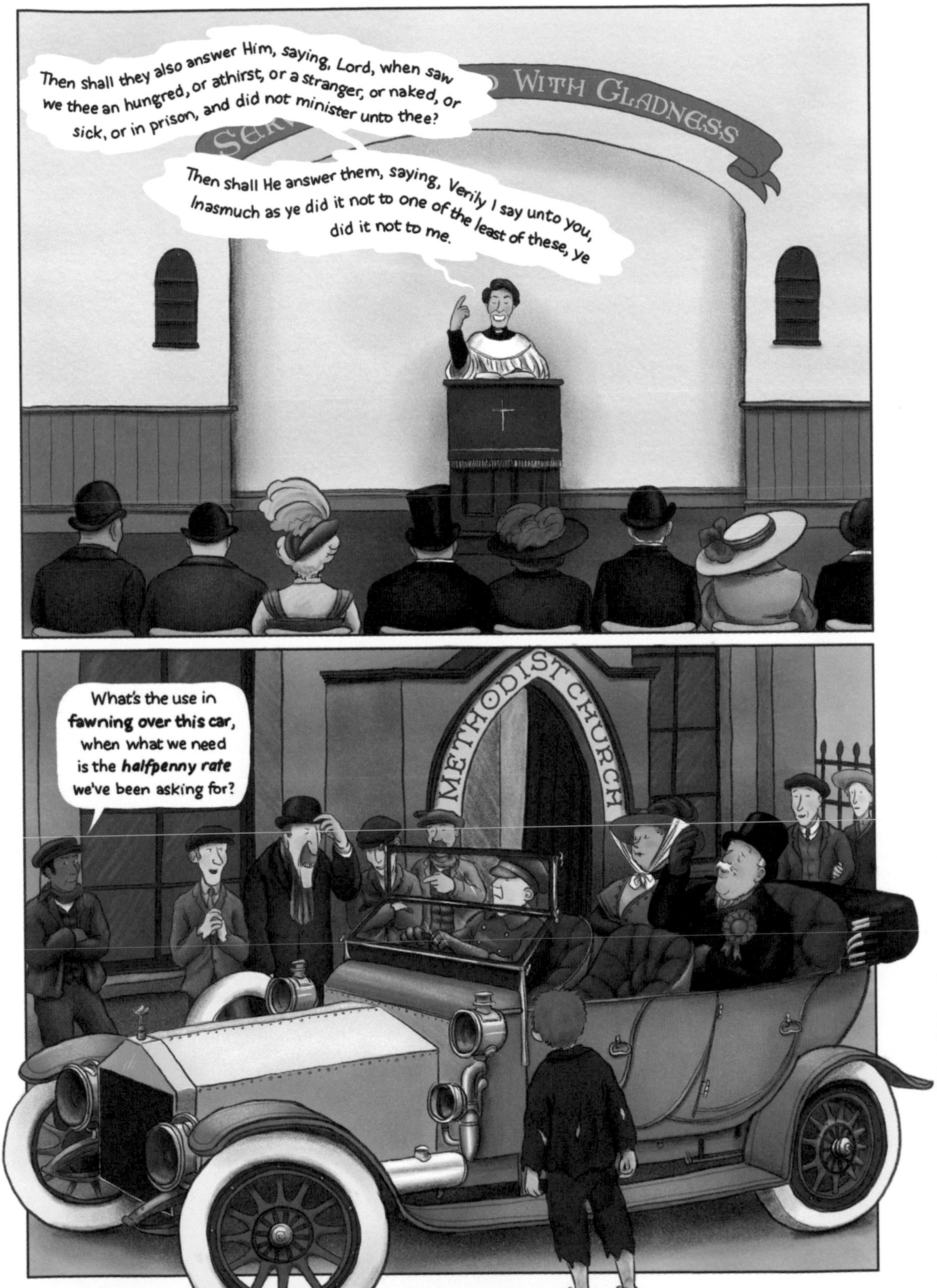
Then shall they also answer Him, saying, Lord, when saw we thee an hungred, or athirst, or a stranger, or naked, or sick, or in prison, and did not minister unto thee?
WITH GLADNESS
Then shall He answer them, saying, Verily I say unto you, Inasmuch as ye did it not to one of the least of these, ye did it not to me.
METHODIST CHURCH
What's the use in **fawning over this car**, when what we need is the ***halfpenny rate*** we've been asking for?

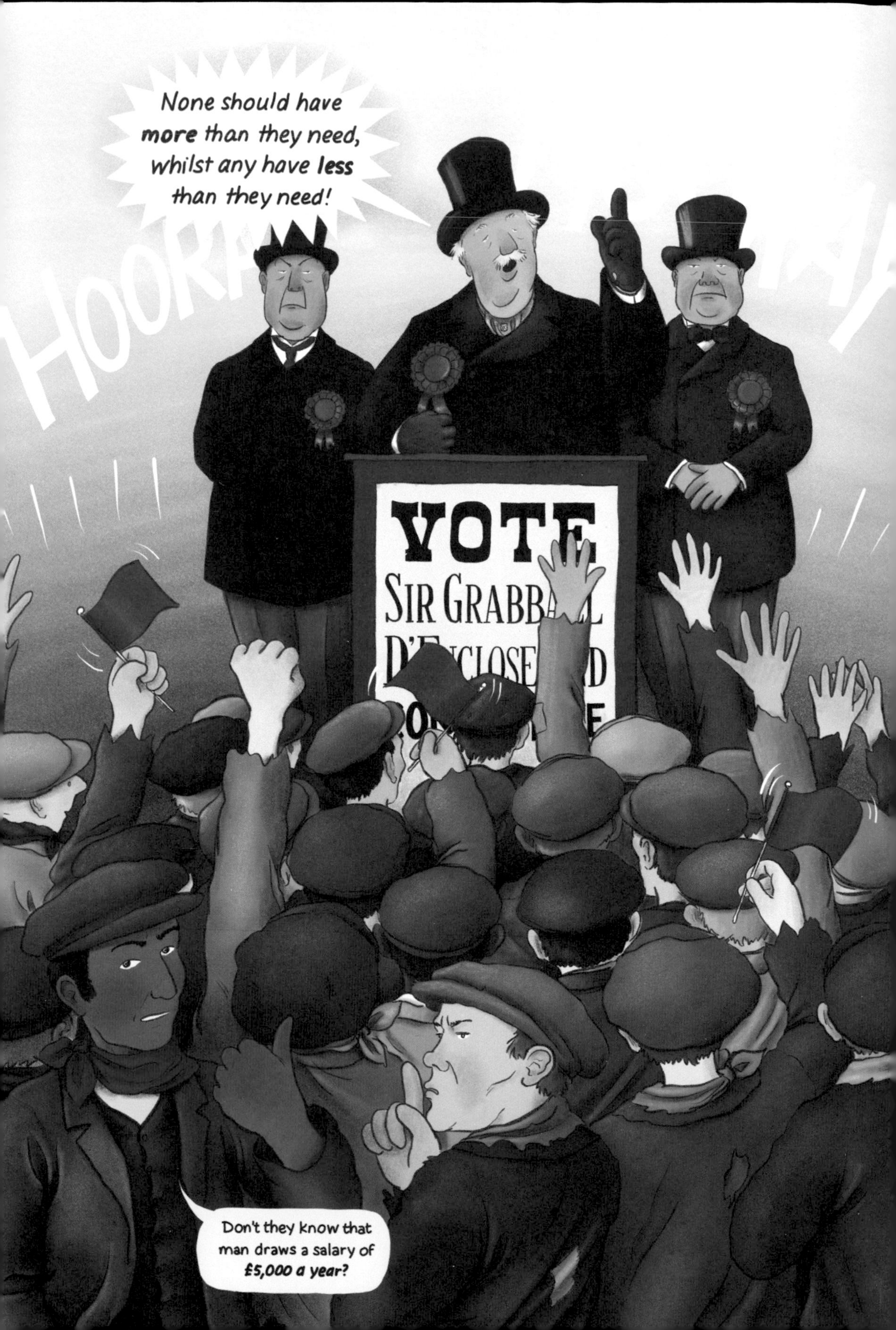
None should have **more** than they need, whilst any have **less** than they need!
VOTE
Don't they know that man draws a salary of ***£5,000 a year?***

14

THE
MEETINGS

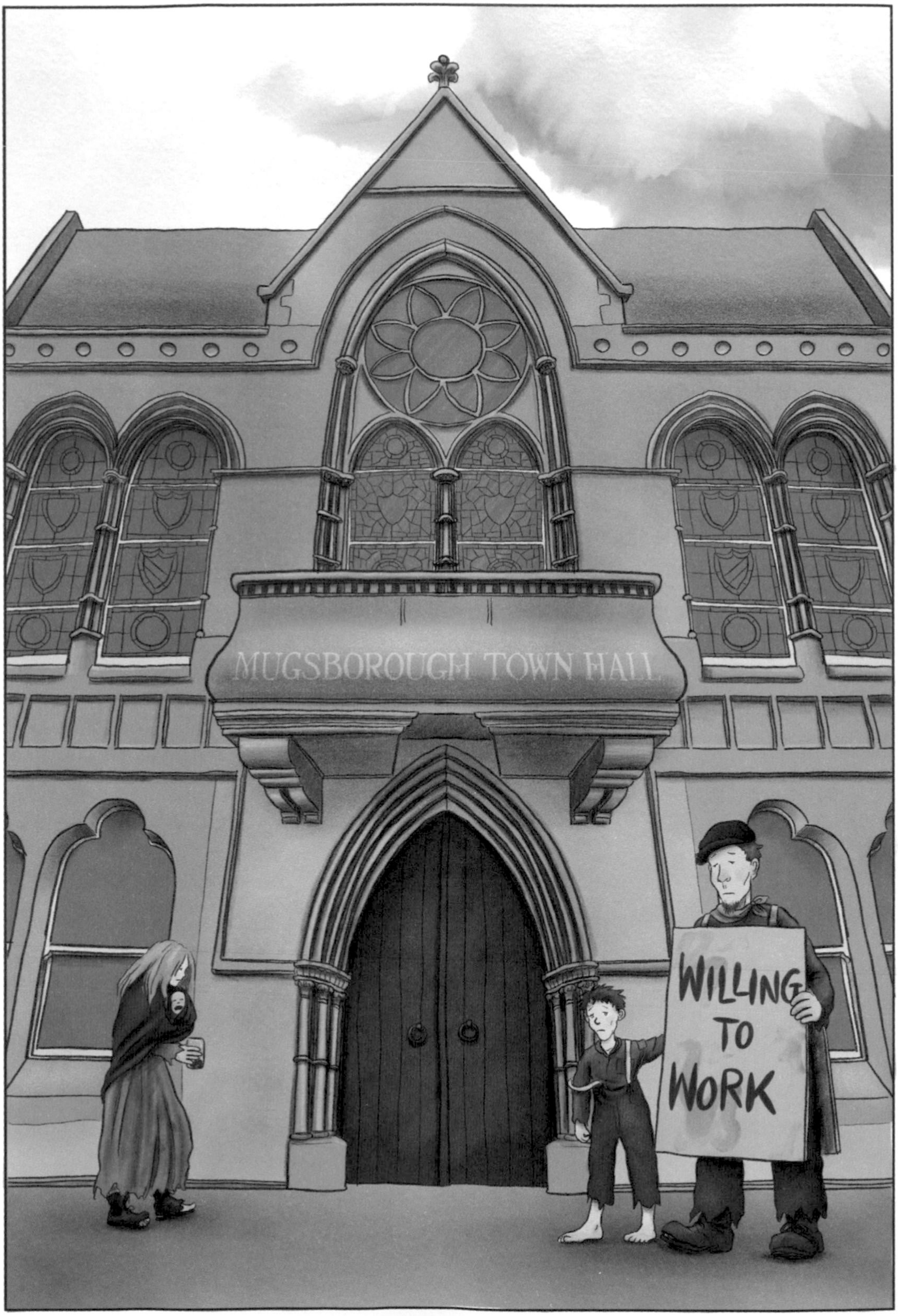
MUGSBOROUGH TOWN HALL
WILLING
TO
WORK

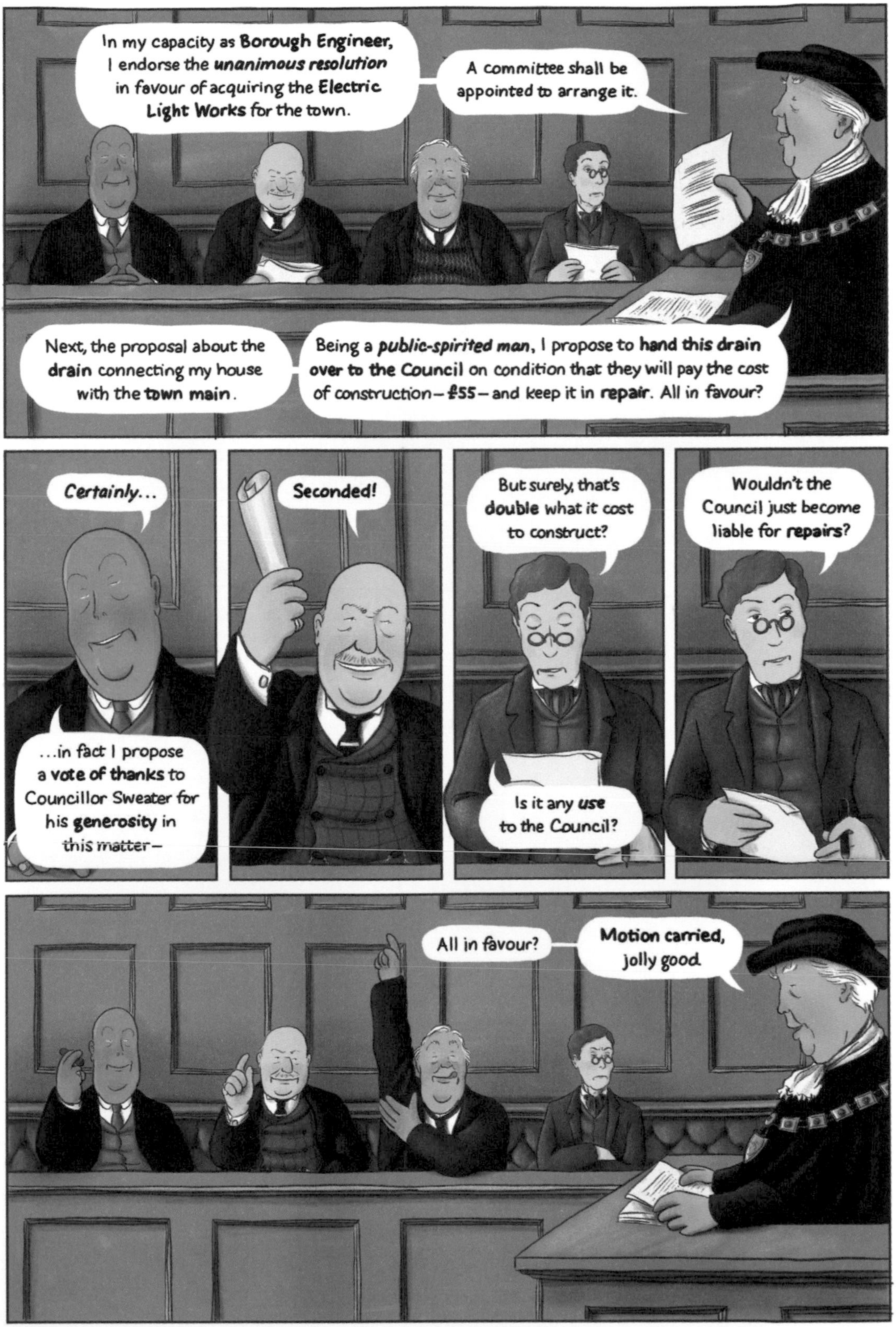
In my capacity as Borough Engineer, I endorse the unanimous resolution in favour of acquiring the Electric Light Works for the town.
A committee shall be appointed to arrange it.
Next, the proposal about the drain connecting my house with the town main.
Being a public-spirited man, I propose to hand this drain over to the Council on condition that they will pay the cost of construction – £55 – and keep it in repair. All in favour?
Certainly...
...in fact I propose a vote of thanks to Councillor Sweater for his generosity in this matter –
Seconded!
But surely, that's double what it cost to construct?
Is it any use to the Council?
Wouldn't the Council just become liable for repairs?
All in favour?
Motion carried, jolly good.

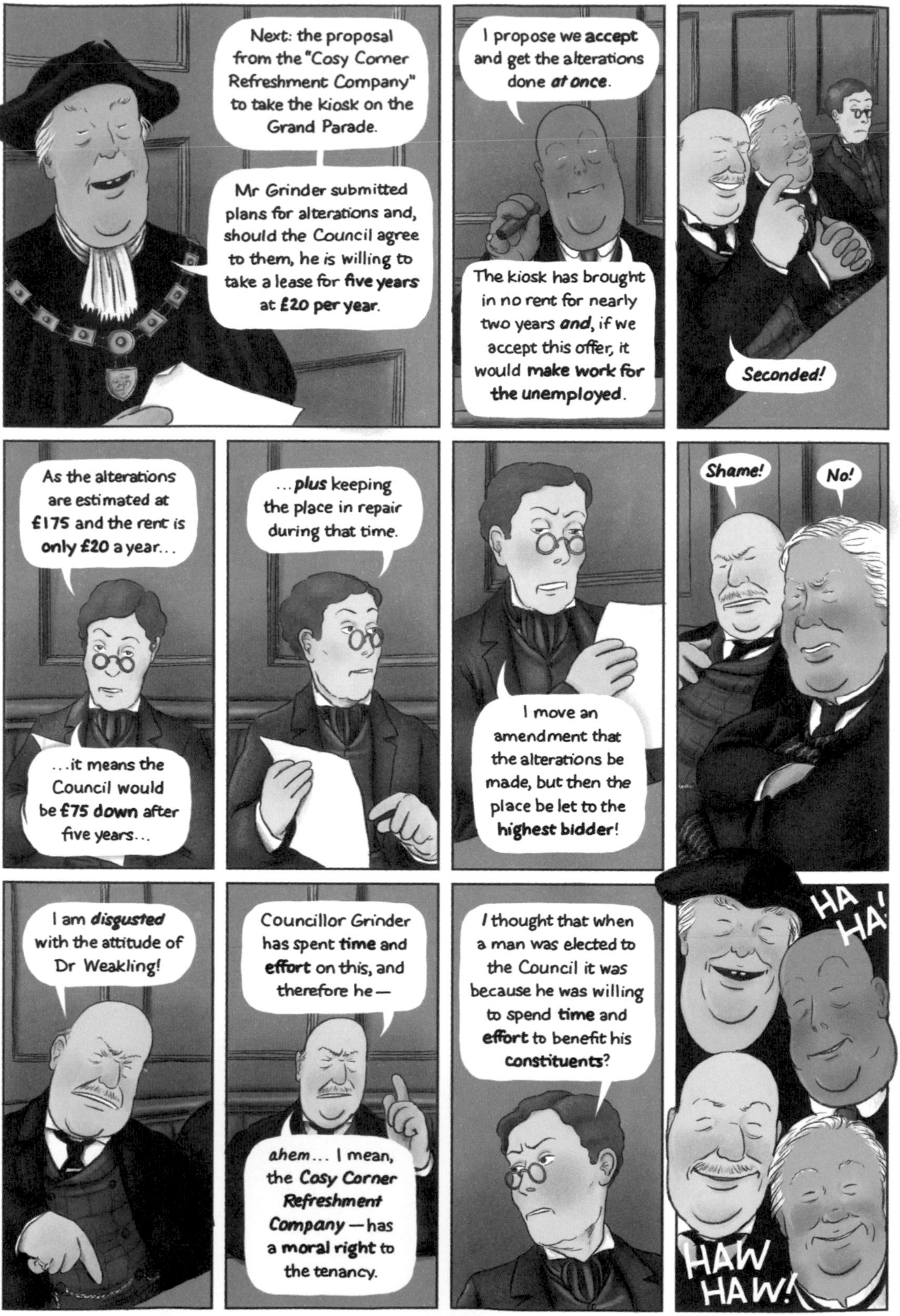
Next: the proposal from the "Cosy Corner Refreshment Company" to take the kiosk on the Grand Parade.
Mr Grinder submitted plans for alterations and, should the Council agree to them, he is willing to take a lease for five years at £20 per year.
I propose we accept and get the alterations done at once.
The kiosk has brought in no rent for nearly two years and, if we accept this offer, it would make work for the unemployed.
Seconded!
As the alterations are estimated at £175 and the rent is only £20 a year...
...it means the Council would be £75 down after five years...
...plus keeping the place in repair during that time.
I move an amendment that the alterations be made, but then the place be let to the highest bidder!
Shame!
No!
I am disgusted with the attitude of Dr Weakling!
Councillor Grinder has spent time and effort on this, and therefore he—
ahem... I mean, the Cosy Corner Refreshment Company—has a moral right to the tenancy.
I thought that when a man was elected to the Council it was because he was willing to spend time and effort to benefit his constituents?
HA HA!
HAW HAW!

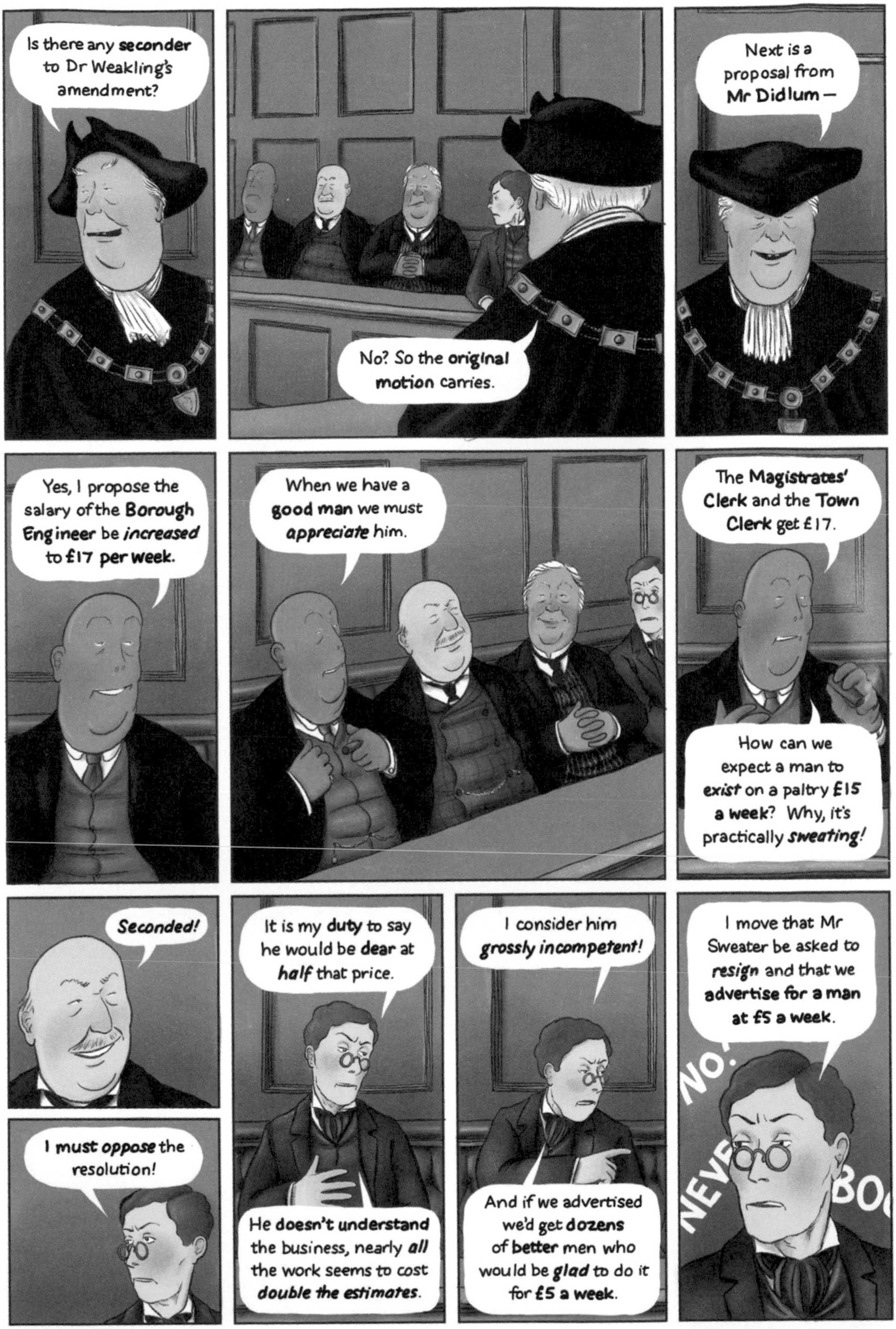
Is there any seconder to Dr Weakling's amendment?
No? So the original motion carries.
Next is a proposal from Mr Didlum —
Yes, I propose the salary of the Borough Engineer be increased to £17 per week.
When we have a good man we must appreciate him.
The Magistrates' Clerk and the Town Clerk get £17.
How can we expect a man to exist on a paltry £15 a week? Why, it's practically sweating!
Seconded!
I must oppose the resolution!
It is my duty to say he would be dear at half that price.
He doesn't understand the business, nearly all the work seems to cost double the estimates.
I consider him grossly incompetent!
And if we advertised we'd get dozens of better men who would be glad to do it for £5 a week.
I move that Mr Sweater be asked to resign and that we advertise for a man at £5 a week.

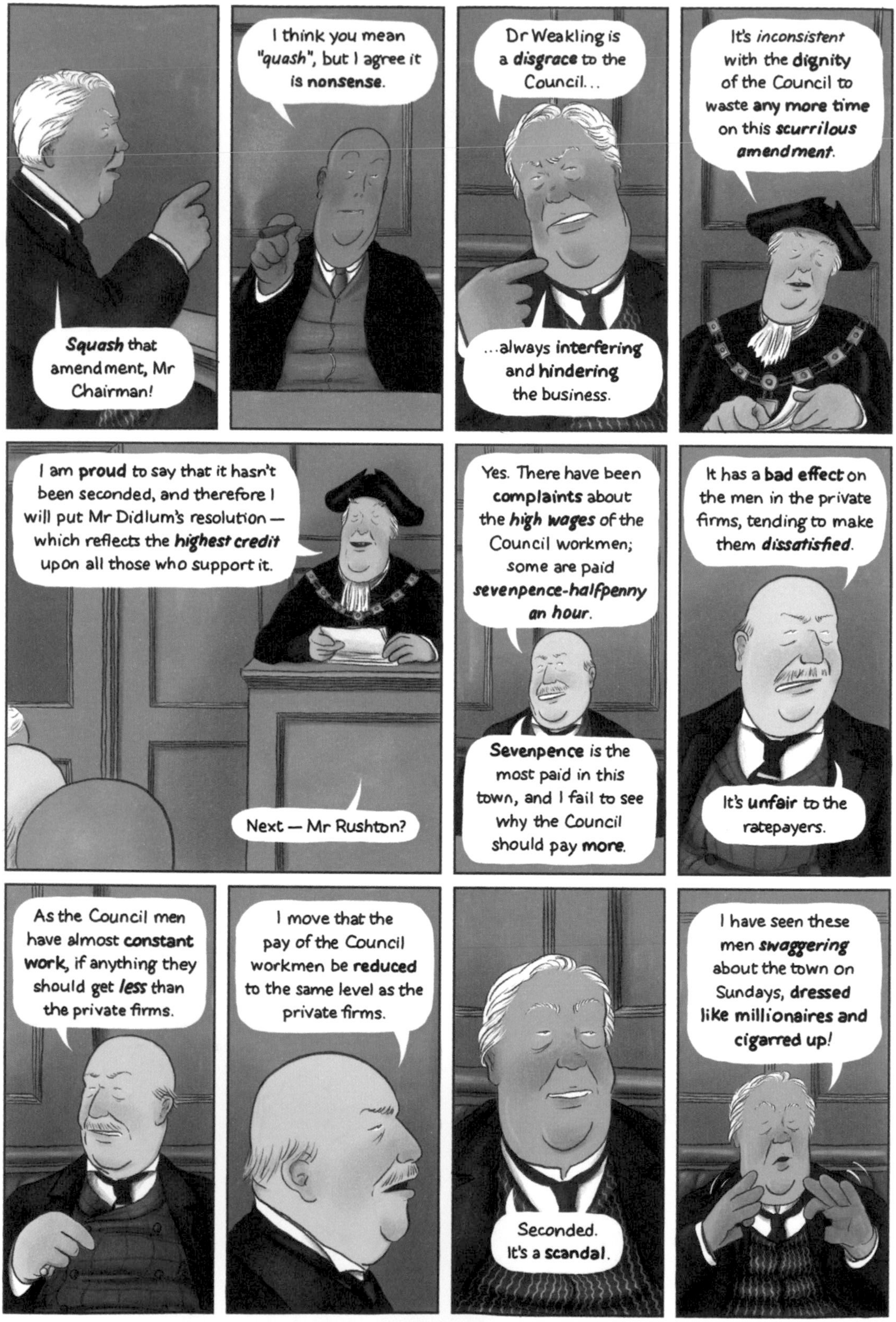

Squash that amendment, Mr Chairman!
I think you mean "quash", but I agree it is nonsense.
Dr Weakling is a disgrace to the Council...
...always interfering and hindering the business.
It's inconsistent with the dignity of the Council to waste any more time on this scurrilous amendment.
I am proud to say that it hasn't been seconded, and therefore I will put Mr Didlum's resolution — which reflects the highest credit upon all those who support it.
Next — Mr Rushton?
Yes. There have been complaints about the high wages of the Council workmen; some are paid sevenpence-halfpenny an hour.
Sevenpence is the most paid in this town, and I fail to see why the Council should pay more.
It has a bad effect on the men in the private firms, tending to make them dissatisfied.
It's unfair to the ratepayers.
As the Council men have almost constant work, if anything they should get less than the private firms.
I move that the pay of the Council workmen be reduced to the same level as the private firms.
Seconded. It's a scandal.
I have seen these men swaggering about the town on Sundays, dressed like millionaires and cigarred up!

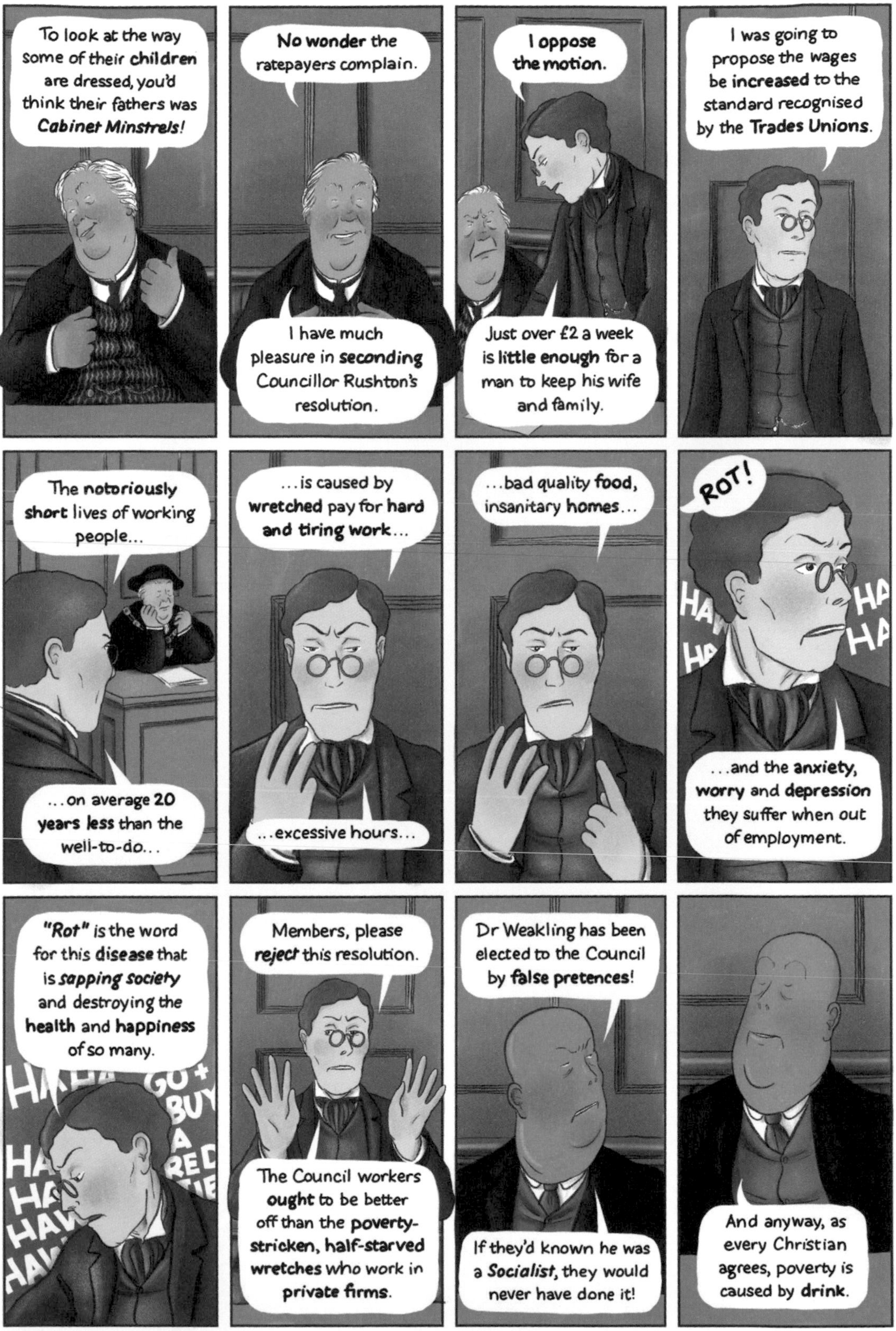
To look at the way some of their **children** are dressed, you'd think their fathers was ***Cabinet Minstrels***!
No wonder the ratepayers complain.
I have much pleasure in **seconding** Councillor Rushton's resolution.
I oppose the motion.
Just over £2 a week is **little enough** for a man to keep his wife and family.
I was going to propose the wages be **increased** to the standard recognised by the **Trades Unions**.
The **notoriously short** lives of working people...
...on average **20 years less** than the well-to-do...
...is caused by **wretched** pay for **hard and tiring work**...
...excessive hours...
...bad quality **food**, insanitary **homes**...
ROT!
...and the **anxiety**, **worry** and **depression** they suffer when out of employment.
"Rot" is the word for this **disease** that is ***sapping society*** and destroying the **health** and **happiness** of so many.
Members, please ***reject*** this resolution.
The Council workers **ought** to be better off than the **poverty-stricken**, **half-starved wretches** who work in **private firms**.
Dr Weakling has been elected to the Council by **false pretences**!
If they'd known he was a ***Socialist***, they would never have done it!
And anyway, as every Christian agrees, poverty is caused by **drink**.

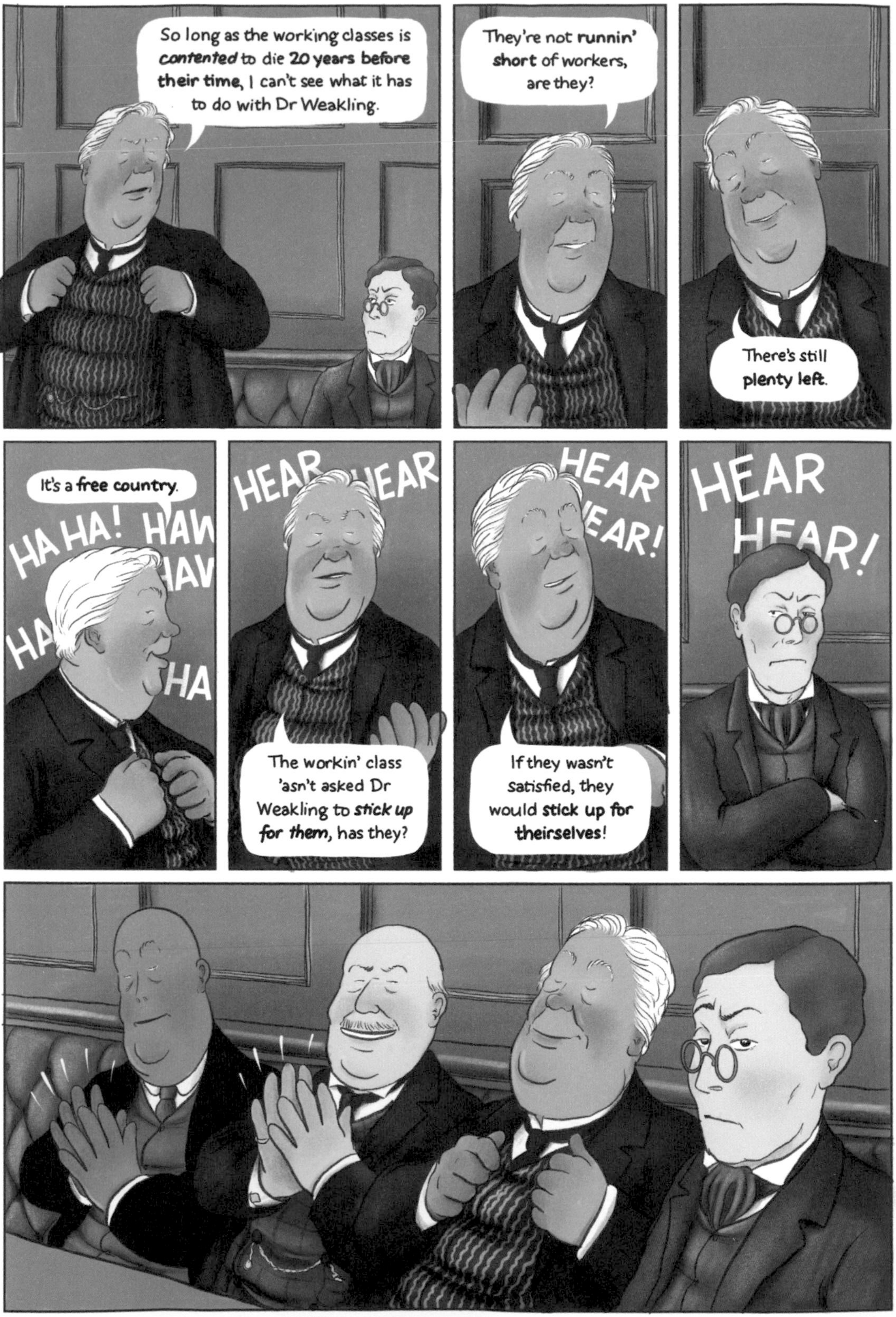
So long as the working classes is contented to die 20 years before their time, I can't see what it has to do with Dr Weakling.
They're not runnin' short of workers, are they?
There's still plenty left.
It's a free country.
HA HA! HAW HAW
HA
HA
HEAR HEAR
The workin' class 'asn't asked Dr Weakling to stick up for them, has they?
HEAR HEAR!
If they wasn't satisfied, they would stick up for theirselves!
HEAR HEAR!

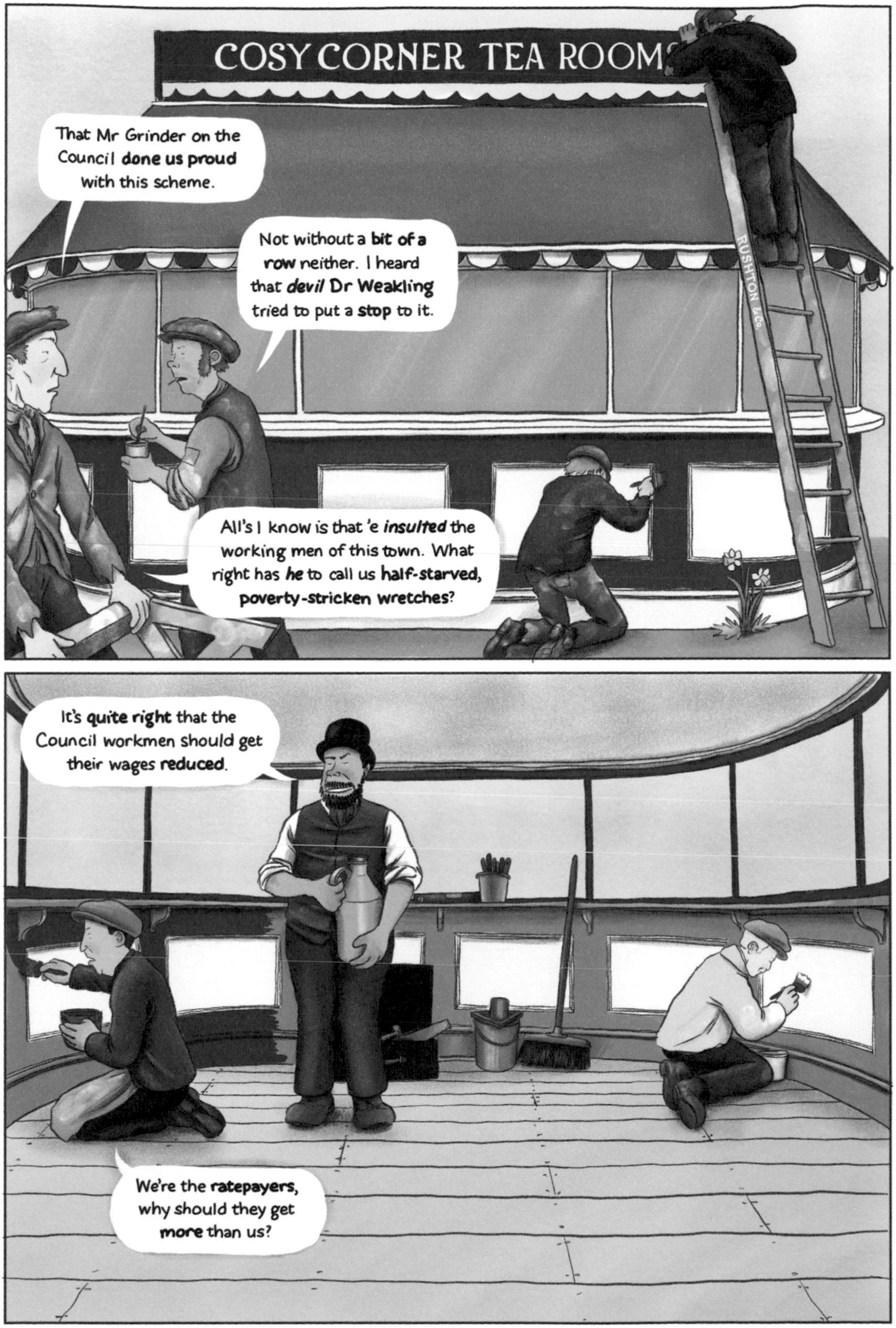
COSY CORNER TEA ROOMS
That Mr Grinder on the Council done us proud with this scheme.
Not without a bit of a row neither. I heard that devil Dr Weakling tried to put a stop to it.
RUSHTON &Co.
All's I know is that 'e insulted the working men of this town. What right has he to call us half-starved, poverty-stricken wretches?
It's quite right that the Council workmen should get their wages reduced.
We're the ratepayers, why should they get more than us?

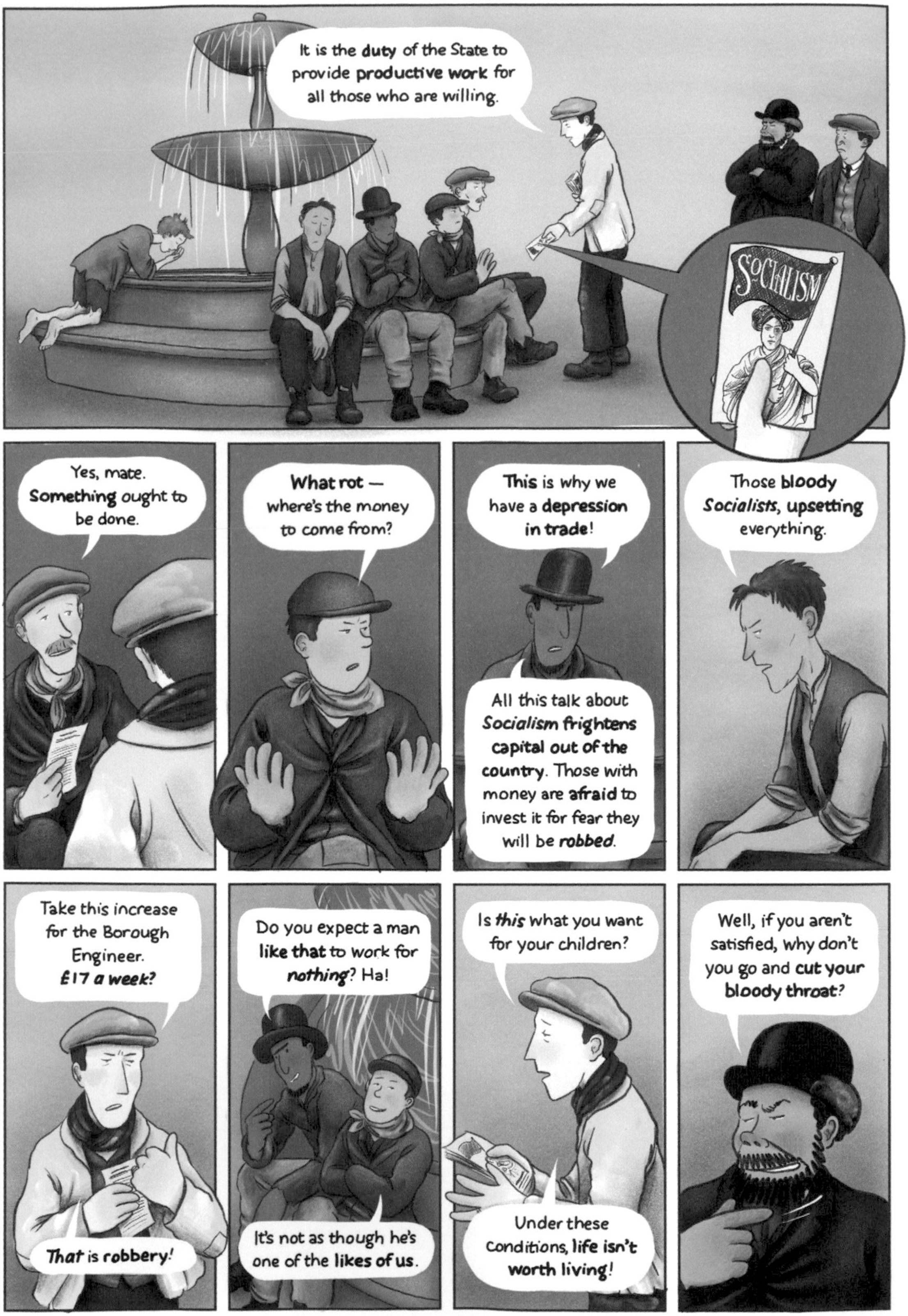
It is the duty of the State to provide productive work for all those who are willing.
SOCIALISM
Yes, mate. Something ought to be done.
What rot — where's the money to come from?
This is why we have a depression in trade!
All this talk about Socialism frightens capital out of the country. Those with money are afraid to invest it for fear they will be robbed.
Those bloody Socialists, upsetting everything.
Take this increase for the Borough Engineer. £17 a week?
That is robbery!
Do you expect a man like that to work for nothing? Ha!
It's not as though he's one of the likes of us.
Is this what you want for your children?
Under these conditions, life isn't worth living!
Well, if you aren't satisfied, why don't you go and cut your bloody throat?

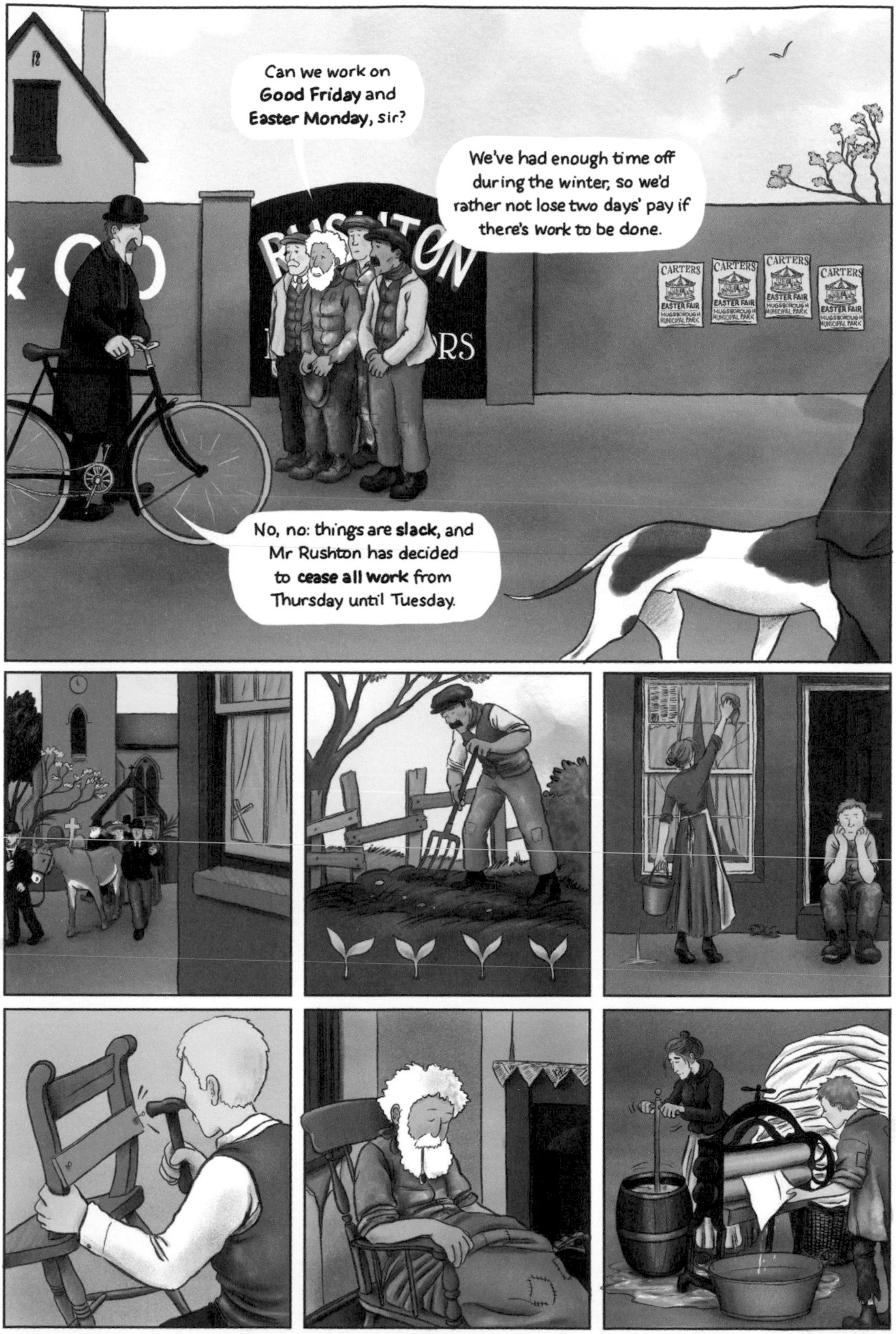
Can we work on Good Friday and Easter Monday, sir?
We've had enough time off during the winter, so we'd rather not lose two days' pay if there's work to be done.
No, no: things are slack, and Mr Rushton has decided to cease all work from Thursday until Tuesday.
RUSHTON
CARTERS EASTER FAIR MUGSBOROUGH MUNICIPAL PARK

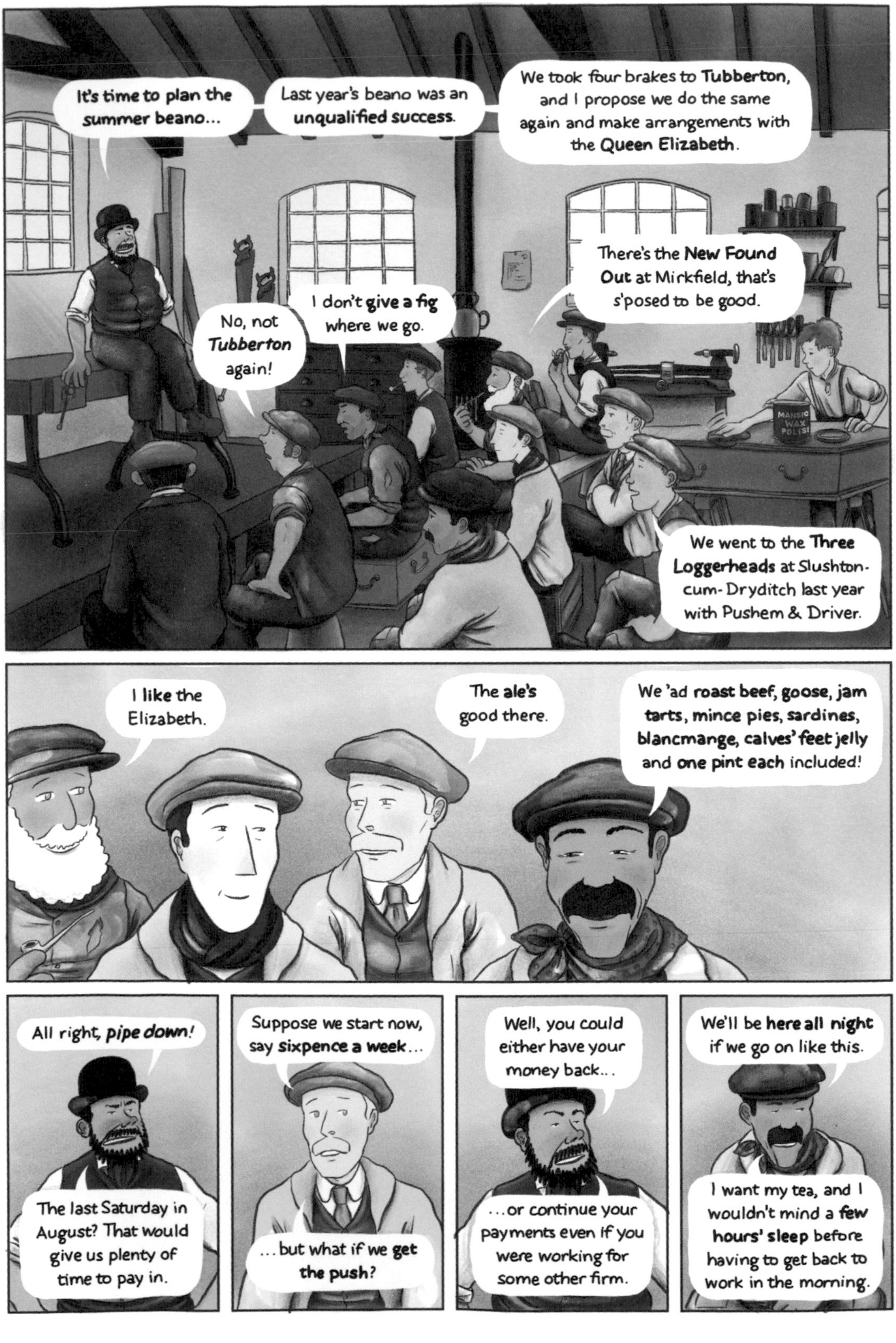
It's time to plan the summer beano...
Last year's beano was an unqualified success.
We took four brakes to Tubberton, and I propose we do the same again and make arrangements with the Queen Elizabeth.
No, not Tubberton again!
I don't give a fig where we go.
There's the New Found Out at Mirkfield, that's s'posed to be good.
MANSIO WAX POLISH
We went to the Three Loggerheads at Slushton-cum-Dryditch last year with Pushem & Driver.
I like the Elizabeth.
The ale's good there.
We 'ad roast beef, goose, jam tarts, mince pies, sardines, blancmange, calves' feet jelly and one pint each included!
All right, pipe down!
The last Saturday in August? That would give us plenty of time to pay in.
Suppose we start now, say sixpence a week...
...but what if we get the push?
Well, you could either have your money back...
...or continue your payments even if you were working for some other firm.
We'll be here all night if we go on like this.
I want my tea, and I wouldn't mind a few hours' sleep before having to get back to work in the morning.

CHAPTER

THE SUMMER

Fifteen

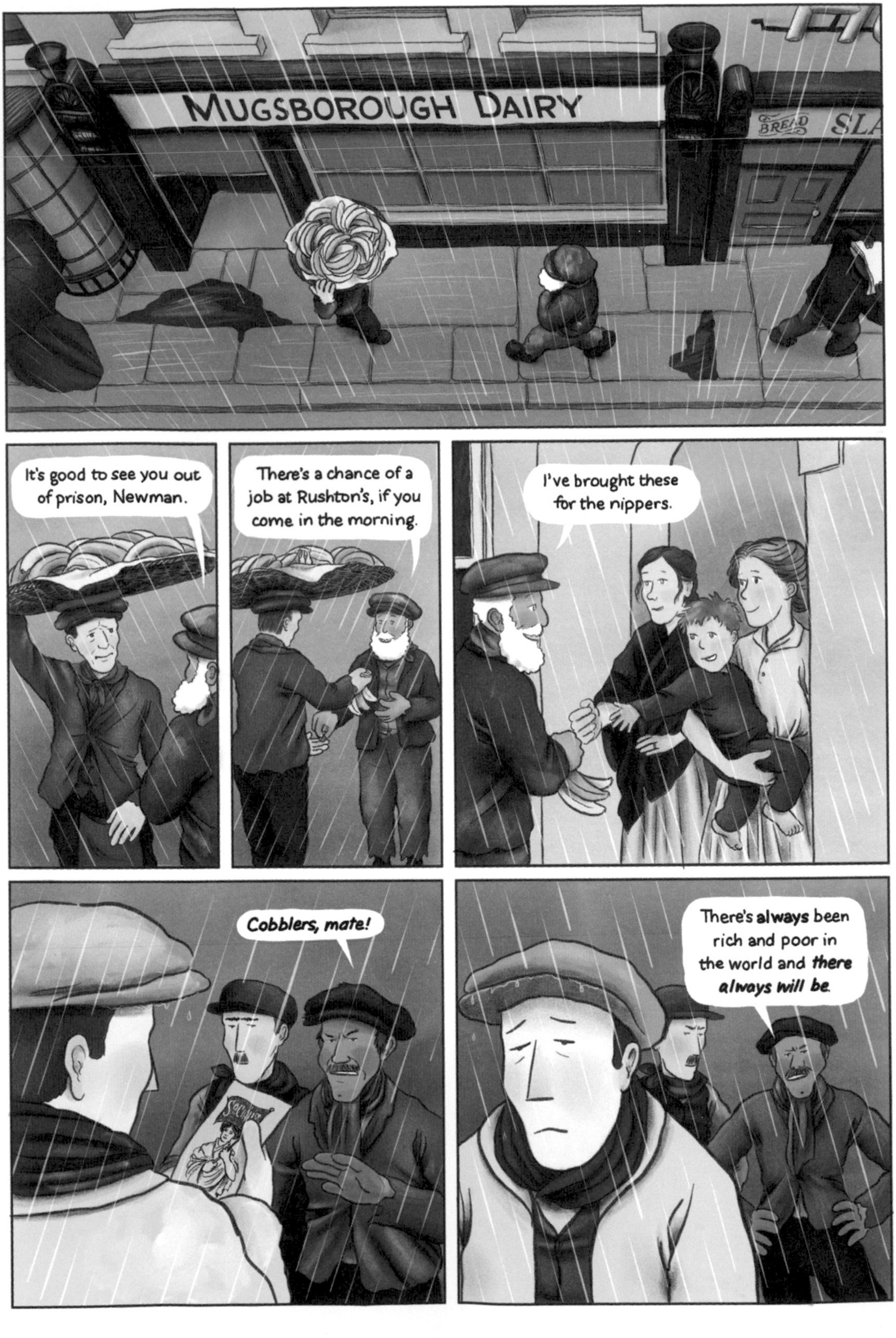
MUGSBOROUGH DAIRY
BREAD
It's good to see you out of prison, Newman.
There's a chance of a job at Rushton's, if you come in the morning.
I've brought these for the nippers.
Cobblers, mate!
There's always been rich and poor in the world and there always will be.

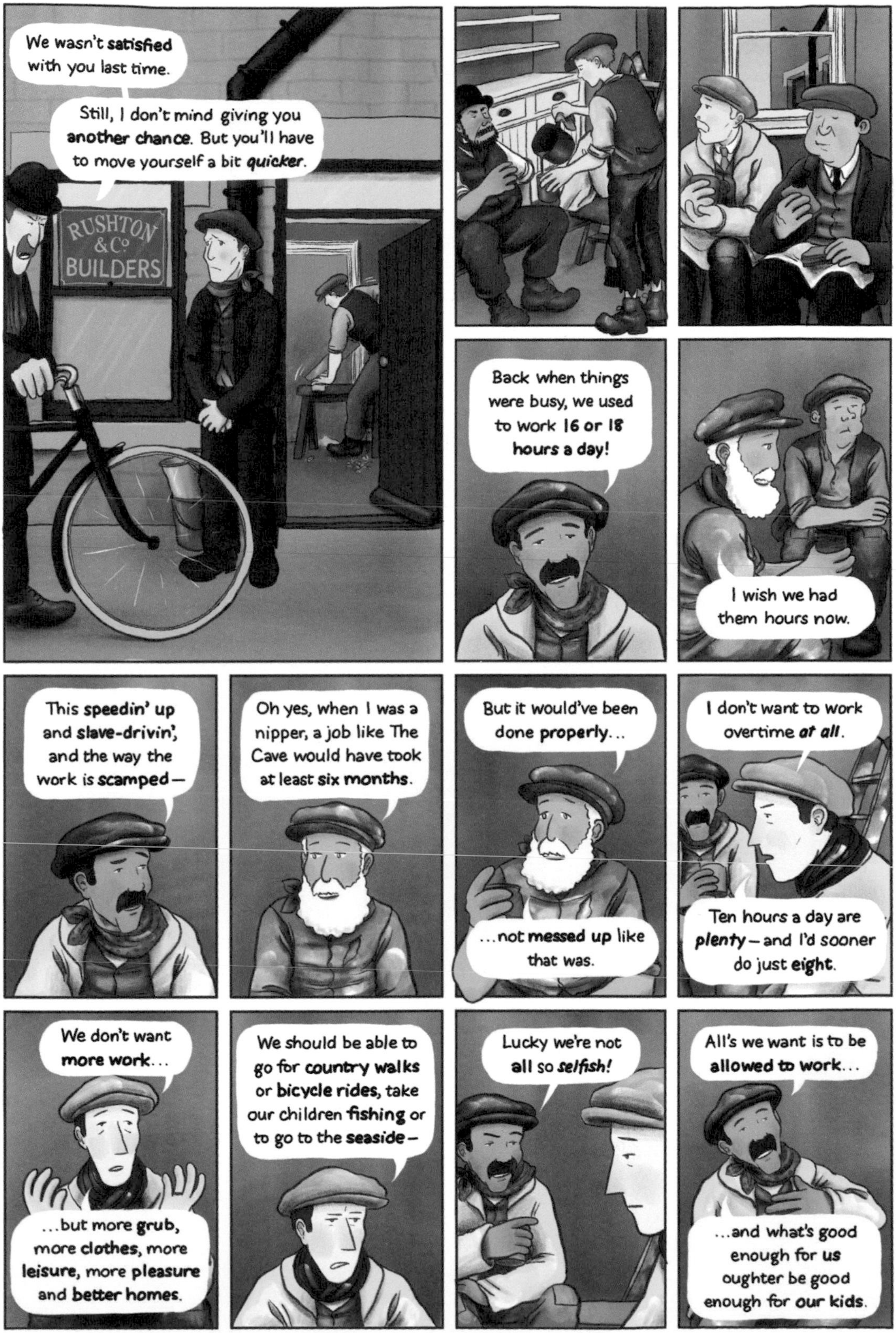
We wasn't satisfied with you last time.
Still, I don't mind giving you another chance. But you'll have to move yourself a bit quicker.
RUSHTON & Co BUILDERS
Back when things were busy, we used to work 16 or 18 hours a day!
I wish we had them hours now.
This speedin' up and slave-drivin', and the way the work is scamped—
Oh yes, when I was a nipper, a job like The Cave would have took at least six months.
But it would've been done properly...
...not messed up like that was.
I don't want to work overtime at all.
Ten hours a day are plenty—and I'd sooner do just eight.
We don't want more work...
...but more grub, more clothes, more leisure, more pleasure and better homes.
We should be able to go for country walks or bicycle rides, take our children fishing or to go to the seaside—
Lucky we're not all so selfish!
All's we want is to be allowed to work...
...and what's good enough for us oughter be good enough for our kids.

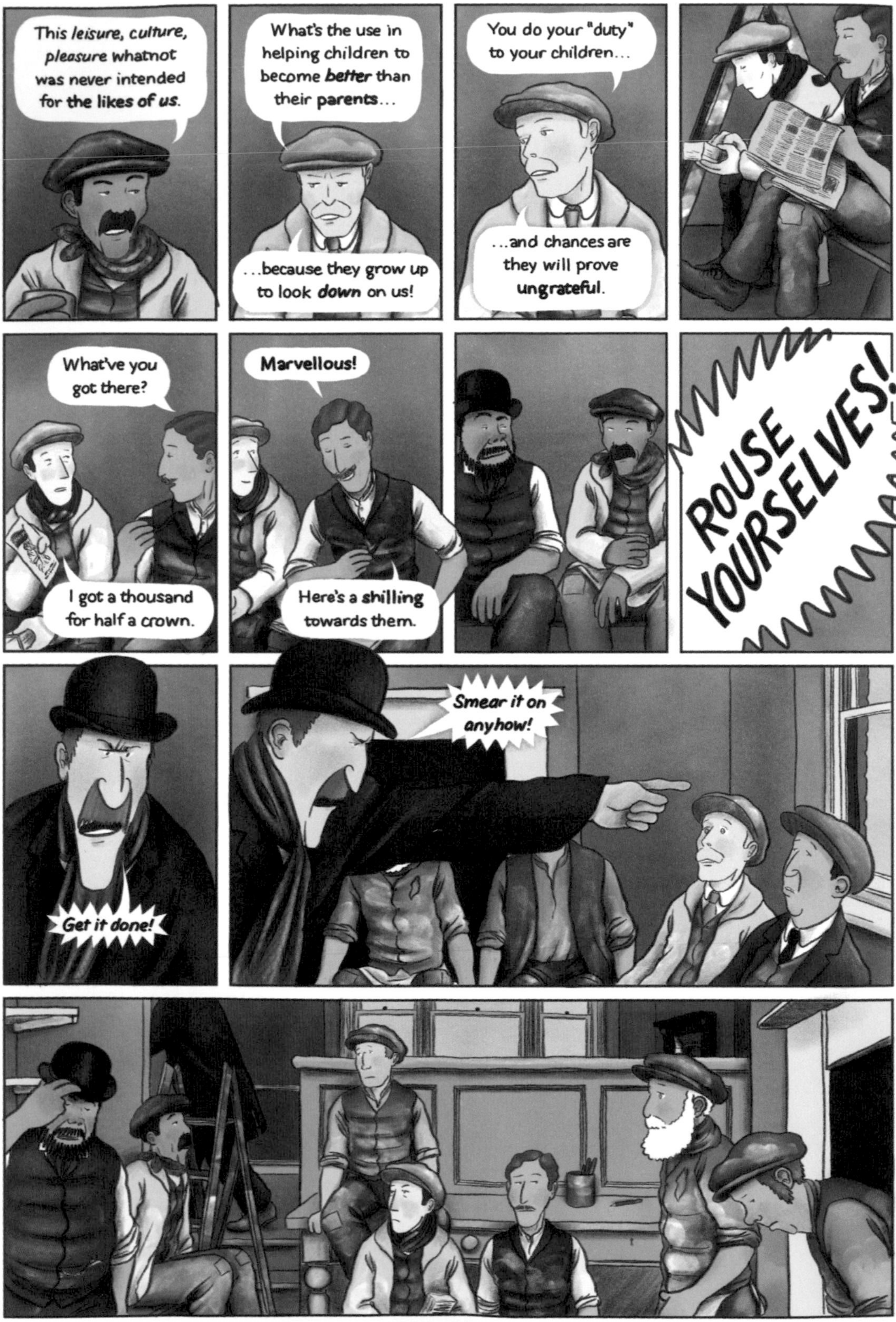
This leisure, culture, pleasure whatnot was never intended for the likes of us.
What's the use in helping children to become better than their parents...
...because they grow up to look down on us!
You do your "duty" to your children...
...and chances are they will prove ungrateful.
What've you got there?
I got a thousand for half a crown.
Marvellous!
Here's a shilling towards them.
ROUSE YOURSELVES!
Get it done!
Smear it on anyhow!

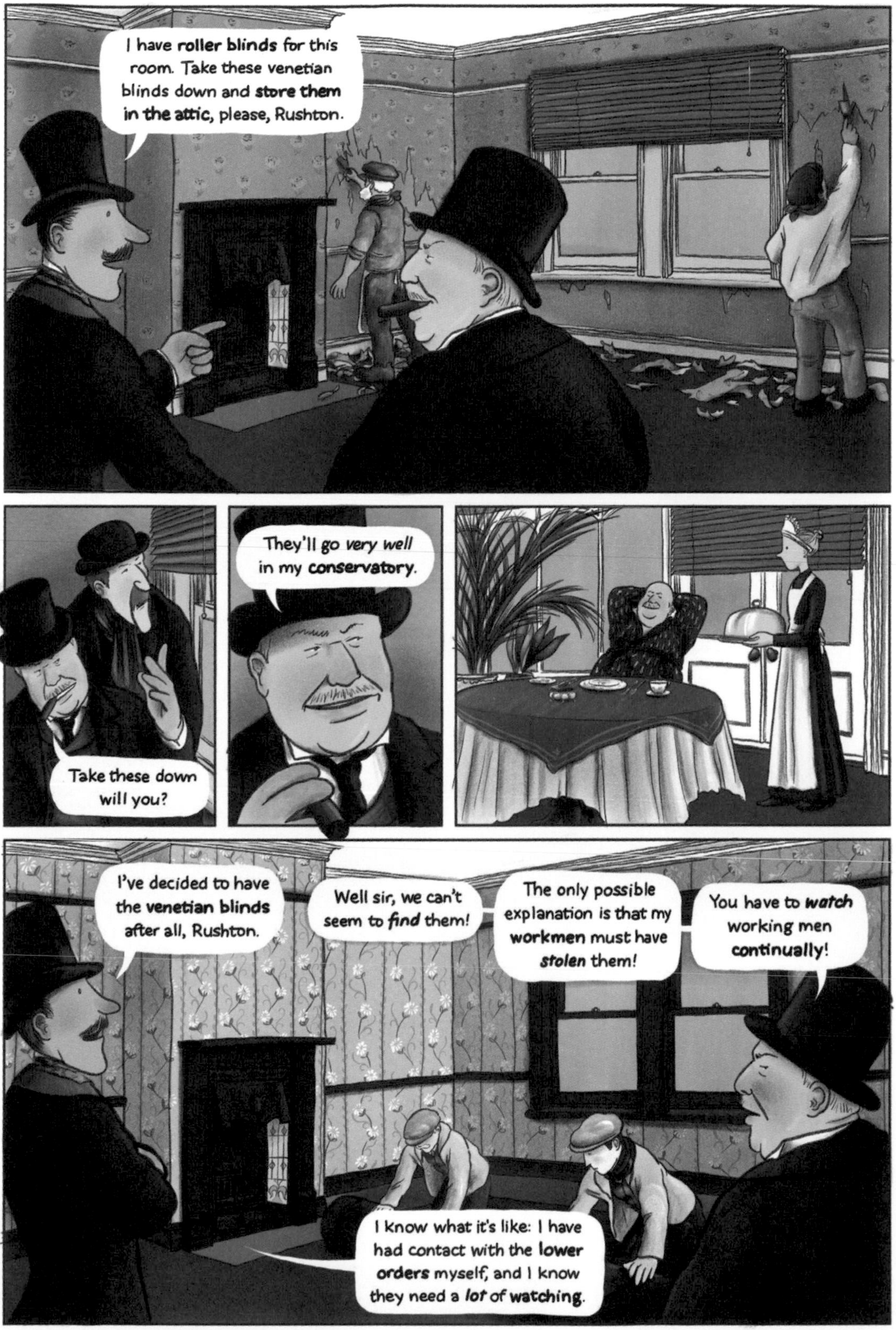
I have **roller blinds** for this room. Take these venetian blinds down and **store them in the attic**, please, Rushton.
Take these down will you?
They'll go *very well* in my **conservatory**.
I've decided to have the **venetian blinds** after all, Rushton.
Well sir, we can't seem to *find* them!
The only possible explanation is that my **workmen** must have *stolen* them!
You have to *watch* working men **continually**!
I know what it's like: I have had contact with the **lower orders** myself, and I know they need a *lot* of **watching**.

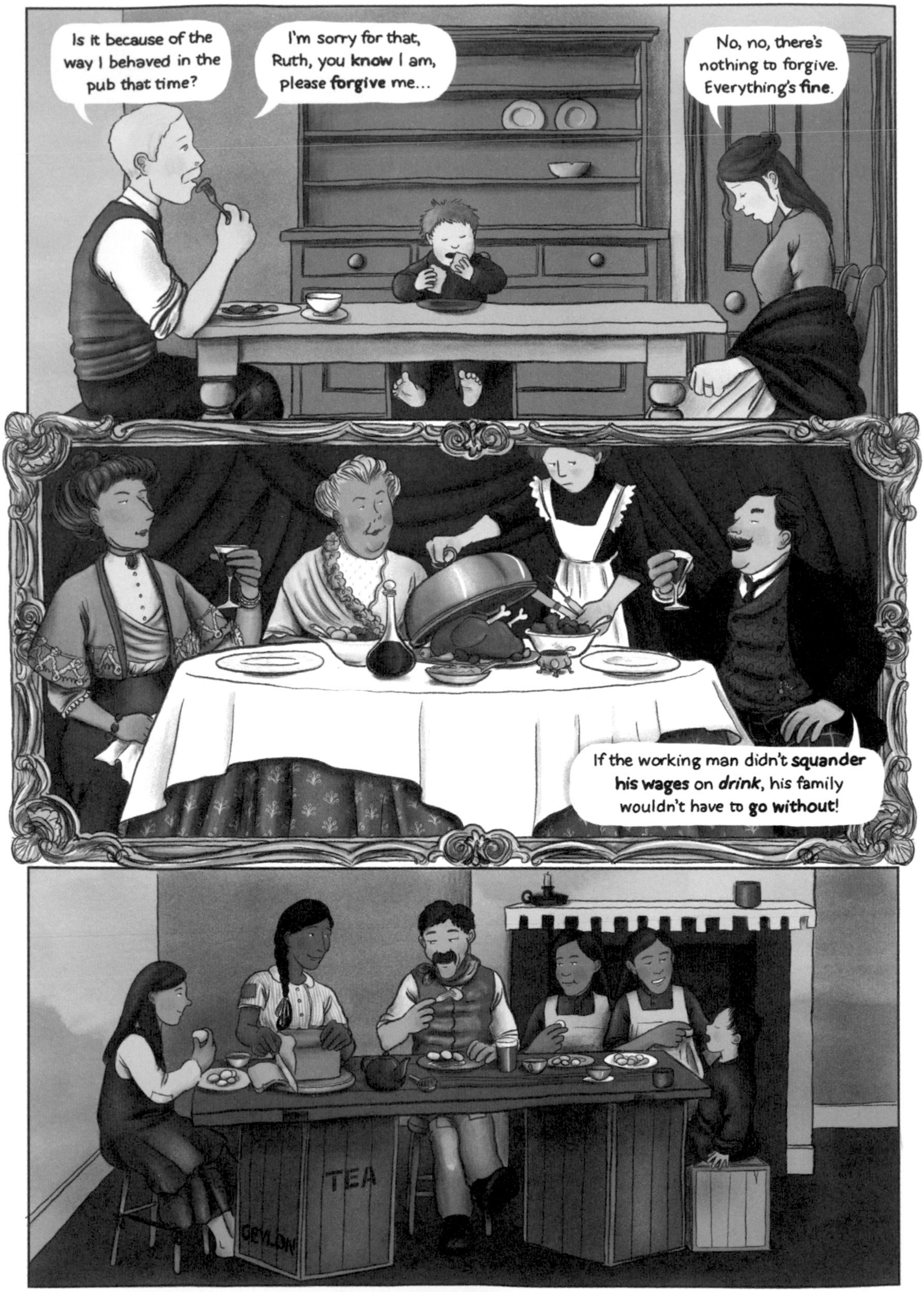
Is it because of the way I behaved in the pub that time?
I'm sorry for that, Ruth, you know I am, please forgive me...
No, no, there's nothing to forgive. Everything's fine.
If the working man didn't squander his wages on drink, his family wouldn't have to go without!
TEA
CEYLON

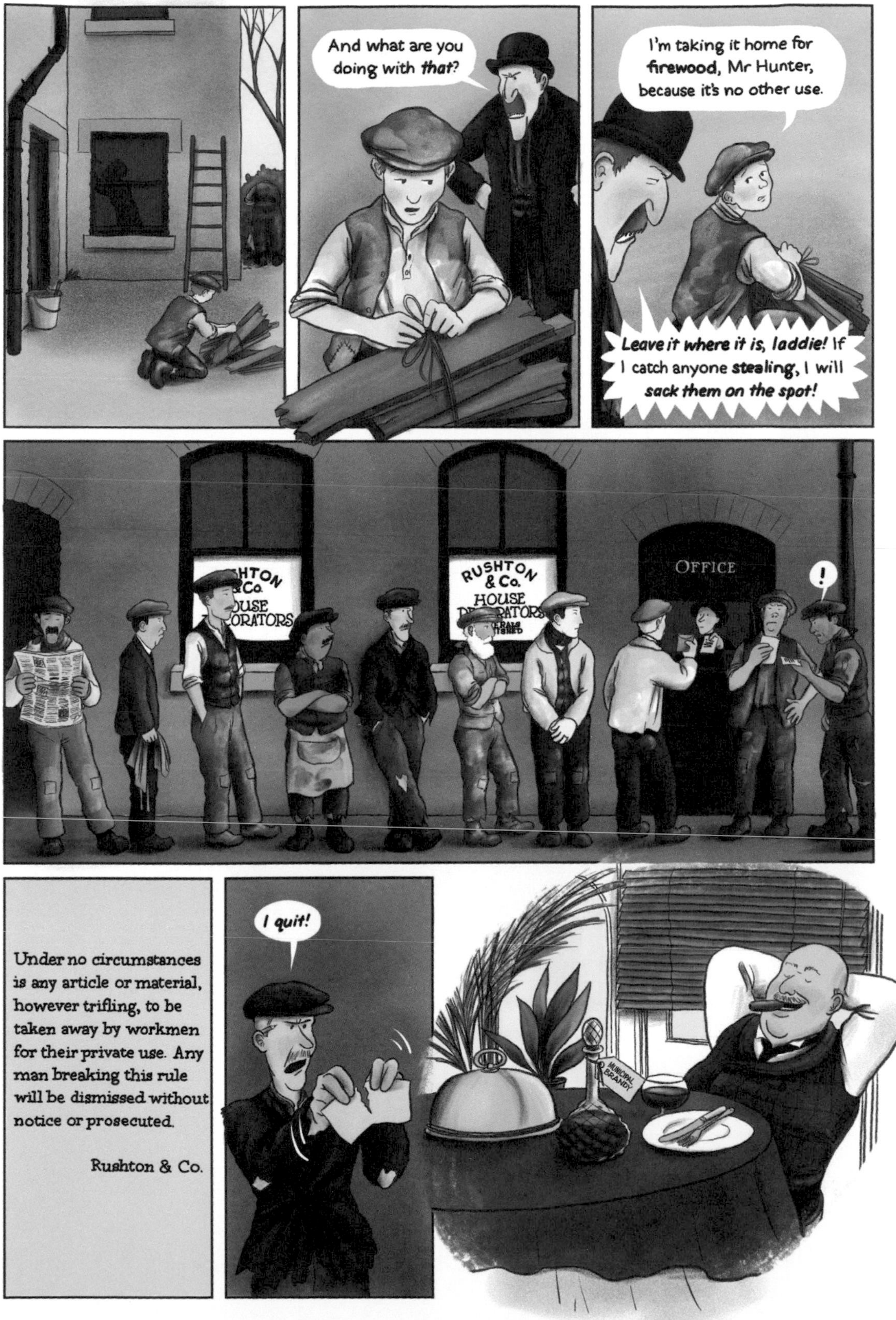
And what are you doing with *that*?
I'm taking it home for **firewood**, Mr Hunter, because it's no other use.
Leave it where it is, laddie! If I catch anyone **stealing**, I will ***sack them on the spot!***
RUSHTON & Co. HOUSE DECORATORS
OFFICE
!
Under no circumstances is any article or material, however trifling, to be taken away by workmen for their private use. Any man breaking this rule will be dismissed without notice or prosecuted.
Rushton & Co.
I quit!
MUNICIPAL BRANDY

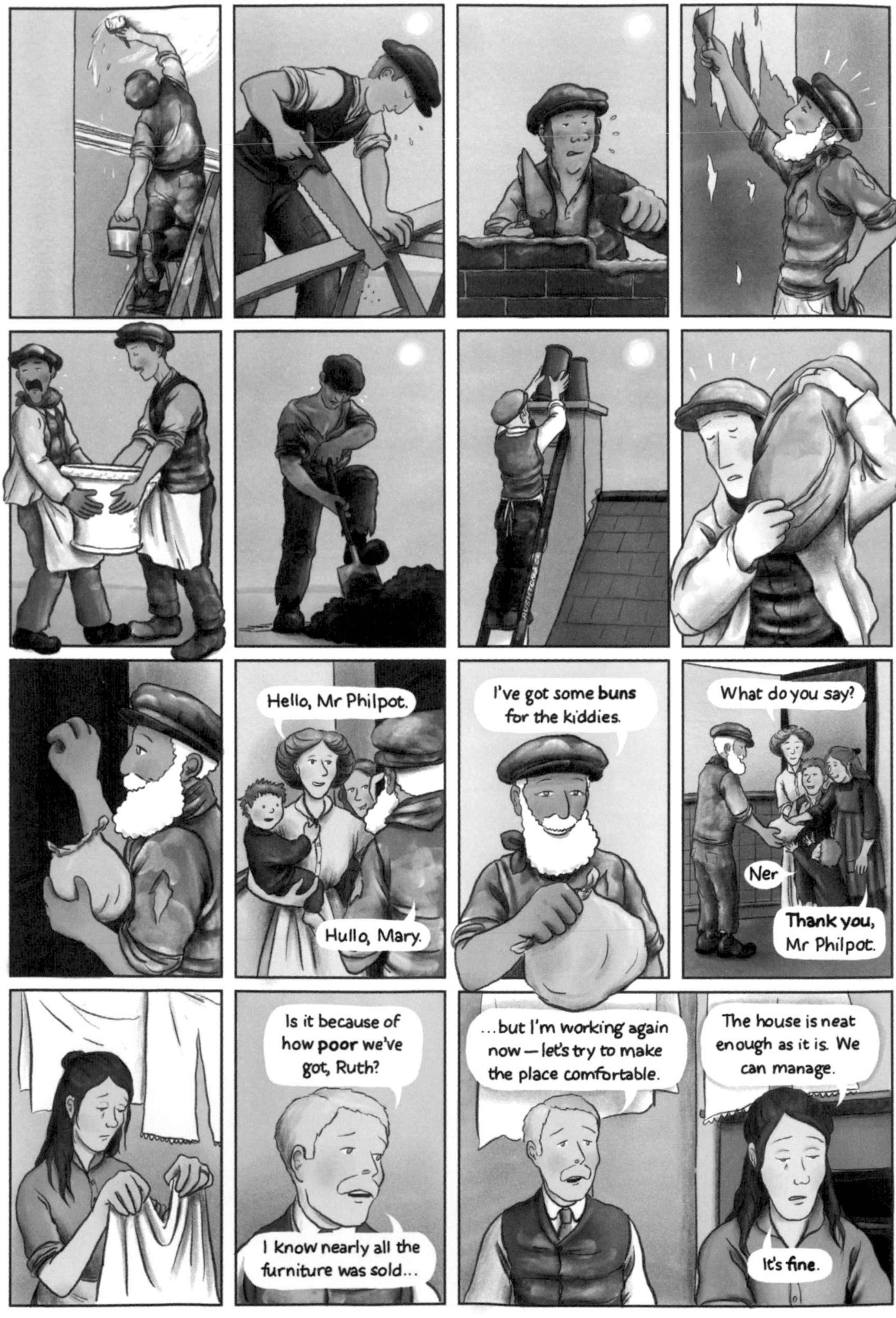
Hello, Mr Philpot.
Hullo, Mary.
I've got some buns for the kiddies.
What do you say?
Ner
Thank you, Mr Philpot.
Is it because of how poor we've got, Ruth?
I know nearly all the furniture was sold...
...but I'm working again now — let's try to make the place comfortable.
The house is neat enough as it is. We can manage.
It's fine.

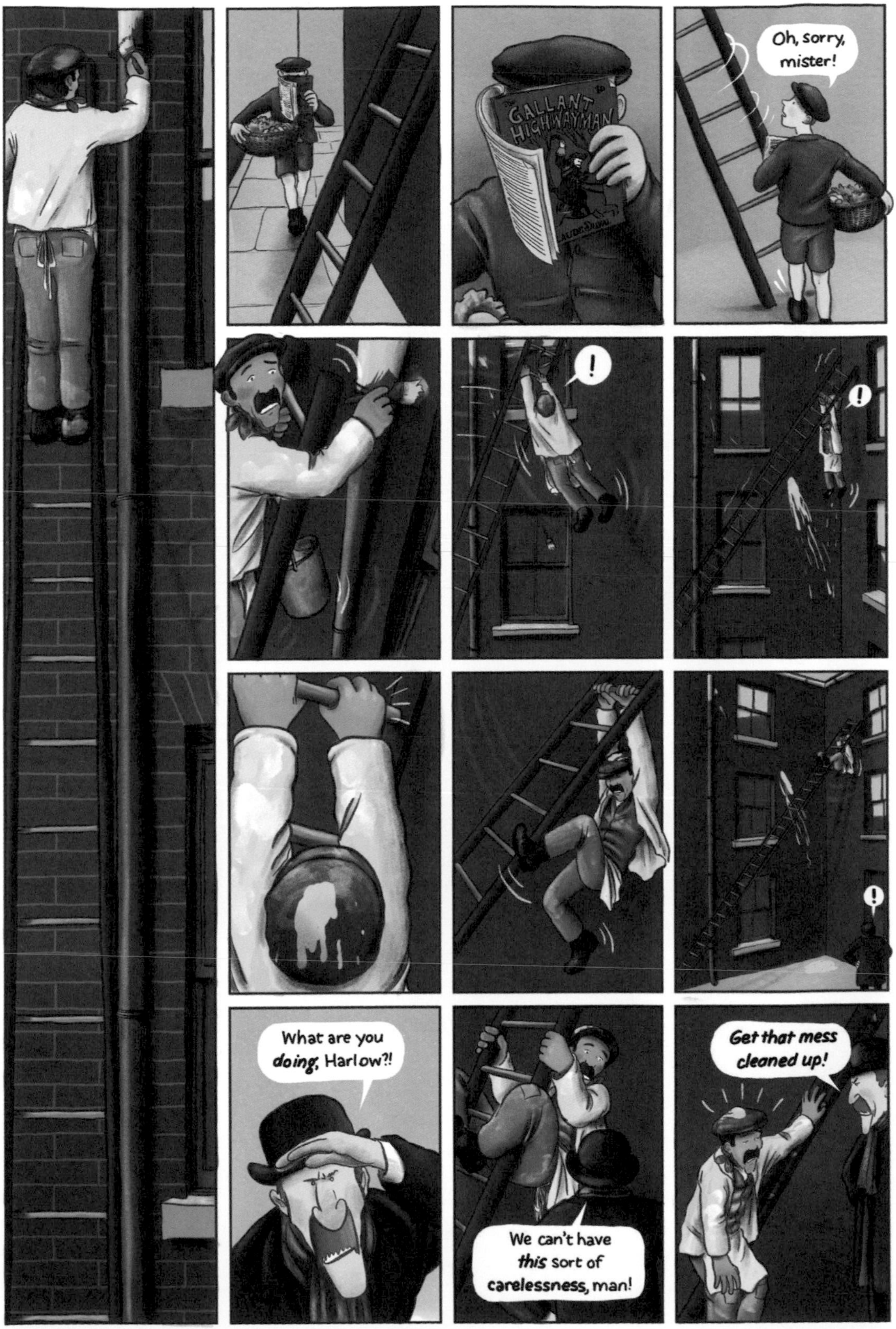
GALLANT HIGHWAYMAN
Oh, sorry, mister!
!
!
!
What are you doing, Harlow?!
We can't have this sort of carelessness, man!
Get that mess cleaned up!

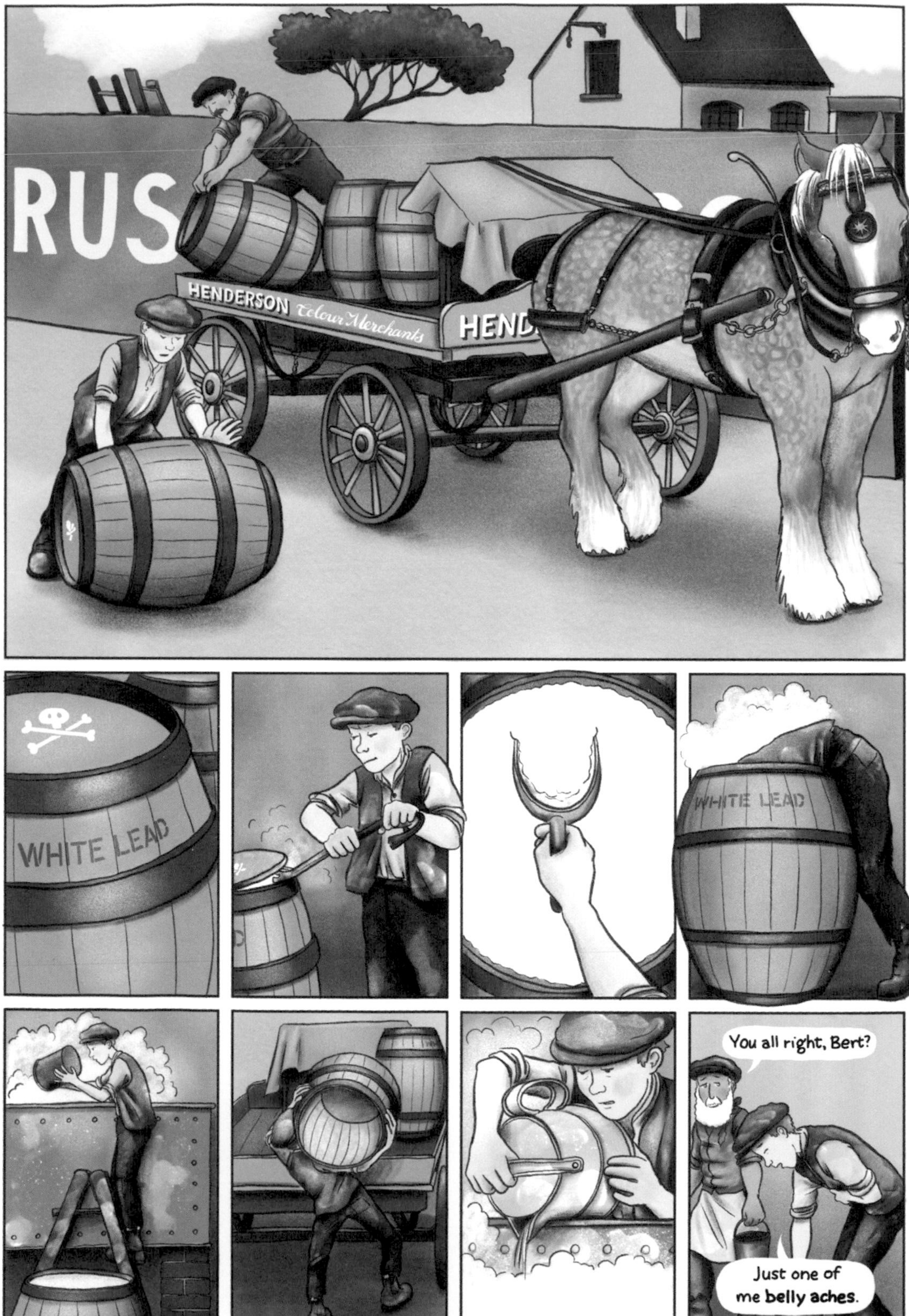
RUS
HENDERSON Colour Merchants
HEND
WHITE LEAD
WHITE LEAD
You all right, Bert?
Just one of me belly aches.

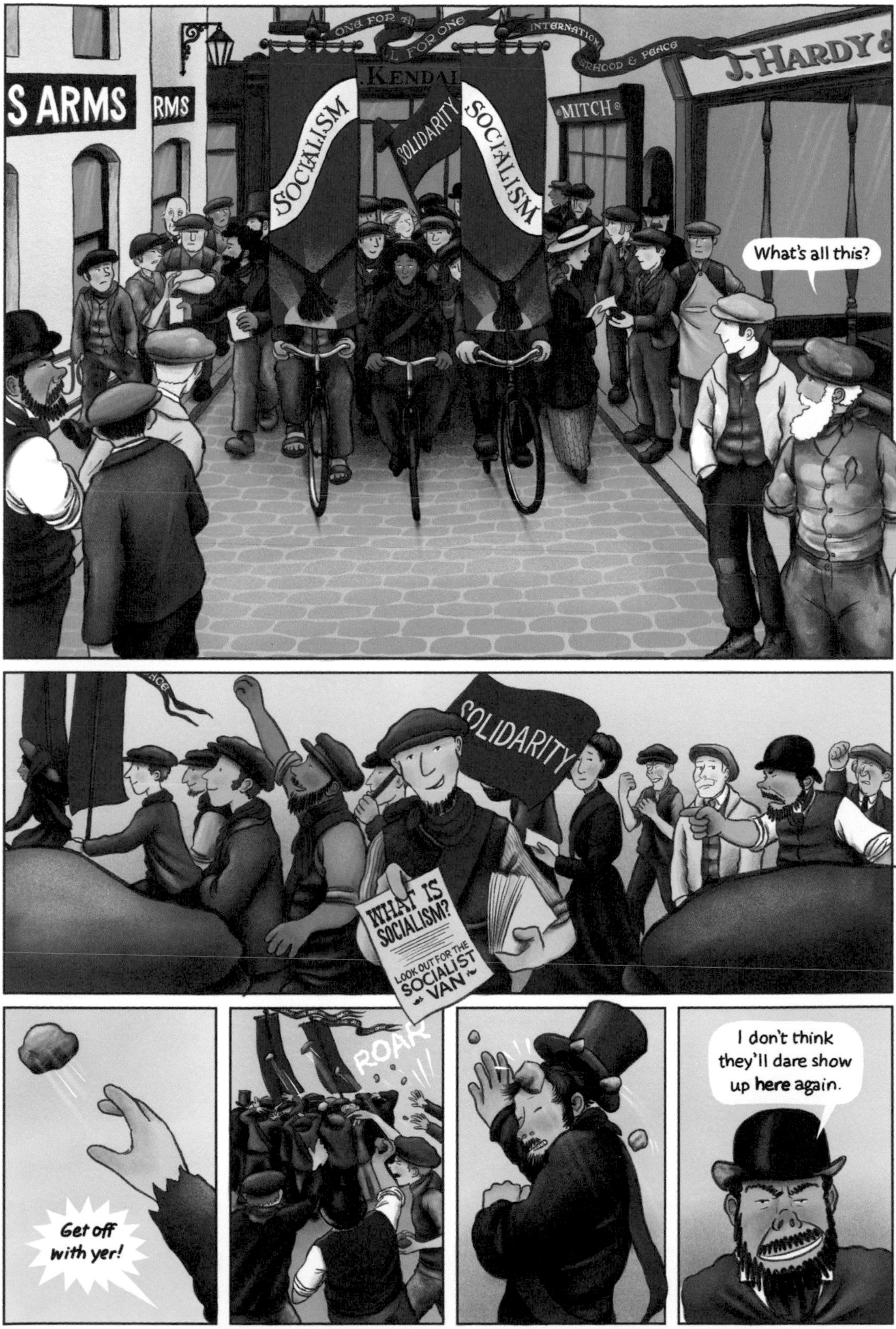
S ARMS
SOCIALISM
SOLIDARITY
SOCIALISM
J. HARDY &
What's all this?
SOLIDARITY
WHAT IS SOCIALISM?
LOOK OUT FOR THE SOCIALIST VAN
Get off with yer!
ROAR
I don't think they'll dare show up here again.

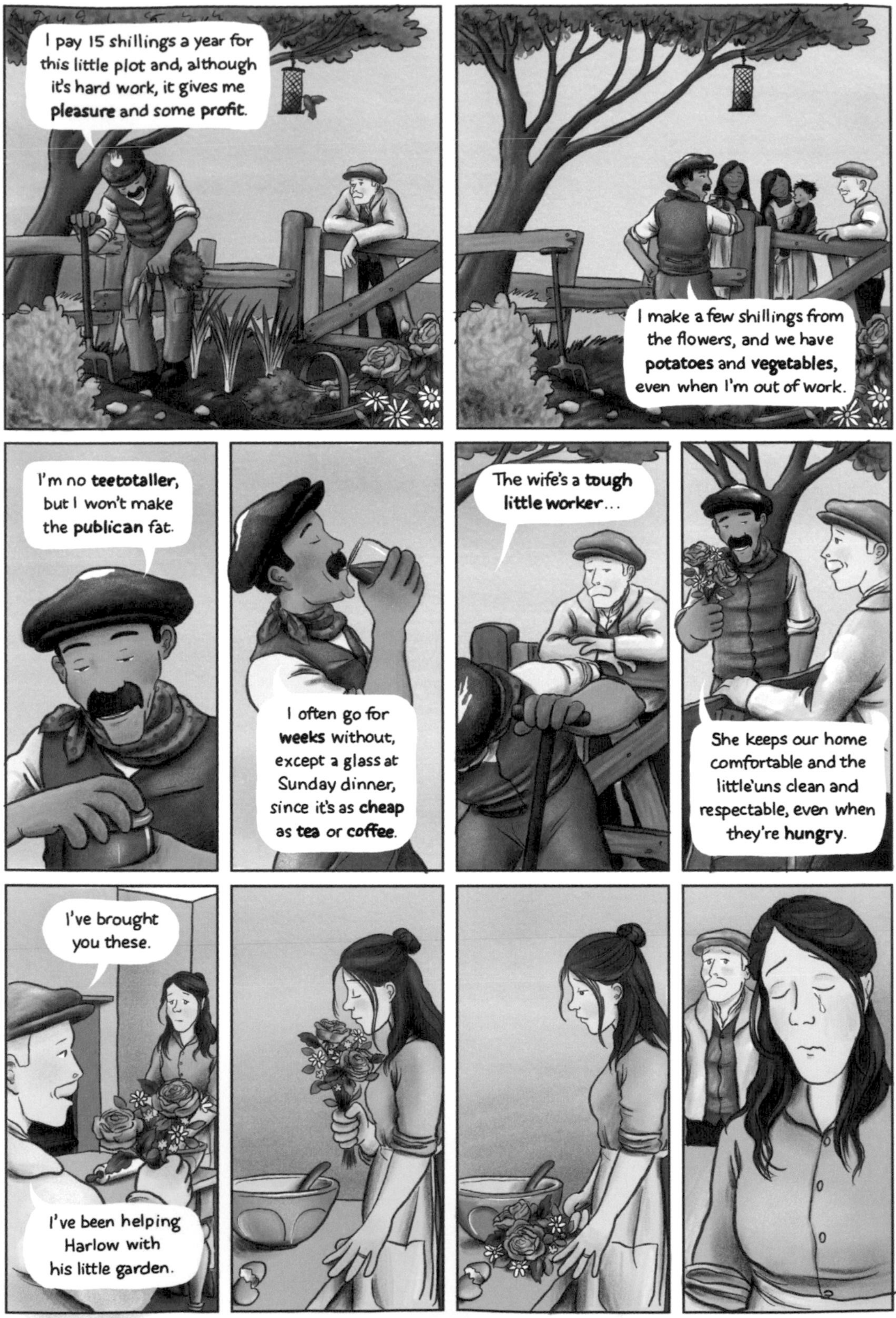
I pay 15 shillings a year for this little plot and, although it's hard work, it gives me **pleasure** and some **profit**.
I make a few shillings from the flowers, and we have **potatoes** and **vegetables**, even when I'm out of work.
I'm no **teetotaller**, but I won't make the **publican** fat.
I often go for **weeks** without, except a glass at Sunday dinner, since it's as **cheap** as **tea** or **coffee**.
The wife's a **tough little worker**...
She keeps our home comfortable and the little'uns clean and respectable, even when they're **hungry**.
I've brought you these.
I've been helping Harlow with his little garden.

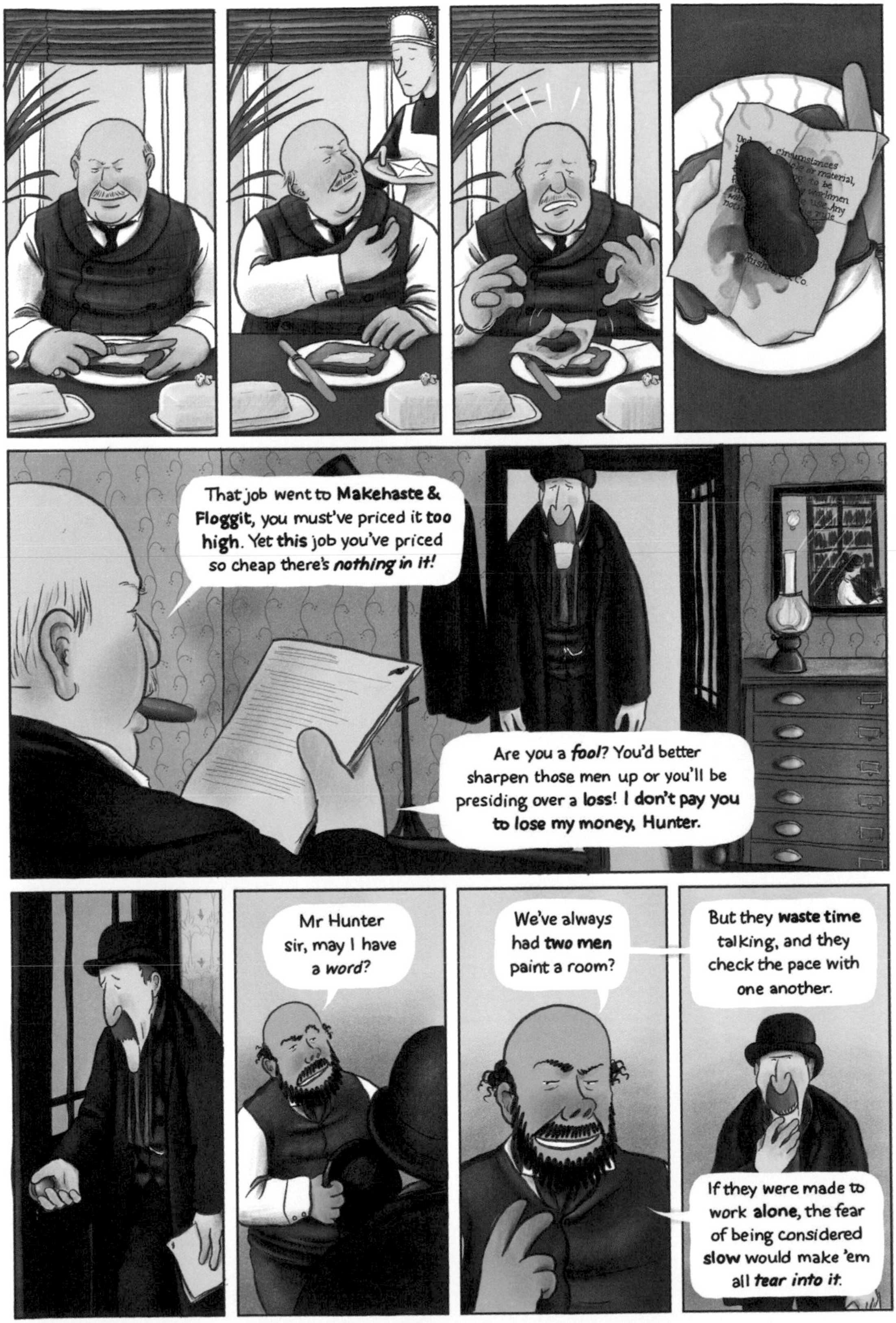
That job went to Makehaste & Floggit, you must've priced it too high. Yet this job you've priced so cheap there's nothing in it!
Are you a fool? You'd better sharpen those men up or you'll be presiding over a loss! I don't pay you to lose my money, Hunter.
Mr Hunter sir, may I have a word?
We've always had two men paint a room?
But they waste time talking, and they check the pace with one another.
If they were made to work alone, the fear of being considered slow would make 'em all tear into it.

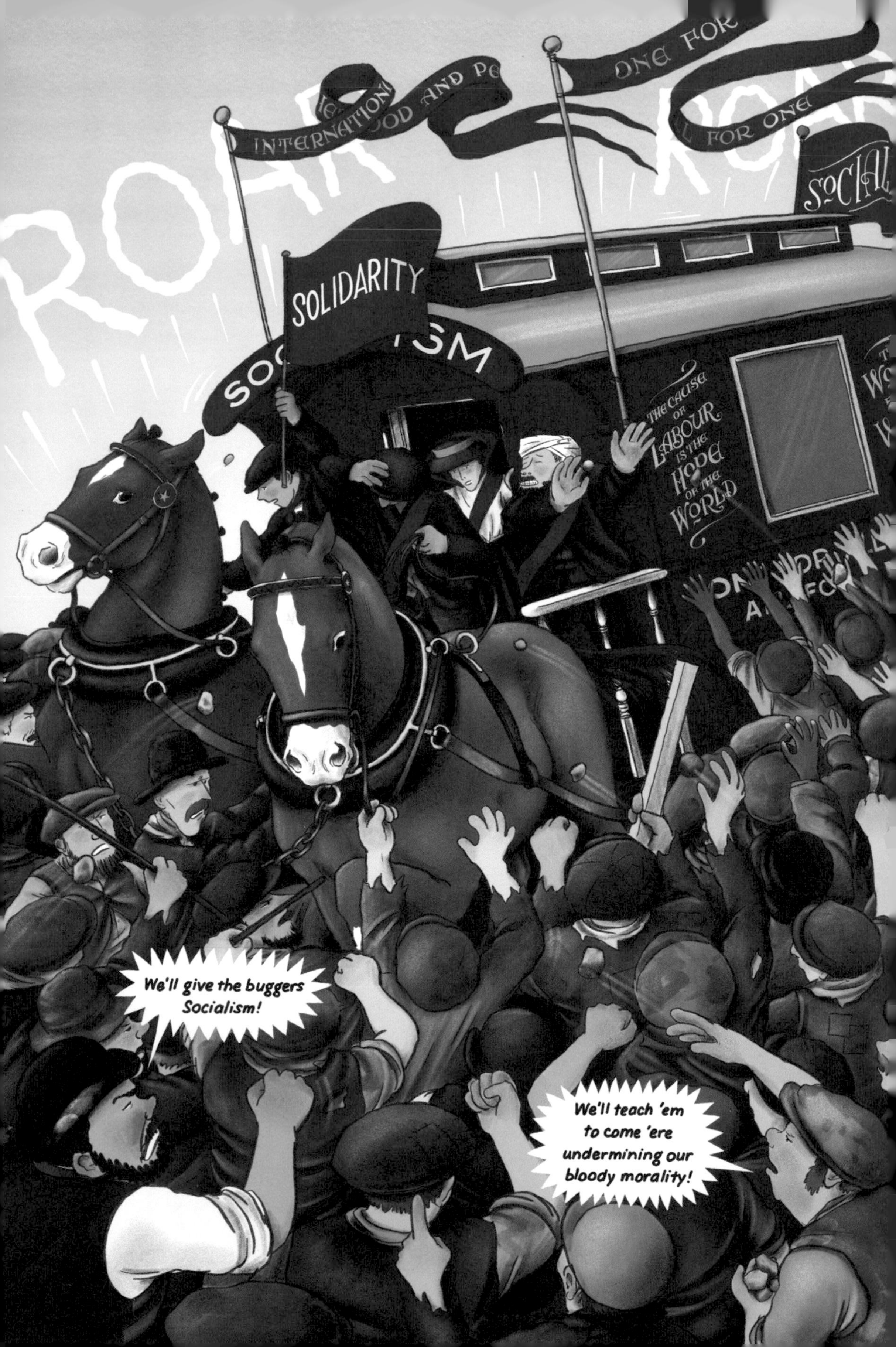
ROAR
ONE FOR
FOR ONE
SOLIDARITY
THE CAUSE OF LABOUR IS THE HOPE OF THE WORLD
We'll give the buggers Socialism!
We'll teach 'em to come 'ere undermining our bloody morality!

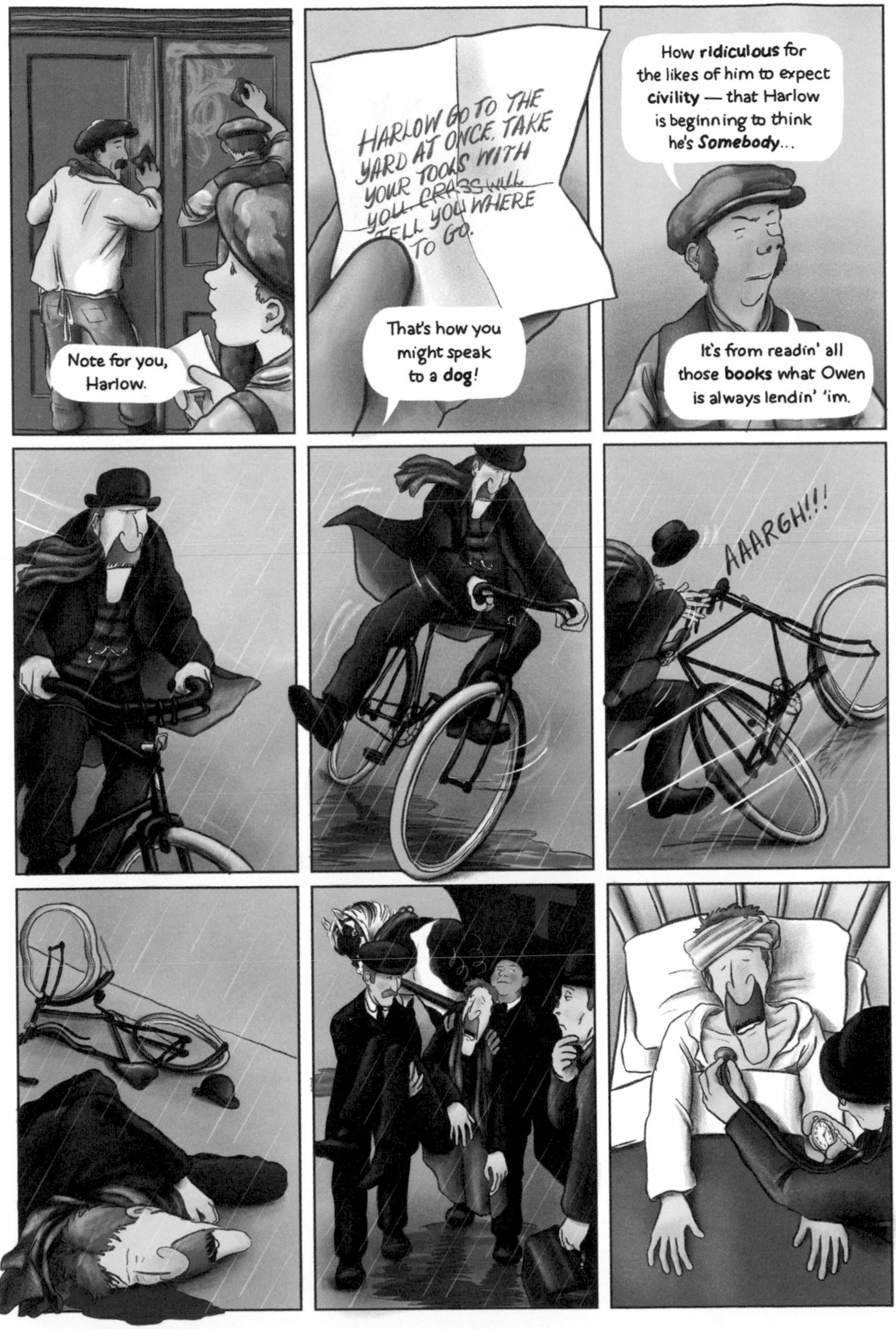
Note for you, Harlow.
HARLOW GO TO THE YARD AT ONCE. TAKE YOUR TOOLS WITH YOU CRASS WILL TELL YOU WHERE TO GO.
That's how you might speak to a dog!
How ridiculous for the likes of him to expect civility — that Harlow is beginning to think he's Somebody...
It's from readin' all those books what Owen is always lendin' 'im.
AAARGH!!!

What a thing about ol' 'Unter, eh? 'E'll be out for **weeks**.

Why Ruth, whatever's wrong?

SOB

SOB

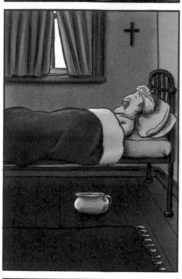

I don't know!

Do whatever **Mr Hunter** would have done.

ROUSE YERSELVES!

Never thought I'd say this, but I'll be **glad** to see Hunter return.

Mr Rushton sent these **figures** for you to look over, sir.

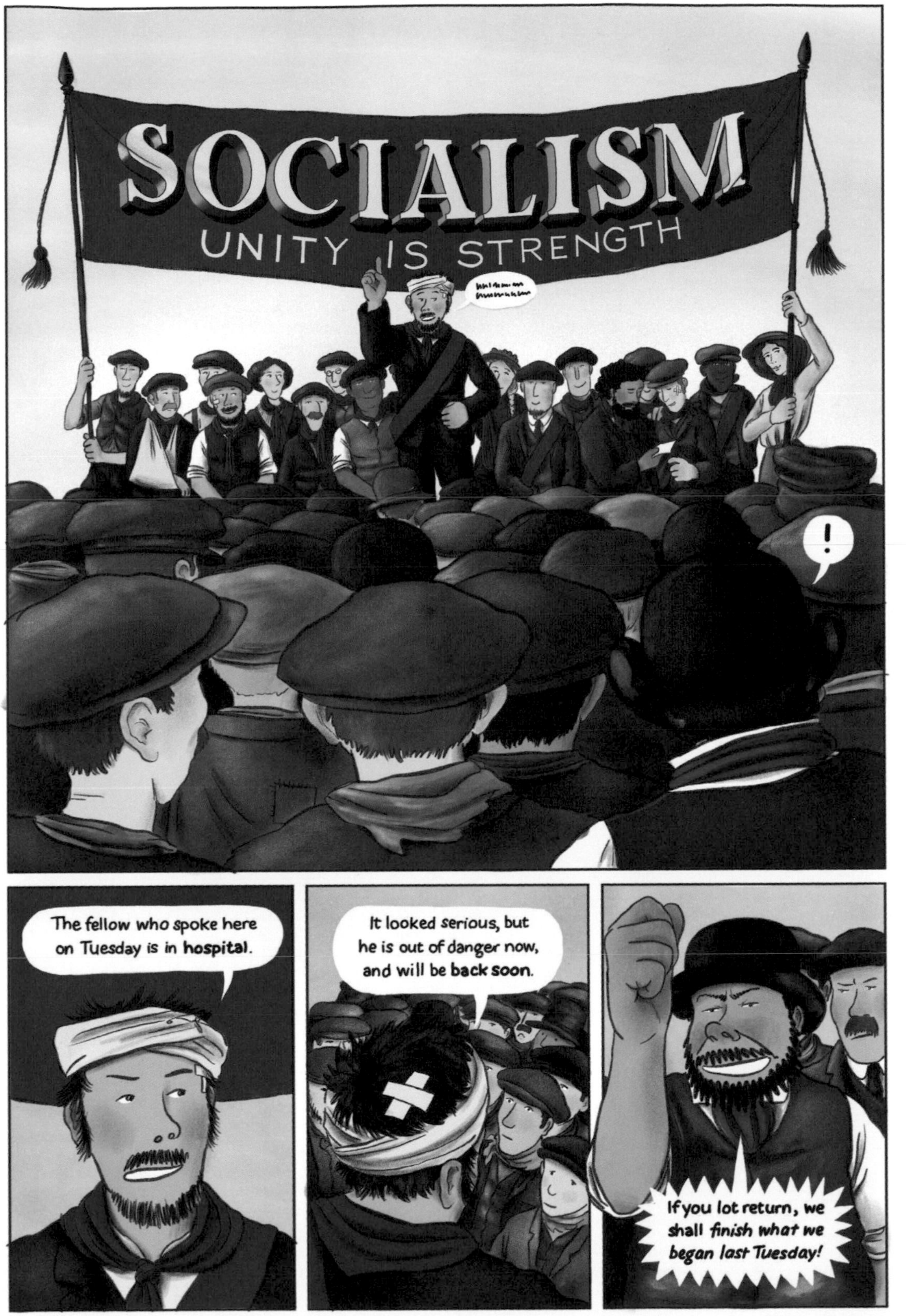
SOCIALISM
UNITY IS STRENGTH
!
The fellow who spoke here on Tuesday is in hospital.
It looked serious, but he is out of danger now, and will be back soon.
If you lot return, we shall finish what we began last Tuesday!

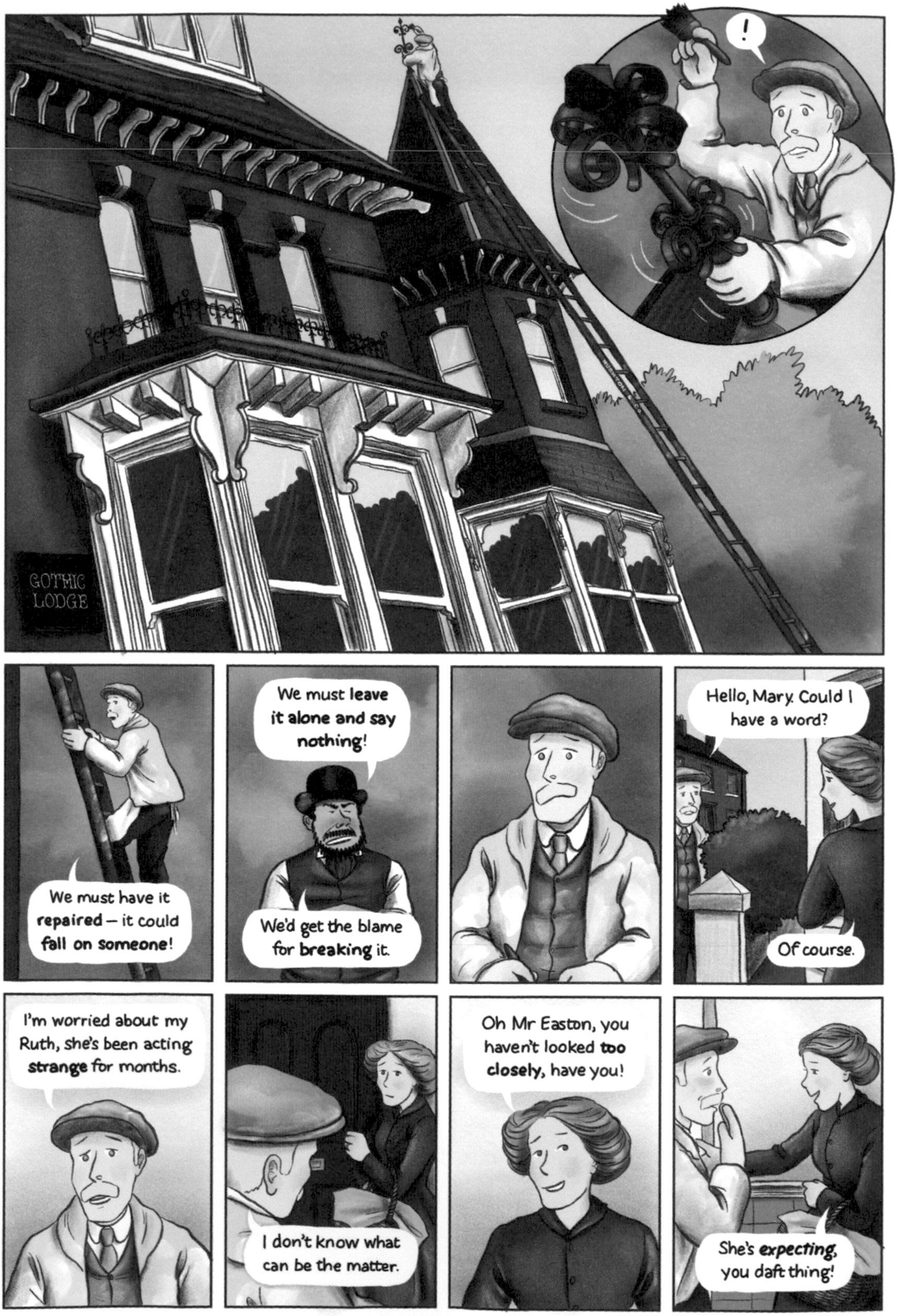
GOTHIC LODGE
!
We must have it repaired – it could fall on someone!
We must leave it alone and say nothing!
We'd get the blame for breaking it.
Hello, Mary. Could I have a word?
Of course.
I'm worried about my Ruth, she's been acting strange for months.
I don't know what can be the matter.
Oh Mr Easton, you haven't looked too closely, have you!
She's expecting, you daft thing!

THE BEANO

CHAPTER 16

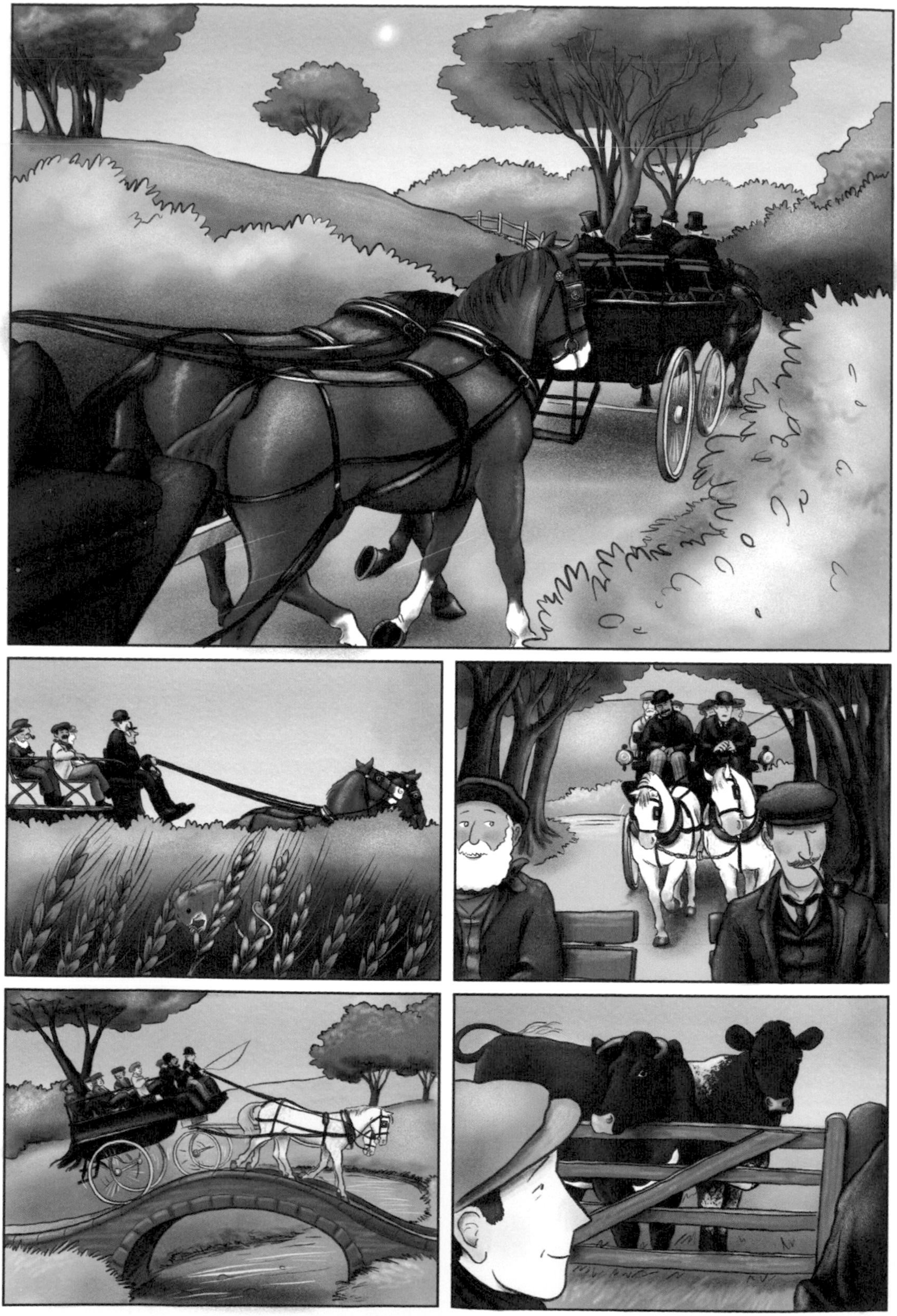

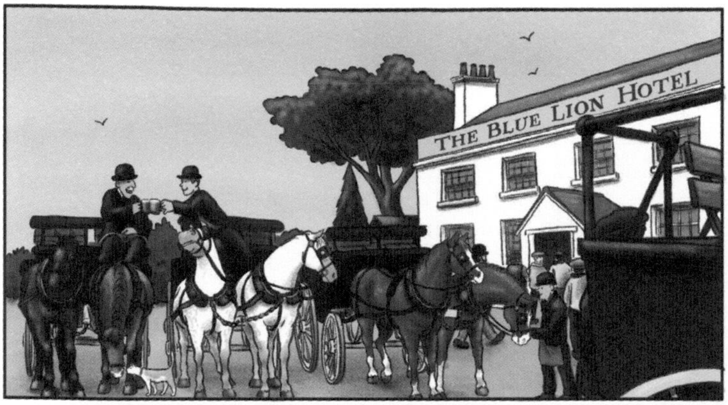
THE BLUE LION HOTEL

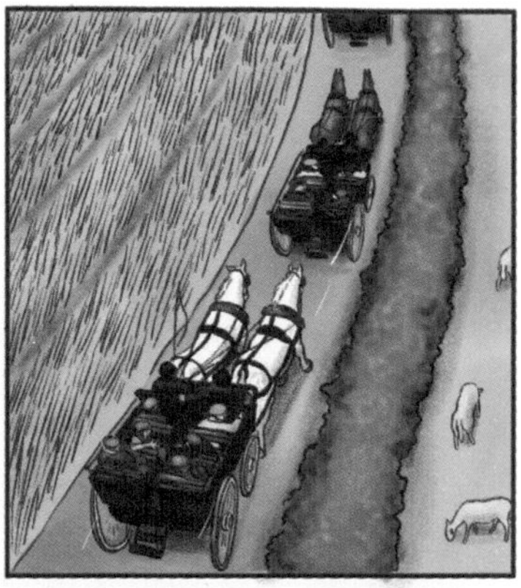

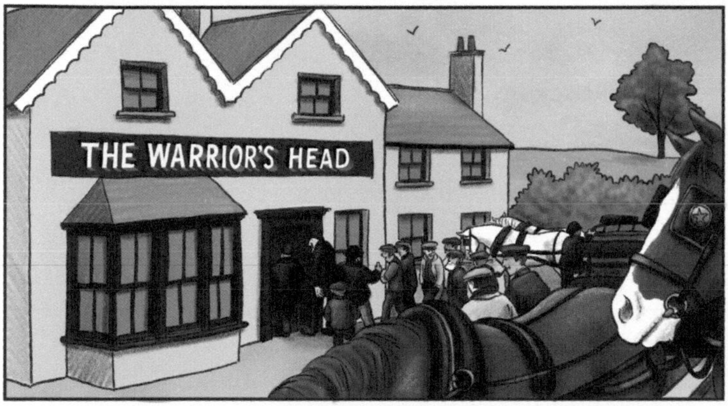
THE WARRIOR'S HEAD

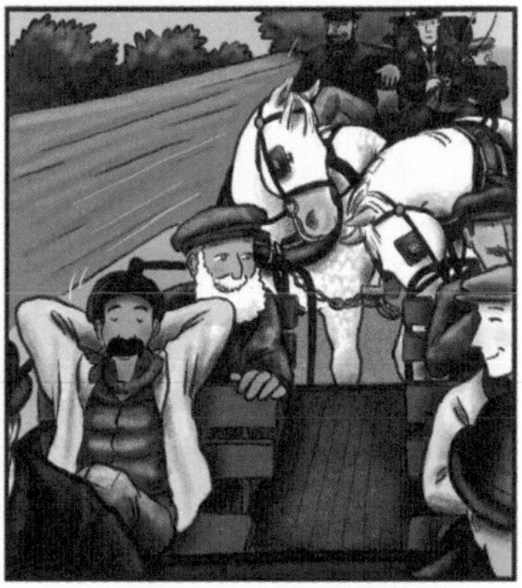

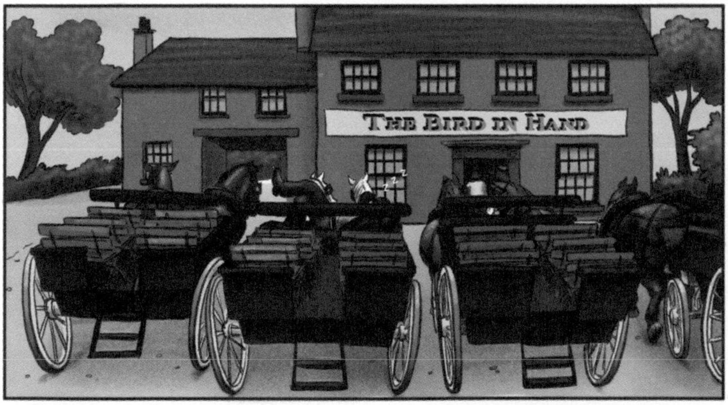
THE BIRD IN HAND

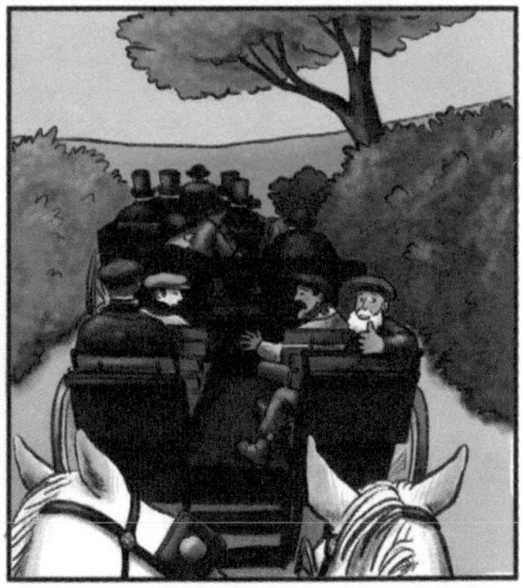

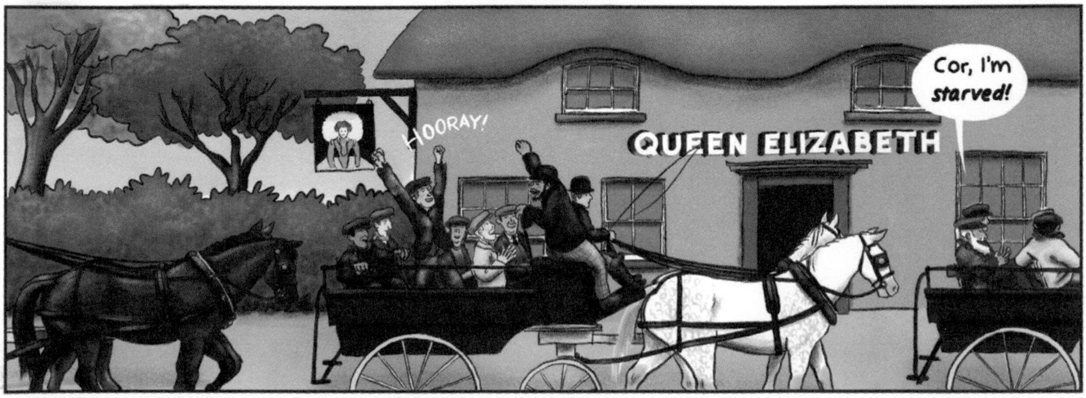
HOORAY!
QUEEN ELIZABETH
Cor, I'm *starved!*

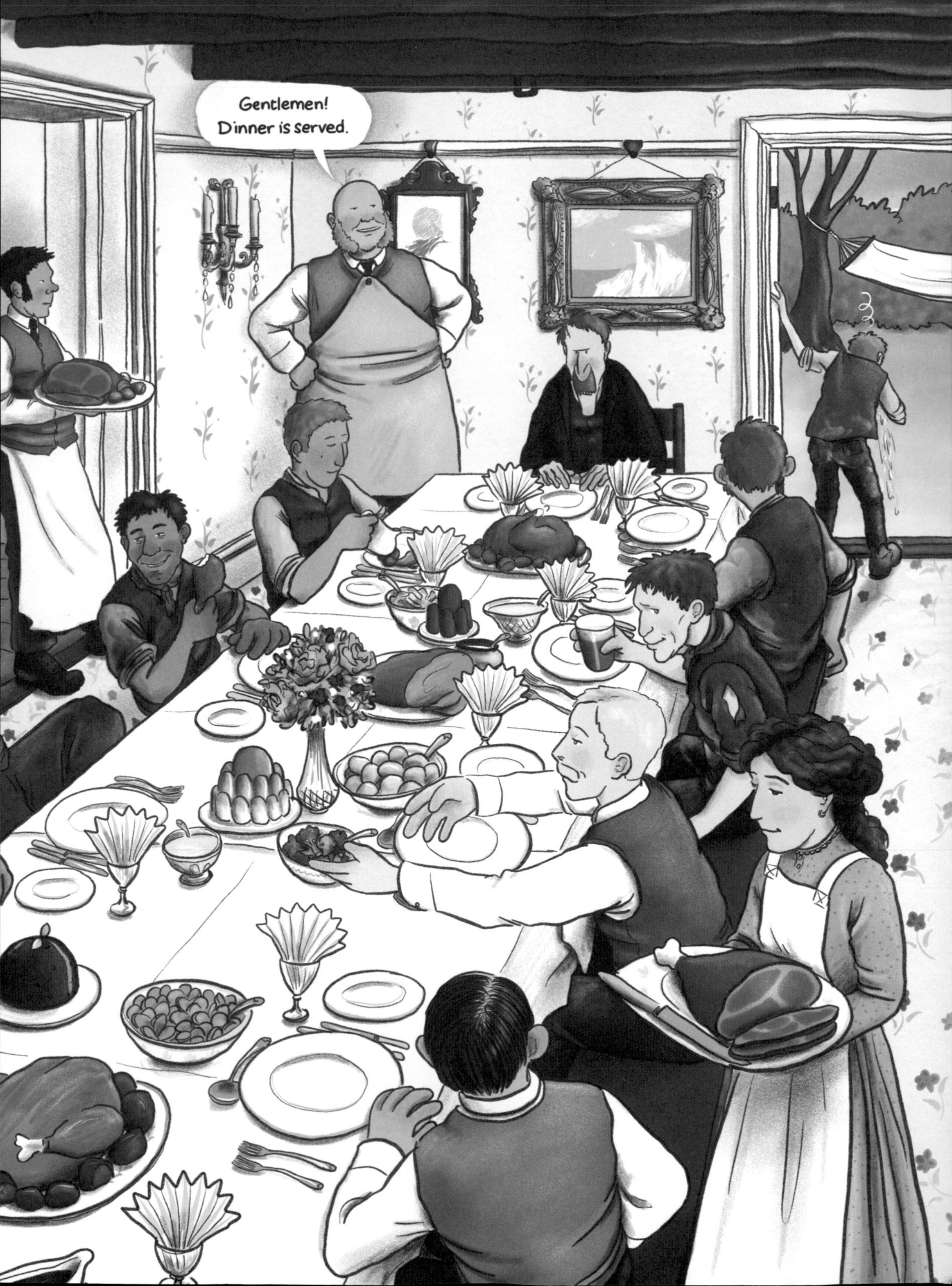
Gentlemen! Dinner is served.

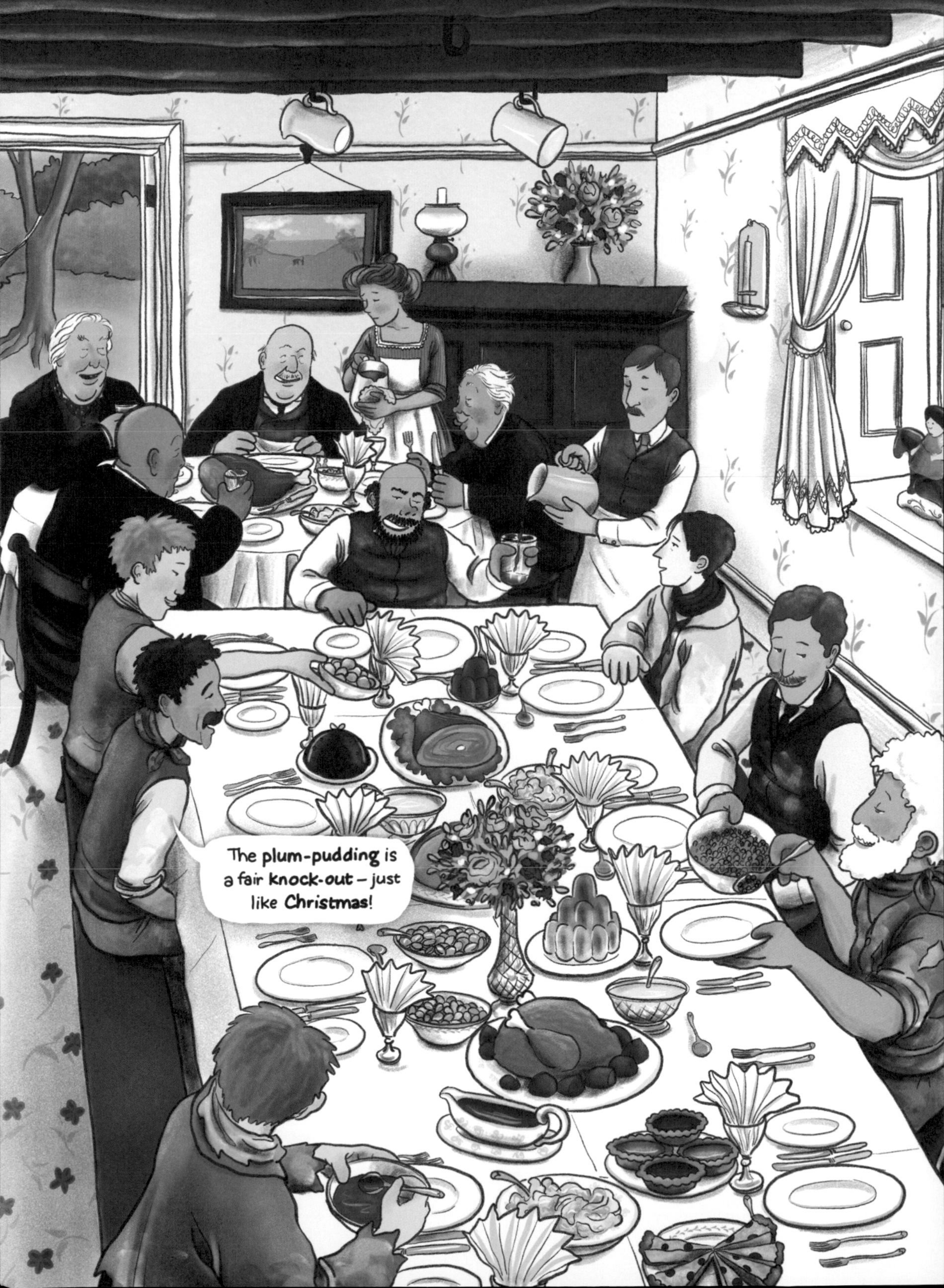
The plum-pudding is a fair knock-out – just like Christmas!

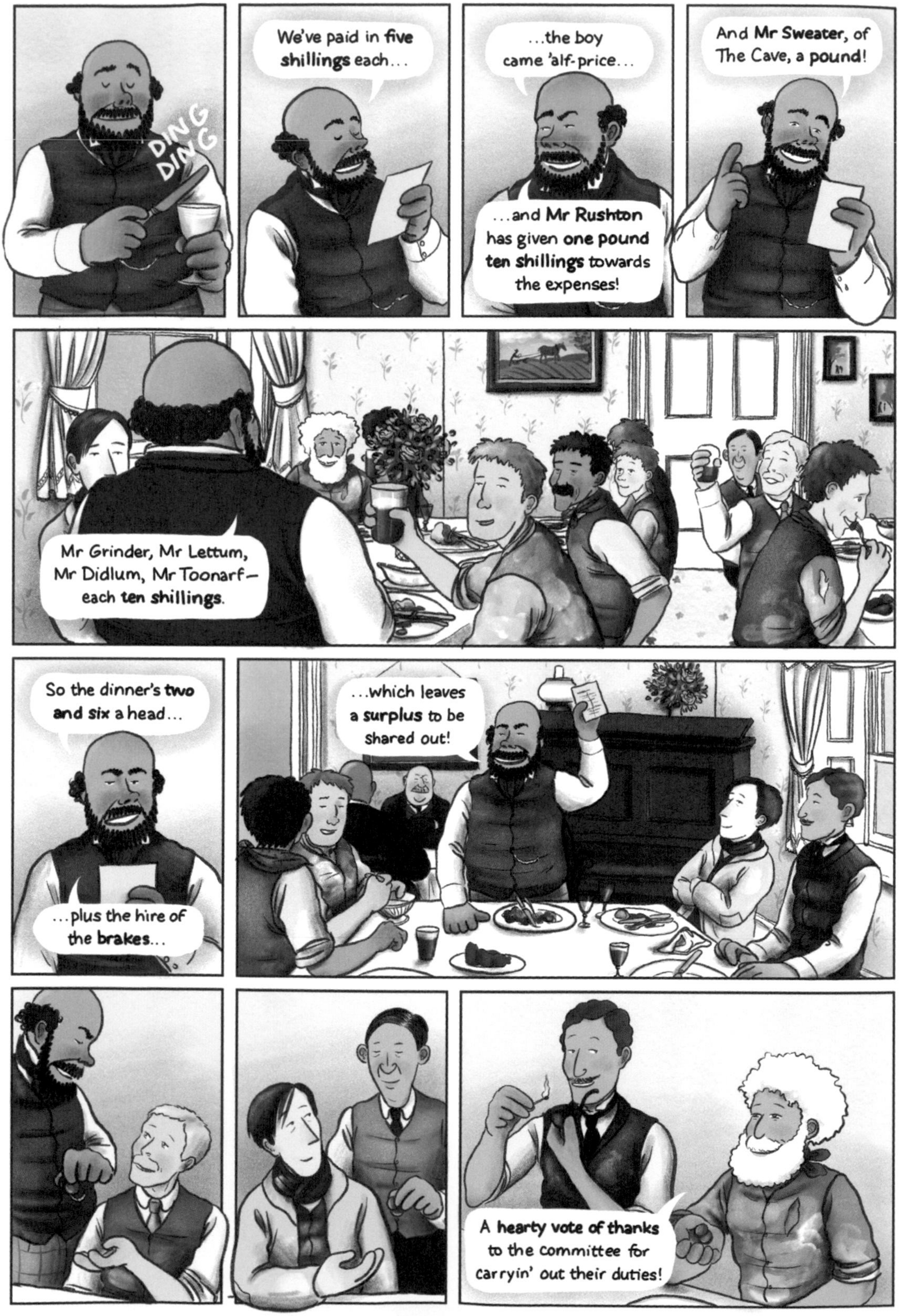
DING DING
We've paid in five shillings each...
...the boy came 'alf-price...
...and Mr Rushton has given one pound ten shillings towards the expenses!
And Mr Sweater, of The Cave, a pound!
Mr Grinder, Mr Lettum, Mr Didlum, Mr Toonarf— each ten shillings.
So the dinner's two and six a head...
...plus the hire of the brakes...
...which leaves a surplus to be shared out!
A hearty vote of thanks to the committee for carryin' out their duties!

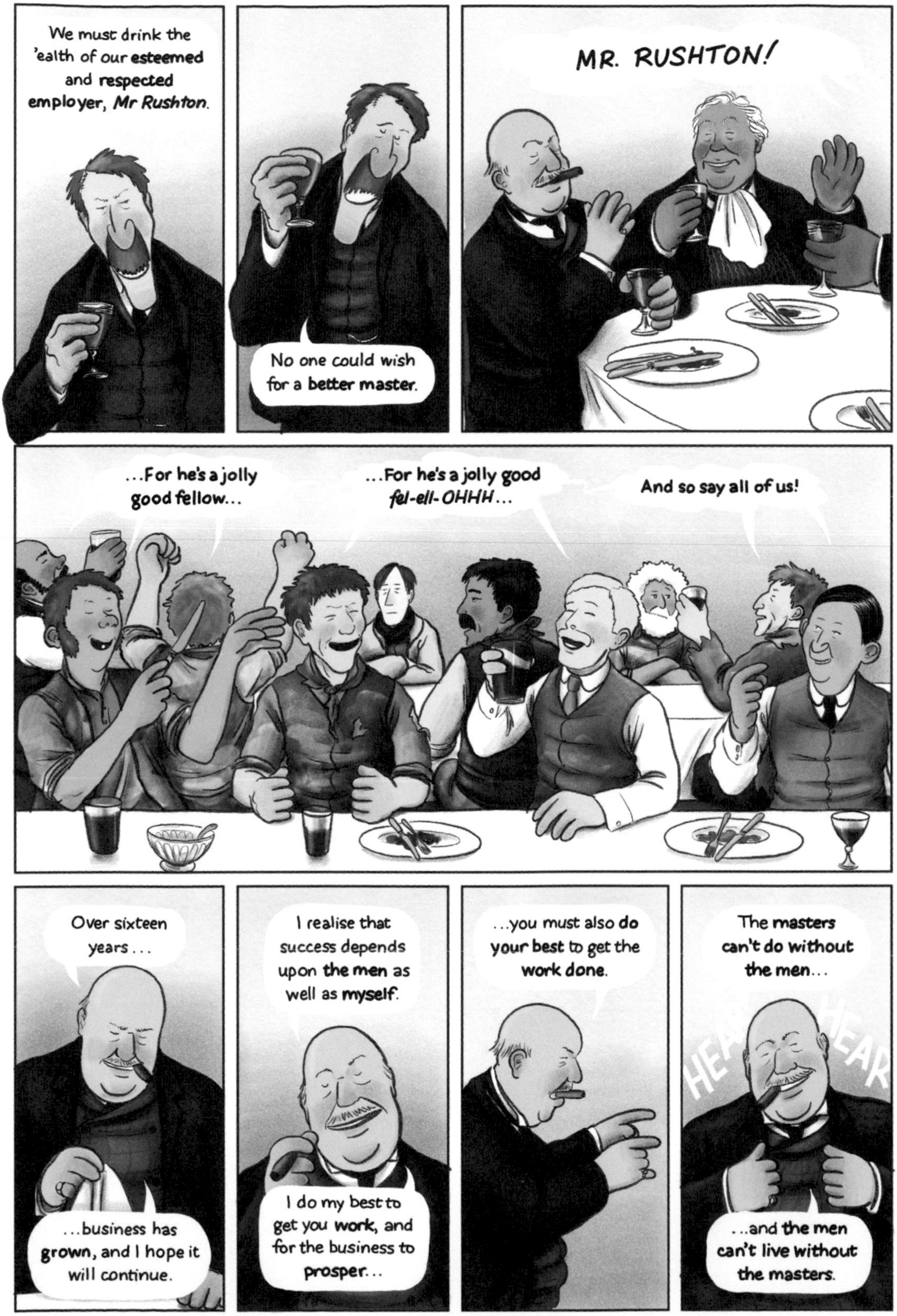
We must drink the 'ealth of our esteemed and respected employer, Mr Rushton.
No one could wish for a better master.
MR. RUSHTON!
...For he's a jolly good fellow...
...For he's a jolly good fel-ell-OHHH...
And so say all of us!
Over sixteen years...
...business has grown, and I hope it will continue.
I realise that success depends upon the men as well as myself.
I do my best to get you work, and for the business to prosper...
...you must also do your best to get the work done.
The masters can't do without the men...
HEAR
...and the men can't live without the masters.

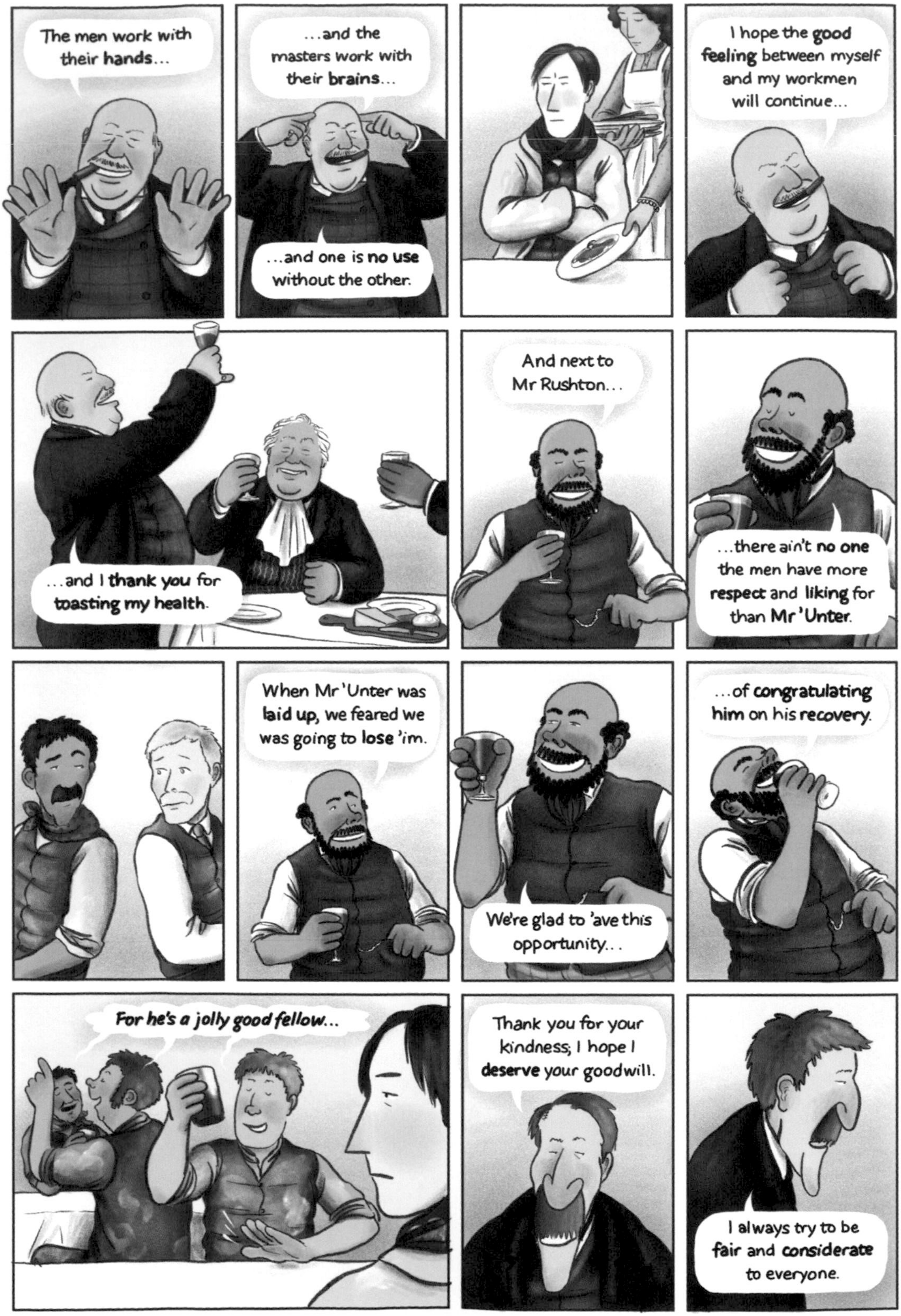
The men work with their hands...
...and the masters work with their brains...
...and one is no use without the other.
I hope the good feeling between myself and my workmen will continue...
...and I thank you for toasting my health.
And next to Mr Rushton...
...there ain't no one the men have more respect and liking for than Mr 'Unter.
When Mr 'Unter was laid up, we feared we was going to lose 'im.
We're glad to 'ave this opportunity...
...of congratulating him on his recovery.
For he's a jolly good fellow...
Thank you for your kindness; I hope I deserve your goodwill.
I always try to be fair and considerate to everyone.

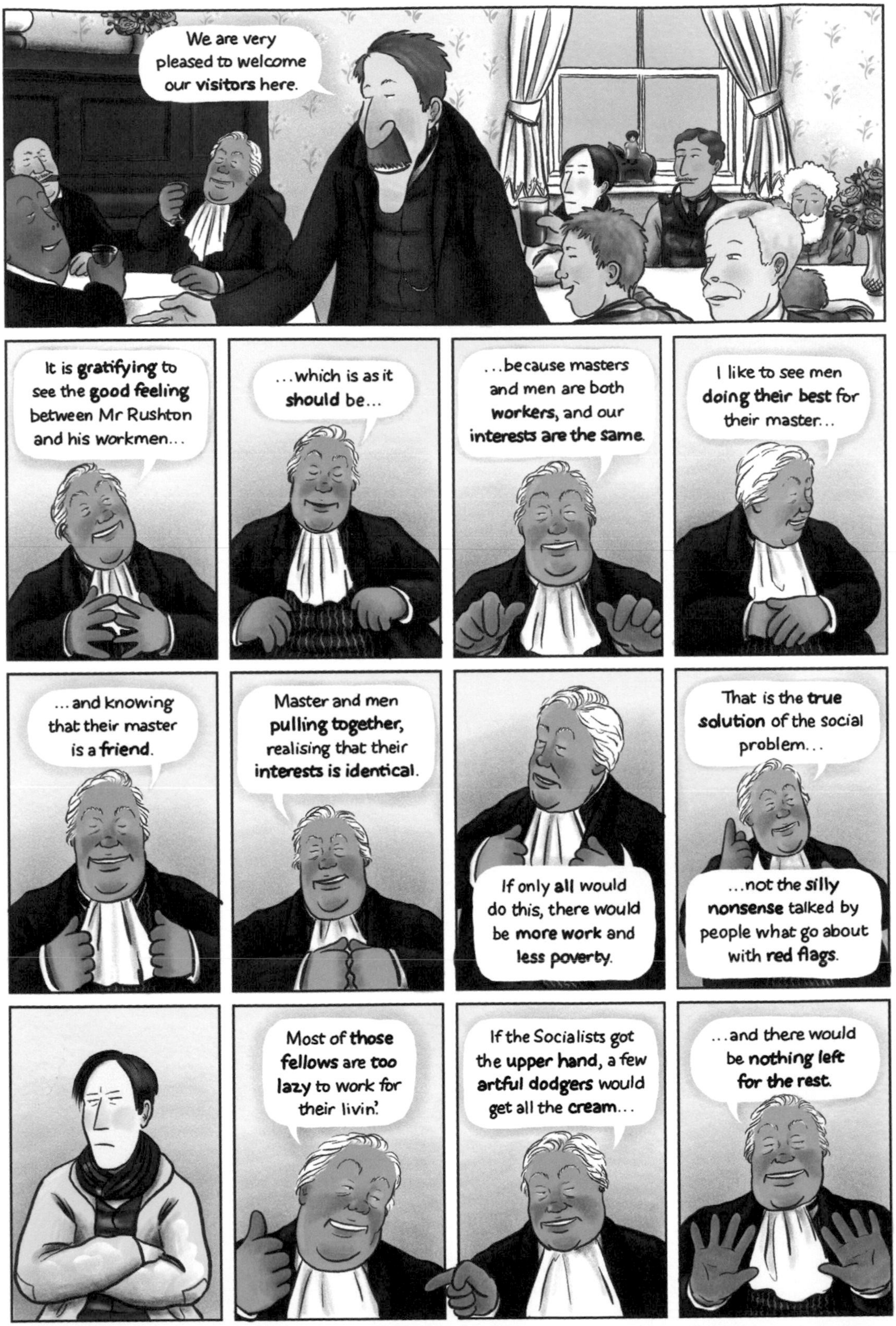
We are very pleased to welcome our visitors here.
It is gratifying to see the good feeling between Mr Rushton and his workmen...
...which is as it should be...
...because masters and men are both workers, and our interests are the same.
I like to see men doing their best for their master...
...and knowing that their master is a friend.
Master and men pulling together, realising that their interests is identical.
If only all would do this, there would be more work and less poverty.
That is the true solution of the social problem...
...not the silly nonsense talked by people what go about with red flags.
Most of those fellows are too lazy to work for their livin'.
If the Socialists got the upper hand, a few artful dodgers would get all the cream...
...and there would be nothing left for the rest.

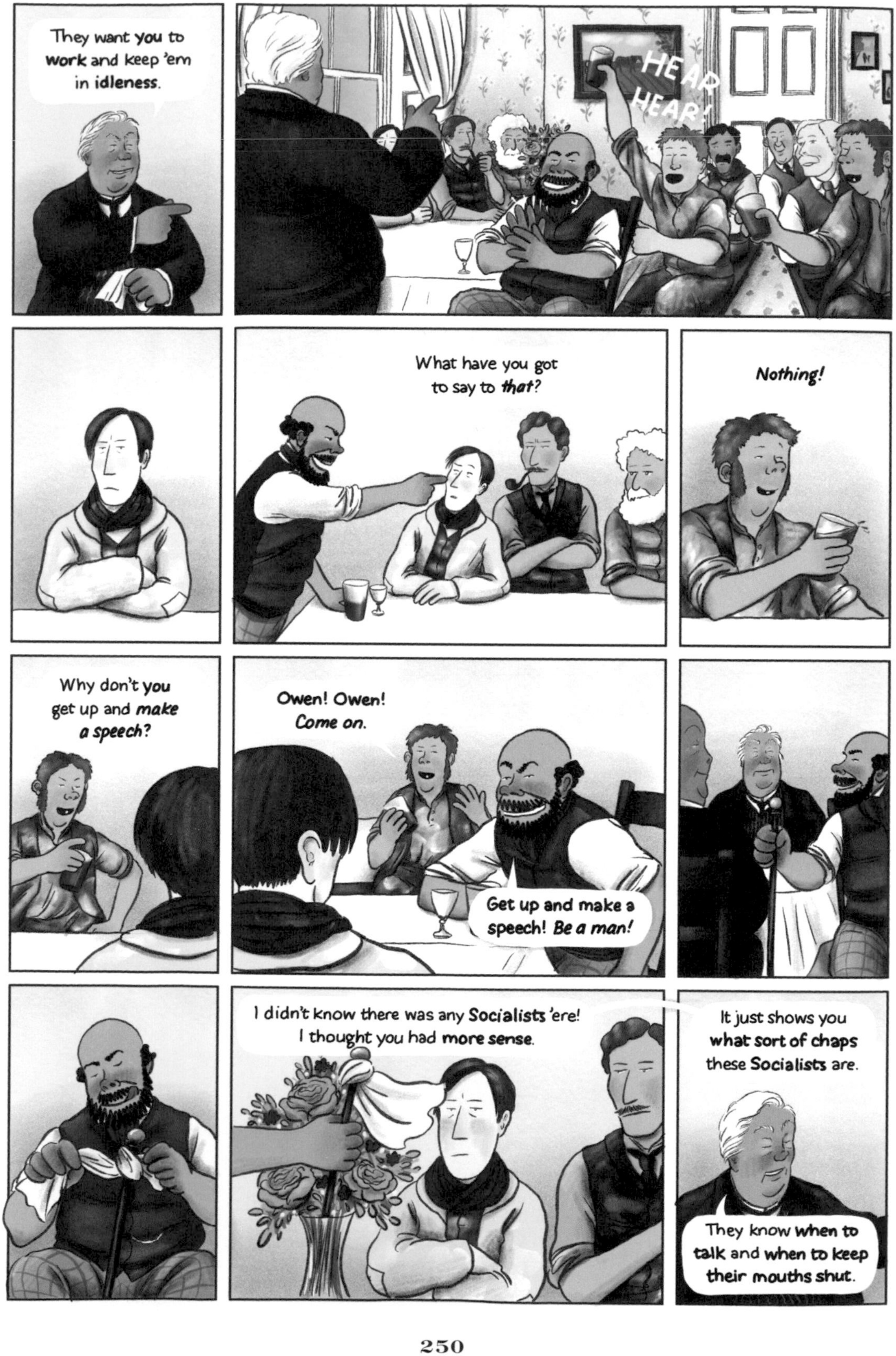
They want **you** to **work** and keep 'em in **idleness**.
HEAR HEAR!
What have you got to say to ***that***?
Nothing!
Why don't **you** get up and ***make a speech***?
Owen! Owen! *Come on.*
Get up and make a speech! *Be a man!*
I didn't know there was any **Socialists** 'ere! I thought you had **more sense**.
It just shows you **what sort of chaps** these **Socialists** are.
They know **when to talk** and **when to keep their mouths shut**.

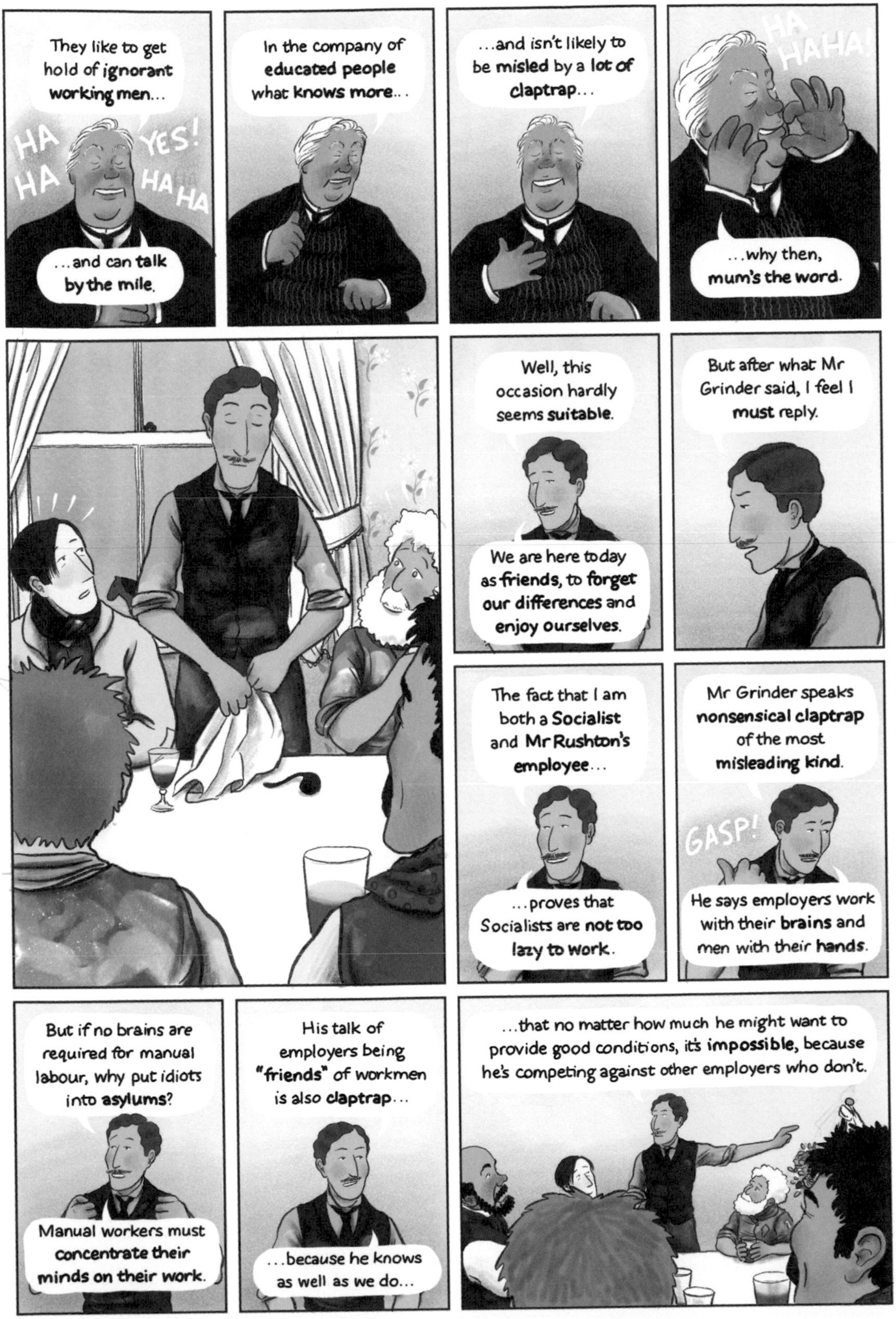

They like to get hold of ignorant working men...
HA HA
YES!
HA HA HA
...and can talk by the mile.
In the company of educated people what knows more...
...and isn't likely to be misled by a lot of claptrap...
HA HAHA!
...why then, mum's the word.
Well, this occasion hardly seems suitable.
We are here today as friends, to forget our differences and enjoy ourselves.
But after what Mr Grinder said, I feel I must reply.
The fact that I am both a Socialist and Mr Rushton's employee...
...proves that Socialists are not too lazy to work.
Mr Grinder speaks nonsensical claptrap of the most misleading kind.
GASP!
He says employers work with their brains and men with their hands.
But if no brains are required for manual labour, why put idiots into asylums?
Manual workers must concentrate their minds on their work.
His talk of employers being "friends" of workmen is also claptrap...
...because he knows as well as we do...
...that no matter how much he might want to provide good conditions, it's impossible, because he's competing against other employers who don't.

It's the **bad employer**...

...the **sweating slave-driver**...

...who **sets the pace**, and the others must **keep up**, against their inclinations.

He says the interests of masters and men are **identical**...

...but the **sooner** work gets done, the **more profit** he makes...

...yet the **faster** it is done, the **sooner** the men will be out of work.

After 20 years, an employer has made enough to live the **rest of his life in comfort**.

But what about the **workman**?

After 20 years, they are either **dead** or **broken**.

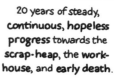

20 years of steady, **continuous, hopeless progress** towards the scrap-heap, the workhouse, and early death.

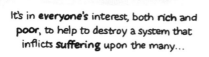

It's in **everyone's** interest, both **rich** and **poor**, to help to destroy a system that inflicts **suffering** upon the many...

...and allows true **happiness** to none.

We must try to find a **better way**.

We haven't come here to listen to a lot of **speechmaking**.

Hear, hear!

Let's sing a song!

Come, come, come an' 'ave a drink with me, Down by the old Bull and Bush, Bush! Bush!

Altogether, boys!

252

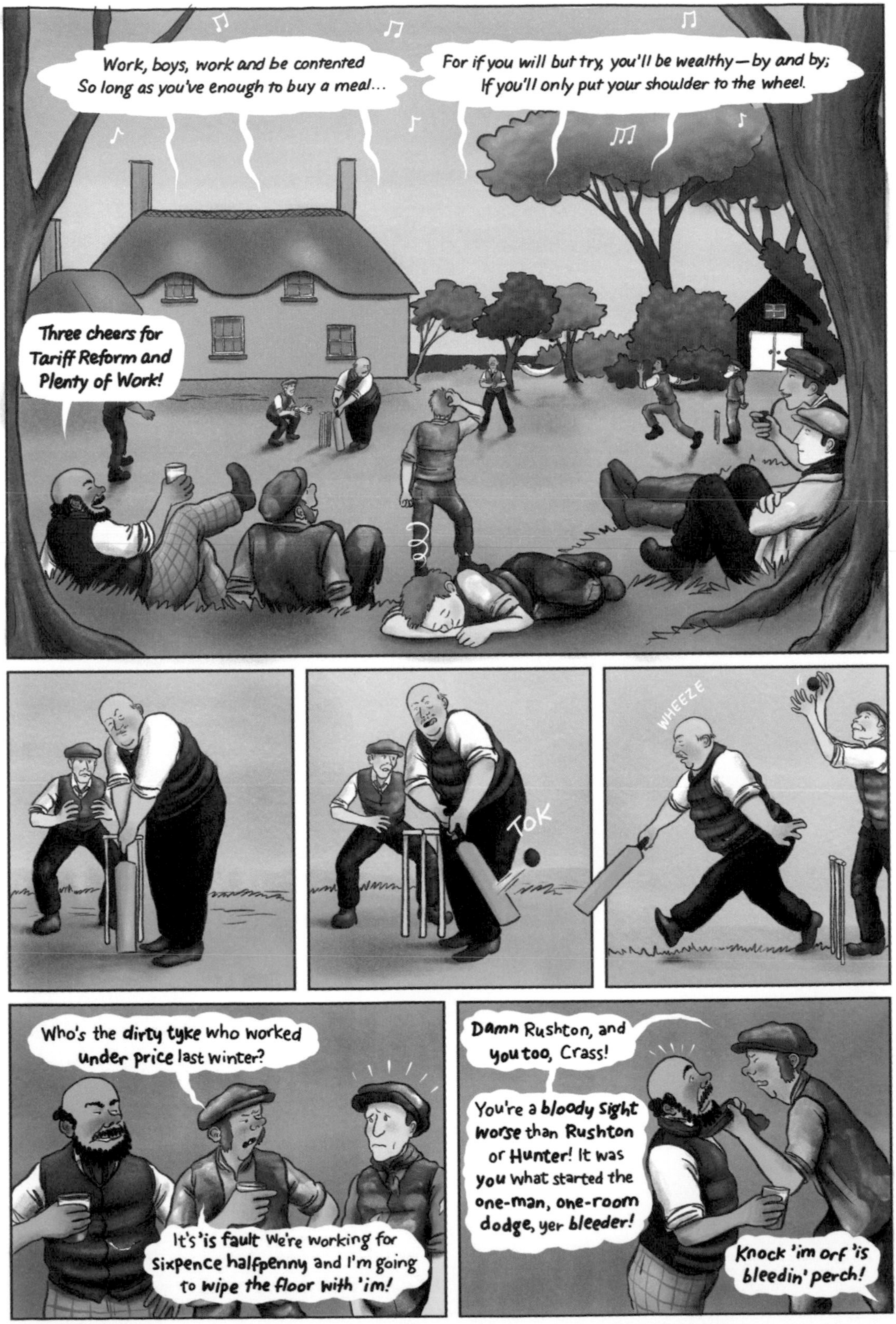
Work, boys, work and be contented
So long as you've enough to buy a meal...
For if you will but try, you'll be wealthy—by and by;
If you'll only put your shoulder to the wheel.
Three cheers for Tariff Reform and Plenty of Work!
TOK
WHEEZE
Who's the dirty tyke who worked under price last winter?
It's 'is fault we're working for Sixpence halfpenny and I'm going to wipe the floor with 'im!
Damn Rushton, and you too, Crass!
You're a bloody sight worse than Rushton or Hunter! It was you what started the one-man, one-room dodge, yer bleeder!
Knock 'im orf 'is bleedin' perch!

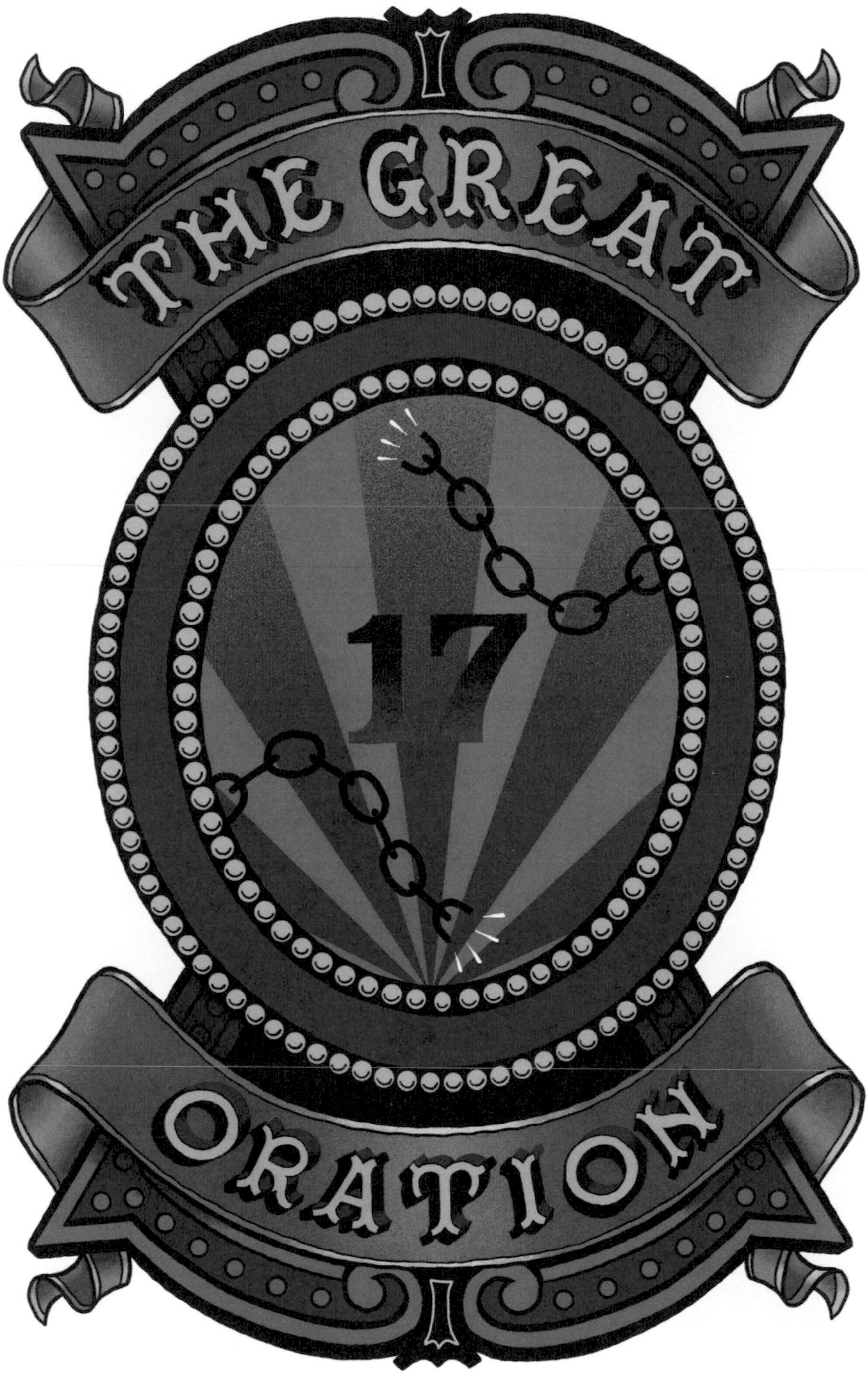
THE GREAT
17
ORATION

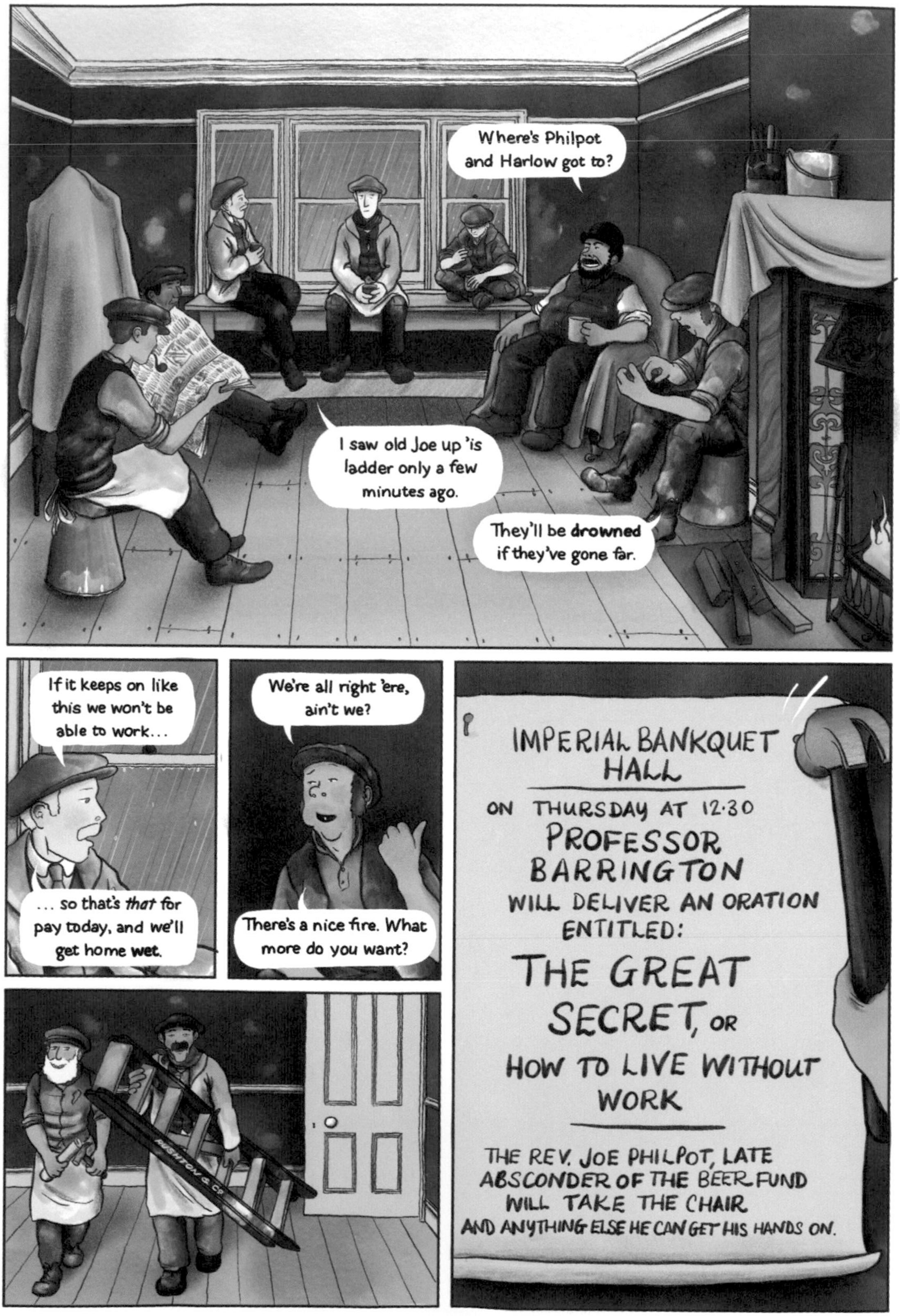
Where's Philpot and Harlow got to?
I saw old Joe up 'is ladder only a few minutes ago.
They'll be **drowned** if they've gone far.
If it keeps on like this we won't be able to work...
... so that's *that* for pay today, and we'll get home **wet**.
We're all right 'ere, ain't we?
There's a nice fire. What more do you want?
IMPERIAL BANKQUET HALL
ON THURSDAY AT 12·30
PROFESSOR BARRINGTON
WILL DELIVER AN ORATION ENTITLED:
THE GREAT SECRET, OR
HOW TO LIVE WITHOUT WORK
THE REV. JOE PHILPOT, LATE ABSCONDER OF THE BEER FUND WILL TAKE THE CHAIR
AND ANYTHING ELSE HE CAN GET HIS HANDS ON.

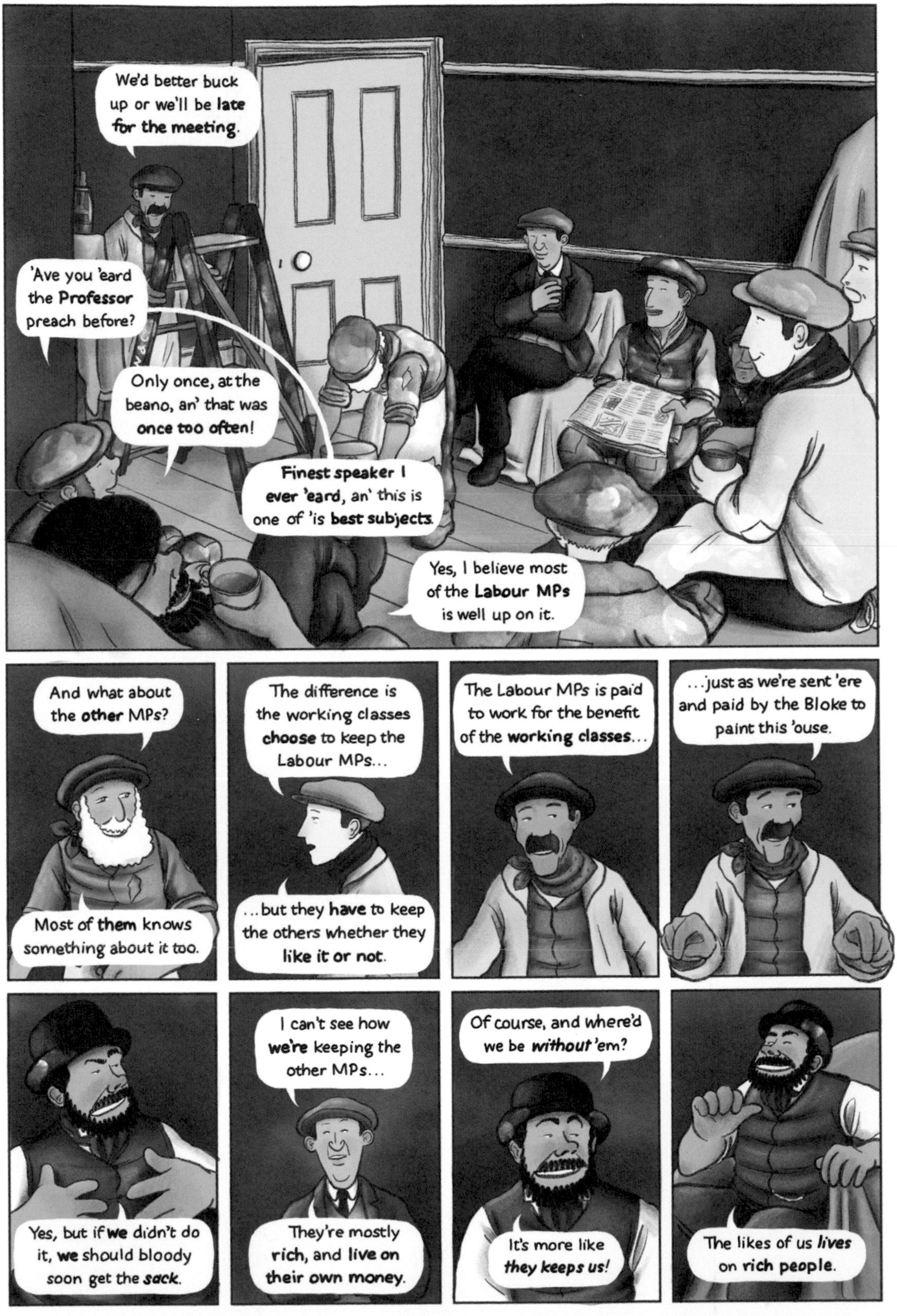
We'd better buck up or we'll be late for the meeting.
'Ave you 'eard the Professor preach before?
Only once, at the beano, an' that was once too often!
Finest speaker I ever 'eard, an' this is one of 'is best subjects.
Yes, I believe most of the Labour MPs is well up on it.
And what about the other MPs?
Most of them knows something about it too.
The difference is the working classes choose to keep the Labour MPs...
...but they have to keep the others whether they like it or not.
The Labour MPs is paid to work for the benefit of the working classes...
...just as we're sent 'ere and paid by the Bloke to paint this 'ouse.
Yes, but if we didn't do it, we should bloody soon get the sack.
I can't see how we're keeping the other MPs...
They're mostly rich, and live on their own money.
Of course, and where'd we be without 'em?
It's more like they keeps us!
The likes of us lives on rich people.

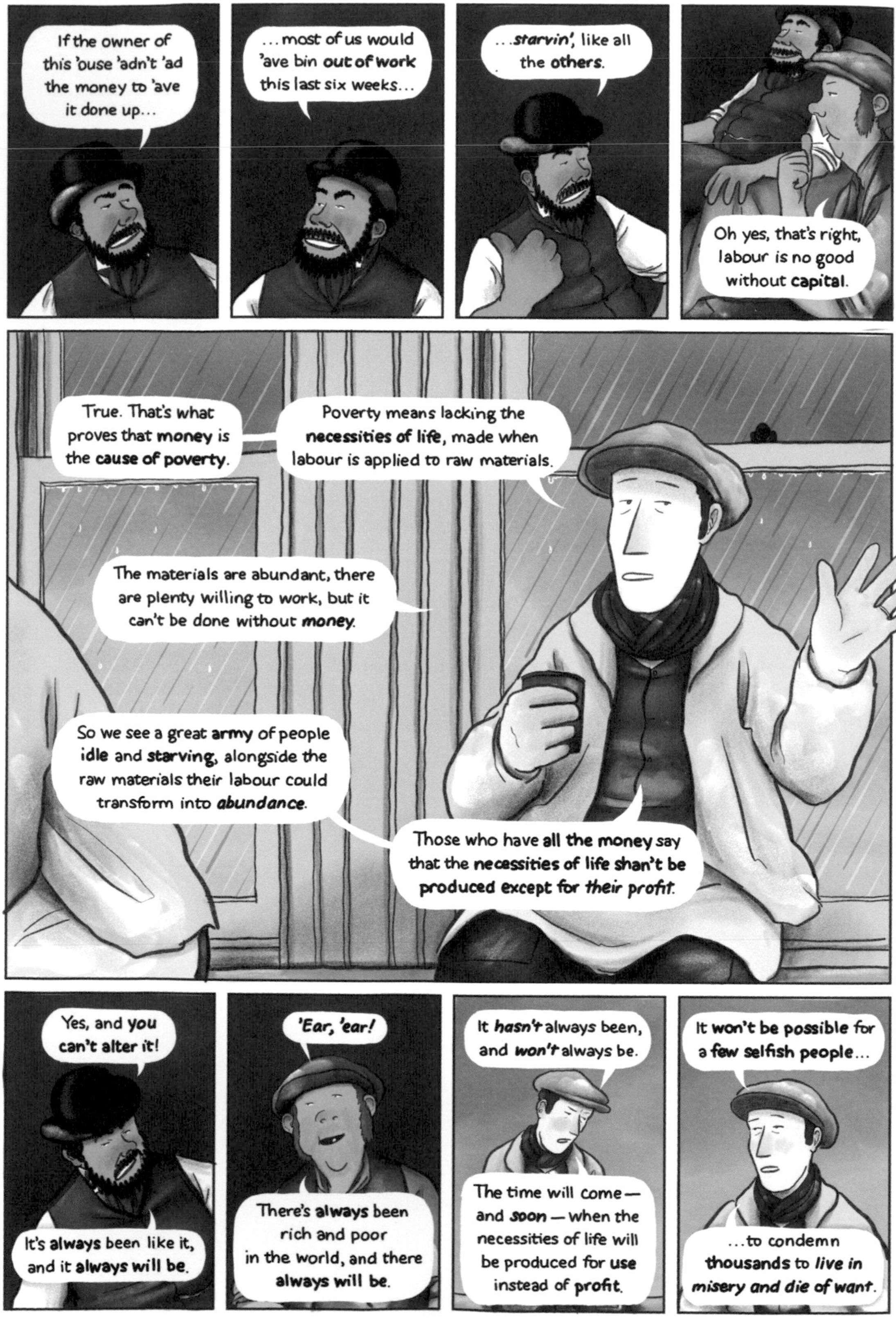
If the owner of this 'ouse 'adn't 'ad the money to 'ave it done up...
...most of us would 'ave bin out of work this last six weeks...
...starvin', like all the others.
Oh yes, that's right, labour is no good without capital.
True. That's what proves that money is the cause of poverty.
Poverty means lacking the necessities of life, made when labour is applied to raw materials.
The materials are abundant, there are plenty willing to work, but it can't be done without money.
So we see a great army of people idle and starving, alongside the raw materials their labour could transform into abundance.
Those who have all the money say that the necessities of life shan't be produced except for their profit.
Yes, and you can't alter it!
It's always been like it, and it always will be.
'Ear, 'ear!
There's always been rich and poor in the world, and there always will be.
It hasn't always been, and won't always be.
The time will come— and soon — when the necessities of life will be produced for use instead of profit.
It won't be possible for a few selfish people...
...to condemn thousands to live in misery and die of want.

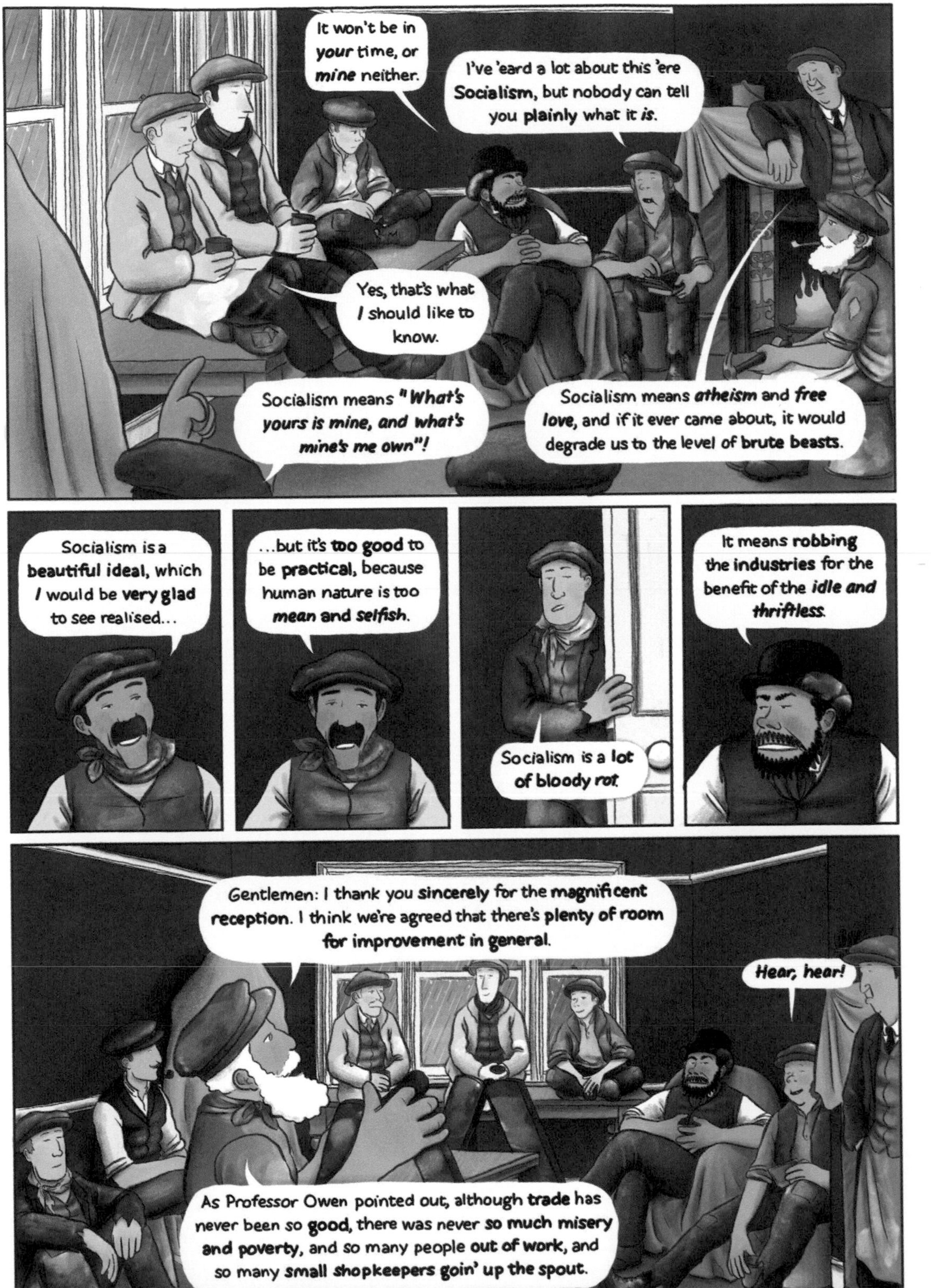
It won't be in *your* time, or *mine* neither.
I've 'eard a lot about this 'ere **Socialism**, but nobody can tell you **plainly** what it *is*.
Yes, that's what *I* should like to know.
Socialism means ***"What's yours is mine, and what's mine's me own"!***
Socialism means ***atheism*** and ***free love***, and if it ever came about, it would degrade us to the level of **brute beasts**.
Socialism is a **beautiful ideal**, which *I* would be **very glad** to see realised...
...but it's **too good** to be **practical**, because human nature is too ***mean*** and ***selfish***.
Socialism is a **lot of bloody** ***rot***.
It means **robbing the industries** for the benefit of the ***idle and thriftless***.
Gentlemen: I thank you **sincerely** for the **magnificent reception**. I think we're agreed that there's **plenty of room for improvement in general**.
Hear, hear!
As Professor Owen pointed out, although **trade** has never been so **good**, there was never **so much misery and poverty**, and so many people **out of work**, and so many **small shopkeepers goin' up the spout**.

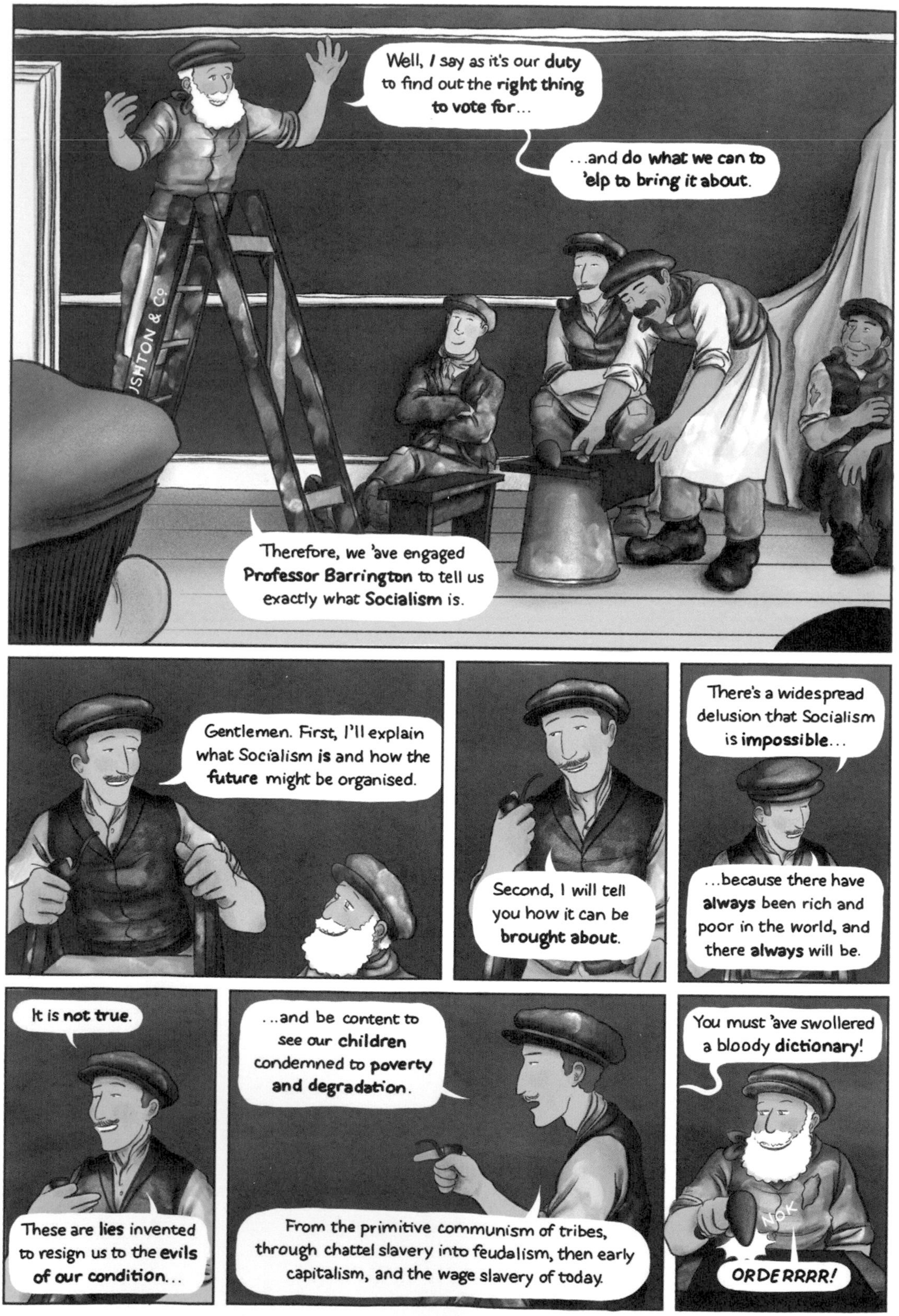
Well, I say as it's our duty to find out the right thing to vote for...
...and do what we can to 'elp to bring it about.
Therefore, we 'ave engaged Professor Barrington to tell us exactly what Socialism is.
Gentlemen. First, I'll explain what Socialism is and how the future might be organised.
Second, I will tell you how it can be brought about.
There's a widespread delusion that Socialism is impossible...
...because there have always been rich and poor in the world, and there always will be.
It is not true.
These are lies invented to resign us to the evils of our condition...
...and be content to see our children condemned to poverty and degradation.
From the primitive communism of tribes, through chattel slavery into feudalism, then early capitalism, and the wage slavery of today.
You must 'ave swollered a bloody dictionary!
NOK
ORDERRRR!

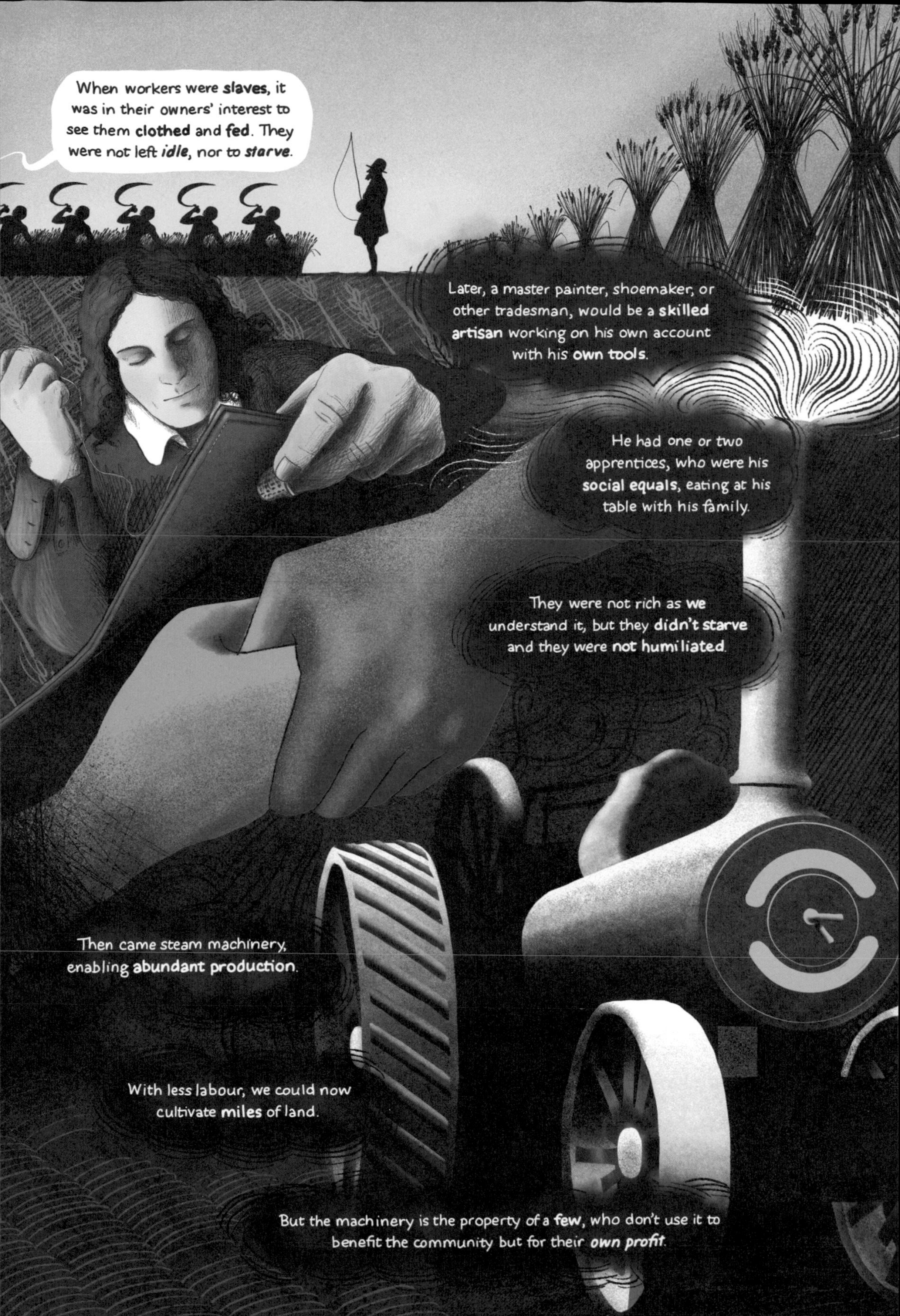
When workers were **slaves**, it was in their owners' interest to see them **clothed** and **fed**. They were not left ***idle***, nor to ***starve***.
Later, a master painter, shoemaker, or other tradesman, would be a **skilled artisan** working on his own account with his **own tools**.
He had one or two apprentices, who were his **social equals**, eating at his table with his family.
They were not rich as **we** understand it, but they **didn't starve** and they were **not humiliated**.
Then came steam machinery, enabling **abundant production**.
With less labour, we could now cultivate **miles** of land.
But the machinery is the property of a **few**, who don't use it to benefit the community but for their ***own profit***.

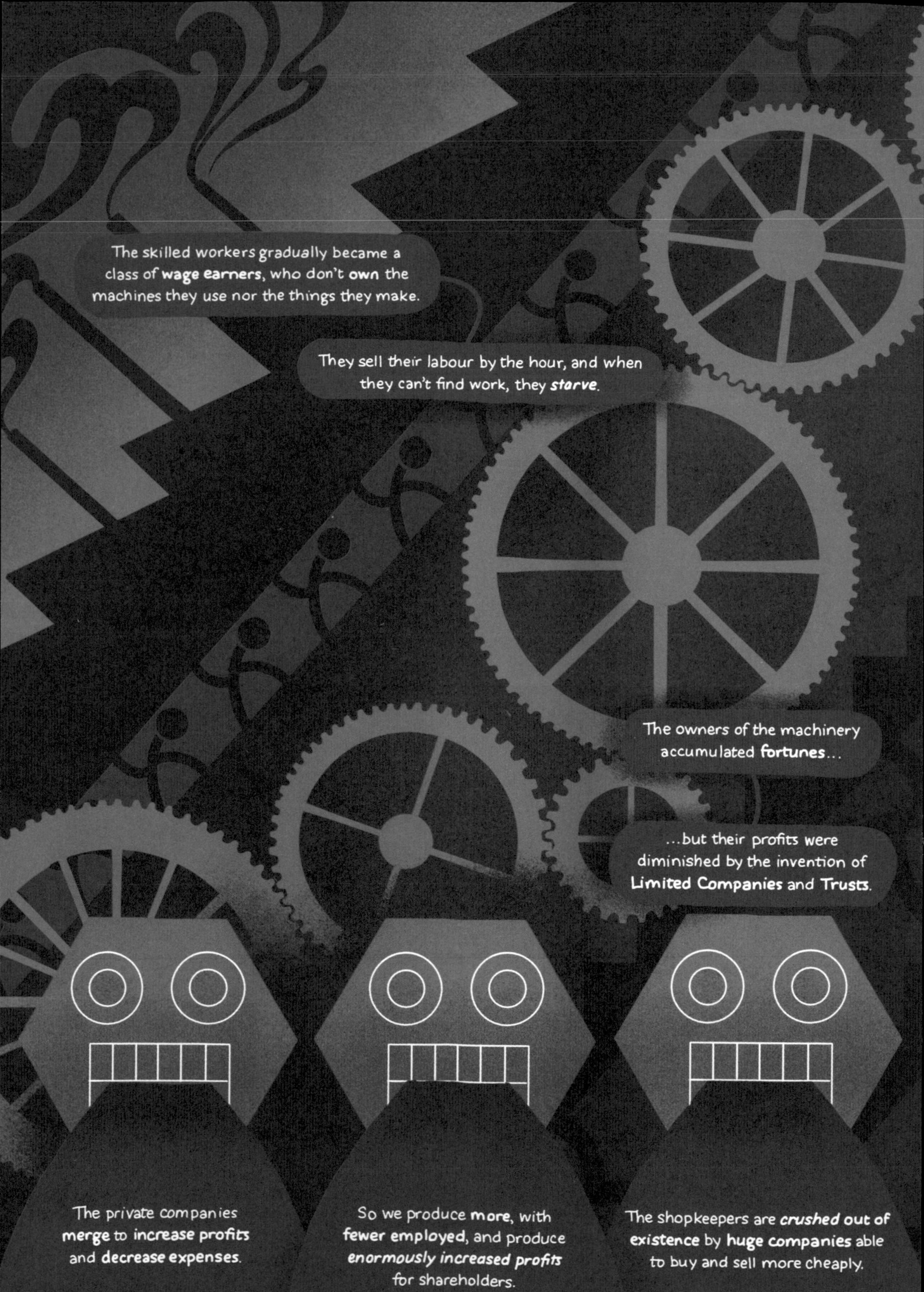
The skilled workers gradually became a class of **wage earners**, who don't **own** the machines they use nor the things they make.
They sell their labour by the hour, and when they can't find work, they ***starve***.
The owners of the machinery accumulated **fortunes**...
...but their profits were diminished by the invention of **Limited Companies** and **Trusts**.
The private companies **merge** to *increase profits* and **decrease expenses**.
So we produce **more**, with **fewer employed**, and produce ***enormously increased profits*** for shareholders.
The shopkeepers are ***crushed out of existence*** by **huge companies** able to buy and sell more cheaply.

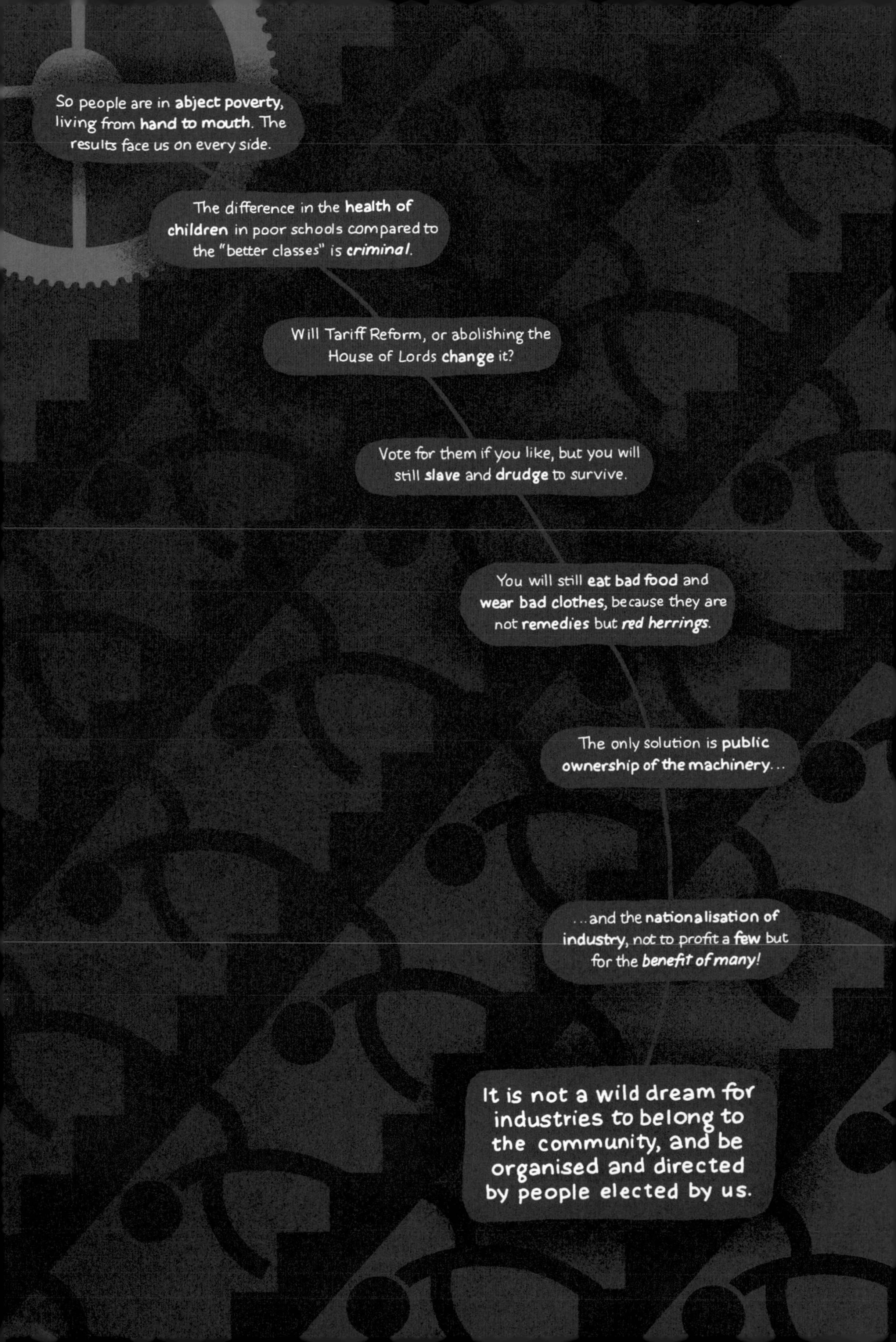
So people are in abject poverty, living from hand to mouth. The results face us on every side.
The difference in the health of children in poor schools compared to the "better classes" is criminal.
Will Tariff Reform, or abolishing the House of Lords change it?
Vote for them if you like, but you will still slave and drudge to survive.
You will still eat bad food and wear bad clothes, because they are not remedies but red herrings.
The only solution is public ownership of the machinery...
...and the nationalisation of industry, not to profit a few but for the benefit of many!
It is not a wild dream for industries to belong to the community, and be organised and directed by people elected by us.

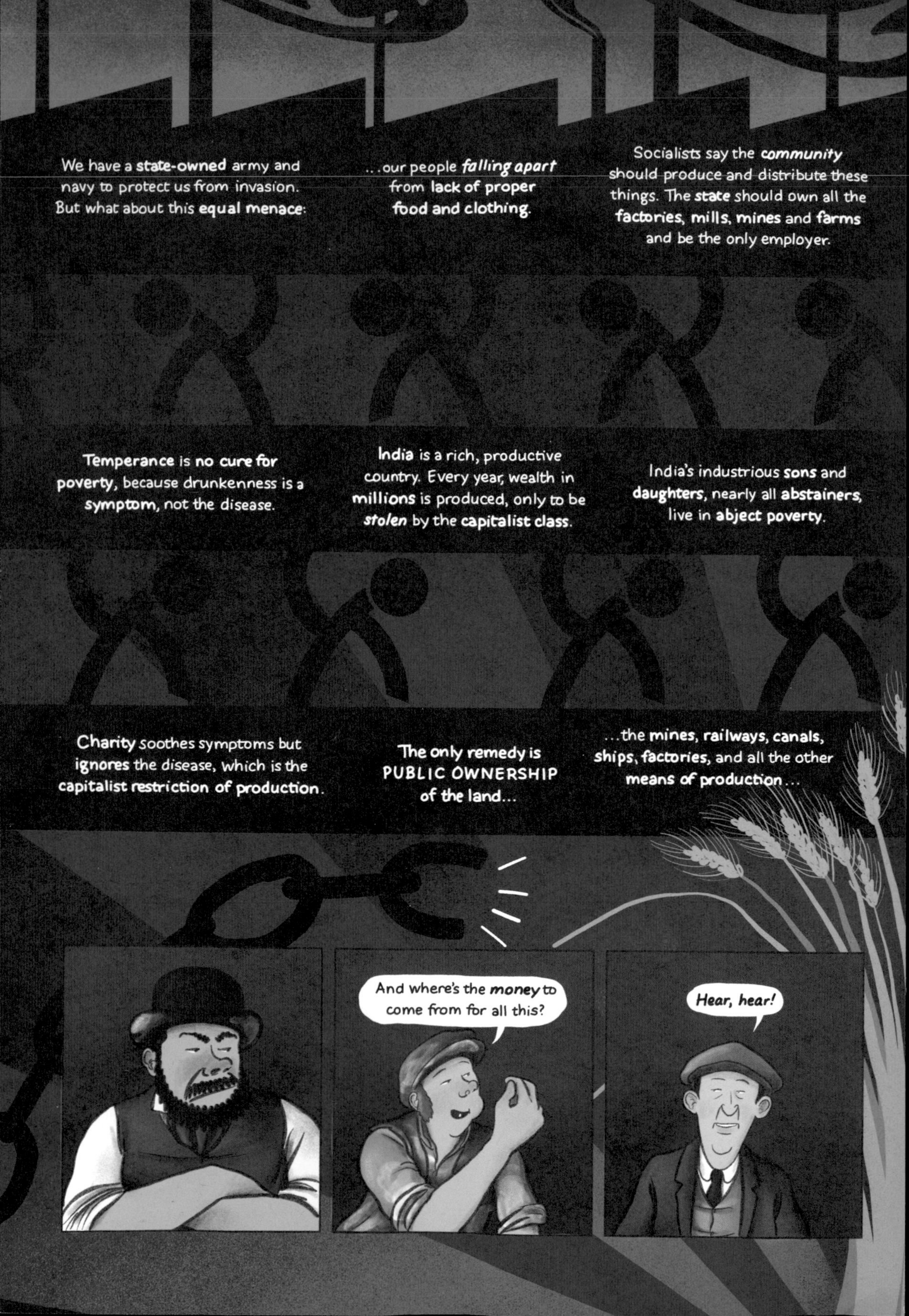
We have a **state-owned** army and navy to protect us from invasion. But what about this **equal menace**:
...our people ***falling apart*** from **lack of proper food and clothing**.
Socialists say the ***community*** should produce and distribute these things. The **state** should own all the **factories, mills, mines** and **farms** and be the only employer.
Temperance is **no cure for poverty**, because drunkenness is a **symptom**, not the disease.
India is a rich, productive country. Every year, wealth in **millions** is produced, only to be ***stolen*** by the **capitalist class**.
India's industrious **sons** and **daughters**, nearly all **abstainers**, live in **abject poverty**.
Charity soothes symptoms but **ignores** the disease, which is the **capitalist restriction of production**.
The only remedy is PUBLIC OWNERSHIP of the land...
...the **mines, railways, canals, ships, factories**, and all the other **means of production**...
And where's the ***money*** to come from for all this?
Hear, hear!

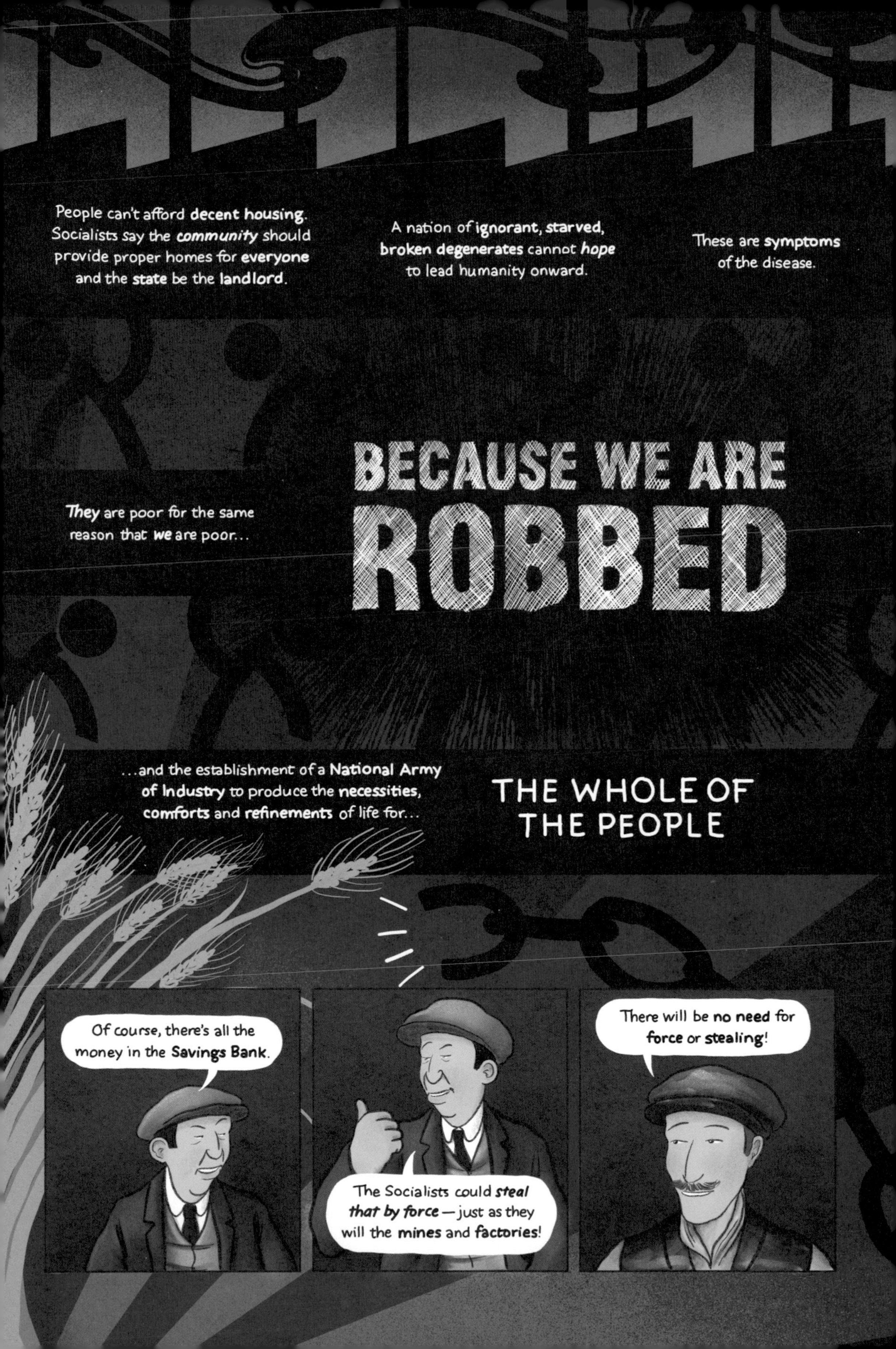

People can't afford **decent housing**. Socialists say the ***community*** should provide proper homes for **everyone** and the **state** be the **landlord**.
A nation of **ignorant, starved, broken degenerates** cannot ***hope*** to lead humanity onward.
These are **symptoms** of the disease.
They are poor for the same reason that ***we*** are poor...
BECAUSE WE ARE ROBBED
...and the establishment of a **National Army of Industry** to produce the **necessities, comforts** and **refinements** of life for...
THE WHOLE OF THE PEOPLE
Of course, there's all the money in the **Savings Bank**.
The Socialists could ***steal that by force*** — just as they will the **mines** and **factories**!
There will be **no need** for **force** or **stealing**!

You talk about **ignorance**: what about all the money spent on **education**?

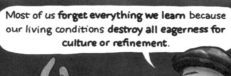

Most of us **forget everything we learn** because our living conditions **destroy all eagerness for culture or refinement**.

We must see children **properly clothed, fed and forbidden to work**. They must be cared for **and** be educated.

All right.

But **how**, when all the land, railways and factories belongs to **private capitalists**?

If you ain't goin' to take 'em by force, I'd like to know how the bloody 'ell you **are** goin' to get 'em?

We don't propose to buy them with **money**.

The people who own them never really **paid** for them — they got them by the "*Money Trick*".

They got 'em by usin' their *brains*.

Exactly.

They call profits the "*wages of intelligence*".

While **we** work, **they** use their brains to **take the things we make**.

The time has come for us to use our brains to **get them back**...

...and stop them from **robbing** us any more.

When a thief is caught with stolen property, is it **robbery** to return it to the **rightful owners**?

The present holders could be allowed to keep it for their lifetime, then it should revert to the **state**, to be used for the **benefit of all**.

There will be plenty of tuneropperty for questions at the **end** of the horation.

Anyone what interrupts again will get a **lick under the ear-'ole with this**.

266

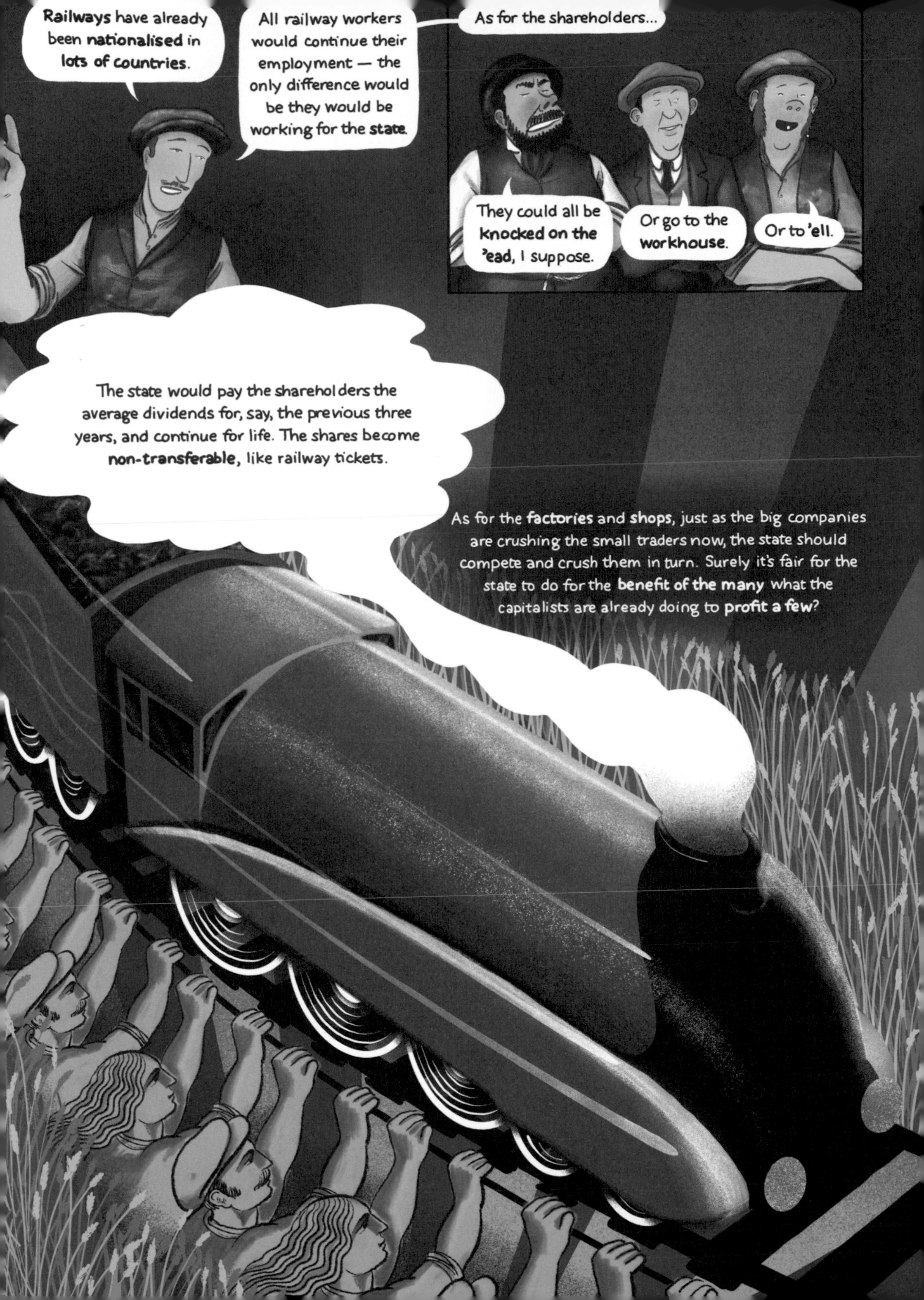
Railways have already been nationalised in lots of countries.
All railway workers would continue their employment — the only difference would be they would be working for the state.
As for the shareholders...
They could all be knocked on the 'ead, I suppose.
Or go to the workhouse.
Or to 'ell.
The state would pay the shareholders the average dividends for, say, the previous three years, and continue for life. The shares become non-transferable, like railway tickets.
As for the factories and shops, just as the big companies are crushing the small traders now, the state should compete and crush them in turn. Surely it's fair for the state to do for the benefit of the many what the capitalists are already doing to profit a few?

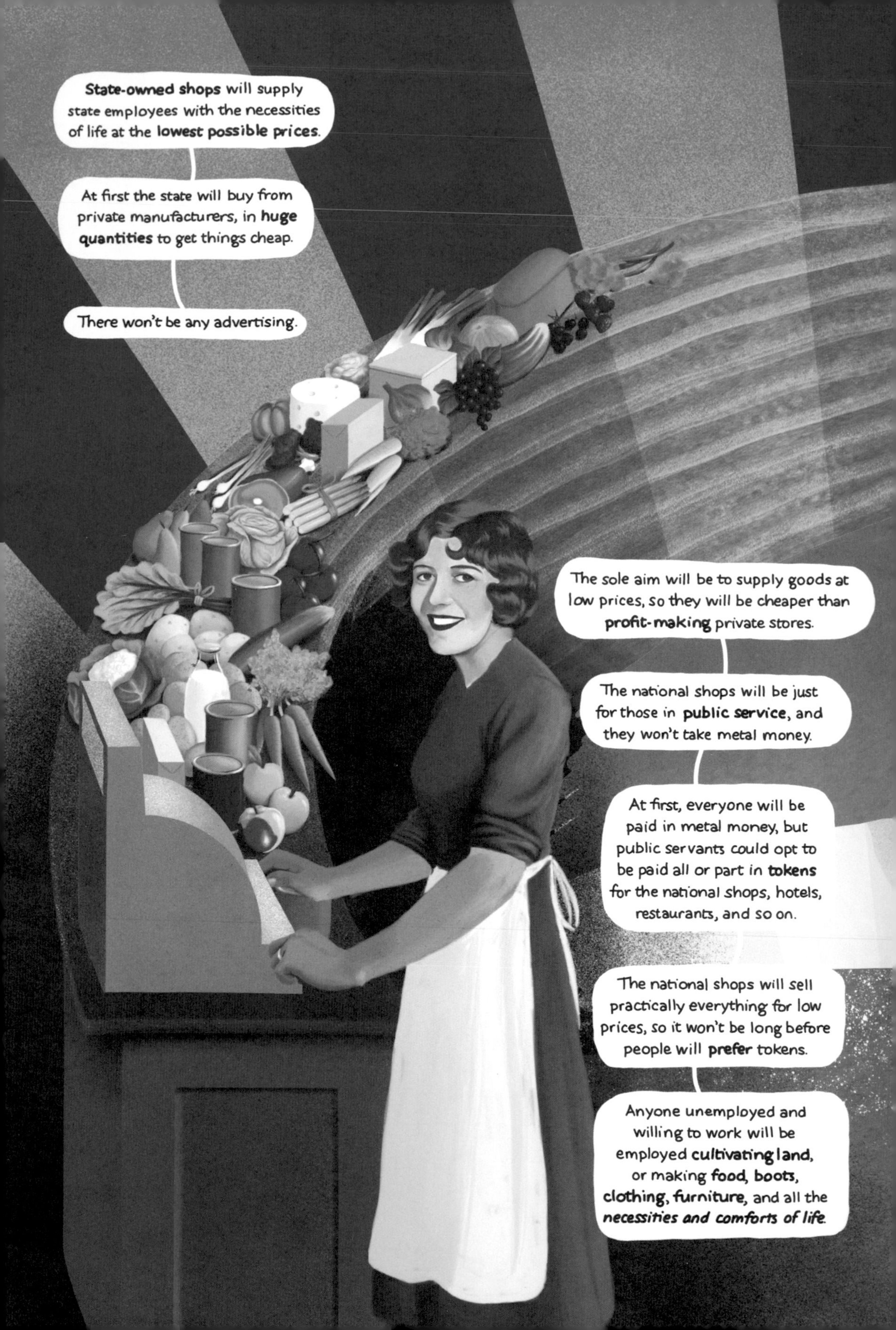

State-owned shops will supply state employees with the necessities of life at the **lowest possible prices**.
At first the state will buy from private manufacturers, in **huge quantities** to get things cheap.
There won't be any advertising.
The sole aim will be to supply goods at low prices, so they will be cheaper than **profit-making** private stores.
The national shops will be just for those in **public service**, and they won't take metal money.
At first, everyone will be paid in metal money, but public servants could opt to be paid all or part in **tokens** for the national shops, hotels, restaurants, and so on.
The national shops will sell practically everything for low prices, so it won't be long before people will **prefer** tokens.
Anyone unemployed and willing to work will be employed **cultivating land**, or making **food**, **boots**, **clothing**, **furniture**, and all the ***necessities and comforts of life***.

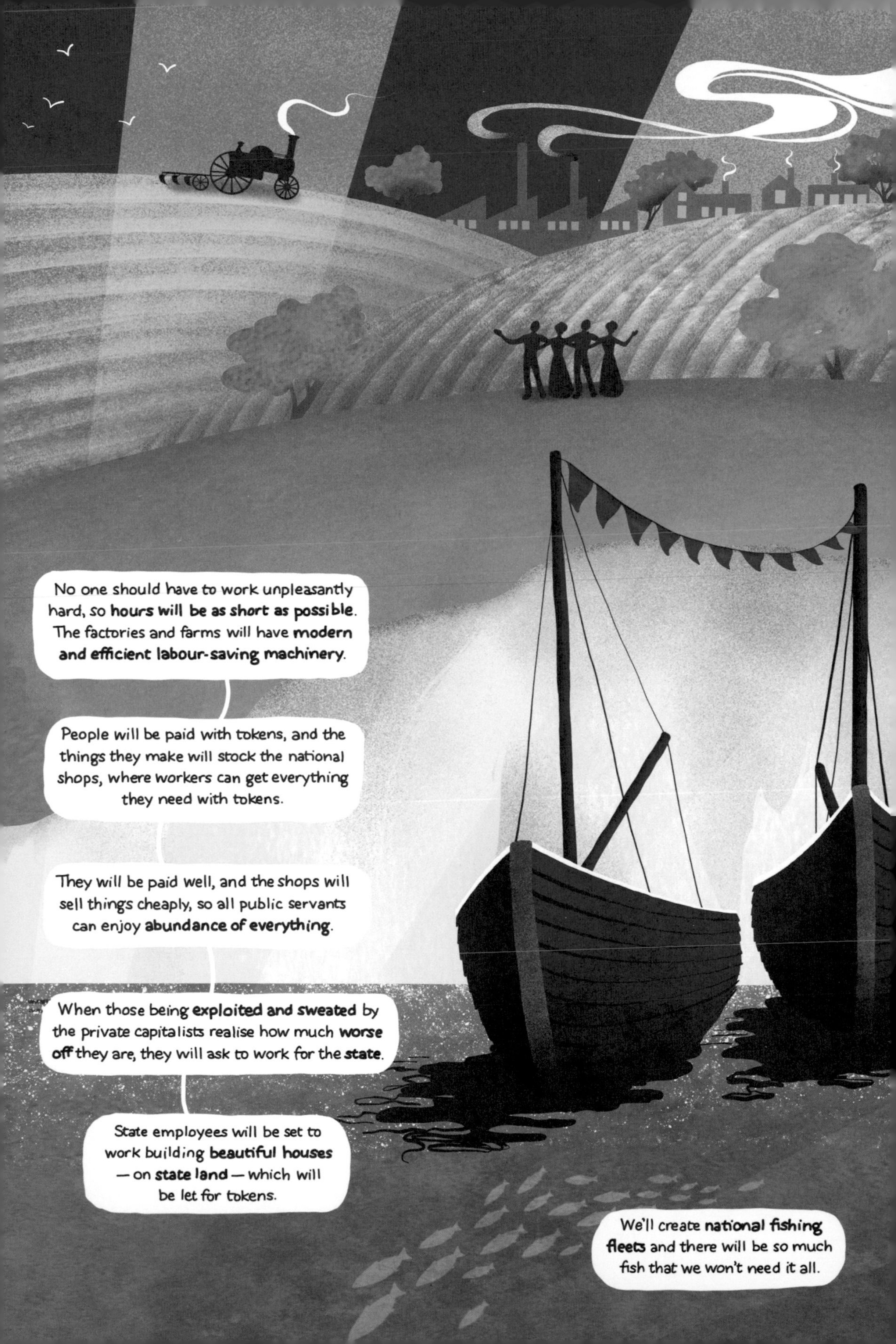
No one should have to work unpleasantly hard, so **hours will be as short as possible**. The factories and farms will have **modern and efficient labour-saving machinery**.
People will be paid with tokens, and the things they make will stock the national shops, where workers can get everything they need with tokens.
They will be paid well, and the shops will sell things cheaply, so all public servants can enjoy **abundance of everything**.
When those being **exploited and sweated** by the private capitalists realise how much **worse off** they are, they will ask to work for the **state**.
State employees will be set to work building **beautiful houses** — on **state land** — which will be let for tokens.
We'll create **national fishing fleets** and there will be so much fish that we won't need it all.

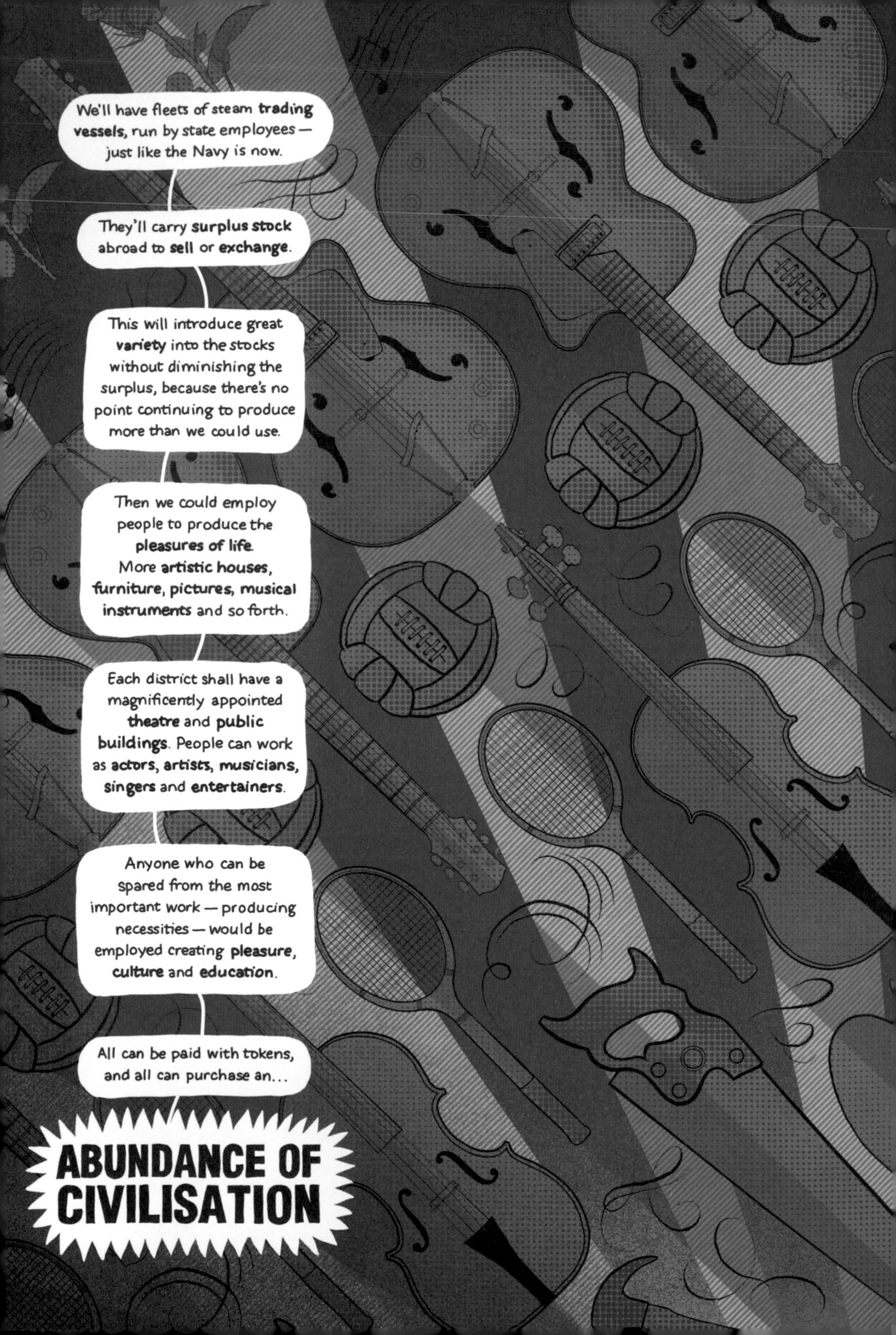
We'll have fleets of steam trading vessels, run by state employees — just like the Navy is now.
They'll carry surplus stock abroad to sell or exchange.
This will introduce great variety into the stocks without diminishing the surplus, because there's no point continuing to produce more than we could use.
Then we could employ people to produce the pleasures of life. More artistic houses, furniture, pictures, musical instruments and so forth.
Each district shall have a magnificently appointed theatre and public buildings. People can work as actors, artists, musicians, singers and entertainers.
Anyone who can be spared from the most important work — producing necessities — would be employed creating pleasure, culture and education.
All can be paid with tokens, and all can purchase an...
ABUNDANCE OF CIVILISATION

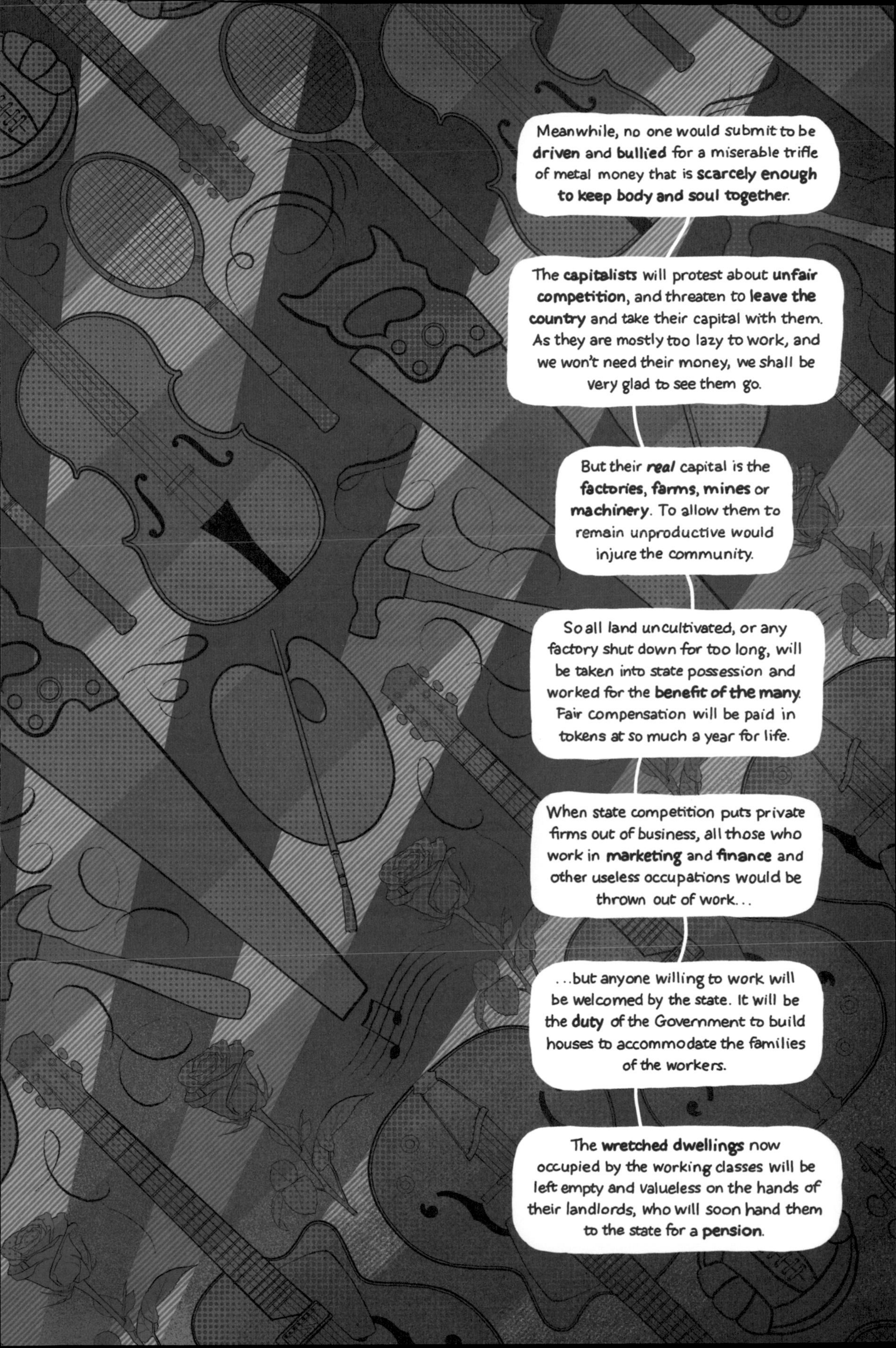
Meanwhile, no one would submit to be **driven** and **bullied** for a miserable trifle of metal money that is **scarcely enough to keep body and soul together**.
The **capitalists** will protest about **unfair competition**, and threaten to **leave the country** and take their capital with them. As they are mostly too lazy to work, and we won't need their money, we shall be very glad to see them go.
But their ***real*** capital is the **factories, farms, mines** or **machinery**. To allow them to remain unproductive would injure the community.
So all land uncultivated, or any factory shut down for too long, will be taken into state possession and worked for the **benefit of the many**. Fair compensation will be paid in tokens at so much a year for life.
When state competition puts private firms out of business, all those who work in **marketing** and **finance** and other useless occupations would be thrown out of work...
...but anyone willing to work will be welcomed by the state. It will be the **duty** of the Government to build houses to accommodate the families of the workers.
The **wretched dwellings** now occupied by the working classes will be left empty and valueless on the hands of their landlords, who will soon hand them to the state for a **pension**.

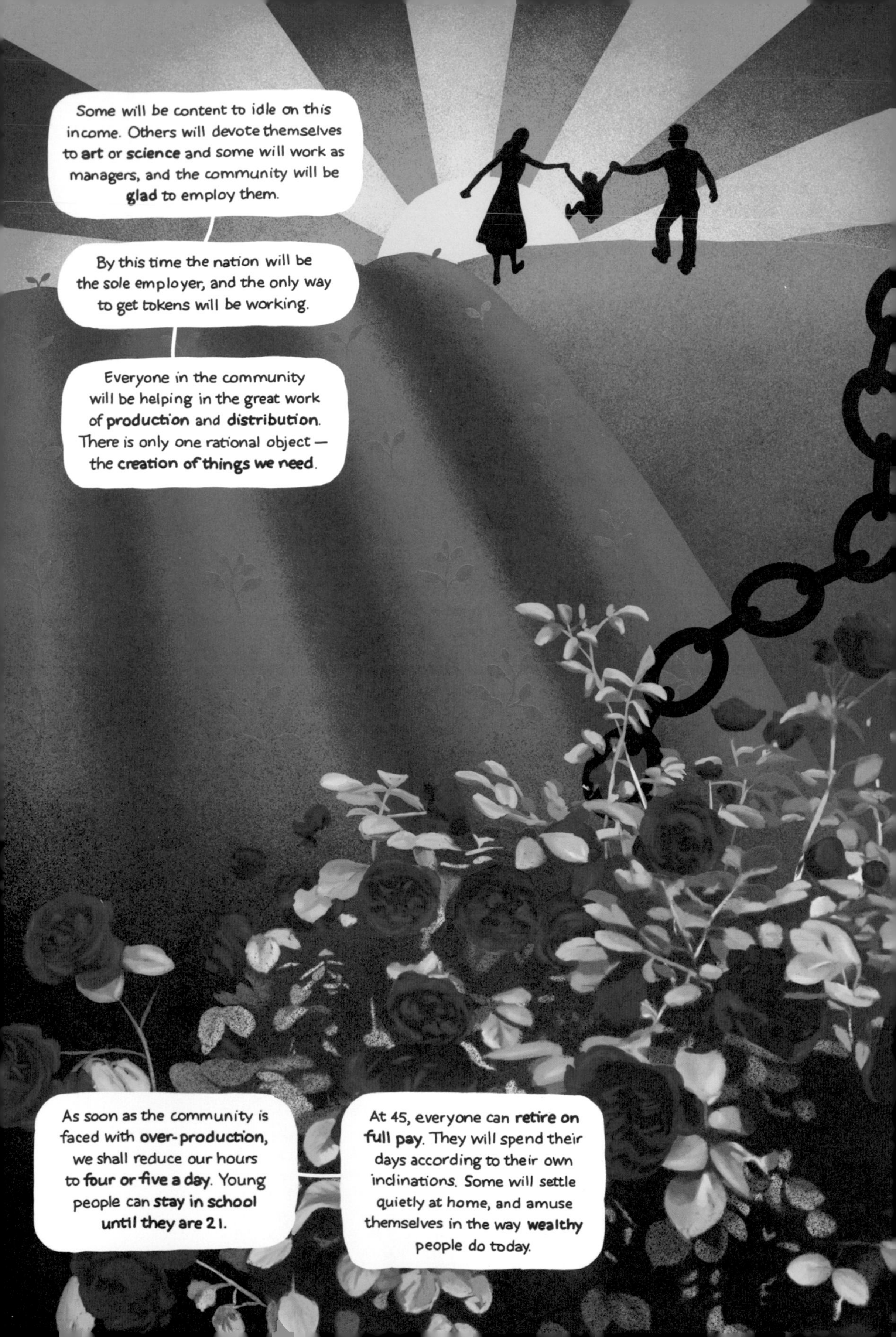
Some will be content to idle on this income. Others will devote themselves to **art** or **science** and some will work as managers, and the community will be **glad** to employ them.
By this time the nation will be the sole employer, and the only way to get tokens will be working.
Everyone in the community will be helping in the great work of **production** and **distribution**. There is only one rational object — the **creation of things we need**.
As soon as the community is faced with **over-production**, we shall reduce our hours to **four or five a day**. Young people can **stay in school until they are 21**.
At 45, everyone can **retire on full pay**. They will spend their days according to their own inclinations. Some will settle quietly at home, and amuse themselves in the way **wealthy** people do today.

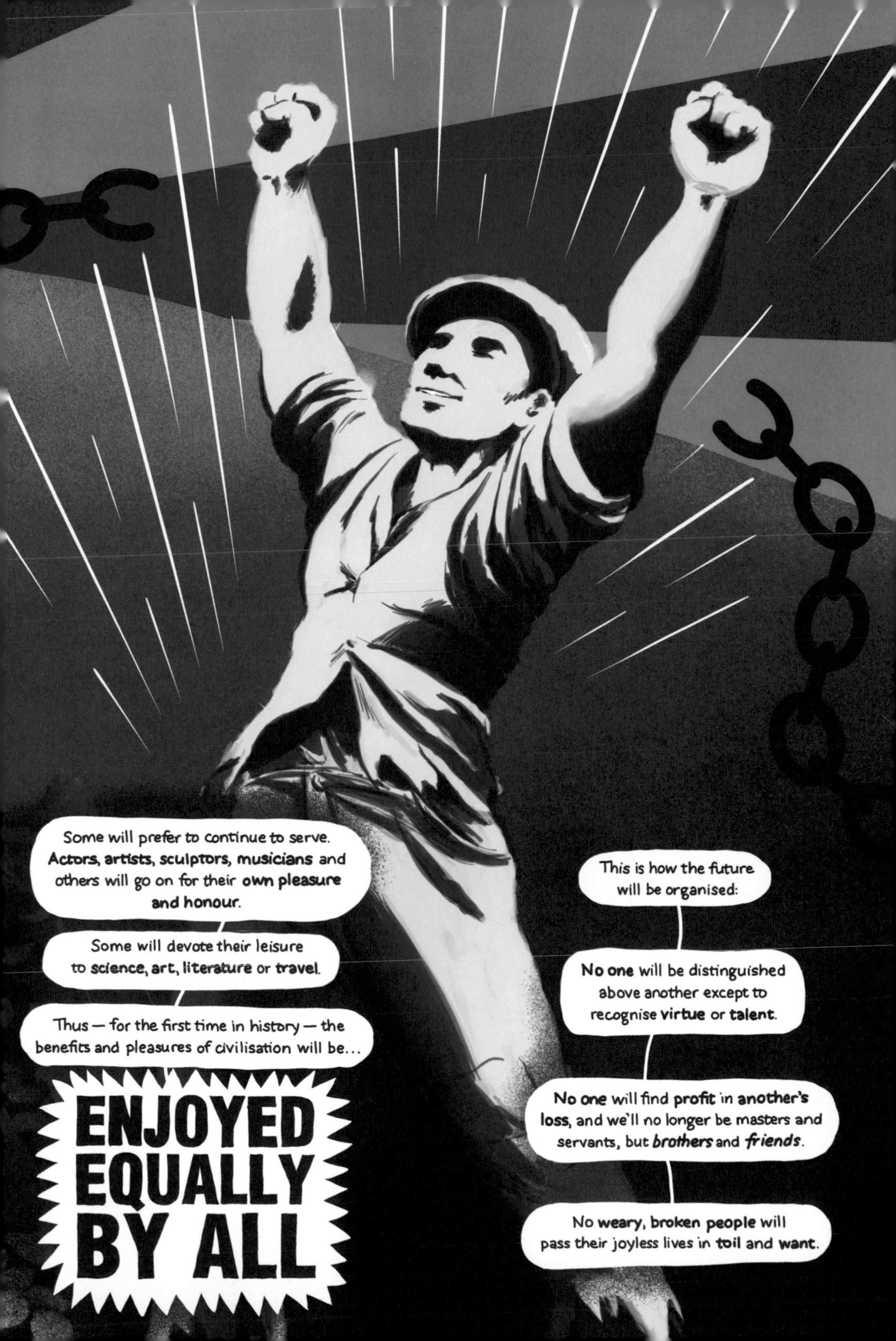

This is how the future will be organised:
No one will be distinguished above another except to recognise virtue or talent.
No one will find profit in another's loss, and we'll no longer be masters and servants, but brothers and friends.
No weary, broken people will pass their joyless lives in toil and want.
Some will prefer to continue to serve. Actors, artists, sculptors, musicians and others will go on for their own pleasure and honour.
Some will devote their leisure to science, art, literature or travel.
Thus — for the first time in history — the benefits and pleasures of civilisation will be...
ENJOYED EQUALLY BY ALL

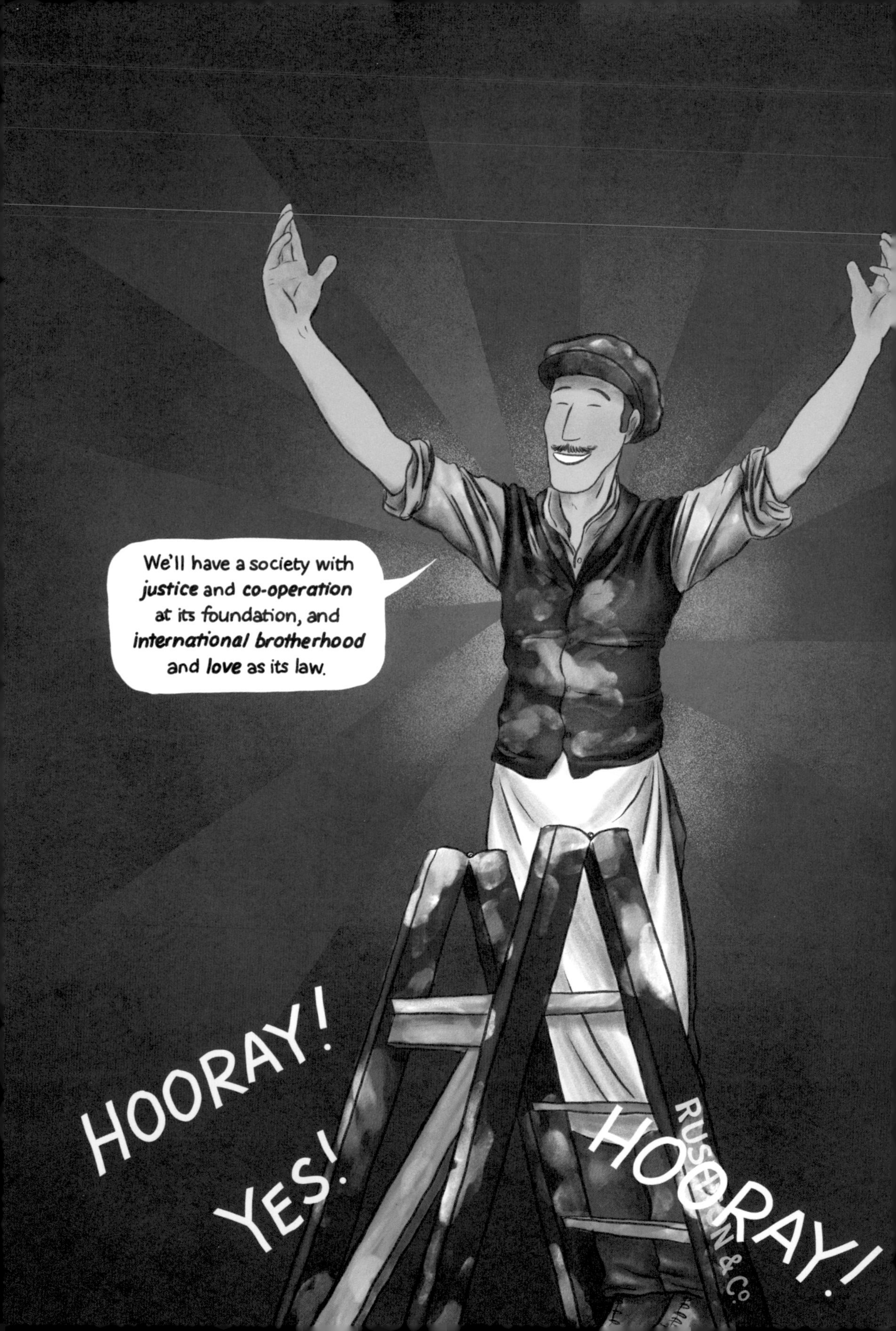
We'll have a society with *justice* and *co-operation* at its foundation, and *international brotherhood* and *love* as its law.
HOORAY!
YES!
HOORAY!

THE 18 OBJECTIONS

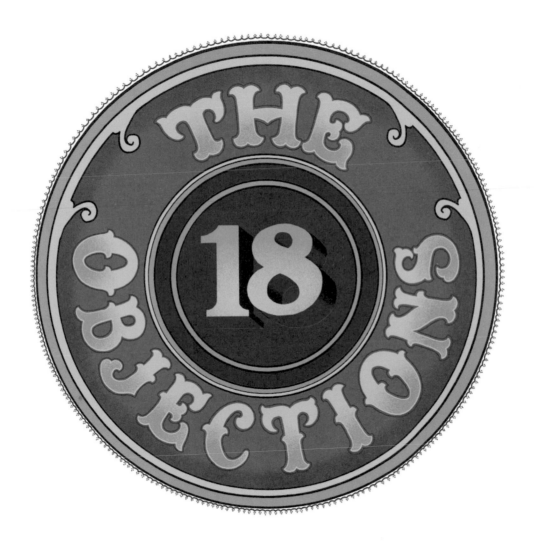

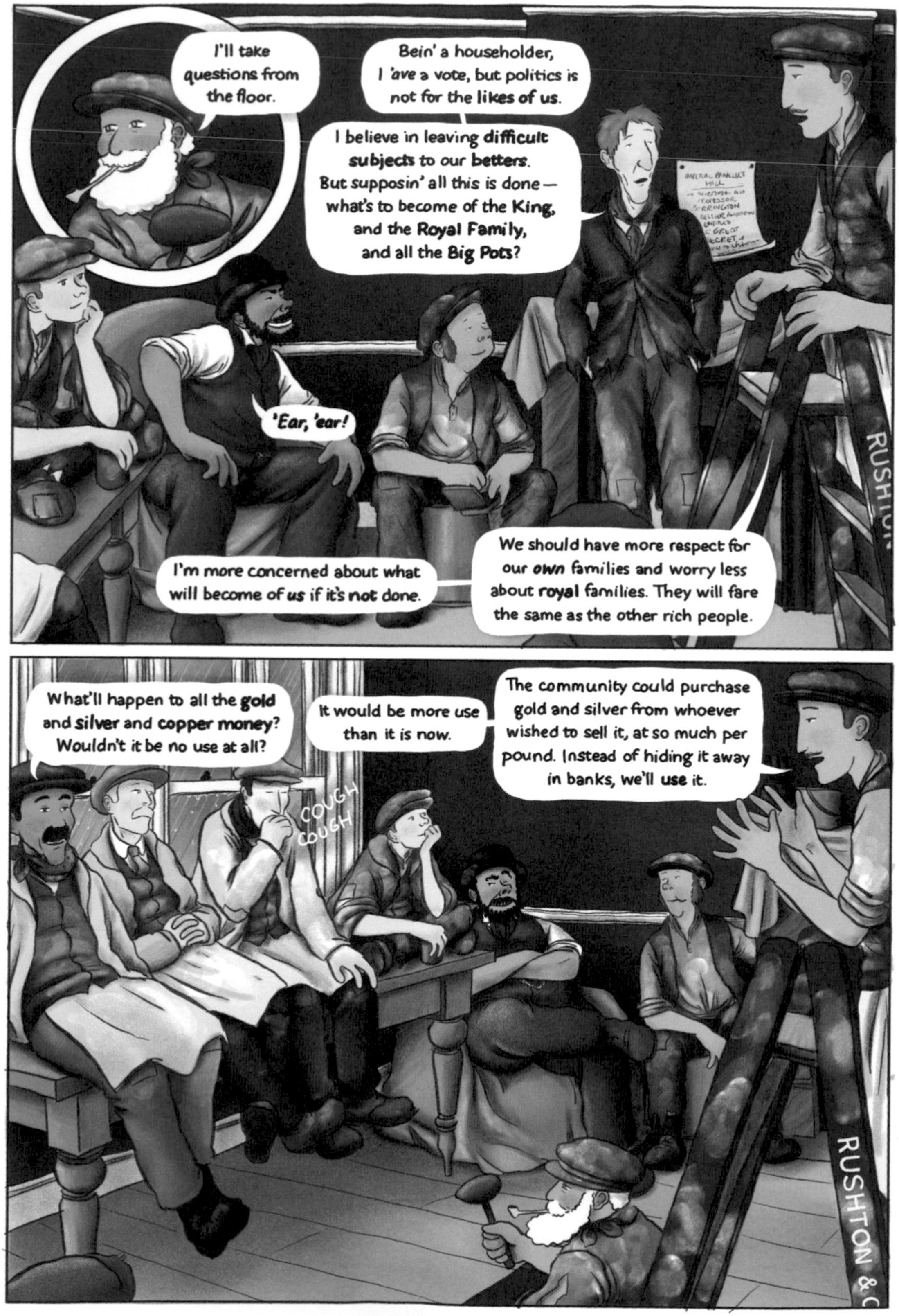
I'll take questions from the floor.
Bein' a householder, I 'ave a vote, but politics is not for the likes of us.
I believe in leaving difficult subjects to our betters. But supposin' all this is done—what's to become of the King, and the Royal Family, and all the Big Pots?
'Ear, 'ear!
I'm more concerned about what will become of us if it's not done.
We should have more respect for our own families and worry less about royal families. They will fare the same as the other rich people.
RUSHTON
What'll happen to all the gold and silver and copper money? Wouldn't it be no use at all?
It would be more use than it is now.
The community could purchase gold and silver from whoever wished to sell it, at so much per pound. Instead of hiding it away in banks, we'll use it.
COUGH COUGH
RUSHTON & C

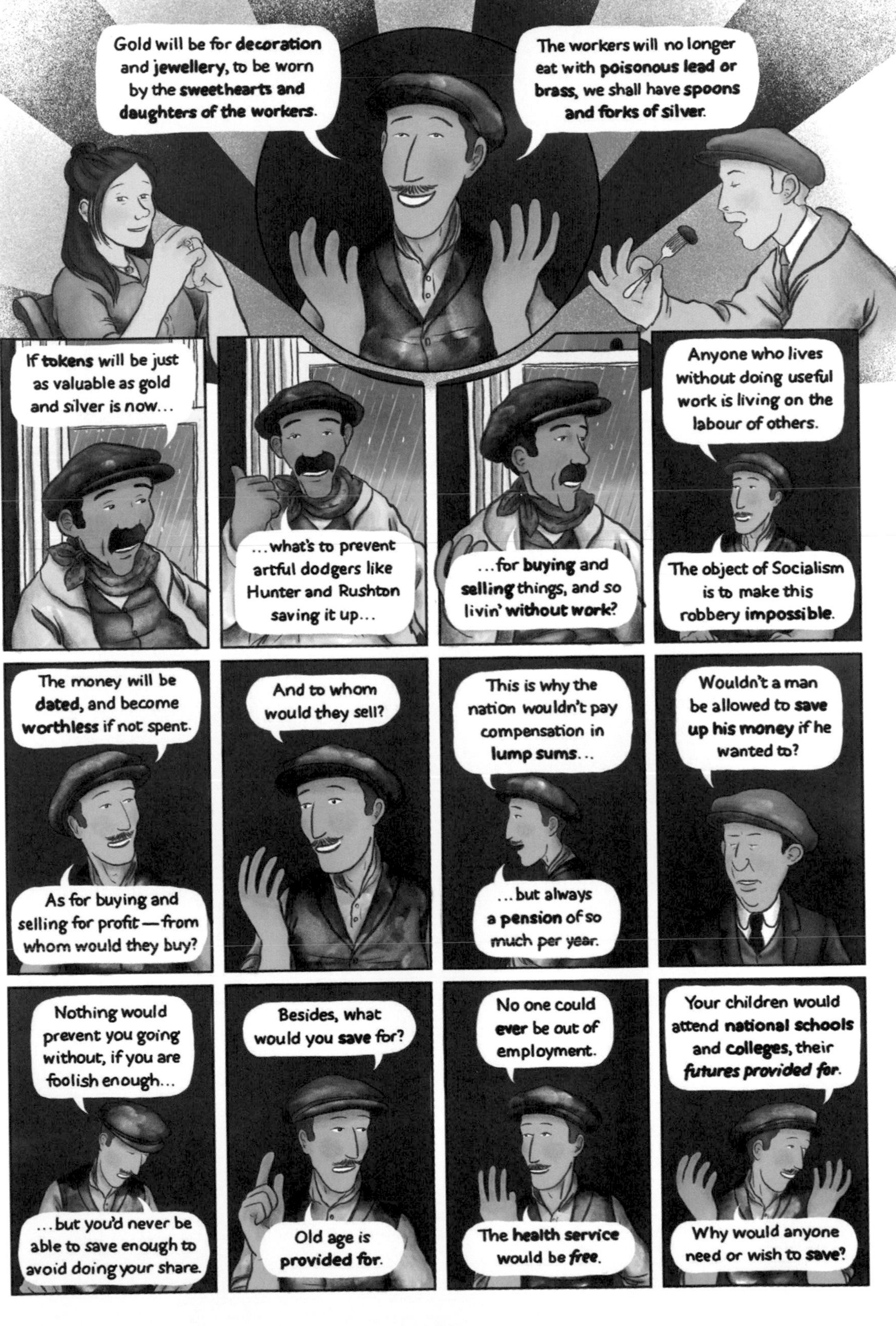
Gold will be for decoration and jewellery, to be worn by the sweethearts and daughters of the workers.
The workers will no longer eat with poisonous lead or brass, we shall have spoons and forks of silver.
If tokens will be just as valuable as gold and silver is now...
...what's to prevent artful dodgers like Hunter and Rushton saving it up...
...for buying and selling things, and so livin' without work?
Anyone who lives without doing useful work is living on the labour of others.
The object of Socialism is to make this robbery impossible.
The money will be dated, and become worthless if not spent.
As for buying and selling for profit—from whom would they buy?
And to whom would they sell?
This is why the nation wouldn't pay compensation in lump sums...
...but always a pension of so much per year.
Wouldn't a man be allowed to save up his money if he wanted to?
Nothing would prevent you going without, if you are foolish enough...
...but you'd never be able to save enough to avoid doing your share.
Besides, what would you save for?
Old age is provided for.
No one could ever be out of employment.
The health service would be free.
Your children would attend national schools and colleges, their futures provided for.
Why would anyone need or wish to save?

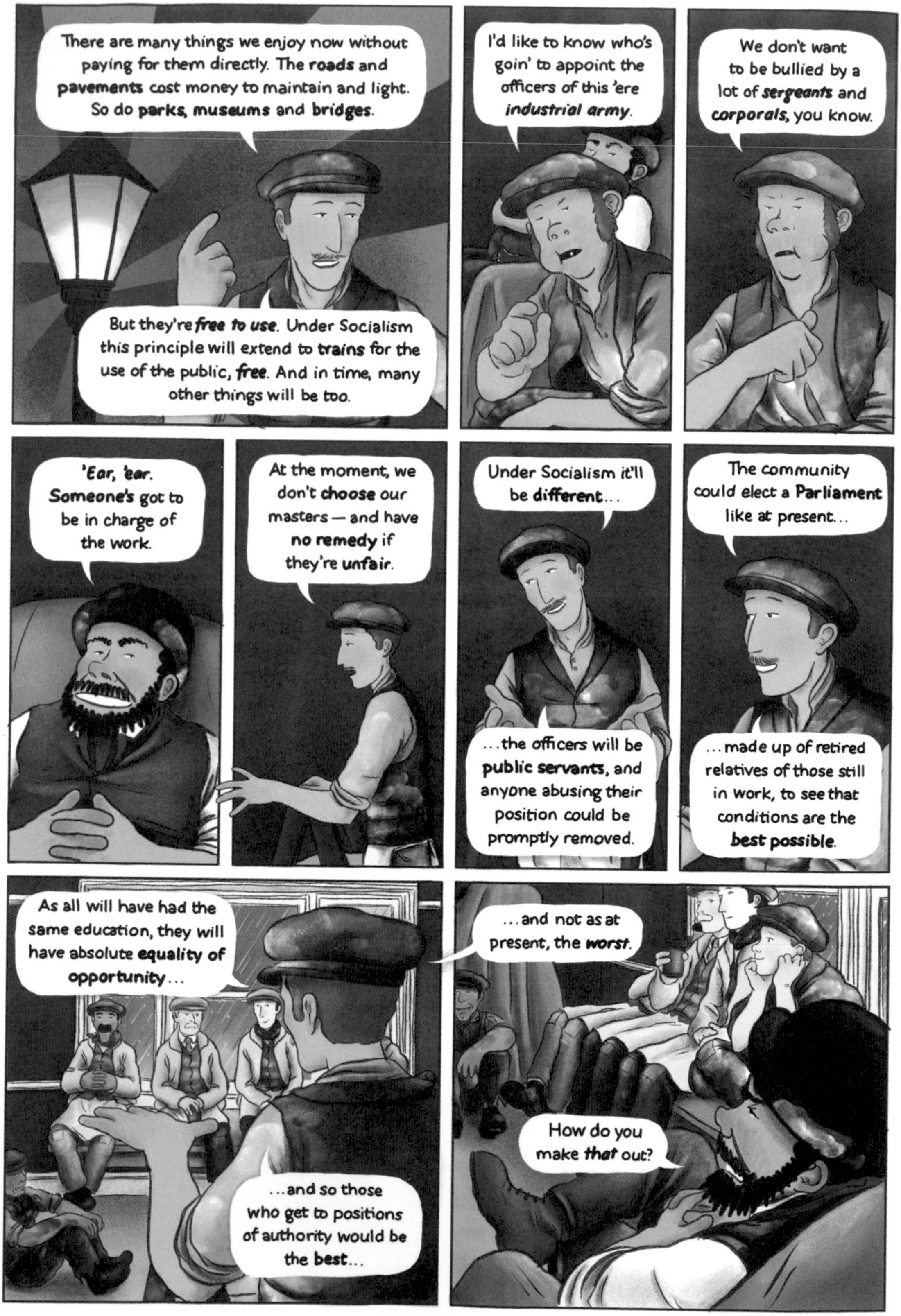
There are many things we enjoy now without paying for them directly. The **roads** and **pavements** cost money to maintain and light. So do **parks, museums** and **bridges**.
But they're ***free to use***. Under Socialism this principle will extend to **trains** for the use of the public, **free**. And in time, many other things will be too.
I'd like to know who's goin' to appoint the officers of this 'ere ***industrial army***.
We don't want to be bullied by a lot of ***sergeants*** and ***corporals***, you know.
'Ear, 'ear. **Someone's** got to be in charge of the work.
At the moment, we don't **choose** our masters — and have **no remedy** if they're **unfair**.
Under Socialism it'll be **different**...
...the officers will be **public servants**, and anyone abusing their position could be promptly removed.
The community could elect a **Parliament** like at present...
...made up of retired relatives of those still in work, to see that conditions are the ***best possible***.
As all will have had the same education, they will have absolute **equality of opportunity**...
...and so those who get to positions of authority would be the **best**...
...and not as at present, the ***worst***.
How do you make ***that*** out?

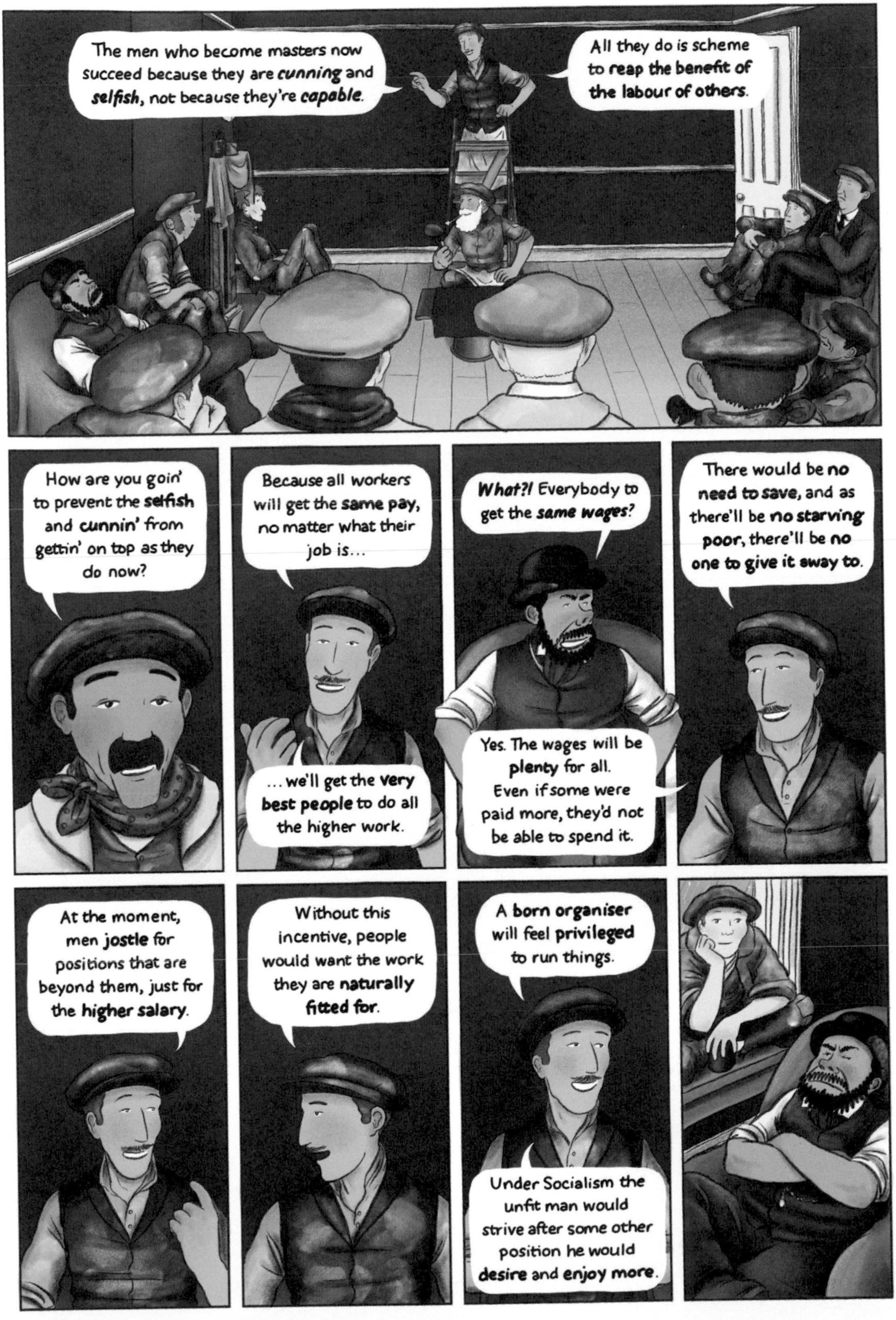
The men who become masters now succeed because they are cunning and selfish, not because they're capable.
All they do is scheme to reap the benefit of the labour of others.
How are you goin' to prevent the selfish and cunnin' from gettin' on top as they do now?
Because all workers will get the same pay, no matter what their job is...
...we'll get the very best people to do all the higher work.
What?! Everybody to get the same wages?
Yes. The wages will be plenty for all. Even if some were paid more, they'd not be able to spend it.
There would be no need to save, and as there'll be no starving poor, there'll be no one to give it away to.
At the moment, men jostle for positions that are beyond them, just for the higher salary.
Without this incentive, people would want the work they are naturally fitted for.
A born organiser will feel privileged to run things.
Under Socialism the unfit man would strive after some other position he would desire and enjoy more.

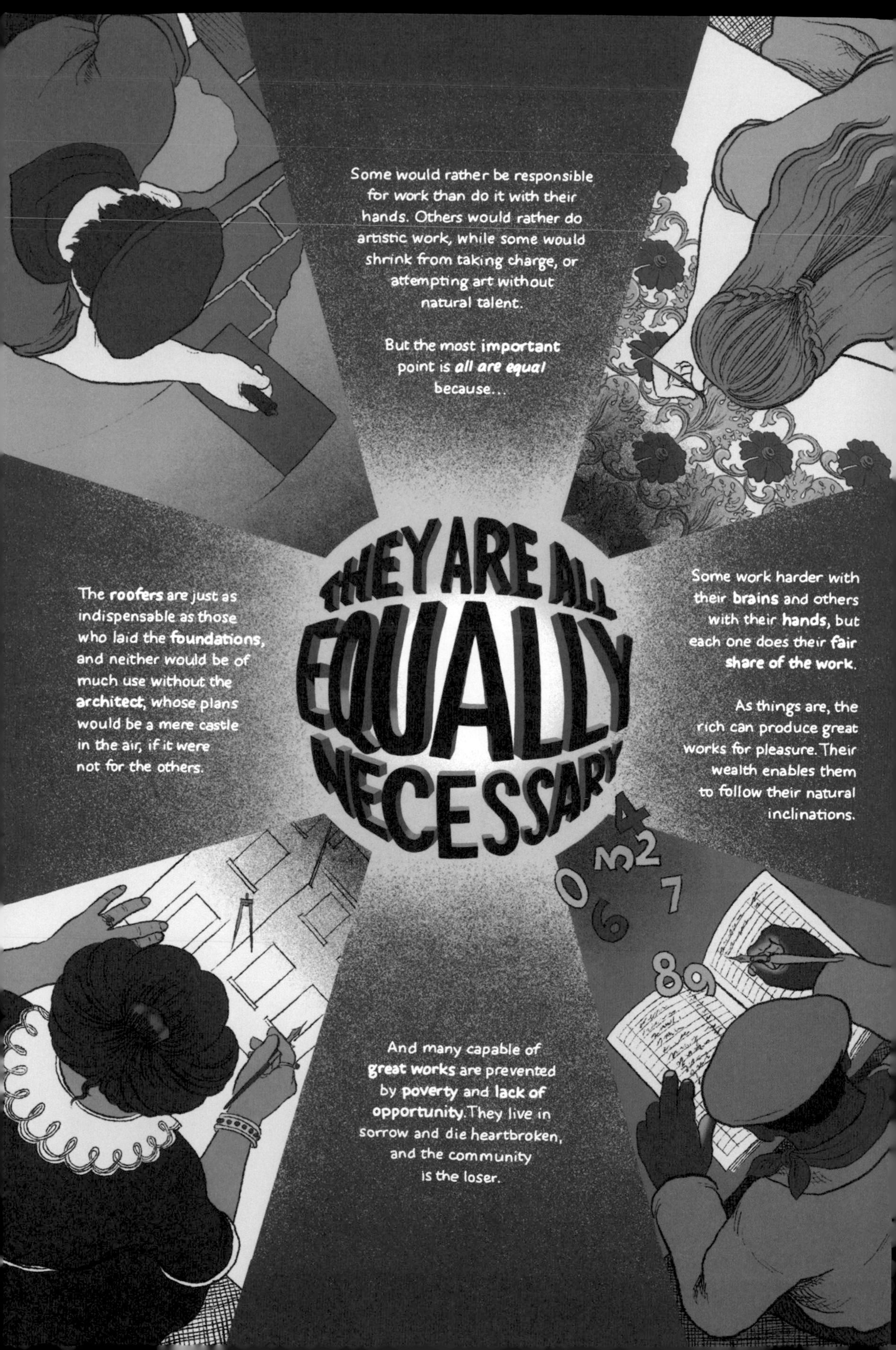
Some would rather be responsible for work than do it with their hands. Others would rather do artistic work, while some would shrink from taking charge, or attempting art without natural talent.
But the most important point is all are equal because...
THEY ARE ALL EQUALLY NECESSARY
The roofers are just as indispensable as those who laid the foundations, and neither would be of much use without the architect, whose plans would be a mere castle in the air, if it were not for the others.
Some work harder with their brains and others with their hands, but each one does their fair share of the work.
As things are, the rich can produce great works for pleasure. Their wealth enables them to follow their natural inclinations.
And many capable of great works are prevented by poverty and lack of opportunity. They live in sorrow and die heartbroken, and the community is the loser.

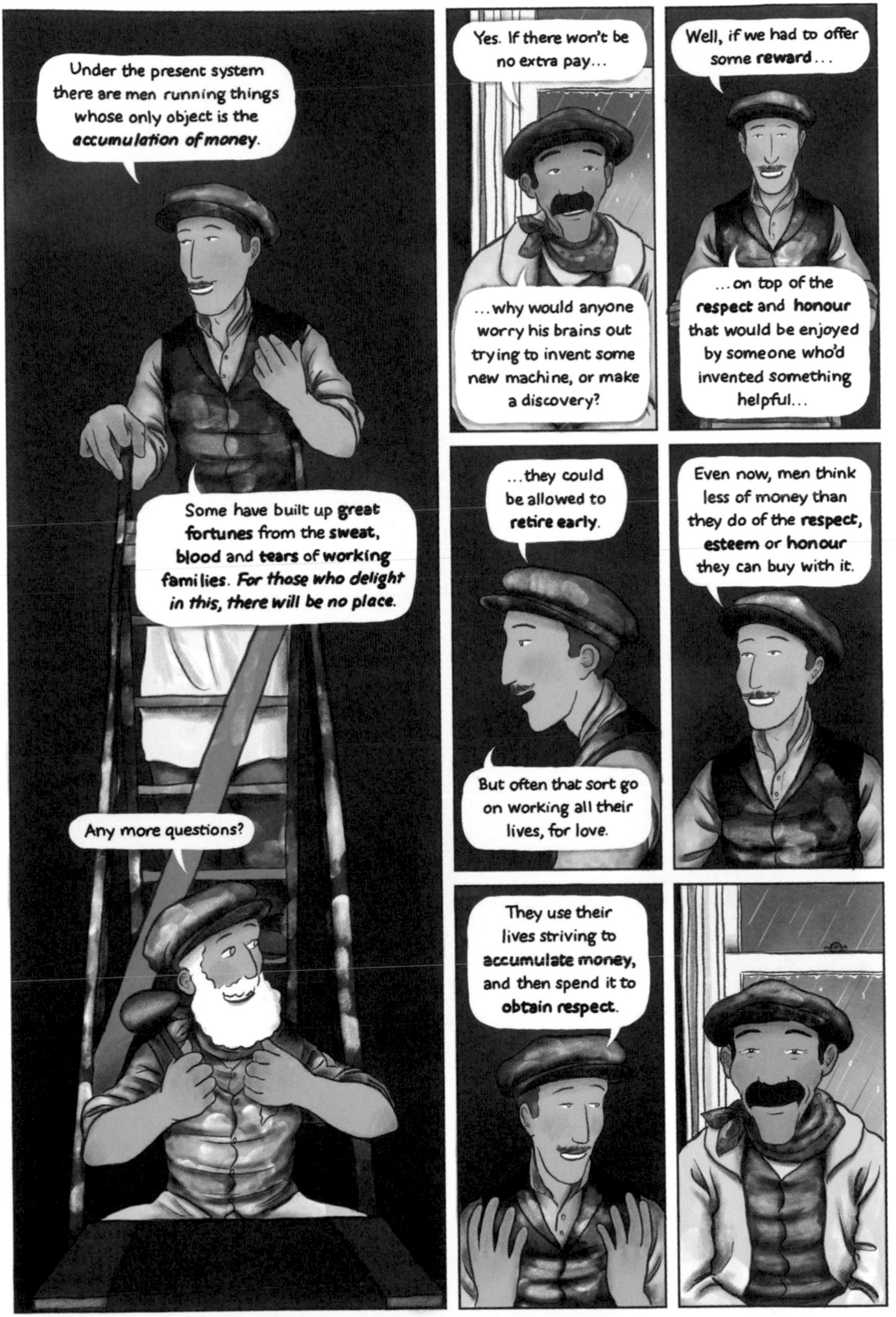
Under the present system there are men running things whose only object is the accumulation of money.
Some have built up great fortunes from the sweat, blood and tears of working families. For those who delight in this, there will be no place.
Any more questions?
Yes. If there won't be no extra pay...
...why would anyone worry his brains out trying to invent some new machine, or make a discovery?
Well, if we had to offer some reward...
...on top of the respect and honour that would be enjoyed by someone who'd invented something helpful...
...they could be allowed to retire early.
But often that sort go on working all their lives, for love.
Even now, men think less of money than they do of the respect, esteem or honour they can buy with it.
They use their lives striving to accumulate money, and then spend it to obtain respect.

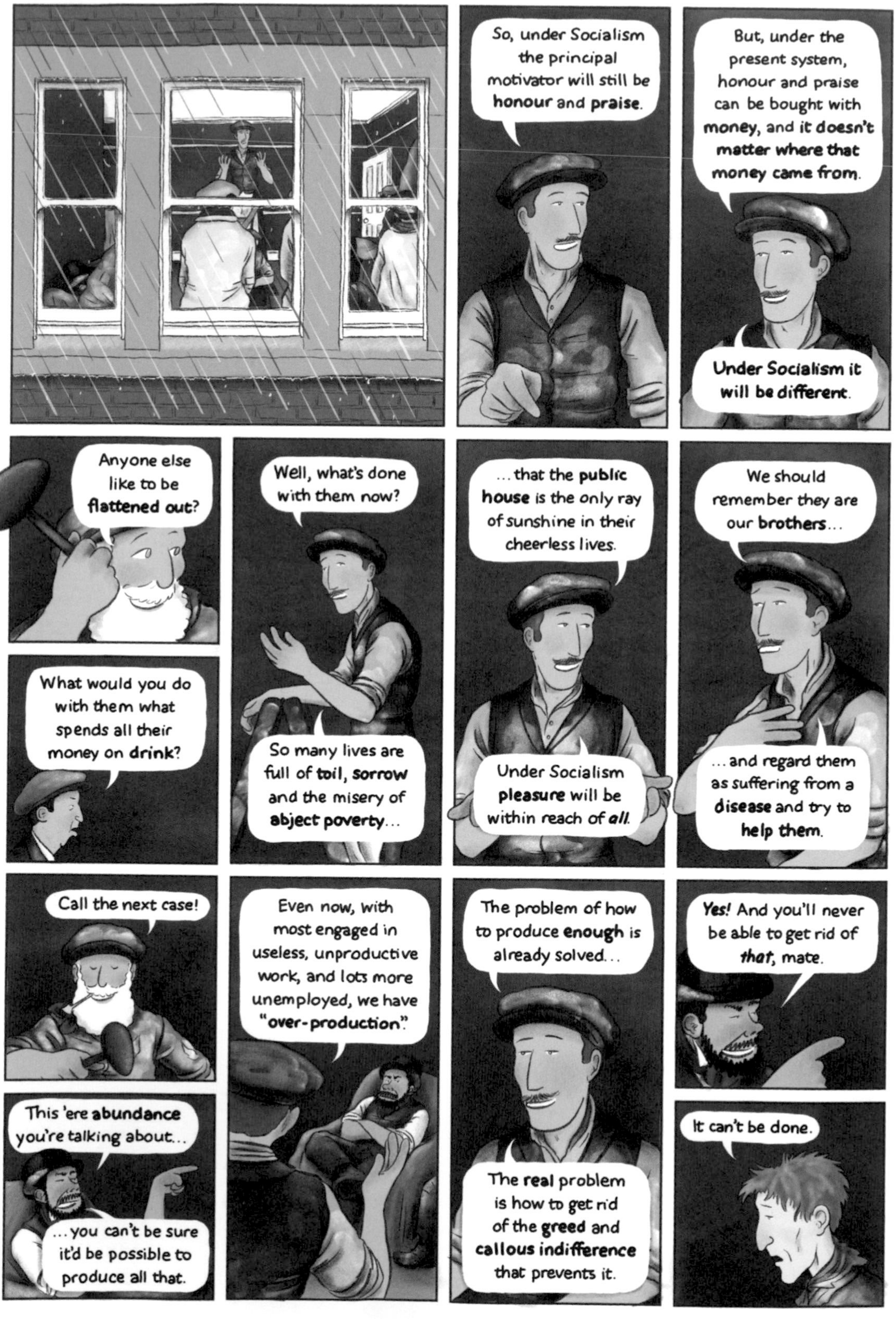
So, under Socialism the principal motivator will still be **honour** and **praise**.
But, under the present system, honour and praise can be bought with **money**, and **it doesn't matter where that money came from**.
Under Socialism it will be different.
Anyone else like to be **flattened out**?
What would you do with them what spends all their money on **drink**?
Well, what's done with them now?
So many lives are full of **toil**, **sorrow** and the misery of **abject poverty**...
...that the **public house** is the only ray of sunshine in their cheerless lives.
Under Socialism **pleasure** will be within reach of ***all***.
We should remember they are our **brothers**...
...and regard them as suffering from a **disease** and try to **help them**.
Call the next case!
This 'ere **abundance** you're talking about...
...you can't be sure it'd be possible to produce all that.
Even now, with most engaged in useless, unproductive work, and lots more unemployed, we have "**over-production**".
The problem of how to produce **enough** is already solved...
The **real** problem is how to get rid of the **greed** and **callous indifference** that prevents it.
Yes! And you'll never be able to get rid of ***that***, mate.
It can't be done.

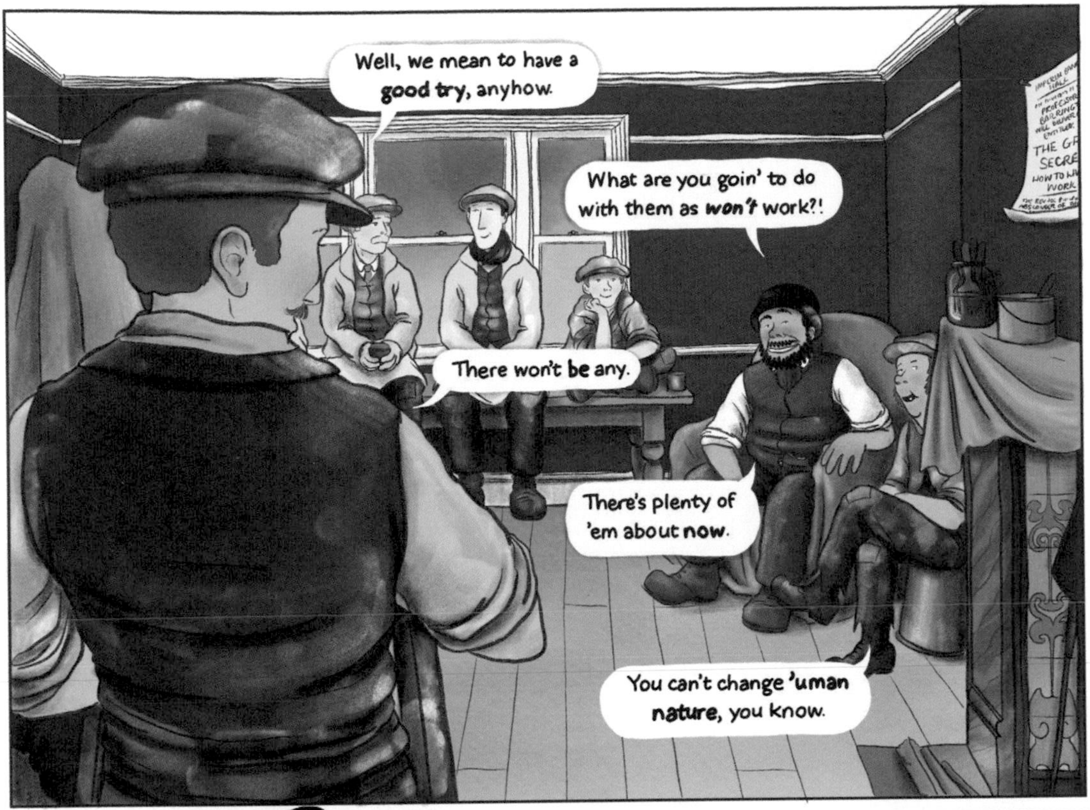
Well, we mean to have a **good try**, anyhow.
What are you goin' to do with them as ***won't*** work?!
There won't **be** any.
There's plenty of 'em about **now**.
You can't change **'uman nature**, you know.

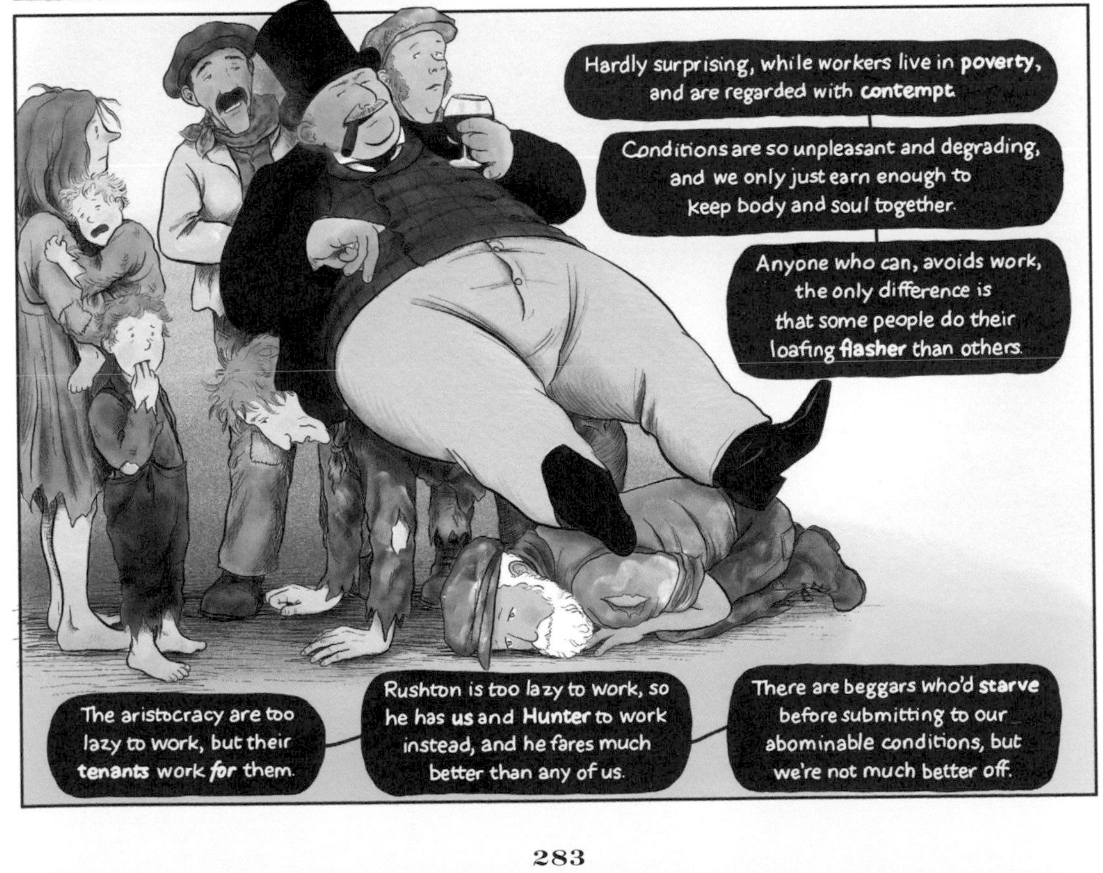
Hardly surprising, while workers live in **poverty**, and are regarded with **contempt**.
Conditions are so unpleasant and degrading, and we only just earn enough to keep body and soul together.
Anyone who can, avoids work, the only difference is that some people do their loafing **flasher** than others.
The aristocracy are too lazy to work, but their **tenants** work ***for*** them.
Rushton is too lazy to work, so he has **us** and **Hunter** to work instead, and he fares much better than any of us.
There are beggars who'd **starve** before submitting to our abominable conditions, but we're not much better off.

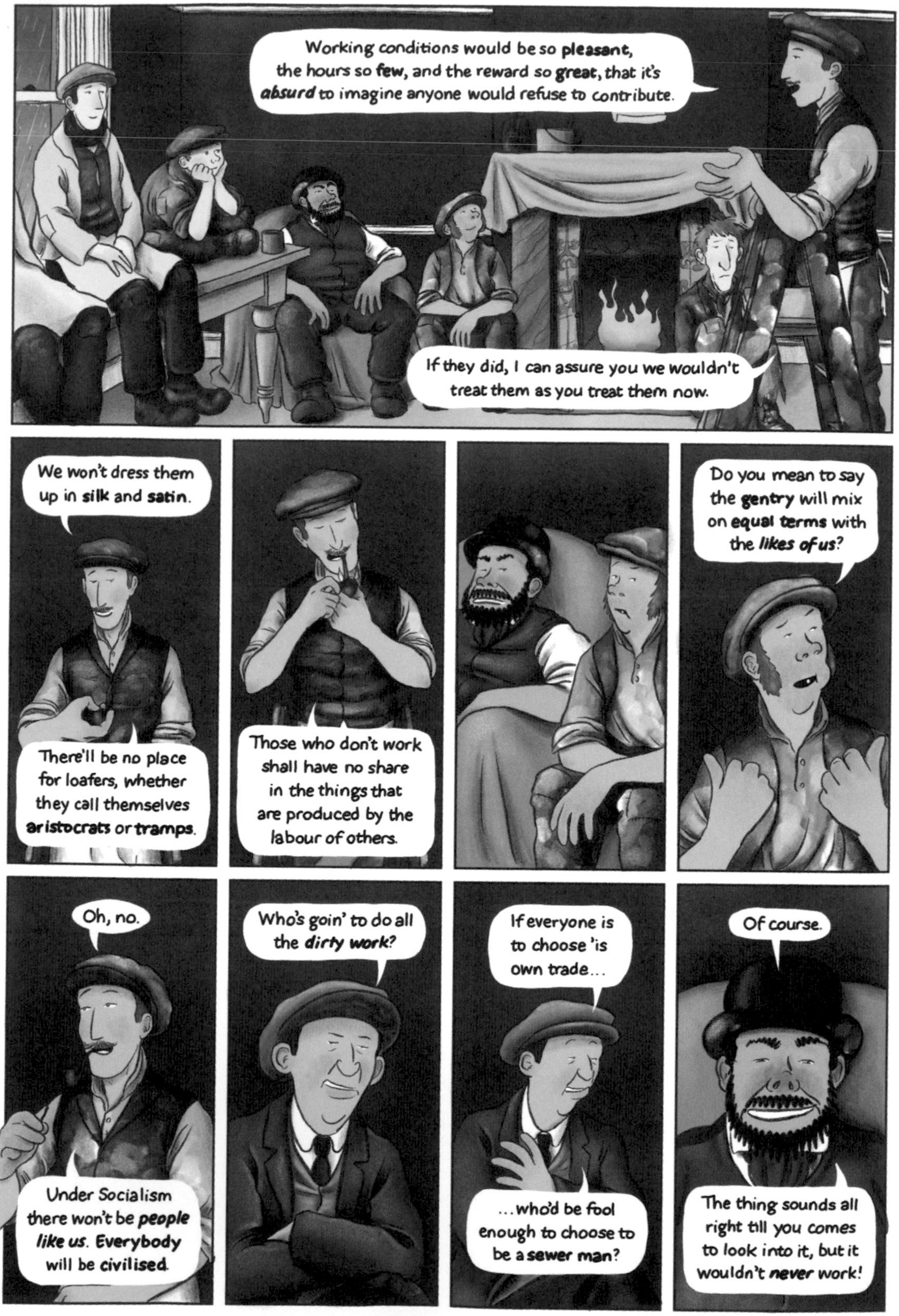
Working conditions would be so pleasant, the hours so few, and the reward so great, that it's absurd to imagine anyone would refuse to contribute.
If they did, I can assure you we wouldn't treat them as you treat them now.
We won't dress them up in silk and satin.
There'll be no place for loafers, whether they call themselves aristocrats or tramps.
Those who don't work shall have no share in the things that are produced by the labour of others.
Do you mean to say the gentry will mix on equal terms with the likes of us?
Oh, no.
Under Socialism there won't be people like us. Everybody will be civilised.
Who's goin' to do all the dirty work?
If everyone is to choose 'is own trade...
...who'd be fool enough to choose to be a sewer man?
Of course.
The thing sounds all right till you comes to look into it, but it wouldn't never work!

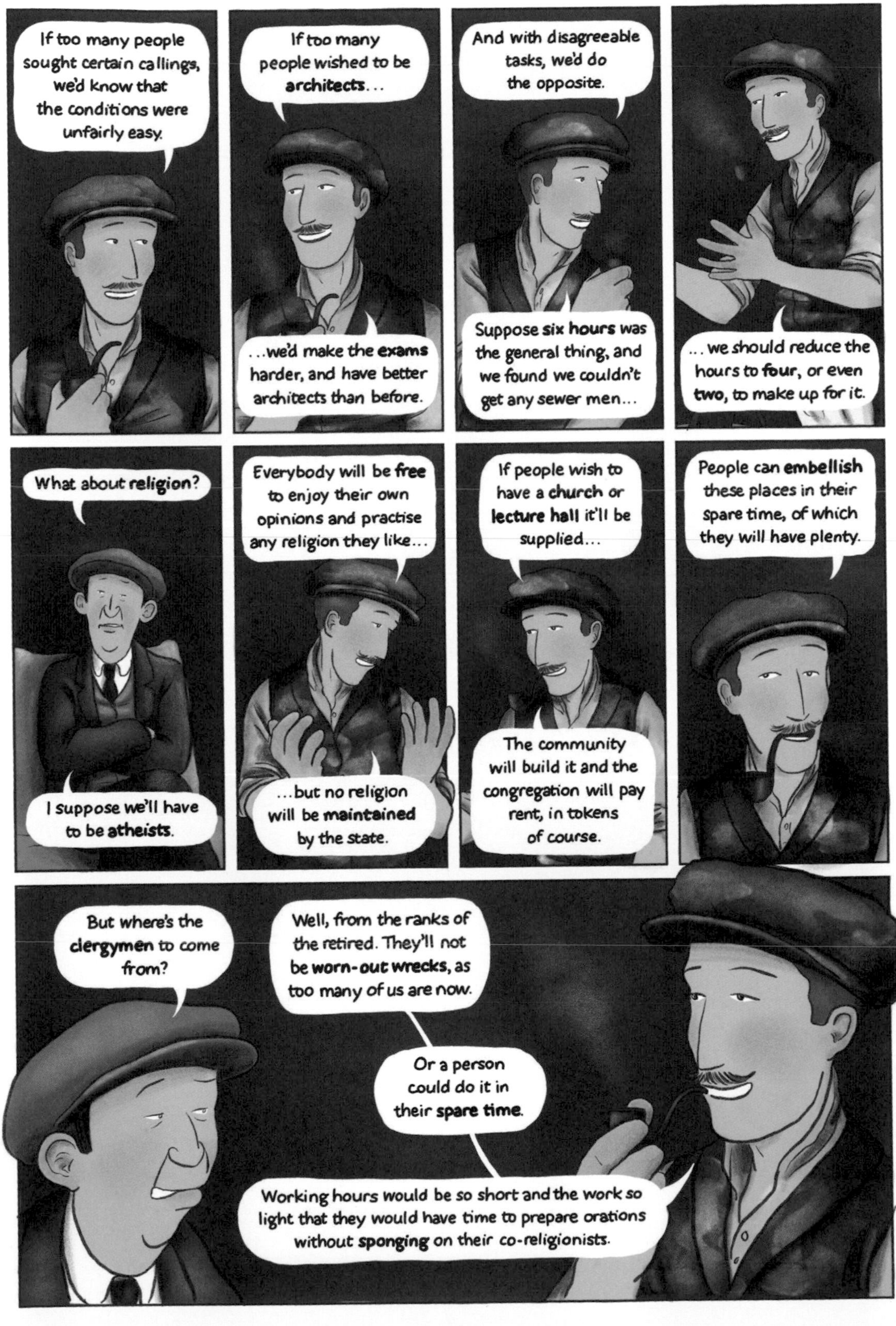
If too many people sought certain callings, we'd know that the conditions were unfairly easy.
If too many people wished to be architects...
...we'd make the exams harder, and have better architects than before.
And with disagreeable tasks, we'd do the opposite.
Suppose six hours was the general thing, and we found we couldn't get any sewer men...
...we should reduce the hours to four, or even two, to make up for it.
What about religion?
I suppose we'll have to be atheists.
Everybody will be free to enjoy their own opinions and practise any religion they like...
...but no religion will be maintained by the state.
If people wish to have a church or lecture hall it'll be supplied...
The community will build it and the congregation will pay rent, in tokens of course.
People can embellish these places in their spare time, of which they will have plenty.
But where's the clergymen to come from?
Well, from the ranks of the retired. They'll not be worn-out wrecks, as too many of us are now.
Or a person could do it in their spare time.
Working hours would be so short and the work so light that they would have time to prepare orations without sponging on their co-religionists.

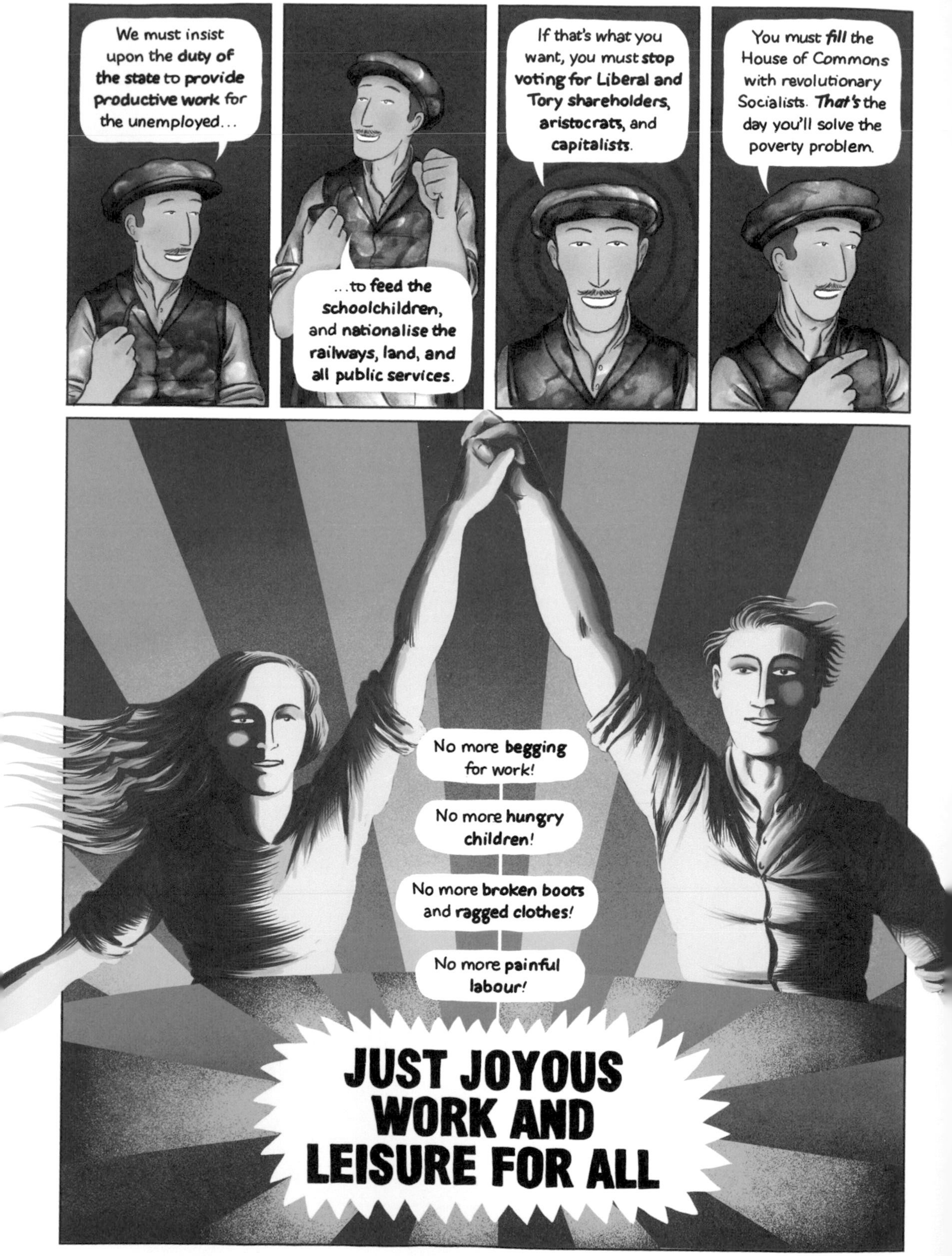
We must insist upon the duty of the state to provide productive work for the unemployed...
...to feed the schoolchildren, and nationalise the railways, land, and all public services.
If that's what you want, you must stop voting for Liberal and Tory shareholders, aristocrats, and capitalists.
You must fill the House of Commons with revolutionary Socialists. That's the day you'll solve the poverty problem.
No more begging for work!
No more hungry children!
No more broken boots and ragged clothes!
No more painful labour!
JUST JOYOUS WORK AND LEISURE FOR ALL

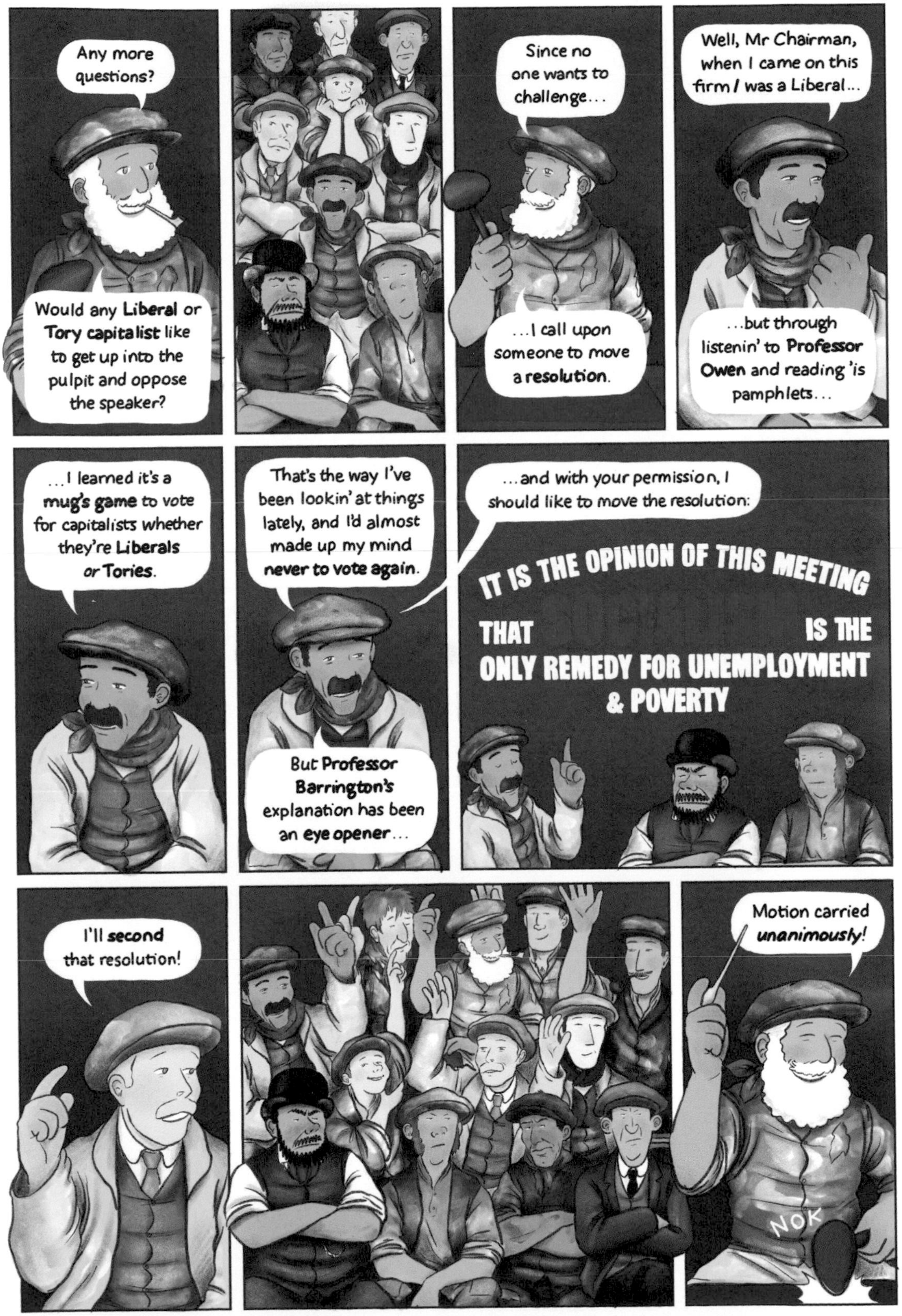
Any more questions?
Would any Liberal or Tory capitalist like to get up into the pulpit and oppose the speaker?
Since no one wants to challenge…
…I call upon someone to move a resolution.
Well, Mr Chairman, when I came on this firm I was a Liberal…
…but through listenin' to Professor Owen and reading 'is pamphlets…
…I learned it's a mug's game to vote for capitalists whether they're Liberals or Tories.
That's the way I've been lookin' at things lately, and I'd almost made up my mind never to vote again.
But Professor Barrington's explanation has been an eye opener…
…and with your permission, I should like to move the resolution:
IT IS THE OPINION OF THIS MEETING
THAT IS THE
ONLY REMEDY FOR UNEMPLOYMENT & POVERTY
I'll second that resolution!
Motion carried unanimously!
NOK

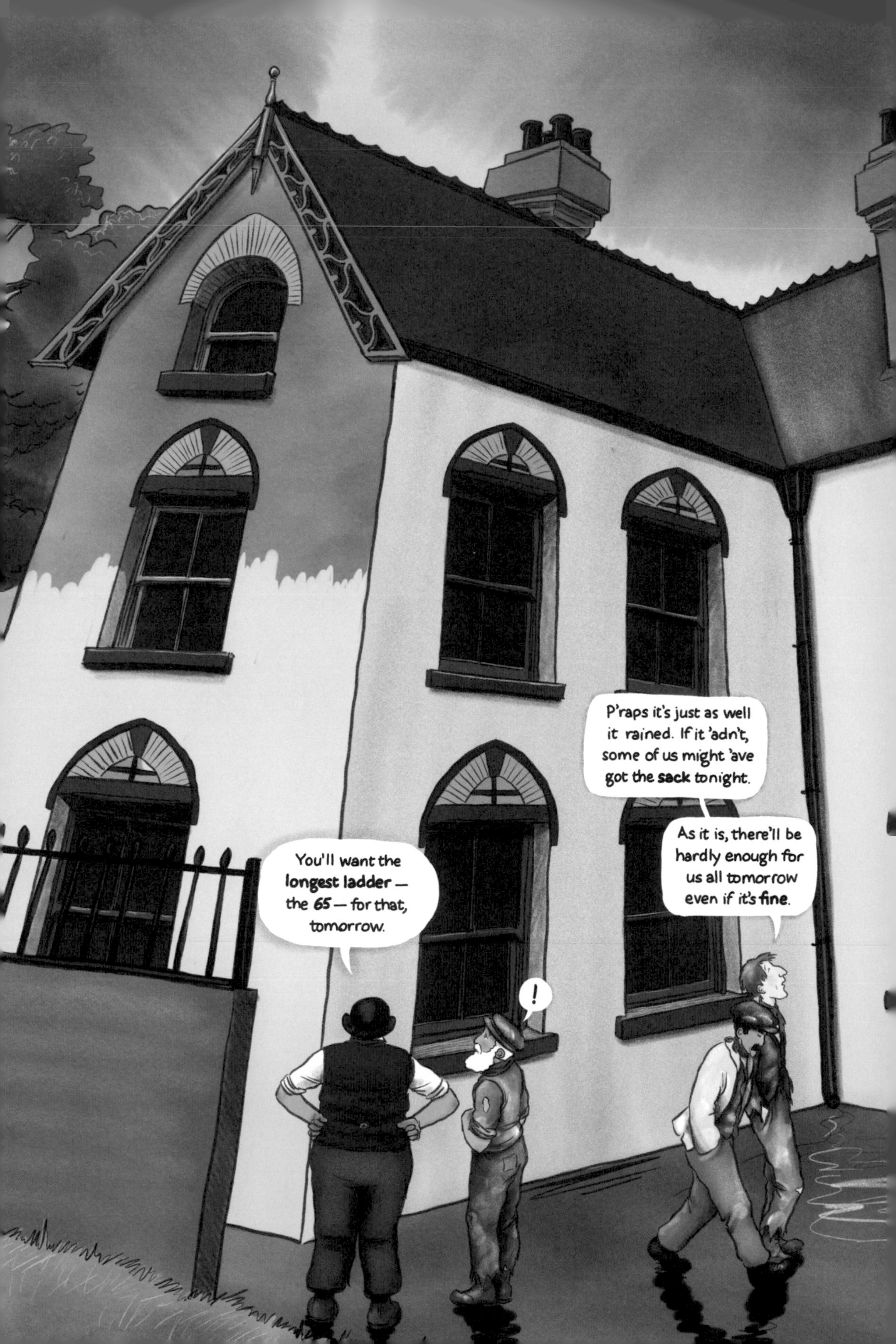
P'raps it's just as well it rained. If it 'adn't, some of us might 'ave got the sack tonight.
As it is, there'll be hardly enough for us all tomorrow even if it's fine.
You'll want the longest ladder — the 65 — for that, tomorrow.
!

THE

ROPE

CHAPTER

19

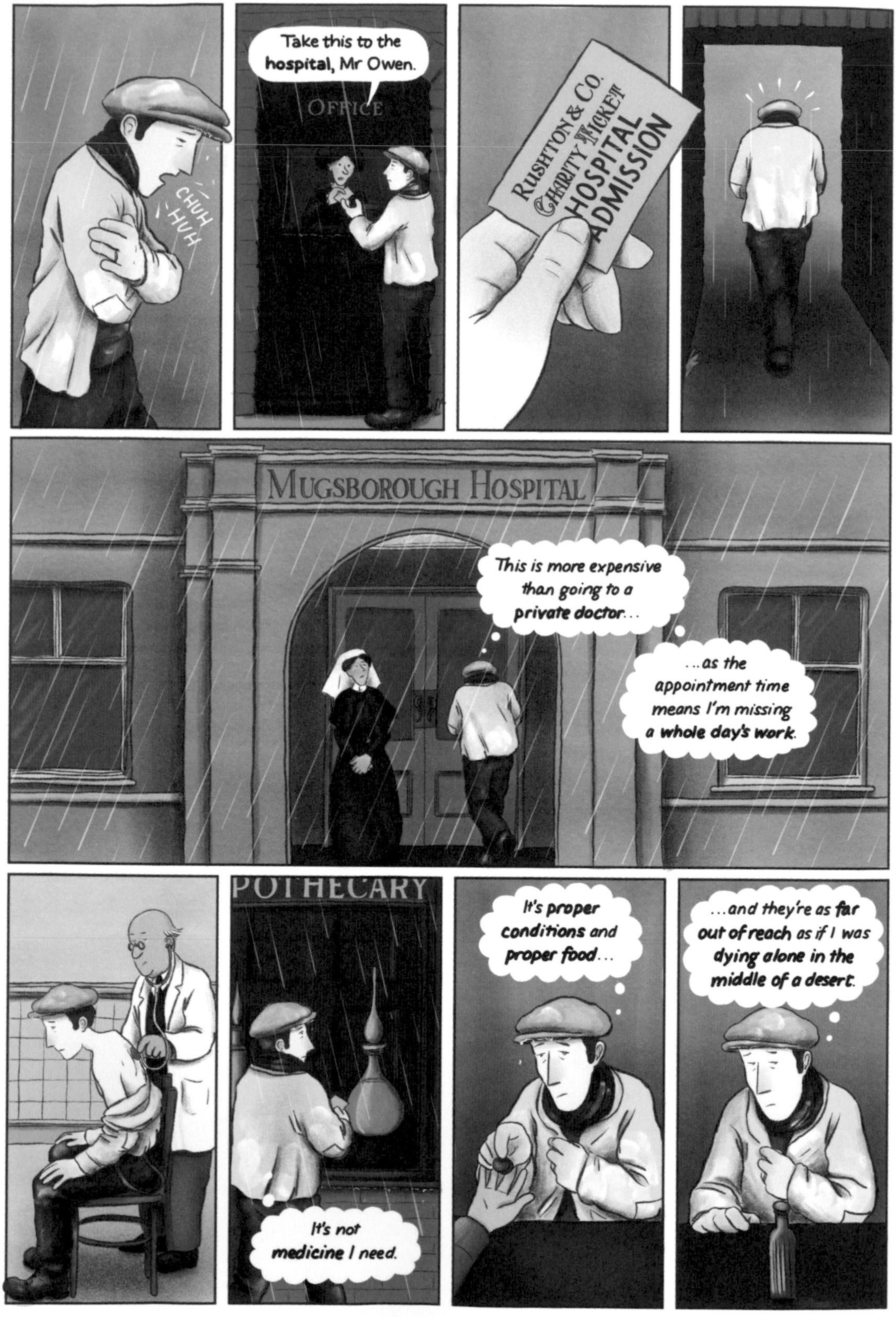
CHUH HUH
Take this to the hospital, Mr Owen.
OFFICE
RUSHTON & CO.
CHARITY TICKET
HOSPITAL ADMISSION
MUGSBOROUGH HOSPITAL
This is more expensive than going to a private doctor...
...as the appointment time means I'm missing a whole day's work.
POTHECARY
It's not medicine I need.
It's proper conditions and proper food...
...and they're as far out of reach as if I was dying alone in the middle of a desert.

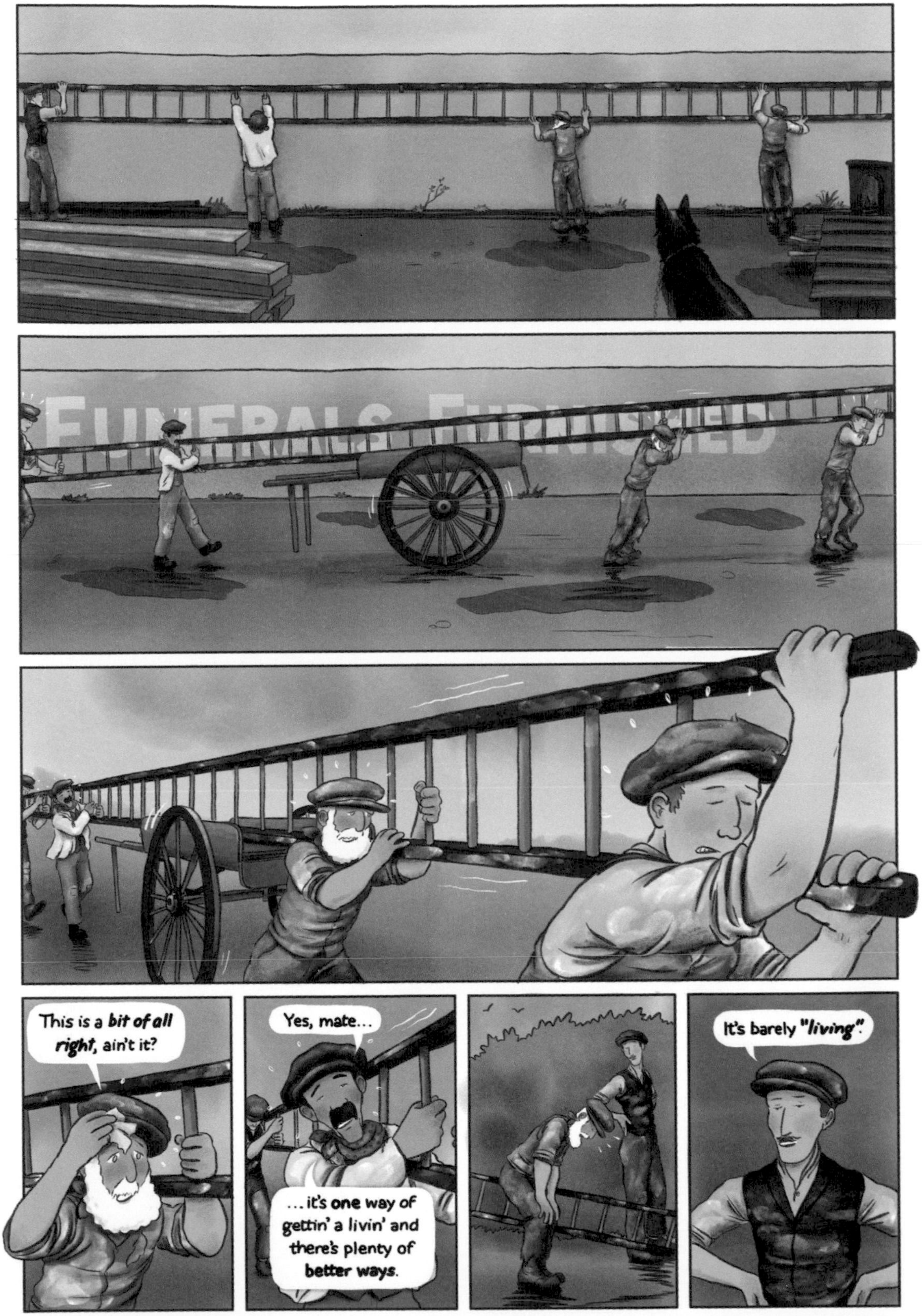
FUNERALS FURNISHED
This is a bit of all right, ain't it?
Yes, mate...
...it's one way of gettin' a livin' and there's plenty of better ways.
It's barely "living".

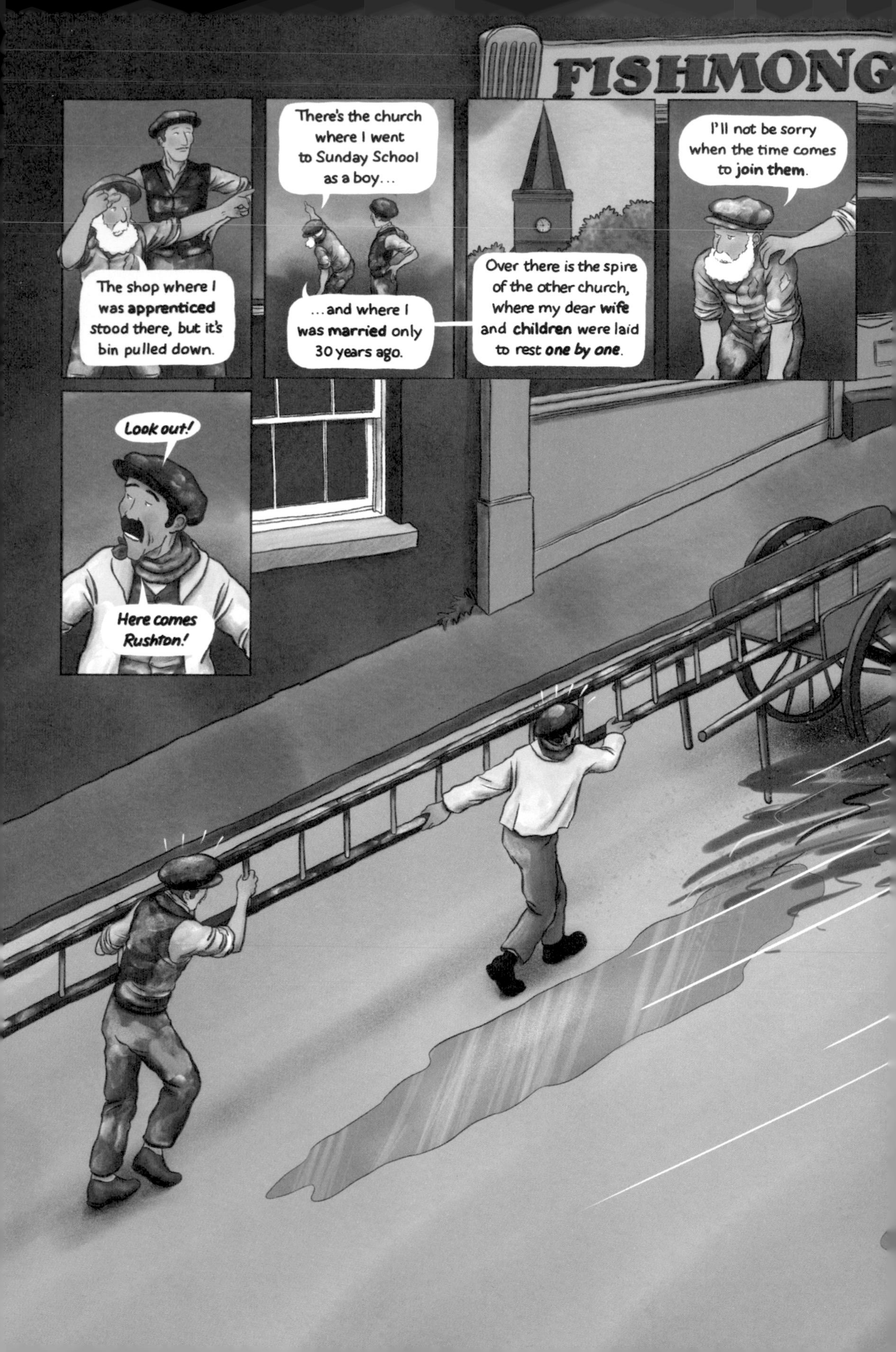
FISHMONG
The shop where I was apprenticed stood there, but it's bin pulled down.
There's the church where I went to Sunday School as a boy...
...and where I was married only 30 years ago.
Over there is the spire of the other church, where my dear wife and children were laid to rest one by one.
I'll not be sorry when the time comes to join them.
Look out!
Here comes Rushton!

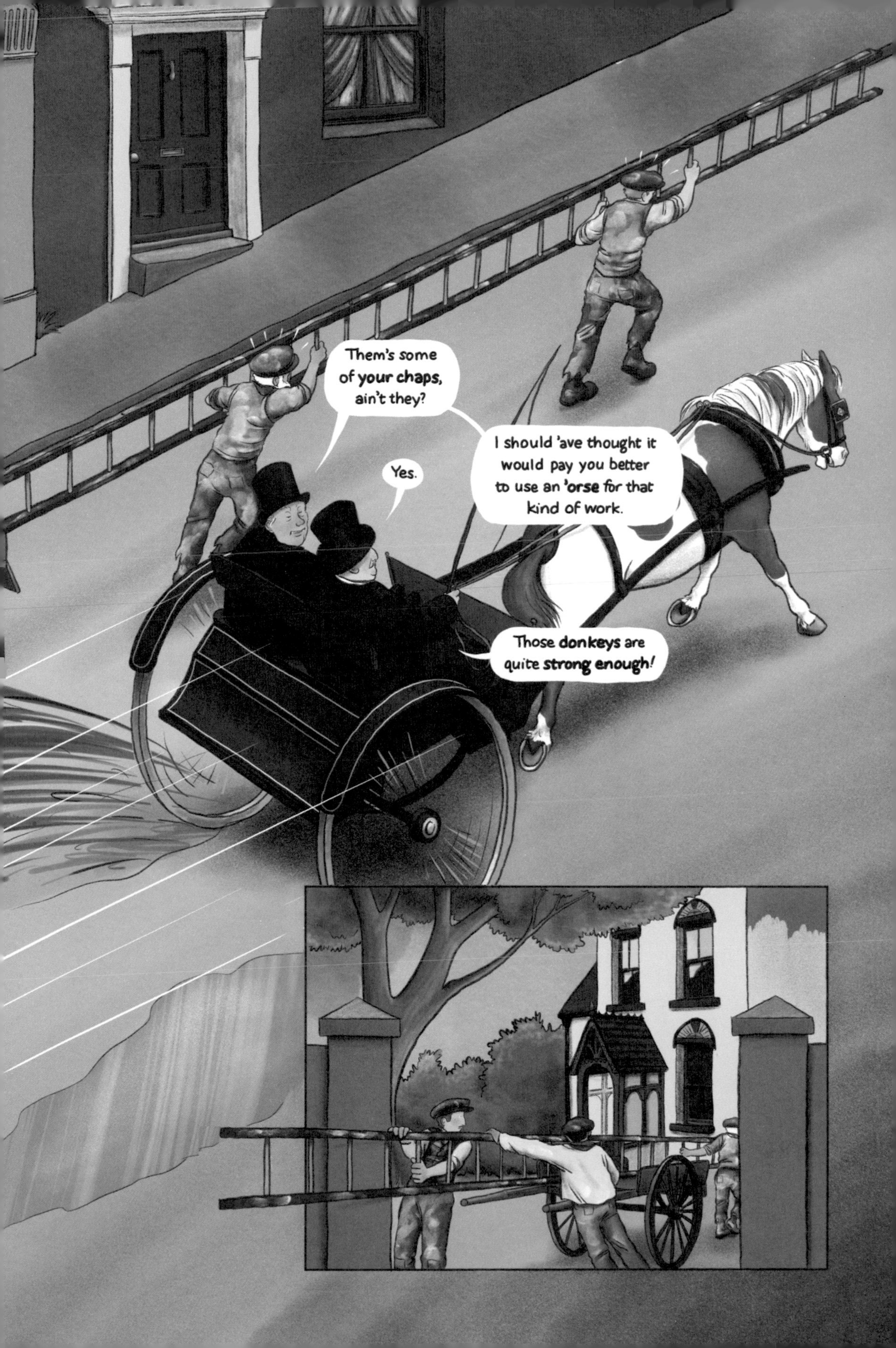
Them's some of your chaps, ain't they?
Yes.
I should 'ave thought it would pay you better to use an 'orse for that kind of work.
Those donkeys are quite strong enough!

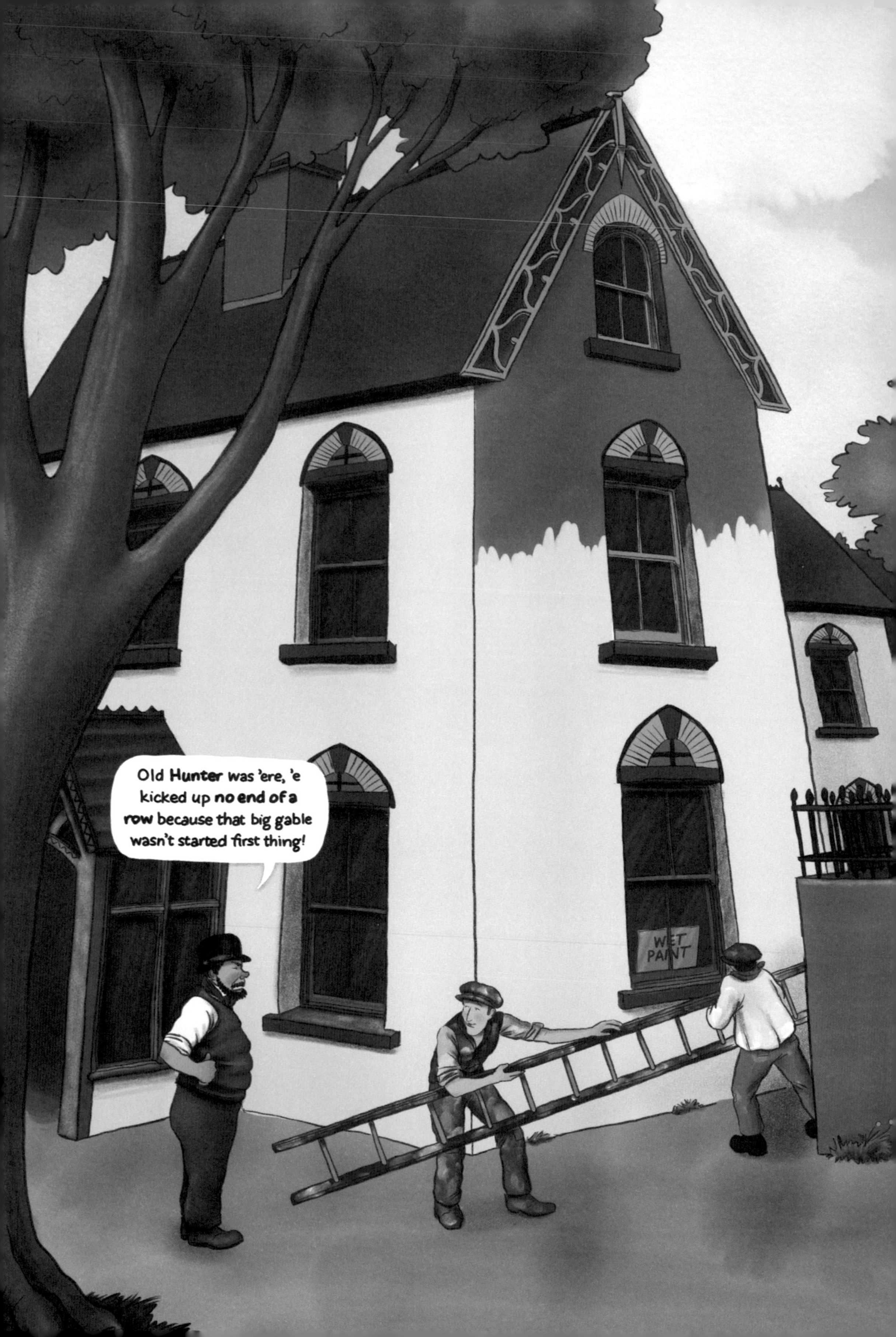
Old Hunter was 'ere, 'e kicked up no end of a row because that big gable wasn't started first thing!
WET PAINT

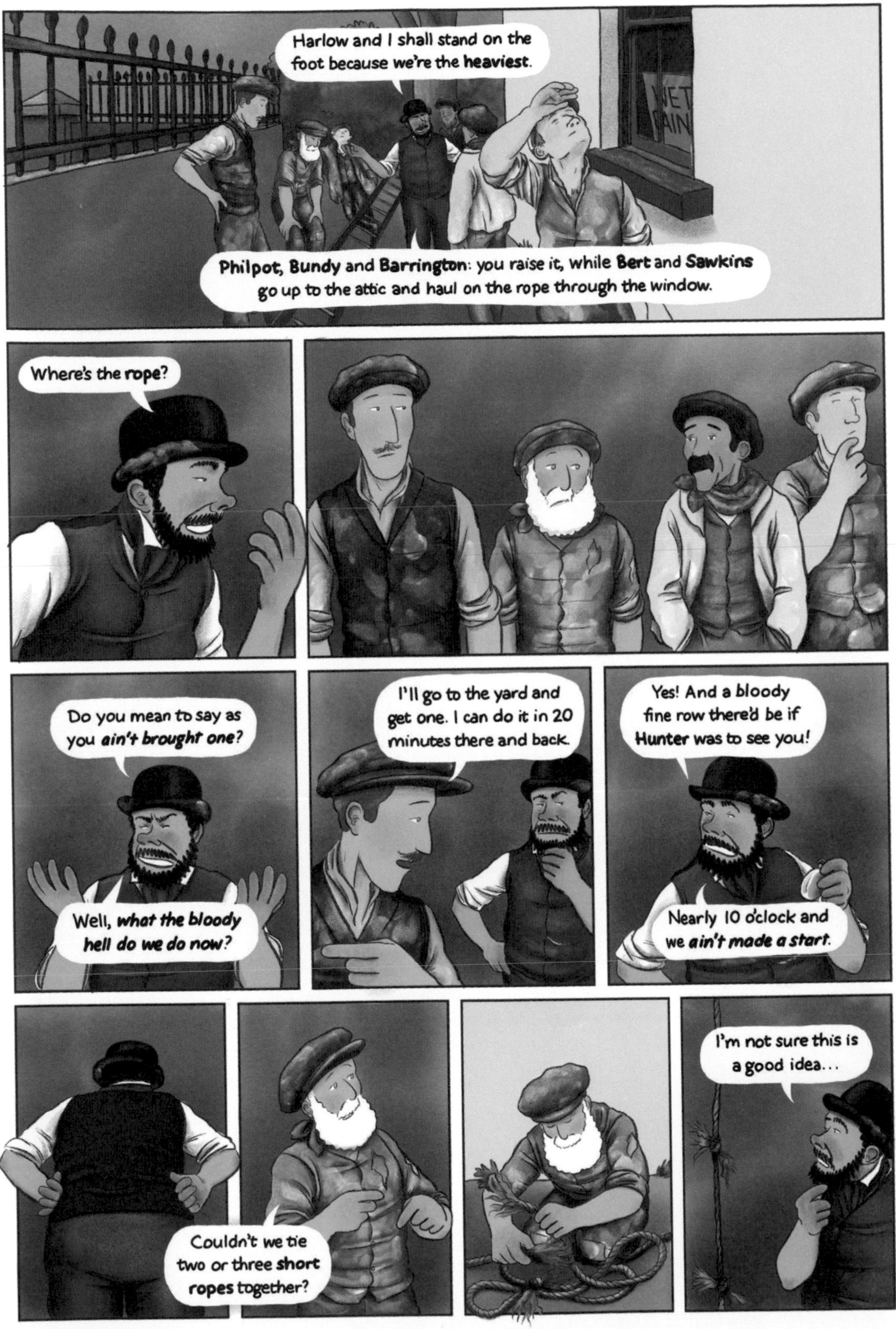
Harlow and I shall stand on the foot because we're the **heaviest**.
WET PAIN
Philpot, **Bundy** and **Barrington**: you raise it, while **Bert** and **Sawkins** go up to the attic and haul on the rope through the window.
Where's the **rope**?
Do you mean to say as you ***ain't brought one***?
Well, ***what the bloody hell do we do now***?
I'll go to the yard and get one. I can do it in 20 minutes there and back.
Yes! And a bloody fine row there'd be if **Hunter** was to see you!
Nearly 10 o'clock and we ***ain't made a start***.
Couldn't we tie two or three **short ropes** together?
I'm not sure this is a good idea...

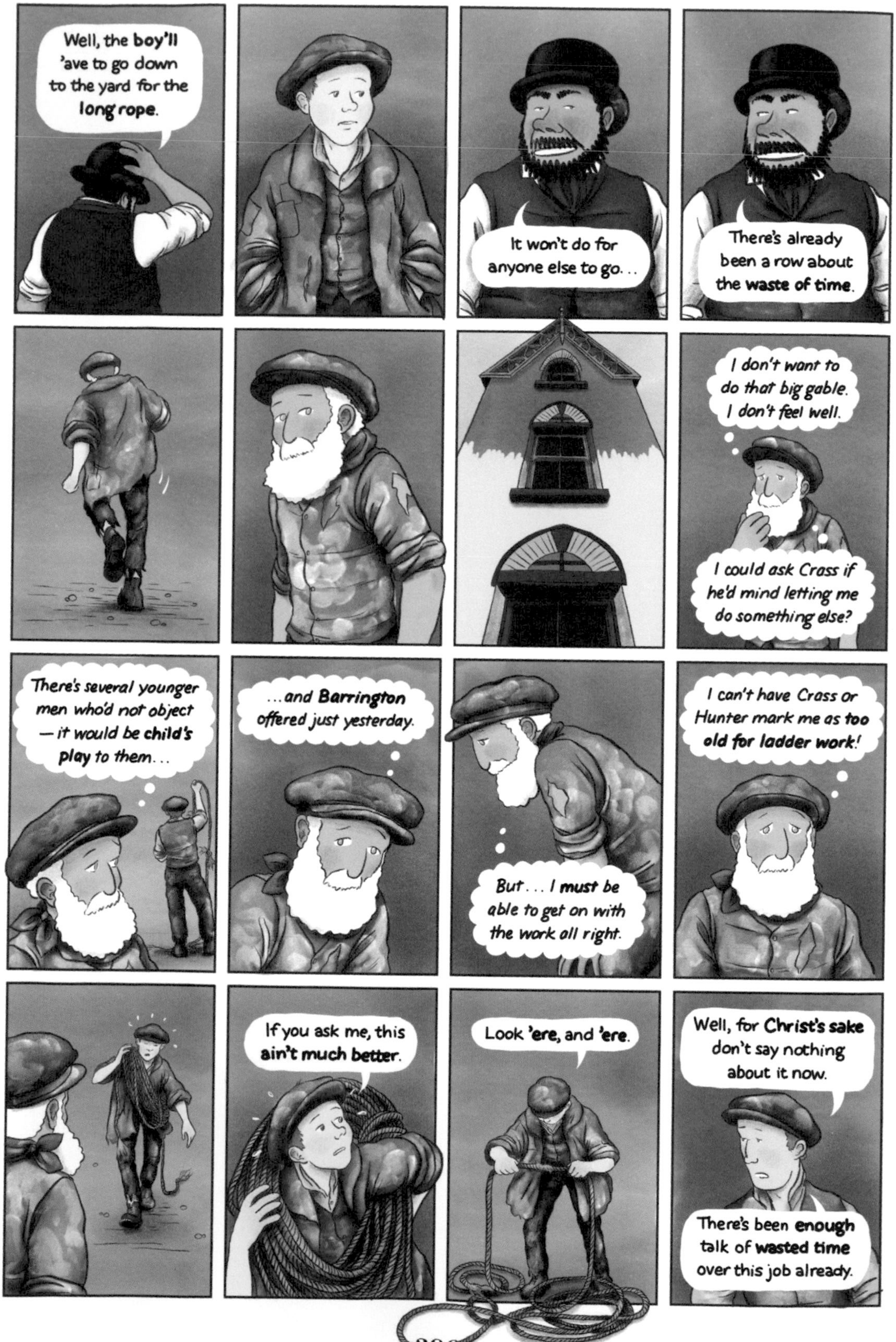
Well, the boy'll 'ave to go down to the yard for the long rope.
It won't do for anyone else to go...
There's already been a row about the waste of time.
I don't want to do that big gable. I don't feel well.
I could ask Crass if he'd mind letting me do something else?
There's several younger men who'd not object — it would be child's play to them...
...and Barrington offered just yesterday.
But... I must be able to get on with the work all right.
I can't have Crass or Hunter mark me as too old for ladder work!
If you ask me, this ain't much better.
Look 'ere, and 'ere.
Well, for Christ's sake don't say nothing about it now.
There's been enough talk of wasted time over this job already.

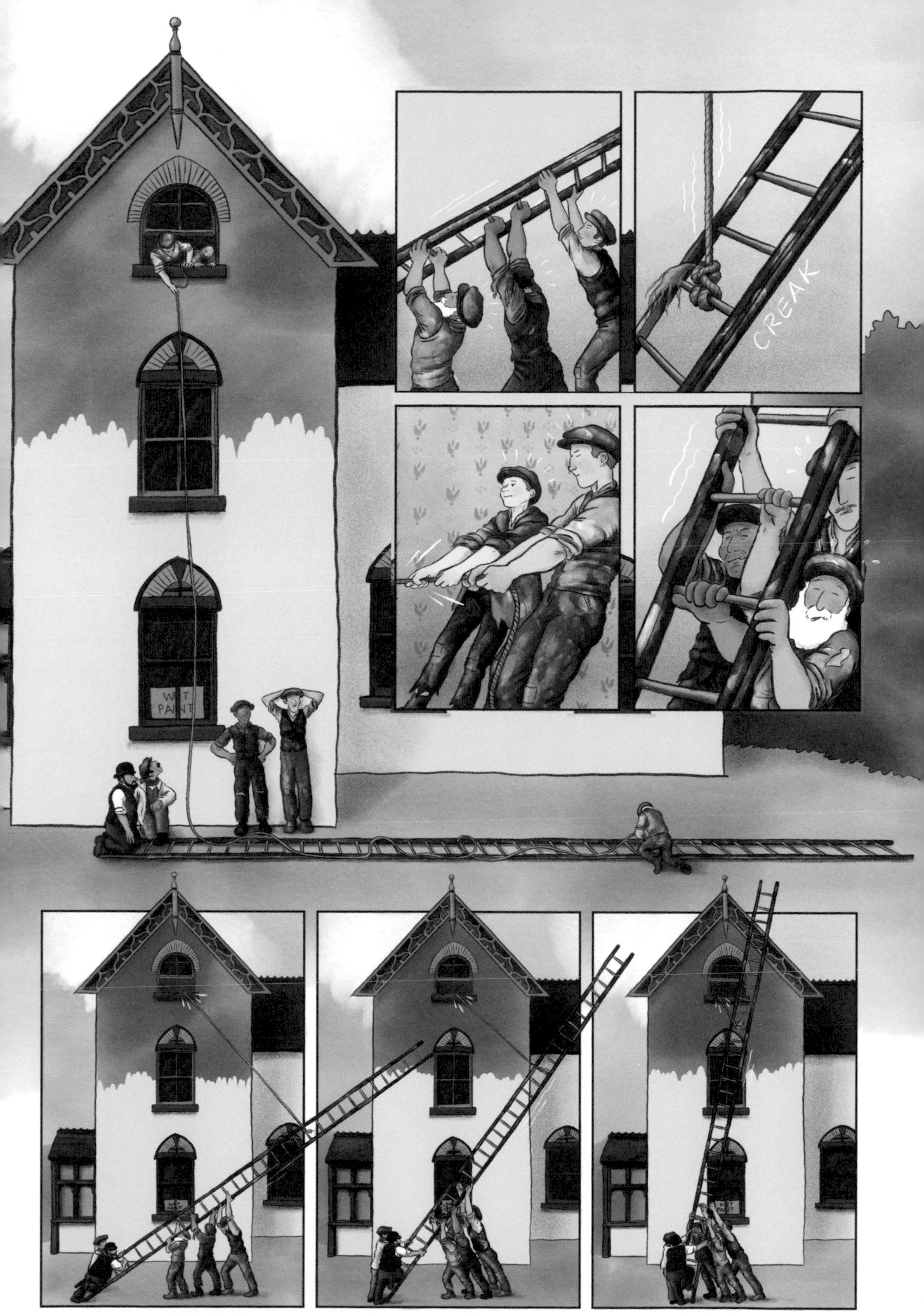
CREAK

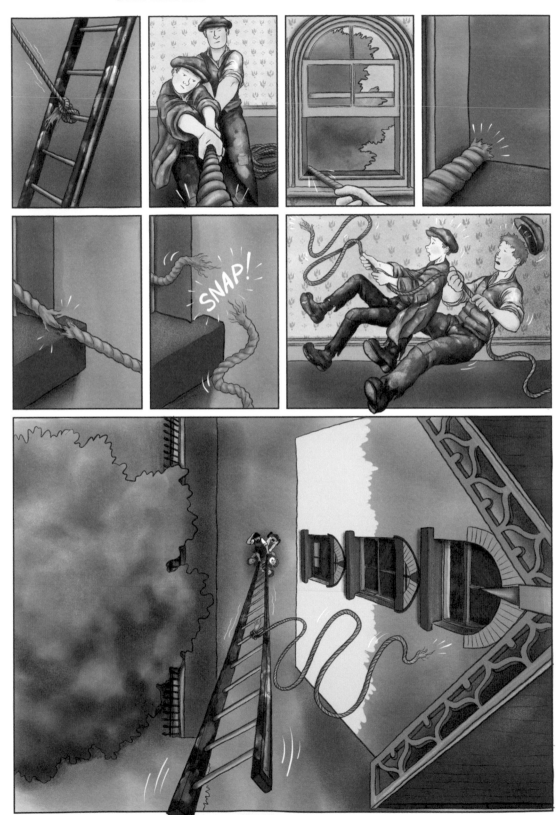

SNAP!

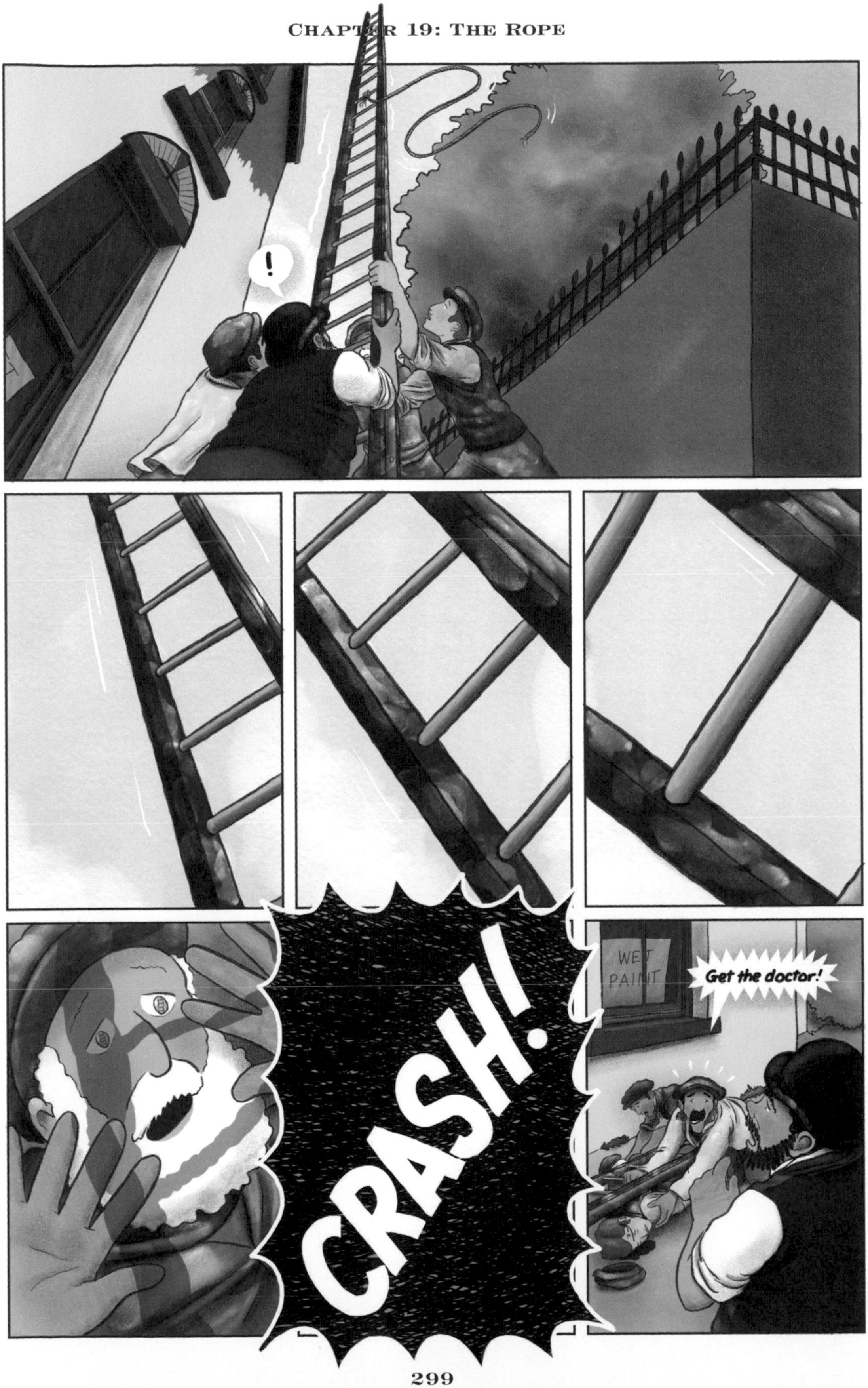
!
CRASH!
WET PAINT
Get the doctor!

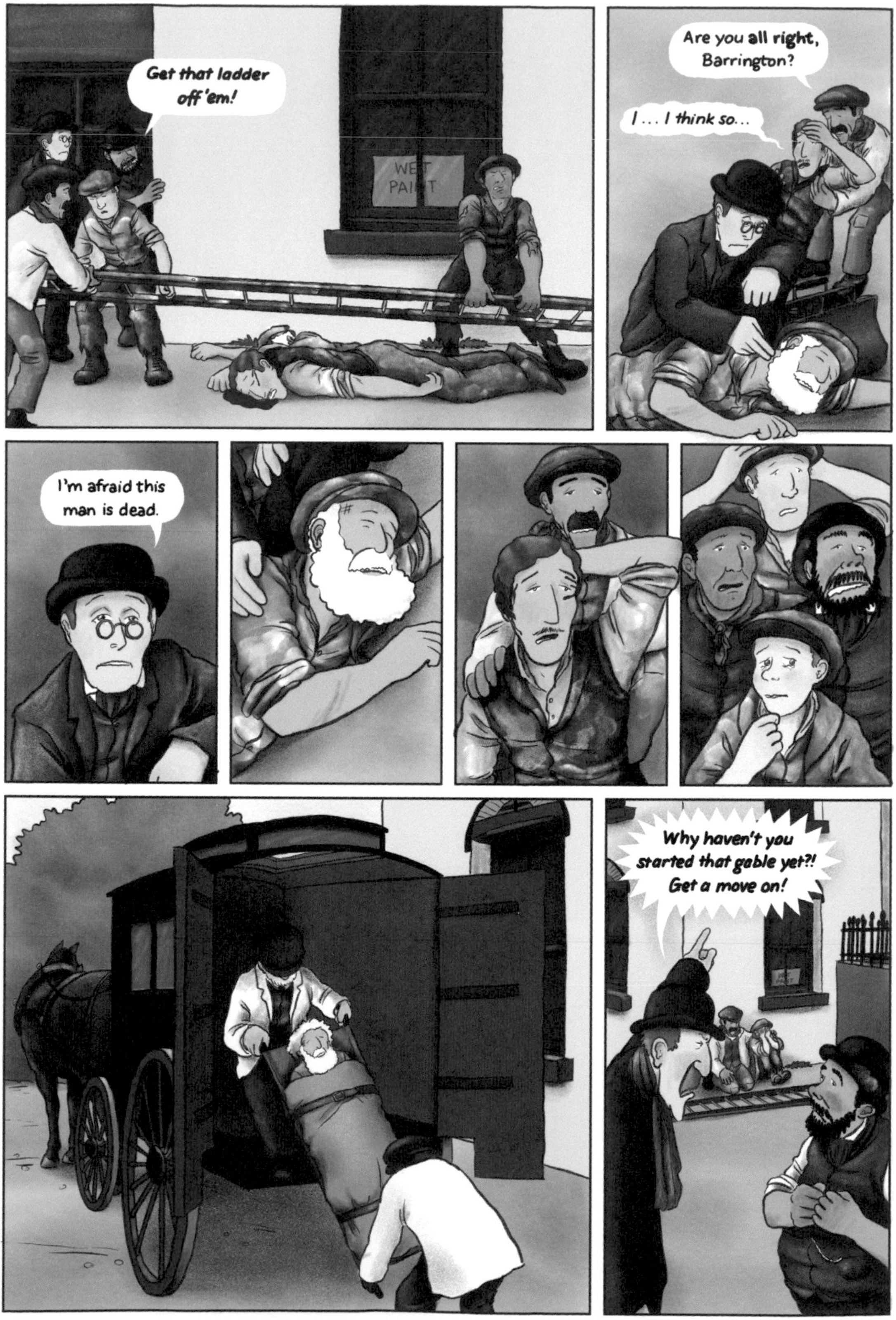
Get that ladder off 'em!
Are you all right, Barrington?
I ... I think so...
I'm afraid this man is dead.
Why haven't you started that gable yet?! Get a move on!

There's been an **accident**, Mr Hunter.

What did you use that **old rope** for?

You should've asked for a **new one!**

...

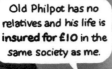

Old Philpot has no relatives and his life is **insured for £10** in the same society as me.

I know that 'e had arranged the money was to be paid to the **old woman** where he lodges.

I should think she would be **very glad** to be relieved of the **trouble** of arranging the funeral.

As a **close friend** of Philpot's, and a fellow member of the **society**...

...p'raps **you** are the most suitable person to take charge of the business for her?

Well, I'll go to see her at once.

O' course, we'll not be able to do much until after the **inquest**, but we can get the **coffin** made...

...and as you know the **mortuary keeper** there will be no **difficulty?**

Don't worry, Harlow, I've got you.

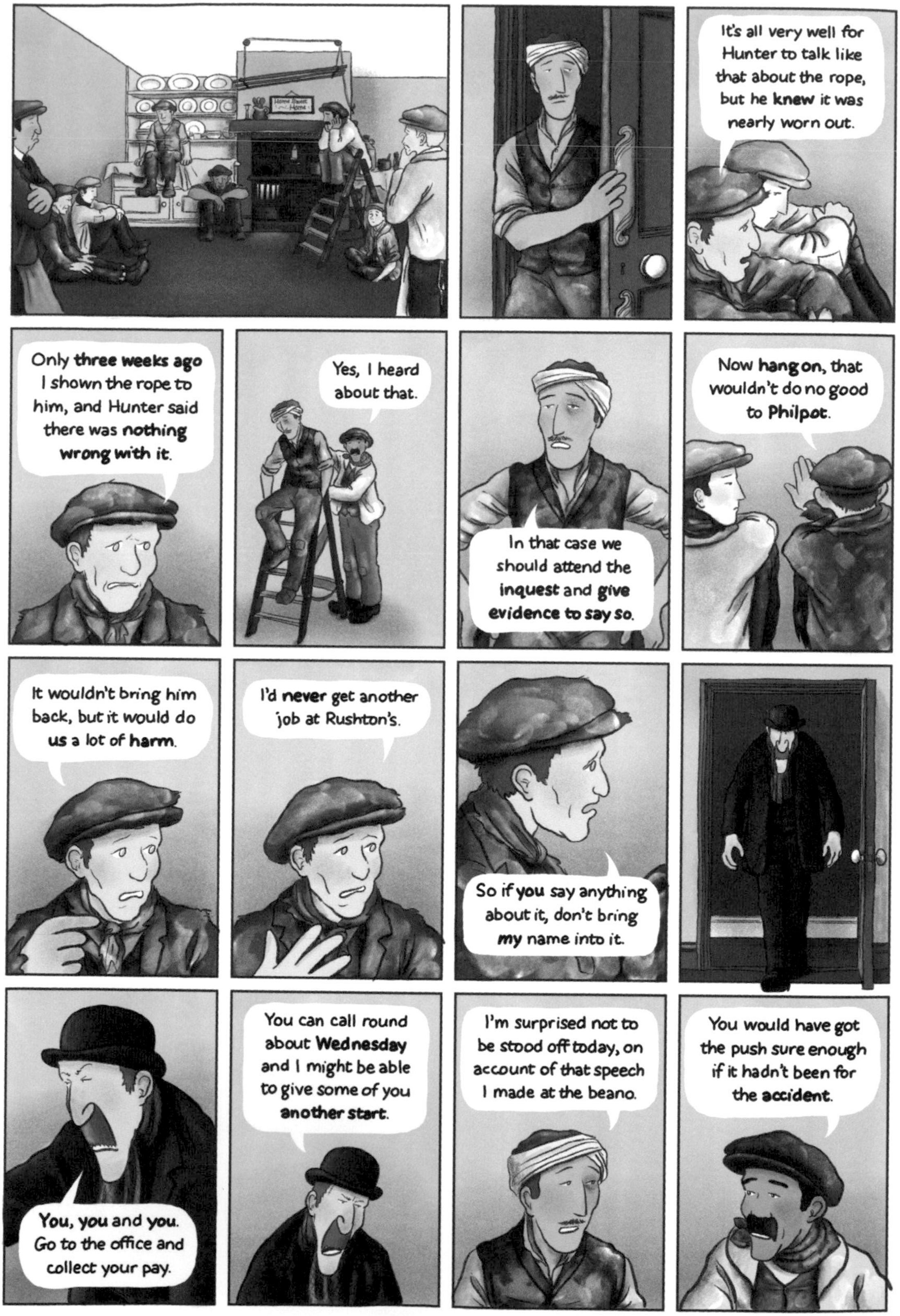
It's all very well for Hunter to talk like that about the rope, but he knew it was nearly worn out.
Only three weeks ago I shown the rope to him, and Hunter said there was nothing wrong with it.
Yes, I heard about that.
In that case we should attend the inquest and give evidence to say so.
Now hang on, that wouldn't do no good to Philpot.
It wouldn't bring him back, but it would do us a lot of harm.
I'd never get another job at Rushton's.
So if you say anything about it, don't bring my name into it.
You, you and you. Go to the office and collect your pay.
You can call round about Wednesday and I might be able to give some of you another start.
I'm surprised not to be stood off today, on account of that speech I made at the beano.
You would have got the push sure enough if it hadn't been for the accident.

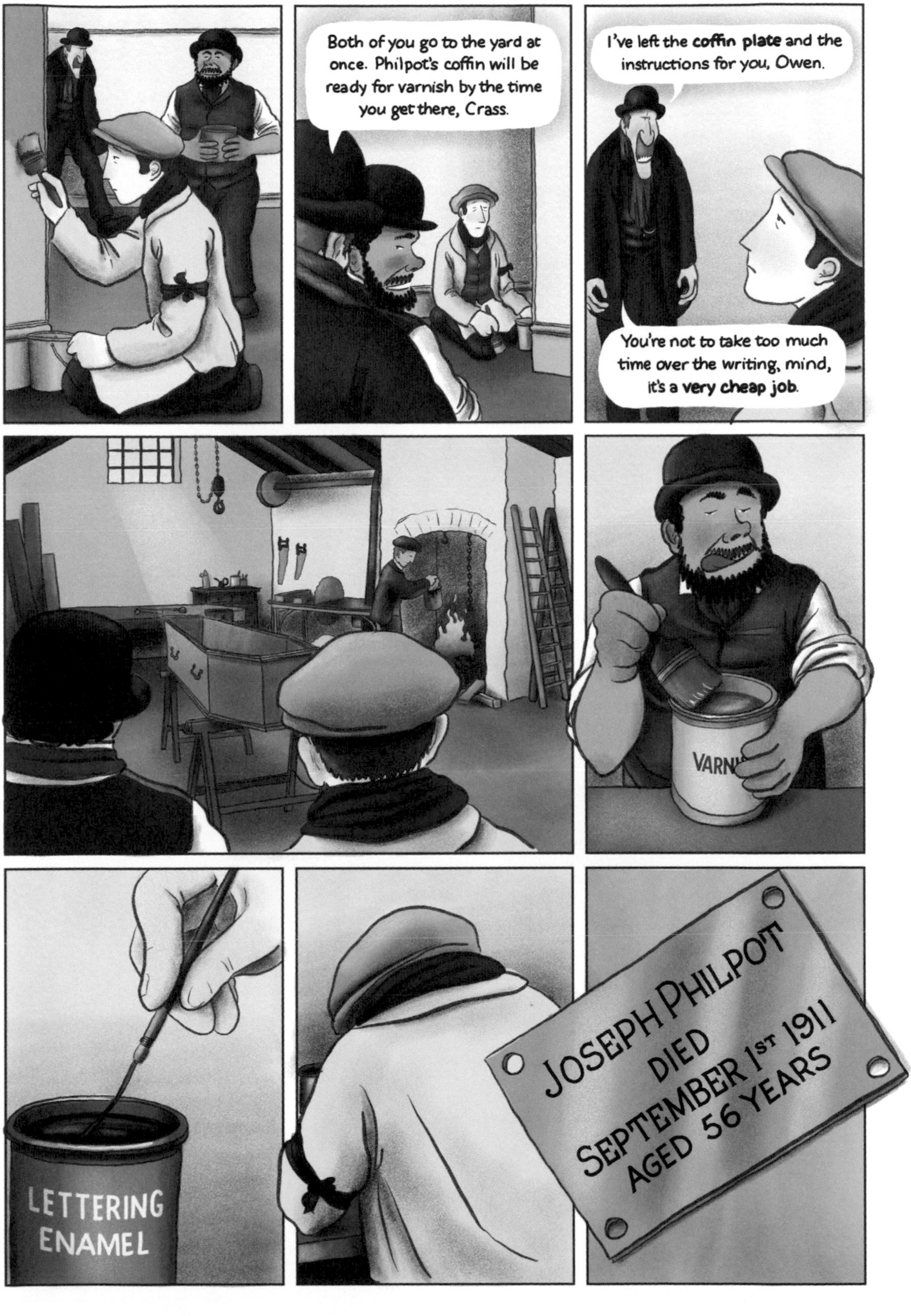
Both of you go to the yard at once. Philpot's coffin will be ready for varnish by the time you get there, Crass.
I've left the **coffin plate** and the instructions for you, Owen.
You're not to take too much time over the writing, mind, it's a **very cheap job**.
VARNI
LETTERING ENAMEL
JOSEPH PHILPOT
DIED
SEPTEMBER 1ST 1911
AGED 56 YEARS

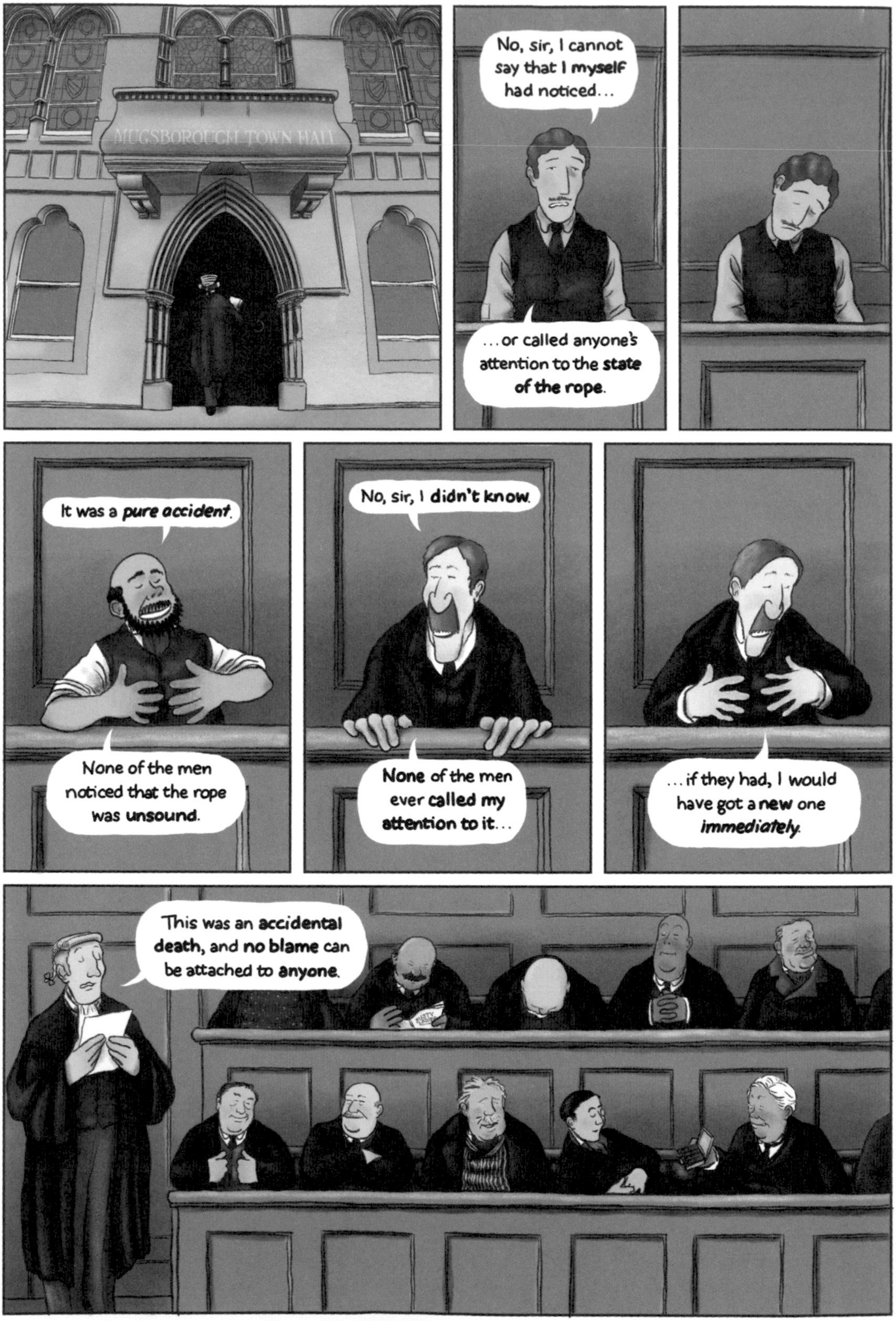
MUGSBOROUGH TOWN HALL
No, sir, I cannot say that I myself had noticed...
...or called anyone's attention to the state of the rope.
It was a pure accident.
None of the men noticed that the rope was unsound.
No, sir, I didn't know.
None of the men ever called my attention to it...
...if they had, I would have got a new one immediately.
This was an accidental death, and no blame can be attached to anyone.

CHAPTER TWENTY

IN MEMORIAM

THE
FUNERAL

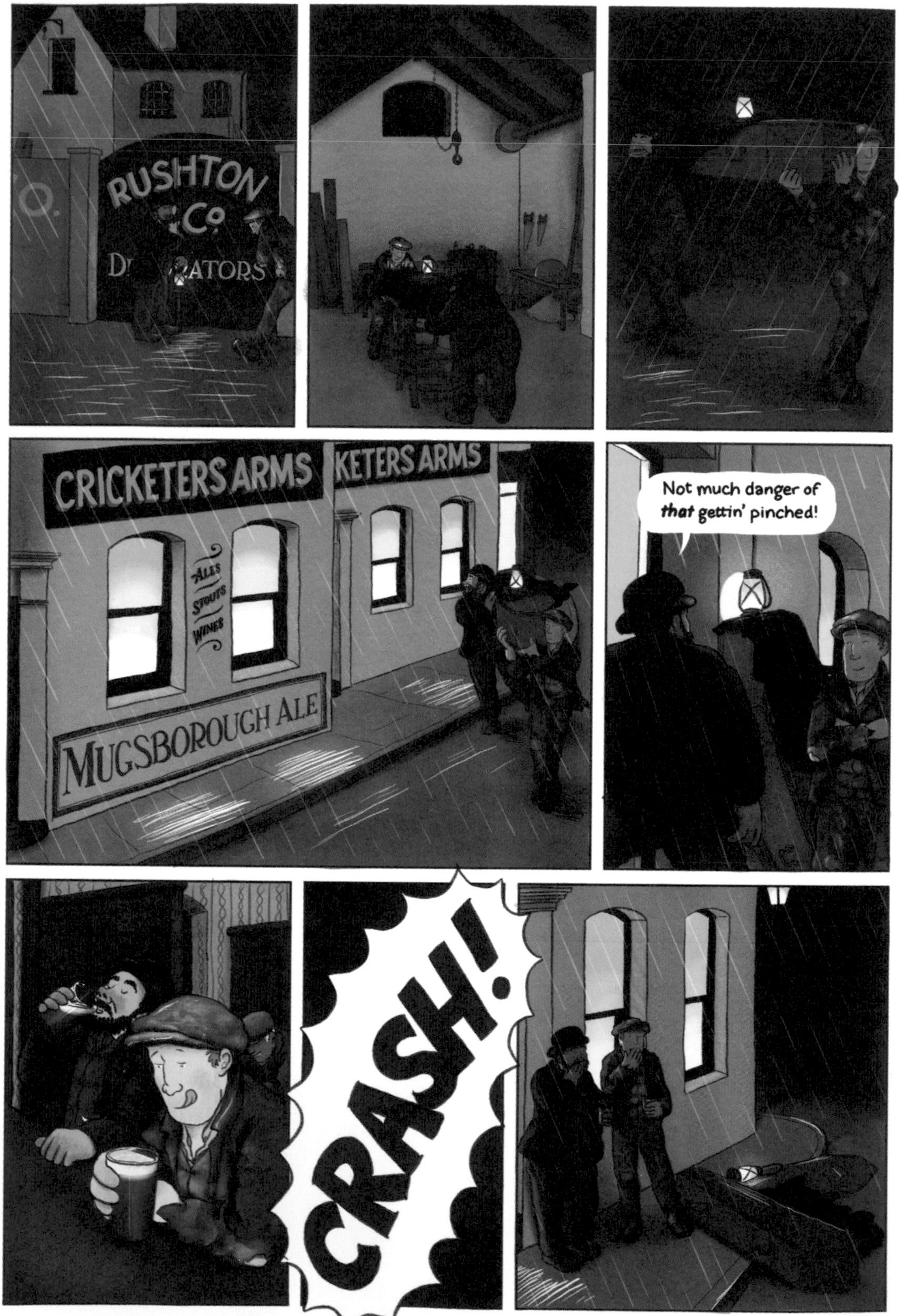

RUSHTON & Co
DECORATORS
CRICKETERS ARMS
KETERS ARMS
ALES STOUTS WINES
MUGSBOROUGH ALE
Not much danger of *that* gettin' pinched!
CRASH!

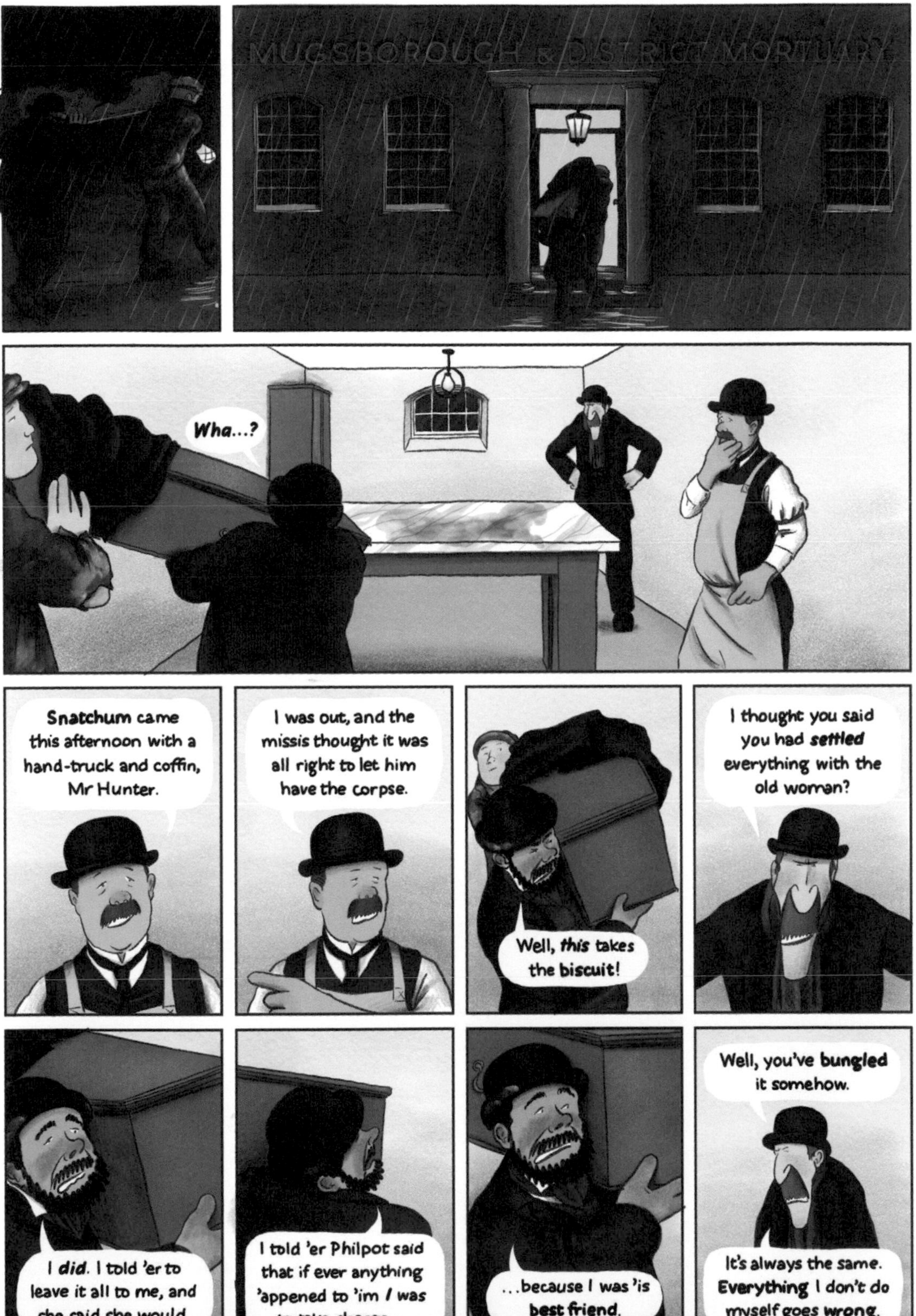
MUGSBOROUGH & DISTRICT MORTUARY
Wha...?
Snatchum came this afternoon with a hand-truck and coffin, Mr Hunter.
I was out, and the missis thought it was all right to let him have the corpse.
Well, *this* takes the biscuit!
I thought you said you had *settled* everything with the old woman?
I *did*. I told 'er to leave it all to me, and she said she would.
I told 'er Philpot said that if ever anything 'appened to 'im *I* was to take charge...
...because I was 'is **best friend**.
Well, you've **bungled** it somehow.
It's always the same. **Everything** I don't do myself goes **wrong**.

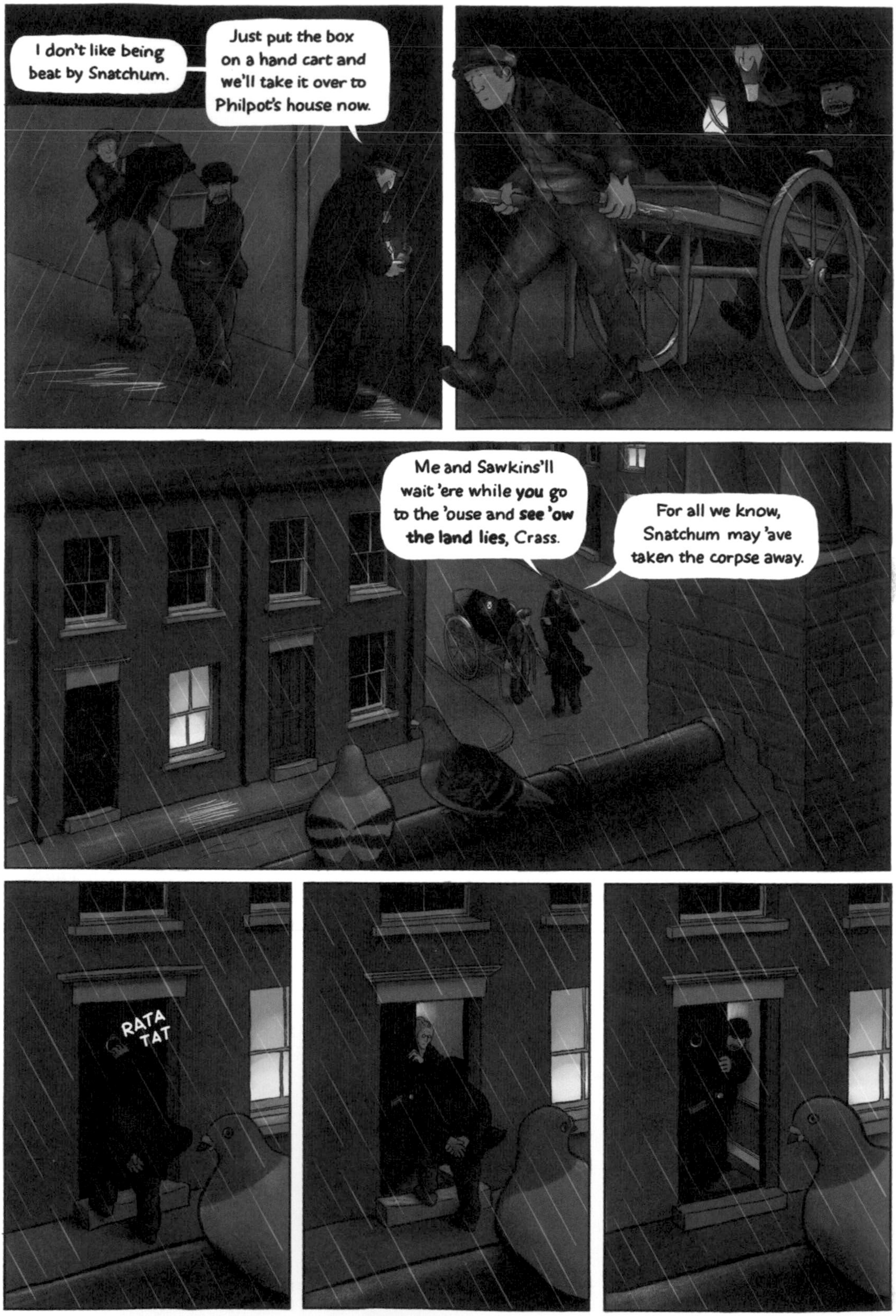
I don't like being beat by Snatchum.
Just put the box on a hand cart and we'll take it over to Philpot's house now.
Me and Sawkins'll wait 'ere while you go to the 'ouse and **see 'ow the land lies**, Crass.
For all we know, Snatchum may 'ave taken the corpse away.
RATA TAT

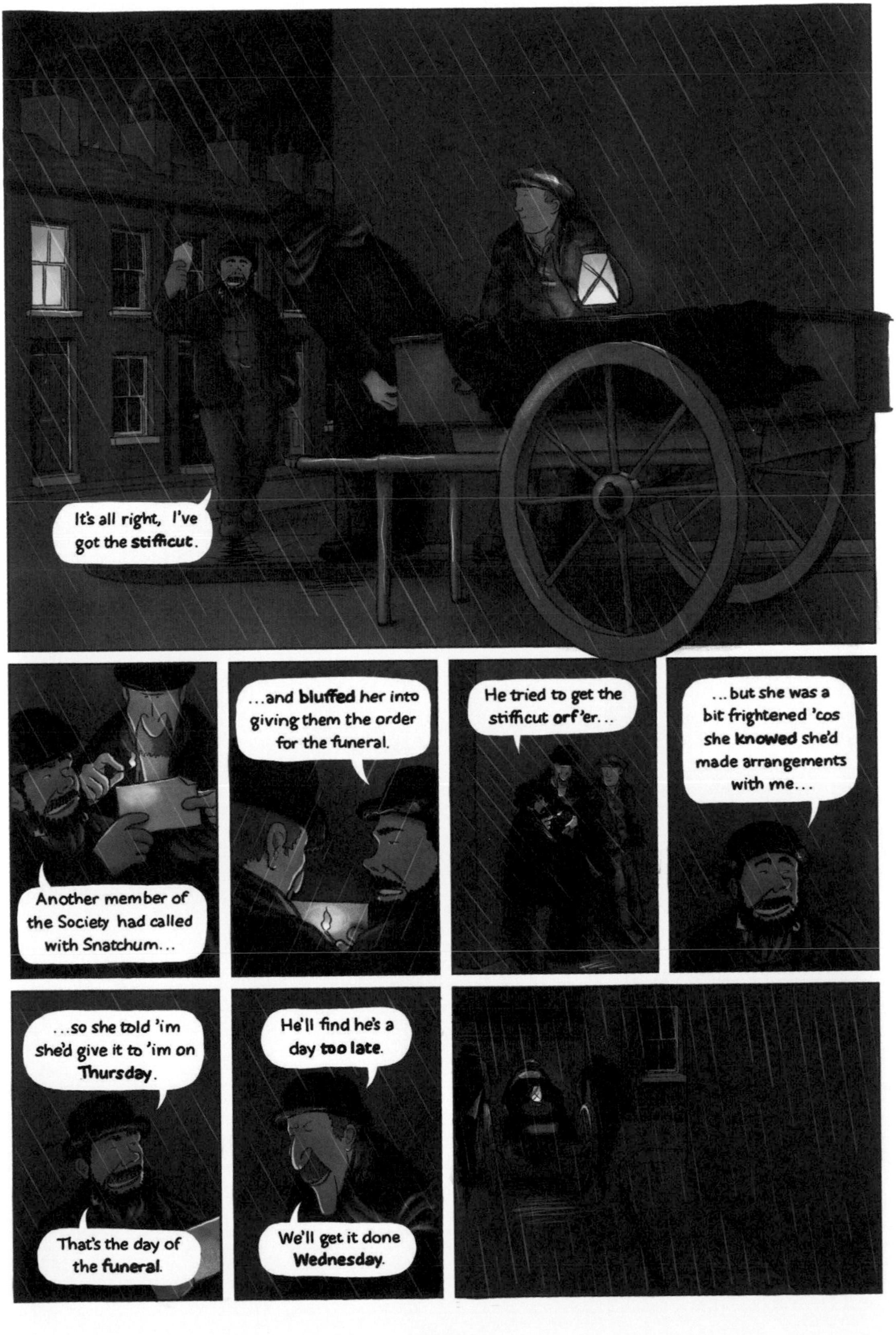
It's all right, I've got the **stifficut**.
Another member of the Society had called with Snatchum...
...and **bluffed** her into giving them the order for the funeral.
He tried to get the stifficut orf 'er...
...but she was a bit frightened 'cos she **knowed** she'd made arrangements with me...
...so she told 'im she'd give it to 'im on **Thursday**.
That's the day of the **funeral**.
He'll find he's a day **too late**.
We'll get it done **Wednesday**.

I shall be glad when it's all over.

I'm sick and tired of answerin' the door to undertakers.

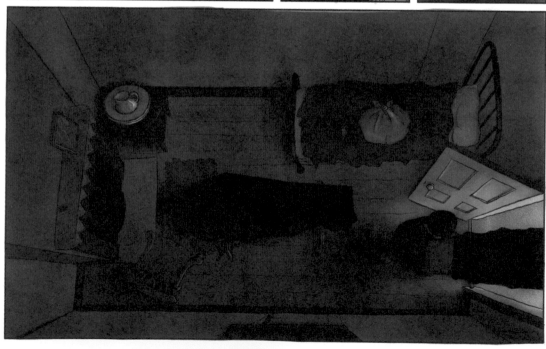

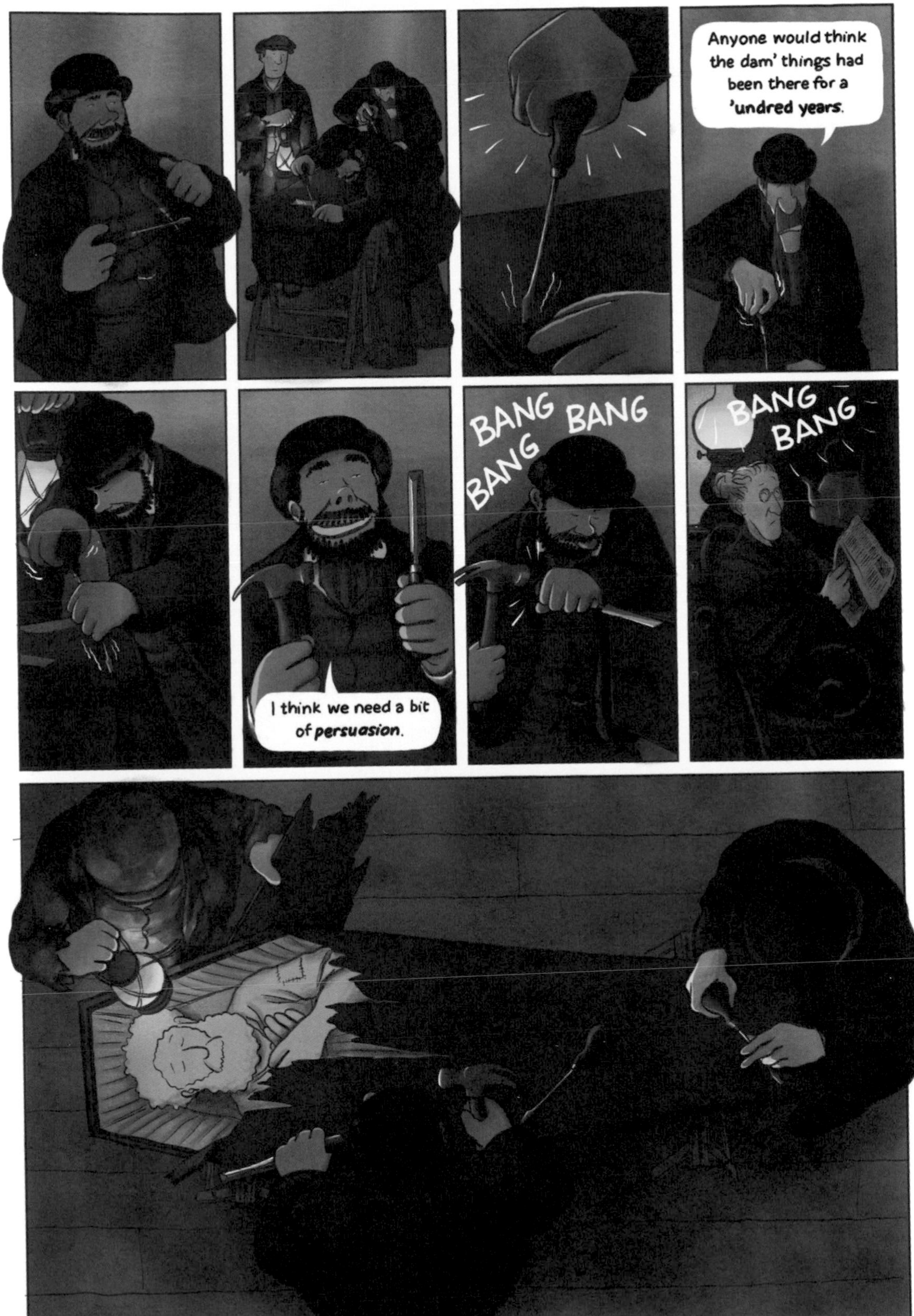
Anyone would think the dam' things had been there for a 'undred years.
I think we need a bit of *persuasion*.
BANG BANG BANG
BANG BANG

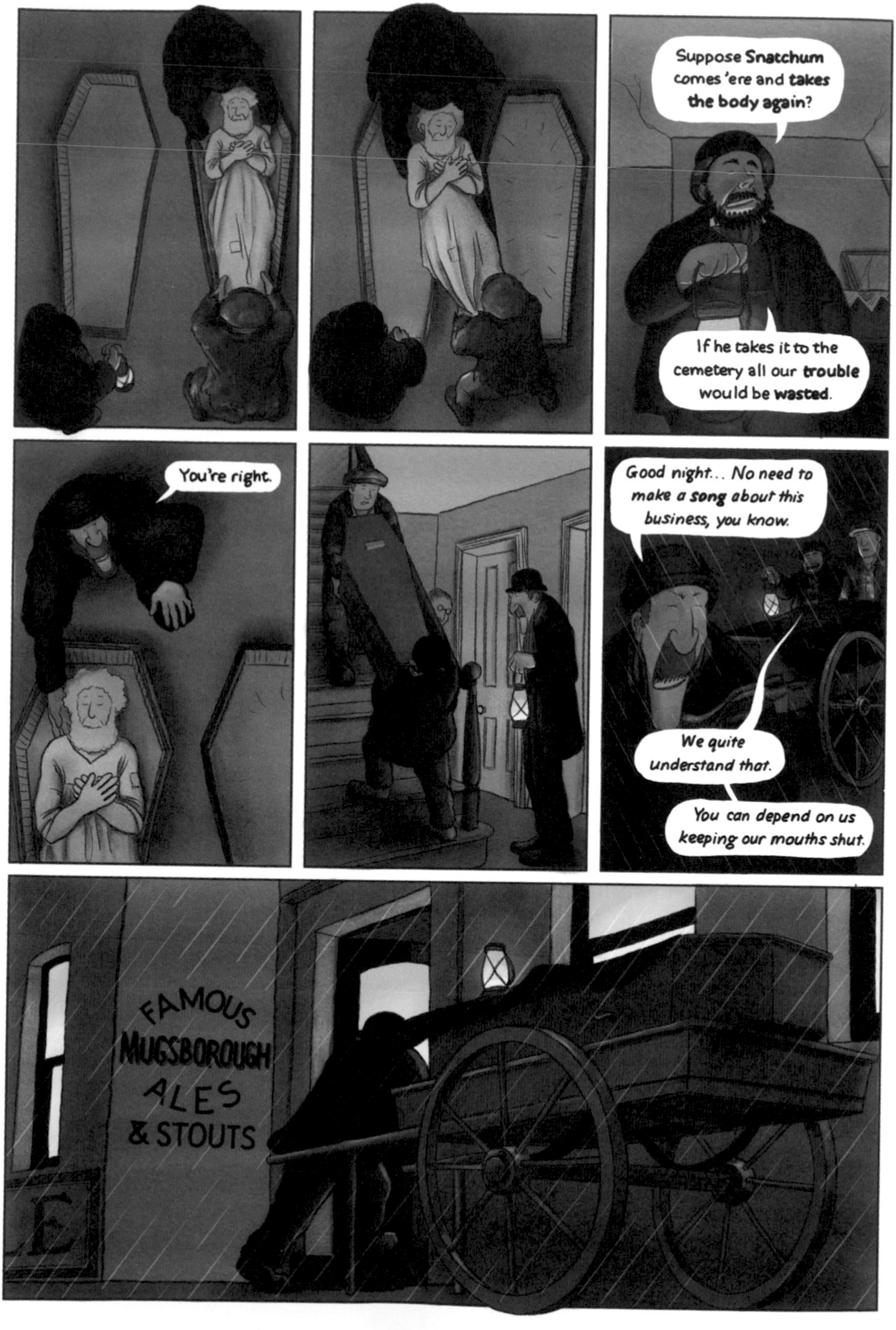
Suppose Snatchum comes 'ere and takes the body again?
If he takes it to the cemetery all our trouble would be wasted.
You're right.
Good night... No need to make a song about this business, you know.
We quite understand that.
You can depend on us keeping our mouths shut.
FAMOUS MUGSBOROUGH ALES & STOUTS

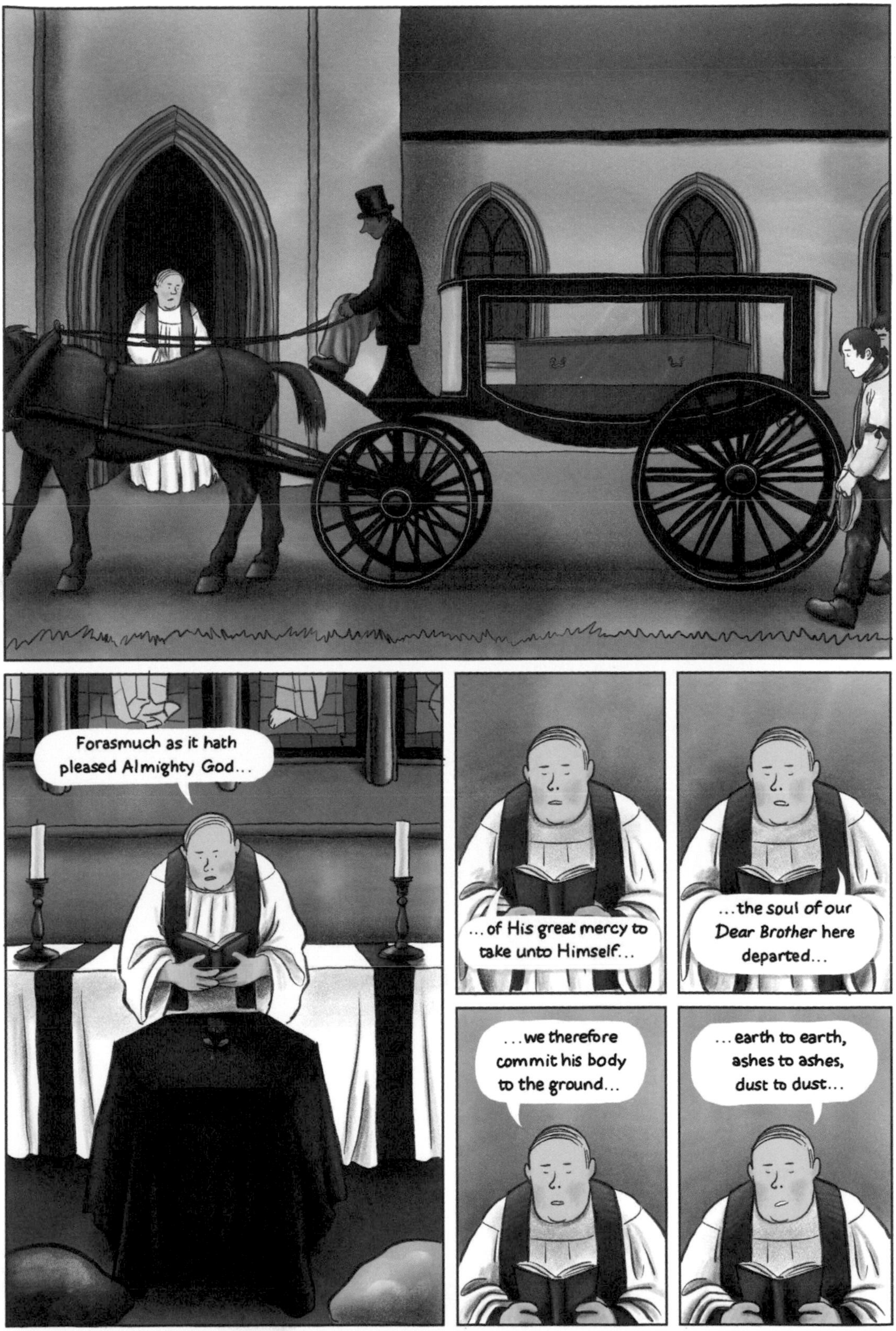
Forasmuch as it hath pleased Almighty God...
...of His great mercy to take unto Himself...
...the soul of our Dear Brother here departed...
...we therefore commit his body to the ground...
...earth to earth, ashes to ashes, dust to dust...

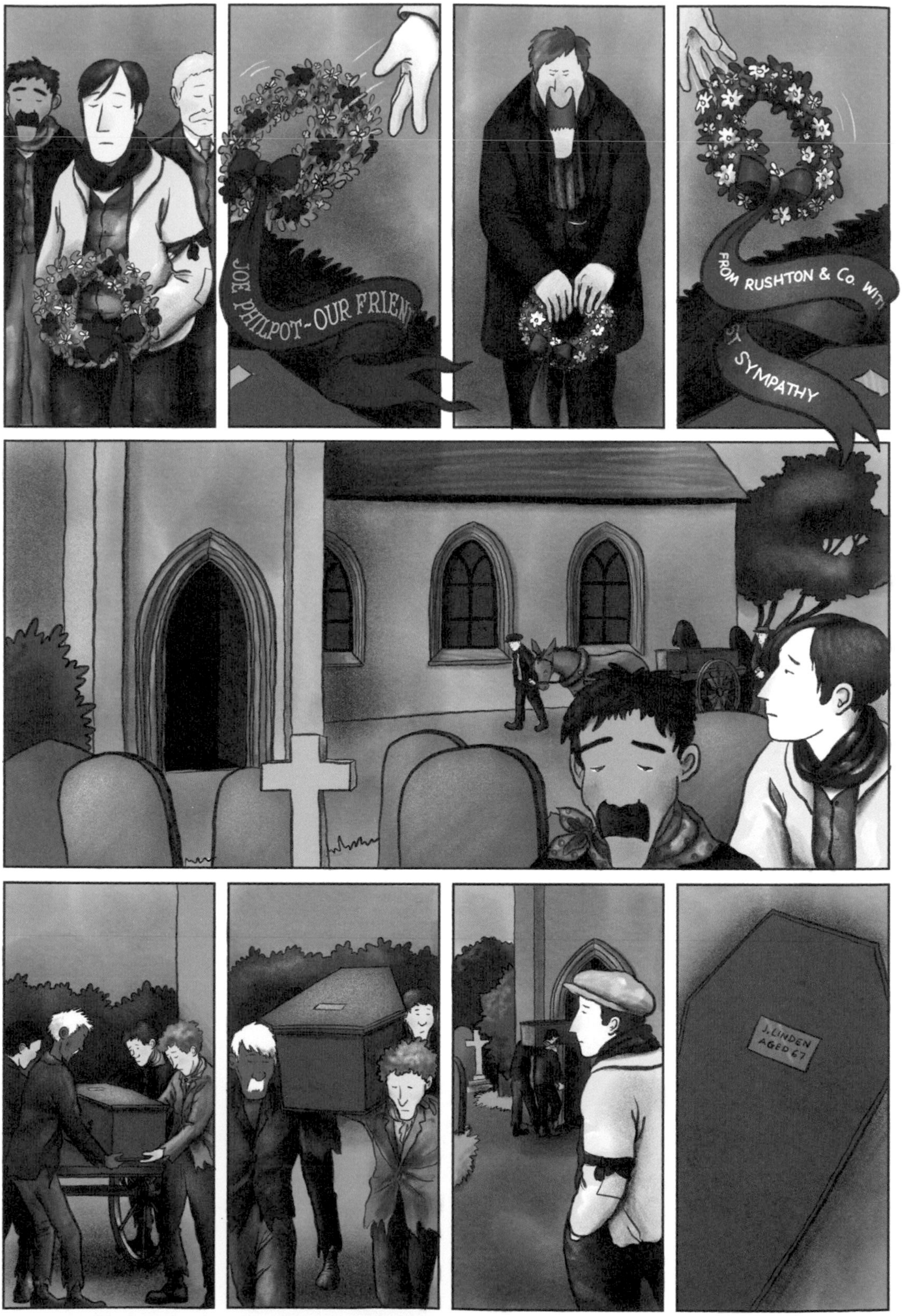
JOE PHILPOT - OUR FRIEN
FROM RUSHTON & Co. WIT
T SYMPATHY
J. LINDEN
AGED 67

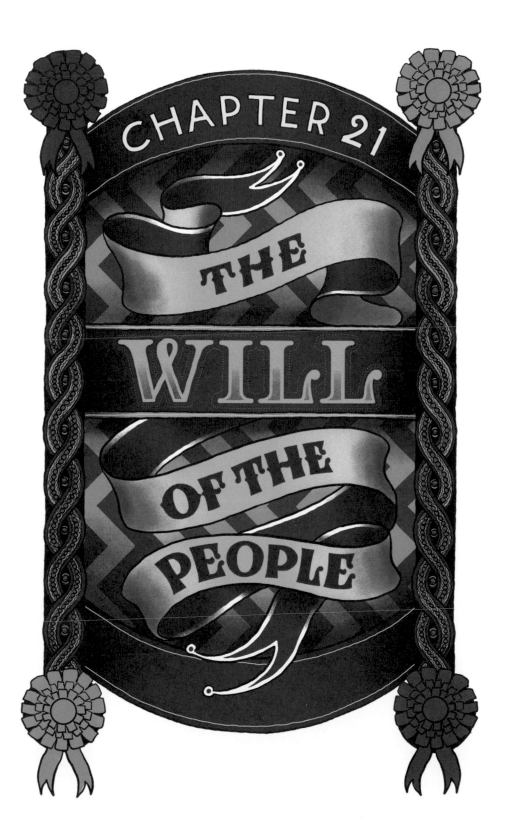

CHAPTER 21

THE WILL OF THE PEOPLE

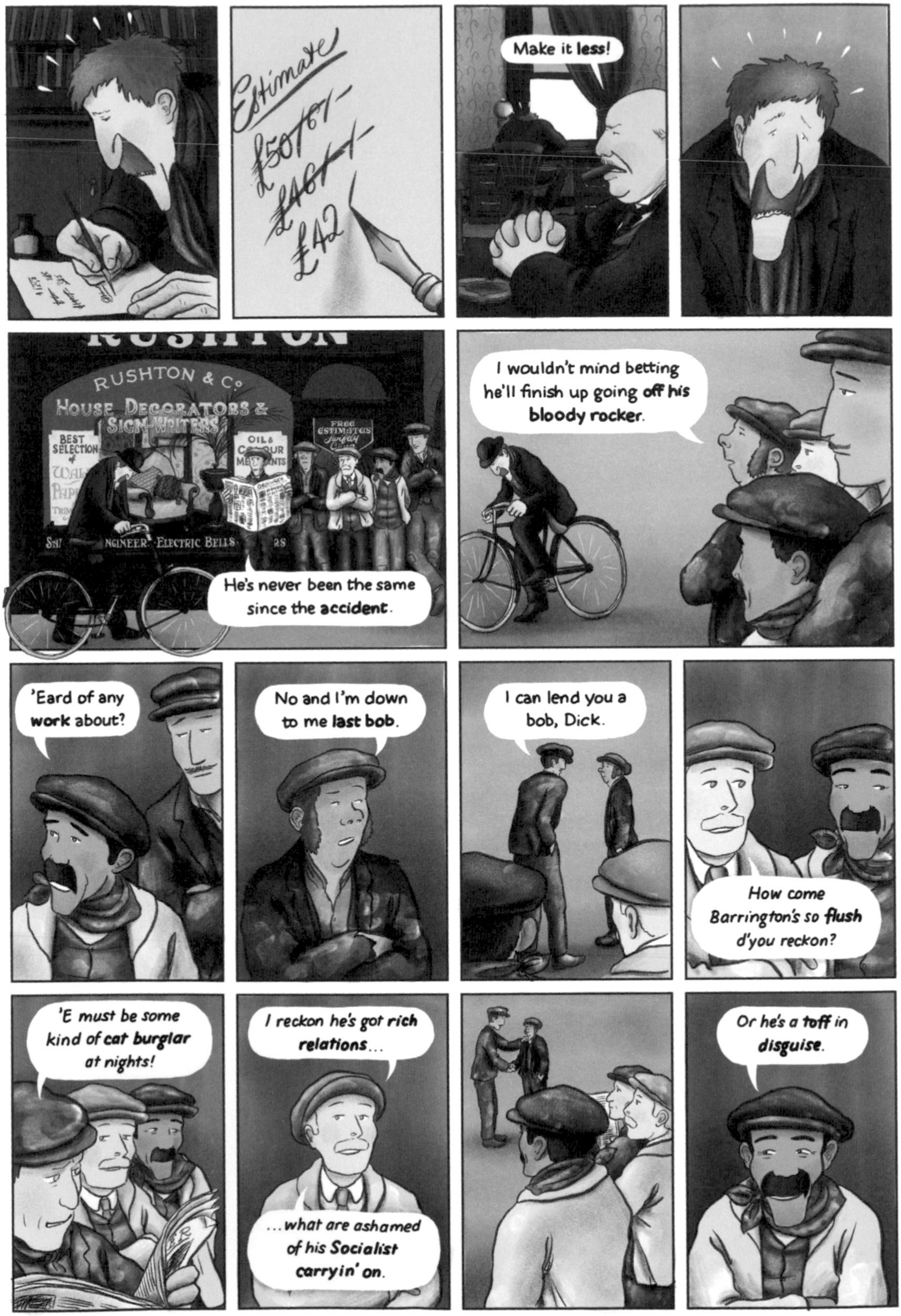
Estimate
£50/6/-
£46/-/-
£42
Make it less!
RUSHTON & Co
HOUSE DECORATORS & SIGN-WRITERS
BEST SELECTION of
OIL & COLOUR
FREE ESTIMATES
ELECTRIC BELLS
He's never been the same since the accident.
I wouldn't mind betting he'll finish up going off his bloody rocker.
'Eard of any work about?
No and I'm down to me last bob.
I can lend you a bob, Dick.
How come Barrington's so flush d'you reckon?
'E must be some kind of cat burglar at nights!
I reckon he's got rich relations...
...what are ashamed of his Socialist carryin' on.
Or he's a toff in disguise.

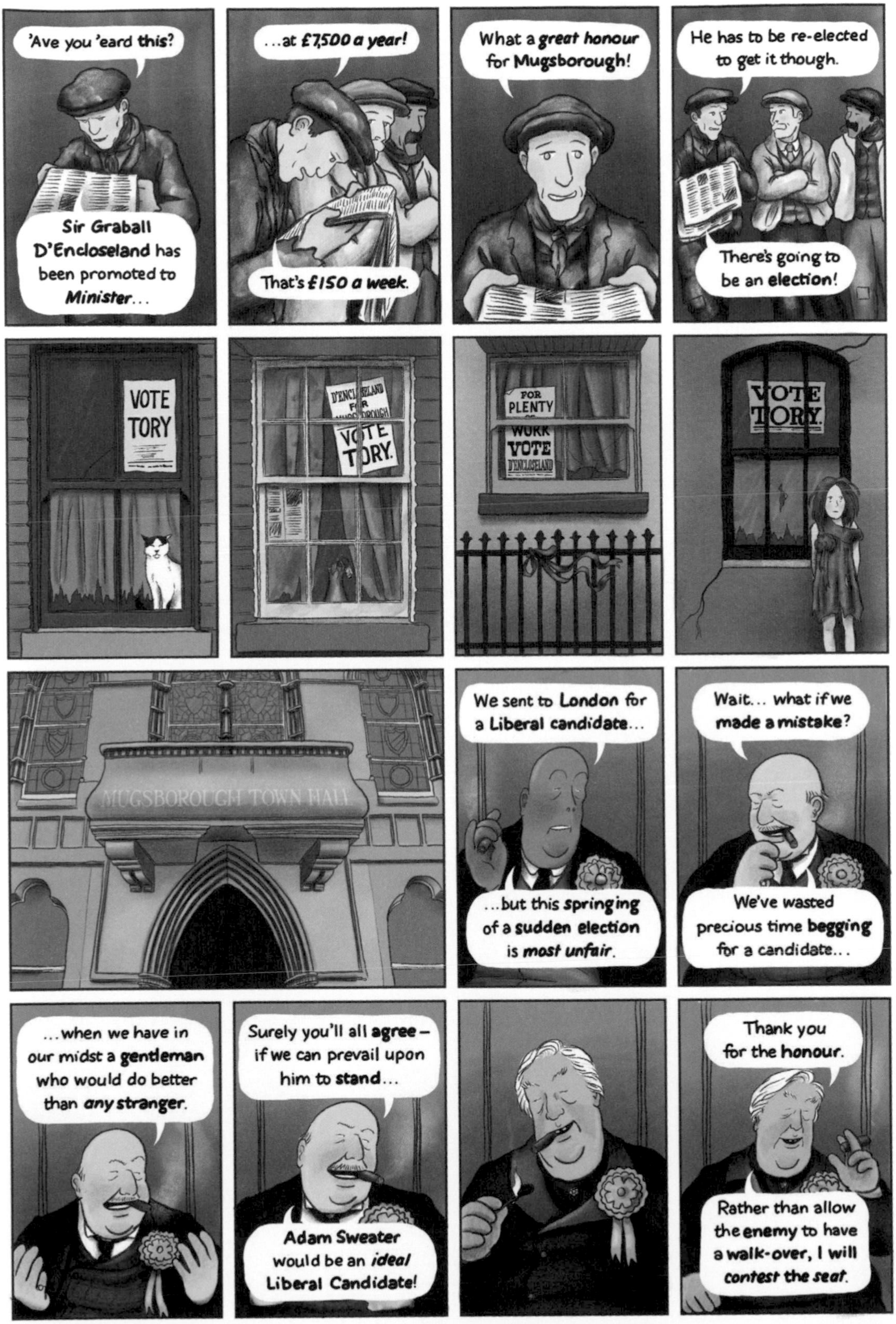
'Ave you 'eard this?
Sir Graball D'Encloseland has been promoted to Minister...
...at £7,500 a year!
That's £150 a week.
What a great honour for Mugsborough!
He has to be re-elected to get it though.
There's going to be an election!
VOTE TORY
D'ENCLOSELAND FOR MUGSBOROUGH
VOTE TORY.
FOR PLENTY OF WORK
VOTE D'ENCLOSELAND
VOTE TORY.
MUGSBOROUGH TOWN HALL
We sent to London for a Liberal candidate...
...but this springing of a sudden election is most unfair.
Wait... what if we made a mistake?
We've wasted precious time begging for a candidate...
...when we have in our midst a gentleman who would do better than any stranger.
Surely you'll all agree – if we can prevail upon him to stand...
Adam Sweater would be an ideal Liberal Candidate!
Thank you for the honour.
Rather than allow the enemy to have a walk-over, I will contest the seat.

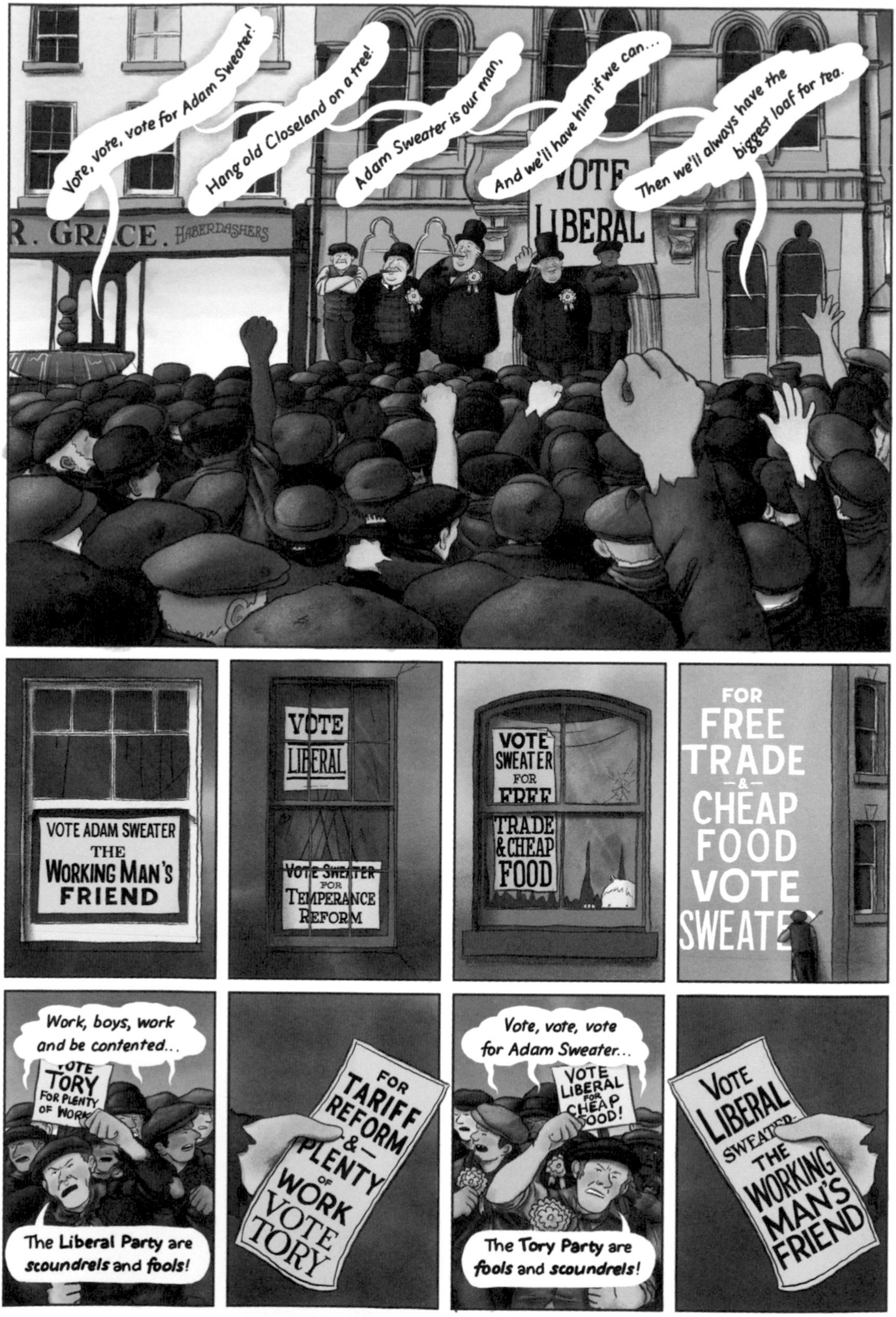
Vote, vote, vote for Adam Sweater!
Hang old Closeland on a tree!
Adam Sweater is our man,
And we'll have him if we can...
Then we'll always have the biggest loaf for tea.
R. GRACE. HABERDASHERS
VOTE LIBERAL
VOTE ADAM SWEATER THE WORKING MAN'S FRIEND
VOTE LIBERAL
VOTE SWEATER FOR TEMPERANCE REFORM
VOTE SWEATER FOR
TRADE & CHEAP FOOD
FOR FREE TRADE & CHEAP FOOD VOTE SWEATE
Work, boys, work and be contented...
TORY FOR PLENTY OF WORK
The Liberal Party are scoundrels and fools!
FOR TARIFF REFORM & PLENTY OF WORK VOTE TORY
Vote, vote, vote for Adam Sweater...
VOTE LIBERAL FOR CHEAP FOOD!
The Tory Party are fools and scoundrels!
VOTE LIBERAL
THE WORKING MAN'S FRIEND

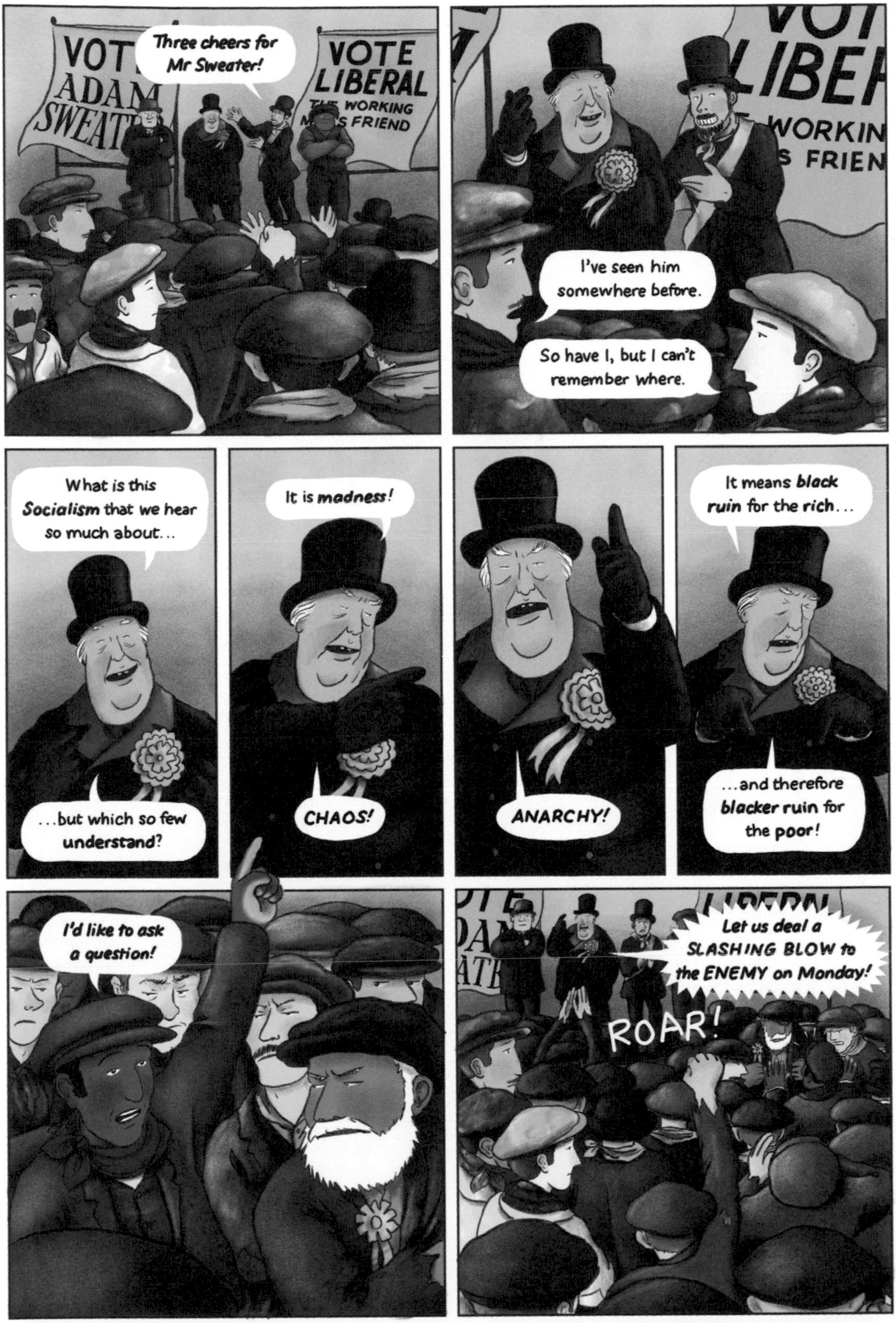
VOTE
ADAM
SWEAT
Three cheers for Mr Sweater!
VOTE LIBERAL
THE WORKING
S FRIEND
I've seen him somewhere before.
So have I, but I can't remember where.
What is this *Socialism* that we hear so much about...
...but which so few understand?
It is *madness*!
CHAOS!
ANARCHY!
It means *black ruin* for the rich...
...and therefore *blacker* ruin for the poor!
I'd like to ask a question!
Let us deal a SLASHING BLOW to the ENEMY on Monday!
ROAR!

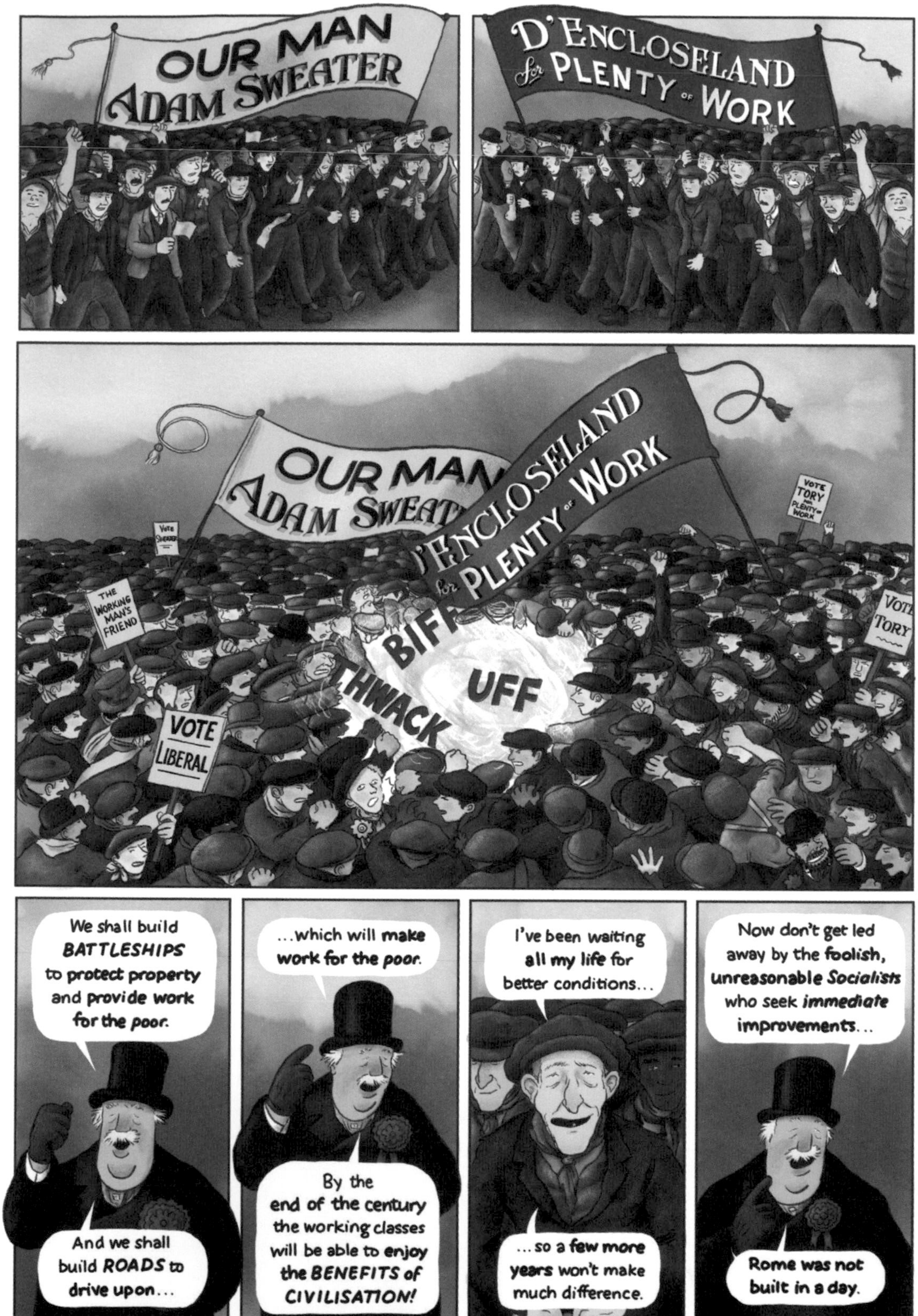
OUR MAN ADAM SWEATER
D'ENCLOSELAND for PLENTY of WORK
OUR MAN ADAM SWEAT
D'ENCLOSELAND for PLENTY of WORK
VOTE TORY
THE WORKING MAN'S FRIEND
VOTE LIBERAL
BIFF
UFF
THWACK
We shall build BATTLESHIPS to protect property and provide work for the poor.
And we shall build ROADS to drive upon...
...which will make work for the poor.
By the end of the century the working classes will be able to enjoy the BENEFITS of CIVILISATION!
I've been waiting all my life for better conditions...
...so a few more years won't make much difference.
Now don't get led away by the foolish, unreasonable Socialists who seek immediate improvements...
Rome was not built in a day.

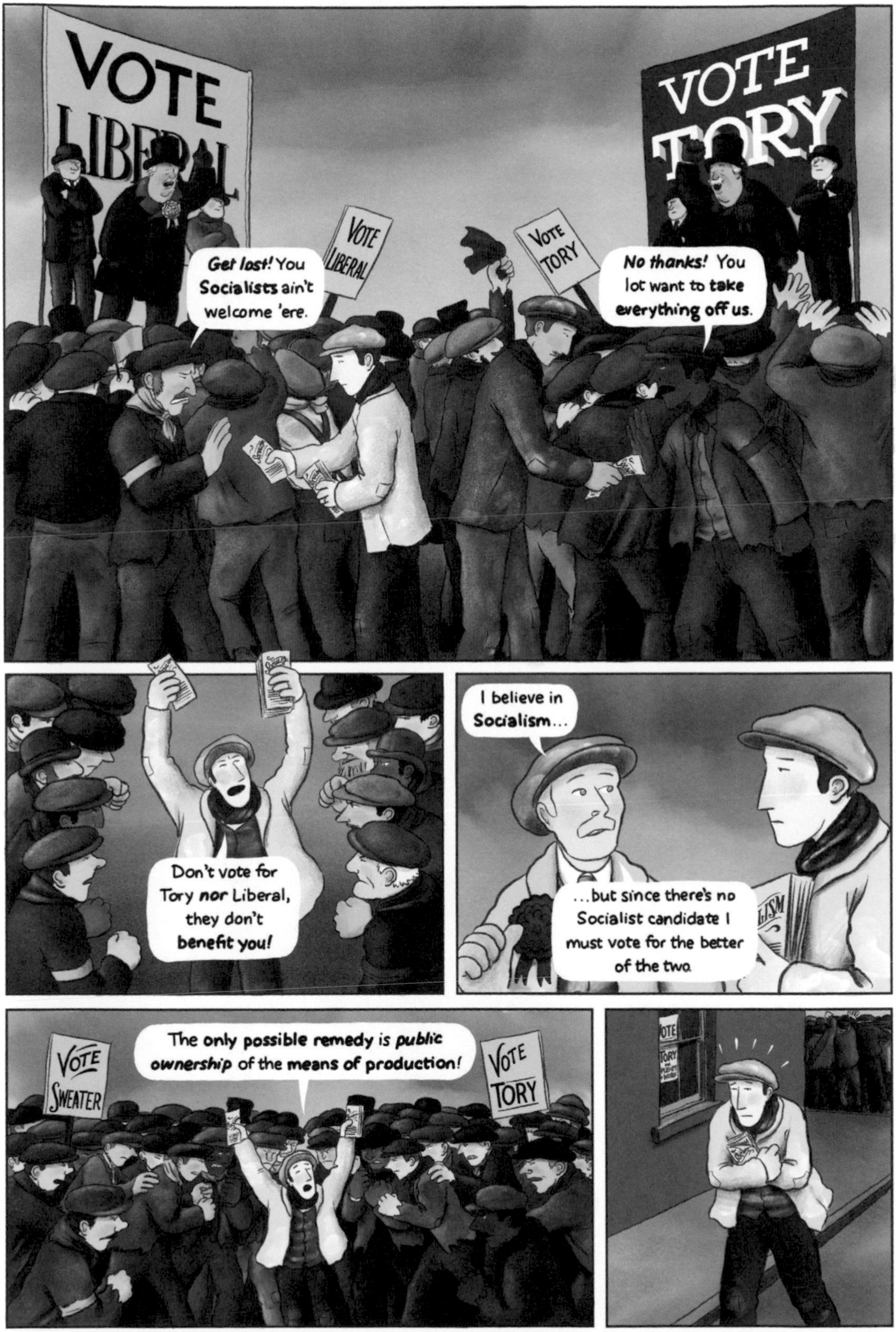
VOTE LIBERAL
VOTE TORY
VOTE LIBERAL
VOTE TORY
Get lost! You Socialists ain't welcome 'ere.
No thanks! You lot want to take everything off us.
Don't vote for Tory nor Liberal, they don't benefit you!
I believe in Socialism...
...but since there's no Socialist candidate I must vote for the better of the two.
VOTE SWEATER
The only possible remedy is public ownership of the means of production!
VOTE TORY

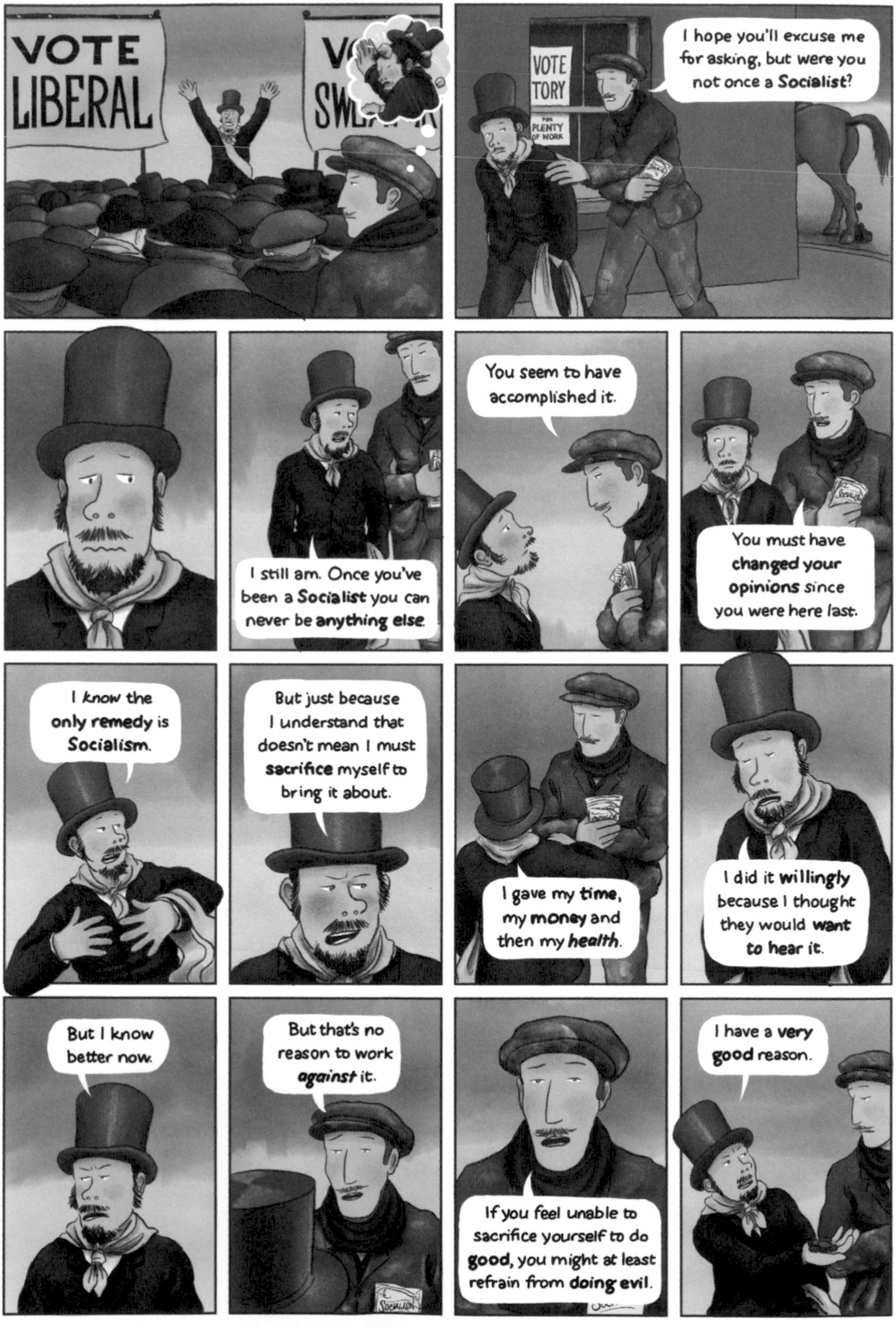
VOTE LIBERAL
VOTE TORY
FOR PLENTY OF WORK
I hope you'll excuse me for asking, but were you not once a **Socialist**?
I still am. Once you've been a **Socialist** you can never be **anything else**.
You seem to have accomplished it.
You must have **changed your opinions** since you were here last.
I *know* the **only remedy** is **Socialism**.
But just because I understand that doesn't mean I must **sacrifice** myself to bring it about.
I gave my **time**, my **money** and then my ***health***.
I did it **willingly** because I thought they would **want to hear it**.
But I know better now.
But that's no reason to work ***against*** it.
If you feel unable to sacrifice yourself to do **good**, you might at least refrain from **doing evil**.
I have a **very good** reason.

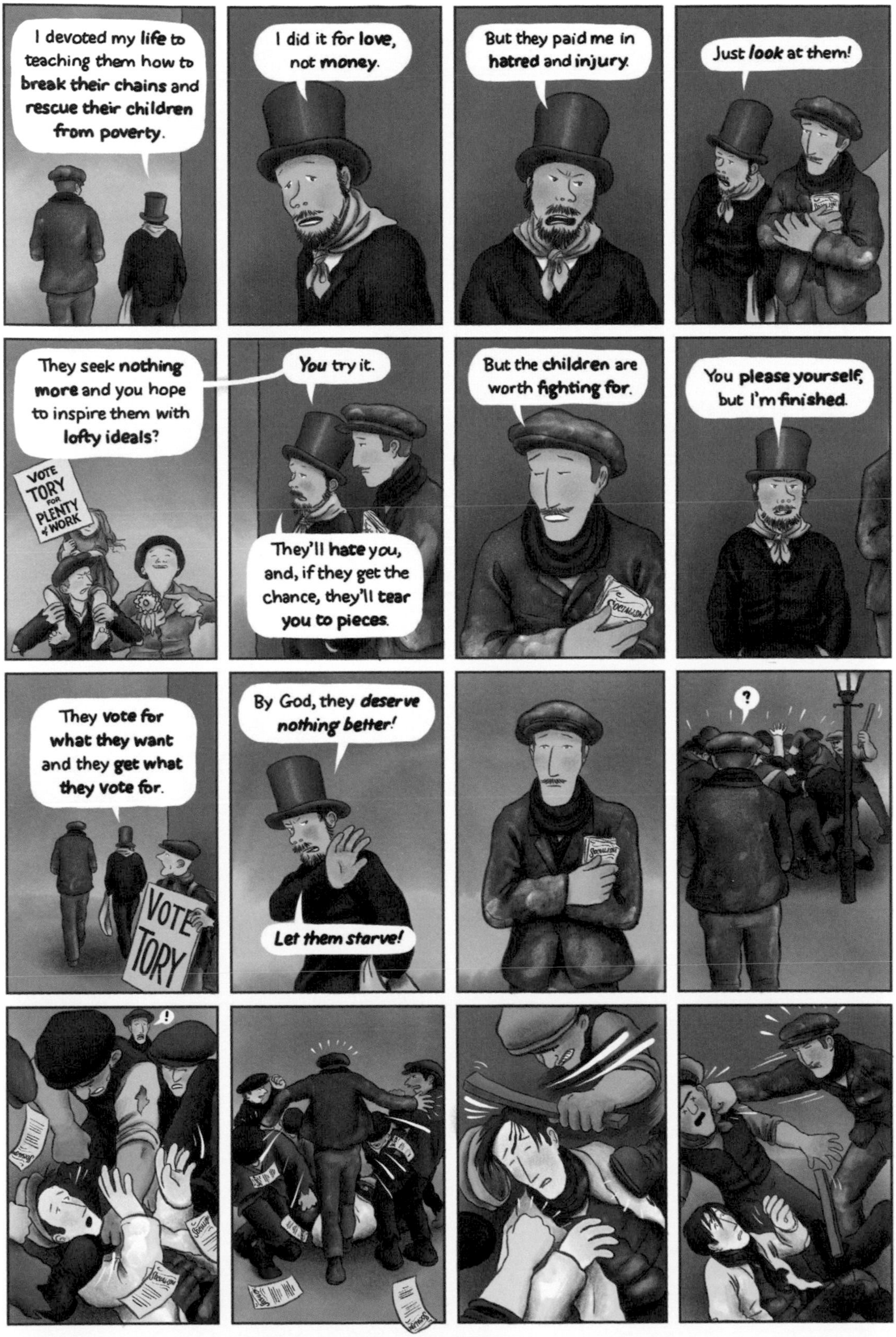
I devoted my life to teaching them how to break their chains and rescue their children from poverty.
I did it for love, not money.
But they paid me in hatred and injury.
Just look at them!
They seek nothing more and you hope to inspire them with lofty ideals?
VOTE TORY FOR PLENTY of WORK
You try it.
They'll hate you, and, if they get the chance, they'll tear you to pieces.
But the children are worth fighting for.
You please yourself, but I'm finished.
They vote for what they want and they get what they vote for.
VOTE TORY
By God, they deserve nothing better!
Let them starve!
?
!

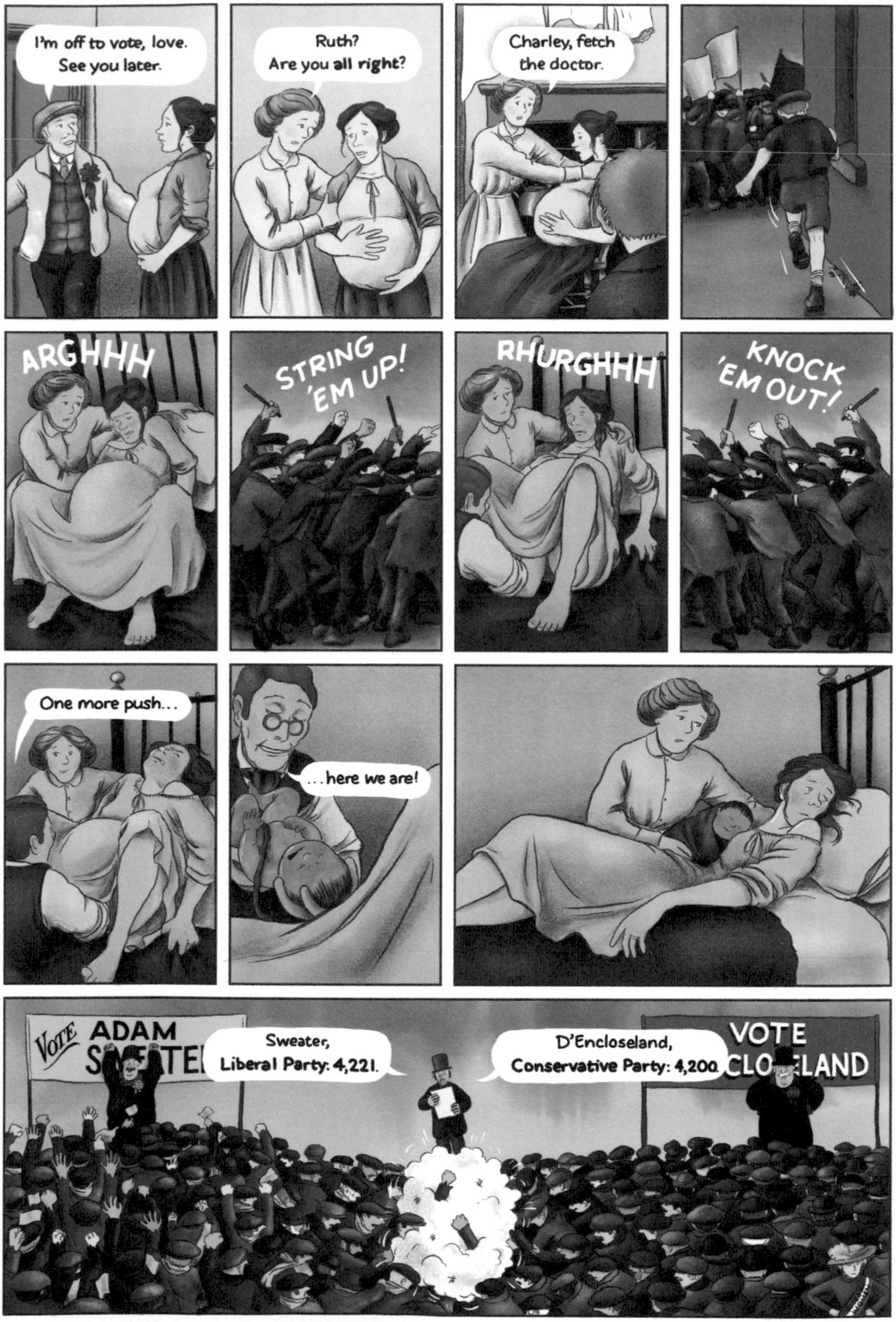
I'm off to vote, love.
See you later.
Ruth?
Are you all right?
Charley, fetch
the doctor.
ARGHHH
STRING
'EM UP!
RHURGHHH
KNOCK
'EM OUT!
One more push...
...here we are!
VOTE ADAM SWEATER
Sweater,
Liberal Party: 4,221.
D'Encloseland,
Conservative Party: 4,200.
VOTE
CLOSELAND

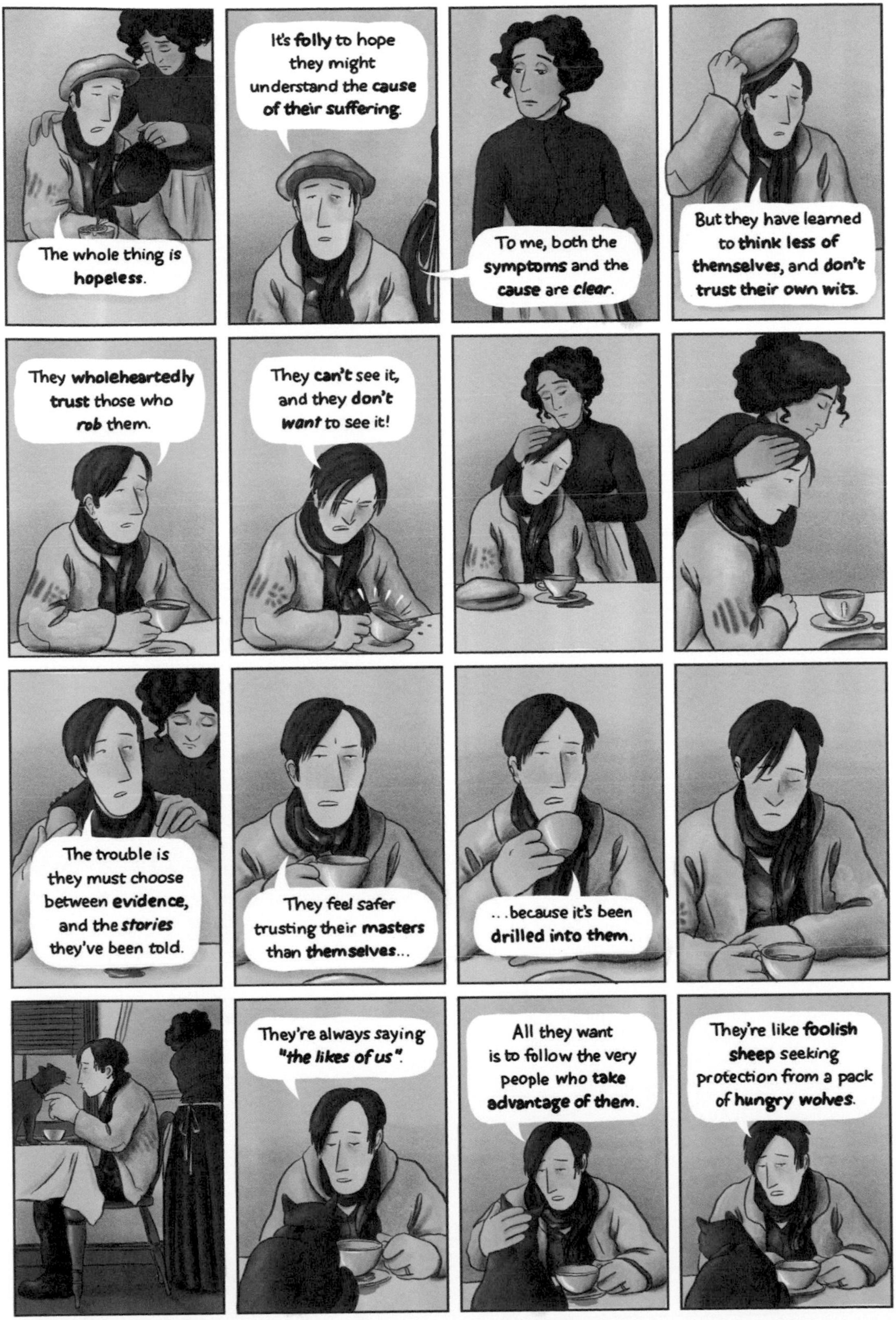
The whole thing is hopeless.
It's folly to hope they might understand the cause of their suffering.
To me, both the symptoms and the cause are clear.
But they have learned to think less of themselves, and don't trust their own wits.
They wholeheartedly trust those who rob them.
They can't see it, and they don't want to see it!
The trouble is they must choose between evidence, and the stories they've been told.
They feel safer trusting their masters than themselves...
...because it's been drilled into them.
They're always saying "the likes of us".
All they want is to follow the very people who take advantage of them.
They're like foolish sheep seeking protection from a pack of hungry wolves.

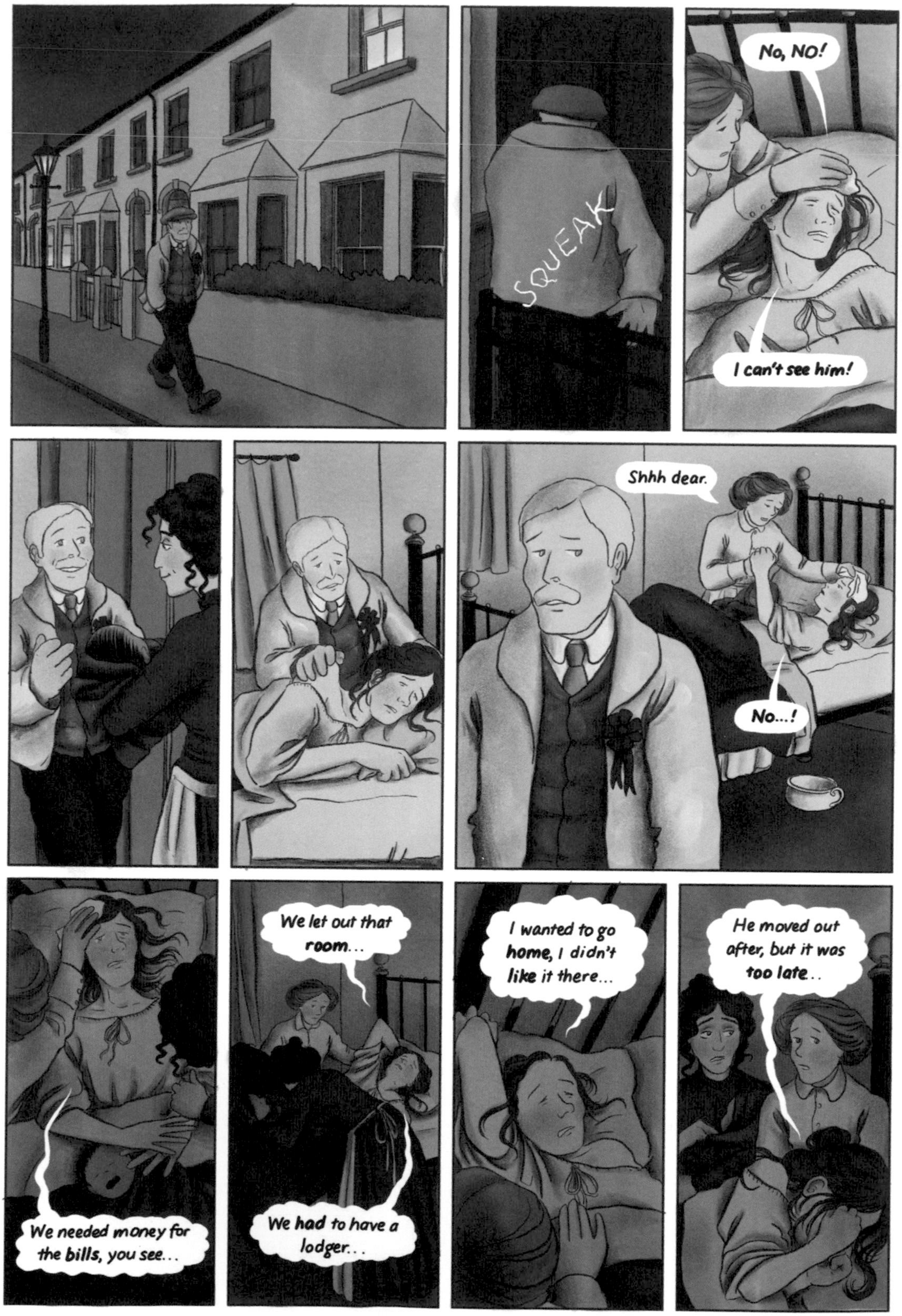
SQUEAK
No, NO!
I can't see him!
Shhh dear.
No...!
We needed money for the bills, you see...
We let out that room...
We had to have a lodger...
I wanted to go home, I didn't like it there...
He moved out after, but it was too late...

22

THE
SUNDERED

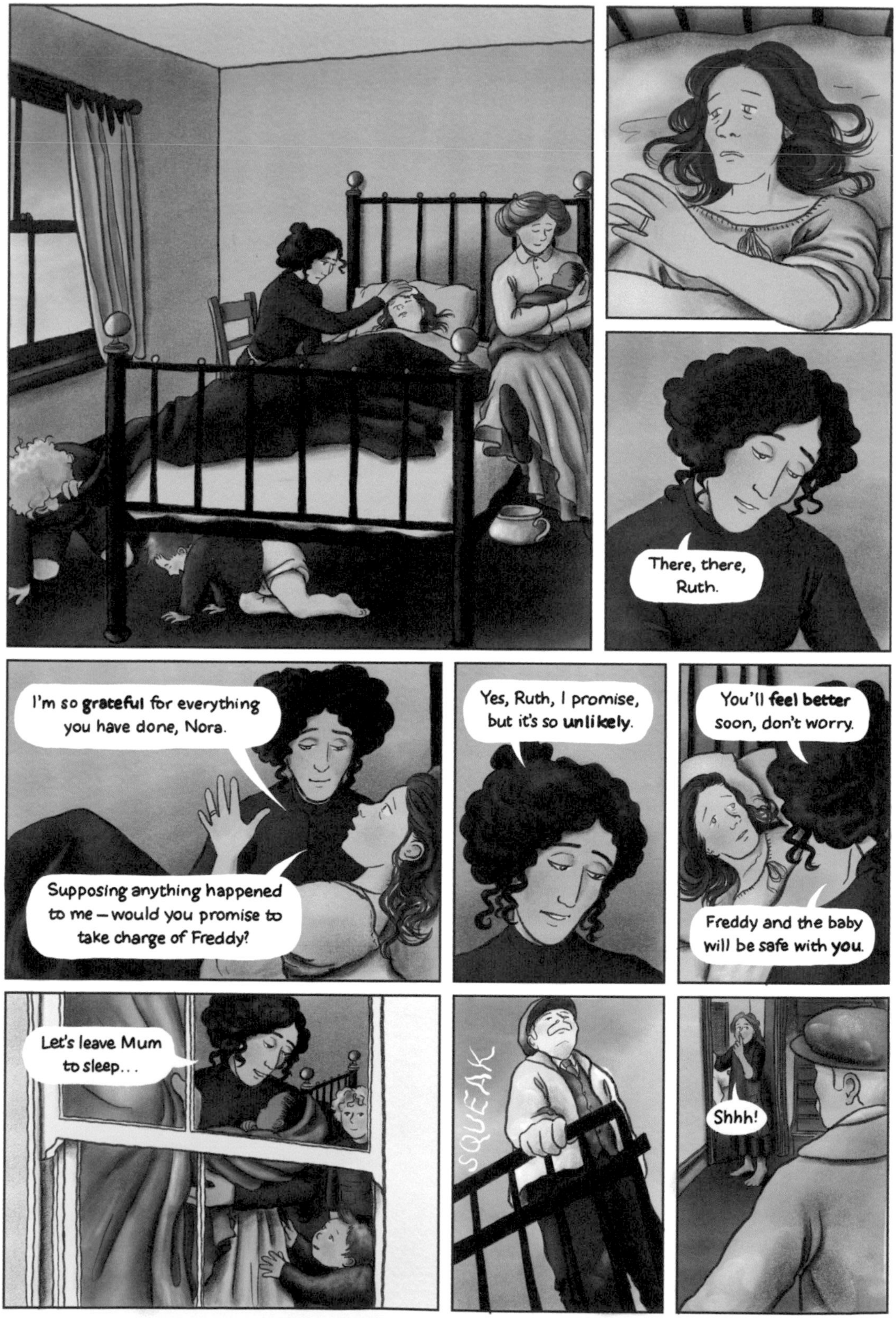
There, there, Ruth.
I'm so grateful for everything you have done, Nora.
Supposing anything happened to me – would you promise to take charge of Freddy?
Yes, Ruth, I promise, but it's so unlikely.
You'll feel better soon, don't worry.
Freddy and the baby will be safe with you.
Let's leave Mum to sleep...
SQUEAK
Shhh!

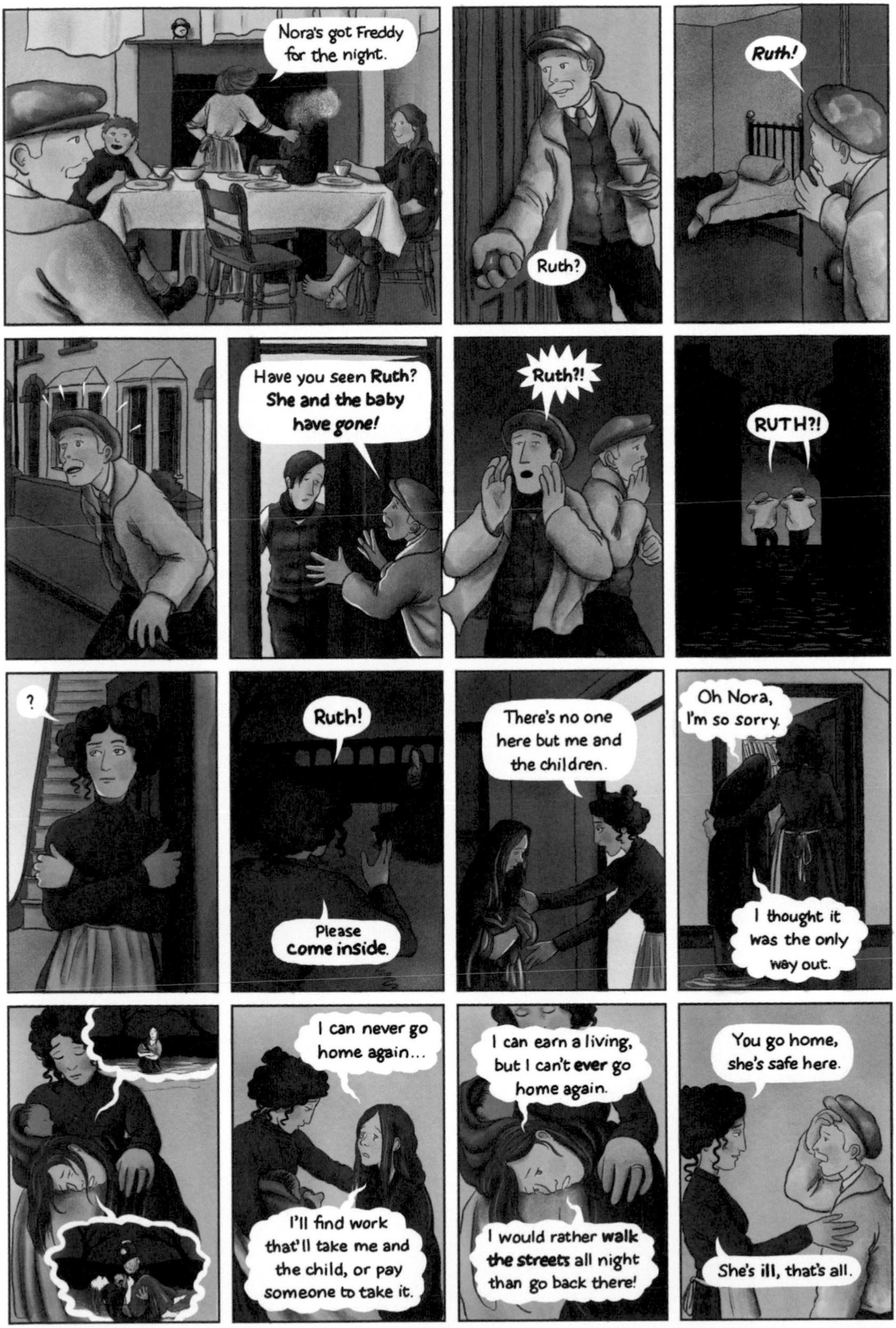
Nora's got Freddy for the night.
Ruth?
Ruth!
Have you seen Ruth? She and the baby have gone!
Ruth?!
RUTH?!
?
Ruth!
Please come inside.
There's no one here but me and the children.
Oh Nora, I'm so sorry.
I thought it was the only way out.
I can never go home again...
I'll find work that'll take me and the child, or pay someone to take it.
I can earn a living, but I can't ever go home again.
I would rather walk the streets all night than go back there!
You go home, she's safe here.
She's ill, that's all.

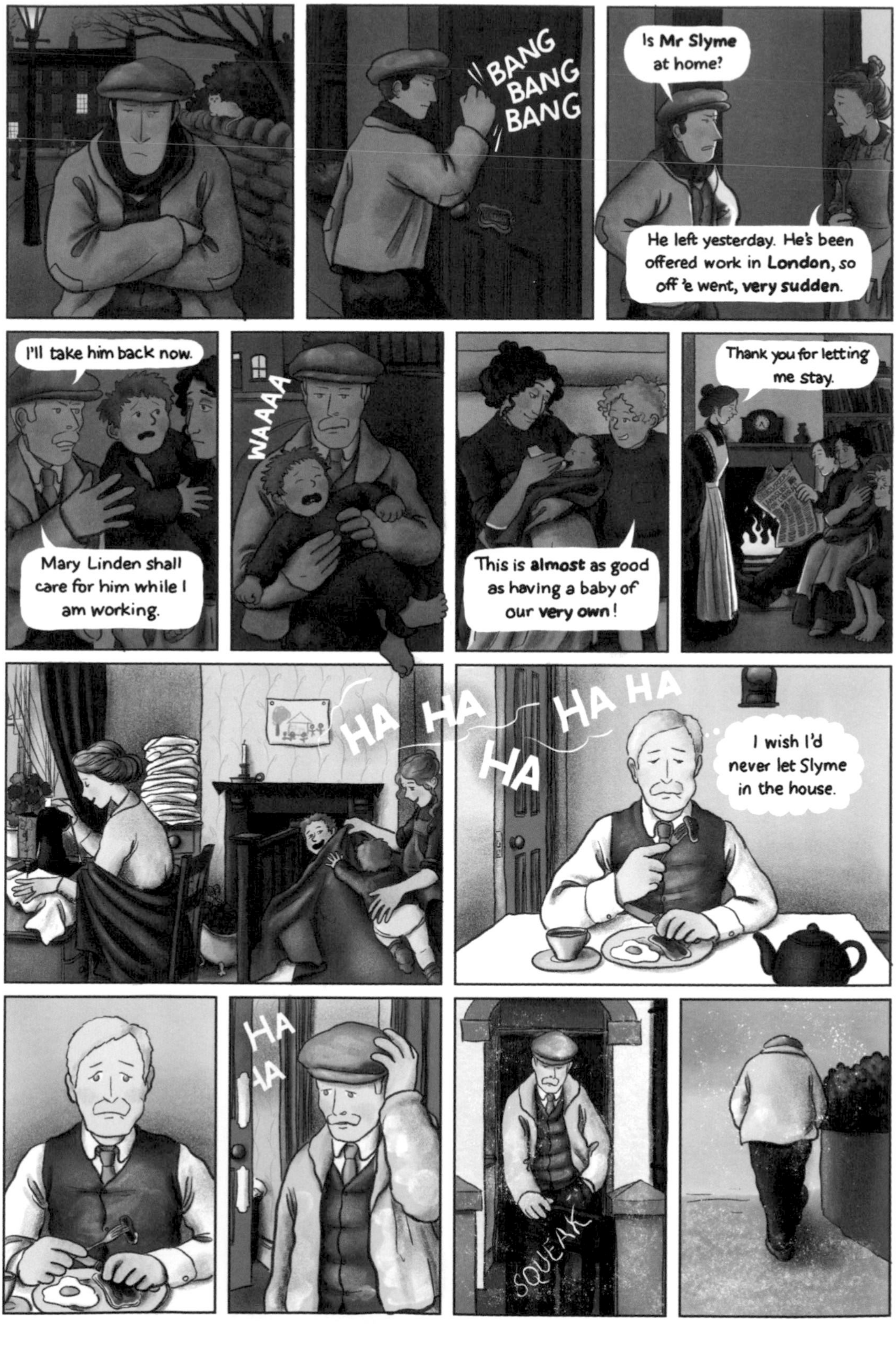
BANG
BANG
BANG
Is Mr Slyme at home?
He left yesterday. He's been offered work in London, so off 'e went, very sudden.
I'll take him back now.
Mary Linden shall care for him while I am working.
WAAAA
This is almost as good as having a baby of our very own!
Thank you for letting me stay.
HA HA
HA HA HA
HA
I wish I'd never let Slyme in the house.
HA
HA
SQUEAK

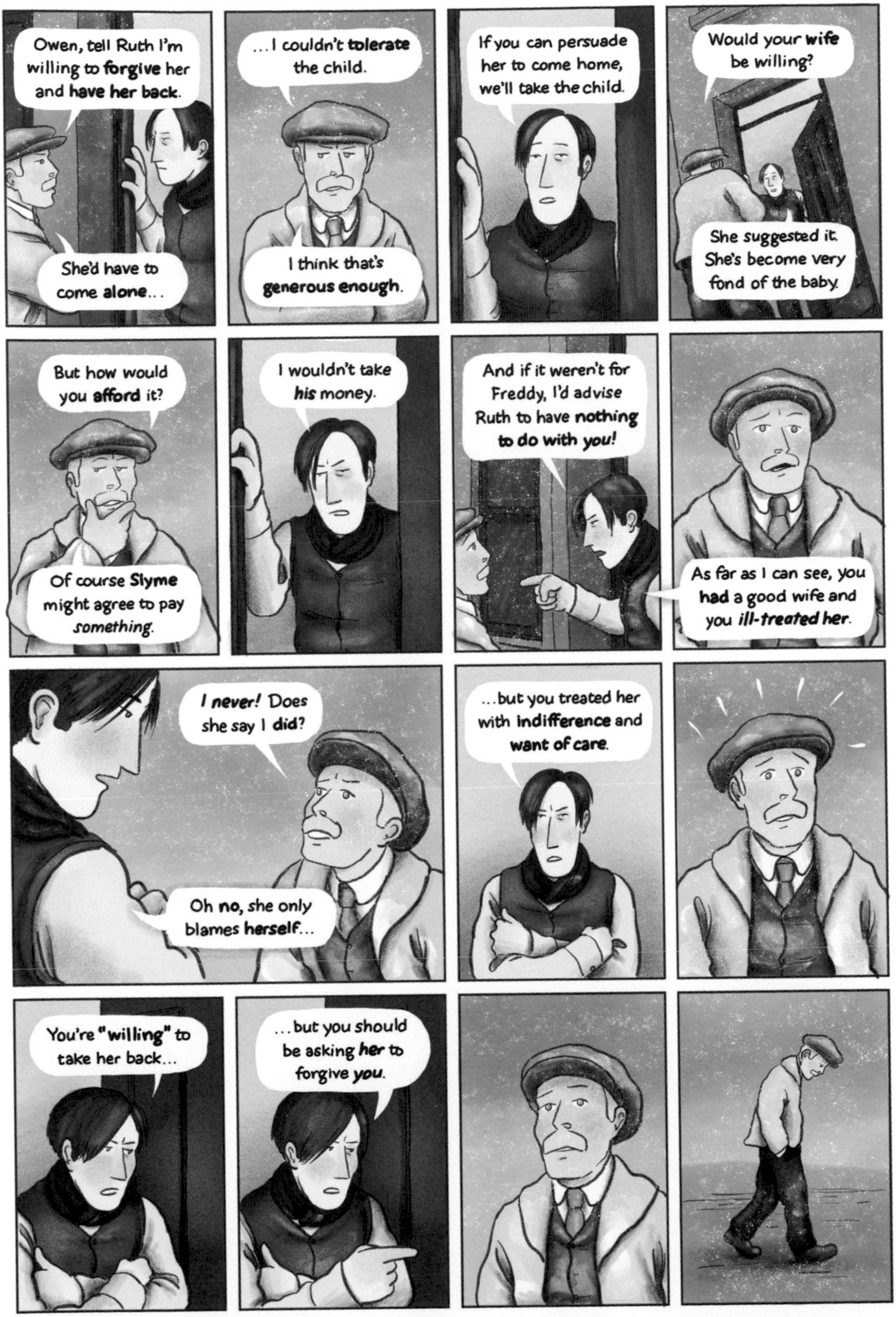
Owen, tell Ruth I'm willing to forgive her and have her back.
She'd have to come alone...
...I couldn't tolerate the child.
I think that's generous enough.
If you can persuade her to come home, we'll take the child.
Would your wife be willing?
She suggested it. She's become very fond of the baby.
But how would you afford it?
Of course Slyme might agree to pay something.
I wouldn't take his money.
And if it weren't for Freddy, I'd advise Ruth to have nothing to do with you!
As far as I can see, you had a good wife and you ill-treated her.
I never! Does she say I did?
Oh no, she only blames herself...
...but you treated her with indifference and want of care.
You're "willing" to take her back...
...but you should be asking her to forgive you.

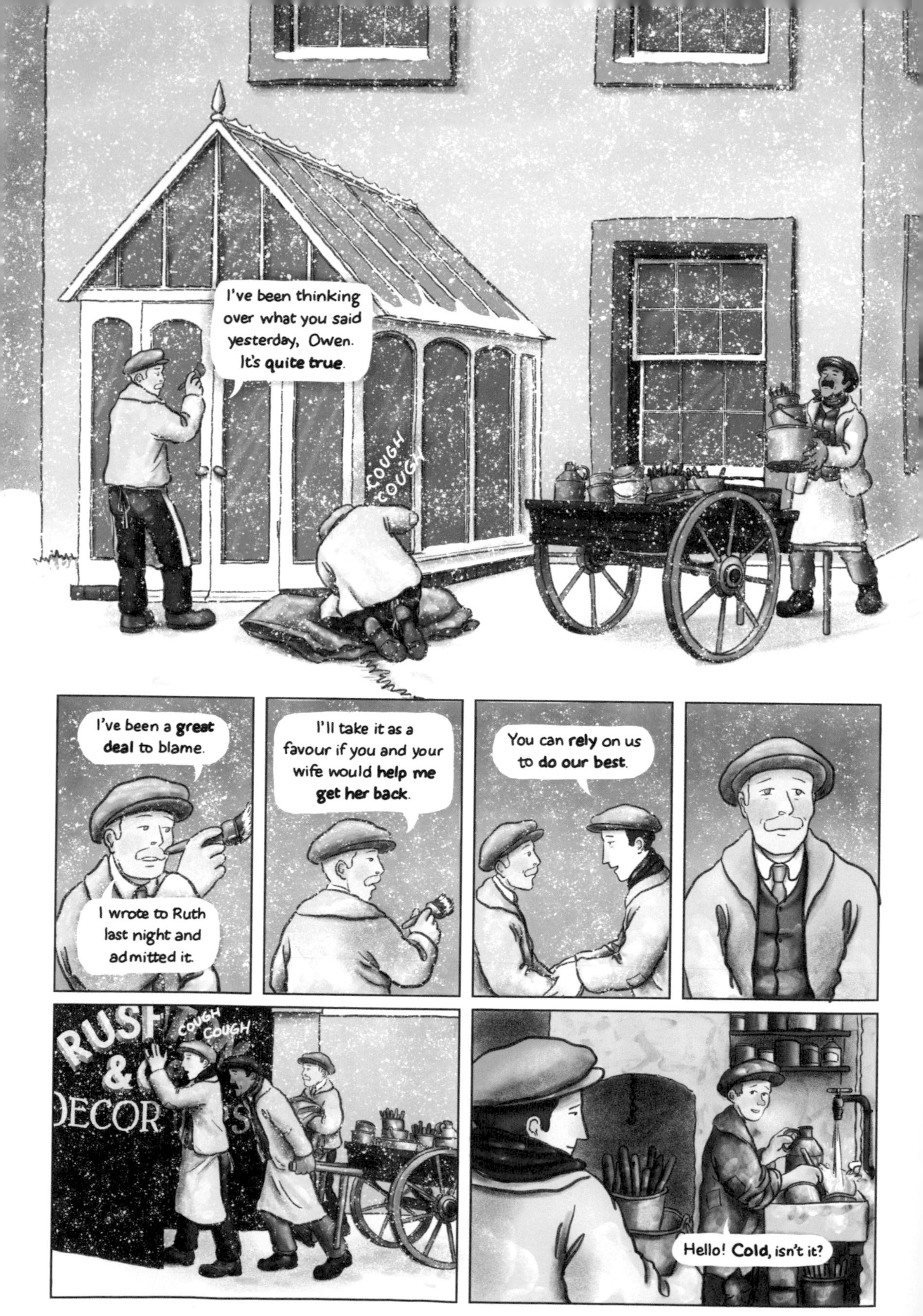
I've been thinking over what you said yesterday, Owen. It's quite true.
COUGH COUGH
I've been a great deal to blame.
I wrote to Ruth last night and admitted it.
I'll take it as a favour if you and your wife would help me get her back.
You can rely on us to do our best.
RUSH &
DECOR
COUGH COUGH
Hello! Cold, isn't it?

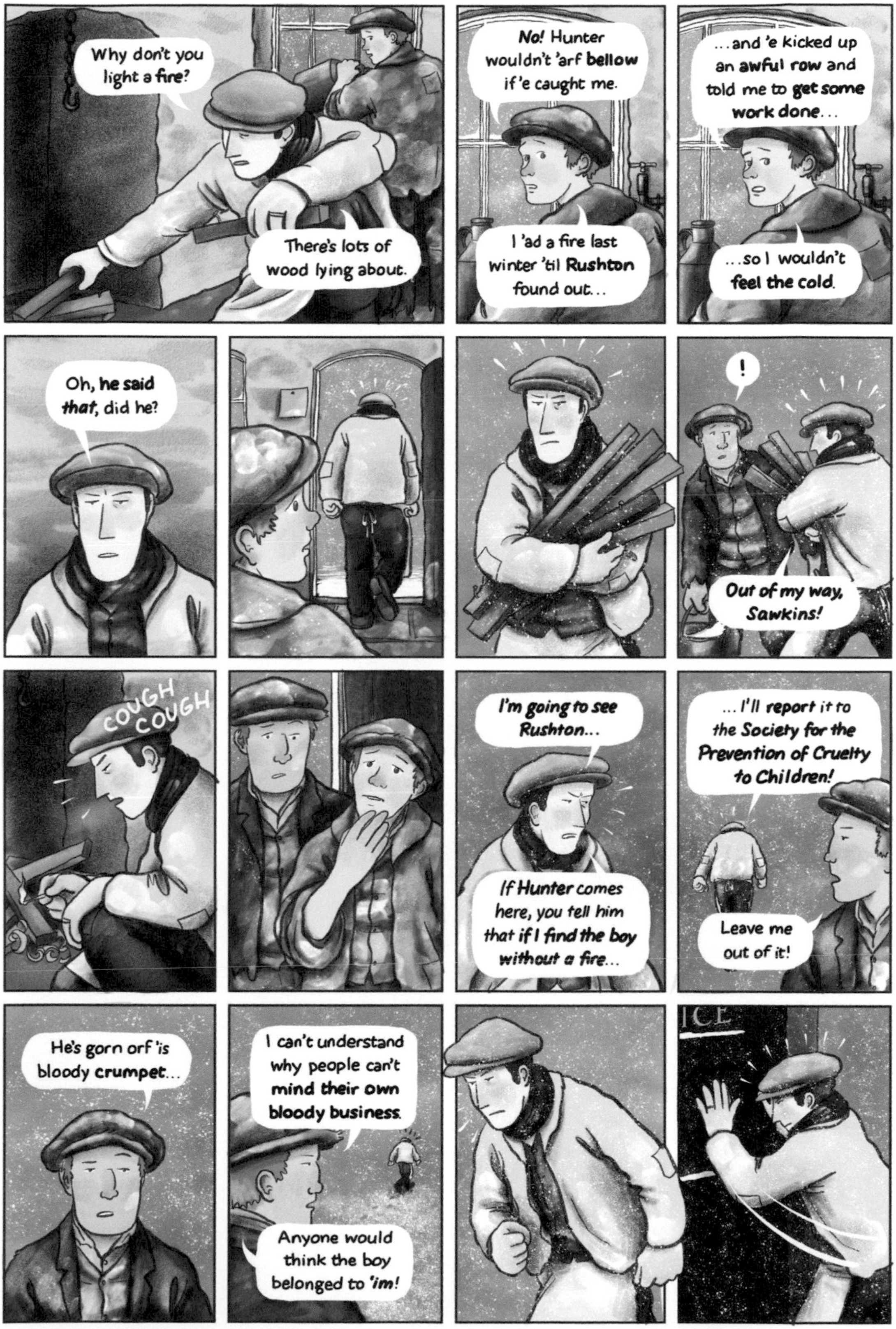
Why don't you light a fire?
There's lots of wood lying about.
No! Hunter wouldn't 'arf bellow if 'e caught me.
I 'ad a fire last winter 'til Rushton found out...
...and 'e kicked up an awful row and told me to get some work done...
...so I wouldn't feel the cold.
Oh, he said that, did he?
!
Out of my way, Sawkins!
COUGH COUGH
I'm going to see Rushton...
If Hunter comes here, you tell him that if I find the boy without a fire...
...I'll report it to the Society for the Prevention of Cruelty to Children!
Leave me out of it!
He's gorn orf 'is bloody crumpet...
I can't understand why people can't mind their own bloody business.
Anyone would think the boy belonged to 'im!

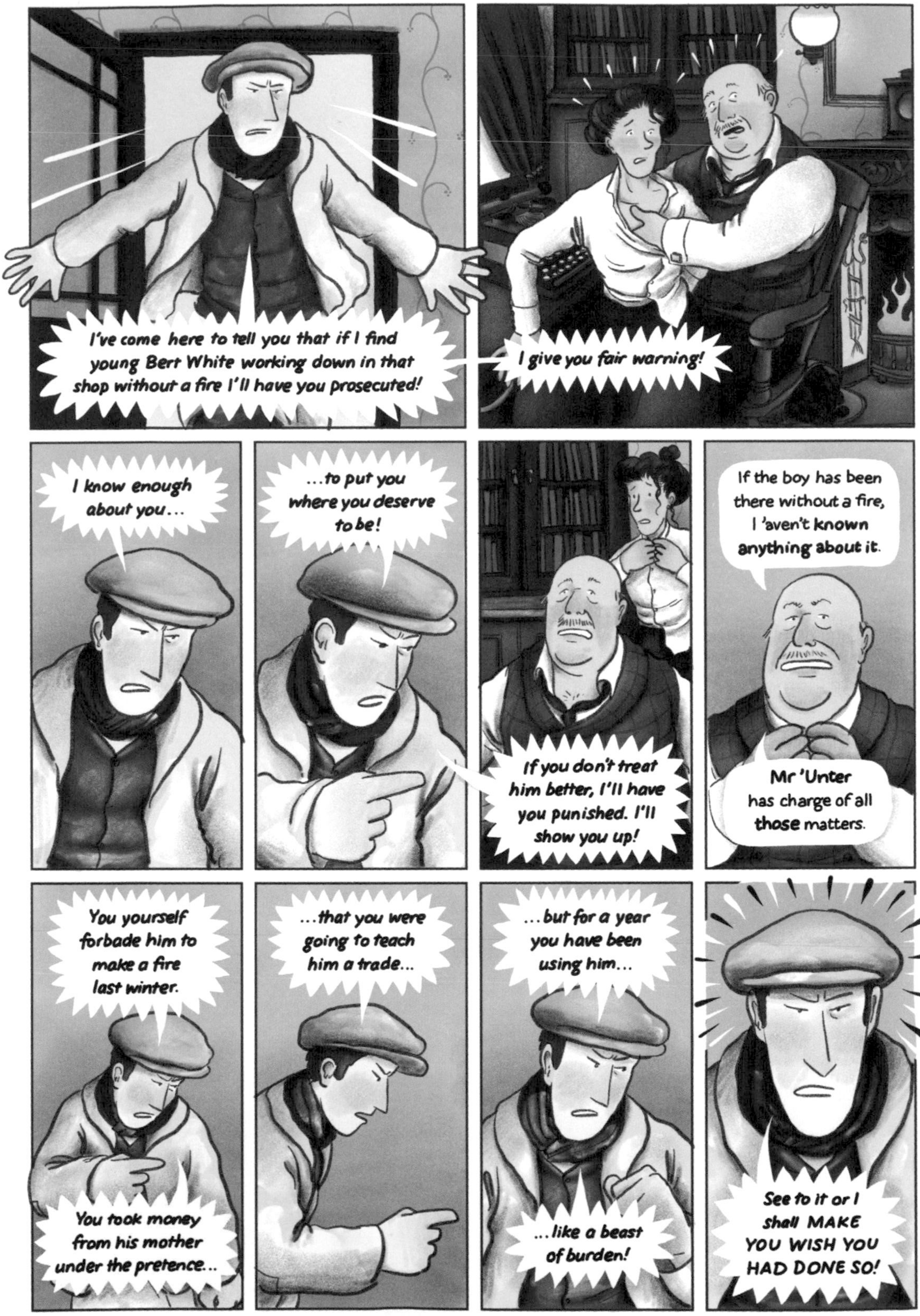

I've come here to tell you that if I find young Bert White working down in that shop without a fire I'll have you prosecuted!
I give you fair warning!
I know enough about you...
...to put you where you deserve to be!
If you don't treat him better, I'll have you punished. I'll show you up!
If the boy has been there without a fire, I 'aven't known anything about it.
Mr 'Unter has charge of all those matters.
You yourself forbade him to make a fire last winter.
You took money from his mother under the pretence...
...that you were going to teach him a trade...
...but for a year you have been using him...
...like a beast of burden!
See to it or I shall MAKE YOU WISH YOU HAD DONE SO!

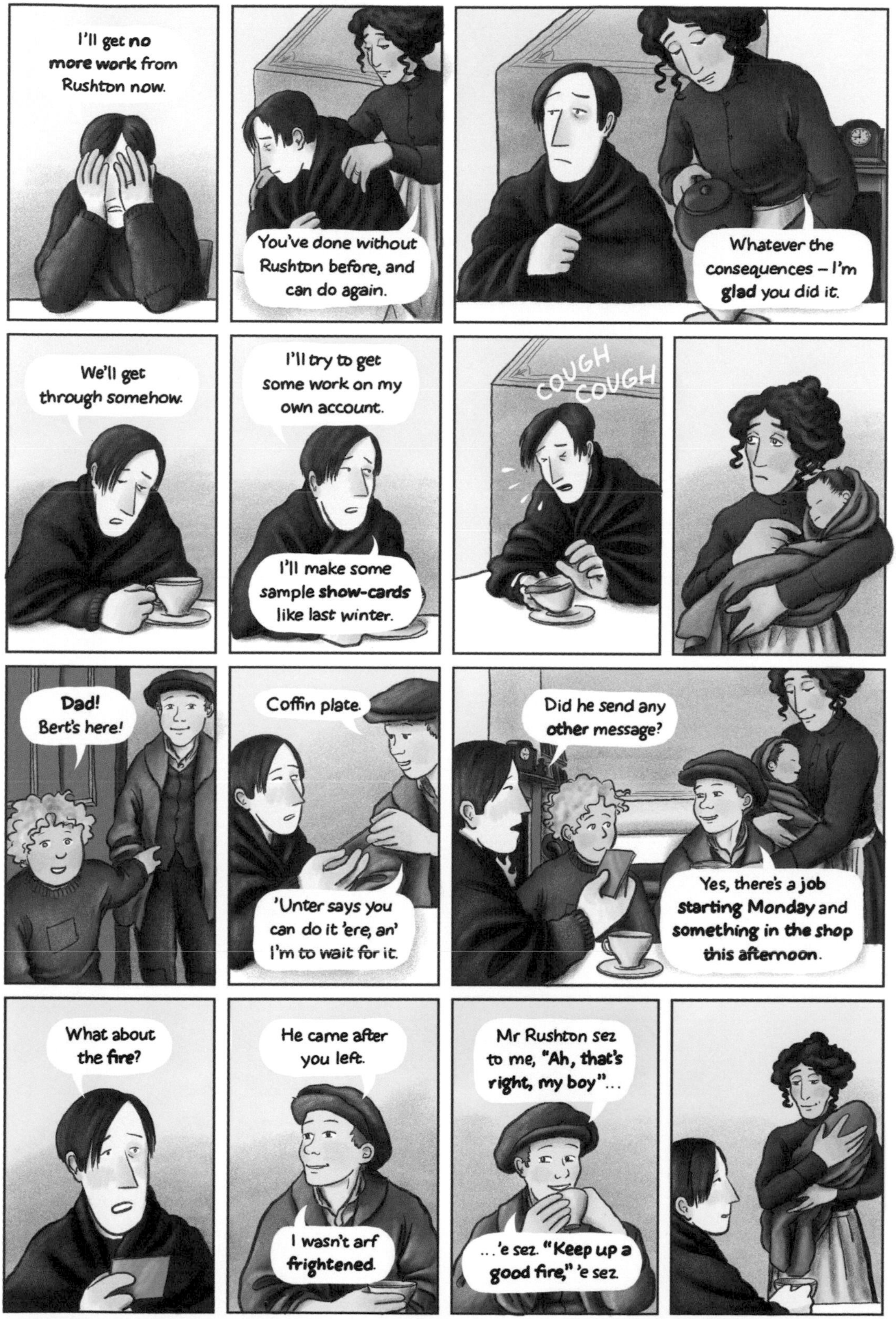
I'll get no more work from Rushton now.
You've done without Rushton before, and can do again.
Whatever the consequences – I'm glad you did it.
We'll get through somehow.
I'll try to get some work on my own account.
I'll make some sample show-cards like last winter.
COUGH COUGH
Dad! Bert's here!
Coffin plate.
'Unter says you can do it 'ere, an' I'm to wait for it.
Did he send any other message?
Yes, there's a job starting Monday and something in the shop this afternoon.
What about the fire?
He came after you left.
I wasn't arf frightened.
Mr Rushton sez to me, "Ah, that's right, my boy"...
...'e sez. "Keep up a good fire," 'e sez.

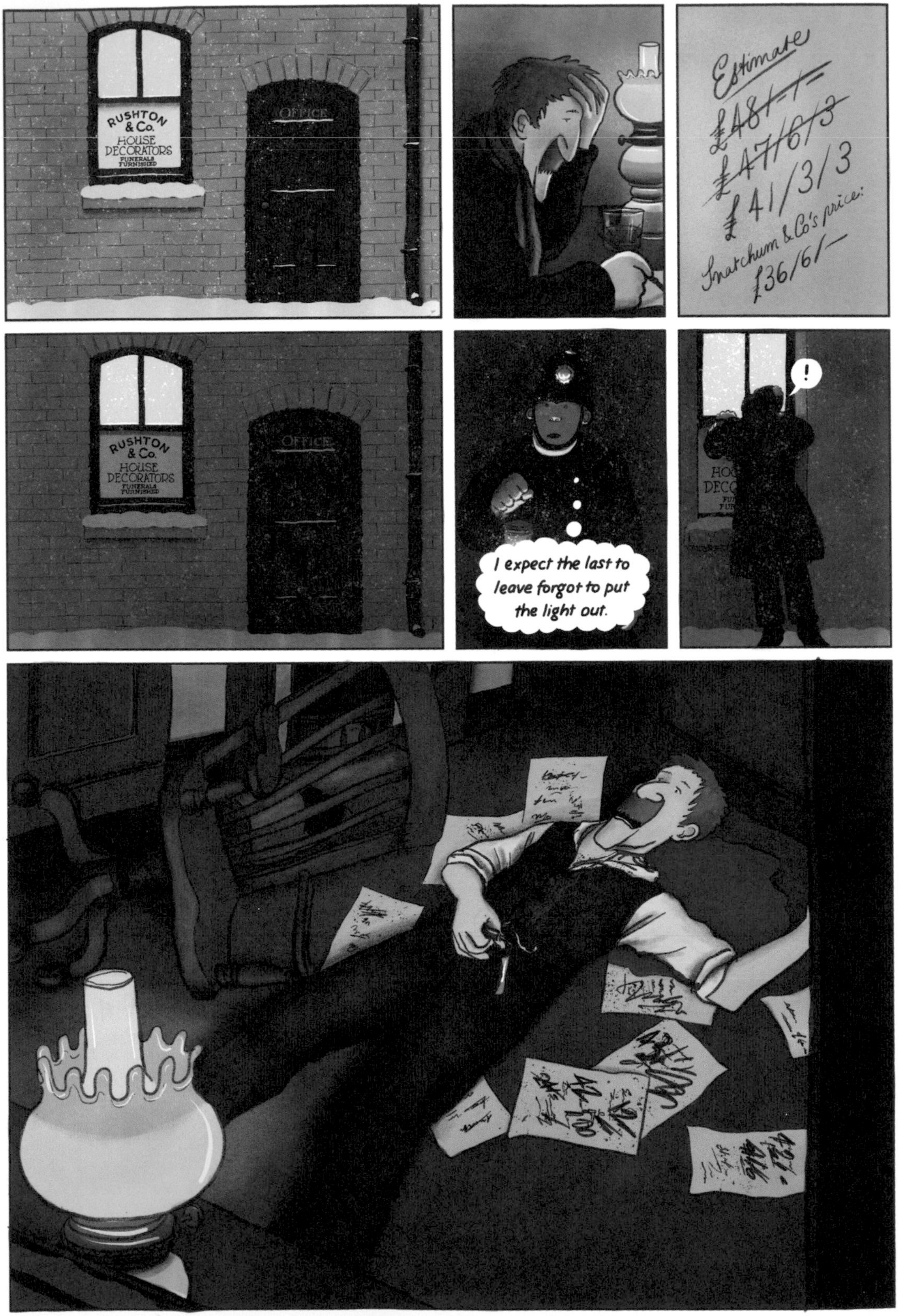
RUSHTON & Co.
HOUSE DECORATORS
FUNERALS FURNISHED
OFFICE
Estimate
£48/-/-
£47/6/3
£41/3/3
Snatchum & Co's price:
£36/6/-
RUSHTON & Co.
HOUSE DECORATORS
FUNERALS FURNISHED
OFFICE
I expect the last to leave forgot to put the light out.
!

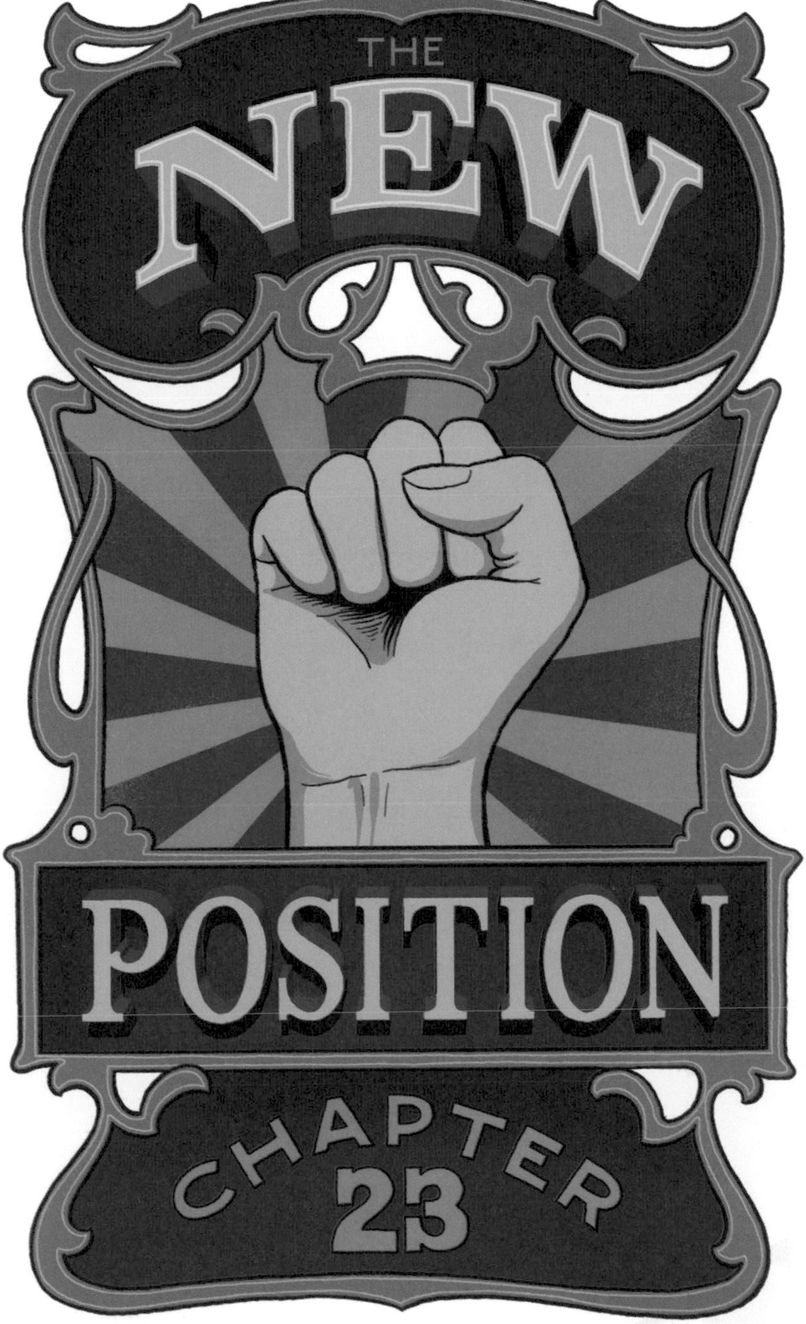
THE
NEW
POSITION
CHAPTER
23

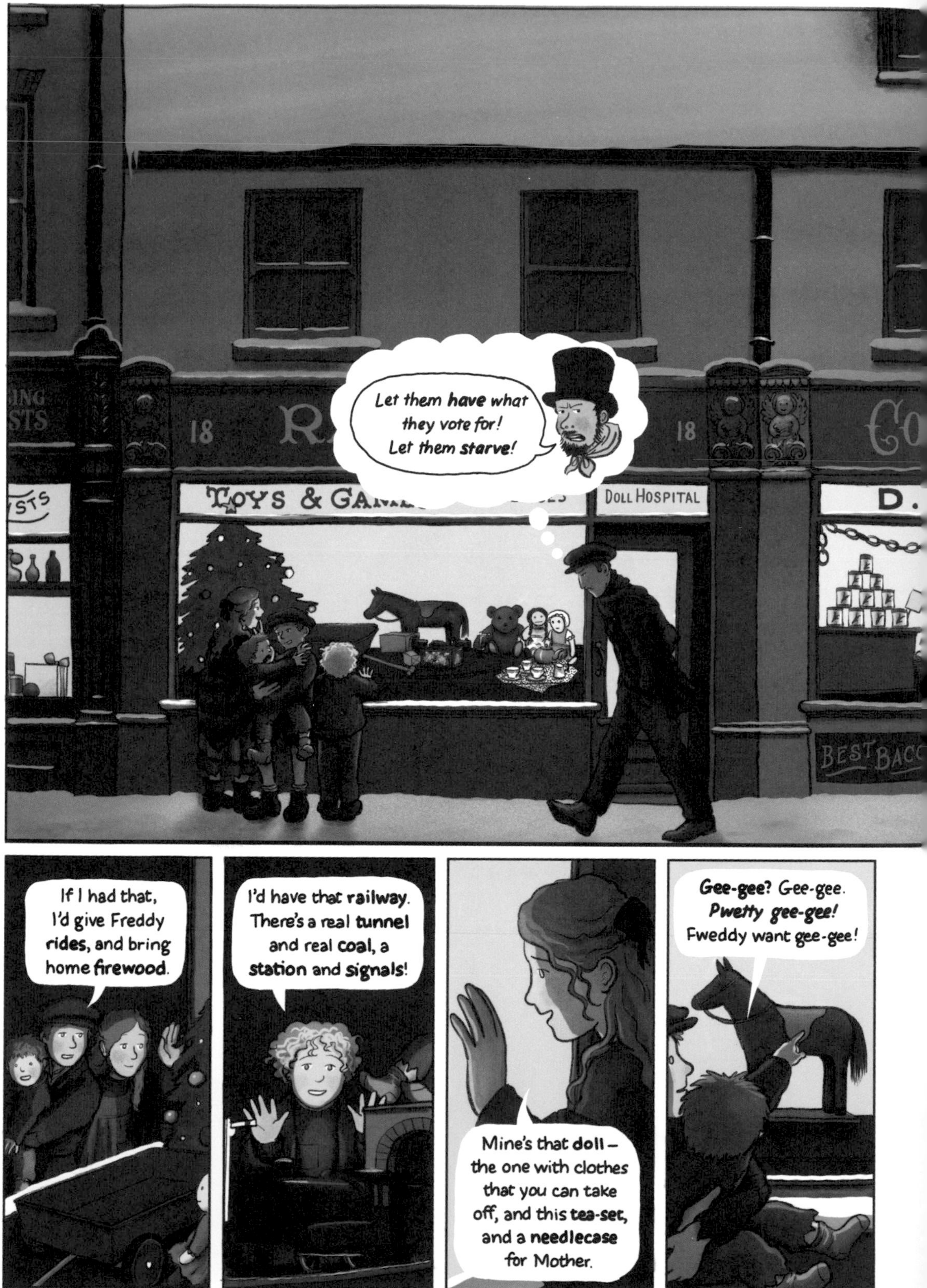
Let them have what they vote for! Let them starve!
DOLL HOSPITAL
If I had that, I'd give Freddy rides, and bring home firewood.
I'd have that railway. There's a real tunnel and real coal, a station and signals!
Mine's that doll – the one with clothes that you can take off, and this tea-set, and a needlecase for Mother.
Gee-gee? Gee-gee. Pwetty gee-gee! Fweddy want gee-gee!

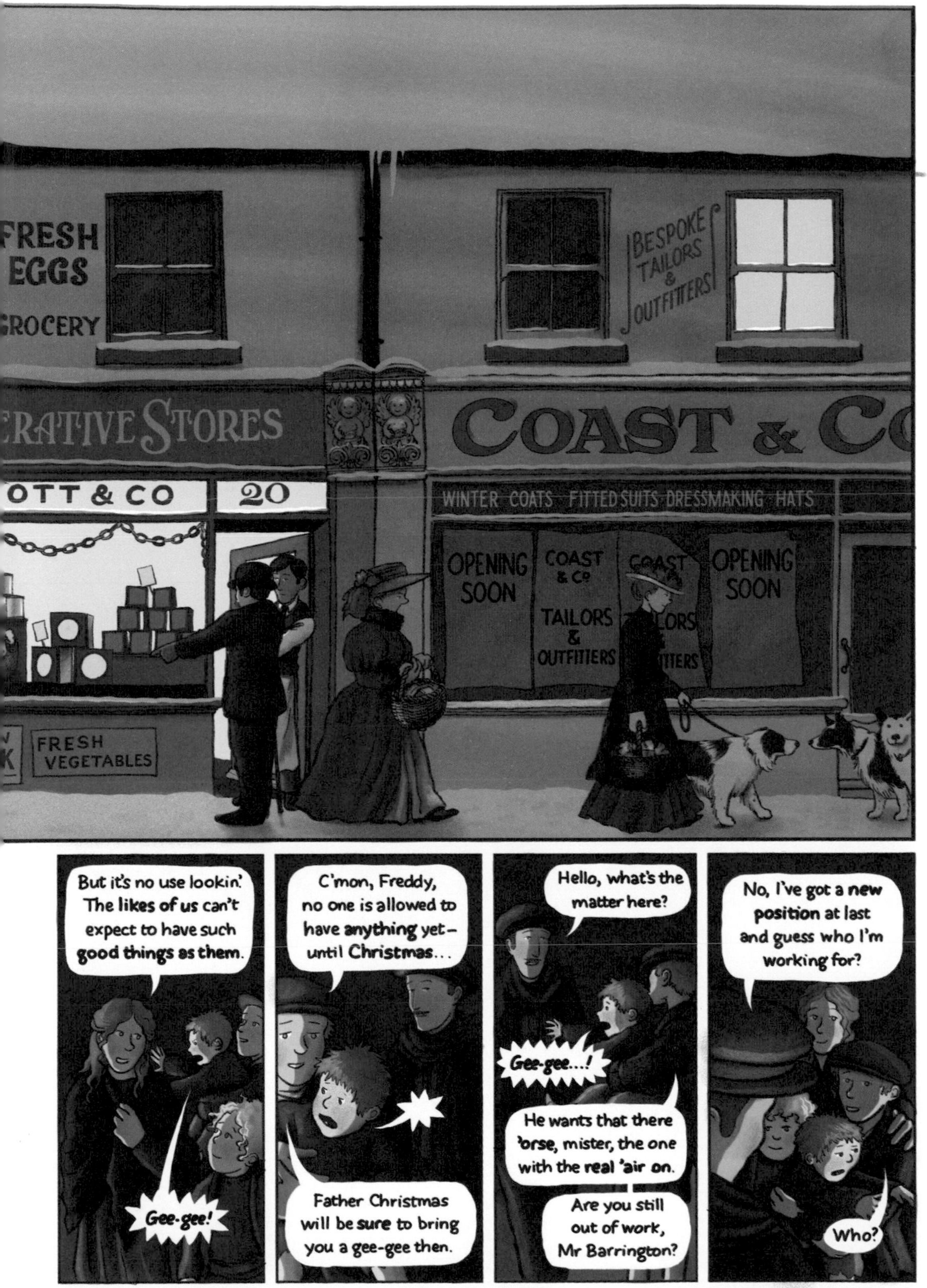
FRESH EGGS
GROCERY
BESPOKE TAILORS & OUTFITTERS
ERATIVE STORES
COAST & C
OTT & CO
20
WINTER COATS FITTED SUITS DRESSMAKING HATS
OPENING SOON
COAST & Co TAILORS & OUTFITTERS
OPENING SOON
FRESH VEGETABLES
But it's no use lookin'. The likes of us can't expect to have such good things as them.
Gee-gee!
C'mon, Freddy, no one is allowed to have anything yet – until Christmas...
Father Christmas will be sure to bring you a gee-gee then.
Hello, what's the matter here?
Gee-gee...!
He wants that there 'orse, mister, the one with the real 'air on.
Are you still out of work, Mr Barrington?
No, I've got a new position at last and guess who I'm working for?
Who?

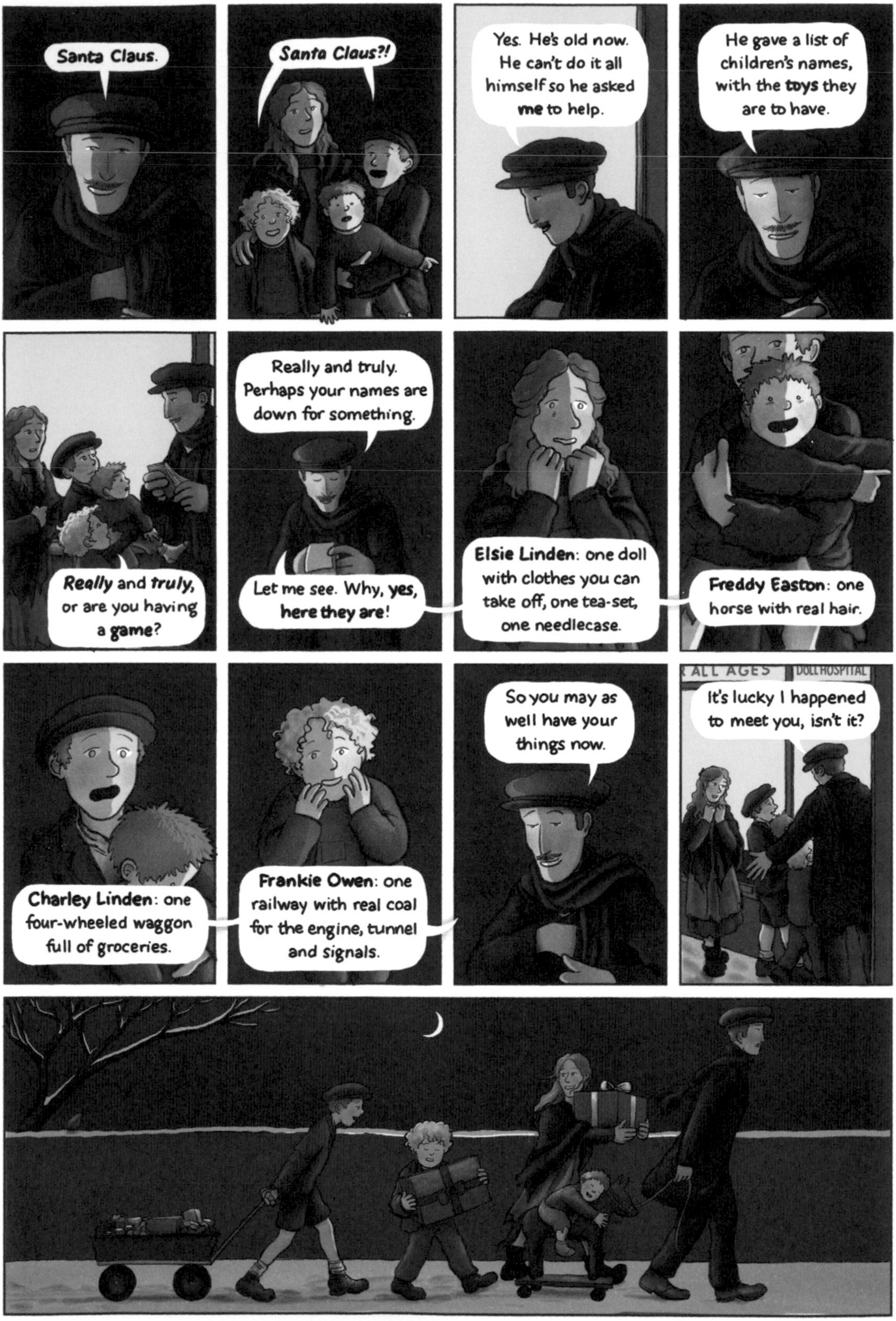
Santa Claus.
Santa Claus?!
Yes. He's old now. He can't do it all himself so he asked me to help.
He gave a list of children's names, with the toys they are to have.
Really and truly, or are you having a game?
Really and truly. Perhaps your names are down for something.
Let me see. Why, yes, here they are!
Elsie Linden: one doll with clothes you can take off, one tea-set, one needlecase.
Freddy Easton: one horse with real hair.
Charley Linden: one four-wheeled waggon full of groceries.
Frankie Owen: one railway with real coal for the engine, tunnel and signals.
So you may as well have your things now.
ALL AGES
DOLL HOSPITAL
It's lucky I happened to meet you, isn't it?

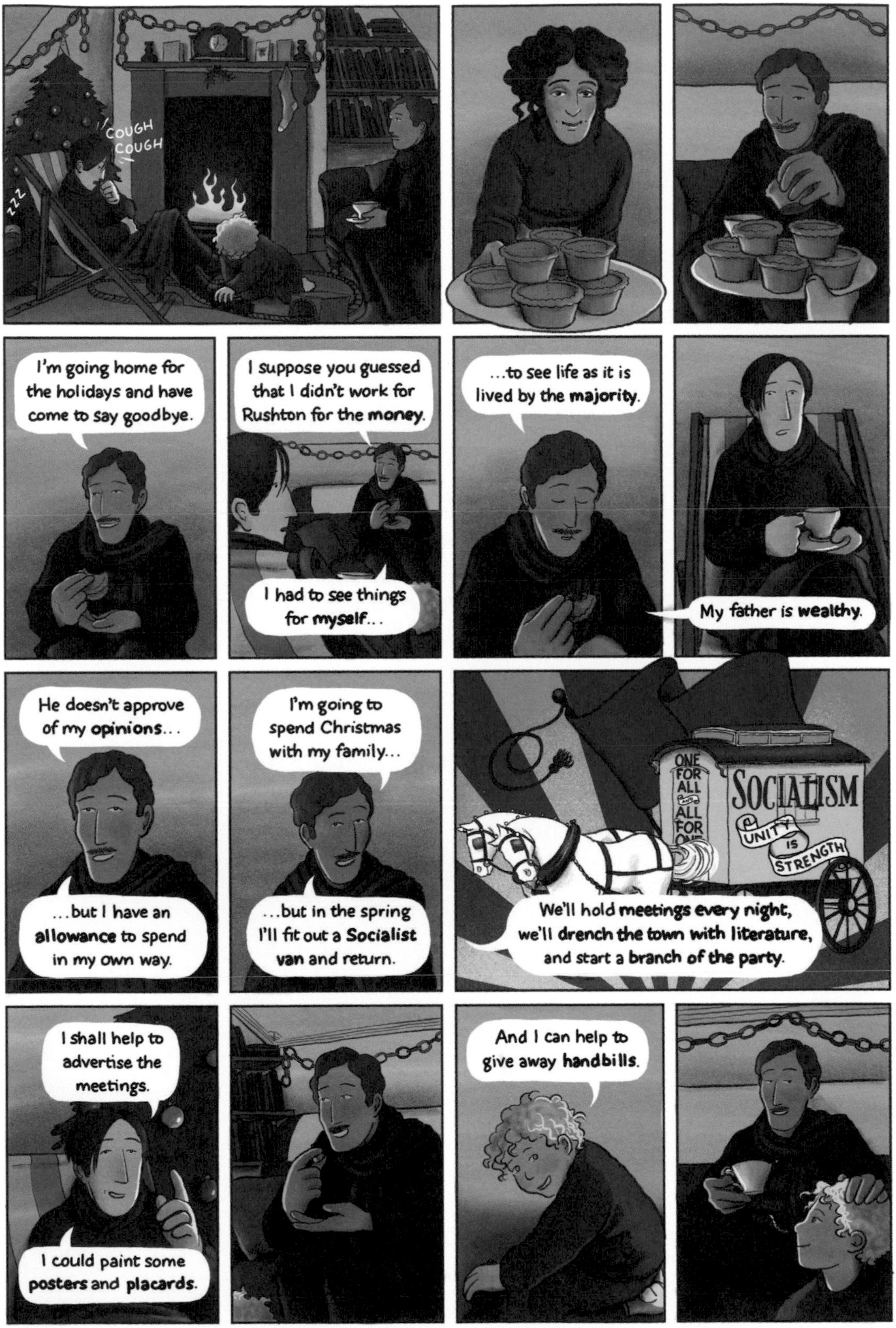
COUGH
COUGH
ZZZ
I'm going home for the holidays and have come to say goodbye.
I suppose you guessed that I didn't work for Rushton for the money.
I had to see things for myself...
...to see life as it is lived by the majority.
My father is wealthy.
He doesn't approve of my opinions...
...but I have an allowance to spend in my own way.
I'm going to spend Christmas with my family...
...but in the spring I'll fit out a Socialist van and return.
ONE FOR ALL AND ALL FOR ONE
SOCIALISM
UNITY IS STRENGTH
We'll hold meetings every night, we'll drench the town with literature, and start a branch of the party.
I shall help to advertise the meetings.
I could paint some posters and placards.
And I can help to give away handbills.

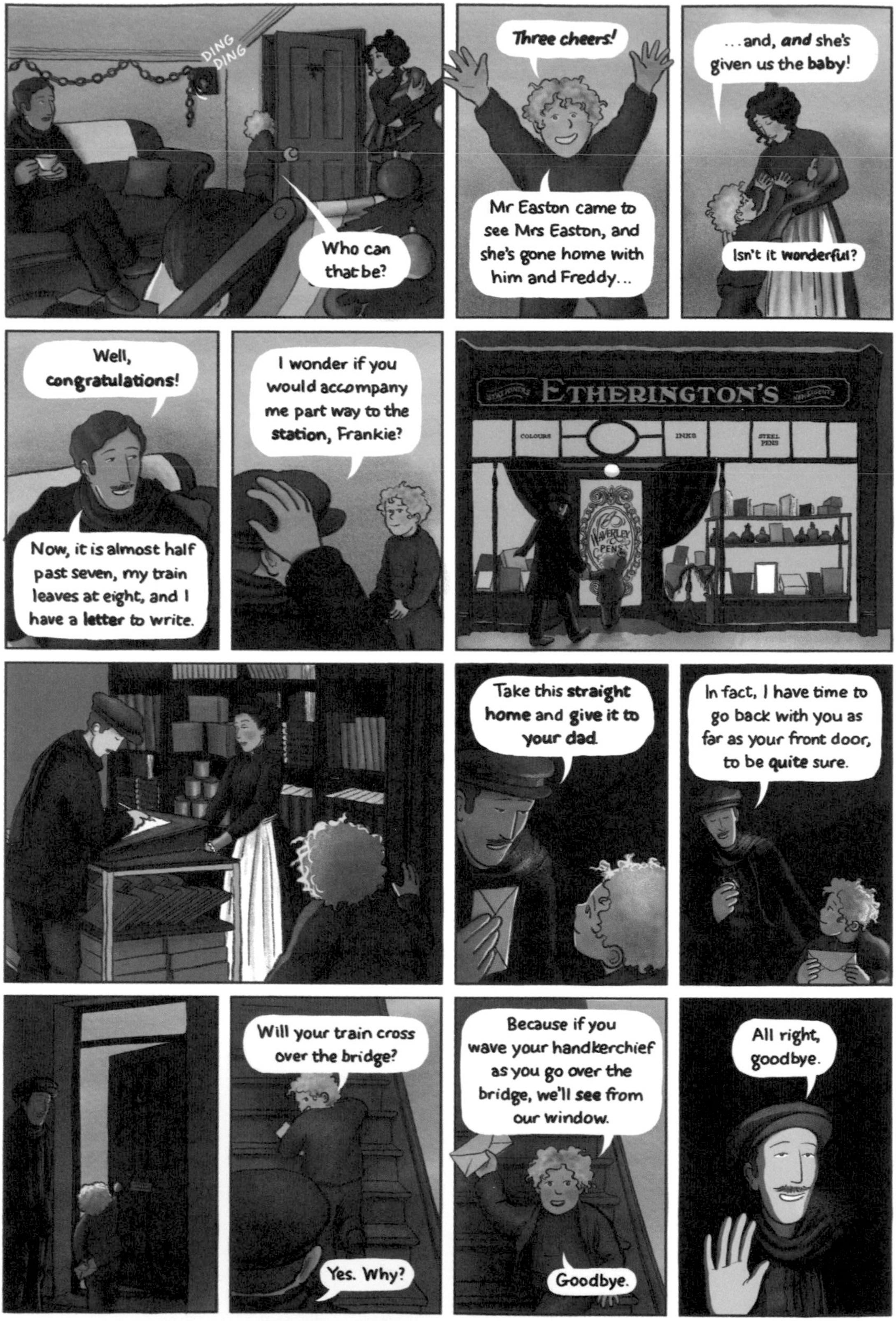
DING DING
Who can that be?
Three cheers!
Mr Easton came to see Mrs Easton, and she's gone home with him and Freddy...
...and, and she's given us the baby!
Isn't it wonderful?
Well, congratulations!
Now, it is almost half past seven, my train leaves at eight, and I have a letter to write.
I wonder if you would accompany me part way to the station, Frankie?
ETHERINGTON'S
COLOURS
INKS
STEEL PENS
WAVERLEY PENS
Take this straight home and give it to your dad.
In fact, I have time to go back with you as far as your front door, to be quite sure.
Will your train cross over the bridge?
Yes. Why?
Because if you wave your handkerchief as you go over the bridge, we'll see from our window.
Goodbye.
All right, goodbye.

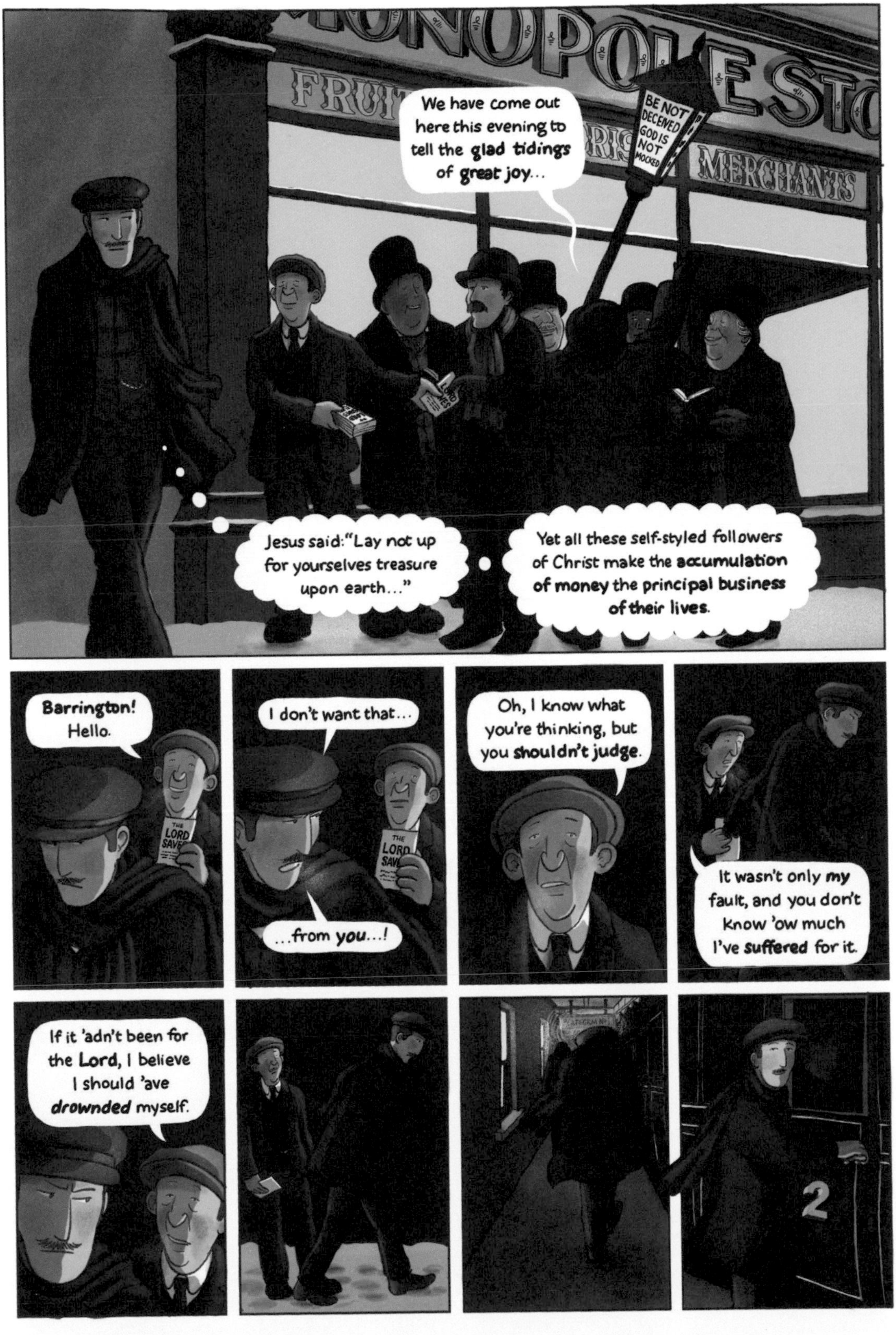
MERCHANTS
BE NOT DECEIVED GOD IS NOT MOCKED
We have come out here this evening to tell the **glad tidings** of **great** joy...
Jesus said: "Lay not up for yourselves treasure upon earth..."
Yet all these self-styled followers of Christ make the **accumulation of money** the principal business of their **lives**.
Barrington! Hello.
I don't want that...
...from **you**...!
Oh, I know what you're thinking, but you **shouldn't judge**.
It wasn't only **my** fault, and you don't know 'ow much I've **suffered** for it.
If it 'adn't been for the **Lord**, I believe I should 'ave ***drownded*** myself.
2

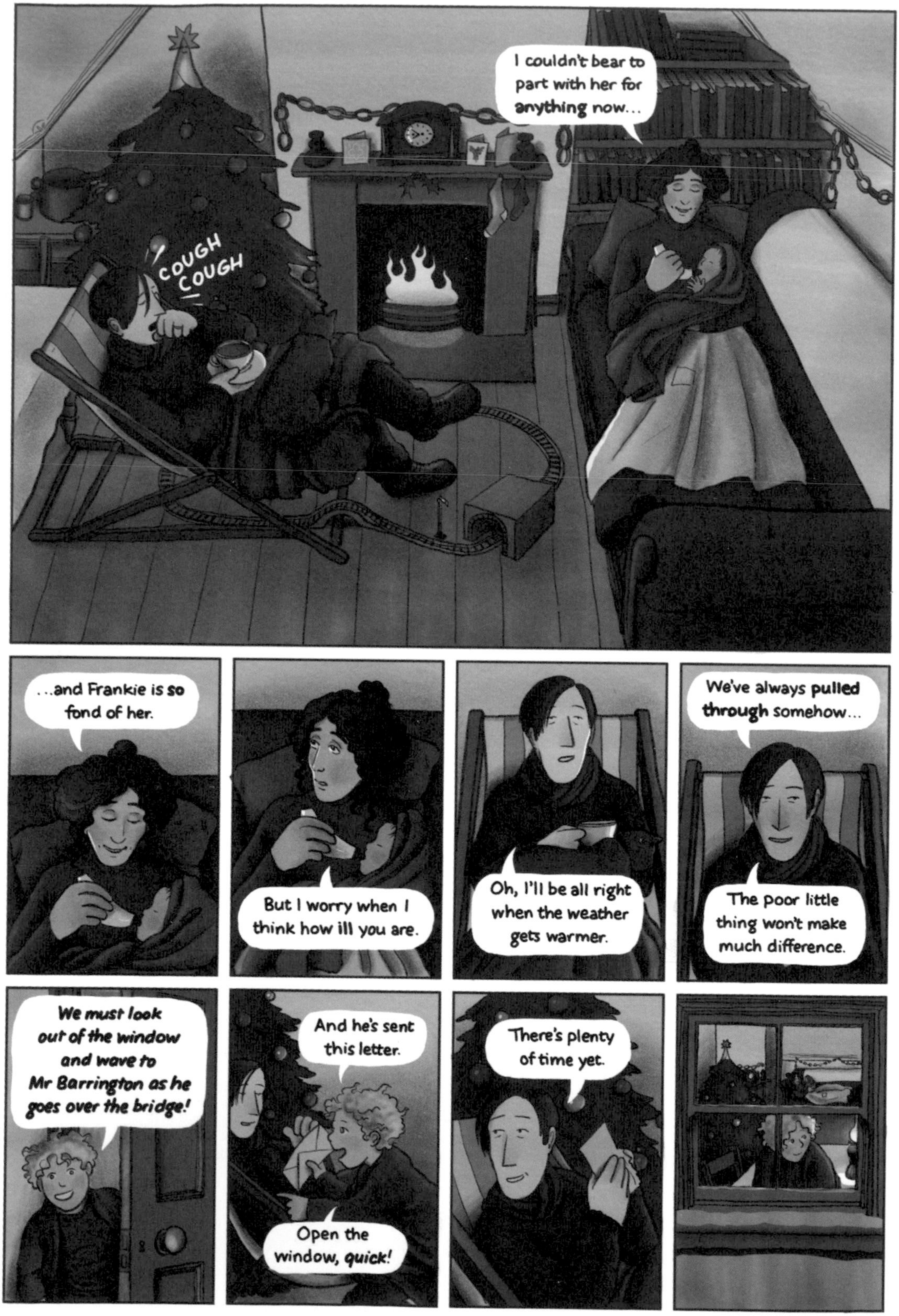
I couldn't bear to part with her for anything now...
COUGH COUGH
...and Frankie is so fond of her.
But I worry when I think how ill you are.
Oh, I'll be all right when the weather gets warmer.
We've always pulled through somehow...
The poor little thing won't make much difference.
We must look out of the window and wave to Mr Barrington as he goes over the bridge!
And he's sent this letter.
Open the window, quick!
There's plenty of time yet.

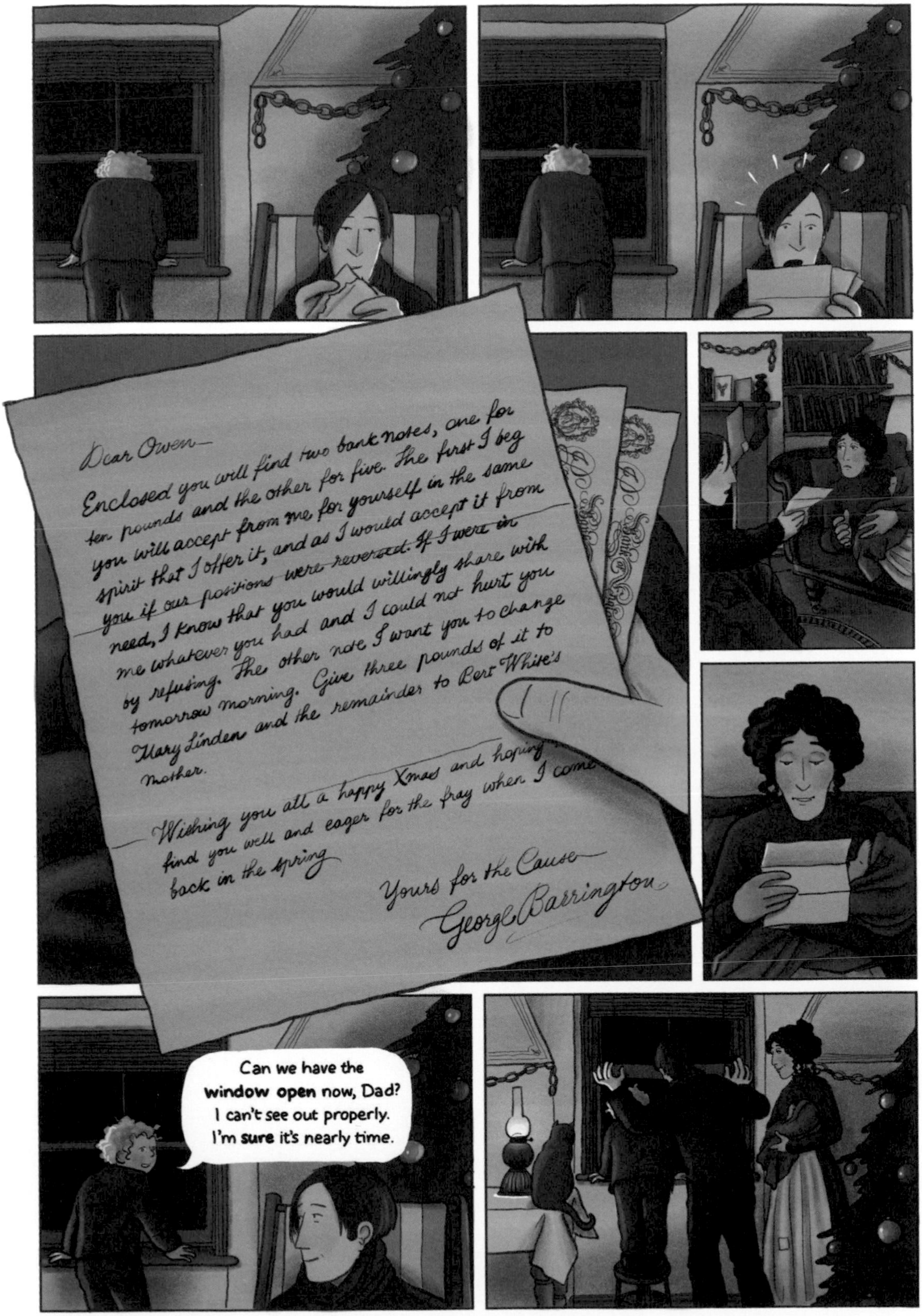
Dear Owen—
Enclosed you will find two bank notes, one for
ten pounds and the other for five. The first I beg
you will accept from me for yourself in the same
spirit that I offer it, and as I would accept it from
you if our positions were reversed. If I were in
need, I know that you would willingly share with
me whatever you had and I could not hurt you
by refusing. The other note I want you to change
tomorrow morning. Give three pounds of it to
Mary Linden and the remainder to Bert White's
mother.
—Wishing you all a happy Xmas and hoping
find you well and eager for the fray when I come
back in the spring
Yours for the Cause—
George Barrington
Can we have the window open now, Dad? I can't see out properly. I'm sure it's nearly time.

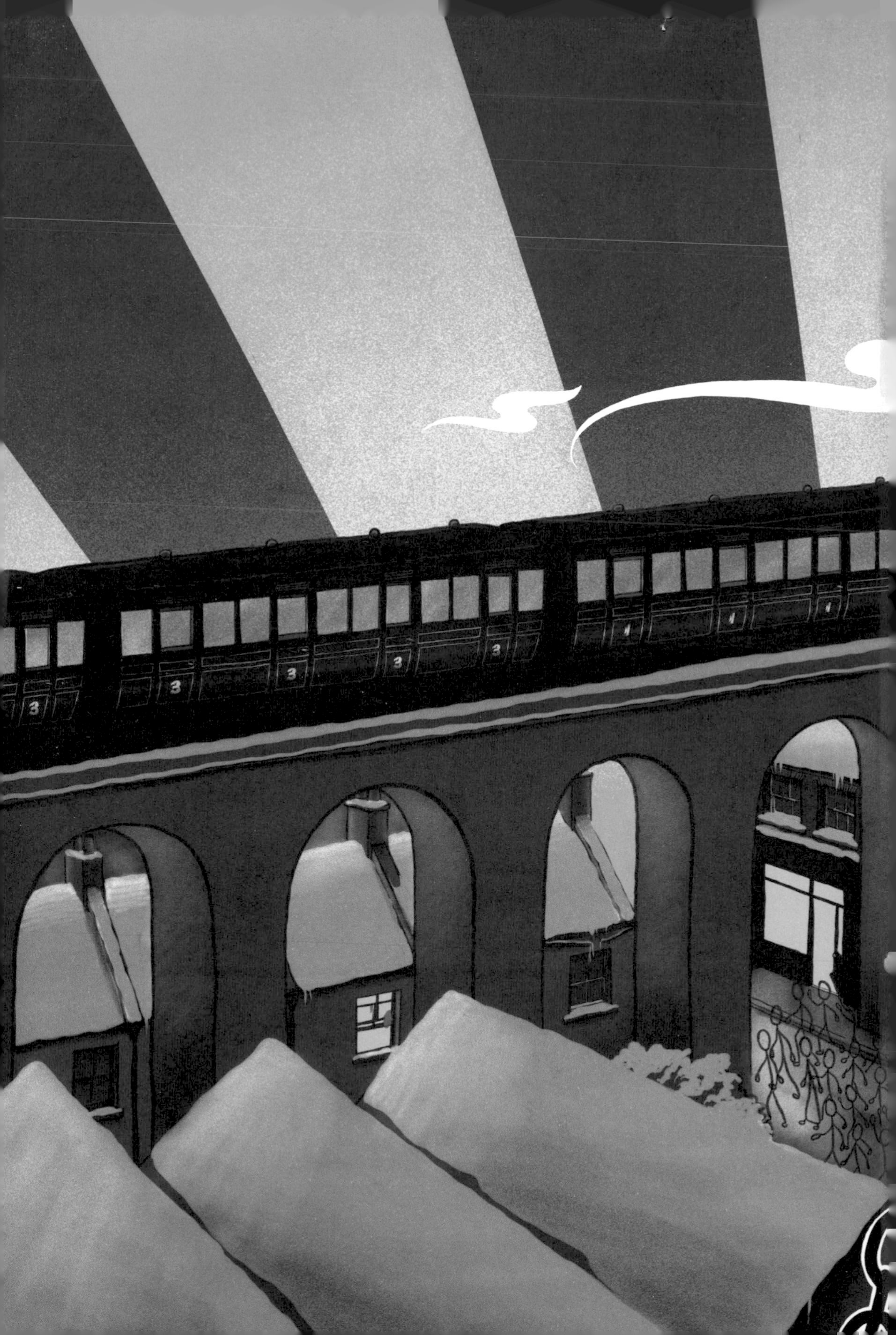